RATIONALISM
VS.
MYSTICISM

Schisms in Traditional Jewish Thought

RATIONALISM
VS.
MYSTICISM

Schisms in Traditional Jewish Thought

Natan Slifkin

The Torah and Nature Foundation
Gefen Books

ISBN 978-965-7023-62-4

Published by:

The Torah and Nature Foundation

Distributed by:

The Biblical Museum of Natural History
Rechov Choshen, Har Tuv
www.BiblicalNaturalHistory.org
office@BiblicalNaturalHistory.org

Gefen Books
www.gefenpublishing.com

Printed in Israel

לזכר נשמת ר' אהרן שמואל בן מנחם מנוס ז"ל

נפטר י'ג אדר ראשון תשע"א

In memory of Samuel Stern

*and all the many members of the Stern and
Ferster families murdered in the Holocaust*

Sam Stern, aged 15 and the youngest of his family, escaped from Vienna in late 1938 on a Kindertransport thanks to Rabbi Solomon Schonfeld *z"l*. He arrived in England with no money, no family and little knowledge of English. By 1949 he was the only male survivor, and his sister the only female survivor of their and previous generations; the last surviving brother had died fighting for Israel.

His wife Mania Ferster נ"י was born in Sosnowiec, south-western Poland, to a Gerer family. She was 13 years old when the war started. She survived the Sosnowiec-Bedzin Ghetto, years in the Gräben slave labour camp and a death march, to be liberated in Bergen Belsen in 1945 by British forces. Only her brother and a cousin survived with her from a large family besides an uncle in England and another in Israel.

They married in 1947 and despite a lack of resources tried various business ventures until, with *siyata d'Shmaya* and herculean efforts, they prospered. Today a large family of children, grandchildren and great-grandchildren provide testimony to their efforts and *chasdei Hashem*.

Dedicated by Michael Stern & Family

Contents

Acknowledgments

This book describes two very different worldviews within traditional Judaism. But what makes a person subscribe to one or the other? Is it nature or nurture?

Perhaps both may play a role. My own rationalist tendencies were clearly bequeathed to me by my parents. My father, Professor Michael Slifkin of blessed memory, was an outstanding scientist, and very much inclined towards reconciling Torah with science. Along with my mother, may she live long, they lived most of their lives and raised me in Manchester, in the north of England—an area known for its plain-talking, unpretentious approach. This meant that despite several years during which I was a passionate advocate of the mystical approach, ultimately the rationalist approach turned out to be far more in line with my natural tendencies.

My mentor for Torah and science topics in the formative years of my yeshivah education was Rav Aryeh Carmell, of blessed memory. He was the one who instilled in me Rambam's approach that one should accept the truth from whatever the source, along with the rationalist approach to the laws of nature and other topics. I feel truly blessed to have been guided by so great a person.

A number of other distinguished Torah scholars in Jerusalem (and one in Bnei Brak) also guided me in several areas of the rationalist approach. Given the dynamics of the communities in which they live, it may cause problems to identify them by name, and so I must thank them without naming them.

Many years later, I entered academia, in the field of Jewish intellectual history. This broadened my intellectual horizons tremendously, and enabled me to understand the historical roots of the Torah-science controversies in which I had become engaged. I am deeply grateful to all my teachers at Machon Lander and Bar-Ilan University, especially Rabbi Profs. Carmi Horowitz, Yosef Tabory and David Malkiel.

The works of many scholars of Jewish intellectual history have benefited me greatly, along with my correspondence with these scholars. In particular, Professor Menachem Kellner's wonderful studies of different aspects of Rambam's thought were enormously enlightening, as were my extensive discussions with him. I am very grateful to Professor Kellner and also to Rabbi Dr. David Shatz for reviewing the manuscript for this book and providing incisive suggestions.

Over the years, there have been many esteemed friends whose insights, knowledge of sources and criticisms have helped me develop the material in this work. I would particularly like to thank Rabbi David Bar-Cohn, Rabbi Scott Kahn, Rabbi Nesanel Neuman, H. Newman, David Ohsie, David Sidney, and Rabbi Dr. Josh Waxman. I would also like to thank all the readers and commenters on my blog www.RationalistJudaism.com who helped me refine the material (sometimes by harshly disputing it) and supported my work.

When I announced my plans to publish a collection of my writings on this topic, Mr. Michael Stern, a man that I had not seen since leaving his *shul* in Manchester nearly thirty years ago, reached out to me to enable the book's publication. I am grateful not only for his financial support of the project, but also for his encouragement and his incisive comments on my essays.

I am deeply grateful to my father-in-law, Mr. Lee Samson, for his constant support of my work, stimulating discussions, and especially for encouraging me to enter academia. My late mother-in-law, Anne Samson, aside from her love and support, always enjoyed listening to my talks on these topics, and I miss her dearly.

My beloved wife Tali has always been a rock of support for me. The turbulent years of controversy which sparked this book were immensely challenging, and I could not have survived them without her strength. May we enjoy continued blessings from our children.

Finally, I would like to express my humble appreciation to the Creator, Who made a universe with mysteries and wonders which excite me every day of my life, and from Whom I feel that I have benefited with the most extraordinary providence. The latter sentiment may not be strictly in line with rationalist philosophy, but that is how I feel.

N. S.

Preface

It might seem odd that someone such as myself is studying and writing and teaching about rationalism vs. mysticism. After all, my lifelong passion is for the animal kingdom, and my regular job is director of the Biblical Museum of Natural History. What is the connection between animals and a schism in Jewish theology?

In fact, there was a direct trajectory from one to the other. The fascination that the animal kingdom holds for many people, including myself, is that it is extraordinary, and simultaneously real. It is extraordinary in its diversity of shapes and sizes and colors and forms and behaviors. Like many people, I am therefore drawn to the more unusual and exotic animals. At the same time, there is the fascination of these creatures being real. Animals are not abstract concepts—they are living and breathing creatures.

Therefore, while I was always interested in virtually all animals, there were some that were particularly interesting. Dinosaurs, for example, while no longer living, are extraordinary creatures that are still very real in that their bones can be seen and touched. And I have also long been interested in the distinction between real and imaginary creatures. Is there such a thing as Bigfoot? The Loch Ness Monster? There are some cryptozoological creatures whose existence cannot be absolutely determined one way or the other, but with others we can be sure that they do not exist.

Because of these interests, when I began exploring the intersection between Torah and the animal kingdom, I was particularly drawn to certain topics. Dinosaurs are real and exciting—how do we reconcile them with the Jewish calendar? There is overwhelming evidence that all animals are descended from a common ancestor—how do we reconcile this with the Torah? Salamanders that are generated from fire and mice that grow from dirt are captivating notions, but they certainly do not exist—how do we account for the Gemara's descriptions of them? I was naturally fascinated and disturbed by these questions. In addition, I had inherited a deep appreciation for science from my father, of blessed memory, who was an outstanding scientist, as well as his intellectual honesty. Thus, I couldn't accept that dinosaurs never existed, or that they lived just a few thousand years ago; nor could I accept either that spontaneous generation really does take place, or that the Sages never actually believed in it. I was intensely bothered by these questions, and by the inability of my teachers in yeshivah to deal with them.

And so I was thrilled when I got to know Rabbi Aryeh Carmell, of blessed memory, and when he and others introduced me to the approaches of Rambam, Rav Hirsch and others who provided reasonable approaches to such topics. They stated that the account of Creation need not be taken entirely literally, and that the Sages of the Talmud, notwithstanding their greatness in Torah, held the beliefs about the natural world that were common to their era. I shared these approaches with others, who were likewise fascinated by the subject matter and relieved to find an authentic and reasonable approach.

Then, as is well known, my books on these topics were banned by numerous leading rabbis in the *charedi* sector of Orthodoxy.[1] This came as a great shock to many people, including myself. To be sure, I knew that these approaches were not exactly common in the yeshivah world. But how could they be branded as unacceptable heresy? To my mind, these approaches were (a) of impeccable credentials in rabbinic scholarship, (b) unobjectionable, and (c) obviously true! How could my ideological opponents, who were far greater in Torah learning and intelligence than me, believe these approaches to be inauthentic, entirely unacceptable, and absolutely false? How could they deny that there was an age of dinosaurs,

---

[1] A full library of documentation relating to this event can be found online at www.zootorah.com/controversy.

and not even be interested in thinking about this question? How could they insist that there are creatures that spontaneously generate?

I embarked upon a long process of analysis, study and reflection in order to understand this. What I finally understood was that there are two fundamentally different worldviews regarding such things as epistemology (the nature of knowledge and where it comes from) and the relative roles of natural law and the supernatural. These are the rationalist and the (for want of a better word) mystical approaches. They are so far apart from each other that if a person is embedded in the mystical approach, then no matter how learned and intelligent he is, the rationalist approach will seem to be entirely false and heretical.

And yet, as I discovered in the course of my studies, the rationalist approach has a rich heritage to it. It was most prominently presented by Rambam, but it was dominant amongst the Rishonim in many ways. And it is fascinating to see how an approach that was once dominant in Jewish thought has declined over time to the point that there are great Talmudic scholars of today who do not realize that it ever even existed.

The goal of this book is not to delegitimize the mystical approach (for reasons that I shall later explain). Rather, it is to preserve and present the rationalist approach for this generation.

PART ONE:

An Overview of Rationalism vs. Mysticism

Introduction

The Importance of Distinguishing between Rationalism and Mysticism

There are various ways of characterizing different groups of Jews. Ashkenazi/Sefardi is one method of differentiation, Hassidic/Litvak, Charedi vs. Modern Orthodox, Israeli vs. Diaspora Jew. Each of these categorizations is useful for understanding a wide range of differences between the people in each category. Drawing this distinction also often has the benefit of minimizing friction between members of each group. A yeshivah student might be infuriated to discover that his roommate does not follow the rulings of "the Gadol HaDor"; but if he discovers that his room-mate is Sefardic, he accepts that obviously he is taking guidance from a Sefardic rabbinic authority instead.

But there is another way of dividing the Jewish People into two categories. It is a division that is not commonly used, and yet it is exceedingly useful. It ties together a whole group of beliefs and attitudes. That is the division between rationalists and non-rationalists, the latter of which we shall refer to as mystics.

The goal here is not to delegitimize any particular approach. Rather, it is to clarify the fact that there are indeed several distinct approaches, which are not all acceptable to everyone. This is important, because we live in an era where different schools of thought in Jewish history are forced together, even when they are at odds with each other. Judaism is often presented as a single, homogenous outlook. This leads people who identify with a particular historical approach to be confused, and feel disen-franchised, when they are expected to conform to a different approach.

Studying this topic, as with many others, reveals that there have been many different voices in our tradition.

In Orthodoxy today, many are averse to pointing out deep differences between great rabbinic figures of history. There is an effort to portray Torah and Judaism as a single, monolithic entity. But the fact is that there is a long history of deeply divergent approaches to some of the most basic aspects of Judaism.

Understanding and implementing rationalist Judaism is hampered by the fact that it has been very much on the decline for hundreds of years, and some people today deny its legitimacy altogether. We will see how in many cases, there was originally a widespread rationalist approach in these areas, which gradually declined over the last few centuries. Documenting this decline is important in order to show how Judaism used to be far more rationalistically inclined, and how the form of Orthodoxy practiced today, viewed by its adherents as the sole authentic form of Judaism, is actually very often a corruption of the approach to Judaism in medieval and ancient times. Often, this involves a great deal of historical revisionism regarding the approach to Judaism in medieval times.

In the cases that we shall study where rationalist versus mystical approaches can be discerned, we see the following pattern occurring over history:

Stage One: Rationalist approach dominant;

Stage Two: Steady increase of mystical approach;

Stage Three: Marginalization of rationalists;

Stage Four: Declaration of rationalism as unacceptable;

Stage Five: Denial that rationalist approach ever existed.

One goal of this study, then, is to breathe new life into the rationalist approach; to explain it, and restore its legitimacy via showing its ancient heritage. But, on the other hand, it is not my goal to de-legitimize the anti-rationalist approach. On the contrary; when we explore the reasons for the decline of rationalism, we shall see that anti-rationalism has great value and that the Jewish People cannot survive without both approaches.

Some Notes on Definitions

In this work, we are not using the definition of rationalism that is found in many historical studies, where it refers to the medieval philosophical belief that truths can be arrived by philosophical contemplation and need not be measured against empirical observation. Instead, we are using a definition frequently adopted in the study of intellectual Jewish history, whereby rationalism refers to a particular school of thought with regard to epistemology, nature and the supernatural, and the service of God.

It is likewise important to clarify that the term "rationalist" is different from the term "rational"—and thus the antonym is not "irrational" but "non-rationalist." Rationalism encompasses a worldview on a range of different matters, and it is not always about whether something is rational or illogical. For example, the differing views about whether God prefers to work through nature or to work through miracles have little to do with being rational or irrational, but rather reflect differing theological worldviews. And aside from the inaccuracy of using the terms rational vs. irrational, it is also extremely offensive!

It is also important to note that there are plenty of ideas and arguments that seemed perfectly rational in the twelfth century, but which would not be rated that way in the twenty-first century. So, for example: Rambam believed that only a fool would deny spontaneous generation. That was a reflection of the scientific beliefs of his era, which a rationalist today should not accept. The same goes for the prevalent medieval rationalist belief that the tenets of Judaism can all be logically and philosophically proven, as we shall discuss in the next section. In the same way, as we shall discuss, the fact that a medieval scholar believed in certain specific supernatural phenomena, such as astrology or demons, does not at all necessarily mean that they were not rationalist, as the available evidence and knowledge at that time may have meant this was a rational conclusion.

There is a distinct group of people who consider themselves loyal followers of the Rambam, but they are medieval rationalists living in the 21st century. And as Rambam says, "A man should never cast his reason behind him, for the eyes are set in the front, not behind." Rambam did not believe Chazal to be infallible, and he would certainly not have rated himself that way, either. A rationalist today should follow Rambam's underlying guiding principles, not necessarily his specific application of them.

Finally, it should be noted that, consistent with common usage today, we shall sometimes use the term "metaphysical" not to refer to the Greco-Muslim metaphysics that Rambam discussed, but rather to its opposite—the supernatural hypostasized forces and reality of the mystical worldview.

The Differences between Rationalism and Mysticism

The differences between rationalists and non-rationalists fall into several related areas:

I. KNOWLEDGE

Rationalists believe that knowledge is legitimately obtained by man via his reasoning and senses, and should preferably be based upon evidence/reason rather than faith, especially for far-fetched claims.

Mystics are skeptical of the ability of the human mind to arrive at truths, and prefer to base knowledge on revelation, or—for those who are not worthy of revelation—on faith in those who do experience revelation.

This relates to how, as we shall now discuss, rationalists see the universe as essentially following a natural order, and hence we can understand it via our senses and reasoning. According to mystics, the supernatural order is dominant, and thus truths about existence require revelation.

II. THE ORDER OF NATURE

Rationalists value a naturalistic rather than supernatural interpretation of events, and perceive a consistent natural order over history, past present and future.

Mystics prefer miracles, and believe them to be especially dominant in ancient history and the future messianic era. They tend to maximize the number of supernatural entities and forces.

III. SUPERNATURAL ENTITIES

Rationalists minimize the number of supernatural entities and forces, seeing them as threatening monotheism. They believe in God, and depending on where on the rationalist spectrum they fall, they may believe in a small number of other supernatural entities or none at all. Discussions of apparent supernatural entities in classical literature are reinterpreted or rejected.

Mystics tend to maximize the number of supernatural entities and forces. They can be either forces of holiness, or forces of evil. These include all kinds of angels and demons, astrological forces, *sefirot* (emanations), *olamot* (spiritual worlds), and an infinite number of other metaphysical entities.

IV. THE FUNCTION OF *MITZVOT*

Rationalists understand the purpose of *mitzvot* and one's religious life in general as furthering intellectual and/or moral goals for the individual and society. Even *chukkim* serve to accomplish these functions, albeit in a way that is not immediately obvious.

Mystics accept that *mitzvot* serve intellectual and moral goals, but see the primary function of *mitzvot* as performing mechanistic manipulations of spiritual metaphysical forces. The reasons for *mitzvot* are either to accomplish these manipulations, or are ultimately incomprehensible.

V. THE NATURE OF TORAH

Rationalists consider the Torah to be the divine instruction book for life—teaching us concepts that improve our minds, character and society, based on the requirements.

Mystics believe the Torah to be the genetic blueprint of creation, possessing all kinds of metaphysical qualities, which only on its most superficial level is an instructional text.

The rest of Part One of this book contains a more comprehensive review of the differences between the rationalist and mystical worldviews, with several examples in each case. Part Two of this work presents an analysis of some of these examples in much greater detail.

Were the Sages Rationalists or Mystics?

Out study primarily focuses on analyzing the differences between rationalist and mystical perspectives beginning from the period of the Rishonim, the great Torah scholars of the medieval period. But what about Chazal,[1] the Sages of the Talmud? Were they rationalists or mystics?

We should first bear in mind that Chazal is not a person; Chazal were lots of people living over different periods in different places. With regard to one aspect of the rationalist/mystic divide—that of preferring to see God operating through nature vs. maximizing the supernatural—there are those who argue that the two opposing viewpoints can already both be found amongst the Sages, specifically with the school of Rabbi Yishmael versus that of Rabbi Akiva.[2]

Rabbi Akiva sought to maximize the supernatural. For example, in the account of the plague of frogs in Egypt, the Torah states that the "frog" came up over Egypt, in the singular form. In the oft-forgotten *peshat* explanation provided by Rashi, this simply reflects it being a collective noun, just as in English we would say "the frog plague" and not "the frogs plague." But Rabbi Akiva explained it to mean that there was one frog which miraculously multiplied into millions.[3] Elsewhere, Rabbi Akiva expounds that the Ten Plagues were actually fifty, and that there were 250 plagues at the Sea of Reeds.[4]

---

[1] An acronym for *Chachameinu, zichronom l'vr*acha – "Our sages, may their memory be for a blessing."

[2] This is developed at length by R. Abraham Joshua Heschel, *Heavenly Torah: As Refracted through the Generations* (New York: Continuum 2005), Chapter Three, pp. 66-70.

[3] Talmud, Sanhedrin 67b. Note that this earned him a rebuke from others: "Rabbi Elazar ben Azarya said, Akiva, Why do you involve yourself with *aggadata*? Finish with your words and go to study *nega'im* and *ohelos*. There was one frog, it called to the others, and they came."

[4] *Haggadah Shel Pesach; Mechilta d'Rabbi Yishmael, Beshalach* 6.

Rabbi Yishmael, on the other hand, minimized the supernatural aspect of miracles. For example, the Torah relates that after bringing an offering at the base of Mount Sinai, Moshe divided the blood in half. The Midrash asks how he was able to divide it exactly in half, and several Tannaim provide supernatural explanations, such as that the blood miraculously divided by itself, or that an angel divided it. But R. Yishmael answers simply that Moshe possessed expertise in the rules of blood and its divisions.[5] Likewise, with regard to the account of the Jewish People prevailing against Amalek when Moshe raised his hands, it was R. Yishmael who first voiced the explanation (subsequently adopted by the Mishnah) that this does not refer to a supernatural effect of Moshe's hands, but rather to the Jewish People looking Heavenwards and receiving Divine aid.[6] And whereas the account of the manna being "bread from the Heavens" was understood by many Sages (including Rabbi Akiva) to refer to the manna being food of the angels that spatially descended from above, Rabbi Yishmael interpreted it to mean that it was physical food which came via God's agency.[7]

Accordingly, the differing approaches between rationalist and mystics with regard to the supernatural can already be traced back to the era of the Tannaim.[8] On the other hand, the difference between R. Yishmael and R.

---

[5] *Midrash Rabbah, Vayikra* 6:5.

[6] *Mechilta D'Rabbi Yishmael, Parashat Amalek* 1.

[7] Yoma 75b; *Midrash Tannaim* to Deuteronomy 26:15.

[8] "…Mystical Judaism *was*, and *is*, normative. Rational Judaism, too, was, and is, normative… However, as Heschel showed in *Heavenly Torah as Refracted through the Generations*, *both* mystical *and* rational Judaism were normative forms within the rabbinic aggadic and halakhic worldview already in early rabbinic times. Both have clearly continued, side by side, even if sometimes in tension. Neither, then, can be favored in a historical or in an ideological sense though each person makes his or her choice, or her or his balance, between these approaches. Jewish religion has not lived, and cannot live, without this co-existence." David R. Blumenthal, Review of Menachem Kellner, *Maimonides' Confrontation with Mysticism*, in *Reviews in Religion and Theology*, 14:2 (2007) 253-57, available online at http://www.js.emory.edu/BLUMENTHAL/-Kellner.htm.

Akiva with regard to the supernatural does not necessarily mean that they took the full rationalist/mystical approaches in other areas.[9]

There is also a marked difference in attitudes to the supernatural between the Babylonian and Jerusalem Talmuds. While the Babylonian Talmud has extensive references and discussions about angels, demons, and all kinds of magical and supernatural forces, these are much less common in the Jerusalem Talmud.[10] In fact, there is a reference in the Babylonian Talmud to a certain verse which was translated in Babylon as referring to male and female demons, but which in the west (i.e. in the Land of Israel) was translated as referring to carriages.[11] The Babylonian Talmud further notes that the demonic risk involved in pairs, which was a subject of great concern in Babylon, was not an issue for their counterparts in the Land of Israel:

> In the West, they are not cautious about having things in pairs... The rule of the matter is that for those who take note of the pairs, the pairs take note of them; those who do not take note of the pairs are not bothered by

---

[9] "...The line that divides the Akivan from the Ishmaelian worldview is not the line between rationality and mysticism"—Gordon Tucker, in Heschel, *Heavenly Torah*, Translator's Introduction to Chapter 4, p. 71.

[10] Louis Ginzberg, *The Palestinian Talmud* (New York, 1941), pp. xxxiii-xxxvi: "Palestinian authors of the Talmud excluded, almost entirely, the popular fancies about angels and demons, while in Babylonia angelology and demonology gained scholastic recognition and with it entrance into the Talmud... A similar observation can be made in regard to the difference in the attitudes of the two Talmuds toward sorcery, magic, astrology, and other kinds of superstitions." See too R. Zvi Hirsch Chajes: "Concerning the subject of demons, the evil eye, and the evil spirits referred to in the Talmud, there can be no doubt that the Rabbis believed in their existence, and consequently we should not attempt to offer other interpretations which will explain them in a sense remote from the literal... We do, however, observe a substantial difference in regard to this matter between the Babylonian and the Palestinian sages, although both believed in the existence of these beings and both tell us of conversations which they held with them, and of the marvelous things which these demons sometimes performed... Yet these Palestinian sages did not elaborate these tales at such inordinate length as is done in the Babylonian Talmud, where they are told with great detail" (Zvi Hirsch Chajes, *Mevo HaTalmud: The Students Guide through the Talmud*, translated by Jacob Shachter. Chapter 31, page 233).

[11] Babylonian Talmud, Gittin 68a.

them. Nonetheless, it is good to show a modicum of concern. (Babylonian Talmud, Pesachim 110b)

The way in which the Babylonian Talmud differs from the Jerusalem Talmud in this regard can be attributed to the influence of Zoroastrianism, the official religion of the Persian Empire, which included Babylon during the Talmudic period.[12] And thus, as with Rabbi Yishmael vs. Rabbi Akiva, the different attitudes to the supernatural do not necessarily reflect a wider difference between rationalism and mysticism.

It is difficult to pin Chazal down into the categories of rationalists and mystics. Their statements are very terse and are open to multiple interpretations. Furthermore, the categories of rationalism and mysticism are not necessarily so relevant to that era, when both philosophy and mysticism were less developed. Still, at the very least, we can perhaps see the roots of both approaches.

The Development of the Rationalist vs. Mystical Divide

The rationalist approach flowered in the Golden Age of Spain. The dramatic spread of Islamic civilization in the medieval period enabled it to absorb the scholarly products of other cultures. The great works of medicine, astronomy, mathematics, and especially the Greek works of natural philosophy were all translated into Arabic. The Jews of Spain, as a literate and wealthy community living under fairly reasonable conditions, were in turn able to absorb this.

The ultimate product of the union of Jews with Greco-Muslim philosophy was, of course, Rambam. His *Moreh Nevuchim*, the *Guide for the Perplexed*, is still the pre-eminent text for the rationalist approach. But Rambam, while foremost of the rationalists, was certainly not the only one. Meiri, Ibn Ezra, and others were also firmly in this camp, and even quasi-mystical figures such as Ramban (Nachmanides) also expressed several clear rationalist tendencies. These towering scholars presented an

---

[12] Studies in this area have been published by Rabbi Dr. Yaakov Elman and Dr. Shai Secunda.

approach to Torah and Judaism which valued the scientific enterprise and maximized the role of nature.

Yet it was precisely the success of the rationalist movement in general, and Rambam in particular, which galvanized the non-rationalist forces into action. Ancient mystical approaches coalesced and evolved into a broad approach. The publication of the Zohar in the fourteenth century—a phenomenon that we shall later discuss in more detail—was even more significant than the publication of the *Guide*. Rationalism went on the decline, and mysticism was on the rise.

After the expulsion of the Jews from Spain, it was in Christian Europe that Jewish culture flourished. But, unlike the Jews in medieval Spain, the Jews in Christian Europe had little exposure to science and philosophy. Meanwhile, in the sixteenth century, the Christians were making enormous strides in astronomy. Embarrassed at the obsolete statements about astronomy in traditional rabbinic texts, rabbinic apologists turned to mysticism as a solution. They insisted that the Sages of the Talmud were privy to supernatural sources of knowledge, and that their seemingly incorrect statements should not be interpreted literally.

With the Enlightenment and Emancipation, the pendulum started to swing back to rationalism. While many Jews sailed the rationalist ship out of Judaism altogether, others, such as Rabbi Samson Raphael Hirsch, incorporated its approach. But then, as a reaction to the emancipation, many traditionalists dug in their heels and became even more anti-rationalist. The rise of Hassidism strengthened the mystical approach to hitherto unseen proportions. And even the backlash to Hassidism, epitomized by R. Chaim of Voloshin, relied heavily upon Zoharic mysticism to present its approach.

In the Afterword, we shall explore the further development of the rationalist-mystic divide in recent history. For now, let us proceed to explore the five aspects of the difference between rationalism and mysticism.

I: Knowledge

Introduction

Rationalists believe that knowledge is legitimately obtained by man via his reasoning and senses. Of course, human beings are finite and fallible. Still, the human brain is a marvelous thing, and it can obtain powerful insights. And the combined efforts of many human minds over time—the scientific enterprise—is particularly effective at discovering truths.

Rationalists further take the position that knowledge should preferably be based upon evidence/reason rather than faith. This is especially true for far-fetched claims.

The rationalist approach certainly acknowledges that there are matters beyond human understanding. It also acknowledges that sometimes, matters should be taken on trust, for reasons such as that there is reason to consider the source of the information to be a reliable authority. Still, in general, the rationalist approach values the ability of mankind to figure things out.

The rationalist approach to knowledge is perfectly expressed in Rambam's view on the falsehood of astrology:

> The summary of the matter is that our mind cannot grasp how the decrees of the Holy One, blessed be He, work upon human beings in this world and in the world to come. What we have said about this from the beginning is that the entire position of the star gazers is regarded as a falsehood by all men of science. I know that you may search and find sayings of some individual sages in the Talmud and Midrashim whose words appear to maintain that at the moment of a man's birth, the stars will cause such and such to happen to him. Do not regard this as a difficulty, for it is not fitting for a man to abandon the prevailing law and raise once again the counterarguments and replies (that preceded its

13

enactment). Similarly it is not proper to abandon matters of reason that have already been verified by proofs, shake loose of them, and depend on the words of a single one of the sages from whom possibly the matter was hidden. Or there may be an allusion in those words; or they may have been said with a view to the times and the business before him... A man should never cast his reason behind him, for the eyes are set in front, not in back. (*Letter to the Sages of Montpellier*)

Rambam exerts great effort to be respectful of the Sages of old, but his approach is nevertheless clear. If reason or logic compels a certain position, one should not reject that position merely because great people in the past held a different view. Rambam also writes about this elsewhere:

Such is the mentality of even the elect of our times, that they do not test the veracity of an opinion upon the merit of its own content, but rather upon its agreement with the words of some preceding authority, without troubling to examine that preceding source itself. (Introduction to *Sefer HaMitzvot*)

Mystics, on the other hand, prefer to base knowledge on supernatural revelation, or—for those who are not worthy of revelation—on faith in those who do experience revelation. They further maintain that such supernatural revelations of knowledge are not limited to Sinai, but rather that they happen quite often. Mystics will thus attribute much great supernatural content to Rabbinic works than do rationalists. They also have a different view of the nature of the wisdom embedded in the Torah itself, as we shall see. Since there are often clashes between knowledge professed to come from revelation and knowledge obtained from philosophy of science, mystics profess skepticism of the ability of the human mind, and even the collective efforts of many human minds over time, to arrive at truths. In addition, because (as we shall later see) mystics are of the view that much of existence involved invisible supernatural phenomena, they believe that true knowledge of existence can only be obtained via supernatural means.

It must be said that the while the rationalist approach to knowledge is more compatible with contemporary attitudes to epistemology, it does run counter to the general thrust of Jewish society. As historian Jacob Katz points out, "Jewish society is traditional—it bases itself on values and knowledge drawn from the past."[1] While there certainly is plenty of historical precedent for the rationalist approach to knowledge, it can destabilize Judaism for many people.

Faith

● *For further discussion, see Appendix I*

The area of faith is one in which there is a great divide between medieval rationalism and contemporary rationalism. The rationalist Rishonim believed that God's existence can be logically proven, along with the other tenets of Judaism. But in the world of modern philosophy, that is no longer true. It can be argued to be rational to accept God's existence, and even that the universe (in terms of the remarkable laws and constants of nature[2]) points towards some sort of Creator, but not that His existence can be conclusively proven with the tools of logic and philosophy.

The other tenets of Judaism are even more challenging. They likewise do not have logical or philosophical proofs (contrary to popular wishful thinking and the claims made by some). There are arguments to be made in their favor, based on history and suchlike, but they are disputable, and there are certainly not logical proofs. Whether these tenets can be accepted on a rational basis, or only on faith, is disputed.[3]

According to the perspective that the rationalist approach can no longer be applied to the fundamental tenets of Jewish faith, is there a point to exploring the application of the rationalist approach to any aspect of

---

[1] Jacob Katz, *Tradition and Crisis: Jewish Society at the End of the Middle Ages*, trans. Bernard Dov Cooperman (New York: NYU Press, 1993), p. 156.

[2] As discussed at length in my book *The Challenge Of Creation*.

[3] Consider the following from Rabbi Dr. David Shatz: "My commitment is not rooted in the (naive) notion that reason vindicates my beliefs. It is rooted rather in what Judaism provides me with: intellectual excitement, feeling, caring for others, inspiration, and a total perspective that is evocative and affecting." This is from his fascinating essay, "The Overexamined Life Is Not Worth Living," printed as a conclusion to his philosophical work *Jewish Thought in Dialogue: Essays on Thinkers, Theologies, and Moral Theories* (Academic Studies Press 2009).

Judaism? The answer is yes. Many people who consider their own faith to lack rational justification may still feel that the rest of Judaism should be as rational as possible. Faith is often a very personal matter that is rooted deep in one's psyche or personal experiences, quite separate from one's approach to the rest of Judaism.

There are also some people who do not have faith in the tenets of Judaism at all, but are nevertheless members of the Orthodox community. In some cases, this is because it is too difficult for them to leave; in other cases, it is because they appreciate the lifestyle and the community. For such people, it is valuable to understand how there is a rationalist approach which makes so many areas of Judaism make more rational sense than they do with the mystical approach that is commonly taught today.

Sources of Faith

What is the source of one's belief in God in general, and in the God of the Jewish People in particular? How does one strengthen one's faith in Judaism?

Mystics are inspired by stories of supernatural phenomena. This is obviously true of most Chassidic approaches, along with many Sephardic communities. But it is also true of many Litvaks, who are likewise often of a non-rationalist mindset. An extreme example is found in a recent book by Rabbi Reuven Schmelczer, *The Heart of Emunah: The Torah Approach for Conveying Yiddishkeit to our Children,*[4] which relates countless stories about the supernatural powers of great rabbis, the truth of miraculous phenomena, and suchlike.

Rabbi Schmelczer saves the best one, a second-hand story allegedly told by the Chafetz Chaim, for the final chapter. In the city of Shavel (Šiauliai), a pig once forced its way into a synagogue, went to the *ammud*, and stood up on its hind legs. Demonstrating a level of intelligence, eyesight, and dexterity not normally seen in this species, it opened up the *siddur*, and

---

[4] The book has glowing endorsements from Rabbi Moshe Shapiro, Rabbi Mattisyahu Salomon, Rabbi Elya Ber Wachtfogel, Rabbi Yaakov Hillel and Rabbi Aryeh Malkiel Kotler. (Rabbi Schmelzcer, along with some of these rabbis, were the driving forces behind the ban on my books.)

began turning pages. It found its way to a *piyut* that mentioned pigs, tore that page out of the *siddur*, and ran out of the synagogue. The rabbi explained that this pig was a *gilgul* of Eisav, and that this was a bad sign. Accordingly, a few days later, the entire city was destroyed in a fire. Rabbi Schmelczer concludes by noting that "stories such as these, told by *tzaddikim* and *gedolim* who personify trustworthiness.... are proof to our *emunah* that there is always a spiritual dimension above what we can see and understand."

Rationalists, on the other hand, would be extremely skeptical about stories involving sentient pigs. And in general, they do not look for supernatural phenomena to boost their faith. As noted earlier, for medieval rationalists, faith was believed to be an intellectual conclusion from philosophical proofs. Today, rationalists are inspired by phenomena which do not break the laws of nature. For example, the extraordinary nature of the laws of science, which result in an orderly universe with intelligent life, is a source of faith.[5] Another is the extraordinary history of the Jewish People, culminating in the return to sovereignty in the Land of Israel. At a more general level, rationalists are inspired by stories of people's human greatness, not their alleged superhuman greatness.

Forming Conclusions Vs. Confessing Ignorance

As discussed earlier, the rationalist approach encourages one to draw conclusions, sometimes even uncomfortable ones, based on the dictates of logic and reason. While nobody is infallible, there are certainly cases where one has reason to be more confident in the conclusions of contemporary epistemology than in positions taken by people in the past. The mystical approach, however, prefers that people do not form conclusions which threaten existing beliefs:

> *Shas* is faith-based knowledge. When faced with the most difficult questions, we don't take the easy way out. We would rather wait for Eliyahu to come! Why settle for a makeshift answer, if we will be handed the reliable solution at a later date? *Teyku* is the answer! From the graves of these giants of wisdom and purity, Abaya and Rava, emerges the truth

---

[5] See my book *The Challenge Of Creation* for an extensive presentation of this topic.

that can never be repudiated by the midgets of our generation. (Rabbi Mattisyahu Solomon, address at the 2004 Siyum HaShas in Madison Square Garden[6])

This approach does have its place. We should not expect, with our limited knowledge and experience, to be able to resolve every difficult question that arises. Often, the most honest, accurate and suitable response is to simply admit and accept that one does not have the solution. At such times, there is an important Yiddish expression to bear in mind: *Fun a kasha shtarbt mon nisht* — "From a question, a person doesn't die." It conveys the advice that we should not be overly distressed when we do not find answers for all our questions.

Nevertheless, this approach is widely misused and abused. It is legitimate to adopt this approach for oneself whenever one wants. It is unreasonable, however, to always expect other people to accept it. All too often, this approach is used to brush off important questions that should be answered and for which the answers are indeed available (albeit unpopular in certain circles).

Aside from the issue of using this approach with others, there is also the more fundamental matter about employing it with regard to oneself. The great rationalist Torah scholars certainly admitted that there were matters that were beyond their comprehension. However, where there were matters for which they could figure out a logical and reasonable approach, they did so, even if it caused some unsavory conclusions. A perfect example is with Rambam's aforementioned letter on astrology, in which he takes the uncomfortable position of rejecting the Sages' views, but explains that "a man should never cast his reason behind him, for the eyes are set in front, not in back." This is in contrast to the non-rationalist approach, which often prefers to state that "we do not understand this" and will not attempt to figure out a conclusion.

---

[6] From a transcript in *Mishpachah* magazine. This is following the popular yeshivah concept of *teyku* as an acronym for *Tishbi yetaretz kushyot ve-ibayot,* "The Tishbite (Eliyahu) will answer the difficulties and questions," i.e. that we confess ignorance. In fact, the original term *teyku* means "let it stand," and it means that there are competing perspectives of equal merit and the matter is thus deadlocked.

When Rambam encountered people who were grappling with the questions raised by Aristotelian philosophy, he did not simply say, "You don't die from a question." Instead, he wrote his *Guide for the Perplexed*, and provided answers wherever possible—even though these answers were not popular with many segments of Jewry, and often went against certain traditional positions.

Science and the Sages

- *Expanded upon in Part Two, "Sod Hashem Liyreyav—When God Reveals His Scientific Secrets"*

One significant ramification of the differing conceptions of the nature of Torah is that according the mystical approach, great Torah scholars are presumed to know much more than merely the texts that they have studied. Rather, they are believed to have supernaturally-sourced insight into the working of the universe and history.

Rationalists, on the other hand, take the approach that when rabbinic scholars, including the great sages of the Talmud, make statements about the natural world, these are not based on supernatural revelation. Rather, they are based on what they, or those upon whom they relied, believed about the world. This position can be found, either explicitly or implicitly, in the writings of many Geonim and Rishonim. Here are but a few examples:

> We must inform you that our Sages were not physicians. They may mention medical matters which they noticed here and there in their time, but these are not meant to be a mitzvah. Therefore you should not rely on these cures and you should not practice them at all unless each item has been carefully investigated by medical experts who are certain that this procedure will do no harm and will cause no danger. (Rav Sherira Gaon, *Otzar HaGeonim*, Gittin 68, #376)

> Do not ask of me to reconcile everything that they [the Sages] stated about astronomy with the actual reality, for the science of those days was deficient, and they did not speak out of traditions from the prophets regarding these matters… (Rambam, *Guide for the Perplexed* 3:14)

> We are not obliged, on account of the great superiority of the sages of the Talmud, and their expertise in their explanations of the Torah and its details, and the truth of their sayings in the explanation of its general principles and details, to defend them and uphold their views in all of their sayings in medicine, in science and in astronomy, or to believe them [in those matters] as we believe them regarding the explanation of the Torah, which they had completely mastered and which it was their role to teach. (Rabbeinu Avraham ben HaRambam, *Ma'amar al Odot Derashot Chazal*)

Rationalists further believe that, notwithstanding its shortcomings, modern science is in general an effective system for determining truths. True, the human brain is certainly fallible. However, the collective enterprise of human minds, using the scientific method, is an effective, albeit not flawless, method for revealing truths about the physical universe. Mystics, on the other hand, profess to be skeptical about the ability of modern science to obtain truths about the universe.

Putting these two aspects together, we can see the relevance with regard to conflicts between modern science and statements about the natural world that are found in rabbinic texts. Rationalists accord a high value to conclusions reached via the modern scientific method, and a low value to statements found in ancient texts. Mystics, on the other hand, take the approach that statements found in ancient texts are unquestionable, while professing skepticism about the conclusions of modern science.

An excellent presentation of the mystical position was presented by Rabbi Uren Reich, Rosh haYeshiva of Yeshiva of Woodlake Village in Lakewood, in a speech about this author's books:

> ...If the Gemara tells us a *metziyus* (a statement about physical reality), it's *emes veyatziv* (true and certain). There's nothing to think about. Anything we see with our eyes is less of a reality than something we see in the Gemara. That's the *emunah* that a *yid* has to have. Unfortunately, I don't know where or why this is, but recently there's been a spate of all kinds of publications—I don't know where they've come from— questioning things that have been *mekubel midor dor* (accepted throughout the generations), that every child learns, together with his mother's milk, *al titosh Toras imecha* (do not depart from your mother's teachings), we learn that every word of Torah is *emes*, every word of *Chazal*

hakedoshim is *emes*. We have come to hear new kinds of concepts, that we have to figure out a way to make Torah compatible with modern day science—it's an *emunah mezuyefes* (perversion of faith)! There's a tremendous *emunah* that these people have for scientists in the outside world—everything they say is *kodesh kadoshim*! And then we have to figure out according to what they say, how to fit in the Gemara with these newfangled discoveries that the scientists have taught us?! These same scientists who tell you with such clarity what happened sixty-five million years ago—ask them what the weather will be like in New York in two weeks' time! "Possibly, probably, it could be, maybe"—*ain itam hadavar*, they don't know. They know everything that happened 65 million years ago, but from their *madda*, and their *wissenschaft*, we have to be *mispoel* (stirred up)?! (Extract from address at Agudath Israel of America's 82nd National Convention)

The gulf between the two approaches is vast and unbridgeable.

There is a very important qualification that must be made, however. The rationalist approach, that the Sages may have been in error with regard to some of their beliefs about the natural world, is often believed and sometimes feared to necessarily lead to rulings in Jewish law having to be revised. This is not the case at all. There are excellent, rational reasons for maintaining that the Sages' rulings are binding even if there is reason to believe that they are based on errant beliefs about the world. This is discussed in detail in the final chapter of *Sacred Monsters* by this author.

The Sun's Path at Night

- *Expanded upon in Part Two, "The Sages vs. Science: The Sun's Path at Night"*

Without doubt, the most prominent example of the difference between rationalist and mystical views regarding the Sages and science is the topic of the sun's path at night. It is also an astonishing example of how the rationalist approach was dominant and then declined so much that today, many learned Torah scholars do not even believe that it ever existed, and are certainly unaware of how dominant it was.

The Talmud (Pesachim 94b) records a dispute between the Jewish Sages and the gentile astronomers regarding the path taken by the sun after it disappears from the horizon in the evening. According to the Jewish Sages, when the sun disappears from sight, it then changes direction, doubling back behind the opaque "dome of the sky" in order to return to the place where it will rise the next morning. (While this may sound bizarre today, it was the prevalent ancient Babylonian cosmological model.) According to the gentile astronomers, on the other hand, when the sun sinks below the horizon in the evening, it continues on the same path to travel beneath us, making a full circuit around the world. The Talmud then quotes Rabbi Yehudah HaNasi as saying that he finds the opinion of the gentile astronomers to be more convincing.

All the Geonim and Rishonim, without exception, explained the Talmud according to its straightforward meaning—namely, that the Talmud is discussing where the sun goes at night, and that Rabbi Yehudah HaNasi was acknowledging the Jewish Sages to have been mistaken in their view that it travels behind the sky. A few Rishonim maintained that the Sages of Israel were nevertheless correct and that the sun really does go behind the sky at night, but the majority of Rishonim acknowledged that they were mistaken in this view, and were apparently not bothered by this.

Beginning in the 16th century, however, this understanding of the Talmud was rejected. In its place, a variety of different readings of this passage were contrived. Today, in communities that adopt the mystical worldview, it is generally considered to be inconceivable to explain the Talmud according to the straightforward explanation of the Geonim and Rishonim. It is presumed that, with access to supernatural sources of knowledge, it is impossible that the Sages of Israel could have subscribed to such a mistaken view of the sun's path at night. As for the many dozens of rabbinic sources stating precisely this, contemporary non-rationalists are either unaware of them, ignore them, or dismiss them as forgeries or otherwise unacceptable.

Rav Yochanan's Teachings

- *Expanded upon in Part Two, "Messianic Wonders and Skeptical Rationalists"*

Another striking example of the gulf between the rationalist and mystical worldviews regarding the Sages' statements about the world relates to a story about Rav Yochanan. The Talmud records Rav Yochanan as expounding that in the Messianic Era, the city of Jerusalem will be rebuilt with windows made from gemstones and pearls that are thirty cubits (about 45 feet) in size. One of Rav Yochanan's students reacts with skepticism, pointing out that no gemstones of such dimensions exist. Subsequently, states the Talmud, this student embarked on an ocean voyage, during which he saw angels hewing out gemstones of these dimensions. He returned to Rav Yochanan and apologetically accepted his statement. Rav Yochanan responded by castigating him for only accepting his teaching based upon empirical confirmation, and not based on innate trust in the validity of whatever he teaches. (A parallel passage has Rabban Gamliel teaching that in the Messianic Era, clothing and bread will grow from the ground.)

For mystics, this passage presents a perfect condemnation of the rationalist approach. Scientific, empirically-based knowledge is being condemned. The student should have accepted Rav Yochanan's teachings on faith, relying on the supernatural source of his wisdom.

However, we must bear in mind that Rambam and the other rationalist Torah scholars also studied this passage in the Talmud. They did not see it as a condemnation of rationalism. Rather, they interpreted it differently.

According to the rationalist approach, when Rav Yochanan spoke about Jerusalem being rebuilt with gemstones of thirty cubits, and Rabban Gamliel spoke about clothing and bread growing from the ground, of course they were not speaking literally—because there is no such thing! The error of the student was in thinking that they were speaking literally. It was only when the student sailed out on the sea of knowledge, and realized that his teacher was not speaking literally, that he accepted his error.

Thus, the very story that non-rationalists use as a condemnation of rationalism is itself used by the rationalist Rishonim as a confirmation of the rationalist approach!

The Size of a *Kezayit*

- *Expanded upon in Part Two, "The Evolution of the Olive"*

During the Pesach seder, there is a mitzvah to eat matzah. The minimum amount of food that is defined as an act of eating is a *kezayit*—the volume of an olive. However, today many people insist on consuming a piece of matzah many, many times this size—up to half the size of an egg. Why?

If we look at the history of the halachic discussion of the *kezayit*, an interesting pattern emerges. All the halachic discussion about the size of the *kezayit* is built upon the writings of the medieval Tosafists from Ashkenaz. The Rishonim of Sefard do not engage in any discussion as to the size of a *kezayit*. It is only by scouring their writings very carefully, including newly discovered manuscripts, that one comes across passing references to the size of a *kezayit*—and they give it as about one-ninth the volume of an egg (which is the size of an olive).

The simple explanation for these two differences is that olives only grow in the Mediterranean basin. The Rishonim of Sefarad did not have to discuss how big olives were, since they were familiar with them. It was only the Rishonim of Ashkenaz who had to discuss the size of the *kezayit*, since they were not familiar with olives. They were forced to draw inferences from various texts, and were misled into giving it a much larger size.

Such an analysis sits will with rationalists, according to whom rabbinic scholars had to work with the information available to them. However, advocates of the mystical approach, even if they formally only ascribe scientific inerrancy to the Sages of the Talmud, are often uncomfortable even with ascribing error to the medieval Rishonim.

The Zohar

- *Expanded upon in Appendix II, "The Authenticity and Authority of the Zohar"*

In the 14th century, a Spanish scholar by the name of Moses de Leon issued a startling proclamation. He announced that he had a long-hidden manuscript from none other than Rabbi Shimon bar Yochai. It was a work of profound mysticism, called the Zohar.

How much authority does one confer upon the Zohar? The question of the authority of the Zohar has profound ramifications for rationalism vs. mysticism, due to the far-ranging mystical teachings present in the Zohar. But how one views the authority of the Zohar itself depends upon one's approach in these areas.

Mystics are enthusiastic about positing supernatural revelation. They are also, by definition, enthusiastic about mystical teachings. And they also place great trust in the rabbis of the past. Thus, they readily accept the authenticity of the supernaturally-revealed Zohar, which was endorsed by many great mystical scholars of the past, and which is a primary resource for mystical teachings.

Rationalists, on the other hand, are reluctant to posit supernatural revelation outside of Sinai. They also maintain a worldview of Judaism which is at odds with many concepts found in the Zohar. Furthermore, they are less likely to accept its authority merely because others did, and they are more likely to critically assess it. Accordingly, they tend to be skeptical of the idea that the Zohar is the secret revelation of Rabbi Shimon bar Yochai, and they view it as the creation of Moses de Leon, albeit based upon a core of older mystical teachings.

Today, the Zohar is widely regarded as a foundational work in Judaism, second only to Tanach and (perhaps) the Talmud. To many people, the idea that the Zohar is largely a 14th century forgery sounds shocking, even heretical. However, it is important to realize that there are countless arguments for this. The Zohar contains numerous words and concepts which are characteristic of texts from 14th century Spain but would be entirely anachronistic for a text from 2nd century Judea.

Furthermore, this view of the Zohar was held by many great rabbinic scholars of impeccable credentials, such as Chatam Sofer. And even some of those who passionately believe in the Tannaic authority of the Zohar, such as Rav Ovadia Yosef, acknowledge that those who reject it do so for serious reasons, and thus should not be written out of Orthodoxy. (For an extensive discussion of the authenticity and authority of the Zohar, see the appendix.)

This does not necessarily mean that contemporary rationalists reject the Zohar entirely. As noted, it does contain a core of older, more authentic, material. Furthermore, even the more recent parts of it may contain valuable insights. Finally, the Zohar has certainly become embedded in the basic library of Jewish literature.

Intellectual Submissions to Authority

- *Expanded upon in Part Two, "Arguing with God: When May Students Dispute Teachers?"*

May one disagree with one's teachers, or with the greatest Torah scholars of the generation? Historically, this was not necessarily related to the rationalist-mystic divide. The recent emphasis upon being *mevatel* one's *da'at*—negating one's own thoughts and conclusions in favor of those of respected authorities—has more to do with sociology. The modern era's emphasis on personal autonomy caused a reactionary movement in the Hassidic world, and this spread to the Lithuanian community in the early twentieth century. Still, the contemporary arguments in each direction certainly relate to the rationalist/mystic divide, and are similar to those regarding disputing the Sages' statements about the natural world.

In the rationalist approach, one may well submit to authority in terms of *halachah* and practical action, for a variety of excellent reasons. However, one does not submit one's intellect. Much like the *zaken mamre*, the rebellious elder, the problem is not holding a different view, but rather translating that view into action in such a way as to undermine the stability of the system of authority. As long as there is no undermining the system of authority in the practical realm, one is free to form one's own conclusions—and one should indeed do so.

The other approach maintains that one should attempt to "brainwash" oneself into rejecting one's own conclusions in favor of the thought processes of people who are believed to be greater Torah scholars. The justification for this is sometimes presented as non-mystical, and based merely on the fact that the greater scholar is far more likely to be correct. However, in fact it is often based on the mystical approach that such people have greater supernatural assistance and insight.

To illustrate this point, let us consider as example often given by proponents of the non-rationalist approach—that it would be ludicrous for a first-year physics student to disagree with Einstein. Superficially, this sounds like a rational (and rationalist) argument. However, upon further reflection, one sees otherwise. A first-year physics student would (at least, in the ideal world) always be welcomed to disagree with Einstein. He would put forth his arguments, and people would weigh these up. And it is even perfectly theoretically conceivable, albeit unlikely, that he would be correct.

In non-rationalist circles, on the other hand, people are discouraged from *ever* disagreeing with Torah scholars of renown, and the presumption is that they could never be correct. Yet there is no scientific or rationalist reason why this should be so. The only justification would be if the Torah sage is presumed to possess greater supernatural input to his positions.

II: The Order of Nature

Introduction

Do the laws of nature function all (or virtually all) of the time, or are there frequently times when God (or man) overrides them? Is it preferable to perceive God as running the world via the laws of nature, or via supernatural acts? What exactly is a "miracle"?

Rationalists and mystics have radically opposed answers to these questions, and it is fundamental to their different outlooks. These differences are expressed in their differing attitudes to the creation of the universe, to Biblical events, to providence, medicine, alleged miracles, the value of work, and the Messianic Era.

Creation

Arguments often rage about the antiquity of the world and the universe, whether there was an age of dinosaurs, and the validity of an evolutionary explanation for the development of life. Allegedly, these are scientific debates, based upon disputing the merits of the scientific evidence. In fact, they stem from underlying different epistemologies and worldviews. One of these relates to the rationalist vs. mystic divide.

People who follow the mystical approach dispute the notion that the universe developed in any kind of naturalistic manner. They prefer to posit that everything came into existence via supernatural means, and thus everything in the universe directly attests to supernatural creation. Mystics object to the very endeavor of attempting to scientifically understand how any aspect of the universe developed, believing it to be something that is infinitely beyond rational human comprehension, aside perhaps via mystical sources of wisdom:

Kavod Elokim haster davar ("The glory of God is in the concealment of the matter")… There is that which is beyond our pare. That which is not for us to dwell into. And that's the *briyah*… It's not our assignment to know *briyas ha-olam*… It's a hidden area. (Rabbi Aharon Schechter, Presentation at Bnei Yeshurun in Teaneck on March 5th, 2006)

Mystics thus regard all scientific challenges to the literal reading of the creation account as being baseless, and all attempts to reconcile science with Genesis to be at best a fool's endeavor, and at worst a heretical perversion of Torah:

…[people such as Natan Slifkin] are trying to make our holy Torah compatible with the views of scientists that everything that occurs is the result of mechanical natural processes… to minimize the role of miracle and maximize the role of nature. This is entirely to minimize the acknowledgment of G-d's power and to move instead in the direction of heresy. (Rabbi Moshe Sternbuch, "Letter Regarding the Works of Natan Slifkin"[1])

The rationalist approach, on the other hand, maintains that the laws of nature that govern the universe are one of God's greatest creations. They also serve to illustrate the lawful nature of God. Accordingly, He works through natural law wherever possible:

…Judaism is most anxious to make its adherents aware that all the phenomena of nature are subject to certain unchanging laws. Since Judaism itself is a system of laws through and through, it attaches a profound ethical value to the study of the natural sciences. Judaism considers it vitally important for its adherents to become aware that their entire universe is governed by well-defined laws, that every creature on earth becomes what it is only within the framework of fixed laws, and that every force in nature can operate only within specified limits. Not by his whims of the moment but only by his own detailed knowledge of, and regard for, these laws can man make nature serve his purposes. Man himself, then, can exercise power only if he, in turn, obeys the laws set down for him and for his world. (Rabbi Samson Raphael Hirsch, "The Educational Value of Judaism," in *Collected Writings* vol. VII p. 263)

---

[1] Available online at www.zootorah.com/contoversy.

The very first moment of creation *ex nihilo* may have been an entirely supernatural act, that cannot be explained naturalistically. But after that moment, the subsequent development of the universe would presumably have followed some sort of process based on the laws of nature. Accordingly, it may be possible for mankind to discover and comprehend how the universe developed in a naturalistic way.

Following the above approach, when Rabbi Hirsch was faced with the publication of Darwin's *Origin of Species*, although he considered that this new theory was as yet "a vague hypothesis still unsupported by fact," he declared that it is by no means incompatible with Judaism:

> ...if this notion were ever to gain complete acceptance by the scientific world... Judaism in that case would call upon its adherents to give even greater reverence than ever before to the one, sole God Who, in His boundless creative wisdom and eternal omnipotence, needed to bring into existence no more than one single, amorphous nucleus, and one single law of "adaptation and heredity" in order to bring forth, from what seemed chaos but was in fact a very definite order, the infinite variety of species we know today, each with its unique characteristics that sets it apart from all other creatures. (Rabbi Hirsch, "The Educational Value of Judaism," *Collected Writings*, vol. VII, p. 264)

Rabbi Hirsch makes it clear that a naturalistic explanation is not something that stands in opposition to divine creation. On the contrary— in this case, it testifies all the more to the genius of the Creator, to His "creative wisdom."[2]

Miracles

The mystical view of miracles is by far the best-known today. In this view, miracles are acts which are supernatural in the most blatant sense. They are acts of God in which He overrides and breaks the laws of nature. They thereby demonstrate His ultimate power and attest to His glory.

Many people are surprised that there could be any other approach. And yet there is. The rationalist view is opposed to perceiving an event as

---

[2] For further discussion of the different approaches to reconciling science with Creation, see my book *The Challenge of Creation*.

representing a supernatural breaking of natural law. Rambam states this explicitly:

> …Our efforts, and the efforts of select individuals, are in contrast to the efforts of the masses. For with the masses who are people of the Torah, that which is beloved to them and tasty to their folly is that they should place Torah and rational thinking as two opposite extremes, and will derive everything impossible as distinct from that which is reasonable, and they say that it is a miracle, and they flee from something being in accordance with natural law, whether with something recounted from past events, with something that is in the present, or with something which is said to happen in the future. But we shall endeavor to integrate the Torah with rational thought, leading events according to the natural order wherever possible; only with something that is clarified to be a miracle and cannot be otherwise explained at all will we say that it is a miracle. (Rambam, *Treatise Concerning the Resurrection of the Dead*)

Ralbag (Gersonides) explains that the problem of miracles is that they indicate that God's system of natural laws is not good enough to accomplish what He wants to happen:

> When God wishes to perform miracles, He does so via causes that are the most appropriate according to natural laws…. This is because the natural order of existence was set by God in the most perfect way possible, and when necessity, due to providence, requires a change from this order, it is appropriate that God should divert from this as little as possible. Therefore God does not perform these miracles except via causes that divert very little from nature. (Ralbag, Commentary to Genesis, 6-9, *HaTo'elet HaShevi'i*)

According, miraculous events would be less prestigious displays of God's wisdom than nature itself. Interestingly, the same view is also found in the writings of the fourteenth century kabbalist Rabbeinu Bachya ben Asher:

> God does not force nature not to pursue its assigned tasks unless there is an overwhelming and urgent need for this. The reason that He does not destroy the system is simply that He Himself created it. Why should God uproot His own handiwork? (Rabbeinu Bachya, commentary to Exodus 17:13)

In this vein, Rabbi Joseph Soloveitchik notes that the Torah strongly downplays any supernatural aspect of miracles:

> What is a miracle in Judaism? The word "miracle" in Hebrew does not possess the connotation of the supernatural. It has never been placed on a transcendental level. "Miracle" (*pele, nes*) describes only an outstanding event which causes amazement. A turning point in history is always a miracle, for it commands attention as an event which intervened fatefully in the formation of that group or that individual. (Rabbi Joseph B. Soloveitchik, *The Emergence of Ethical Man*, p. 187)

Does the rationalist approach completely negate supernatural miracles, or just minimize them? The answer is that there is no such thing as "the" rationalist approach—there is a spectrum. The rationalist *tendency* is to minimize supernatural miracles—whether they are entirely minimized to the point of non-existence will depend on the rationalist. It should be noted that there is dispute regarding the extent of Rambam's minimization of supernatural miracles. He addressed this topic in several places in his writings, and it is very difficult to reconcile all his statements, leading some to believe that he changed his views on this matter.[3]

The Plagues of Egypt

The Ten Plagues provide an excellent example of the stark difference between the rationalist and mystical approaches. There are those who explain them in the most supernatural way possible, while others seek to explain them as unusual but naturalistic events. Indeed, some authorities note that the plagues of Egypt did not fully convince the Jewish People that Moses was a messenger of God, since they could have been attributed to either sorcery or natural causes.[4]

Let us consider the second plague, of frogs. Many contemporary illustrated haggadot depict a single giant frog, being struck by the Egyptians, which has further frogs showering from it. This is based upon

---

[3] For a thorough study, see the chapter in Part Two, "Rambam's Naturalizations of Miracles."

[4] See Rambam, *Yad HaChazakah, Hilchot Yesodei HaTorah* 8:1-2 as explained by Rashba, Responsa 4:234.

a very well-known Midrash cited by Rashi, which seeks to address why the Torah states that "the frog came up" in the singular (Ex. 8:2). The given explanation is that the plague began as a single frog, which then miraculously produced countless further frogs. Such is the mystical approach, which seeks to maximize the supernatural aspects of the plague.

Less well-known is Rashi's other explanation, presented as the *peshat* (straightforward meaning). In this, he states simply that "frog" is written in the singular because with a swarm, the noun is used as a collective noun. It is remarkable how many people only recall Rashi's non-*peshat* explanation!

Or consider the fourth plague, that of *arov*. It is commonly explained today to refer to a mix of wild animals. But which animals? Some popular illustrated Haggadot also depict giant octopuses using their tentacles to break into Egyptian houses and open them from the inside, and polar bears arriving on blocks of ice. These illustrations, based on Midrashic insights,[5] accord with the mystical approach, in which the plagues are as supernatural as possible. At the other end of the spectrum, one could explain that it was simply the local Egyptian wild animals, such as lions and wolves. And there are opinions in the Midrash that it was simply a mix of insects.[6]

The seventh plague, of hail, is generally presented as the ultimate example of a supernatural phenomenon, since it had two diametrically opposed elements: fire burning inside ice. This is widely believed to be the explicit and unambiguous description of the verse itself, which states that there was "fire flashing in the hail" (Ex. 9:24). However, if we recall that the account of the "frog" rising up was a collective noun, then the same may well be true of the hail. Accordingly, the description of "fire flashing in the hail" would refer not to fire flashing inside the individual hail*stones*, but rather to fire flashing inside the hail*storm*—and it refers to lightning.

At a more general level, Rabbi Soloveitchik observes that the account of the plagues is clearly not intended to be greatly supernatural:

---

[5] See *Sacred Monsters* by this author, Chapter Two: Mermaids, Krakens and Wild Men.

[6] *Midrash Shemot Rabba* 11:12.

As we read the story of the exodus from Egypt, we are impressed by the distinct tendency of the Bible to relate the events in natural terms. The frogs came out of the river when the Nile rose, the wind brought the locusts and split the sea. All archaeologists agree that the plagues as depicted by the Bible are very closely related to the geographical and climatic conditions that prevail in Egypt. Behind the passages in the Bible we may discern a distinct intention to describe the plagues as naturally as possible. The Bible never emphasizes the unnaturalness of the events; only its intensity and force are emphasized. The reason for that is obvious. A philosophy which considers the world-drama as a fixed, mechanical process governed by an unintelligent, indifferent principle, may regard the miracle as a supernatural transcendental phenomenon which does not fit into the causalistic, meaningless monotony. Israel, however, who looked upon the universal occurrence as the continuous realization of a divine ethical will embedded into dead and live matter, could never classify the miracle as something unique and incomprehensible. Both natural monotony and the surprising element in nature express God's word. Both are regular, lawful phenomena; both can be traced to an identical source. In the famous Psalm 104, *Barkhi nafshi* ("My soul will bless"), the psalmist describes the most elementary natural phenomena like the propagation of light in terms of wonder and astonishment—no different from Moses' Song of the Sea. The whole cosmos unfolds itself as a miraculous revelation of God. The demarcation line between revelation and nature is almost non-existent! (Rabbi Joseph B. Soloveitchik, *The Emergence of Ethical Man*, pp. 187-188)

Rabbi Soloveitchik concludes that the wonder of miracle is not in it departing from the natural order, but in it matching the natural order to the historical context:

In what, then, does the uniqueness of the miracle assert itself? In the correspondence of the natural and historical orders. The miracle does not destroy the objective scientific nexus in itself, it only combines natural dynamics and historical purposefulness. Had the plague of the firstborn, for instance, occurred a year before or after the exodus, it would not have been termed "with a strong hand" (*be-yad hazakah*). Why? God would have been instrumental in a natural children's plague. Yet God acts just as the world rule. On the night of Passover He appeared as the God of the cosmos acting along historical patterns. The intervention of nature in the historical process is a miracle. Whether God planned that history adjust itself to natural catastrophes or, vice versa, He commands nature to cooperate with the historical forces, is irrelevant. Miracle is simply a natural event which causes a historical metamorphosis. Whenever history is transfigured under the impact of cosmic dynamics, we encounter a miracle. (Ibid., p. 188)

Medicine

The Mishnah (Pesachim 4:9) states that there was a certain "Book of Remedies" which King Hezekiah hid, and the rabbis praised him for doing so. Why? Rashi says that people were using it to effectively cure disease, whereas the ideal approach is to turn to God for a supernatural cure. In line with this approach, Ramban says that in an ideal world, a righteous person would not go to the doctor if he became sick. Instead, he would engage in repentance, good deeds and prayer, which would supernaturally effect his cure.[7] Visiting doctors is a concession to the low spiritual state in which we find ourselves.

Rambam, on the other hand, vehemently opposes this approach.[8] He says that the problem with the "Book of Remedies" was that it contained cures that were based on astrology, and were thus false and potentially harmful; in addition, it contained information about toxicology that could be advantageous to planning murders. Had it simply been a book of effective medicine, there would have been no reason to conceal it. The notion that one would do so in order to make sure that people are turning to God rather than science is "misguided and foolish," he says, and if one were to take that line of thought to its logical conclusion, it would mean that it would be better to turn to God to satisfy one's hunger, rather than to eat food!

Here we see how the mystical approach is that the ideal is to turn to God to cure sickness through supernatural means, whereas the rationalist

---

[7] Ramban, commentary on Leviticus 26:11.

[8] Rambam, *Commentary on the Mishnah, Pesachim* 4:10.

approach is that turning to physicians and medicine is the only legitimate approach.[9]

Providence

The rationalist approach of perceiving God as ideally working through nature does raise a fundamental question. What does this mean in terms of daily providence—God's adjusting each person's circumstances, either as reward or retribution for their deeds, or to present them with the requisite spiritual challenges? Surely that means constant supernatural involvement?

Interestingly, in contemporary times, this may not be a difficulty. Modern physics may provide ways in which God can effect providence without overriding the laws of nature.[10] But how did the rationalist scholars of the medieval period approach this topic?

The answer is that among the Torah scholars of the tenth to fifteenth centuries we find prominently the view that Divine providence is of very limited application. Despite the very common belief that normative Judaism mandates acknowledging that "there's no such thing as coincidence" and "it's all *bashert* (divinely ordained for one's own maximal growth)," such concepts are of relatively recent propagation and have only minor support in classical Jewish philosophy.

Rambam's view was subject to considerable dispute as to its true nature, and this was one of the topics of the fiery Maimonidean controversies of the thirteenth century.[11] Certainly Rambam greatly limits providence, to only functioning with people that maintain a certain intellectual relationship with God. But according to the more extreme

---

[9] For further discussion, see Daniel Sinclair, "Maimonides' Rational and Empirical Epistemology and its Influence on Bio-Medical Halakhah," in K. E. Collins, *Moses Maimonides and his Practice of Medicine* (Haifa 2013) pp. 135-151.

[10] See my book *The Challenge Of Creation*, chapter four.

[11] *Guide For The Perplexed* 3:17-18,22-23,51. For extensive discussion, see Dov Schwartz, "The Debate over the Maimonidean Theory of Providence in Thirteenth-Century Jewish Philosophy." See too the essay by Menachem Kellner on "Maimonides on Reward and Punishment" printed as an appendix to his book *Must a Jew Believe Anything?*

rationalist interpreters of Rambam, such as Shmuel Ibn Tibbon, Rambam was of the view that providence does not refer to God changing a person's circumstances at all. Instead, it refers to a person focusing his thoughts on spiritual (which means intellectual) matters, so that the misfortunes of the world simply do not concern him.

Even Ramban (Nachmanides), although popularly thought to maintain a view that miraculous providence is all-encompassing, is actually of a very different view. His opinion is that the continuous miraculous providence which functions at a national level is only when the nation is of a high spiritual caliber. And barring the absolutely righteous and the absolutely wicked, most people's lives follow natural law, except with regard to reward and punishment which take place via hidden miracles.[12] Rabbi Ovadiah Seforno explicitly states that the majority of the Jewish People are governed by natural law and do not enjoy specific divine providence.[13]

It was primarily due to the advent of Hassidism that an apparently different view developed, first propounded by Rabbi Yisrael Baal Shem Tov (1698-1760) and subsequently elaborated upon by the Habad movement.[14] This view stated that specific divine providence applies to all beings—even animals. It has been suggested that the propagation of this view may have been a reaction against the acceptance in the general culture of the deterministic scientific view.[15] But today it is probably due to the

---

[12] See Ramban to Genesis 17:1, 46:15, Exodus 6:2, Leviticus 26:11, Job 36:7, and the important essay by Rabbi Dr. David Berger, "Miracles and the Natural Order in Nahmanides." A different view is found in Rabbeinu Bachya, in his introduction to Exodus 30:12. Rabbi Chaim Friedlander, in *Sifsei Chaim, Emunah VeHashgachah* vol. 1, interprets Ramban in line with the current mainstream outlook on divine providence, but his explanation appears somewhat forced.

[13] Seforno, Commentary to Leviticus 13:47. See too *Sefer haIkkarim* 4:10 and Chafetz Chaim, in *Shem Olam, Nefutzas Yisrael* 8.

[14] See too Rabbi Tzaddok HaCohen, *Sefer HaZichronos* 3, *Yichud Hashem*.

[15] See Chofetz Chaim, *Shem Olam* 1:3 and 1:24.

emotional comfort provided by universal providence ("there was a reason why I missed the train!") that it has become so widely accepted.[16]

Sages, Rebbes and Miracle Workers

- *Expanded upon in Part Two, "The Sages' Powers of Life and Death"*

The Talmud contains numerous accounts of the sages performing wonders, to the extent of being able to resurrect the dead. Many continue to ascribe such powers to the great rabbis of later history. For adherents of the mystical worldview, such stories provide proof of the reality of this approach:

> ...If the Gemara tells us a *metziyus* (a statement about physical reality), it's *emes veyatziv*. There's nothing to think about. Anything we see with our eyes is less of a reality than something we see in the Gemara. That's the *emunah* that a *yid* has to have... *Chazal HaKedoshim—hakatan shebetalmidei Rabbeinu haKadosh mechayeh meisim* (With the holy sages, the least of Rabbi Yehudah's disciples were able to resurrect the dead)! If the Gaon says that he could bring down *kol galgal hachamah* on this table and show it to Aristo[17]—do we have a doubt that what *Chazal HaKedoshim* said is *emes*? *Ra'u mi'sof ha-olam ve'ad sofo* (they saw from one end of the world to the other)—*ain leharher achar divrei haGemara* (one may not doubt the words of the Gemara). (Rabbi Uren Reich, extract from address at Agudath Israel of America's 82nd National Convention)

Of course, there is no way that Rambam and other rationalists accepted such Talmudic accounts at face value. Considering how Rambam and others would naturalize even seemingly supernatural stories in Scripture, there is no doubt that they would do the same with the Talmud. Miracle stories in the Talmud were variously either allegorized, described as exaggerations, or would simply be dismissed, following the Geonic principle that aggadata is not binding dogma and its authority can be

---

[16] In non-Hassidic circles, one can still find expression of the traditional view limiting providence to select individuals. See *Michtav Me-Eliyahu* vol. II p. 75.

[17] The reference is to R. Menachem Mendel of Shklov, Introduction to the Commentary of the Gra on Avot. R. Menachem Mendel writes that the Gra once mentioned that Aristotle was a heretic, and added that if Aristotle was present, he would recite a Divine Name and cause the heavenly spheres to shine on the table and disprove Aristotle's views.

rejected if it conflicts with reason. Even a more recent and less rationalist authority such as Rabbi Hirsch acknowledges the legitimacy of this approach:

> I tend to think it not at all farfetched that even in Talmudic times, the Holy One performed miracles—in special circumstances—for the greatest and most pious of Chazal... But if one of our contemporary rabbinical scholars should say to me, "Brother, I believe wholeheartedly like you that the Holy One has the power and the ability to change nature at His will... But my feeling is that the Holy One changes nature only for some great need or to publicize some lofty matter, for the order of nature is His will, which was ordained and is maintained by Him. So if I know for sure that Chazal intended the miracle stories related in their aggados to be taken literally, God forbid that I should doubt their veracity, and I would believe as you do that these incidents really took place. But I wonder: Are we to understand these stories as having really taken place or are they analogies or parables? I personally tend to accept the opinion of those who say that aggadic miracle stories are not to be taken literally," —may I push this person away? May I grow angry at him? May I consider myself a greater believer than he? Both of us are equally firmly rooted in the principles of Jewish faith. (Letter to R. Hile Wechsler, published by Mordechai Breuer in *HaMa'ayan* 16:2 (Tevet 5736/1976) p. 7)

In contemporary times, the rationalist and mystical approaches continue this difference of opinion not only with regard to great figures of history, but also with regard to rabbis and rebbes of today. For those of a mystical inclination, the greatness of contemporary figures is revealed by stories of their performing superhuman feats of divination and other such miracles. Those of a rationalist inclination, on the other hand, are skeptical of such stories, and prefer to see the greatness of people in their humanity rather than their alleged superhumanity.

The Messianic Era

- *Expanded upon in Part Two, "Messianic Wonders and Skeptical Rationalists"*

The dispute between rationalists and mystics regarding whether it is preferable to view God as operating via nature or the supernatural also finds expression with regard to the future—specifically, to the Messianic Era. The Prophets describe the Messianic Era in wondrous terms:

> The wolf shall live with the lamb, and the leopard shall lie down with the kid; and the calf and the young lion and the fatling together; and a small child shall lead them. And the cow and the bear shall graze; their young ones shall lie down together; and the lion shall eat straw like the ox. (Isaiah 11:6-7)

Yet there is a dispute in rabbinic tradition regarding the interpretation of these prophesies. Some explain them literally, to mean that predatory animals will actually change their nature and become herbivorous.[18] This is in line with the mystical approach, which is happy to believe in God completely negating the natural order.

Rambam and others, however, interpret these prophecies metaphorically.[19] Instead of referring to actual animals, these verses refer to wicked people and nations that are symbolized by these animals. Such people will no longer pose a threat, and will live in peace with us.

Another example is with regard to Talmudic teachings regarding the order of nature in the Messianic Era. As discussed above, the Sages speak about how in the Messianic Era, Jerusalem will be rebuilt with enormous gemstones, and fine garments and bread will grow from the ground. For mystics, this reflects the entirely supernatural conduct of the Messianic Era. For rationalists, on the other hand, such teachings of the Sages are most certainly not intended literally.

The Decline of Generations

The popular notion of *yeridat hadorot*, the "decline of generations," is that as one goes back further in history, people were greater spiritually, intellectually, and even physically. Every moment of their lives was lived

---

[18] Metzudos and Malbim to Isaiah 11:7; Abarbanel to Hosea 2:18.

[19] Rambam, *Mishneh Torah, Hilchot Melachim* 12:1; Ibn Ezra to Isaiah 11:6. Radak to Isaiah 11:6-7 suggests that, as well as the allegorical meaning, it is also referring to actual animals, but it is only stating that the animals in the Land of Israel will not kill, and will satisfy themselves with animals that have died naturally; outside of Israel, however, they will kill as usual.

with a dedication to holiness that we cannot begin to emulate. Their intellectual grasp of Torah was on a level that the greatest genius of today cannot begin to fathom, and thus it is ridiculous to argue with authorities of previous eras. And they were also physically superior in all kinds of ways.

The concept of *yeridat hadorot* is often assumed today to be axiomatic and fundamental to Judaism, and supported by the full gamut of classical sources. In fact, the Talmud is ambivalent; there are a number of sources which indicate that certain earlier generations were superior, but there are also a number of sources which state that certain later generations were equal or even superior.[20]

Yeridat hadorot is relevant to the rationalist/mystic divide in several ways. One is that the medieval rationalist approach of Rambam maintained there to be a basically constant order of nature over history. This which would preclude the notion of humans dramatically changing.

In fact, this is a way in which modern rationalism would differ from medieval rationalism. Rambam's view of an unchanging world, in which species never change or even become extinct, is now known to be mistaken.[21] Yet the fact that Rambam had this belief meant that his view of *yeridat hadorot* was not that it meant a decline in man's intellectual or physical capacity. As we shall see, Rambam had a radically different understanding of the concept of *yeridat hadorot* than the popular view today.[22]

Rationalism further mandates that claims require evidence proportionate to the degree that they are far-fetched. And modern science has

---

[20] *Sukkah* 28b states that Hillel had thirty disciples who were worthy to have the Divine Presence rest upon them as on Moshe Rabbeinu. *Sanhedrin* 21b-22a states that Ezra was great enough to receive the Torah, and the only reason that he didn't was that Moshe had already received it. *Menachot* 29b states that Moshe was given a look at Rabbi Akiva's class and could not follow it. Various other passages are cited by Menachem Kellner, *Maimonides on the "Decline of the Generations" and the Nature of Rabbinic Authority.*

[21] See the chapter on extinction in my book *The Challenge Of Creation*, fourth edition.

[22] For extensive discussion, see Menachem Kellner, *Maimonides on the "Decline of the Generations" and the Nature of Rabbinic Authority.*

rejected the notion that humans in the past were larger, longer-lived, or more intelligent. Until a few centuries ago, all mankind believed that the ancients were more intelligent than us. That's why it was virtually unthinkable to dispute Aristotle. Today, outside of traditionalists, people do not accept that the ancients were more intelligent than us. There is no evidence for it, a lot of evidence against it, and understandable reasons as to why people used to believe it to be the case.

For mystics, on the other hand, there is always the desire to believe in the most supernatural of miracles. Since not too many of these happen today with people like us, they can at least believe that they happened in antiquity, with people who were very different.

The non-rationalist view of *yeridat hadorot* includes a belief that the ancients were physically superior—they were stronger, taller (in the case of the Levites, fifteen feet,[23] and in the case of Biblical giants, hundreds of feet[24]) and longer-lived (as per the Biblical account of various figures).

As an example of this belief, consider R. Yechezkel Landau, author of responsa *Noda B'Yehudah*. He was faced with a discrepancy between the ratio of thumb size to egg size given in the Talmud, and that of his era. There were two possible conclusions: either people's thumbs have become larger, or eggs have become smaller. R. Landau determined that it must have been the latter:

> And it is known that the generations progressively decline, and it is therefore impossible that our thumbs should be larger than the thumbs in the day of the Sages of the Mishnah. (*Tzlach, Pesachim* 120a)

When it comes to matters of the intellect, Maharal of Prague writes that with earlier generations, the intellectual faculty was dominant and enabled people to possess greater understanding, unlike later generations, which have a minimal level of understanding and can never really understand the words of their predecessors.[25] Ramchal writes that the most learned of his generation is no greater than the most insignificant

---

[23] Talmud, Shabbat 92a. See Rabbi Moshe Feinstein, *Iggros Moshe, Yoreh De'ah* 3:66,

[24] See the chapter on giants in *Sacred Monsters* by this author.

[25] Maharal, *Be'er HaGolah*, introduction.

disciple of previous generations.[26] The assumed decline was given as the reason why the Sages of the Talmud did not argue with the Sages of the Mishnah, and why the Rishonim (the medieval rabbinic scholars) did not argue with the Sages of the Talmud, and why the Acharonim did not argue with the Rishonim.[27] The later the generation, the less intelligent and understanding. Even when there gradually grew an awareness that later figures could attain certain valuable insights that earlier generations lacked, this was only delicately granted in a limited sense, by way of the metaphor of "dwarfs standing on the shoulders of giants."[28]

Rambam, on the other hand, did not accept that past generations were superior physically, spiritually or mentally. In contrast to Rashi who explained that Og was hundreds of feet tall, Rambam explained that he was around eight feet tall.[29] In contrast to those who understood that the early generations of man all lived vast lifespans, Rambam took the position that this was an exceptional occurrence for select individuals, perhaps because of some specific nutrition, or perhaps due to a miracle.[30] Other Rishonim presented different explanations of the lifespans: R. Nissim of Marseilles explained that it refers to the way of life instituted by that person,[31] R. Moshe ibn Tibbon explained it to refer to the dynasty, and R. Eliezer Ashkenazi stated that the long lifespans recorded in Scripture are either non-literal figures of speech, or simply a record of popular beliefs. For all these authorities, the idea that there was a broad decline in the physical nature of the human body was inconceivable.

When it comes to intellectual and spiritual matters, Rambam likewise did not see there as being any decline. To be sure, the Mishnah and Talmud possess a special status. But this does not relate to their authors

---

[26] Ramchal, *Mesilat Yesharim* 22.

[27] Chazon Ish, *Letters* 2:24.

[28] See Avraham Melamed's *Al Kitfei Anakim* and the writings of Israel Ta-Shma for further discussion of this.

[29] Rambam, *Guide for the Perplexed* 2:47.

[30] Ibid.

[31] *Ma'aseh Nissim*, p. 274.

being superior types of human beings or anything like that. Rather, it relates to a particular combination of circumstances:

> Ravina and Rav Ashi and their colleagues were the last of the great sages who firmly established the Oral Torah, made decrees, and ordinances and introduced customs. Their decrees, ordinances, and customs obtained universal acceptance among Jews wherever they settled. After the court of Rav Ashi, who compiled the Gemara which was finally completed in the days of his son, an extraordinarily great dispersion of Israel throughout the world took place. The people emigrated to remote parts and distant isles. The prevalence of wars and the march of armies made travel insecure. The study of the Torah declined...
>
> In our days, severe vicissitudes prevail, and all feel the pressure of hard times. The wisdom of our wise men has disappeared, the understanding of our prudent men is hidden. Hence the commentaries of the Geonim and their compilations of laws and responses, which they took care to make clear, have in our times become hard to understand so that only a few individuals properly comprehend them. Needless to add that such is the case in regard to the Talmud itself... (Introduction to the *Mishneh Torah*)

According to Rambam, the decline of generations is circumstantial. The sages of the Talmud had the advantage of relatively comfortable circumstances in which they could flourish. Furthermore, they were geographically concentrated, which enabled their scholarship to be both concentrated and universally binding.

With this in mind, we can understand why Rambam rules that when a Beit Din uses the tools of Scriptural interpretation to produce a ruling, a later Beit Din can dispute and overturn this.[32] Rabbi Yosef Karo explains that Rambam's source for this is the fact that in the Talmud itself, we frequently see the Sages of later generations disputing the conclusions of earlier generations. But, asks Rabbi Karo, if so, then why do the intergenerational disputes between sages only occur within distinct eras? Why do the Sages of the Talmud not dispute the Sages of the Mishnah, and why do later generations not dispute the decisions reached in the

---

[32] Rambam, *Mishneh Torah, Hilchot Mamrim* 2:1.

Talmud? He answers that the Sages of the Talmud accepted the authority of the Sages of the Mishnah, and the later generations accepted the rulings of the Talmud.[33]

Chazon Ish is of the opinion that such acceptances are due to an acknowledgment that the earlier generations were more likely to be correct, due to their being wiser or closer to Sinai.[34] But Rabbi Shlomo Fisher, dean of the Itri Yeshivah in Jerusalem, argues that this does not appear correct.[35] Since within each period, later generations were confident to dispute earlier ones, why would there have been a sudden drop in the intellectual level immediately at the end of each period? Furthermore, later generations have reason to be confident that they are more likely to be correct than earlier generations, since they have all the halachic discussions of the earlier generations available to them as a starting point for their analysis.

Rabbi Fisher thus concludes that when later Torah scholars do not dispute the rulings established by earlier authorities, this does not at all mean that they acknowledge that the earlier authorities are correct. Instead, it is simply a matter that the Jewish People has gradually collectively decided to accord final authority to the sages of earlier eras, even when there is reason to believe that they are mistaken.[36]

We can understand this in light of Rambam's aforementioned statements. The historically unique circumstances of the Talmud, which

---

[33] Rabbi Yosef Karo, *Kesef Mishneh, Hilchot Mamrim* 2:1.

[34] Chazon Ish, *Letters* 2:24. Chazon Ish seems to claim that this is Rabbi Karo's position. Yet if that was the case, one would expect Rabbi Karo to have made some sort of statement to that effect. It appears more likely that Rabbi Karo is simply following Rambam's position in his introduction to *Mishneh Torah*, which grants authority to the Sages based on historical circumstances. Furthermore, claiming that latter Sages did not dispute earlier ones due to an acknowledgment of the superiority of the earlier generations is a difficult interpretation of Rambam, whose position is that even when an earlier Beit Din is superior in wisdom, a latter Beit Din can overrule it.

[35] Rabbi Shlomo Fisher, *Derashot Beit Yishai* 15.

[36] Chacham David Nieto, in *Matteh Dan*, acknowledges that this was R. Karo's understanding, though he personally disagrees. See Michael Berger, *Rabbinic Authority*, for a lengthy and invaluable discussion of this topic.

collected the rulings of the last centralized body of rabbinic scholars, resulted in it possessing canonical status. It has nothing to do with any intrinsic greater intellectual capacity of earlier generations, and according to Rambam there is no reason to believe that any such greater capacity existed.

Cause-and-Effect, and the Value of Endeavor

Related to the mystical preference for the supernatural is that according to the mystical approach, even those phenomena which appear to be following the natural order of cause-and-effect are in fact doing no such thing.

The standard approach taught in many yeshivot today[37] is that there is absolutely no correlation, zero cause-and-effect, between *hishtadlut*

---

[37] Rabbi Dr. Menachem-Martin Gordon attributes much of the recent decline in the rationalist approach to Rabbi Eliyahu Dessler. He describes Rav Dessler's anti-science position as follows: "Rav Dessler's book, *Mikhtav me-Eliyahu*, whose impact on the yeshiva world in recent years has been *enormous*, represents a radical departure from the Talmudic position (*Hullin* 105a, *Niddah* 70b), as well as the medieval philosophic tradition (Rambam, *Moreh Nevuchim*, 3:17), in its denial of the reality of natural law and the cause—and—effect nexus of human initiative (*Mikhtav*, I, pp. 177-206). For Rav Dessler, the study of the sciences—even medicine, for that matter—is pointless, since the exclusive determinate of human welfare is the providential hand of God responding to religious virtue. Similarly, serious financial initiative is unnecessary. The diagnostic skill of the physician (*Mikhtav*, III, p. 172), the financier's business acumen (*Mikhtav*, I, p. 188), ostensibly critical factors in the effectiveness of their efforts, are only illusory causes, argues Rav Dessler. Admittedly, he concedes, one must "go through the motions" of practical activity (the notion of *hishtadlut*, *Mikhtav*, I, pp. 187-88)—visiting a physician, making a phone call for financial support—but such is necessary only as a "cover" for the direct Divine conduct of human affairs, which men of faith are challenged to discern. Recognizing the immediacy of the Divine hand behind the facade of human initiative is the ultimate test of faith. One should be engaged in practical effort only for the purpose, paradoxically, of discovering its pointlessness! Therefore, asserts Rav Dessler, to the degree that a man has already proved his spiritual mettle, his acknowledgment of Divine control, could the extensiveness of his "cover" be reduced. Or, alternatively, to the degree that a man is not yet sufficiently spiritually perceptive— wherefore pragmatic initiative might "blind" him to Divine control—should he limit such recourse. Accordingly, *b'nei yeshiva* are implicitly discouraged from any serious financial initiative—or involvement across the board in any area of resourceful effort, be

(worldly endeavor) and *parnasah* (income). Rather, the *hishtadlut* is simply a fine imposed on those who are far from spirituality, and has no bearing on the actual sustenance received.[38] A corollary of this is that to the extent to which a person is on a higher spiritual level, he has less need to engage in the sham of material endeavor.

(It might appear that this is simply a reflection of Chazal's statements about a person's sustenance being decreed on Rosh Hashanah.[39] But such statements simply express the tension between God's foreknowledge and man's free will. They do not mean that physical endeavor is of no consequence.)

A Scriptural verse often cited in support of this approach is Moshe Rabbeinu's condemnation of those who say that "my strength and the power of my hand made me this great wealth" (Deut. 8:18). It is argued that this shows that wealth comes from God, and has nothing to do with personal effort. However, the very next verse states that "You shall remember God your Lord—that it was He who gave you strength to make wealth." Moshe does not deny that personal effort is involved—rather, he urges the nation to remember that God is the ultimate source of all our strength.

---

it technological, political, etc.—since the circumstances of life are, in reality, a spontaneous Divine miracle. (Note Rav Dessler's necessarily strained interpretation of *Hullin*, ad loc. and *Niddah*, ad loc., where one is advised by Hazal to survey one's property with regularity, and to "abound in business." in the pursuit of wealth! — *Mikhtav*, I, pp. 200-01)... For Rav Dessler, the "natural agency" of medical treatment (III, p. 172), which, admittedly, those of low—faith level must necessarily pursue, is not an effect of natural law as Ramban recognizes it, but, once again, a deceptive expression at every moment of the spontaneous Divine will (see his own reference [ad loc., p. 173] to his basic definition of "nature" in I, pp. 177-206)." (*Modern Orthodox Judaism* p. 31). See too David Shatz, "Practical Endeavor and the Torah u-Madda Debate," *The Torah U-Madda Journal* Vol. 3 (1991-1992), pp. 98-149, especially endnotes 85 and 87.

[38] This would appear to raise the question of why there is a general correlation between working in professional careers and receiving a higher income.

[39] *Mesilat Yesharim*, Chapter 21, towards the end: "But this does not imply that one's effort leads to results. Rather, the effort is a prerequisite. Once one makes the effort his obligation is fulfilled and it becomes possible for the Heavenly blessings to rest upon him."

The culmination of the non-rationalist approach is the complete negation of all material endeavor. This is reflected in the declaration of Rabbi Chaim Kanievsky, as cited by Rabbi Nachum Eisenstein, that one should not talk about the question of how people in Kollel support their families, since it is a miracle which can only function when it is kept secret.[40]

The rise of the non-rationalist approach with regard to the innate worthlessness of material endeavor is not only relevant with regard to working for a living. It also has ramifications for one's attitude towards military defense of Israel. The non-rationalist approach is reflected in the declaration of Shas leader Rabbi Shalom Cohen that Israel does not need an army, since it is protected by prayer.[41] This is in sharp contrast to Rambam's position that it was the neglect of proper military efforts which led to the destruction of the Beit HaMikdash:

> This is what led to the loss of our kingdom, the destruction of our Sanctuary, and extended the duration [of our exile] to the present day: our forefathers sinned and are no longer, in that they found many books concerning these matters of those who gaze at the stars—these things being the essence of idolatry, as we explained in "Laws of Idolatry"—they erred and were attracted to them, thinking that they were splendid sciences, having great utility and thus neglected the study of war and conquest, thinking rather that those [sciences] would be of use to them; for this reason did the prophets call them ignoramuses and fools. (Rambam, *Letter to the Rabbis of Marseilles*)

Thus, the difference between rationalist and mystical approaches to the role of nature are not only theoretical, but can also have significant social ramifications.

---

[40]   http://podcast.headlinesbook.com/e/6317-halachos-of-parnassah-and-the-tuition-crisis/.

[41]   https://www.jpost.com/Operation-Protective-Edge/Shas-leader-Israel-doesnt-need-army-since-ultra-Orthodox-prayers-protect-it-368728.

III: Supernatural Entities

Introduction

Related to the difference between rationalists and mystics with regard to the natural order is their different views regarding metaphysical entities.

Rationalists minimize the number of supernatural entities and forces, seeing them as threatening monotheism. They believe in God, and depending on where on the rationalist spectrum they fall, they may believe in a small number of other supernatural entities or none at all. Discussions of apparent supernatural entities in classical literature are reinterpreted or rejected. And commandments which seem to relate to metaphysical properties of things are explained instead to refer to their historical context or to our designation of them.

Mystics tend to maximize the number of supernatural entities and forces. They can be either forces of holiness, or forces of evil. These include all kinds of angels and demons, *sefirot* (emanations), *olamot* (worlds), and an infinite number of other metaphysical entities. According to this view, many *mitzvot* relate to the metaphysical properties of various things, which are seen as hypostasized entities.

Magic

Perhaps one of the most notable distinctions between the rationalist and mystical approaches is with regard to magic. There are several instances where the Torah prohibits magic and other forms of sorcery. Rambam is well-known for explicitly stating that the basis of this prohibition is that magic is nonsense, with no validity at all. After discussing the prohibitions against sorcery, divination and suchlike, he concludes by stating the following:

All the above matters are falsehood and lies with which the original idolaters deceived the gentile nations in order to lead them after them. It is not fitting for the Jews who are wise sages to be drawn into such emptiness, nor to consider that they have any value as [implied by Num. 23:23]: "No black magic can be found among Jacob, or occult arts within Israel." Similarly, [Deut. 18:14] states: "These nations which you are driving out listen to astrologers and diviners. This is not [what God... has granted] you." Whoever believes in [occult arts] of this nature and, in his heart, thinks that they are true and words of wisdom, but are forbidden by the Torah, is foolish and feebleminded." (*Mishneh Torah, Hilchot Avodah Zarah* 11:16)

Ramban, on the other hand, explains that the prohibitions against sorcery and divination are due to the fact that these are genuinely efficacious procedures which subvert God's preferred system for running the universe.[1]

However, it is not so simple to divide Rambam and Ramban into the rationalist and mystical camps on this point. Ramban justified his belief in the reality of magic at least partially on the grounds of extensive eyewitness testimony. In the medieval period, when many natural phenomena were less well understood, as were tricks of sleight-of-hand and suchlike, there appeared to be rational grounds for accepting the reality of magic. So whereas a person today who believes in magic would be clearly classified as non-rationalist, the same cannot be necessarily be said for Ramban.

Ramban's disciple, R. Shlomo b. Aderet (Rashba) disagreed strongly with Rambam's across-the-board dismissal of all magic and similar phenomena as being nonsense.[2] Rashba points out that the Talmud is full of accounts of such things, which (unlike Rambam) he takes authoritatively, and he stresses that this is even though there is no rational explanation for them. But he does not only invoke the authority of the Sages for this. Rashba argues that it is impossible to claim that only phenomena for there is a rational explanation are real. His reason is that

---

[1] Ramban, Commentary to Deut. 18:9.

[2] Rashba Responsa 1:413.

there are phenomena that undeniably exist, and yet for which there can be no scientific explanation. The example that he brings is the magnet, and its use in a compass. Rashba notes that "the wisest of scholars in the sciences can never grasp the nature" of such things. He describes magnetism as a being part of a class of phenomena called *teva ha-mesugal*, which is intermediate between the fully natural and the utterly supernatural (acts of God).[3]

Now, as we shall discuss in the chapter on demons, one cannot simply assert that those who believed in demons, magic and suchlike were not rationalists. Given the state of knowledge of the world in the medieval period, some people believed in such things for rational reasons. Nevertheless, there is still a gulf separating the rationalist Rishonim of Spain from the mystical Rishonim and from the non-rationalist Rishonim in Ashkenaz.

Superficially, Rashba's discussion appears not too far removed from that of Ralbag. Ralbag was an extreme rationalist, yet he likewise asserts that magnets can only be explained in terms of being a *segulah*. However, the term *segulah* as used by Ralbag (and Rashba) has been borrowed from pharmacology, where it refers to peculiar properties which cannot be explained in terms of its constituent elements.[4] In applying it to magnets, Ralbag is claiming that the nature of the magnet cannot be grasped by the science of his day; but he is not explaining it as a supernatural phenomenon, and he did not see it as reason to accept the validity of magic.

For Rashba, on the other hand, there is no distinction between that which science cannot currently explain, and that which it will *never* explain. Rashba's point is not that there are "empirically tested phenomena work through the principles of science despite the fact that we do not understand these principles." On the contrary; his view is that

---

[3] See *Rashba's Ma'amar al Yishmael shechibber ha-Datot*, in *R. Salomo b. Abraham b. Adereth: Sein Leben und seine Schriften* (Schletter, 1863), p. 11 in the Hebrew section, and the discussion by David Horwitz, "Rashba's Attitude to Science and its Limits," *The Torah u-Madda Journal* vol. 3 (1991-92) pp. 59-60 and 76-77.

[4] See Y. Tzvi Langermann, "Gersonides on the Magnet and the Heat of the Sun," in *Studies on Gersonides*, ed. Gad Freudenthal (Leiden: E.J. Brill, 1992), pp. 267-284.

there are principles *other than* laws of science and nature that operate. Unlike Rambam, who realized that magnets are a solely naturalistic phenomenon, Rashba believed that magnets operate in a different realm—that of *segulah*. According to Rashba, the framework within which *segulot* work is precisely *not* the framework of science and nature. He therefore sees magnets as reason to accept belief in magic and all such phenomena. The lack of any conceivable scientific explanation for a phenomenon is no reason *whatsoever* to doubt its existence.

Now, it is true that even today, we don't really understand what magnetism, or gravity for that matter, actually is. We can measure and describe how it works, but we still don't know what it fundamentally *is*. Nevertheless, we are fully confident that it is a natural, rather than supernatural, phenomenon. Rambam and even Ralbag felt the same way, which is why their inability to comprehend magnetism or other phenomena did not prevent them from dismissing other phenomena as clearly false. Rashba, on the other hand, did not believe that we can ever dismiss phenomena as scientifically impossible and false—and saw magnets as evidence for this. This is the difference between Rambam/Ralbag on the rationalist side, and Rashba on the non-rationalist side.

Still, it is significant to note that contemporary polemicists against the rationalist approach, who sometimes state emphatically that Torah Judaism follows the approach of Rashba in such things, do not cite his proof from magnets!

Demons and Evil Spirits

- *Expanded upon in Part Two, "Wrestling with Demons"*

Related to the topic of magic are the notions of demons and *ru'ach ra'ah* ("evil spirits"). The Talmud has a wide range of statements about demons and other malevolent entities. Demons were described as invisible winged creatures that eat, reproduce, and die, and which exist in untold numbers. They were believed to haunt various places and occasionally to speak to people.

The majority of rabbinic scholars over the centuries accepted the existence of demons. This was partly due to demons forming a clear part of the Talmudic worldview, but also because there was no reason *not* to believe in their existence. In the absence of a scientific explanation as to why things happen in the world, it was reasonable to presume that there were invisible beings that cause things to happen.

Still, there were several prominent rationalist rabbinic scholars who rejected the existence of demons, notwithstanding the prestigious Talmudic support for them. Rambam is the most prominent of these, but there were also several other rationalist rabbinic scholars who either explicitly or implicitly denied the existence of demons.

Demonology does, however, seem to differ from many other topics of the rationalist/mystic divide. With the other topics, the mystical view has been steadily become more pervasive over history. With demons, on the other hand, while many Jews today *profess* to believe in the existence of demons, very few *actually* believe in them.

A similar situation exists with *ruach ra'ah*—"evil spirits." During an extensive discussion about various ailments and their cures and prevention, the Talmud refers to an evil spirit that refuses to depart until one washes one's hands three times.[5] Elsewhere, the Talmud says that eating peeled onions or and garlic or shelled eggs that were left overnight is lethally dangerous, due to the "evil spirit" that rests upon them.

Such beliefs probably reflect a combination of natural and supernatural concerns; in antiquity, where there was little framework for explaining phenomena, people often did not perceive a difference between physical ailments and demonic harm. Rambam, consistent with his rationalist outlook, did not accept the existence of such "evil spirits." But even many non-rationalists were aware that no such dangers appeared to exist. Reluctant to say that the Sages were mistaken, Tosafot instead stated that such evil spirits were no longer to be found.

Today, some non-rationalists will adopt Tosafot's approach and say that the *ruach ra'ah* was a real phenomenon that no longer exists. Others will attempt to reinterpret the Talmud as accurately referring to a scientifically-validated phenomenon. Still others will claim that the

---

[5] *Shabbat* 109b.

Talmud is referring to a supernatural rather than natural phenomenon, though whether this includes measurable effects in the physical world is not usually made clear. The goal is to maintain a professed belief in the inerrancy of the Talmud—but in reality, what has happened is that people have accepted a broad naturalistic view of the universe, and do not believe that evil spirits exist.

Angels

The mystical view of angels is one with which everyone is familiar. They are supernatural sentient beings, possessing intelligence and different personalities. They can manifest in this world in human form, and interact with people in humanlike ways.

Rambam had a very different view. He refused to accept that there could be any angel that has corporeal form. Wherever there are Scriptural references to angels as humanoid characters, these are to be interpreted as visions perceived in a dream or a state of prophetic inspiration.

> …The appearance or speech of an angel mentioned in Scripture took place in a vision or dream…. it is very difficult for people to apprehend, except after strenuous training, that which is absolutely devoid of physicality… Because of the difficulty of this matter, the books of the prophets contain statements whose external sense can be understood as signifying that angels are corporeal, that they move, that they have human form, that they are given orders by God and that they carry out God's orders… (Rambam, *Guide for the Perplexed*, 1:41,49)

Other references to angels in Scripture were understood by Rambam in the framework of Greco-Muslim philosophy. He explained them to refer to that which Aristotle described as "intelligences":

> We have already stated above that the angels are incorporeal. This agrees with the opinion of Aristotle: there is only this difference in the names employed—he uses the term "Intelligences," and we say instead "angels." His theory is that the Intelligences are intermediate beings between the Prime Cause and existing things, and that they effect the motion of the spheres, on which motion the existence of all things depends. This is also the view we meet with in all parts of Scripture: every act of God is described as being performed by angels. But "angel" means "messenger";

hence every one that is entrusted with a certain mission is an angel. (*Guide for the Perplexed* 2:6)

In general, says Rambam, the notion of an "angel" simply means a causative force, which is an emissary of God in the sense that He created it as a means to fulfill His will:

> All forces are angels. How great is the blindness of ignorance and how harmful! If you told a person who is one of those who deem themselves one of Israel's sages that the Deity sends an angel, who enters the womb of a woman and forms the fetus there, he would be pleased with this assertion and would accept it and would regard it as a manifestation of greatness and power on the part of the Deity... But if you tell him that God has placed in the sperm a formative force shaping the limbs ... and that this force is an "angel"... the person would shrink from this opinion... Our Sages have already stated--for him who has understanding--that all forces that reside in a body are angels, much more the forces that are active in the Universe. (Ibid. 2:6)

Since the term "angel" refers to causative forces, it is not limited to being used for forces of nature. Even objects can be the cause of something, and thus be described as angels:

> The early sages said: "Whoever has *tefillin* on his head and arm, *tzitzit* on his garment and a *mezuza* on his entrance is assured that he will not sin," for he has many reminders. And these are the angels that save him from sinning, as it says, "The angel of the Lord encamps around those who fear Him, and rescues them" (Psalms 34:8). (Rambam, *Mishneh Torah, Hilchot Mezuzah* 7:13)

Needless to say, this is not the way that others understood this concept. But it reflects the rationalist approach of minimizing the number of supernatural entities.

The Evil Eye and Astrology

- *Expanded upon in Part Two, "Ayin Hara—Ocular Radiation or Heavenly Accounting?"*

The Evil Eye is something that is risked when things are looked at with desire, jealousy or resentment by others. Several medieval rabbinic authorities explain that drawing attention to someone leads God to examine their deeds more carefully and exactingly, which makes it more likely for them to be found lacking and receive Divine punishment.

This sort of explanation of the Evil Eye, which does not involve any ocular component, is popular today. However, the rationalist Rishonim do not mention such an explanation, and probably would not have agreed with it. The notion that one person's feelings of envy can cause God to re-evaluate the merits of someone else does not really fit with the rationalist view of how God operates. Furthermore, and perhaps more significantly, it is difficult to claim that this is what the Gemara itself means in its various discussions of the Evil Eye, which very clearly refer to an ocular component.

Most of the Rishonim, including most of the rationalists, explained the notion of *ayin hara* to refer to physical damage caused by the eye, when it looks at something with jealousy or resentment. From ancient times, the idea that animals and people can affect their surroundings with their eyes was considered perfectly normal, and even to have a scientific basis in the extramission theory of vision (via which eyes interact with the world by emitting light, rather than by absorbing it). The extramission theory of vision was likewise adopted by scientifically-oriented rabbinic scholars, and it was understood to be a scientific explanation of *ayin hara*. Detailed discussions of its mechanism were given by prominent *rationalist* Rishonim such as Ralbag, along with R. Yitzchak Arama and others. Rabbi Yosef Karo even discussed whether windows can block the transmission of *ayin hara* (he concluded that they can), and others wrote that spectacles would likewise block it!

Rambam, on the other hand, makes it clear in several places that he does not believe that the Evil Eye is something that can harm other people or property. The most he will grant is that one should avoid invading privacy and engendering jealousy, for ethical rather than metaphysical reasons. But Rambam's unique position was not because he was more rationalist and others were less rationalist. His rejection of the notion of the Evil Eye is apparently simply because he followed Aristotle's theory of vision rather than the extramission theory of Plato and Galen.

Belief in the ocular approach to *ayin hara* continued into the nineteenth century, with such figures as Malbim and R. Baruch HaLevi Epstein claiming scientific evidence for the eye emitting dangerous "radiation." It was only in the 20th century that no longer did anyone attempt to provide scientific explanation of vapors or radiation being emitted from the eye. People instead adopted the approach that the Evil Eye refers to damage caused due to jealousy and other such thoughts, without there being any ocular component.

Yet the 20th century did not only see a difference in the explanation of the mechanism of the evil eye. It also saw a dramatic downgrade in the power that people attributed to it. This is presumably because with the increased mechanistic understanding of how the universe works, there was less room to attribute misfortune to supernatural causes. Still, belief in the Evil Eye has not declined to the same extent as belief in demons. This is probably due to the psychological factors involved in people feeling nervous about their good fortune.

For such people, there is often concern about trying to prevent problems caused by the Evil Eye. Many will say "*bli ayin hara*" as a kind of preventative incantation. Others are happy to pay hundreds of dollars to have the effects of *ayin hara* removed via various superstitious techniques such as pouring lead and acquiring amulets.

Most people today, however, seem to prefer to explain *ayin hara* as referring to causing divine judgment via jealousy, with no ocular component. Yet it is difficult for many people to believe in it as being any kind of significantly powerful force. But since classical and medieval authorities clearly saw it as a significant danger, the solution is to claim that it has been on the wane and may have even ceased to exist, or that it only exists if you believe in it. Such is the way that a more rationalist approach spreads in the Orthodox Jewish community, when few people are willing to simply adopt Rambam's approach and entirely deny the existence of *ayin hara* as a damaging force.

Astrology is similar to the Evil Eye in that the medieval authorities who believed in its existence as a genuine power did not necessarily do so for non-rationalist reasons. Ralbag, for example, had a carefully developed approach in which astrology is a quasi-naturalistic phenomenon, involving the effect of the "Active Intellect" upon the world. Rambam, on the other hand, rejected astrology as being unsupported by adequate evidence. Today, however, those who believe in astrology are certainly mystics who do so for non-rationalist reasons.

Impurity and Non-Kosher Food

In the mystical worldview, metaphysical entities are not restricted to the world of angels and demons. Rather, there are hypostasized, metaphysical forces which lie at the core of basic principles of Judaism. Rationalists, on the other hand, understand these principles to be independent of a metaphysical framework, the existence of which they do not accept.

The concept of *tumah*, usually translated as "impurity," lies at the heart of many commandments. Corpses and dead vermin transmit impurity. The emission of certain bodily fluids renders one in a state of impurity, as does childbirth. Animals that are forbidden from consumption are also described as "impure" (the colloquial term "*treife*" is inaccurate).

But what is this "impurity"? According the mystical approach, this impurity is a metaphysical state—a sort of invisible, spiritual "dirt." It has objective existence, regardless of how people relate to it. Here is a letter from the *Yated Ne'eman* newspaper addressing the cause of youths leaving Torah observance, which highlights the non-rationalist approach taken to an extreme:

> Our Chachonim discussed these topics. They said that boys can lose their *yiras Shomayim* by not wearing yarmulkas. They spoke about *timtum halev*, which comes from the wrong things going into one's mouth. When a boy is small as his yarmulka falls off, how quickly do we run to put it back? Do we realize that this can spell difference between whether he will still be in yeshiva at age 17? When we allow our daughters to eat *cholov stam* chocolate bar, do we realize the ramifications down the line and where this can lead? When our toddlers have fever and we give them Tylenol gelcaps with treif in it, why do we wonder that so many of our youth are falling by wayside? These things are not opinions or thoughts.

These are facts, built into Creation since the first six days. (Letter to *Yated Ne'eman*, 7.7.2009)

According to the rationalist approach, on the other hand, impurity is not a metaphysical state. Rather, it is a designation, a state which we (following God's instructions) ascribe to certain people, creatures and objects.[6] And we are forbidden to eat certain foods, in order to accomplish various functions relating to perfecting our characters and our society; there is nothing inherently metaphysically impure about these foods.

The differing views on the nature of impurity are also seen in the laws of accidental and forced transgression.[7] The Torah is explicit that if someone sins by accident, they must nevertheless bring an offering. But why? Ramban, following the mystical approach, explains that even though it was an accident, the impurity has nevertheless tainted one's soul.[8] Rambam, on the other hand, explains that he has to atone for being somewhat negligent, as had he been more careful, the accident would not have happened.[9]

What if someone ate impure food through absolutely no negligence on their behalf, or in a case where it was halachically required (such as for survival)? According to Rambam, there are no negative consequences whatsoever.[10] Indeed, in a situation where kosher food items are mixed up with a non-kosher food item, according to many views one is entitled to rely on the majority of items and eat all the food, because with any given item, the odds are that it is kosher. This is despite the fact that if one eats all the items, one has certainly consumed the non-kosher item! Evidently, there is no concern for metaphysical harm; the only problem of eating non-kosher food is transgressing institutional prohibition.

According to the mystical approach, on the other hand, even if one eats non-kosher food in a situation where it is halachically permissible, or

---

[6] See Rambam, *Mishneh Torah, Hilchot Mikvaot* 11:12. For extensive discussion, see Kellner, *Maimonides' Confrontation with Mysticism*, chapter 4.

[7] See Kellner, *Maimonides' Confrontation with Mysticism*, chapter 2.

[8] Ramban, Commentary to Leviticus 4:2.

[9] Rambam, *Guide for the Perplexed* 3:41.

[10] *Guide* 3:41; *Mishneh Torah, Hilchot Maachalot Issurot* 14:10-13.

where there was no negligence at all, it has nevertheless still harmed one's soul. This was seen in the discussion following the notorious scandal in Monsey in 2006, where a respected butcher was discovered to have been selling non-kosher meat for years. Responsa published after the event made no reference to Rambam's view (they were probably unaware of it). Instead, they quoted numerous opinions from the mystically-inclined Rishonim to demonstrate that even though it was a case of *onnes* (no negligence at all), there would still be metaphysical harm caused to peoples' souls.[11] (The few opinions quoted in opposition stated that the metaphysical harmful characteristics of non-kosher food only come into existence where eating them is a sin, not in a case of *onnes*, but this is far from straightforward. The Rishonim who advocate for non-kosher food possessing metaphysically harmful qualities certainly appear to see this as a property of the food itself, which is the very cause of it being halachically forbidden, rather than being generated as a consequence of the prohibition.)

The differing views of the nature of non-kosher food may also explain the differing approaches with regard to checking vegetables for insects. Those who advocate for a far more intensive search than was traditionally done are usually of the mystical mindset, and are concerned for actual metaphysical harm that will be sustained by eating insects. Those following a rationalist approach, on the other hand, are of the view that following the classical halachic requirements is all that is required, and there is no metaphysical harm about which to be concerned.

What about being *choshesh lechol hedeyos*—being concerned for all opinions? The answer to this also relates to rationalist vs. mystical approaches to Judaism. According to the mystical approach, there is a metaphysical reality to these laws, an objective spiritual state that is "out there". Hence, one would probably want to make absolutely sure to be in line with it, and one would take into account other views; after all, they *might* be right. According to the rationalist approach, on the other had,

---

[11] See Rabbi Gedaliah Oberlander, "*Timtum Halev MeiAchilas Ma'achalos Issuros B'Onnes*," *Ohr Yisrael* 45 pp. 103-109, and the rejoinder by Rabbi Yaakov Dovid Luban, *Ohr Yisrael* 46, pp. 49-52.

there is no independent metaphysical reality. Rather, there are legal conventions as to how to relate to different things.

The Holy Land, the Holy City and the Holy Temple

The Land of Israel is known as the Holy Land, Jerusalem is the Holy City, and the Temple Mount is the holiest place of all. But what does that actually mean?

Do these places possess an intrinsic, metaphysical sanctity, embedded in them since Creation? That is the mystical view presented by R. Yehudah HaLevi in the *Kuzari* (V:23). It is the view taken as a given by countless rabbinic authorities over the ages, and popularly assumed today to be the only conceivable approach.

Rambam, on the other hand, was of the view that the sanctity of these places is not a metaphysical quality. Rather, it is a status that stems from their historical role.[12] When Rambam stresses that the site of the altar must never be moved, the reason that he gives is not that it possesses inherent metaphysical significance. Rather, it is because of the history of the site, in terms of the events that took place there—the placement of the altar there by David and Solomon, the usage of that site by Avraham, and so on.[13]

And the original selection of these sites could have been for relatively mundane reasons. Rambam's explanation for the selection of the Temple Mount will no doubt come as a shock to many:

> It is known that idolaters sought to build their temples and to set up their idols in the highest places they could find there, on the highest mountains. Therefore Avraham Avinu selected Mount Moriah, because of its being the highest mountain there, and proclaimed on it the unity of God. (*Guide for the Perplexed* 3:45)

Within Mount Moriah, Avraham decided that any divine worship would take place facing the west, and the Temple itself was eventually situated there. The reason for this was again not connected to any special

---

[12] For extensive discussion, see Kellner, *Maimonides' Confrontation with Mysticism*, pp. 107-115. He also references numerous studies on this topic.

[13] *Mishneh Torah, Hilchot Beit HaBechirah* 2:1-2.

metaphysical properties of the westernmost part, but for a different reason entirely:

> Avraham designated the western part of it, that the Holy of Holies would be in the west... And it appears to me that the reason for this was that the popular view in the world at that time was to worship the sun as a god, and so people undoubtedly turned in prayer to the east. Therefore, Avraham Avinu turned to the west on Har HaMoriah—that is to say, in the Sanctuary—in order to have his back to the sun. (ibid.)

The consequence of Rambam's view, that the sanctity of the Land is a function of its usage rather than due to any intrinsic metaphysical qualities, is that this sanctity can disappear:

> All territories held by those who came up from Egypt, and consecrated with the first consecration, subsequently lost their sanctity when the people were exiled from there, since it was consecrated at the time due to the conquest alone and was not consecrated for all time. When the exiles returned and seized part of the land, they consecrated it a second time with a permanent consecration, both for that time and the future. (*Mishneh Torah, Hilchot Terumot* 1:5)

This view on the nature of the sanctity of the Land of Israel is not unique to Rambam, nor to the medieval philosophers. The same view is to be found in the writings of Rav Soloveitchik:

> With all my respect to the [views of certain] Rishonim, I must disagree that *kedusha* is an objective metaphysical quality inherent in the land. *Kedusha*... is man-made; more accurately, it is a historical category. Soil is sanctified by historical deeds performed by a sacred people, never by a primordial superiority. *Kedushat Ha'aretz* denotes the consequence of a human act. (Rabbi Joseph B. Soloveitchik, *The Emergence of Ethical Man*, p. 150)

It is crucial to stress that this does not mean that according to the rationalist approach, the Land of Israel or Jerusalem or Mount Moriah are any less holy than according to the mystical approach. Rather, it is simply a different perspective on what the nature of holiness is all about.

The Festivals and Calendar Events

In Judaism, as well as holy places, there are holy times—the Sabbath, the festivals, and so on. There are also times of forces of evil and punishment, such as Tisha B'Av. Just like sanctity in space, sanctity in time is also viewed differently by the rationalist and the mystical schools of thought.

According to the mystical school of thought, there are times and periods which contain innate spiritual powers. This is not only with regard to astrology. Every event on the calendar—all the festivals (whether Biblical or rabbinic), as well as Shabbat, are considered to be manifestations of spiritual forces which exist during those times. This is true even for festivals that are based on historical events, such as Pesach and the Exodus. The spiritual power of renewal that occurs in Nissan is physically manifest in the renewal of nature that occurs in spring and also caused the Exodus to take place at that time.[14]

According to the rationalist approach, on the other hand, dates on the calendar become special due to events that took place upon them. Rambam speaks of the importance of Shabbos not in terms of it manifesting a special spiritual reality of that day, but rather solely in terms of the lessons that it teaches about God having created the universe.[15] Indeed, as Narvoni and other medieval commentaries on Rambam understood, Rambam was of the view that the six days of creation were not 24-hour periods and were not even actual time periods at all, but rather represent hierarchical stages in the natural world.[16] Thus, Shabbos reflects a concept rather than a period of time. Similarly, Meiri writes that Rosh Hashanah is not actually a special time of judgment, since God is above time. Rather, it is declared as such because it is necessary to focus

---

[14] There is an entire book, *Seasons of Life: The Reflection of the Jewish Year in the Natural World*, based on this mystical approach. Ironically, it was written by me, twenty-five years ago.

[15] *Guide for the Perplexed* 2:31. For discussion, see Menachem Kellner, *Maimonides' Confrontation with Mysticism*, pp. 123-125.

[16] See my book *The Challenge of Creation* for further discussion.

on certain themes at specific times, in order to stimulate people to repent.[17]

Since, according to the rationalist approach, the dates of the festivals are special not due to any intrinsic metaphysical significance but rather due to what they commemorate, this means that if for some reason there is an error in the date, no harm has been done. This is an accordance with the Mishnah, which records how Rabbi Yehoshua felt that Rabban Gamliel had declared the new month (and thus the festivals) on the wrong date. Rabbi Akiva pointed out to Rabbi Yehoshua that he need not be overly distressed, based on an exposition of a verse:

> …"These are the convocations of God, the Holy convocations, which you shall declare" (Lev. 23:4)—whether they were declared at their proper time or not, I have no convocations other than these. (Rosh HaShanah 2:9)

Another potential ramification of the difference between the two views is with regard to the international dateline. There are no traditional sources providing guidance as to where the dateline should be located. When authorities in the modern era weighed in on this question, a variety of views were proposed. Some stated that it should be six hours (90°) east of Jerusalem, while others say that it is 180° east/west of Jerusalem. These calculations are, however, based on fairly non-rationalist types of inferences from traditional texts, since in antiquity nobody believed that civilization wrapped around the globe. A more rationalist approach, taken by Rav Isser Zalman Meltzer and Rav Zvi Pesach Frank, is that there is no halachic prime meridian and thus no unique halachic international dateline. Instead, one simply follows global convention with regard to the days of the week. The latter approach only makes sense if one assumes that the calendar has no innate metaphysical reality.

A further relevance of the dateline to the rationalist/mystical divide is with regard how one deals with the alternate views. The dispute has practical ramifications regarding when Shabbos falls in places such as eastern Australia and Hawaii. And Shabbos is an extremely serious matter. Perhaps, then, one should be *choshesh lechol hedeyot*, concerned for all

---

[17] R. Menachem Meiri, *Meshiv Nefesh* 2:1.

opinions, and thus Jews in eastern Australia should avoid work on Sunday, and Jews in Hawaii should avoid work on Friday?

According to the mystical approach, since there is a metaphysical reality to Shabbos, an objective spiritual state that is "out there," one would probably want to make absolutely sure to be in line with it, and one would take into account all views; after all, they *might* be correct. According to the rationalist approach, on the other hand, there is no independent metaphysical reality to Shabbos that one must be concerned about. Rather, Shabbos attains its status as a result of our designation of it.

The Chosen People

> For you are a holy people to the Lord your God, and the Lord has chosen you to be His own treasure out of all peoples that are upon the face of the earth. (Deut. 14:2)

Just as the mystical approach maintains that the special nature of the Holy Land, the Temple, and the festivals relates to actual hypostasized qualities, the same goes for the mystical view regarding the special nature of the Jewish People. R. Yehudah HaLevi, in the *Kuzari*, writes that Jewish souls possess a certain "divine aspect" which is lacking in the souls of non-Jews.[18] This is something that originated in Adam, and was only transmitted to select descendants, ultimately passing only through Avraham's lineage. The Zohar describes the souls of Jews as emanating from God, and therefore possessing special sanctity; the souls of other nations, on the other hand, "emanate from… impure sources."[19] Similar statements are to be found in the writings of other mystics such as Maharal, R. Moshe Chaim Luzzatto, R. Schneur Zalman of Liadi, R. Chaim of Volozhin, and even R. Avraham Yitzchak Kook.[20]

---

[18] *Kuzari* 1:95. This is not, however, quite as racist as is sometimes believed. See H. Norman Strickman, "Misinterpreting Rabbi Judah Ha-Levi," *Hakirah* 20 (2015) pp. 75-90.

[19] Zohar, Bereishit 170.

[20] See Rabbi Hanan Balk, "The Soul of a Jew," *Hakirah* 16 (2013) pp. 47-76.

In contrast to all this is the rationalist approach of Rambam.[21] According to Rambam, there is nothing inherently different about Jews and non-Jews. Instead, the difference is circumstantial and cultural, and results from the particular path in life that Abraham chose to take. It wasn't that Avraham Avinu was born with some kind of special quality which led to God choosing him. Rather, Avraham was the first person to use his mind and free will to realize that there is One God, and to dedicate himself to His service. Consequently, he was rewarded by God giving the Torah to his descendants.[22] The Torah is a guide to improving oneself ethically and ultimately intellectually. Thus, the Jewish People have a cultural advantage, not an intrinsic advantage based on any kind of metaphysical qualities.

The Holy Language

Why is Hebrew called *Lashon HaKodesh*, the Holy Language? What exactly is special about it?

The mystical view is that the Hebrew language is uniquely different from all other languages. Other languages are merely conventions; the letters l-i-o-n are agreed upon to refer to the king of beasts, but they do not intrinsically mean it, and society could just as well agree to call lions "simbas." With Hebrew, on the other hand, when Adam named the lion *aryeh*, he was discerning the very essence of the creature. This is because the Hebrew letters are the raw mystical forces with which God created the universe. The Hebrew language both reflects reality and creates reality. God spoke, and the universe came into being. The Hebrew letters embody supernatural forces, which is why combinations of those letters are a potent source of energy that can affect the world. In particular, the four, twelve and forty-two letter Names of God contain tremendous energy

---

[21] For a full discussion, see Kellner, *Maimonides' Confrontation With Mysticism*, pp. 41, 77-84, and 216-264.

[22] A famous epigram goes, "How odd of God/to choose the Jews." One of several rejoinders that have been offered is, "It's not so odd/the Jews chose God." This reflects the Maimonidean perspective. There is another rejoinder, "It's not so odd/the *goyim* annoy 'im," which is closer to the mystical perspective.

when written and especially when pronounced correctly (but the tradition of how to do so has been lost).

The mystical view of the Hebrew language has become completely normative in Orthodox circles today. Most people do not imagine that any other view has ever existed or could exist. Yet Rambam did not have this understanding of why Hebrew is holy.[23]

In the *Guide for the Perplexed*, Rambam discusses how language sets aside humans from animals.[24] Accordingly, it is a special gift which should be used appropriately. Rambam proceeds to explain why Hebrew is called the Holy Language. He does not say that this is because God created this language, or because He used it for Creation, or because it is a language with intrinsic meaning or metaphysical qualities. Rather, Rambam says that the Hebrew language is holy because it does not contain any words for excretory or sexual organs or functions.

According to Rambam, when Adam named the animals, he was not discerning their essence. Instead, Rambam says that when the Torah states that the animals received their names from Adam (and not from God), this shows that language is a mere human convention.[25]

But what about God uttering Hebrew words to create the universe? Here too Rambam takes a different approach. Rambam explains that God never actually speaks. Rather, when the Torah states in the account of Creation that God said "Let there be light," it does not mean that He spoke, but rather that He desired that there be light.[26]

By the same token, Rambam rejected the notion that uttering combinations of Hebrew letters, even the Names of God, can have metaphysical power with physical effects. Rambam explains that the significance of the Names of God is not in any mystical properties, but rather in the philosophical *lessons* that they conveyed. The forty-two letter

---

[23] For a full discussion, see Kellner, *Maimonides' Confrontation With Mysticism*, chapter five.

[24] *Guide for the Perplexed* 3:8.

[25] *Guide* 2:30. See the commentaries of Narvoni and Shem Tov.

[26] *Guide* 1:65.

Name of God was not an incantation, but rather a phrase of several words, forty-two letters in total, which had a meaning regarding the essence of God.[27] Rambam vehemently condemns those who attribute innate power to these letter combinations:

> You must beware of sharing the error of those who write amulets. Whatever you hear from them, or read in their works, especially in reference to the names which they form by combination, is utterly senseless; they call these combinations *shemot* (names) and believe that their pronunciation demands sanctification and purification, and that by using them they are enabled to work miracles. Rational people should not listen to such men, nor in any way believe their assertions. (*Guide* 1:61)

The difference between the mystical and rationalist view of the Hebrew language is also seen in their respective explanations of a Talmudic passage regarding changing one's name:

> Four things cause an evil decree against a person to be torn up. They are: charity, prayer, the changing of one's name and the changing of one's deeds. (Rosh HaShanah 16b)

According to the mystical approach, this relates to a person's name possessing metaphysical significance and power. Thus, if a person is, God forbid, lying in a coma, changing their name could change their fate.[28] Rambam, on the other hand, has a completely different explanation of this passage:

> Among the ways of repentance are for the penitent to continue to cry out in tearful supplication before God, to give charity according to his means, and to greatly distance himself from the thing in which he sinned, and to change his name, as if to say, "I am now another person, and not that person who perpetrated those sins." (*Mishneh Torah, Hilchot Teshuvah* 2:4)

According to Rambam, changing one's name is a psychological tool to effect character reform. It has no mystical powers and thus it would be useless to do it on a person who is unconscious.

---

[27] *Guide* 1:61-62.

[28] *Sefer Chassidim* 245, Rema to *Shulchan Aruch, Yoreh Deah* 465:10.

The difference between the two worldviews also makes all the difference regarding *gematriyot*, numerical values of letters. According to the mystical approach, *gematriyot*, numerical values of letters, are of great significance; according to the rationalist approach, they are nothing more than wordplay. Likewise, the practice in some circles to evaluate a prospective marital match based on whether the names are mystically "compatible" would be regarded as utterly baseless from a rationalist perspective.

Rambam's view about Hebrew is quite radical. It was not shared by all the other rationalist Rishonim; and it earned the criticism not only of his usual opponents such as Ramban, but even of his defenders such as Ritva.[29] Nevertheless, this was his view, and it is of particular relevance today, when there are developed sciences regarding the history of language.

Spilling Seed

A perhaps unexpected area of difference between the rationalist and mystical schools of thought is with regard to the laws of marital intimacy and the spilling of seed.[30]

The history of Jewish law with regard to the laws of marital intimacy reveals that the earlier sources, i.e. Chazal and the Rishonim, are far more lenient in this regard than are many later halachists—specifically, with regard to permitting forms of intercourse which do not lead to pregnancy. The later stringent approach can be traced to several factors. One is what appears to be a copyist's interpolation into a manuscript of Rambam's *Mishneh Torah*, that alternate sexual positions are only permitted if one does not waste seed. This was later incorporated into halachic discussion as being Rambam's own opinion.[31]

---

[29] *Sefer HaZikaron* 72.

[30] For a thorough discussion, see Rabbi Yaakov Shapiro, *Sexuality and Jewish Law: In Search of a Balanced Approach in Torah, Vol. I: Halachic Positions: What Judaism Really Says About Passion In The Marital Bed.*

[31] See Rav Yehudah Henkin, *Bnei Banim* 4:18, which discusses this textual discrepancy at length.

But the primary factor responsible for the change in halachic trends appears to be the Zohar, which strongly condemned the wasting of seed, and the influence of subsequent mystics, which saw wasted seed as a source of metaphysical harm which creates demonic forces. This is not to say that all contemporary rabbis of a mystical persuasion follow the Zohar in this area, nor that all those who take a stringent approach are relying on the Zohar. However, it is certainly a significant factor. Furthermore, the Zohar also states that someone who wastes their seed has no atonement whatsoever (which enabled unethical kabbalists, who claimed to know secret *tikkunim* for this, to amass fortunes).

The Zohar was not the first source to condemn wasting seed. The Gemara speaks harshly against spilling seed in vain, comparing it to bloodshed.[32] Note, however, that the Gemara does not clarify exactly what "in vain" means. Is it "in vain" when it gives pleasure to the wife, or the husband, even if it cannot lead to pregnancy? There are a range of views in the Rishonim and Acharonim regarding this question. For example, Tosafot (Yevamot 34b) quotes Rabbeinu Yitzchak of Dampierre (Ri) who permits occasional intercourse, performed in a way that does not lead to pregnancy, for the sake of sexual fulfillment. The majority of extant medieval writings that weigh in on the question endorse this approach of Rabbeinu Yitzchak.

But the Zohar goes vastly further than the Gemara in condemning wasting seed, saying that it is worse than *any* other sin. It seems that the Torah's story of the sin of Er and Onan is explained very differently by the Zohar than how it was understood by other Rishonim.[33] And it is the view of the Zohar, rather than the Gemara and other Rishonim, which is endorsed by R. Yosef Karo,[34] where he writes that "had Rabbeinu Yitzchak seen the punishment that the Zohar forewarns for the wasting of seed in

---

[32] Niddah 13a.

[33] See the discussion at www.RationalistMedicalHalacha.blogspot.com.

[34] *Bedek HaBayit, Even HaEzer* 25.

vain, that it is greater than that of any other sin in the Torah, he would not have written what he did."[35]

Interestingly, a prominent rabbi in Israel, Rabbi Eliezer Melamed, takes a relatively lenient approach to the laws of marital relations.[36] Yet he downplays this part of the Zohar in a different way than others. Instead of pointing out that there are other halachic authorities who dispute the Zohar's approach in this area, or R. Karo's interpretation of it, he downplays the Zohar itself; not the authenticity of it, but the meaning of it. Rabbi Melamed says that the fire-and-brimstone expressed by the Zohar against spilling seed in vain is simply an exaggeration. He further points out that the Talmud's severe-sounding comparison of spilling seed to bloodshed is a rhetorical flourish, noting that the Talmud says the same about someone who embarrasses others in public or who does not escort his guests out.[37] Still, while his interpretation of the Talmud is likely correct, it seems that the Zohar really did mean what it said—at least, that is how it has always been understood.

---

[35] It should be noted that other halachic authorities were more lenient than R. Karo. And one *acharon*, R. Shlomo Yehuda Tabak, disputes R. Karo's claim that Rabbeinu Yitzchak would have retracted his view had he seen the Zohar; he argues that the Zohar's severe words about wasting seed apply only to a person whose intent is to avoid having children or who does so constantly.

[36] *Simchat Habayit U-birchato* (see too the companion *Harchavot* volume).

[37] The same interpretation of such condemnations in the Talmud is given by Rivash, as well as by an early Acharon, Rav Yehoshua Heschel of Krakow, specifically in this context.

IV: The Function of *Mitzvot*

Introduction

What is the function of *mitzvot*? Rationalists understand the purpose of *mitzvot* and one's religious life in general as furthering intellectual and/or moral goals for the individual and society. Even *chukkim* serve to accomplish these functions, albeit in a way that is not immediately obvious.

Mystics accept that *mitzvot* serve intellectual and moral goals, but see the primary function of *mitzvot* as performing mechanistic manipulations of spiritual metaphysical forces. The reasons for *mitzvot* are either to accomplish these manipulations, or are ultimately incomprehensible.

In this section, we will discuss several aspects of this difference of opinion, along with several examples of *mitzvot* that are viewed differently by rationalists and mystics.[1]

Kabbala and Halacha

In general, even among non-rationalists, there is widespread reluctance to explicitly involve mystical considerations in halachic matters. Even those who believed that the Zohar was written by R. Shimon bar Yochai, a *tanna*, did not ascribe it with the status of legal rulings presented in the Talmud.[2] In any dispute between the Talmud and the Zohar, the general approach was to follow the Talmud. With regard to changing customs to fit Kabbalistic ideas, R. Shlomo Luria says that "even if Rabbi Shimon bar

---

[1] See too Yair Lorberbaum, "Halakhic Realism," *Shenaton ha-Mishpat ha-Ivri: Annual of the Institute for Research in Jewish Law* 27 (2013), pp. 61–130.

[2] A useful list of sources regarding the halachic authority of the Zohar can be found at www.hamakor.org/metahala/zohar.htm.

Yochai was standing before us screaming to change our ancient custom, we would not listen to him."[3]

There were those who did explicitly involve kabbalistic considerations in halacha. R. Yaakov Chaim Sofer (1870–1939) ruled that one does not recite the prayer on newly blossoming trees on Shabbat, because by separating the "divine sparks" from the tree, one has performed the act of *borer*.[4] But this was rejected by none other than R. Ovadia Yosef, who strongly challenges the notion that one can use kabbalistic considerations in halachic matters.[5] R. Moshe Sofer (Chatam Sofer) writes that anyone who mixes kabbalastic considerations into halachic matters is liable for "sowing *kilayim*" (forbidden mixtures).[6]

A contemporary example of this can be found in the voluminous halachic works of Rabbi Eliezer Melamed from the national-religious community. While Rabbi Melamed himself has a strong background in mysticism, he often relegates that to the sidelines or downplays it when determining halachah, with notable consequences.

Still, as we shall see, there are nevertheless many cases where mystical considerations have indeed influenced halacha. Note, however, that this does not necessarily mean that a rationalist should not follow that halacha. There can be reasons for observing halacha even if they are based on metaphysical assumptions that one disputes, just as there are valid reasons for following halachah even if it appears to be based on mistaken beliefs about the natural world.[7]

Furthermore, the widespread professed position that kabbalah should not affect halacha is with regard to cases where kabbalistic considerations, or kabbalistic texts, are overtly related to halachah. Yet there are many other cases where the relevance of mysticism to the halachah are not as immediately obvious or as well-known. Indeed, as we shall now explain,

---

[3] Maharshal, responsa 98.

[4] *Kaf Ha-Chaim* 226:4.

[5] *Yechaveh Daat* 1:2.

[6] Responsa Chatam Sofer, *Orach Chaim* 51.

[7] See the final chapter of my book *Sacred Monsters*.

the difference between the rationalist and the mystical worldviews are fundamental to what all *mitzvot* are about.

The Controversy over Rationalizing Commandments

Historically, there have been people who stated that the Torah's commandments have no rational reason (or at least, none that can be grasped by man). Some maintained that the true reasons for *mitzvot* are transcendental, and that human explanations for the *mitzvot* degrade them. Thus, even for a mitzvah like Shabbat, with which the Torah explicitly states that its purpose is to attest to Creation, Rashba argued that the real reason, as with all other commandments, is a mystical secret that transcends human understanding. Others stated that the only reasons for fulfilling *mitzvot* are to fulfill God's dictate. Even some of those who approved of giving rationales for commandments stressed that these should not be thought of as the actual reasons, but rather only as a means to make it easier for people to observe them:

> ...All the reasons for *mitzvot* are only to make them appealing to the intellect... but Heaven forbid to think that they are actually the main intent of the Giver of the Torah... (Netziv, *Haamek Davar*, Exodus 20:12)

Rambam, however, harshly condemns such approaches:

> There are people who find it difficult to give a reason for any of the commandments, and consider it right to assume that the commandments and prohibitions have no rational basis whatever. They are led to adopt this theory by a certain disease in their soul, the existence of which they perceive, but which they are unable to discuss or to describe. For they imagine that these precepts, if they were useful in any respect, and were commanded because of their usefulness, would seem to originate in the thought and reason of some intelligent being. But as things which are not objects of reason and serve no purpose, they would undoubtedly be attributed to God, because no thought of man could have produced them. According to the theory of those weak-minded persons, man is more perfect than his Creator. For what man says or does has a certain object, whilst the actions of God are different; He commands us to do what is of no use to us, and forbids us to do what is harmless.

> Far be it to posit this! On the contrary, the sole object of the Law is to benefit us. Thus we explained the Scriptural passage, "for our good always, that He might preserve us alive, as it is this day" (Deut. 6:24). Again, "which shall hear all those statutes, and say, surely this great nation is a wise and understanding people" (ibid. 4:6). He thus says that even every one of these "statutes" convinces all nations of the wisdom and understanding it includes. But if no reason could be found for these statutes, if they produced no advantage and removed no evil, why then should he who believes in them and follows them be wise, reasonable, and so excellent as to raise the admiration of all nations? (Rambam, *The Guide for the Perplexed* 3:31)

The rationalist attempts to present rational reasons for the Torah's commandments as much as possible. Furthermore, the rationalizations themselves are expressed in terms of the functions of the commandments for the human mind, the human body and for society, and not in terms of manipulating mystical forces.

How does this relate to the other three aspects of the rationalist approach? It relates to the first aspect, knowledge, in that the reasons for commandments are considered to be comprehensible, and grasping them is a function of applying the human mind rather than requiring supernatural insights. And it strongly relates to the third aspect, supernatural entities, in that the commandments are seen as spiritually improving the world in terms of peoples' thoughts and behavior, rather than by manipulating alleged metaphysical forces.

It is important to note that being a rationalist does *not* mean that one only fulfills the commandments which one rationally grasps. One might follow a medical recommendation that one does not comprehend, but one does it because one trusts, with good reason, that medical science has reasons for prescribing a course of action. Likewise, having a rationale for observing *mitzvot* in general does not require that one understands the rationale for any given mitzvah.

The Function of *Mitzvot*

What is the function of *mitzvot*? The mystical approach is that they serve to create and manipulate various spiritual energies:

> All the *mitzvot* are attached and dependent at their upper source and root with the elements of the Chariot and the *Shiur Komah* of all the worlds, for every individual mitzvah at its root includes myriads of forces and lights from the order of the *Shiur Komah*... and when a person does the will of his Creator, blessed is His Name, and fulfills on of God's commandments with a particular limb and its power, the tikkun is relevant to the parallel world and upper energy, to rectify it, or to elevate it, or to add light and holiness to its sanctity... (R. Chaim of Volozhin, *Nefesh HaChaim* 1:6)

This is not to say that they have no other function or benefit—mystics would agree that there could be all kinds of benefits. But the effect on spiritual forces is certainly a significant, probably the most significant, function.

In sharp contrast, Rambam explicitly states that the reasons for all *mitzvot* are explicable in terms of rational reasons which do not involve mystical components:

> But the truth is undoubtedly as we have said, that every one of the six hundred and thirteen precepts serves to inculcate some truth, to remove some erroneous opinion, to establish proper relations in society, to diminish evil, to train in good manners or to warn against bad habits. All this depends on three things: opinions, morals, and social conduct... Thus these three principles suffice for assigning a reason for every one of the Divine commandments. (Rambam, *The Guide for the Perplexed* 3:31)

Note that this includes the commandments classified as *chukkim*, which are popularly thought to be *mitzvot* that have no rational reason.

> All of us, the common people as well as the scholars, believe that there is a reason for every precept, although there are commandments the reason of which is unknown to us, and in which the ways of God's wisdom are incomprehensible. This view is distinctly expressed in Scripture; comp. "righteous statutes and judgments" (Deut. 4:8); "the judgments of the Lord are true, and righteous altogether" (Ps. 19:10). There are commandments which are called *chukkim*, "ordinances," like the prohibition of wearing garments of wool and linen (*sha'atnez*), boiling meat and milk together, and the sending of the goat [into the wilderness on the Day of Atonement]. Our Sages use in reference to them phrases like the following: "These are things which I have fully ordained for thee:

and you dare not criticize them"; "Your evil inclination is turned against them"; and "non-Jews find them strange." But our Sages generally do not think that such precepts have no cause whatsoever, and serve no purpose; for this would lead us to assume that God's actions are purposeless. On the contrary, they hold that even these ordinances have a cause, and are certainly intended for some use, although it is not known to us; owing either to the deficiency of our knowledge or the weakness of our intellect. Consequently there is a cause for every commandment: every positive or negative precept serves a useful object; in some cases the usefulness is evident, e.g., the prohibition of murder and theft; in others the usefulness is not so evident, e.g., the prohibition of enjoying the fruit of a tree in the first three years (Lev. 19:73), or of a vineyard in which other seeds have been growing (Deut. 22:9). Those commandments, whose object is generally evident, are called "judgments" (*mishpatim*); those whose object is not generally clear are called "ordinances" (*chukkim*)... the giving of these commandments is not a vain thing and without any useful object; and if it appears so to you in any commandment, it is owing to the deficiency in your comprehension. You certainly know the famous saying that Solomon knew the reason for all commandments except that of the "red heifer." Our Sages also said that God concealed the causes of commandments, lest people should despise them, as Solomon did in respect to three commandments, the reason for which is clearly stated. In this sense they always speak; and Scriptural texts support the idea. (Ibid. 3:26)

According to Rambam, *chukkim* also have a rational reason; it's just that it's harder to figure out what it is. Sometimes, this may be because we lack historical knowledge. According to Rambam, many of the seemingly irrational *mitzvot* are to be understood in the context of the era in which the Torah was given. They serve to modify or negate various pagan practices.

While Rambam is of the firm opinion that the function of the commandments is to be explained in terms of their effects in this world, on our minds, bodies and societies, he takes a very harsh stance against those who would use spiritual matters for physical benefit:

One who whispers over a wound, reciting a verse from the Torah, and likewise one who recites [verses] over an infant so that he will not be frightened, [and] one who places a Torah scroll or tefillin on a child so that he will sleep—not only are they included among sorcerers and practitioners of witchcraft, but they are among those who deny the Torah, for they turn the words of Torah into [a means of achieving] physical health, whereas they are [in truth] but [a means of achieving] spiritual health, as it says, "and they shall be life for your soul" (Prov. 3:22). But a healthy person who recites verses or a paragraph of Psalms so that the merit of their recitation will protect him such that he will be saved from trouble and harm—this is permissible. (*Mishneh Torah, Hilchot Avodat Kokhavim,* 11:12)

According to Rambam, there certainly are *mitzvot* which serve to maintain physical health—such as the commandment to erect a protective wall around a balcony. But *mitzvot* such as the study of Torah, and the writing of a mezuzah, do not serve to provide physical benefits via metaphysical forces; rather, they serve to improve our minds, via teaching us ideas. Rabbi Samson Raphael Hirsch, notwithstanding his condemnations of Rambam for his rationalism in other areas, also makes this point:

> And what wrong and mischievous notions exist concerning the principles, ordinances, and teachings of Judaism? Even that which is known externally and superficially, how little is it known as regards its wondrously profound inner meaning! For instance, the Edoth duties, so useful and indispensable through the lessons they teach, are looked upon by some as mere mechanical *opus operatum*, or as talismanic jugglery for the prevention of physical evils or the erection of mystic supramundane worlds. (Rav Hirsch, *The Nineteen Letters*, Letter 17)

Segulot

Segulot are not *mitzvot* per se. However, like *mitzvot*, they are rated by mystics as suitable actions that are part of religious life. And, like *mitzvot*, they are about manipulating metaphysical forces.

The mystical approach presents all kinds of *segulot*. There are *segulot* for livelihood, such as baking *schlissel challah*, and writing *parashat ketoret* on a parchment and reciting it twice daily. There is even a *segulah* for getting rid of mice: hanging a picture of Rebbe Yeshaya of Kraeastir. There are modern catch-all *segulot*, such as reciting *Perek Shirah*. And there are *segulot* for having children; a book entitled *To Fill The Earth: 277 Segulos and Advice on Fertility Issues, In Personal Consultation with Maran HaRav Chaim Kanievsky, Shlitah*, includes the following:

> A dried pig's testicle, pulverized and ground up, will help a woman conceive. If the right testicle is used, a male child will be born; if the left testicle is used, a female child will be born. (*Segulos Yisrael, ma'areches os ayin*, from the *sefer Mar'eh Yeladim*)

According to the rationalist approach, there are several problems with *segulot*. First is that they simply don't work. *Segulot* are simple superstitions, often based on a pre-scientific understanding of how the universe works.

But the more serious problem is that the idea of using *segulot* goes against the essence of what religious duties are about. The opposition by Rambam and others to using *mezuzot* as a form of amulets applies equally to using amulets as amulets! According to the rationalist approach, our religious life is about learning concepts, refining our intellects, improving our character, and perfecting society. *Segulot* are the antithesis of that.

It is true that from a rationalist perspective *segulot* can nevertheless potentially be beneficial, in terms of psychological benefits. However, they can also very dangerous. They can distract people from engaging in proper ways of attaining their objectives. And the *segulah* mindset causes people who are going through difficult times to be vulnerable to being preyed upon by unscrupulous *segulah*-peddlers.

Mezuzah

Every Jewish home has a *mezuzah*, but what is its function? Rationalists and mystics have very different answers to this simple question.[8] The mystical view is that the *mezuzah* is a form of amulet that serves to

---

[8] An extensive discussion of this topic by Martin Gordon, "*Mezuzah*: Protective Amulet or Religious Symbol?", *Tradition* 13 (1977) pp. 7-40, reprinted in Martin Gordon, *Modern Orthodox Judaism* (but note that the article is written from a clear apologetic stance that seeks to minimize the mystical view as much as possible). See too Hillel Aviezer, "*HaMezuzah – Bein Mitzvah LeKemiya*" (Hebrew), *Maaliyot* 19 (5757) pp. 217-236, available online at http://asif.co.il/?wpfb_dl=413, and Oded Yisraeli, "The Mezuzah as an Amulet: Directions and Trends in the Zohar," *Jewish Studies Quarterly* (2015) 22:2, pp. 137-161.

metaphysically protect the home. The rationalist view is that the *mezuzah* serves as a reminder of the foundations of Judaism, as Rambam explains:

> A person must be meticulous with regard to *mezuza*, because it is everyone's constant obligation. And whenever he enters or leaves he encounters the oneness of the Name of the Holy One, and will recall the love for Him and will awaken from his slumber and preoccupation with the vanities of the time. He will realize that there is nothing that remains forever except the awareness of the "Rock of the World," and will then immediately return to his senses and follow the path of the upright. The early sages said: "Whoever has *tefillin* on his head and arm, *tzitzit* on his garment and a *mezuza* on his entrance is assured that he will not sin," for he has many reminders.... (*Mishneh Torah, Hilchot Mezuza* 6:13)

Rambam vehemently condemns those who seek to turn the mezuzah into an amulet:

> It is a widespread custom to write Shadai on the outside of a mezuzah, opposite the space between the sections. And there is no loss in this, because it is on the outside. But those who write the names of angels, or holy names, or verses or seals on the inside, are in the category of those who have lost their share in the World-to-Come. For it is not enough that these fools have negated the mitzvah, but further that they took a great mitzvah, which is establishing the oneness of the Name of the Holy One, and His love and service, and made it into an amulet for personal benefit, as they foolishly believe that the mezuzah is something beneficial for the vain pleasures of this world. (*Mishneh Torah, Hilchot Mezuzah* 5:4)

The differing views as to the function of the *mezuzah* go back to the Talmud. The Talmud states that the *mezuzah* should be affixed within a handbreadth of the entrance to the house.[9] The rabbis give the reason for this as being that the homeowner should encounter the *mezuzah* immediately, while R. Chanina of Sura gives the reason as being in order that the *mezuzah* should protect the entire house. While R. Chanina is clearly a Talmudic source for the mystical approach, it is reasonable to deduce that the rabbis disagree with the notion of the *mezuzah* providing protective value.

---

[9] Menachot 33b.

Even some passages in the Talmud which appear to clearly side with the mystical approach were explained differently by the Rishonim. The Jerusalem Talmud records how King Artavan sent a priceless jewel to Rabbi Yehudah HaNasi, whereupon the latter reciprocated by sending him a *mezuzah*, telling him that "What you have sent me requires protection, whereas what I have sent you protects you even while you sleep."[10] R. Abba Mari ben Yosef Astruc, who spearheaded the campaign against rationalism and philosophy, nevertheless explains this passage to refer not to the *mezuzah* possessing innate protective power, but rather to it teaching the principles of monotheism to which adherence will bring protection.[11]

Furthermore, several of the laws about *mezuzah*, which exempt one from affixing or checking a *mezuzah* under various circumstances, are perfectly reasonable from the rationalist standpoint, but are difficult to understand within the mystical view. For example, a *mezuzah* need only be checked twice in seven years. But if it ensures the safety of the home, why is it not recommended to check it more often? With smoke alarms, it is recommended to check them monthly, and replace the batteries every year! Furthermore, whereas a regular mezuzah needs to be checked twice in seven years, that of a community need only be checked twice in *fifty* years.[12] The commentaries explain that it is too much to expect anything more, since individuals tend to shirk public responsibility. But if it's a matter of protecting the public, surely the *mezuzot* should be checked at least as often as private *mezuzot*, if not more so! Likewise, the exemption from mezuzah for a short-term rental likewise does not comport with the notion that it serves to protect.

There is a very clear practical difference between the rationalist and mystical views regarding the function of the mezuzah. If, Heaven forbid, one suffers from a burglary, fire or some other tragedy in the home, what should one do? According to the mystical approach, one should check the *mezuzot*. According to the rationalist approach, there would be no

---

[10] Yerushalmi Pe'ah 1:1.

[11] *Minchat Kanaut* (Pressburg 1838) p. 11.

[12] Yoma 11a.

particular relevance to doing so. You would check the security systems, not the *mezuzot*!

Netilat Yadayim

There is a mitzvah of *netilat yadayim*, washing one's hands in the morning. But what is the reason for this washing—what is its purpose? Today, it is widely assumed that the reason is to remove "evil spirits." But an analysis of the sources in the Talmud and Rishonim reveals a much more ambiguous and complex picture.[13]

The Talmud states that there is a mitzvah to wash one's hands in the morning, and one duly recites a blessing.[14] It does not give any explanation for this. Some, but not all, authorities relate the mitzvah of washing one's hands in the morning to another passage in the Talmud. During an extensive discussion about various ailments and their cures and prevention, the Talmud refers to an evil spirit that refuses to depart until one washes one's hands three times.[15] The Talmud may appear to be describing a supernatural problem with a ritual solution. But, given the context of the discussion, it appears that the Talmud is attempting to solve a medical risk; it should be recalled that in antiquity, people often did not perceive a difference between physical ailments and demonic harm.

The earliest authority to explicitly discuss the reason for this mitzvah is the Rosh. He gives the reason as being one of physical hygiene:

> For a person's hands are active, and it is impossible that they would not have touched soiled flesh during the night. (Rosh to Berachot 9:23)

Rashba, seeking to explain why a blessing and a vessel is required, gives an additional reason for the mitzvah:

> In the morning, we are made like a new creation… and so we need to sanctify ourselves with His holiness, and wash our hands from a vessel,

---

[13] For extensive discussion, see Martin Gordon, "*Netilat Yadayim Shel Shaharit:* Ritual of Crisis or Dedication?" *Gesher* 8 (1981), also published in *Modern Orthodox Judaism: Studies and Perspectives.*

[14] Berachot 60b; see too 14b.

[15] Shabbat 109b.

like the Kohen who sanctified his hands from the basin before his service. (Rashba, Responsa 1:191)

This explanation is also rationalist; it relates to commemoration and psychological conditioning.

The Zohar, on the other hand, presents a mystical reason for washing one's hands:

> There is no man who does not experience the taste of death at night… For the holy soul leaves him, and an impure spirit comes to rest on that body, contaminating it. When the soul returns to the body, that uncleanliness passes away. But it is taught that a man's hands retain the contaminating uncleanliness… until he washes them. (Zohar I, 184b, *parashat Vayishlach* 114-115).

According to the Zohar, when a person sleeps, it is not merely that his soul departs—there is an actual impure spirit that descends upon his body. While that spirit departs when he awakens, traces of its effects remain on his hands. These traces are considered to be dangerous, such that the Zohar states that not only must his hands be washed, but even later adds that the water used for that washing must be disposed of carefully, because it contains the impure spirit and could actually harm people. The Zohar further describes the proper method of removing this dangerous spirit: One takes a vessel containing the water in one's right hand and passes it to the left hand. Then one washes the right and left hands three times alternately, beginning with the right each time, in order to empower the *sefirot* of *chessed* (represented by the right hand) over *din* (represented by the left hand).[16]

The differences between the rationalist and mystical explanations of the mitzvah have further practical ramifications. According to the rationalist approach, whereby washing one's hands serves to cleanse oneself physically and symbolically for the work of the day, it need only be done before one gets one's day going. According to the mystical explanation, on the other hand, whereby one is contaminated by

---

[16] Zohar 198b.

impurity, one should get rid of it as soon as possible—preferably before even leaving one's bed.[17]

R. Yosef Karo notes that the Zohar's explanation of this mitzvah introduces novelties that are not mentioned in the *Poskim*.[18] Nonetheless, he incorporated them into the *Shulchan Aruch*, ruling that a person must pour three times on each hand, in order to remove the harmful spirit.[19]

Shiluach HaKein

- *Expanded upon in Part Two, "Shiluach Ha-Kein"*

Shiluach hakein is a combination of two *mitzvot*—the prohibition against taking both a mother bird and her eggs, and the positive commandment to send the mother bird away before taking her eggs. It is a striking example of a mitzvah that in the days of the Rishonim was perceived in a very rationalistic manner, in accordance with the straightforward understanding of Scripture; and which, over time, became interpreted as the ultimate in anti-rationalist belief.

According the majority of Rishonim, *shiluach hakein* is all about compassion. It is cruel to take the mother and her young, because that is destroying two generations of life, and taking advantage of the mother bird's desire to protect her eggs by not flying away. And though one may take just the eggs, one must send away the mother bird first, so that she does not suffer the distress of actually seeing her eggs being taken.

According to the Zohar, on the other hand, *shiluach hakein* has nothing to do with compassion to birds. Just the opposite; it's about cruelty—not for the sake of cruelty, but rather in order to engineer a celestial process. When one sends away the mother bird, the mother bird is chirping in distress. This sets into a motion a metaphysical process in the celestial realm. The angel appointed over the birds becomes distressed in turn, and he goes and complains to God. God responds, Why am I receiving complaints about the pain of birds, and not about the pain of the Jewish

---

[17] See *Mishnah Berurah* 1:2.

[18] *Beit Yosef, Orach Chaim* 4:8.

[19] *Shulchan Aruch, Orach Chaim* 4:2.

People and the *Shechinah* in exile? As a result, He decides to release an outflow of compassion on the Jewish People.

There is a very significant practical difference between these two approaches. According to the rationalist approach, sending away the mother bird is a compassionate way to take the eggs—but if one does not want the eggs, then clearly the best course of action is to just leave them and not do anything. But according the mystical approach, whereby the mitzvah is about causing pain to the bird in order to set a certain metaphysical process into operation, one should send away the mother bird whether one wants the eggs or not.

Prayer

What does petitionary prayer actually do? This is a longstanding philosophical problem. If God is all-knowing, and always acts for the best, then what is the purpose of asking Him to do something? Rationalists and mystics have a different approach to this question.

The general thrust of the rationalist approach is that the function of prayer is to transform *us*. Changing ourselves causes us to be suited to a different level of providence—however providence is understood.[20] The formulations of prayer may not be accurate from a strict philosophical perspective, but they reflect the psychological requirements of human nature.[21]

Mystics, on the other hand, are not particularly bothered by this question. This is because from a mystical perspective, the focus with prayer is not so much on a conversation of some sort with God. Rather, the focus is on the manipulation of various spiritual forces, through the utterances of various formulations and the actualizations of specific intents.

Another difference between the rationalist and mystical approaches is with regard to intermediaries. For rationalists, there is no role for

---

[20] See the earlier discussion of this topic in Section II.

[21] Marvin Fox, "Prayer and the Religious Life," in *Interpreting Maimonides* (University of Chicago Press 1990); Roslyn Weiss, "From Freedom to Formalism: Maimonides on Prayer," *CCAR Journal* (Fall 1997) pp. 29-43.

intermediaries in prayer. For mystics, on the other hand, with whom prayer is about manipulating various spiritual energies, there are all different kinds of intermediaries that can be of help. Rambam's ruling that it is heretical to pray to any intermediary won broad acceptance regarding the letter of his ruling, but not regarding the spirit of it; people simply claimed that they were not asking the intermediaries to intercede on their behalf, but rather to present their case before God.

Thus, for example, the prayer *Machnisei Rachamam*, recited in the liturgy of *selichot*, and *barchuni leshalom*, recited in the *Shalom Aleichem* song, both address requests to angels. As such, there has long been controversy about their recital, with efforts to reinterpret them. Praying at graves is more likely to be done by those of a mystical persuasion than by those of a rationalist persuasion. The practice of praying at special places such as the Western Wall, is understood by mystics as giving special powers to the prayer, while it is understood by rationalists as putting one in a superior frame of mind. And while mystics speak of special powers in praying on specific times, such as in the ninth hour of the ninth day of the ninth month of the ninth year in the *Birkat HaChamah* cycle, rationalists would reject this notion entirely. There are times that are more conducive to putting oneself in a certain frame of mind, but no inherent powers at different times.

Doing *Mitzvot* To Benefit Others

- *Expanded upon in Part Two, "What Can One Do for the Deceased?"*

Can one perform *mitzvot* and direct the credit to other people? Can one perform a mitzvah such as separating challah, reciting a *beracha*, or studying Torah, and say that the reward for that mitzvah should go to a particular designated person, whether they are alive or deceased? Such efforts have become almost completely normative in the Orthodox Jewish community today. However, they are an innovation, and they are not consistent with rationalist or indeed any classical approaches in rabbinic thought.

According to the rationalist approach, the function of *mitzvot* is to teach us ideas, perfect our characters, and improve society. Furthermore, according to the rationalist approach, this is not only the function of *mitzvot*, but also creates their reward. Having transformed our minds, we have created a relationship with God, the positive effects of which we reap in this world and the next. The reward is not some sort of spiritual paycheck that can be transferred to somebody else's account.

The popular notion that one can indeed transfer the merit for one's mitzvah to someone else is only possible within a mystical framework. Mysticism enables one to posit that *mitzvot* create discrete metaphysical "spiritual energies" that can be designated and transferred to others.

V: The Nature of Torah

Introduction

Rationalists understand the purpose of *mitzvot*, and religious life in general, as furthering intellectual and moral goals for the individual and society. Mystics agree that *mitzvot* provide intellectual and moral benefits, but see their primary function as performing mechanistic manipulations of spiritual or celestial forces. We have discussed how these different views have ramifications with regard to *mitzvot* such as mezuzah, *netilat yadayim*, and *shiluach hakein*. But there is another mitzvah in which the difference between the two schools of thought is reflected, and it is perhaps the most significant of all: the mitzvah of learning Torah.

The nature of the mitzvah of Torah study is an extremely complicated topic. Doing full justice to it is well beyond the scope of this chapter.[1] It is also impossible to talk about "the" classical approach to Torah study, since a variety of different approaches are found in the Talmud and the Rishonim. However, there are certain broad points that can be made, in particular vis-a-vis the contrast between rationalist and mystical worldviews with regard to Torah study. These have to do with both the function of Torah study and its status.

The study of Torah is of immense importance in Judaism, as we shall see. Can the importance of something that is tremendously important be over-emphasized? The answer is yes, of course it can. As long as something is not the *only* matter of importance, it is possible to over-emphasize its importance (even if it were to be the *most* important of all things). The

---

[1] Rabbi Dr. Norman Lamm's *Torah Lishmah—Torah for Torah's Sake in the Works of Rabbi Hayyim of Volozhin and his Contemporaries* (Hoboken, NJ: Ktav 1989) is an excellent study of many aspects of this topic.

engine is by far the most important component of a car; but it is possible to over-emphasize the importance of the engine.

Still, when something is enormously important, and is not taken at all seriously enough by many people, and especially if it is something that defines one's social group, then some people will naturally be hostile to the proposal that it is being over-emphasized. As such, the discussion in this chapter is likely to arouse no small amount of opposition.

What is Torah?

The difference between the rationalist and mystical views regarding the mitzvah of learning Torah relates to their fundamentally different view regarding what Torah actually is. Rationalists consider the Torah to be the divine instruction book for life—teaching us concepts that improve our minds, character and society. Mystics, on the other hand, believe the Torah to be the genetic blueprint of creation, possessing all kinds of metaphysical qualities, which only on its most superficial level is an instructional text.

The concept that Torah is the "blueprint" of creation, found in a small number of passages in the Midrash, later became central to mystical thought.[2] It supports the notion that one can derive knowledge about the universe from the Torah, and it also supports the notion that studying Torah provides energy to sustain the universe.

Today, the mystical view that Torah is the blueprint of creation is so thoroughly embedded in Judaism that most people consider it axiomatic to Jewish thought. Yet the concept that Torah is the blueprint of creation is open to multiple interpretations, and the sense in which it is taken today is certainly not what was understood by many early rabbinic authorities. Some of the greatest Rabbinic scholars did not even accept it at all.

The notion that the Torah is the blueprint of the universe presupposes that Torah precedes the universe. Such a statement is found explicitly in

---

[2] Ironically, a series of books that I wrote around two decades ago under the general title "The Torah Universe" was fundamentally based on the mystical understanding of this concept!

some early texts. *Midrash Bereishit Rabbah*[3] speaks about Torah preceding creation by 2000 years. There is also a list of seven things that existed before the creation of the universe, including Torah:

> There were seven things created before the universe: the Torah, Gehinnom, Gan Eden, the Throne of Glory, the Beit HaMikdash, repentance, and the name of the Messiah. (*Midrash Pirkei D'Rebbi Eliezer* 3; Talmud, Pesachim 54a, Nedarim 39b)

Yet many thinkers, including Rav Saadia Gaon[4] and even R. Yehudah HaLevi,[5] referenced this account but did not take it literally.[6] Some explained such statements to refer to the Ten Commandments preceding creation,[7] or to the Torah being the goal of creation.[8] Ran explains that God already knew before creation that it would be necessary to later create these things, because the world could not function properly without them.[9]

Rambam consciously rejected the notion that Torah preceded the universe.[10] Rambam's rejection of this was due to two reasons. First, Rambam's view of God's uniqueness and unity leads him to states that the notion of *anything* existing before creation, alongside God, is heretical.[11]

---

[3] *Midrash Bereishis Rabbah* 8:2.

[4] Rav Saadiah's comments are cited by R. Yehudah Barzilay, Commentary to *Sefer Yetzirah* (Berlin 1885, Halberstam edition) p. 92.

[5] *Kuzari* 3:73.

[6] See Harry A. Wolfson, *Repercussions of the Kalam in Jewish Philosophy* (Cambridge: Harvard University Press, 1979), pp. 85–113.

[7] Mabit, *Beis Elokim*.

[8] Ibn Ezra, introduction to his commentary to the Torah. See Abraham Joshua Heschel, *Heavenly Torah: As Refracted Through the Generations* (New York: Continuum Books 2007), chapter 17, for a discussion of further sources that do not take this statement at face value.

[9] Ran, commentary to Nedarim 39b.

[10] For extensive discussion, see Menachem Kellner, "Rashi and Maimonides on the Relationship Between Torah and the Cosmos," in *Between Rashi and Maimonides: Themes in Medieval Jewish Thought, Literature and Exegesis*, ed. Ephraim Kanarfogel and Moshe Sokolow (Jersey City, NJ, 2010) pp. 23–58; idem, "*Kadma Torah Le-Olam? – Iyun BeRambam*," *Daat* 61 (Summer 5767) pp. 83-96.

[11] See *Guide for the Perplexed* 1:9 and 2:26, and the extensive discussion in Kellner, ibid.

Second, it did not fit with his view that many of the commandments were issued as a response to historical circumstances, and thus could not have preceded these circumstances. Indeed, Judaism itself, in Rambam's view, is a consequence of Avraham's initiative in seeking out his Creator, and thus did not exist before Avraham.

How Did the Forefathers Observe the Torah?

The notion that Torah preceded the universe and is the blueprint of the universe is also related to certain interpretations of the concept that "the forefathers observed the Torah."[12] Some authorities, such as Rashi and Rashba, interpreted this very broadly to mean that the forefathers actually observed all the details of the Torah that was yet to be given at Sinai, including all 613 *mitzvot*. This is related to the mystical view that the Torah preceded creation and is the blueprint of creation; hence, it was possible for the forefathers to "tap into" it, even without having received it at Sinai.

Following this approach, there are all kinds of creative exegeses to illustrate how Biblical figures observed Torah law. The Talmud itself makes reference to the forefathers knowing and observing specific Torah laws, including those of the Oral Law,[13] and later authorities took this to much greater extremes:

> The *pasuk* says that Yaakov gave Eisav bread and lentil stew. Eisav only asked for the lentils, why did Yaakov give him bread? R. Chaim Kanievsky answers that since there is a dispute in the Gemara as to what *bracha* to make on beans that were cooked for a long time (either *Shehakol* or *Ha'adama*), the best way to avoid any problems is to wash on bread. Therefore, Yaakov gave Eisav the bread so he would wash and not worry about which *bracha* to make. (*Derech Sicha Al HaTorah*[14])

---

[12] Yoma 28b, Kiddushin 82a.

[13] Yoma 28b.

[14] See further at http://revach.net/parshas-hashavua/quick-vort/Parshas-Toldos-Rav-Chaim-Kanievsky-Meshech-Chochma-Eisav-and-Lavan-Who-Was-The-Big-Lamdan/1306.

However, other authorities, such as Rambam,[15] Ibn Ezra[16] and Rashbam[17] were not of the view that the forefathers observed any more *mitzvot* than those which were specifically commanded to them. The forefathers observed the Torah only in the sense that they acted righteously according to the code of conduct that was relevant and known in their day.[18]

The Function of Torah Study: In the Talmud

What is the goal and function of studying Torah? There are numerous sources in Chazal which imply that the (primary) function of studying Torah is in order to observe it:

> It is not the exposition that is the main point, but rather the actions. (Mishnah, Avot 1:17; similarly in *Sifra, Acharei Mot* 9)

> Rabbi Eleazar said: What was the blessing that Moses first blessed upon the Torah? Blessed are You, God our Lord, King of the Universe, Who chose this Torah, and sanctified it, and desired those who fulfill it. He did not say "those who toil in it," and he did not say "those who contemplate it," bur rather "those who fulfill it"—those who fulfill the words of the Torah. (*Midrash Rabba, Devarim* 11:6)

> Rava would often comment: The purpose of wisdom is repentance and good deeds—that a person should not read and study and then defy his father, his mother, his rabbi, and those greater than him in wisdom and rank, as it says, "The beginning of wisdom is the fear of the Lord; a good understanding is gained by all those that do them" (Ps. 111:10). It does

---

[15] See *Mishneh Torah, Hilchot Melachim* 9:1, and Kellner ibid.

[16] Commentary to Genesis 26:5.

[17] Commentary to Genesis 26:5.

[18] See too R. Yechiel Yaakov Weinberg, *Seridei Esh* 2:53, and Rav Kook, *Igrot HaRe'iyah*, vol. I, p. 135. An extensive discussion can be found in Isaiah Gafni, "Rabbinic Historiography and Representations of the Past," in *The Cambridge Companion to The Talmud and Rabbinic Literature* (2007) pp. 295-312, and a more accessible discussion can be found in Aqibha Weisinger, "Pre-Sinaitic Halakhic Observance As Interpreted By Medieval Authorities," available online at http://www.academia.edu/20066648/Pre-Sinaitic_Halakhic_Observance_As_Interpreted_By_Medieval_Authorities.

not say, "for all who study," but "for all who do," which implies, those that do them *lishmah* and not *shelo lishmah*. (*Berakhot* 17a[19])

One of the most significant discussions relating to this point is in the Talmud's account of how a group of Sages debated whether studying Torah is greater than fulfilling it:

> Rabbi Tarfon and the Elders were already gathered in the upper chamber of Nitza's house in Lod, when the following question was raised before them: What is greater, study or practice? Rabbi Tarfon answered, saying: Practice is greater. Rabbi Akiva answered, saying: Study is greater. All of them answered, saying: Study is greater, because study leads to practice. (*Kiddushin* 40b[20])

This dispute was resolved with the conclusion that study is greater. That would seem to indeed demonstrate that the study of Torah is an end unto itself, and is the highest form of human endeavor.

And yet matters become more complicated when this is considered carefully. The Talmud's conclusion is not merely that study is greater. It is that study is greater *because it leads to practice*.[21] But if study is greater because it leads to practice, then this effectively means that practice is more important! Rabbi Dr. Norman Lamm, in his comprehensive and excellent study of this topic, notes that many authorities interpret the Talmud to mean that study is "greater" only in the sense that it takes precedence; you have to study the Torah in order to know how to practice it:

> One could thus suggest, as indeed many have, that the assembly's preference for study is meant only in a chronological sense; it is to be propaedeutic to practice. To be sure, it is indispensable to practice and

---

[19] This follows the Munich manuscript of the Talmud; see online at http://daten.digitale-sammlungen.de/~db/bsb00003409/images/index.html?id=00003409-&groesser=&fip=193.174.98.30&no=&seite=287

[20] For extensive discussion of this passage, see Lamm, *Torah Lishmah*, pp. 139-143.

[21] It should be noted that not all Torah study leads to practice. For more on this, see the excellent and very important article by Rabbi Dr. Aaron Hersh Fried, "Is There a Disconnect between Torah Learning and Torah Living? And If So, How Can We Connect Them? A Focus on Middos," *Hakirah: The Flatbush Journal of Law and Thought*, Volume 6 (Summer 2008) pp. 11–56.

therefore has to come first, but it serves only as a means to achieve another end, namely, practice, which remains axiologically superior. (*Torah Lishmah—Torah for Torah's Sake in the Works of Rabbi Hayyim of Volozhin and his Contemporaries*, p. 141)

We see that the greatness of studying Torah is due to it teaching us how to fulfill the Torah, which is the ultimate goal. This is also seen in a passage discussing the form of praise that was set aside for King Chizkiyah:

> "They honored (Chizkiyah) in his death" ...- they put a Torah scroll on his bed, and they said, "This one fulfilled all that is written in this." But surely we do the same today (and thus it is no particular honor)? ...We say that the person fulfilled the Torah, but we do not say that he expounded Torah (whereas with Chizkiyah, it was said that he expounded Torah). But did the master not say that learning Torah is great, because it leads to practice (and thus the praise given today of Torah scholars, that they fulfill the Torah, is even greater than that given to Chizkiyah[22])? This [that the greatness of study is insofar as it leads to practice] refers to one's own learning, and this [that Chizkiyah was honored with] refers to teaching others. (Bava Kama 17a)

Here we see a clear hierarchy. Fulfilling the Torah is greater than studying it; teaching others is even greater, because it leads many people to fulfill it.[23]

The Function of Torah Study: In the Rishonim

Amongst the Rishonim, we likewise find the function of Torah study described in terms of learning how to act. Let us survey the words of several Rishonim, beginning with Rambam:

> The goal of wisdom should not be to receive honor from people or to profit financially. And one should not busy himself with God's Torah in

---

[22] This follows Rashi's explanation. Tosafot cites the alternate explanation of Rabbeinu Tam, that the question is: "But did the master not say that learning Torah is great, because it leads to fulfilling (and thus the praise given today of Torah scholars, that they fulfill the Torah, necessarily implies that they also learned it)!" For a detailed discussion regarding this passage, and possibly errors in its transmission, see Yosef Witztum, "*Kiyyem Zeh Mah Shekatuv Bezeh*," *Netuim* 6:59-72.

[23] See too Tosafot to Kiddushin 40b s.v. *Talmud Gadol*.

order to earn a living from it. The goal of learning wisdom should be for nothing other than knowing it, and likewise the goal of truth is to know that it is true and the Torah is true, and the goal of knowing it is to fulfill it. (Rambam, *Commentary on the Mishnah*, Sanhedrin 10:1)

There is no mitzvah among all the *mitzvot* which can be weighed against the study of Torah; rather, the study of Torah is equal to all the other *mitzvot*, because study brings to action, and therefore study always takes precedence to action. (*Mishneh Torah, Hilchot Talmud Torah* 3:3)

While Rambam here describes the goal of Torah study as being action, elsewhere he writes that the perfection of the intellect is the ultimate goal of human existence.[24] However, the type of perfecting the intellect that Rambam had in mind was that of philosophical contemplation, not learning Gemara. As the Vilna Gaon points out, Rambam was deeply affected by Greco-Islamic thought. In the role that he attributed to philosophical contemplation, Rambam represents an unusual departure from both those who preceded him and those who followed him. But when it comes to regular Torah study, Rambam held that the goal of it was to know how to perform *mitzvot*.

R. Menachem Meiri likewise describes the goal of Torah study as being to lead to *mitzvot*. This is in the context of discussing the principle that for certain *mitzvot*, one should interrupt one's Torah study in order to fulfill them:

Should you ask: How could they be more lenient with the study of Torah than with all other *mitzvot*, in which they said that one who is busy with a mitzvah is exempt from other *mitzvot*?.... The answer is that study is for nothing other than to bring to action, so how could it remove the obligation to act?! (Meiri, Commentary to Shabbat 9a)

The importance of study in terms of its instructional role is also seen in Tosafot.[25] In addressing a certain question, Tosafot states that for a person who does not yet know how to live a mitzvah-observant lifestyle, study takes precedence, but once a person knows how to live such a lifestyle, *mitzvot* are greater than study.

---

[24] *Guide for the Perplexed* 3:54.

[25] Tosafos to Kiddushin 40b s.v. *Talmud Gadol*.

Numerous other Rishonim likewise explain the goal and function of learning Torah in terms of its instructional role:

> This [learning in order to practice] is the highest level; it is achieved by one who studies the Torah with the aim of revealing its principles and viewing its mysteries, so that he may walk in its paths and fulfill its commandments. (R. David b. R. Avraham b. Rambam, Midrash David to Avot 4:5)

> It is not the study that is the main point, but rather it is a man's good deeds that pull and bring him into the next world. (R. Shimshon of Shantz, Comment to Sifri Acharei 9:9)

> "It is not the study that is the main point, but rather the practice"—That is to say, the goal of a person's knowledge and toil in Torah is not that he should study much Torah. The goal is nothing other than that it should bring him to practice. And that is what is written, "And you should study them and guard them to fulfill them"—it comes to teach that the purpose of study is for nothing other than practice. (Rabbeinu Bechaye, Commentary to Avot 1:17; see there at length)

> It is well known that the purpose of the entire Torah is to acquire the fear of Heaven, and not to attain wisdom, for our grasp of wisdom is limited... Our obligation to study in the beginning is only so that we can arrive at the deed, since it is impossible for one who is not knowledgeable of a mitzvah to perform it as well as one who is. (Rabbeinu Nissim ben Reuven, *Derashot HaRan* 7)

> "And one who learns in order to fulfill, is given the opportunity to learn and to teach and to fulfill." This refers to someone who wants to delve into his studies to get to the heart of the matter, and he wants to toil for many days and years in order to attain every minutia, and to conduct himself according to the true path. This is someone who "learns in order to fulfill," for his entire purpose is for nothing other than his actions to be correct, and therefore he is given the opportunity to learn and to teach and to fulfill, since everything is for the sake of his actions. (Rabbeinu Yonah, Commentary to Avot 4:6)

In these views we see that the tremendous value attached to studying Torah is due to its instructional role in teaching us how to live a proper mitzvah-observant life. There is certainly also value in studying Torah even with non-practical applications—indeed, many parts of the Torah do not have practical applications. Nevertheless, the primary value of it is in its role in inspiring and teaching us how to conduct our lives. (Such a role can also be fulfilled by studying non-instructional parts of Torah, since such engagement with Torah generates a commitment to fulfilling the Torah.)

It should be noted that there is a significant difference between the Rishonim of Ashkenaz and the Rishonim of Sefarad in their approach to Torah.[26] The Rishonim of Sefarad wrote codes; the Rishonim of Ashkenaz wrote commentaries. The Rishonim of Sefarad were always concerned with the bottom line, with the practical halachah; the Rishonim of Ashkenaz cared relatively little for that and were more interested in discussing and resolving contradictions in texts.

Nevertheless, even for the Rishonim of Ashkenaz, while there was less of a practical aspect in their Torah studies, the overall significance of the endeavor was still seen in terms of scholarship. In all the discussions of the Gemara and Rishonim as to the value of studying Torah, not one of these mentions any mystical notions of metaphysical energies created by the study of Torah. All the discussions in the Gemara and Rishonim about the particular importance of Torah study are expressed in terms of its instructional and educational value.

The Mystical Function of Torah Study

For the rationalist Rishonim, learning Torah serves to increase one's knowledge, and to refine one's character, via moral lessons and learning the commandments. That is it, and that is all. Which is not, of course, to trivialize these functions—from a rationalist perspective, these are of immense importance!

With the rise of mysticism, on the other hand, came a new and primary function of Torah study. Beginning a few centuries ago, and accelerating in the last few decades, the mitzvah of Torah study has been dramatically transformed not just in the importance attached to it, and in the very

---

[26] See Yehudah Galinsky, "Halakhah, Economics, and Ideology in the Beit Medrash of the Rosh in Toledo," *Zion* 72:4 (2007) pp. 387-419 (Hebrew).

nature and function of the act itself. As expressed by Rabbi Chaim of Volozhin in *Nefesh HaChaim*, the primary function of Torah study was now seen as being to metaphysically sustain the universe, via the creation and nourishment of spiritual forces:

> The entire life and existence of all the worlds is only by way of the Jewish People busying themselves with the Holy Torah. (*Nefesh HaChaim* 1:16)

The seminal study of this topic is that of Rabbi Dr. Norman Lamm, *Torah Lishmah—Torah for Torah's Sake in the Works of Rabbi Hayyim of Volozhin and his Contemporaries*. Rabbi Lamm points out that it is not only that the Kabbalistic view of Torah is different from the rationalist view. Even within the Kabbalistic framework, the approach of R. Chaim was a radical innovation:

> R. Hayyim's emphasis upon the study of Torah in the scheme of religious values exceeds that of his predecessors.... This emphasis issues, in turn, from his concept of Torah... In keeping with the Kabbalists, R. Hayyim hypostatizes Torah: it is a primordial, timeless, organic entity... Most other Kabbalists, before and contemporary with R. Hayyim, located the origin of Torah *within* the process of emanation... the highest source claimed for Torah is that of the world of *Azilut*, after God has already left His inner being and turned outwards. Thus Torah, no matter how lofty its origin, is the product of divine emanation and hence removed from his essence... R. Hayyim, however, did not follow this mainstream kabbalistic doctrine. He took the bold step of removing Torah from the world of divine emanation and assigning its genesis to the infinitely mysterious regions of the *En-Sof...* Torah is thus conceived of as an aspect of God Himself, in His absoluteness and transcendence, rather than as one of the manifestations of the unfolding of His will and creative power.

> A number of important consequences flow from this Torah-concept of R. Hayyim. First, the doctrine of the preexistence of the Torah... is now taken in more than the chronological sense... The Torah's preexistence is primarily an axiological-teleological concept. Torah, as an aspect of God beyond all of existence which issues from Him, in the forms which mortals can perceive it, is the telos of all existence. Torah "is the soul and the life and light and the root of all the worlds." (*Torah Lishmah*, pp. 103-105)

Why did R. Chaim change the nature of the mitzvah of Torah study in this way? As is widely acknowledged, this was in reaction to the rise of Chassidism:

> While the Hasidic masters… never negated the study of Torah, they, so to speak, "naturalized" it. Torah study was viewed as just one of the 613 commandments, and its significance was thus correspondingly reduced from its position of unimpeachable eminence… In the writings of the Rabbi of Layady (R. Shneur Zalman) we find, despite his position as one of the most moderate of the Hasidic camp, the clear formulation of the new movement's valuation in which the study of Torah is relegated to second place and the practice of *mitzvot* becomes the chief instrument whereby man fulfills his divinely ordained function of achieving the redemption of the universe. It is against this background—that of widespread ignorance of Torah in a practical sense, and the devaluation of the supremacy of Torah on the theoretical level by the Hasidic teachers—that we must view the reaffirmation by R. Hayyim of the uncontested superiority of Torah over and above any and all other religious activities. For, indeed, R. Hayyim is unequalled in his valuation of Torah as superior to any other value… R. Hayyim's reaction to the disturbance in the study-practice (and study-prayer) equilibrium by the hasidic initiative was to endow study with a value much greater than was attributed to it before. (*Torah Lishmah*, pp. 146, 152, 169)

The significance of R. Chaim's revolution was not only to increase the value placed upon Torah study, but also to transform the idea of what Torah study actually does. It also led to several traditional statements about Torah being given new meaning. We shall explore several examples of this.

Torah Lishmah

There are countless phrases from classical Jewish sources bandied around which are nearly universally assumed to have a certain meaning, but with which, upon careful study, it is revealed that the contemporary meaning is not actually the classical meaning. Rather, it is based on the mystical outlook, and is being read back into the original wording. This is especially the case with phrases relating to Torah study.

One example of this is with the phrase *Torah lishmah*. This phrase, and its interpretations, crystallizes the difference between rationalists and mystics with regard to the function of Torah study.

It should first be made clear that in general, the translation of *lishmah* certainly does not mean "for its own sake." Rather, it means *leshem Shamayim*, "for the sake of Heaven." This is most clearly seen in the discussion of the concept of *aveira lishmah*. This phrase does not refer to a transgression committed "for its own sake"; rather, it refers to a transgression committed *leshem Shamayim*. By the same token, learning *Torah lishmah* means learning Torah *leshem Shamayim*.

We also find explicit statements from the Sages that *Torah lishmah* refers to learning for the sake of Heaven and not to learning for the sake of learning:

> Rava would often comment: The purpose of wisdom is repentance and good deeds—that a person should not read and study and then defy his father, his mother, his rabbi, and those greater than him in wisdom and rank, as it says, "The beginning of wisdom is the fear of the Lord; a good understanding is gained by all those that do them" (Ps. 111:10). It does not say, "for all who study," but "for all who do," which implies, those that do them *lishmah* and not *shelo lishmah*. (*Berachot* 17a[27])

This explanation is echoed in later rabbinic sources:

> If a man wishes to study *lishmah*, what shall he intend when he studies? "Whatever I study I will practice." (R. Yehudah b. Shmuel, *Sefer Chassidim* 944)

Even some of the early mystics explained *lishmah* in this manner:

> The essence of Torah *lishmah* is the Torah that man learns in order to practice it. (R. Eliyahu de Vidas, *Reishit Chochma*, introduction)

Gradually, however, mystics integrated the notion of the study of the Torah having metaphysical ramifications:

---

[27] This follows the Munich manuscript of the Talmud; see online at http://daten.digitale-sammlungen.de/~db/bsb00003409/images/-index.html?id=00003409&groesser=&fip=193.174.98.30&no=&seite=287

> How good it is if, when one opens a book, one says, "Behold, I wish to study in order that the study bring me to practice and to proper character traits and to the knowledge of Torah, and I do this in order to unity the Holy One with His Shechinah"—this is what is called Torah *lishmah*. (R. Yeshaya Horowitz, *Shnei Luchot HaBrit, masechet Shavuot*)

This culminated with R. Chaim of Volozhin, who writes at length about Torah *lishmah*, and describes it as referring to Torah study for "its own sake"—meaning, not for the sake of knowing how to fulfill the *mitzvot*, and nor for the sake of the religious experience of *devekut*. Rather, it is simply for the sake of learning Torah, which itself is the ultimate mystical-cosmic act of metaphysically sustaining the universe.

R. Chaim is therefore proposing that the *lishmah* of Torah has a different meaning than the usual meaning of the term *lishmah*, which, as noted above, always means "for the sake of Heaven." He bases this radical approach on the words of a single Rishon, R. Asher b. Yechiel (the Rosh).[28] This is with regard to a passage in the Talmud about the proper motivations for Torah study, which includes the following statement:

> R. Eliezer b. R. Tzadok said, Do [good] deeds for the sake of their Maker, and speak of them for their sake. (Nedarim 62a)

On this, the Rosh comments:

> "Do [good] deeds for the sake of their Maker"—for the sake of the Holy One, Who made everything for His sake. "And speak of them for their sake"—all your words and discussions about Torah should be for the sake of Torah, such as to know, to understand, and to increase insight and dialectical skill, and not for chiding others or for vanity." (Commentary of the Rosh ad loc.)

One could explain that Rosh is simply saying that Torah should not be studied for ulterior, nefarious motives. But R. Chaim understands Rosh as stressing the Talmud's differentiation between doing *mitzvot*, which is for the sake of Heaven, and learning Torah, which is for its own sake.

---

[28] See Yehudah Galinsky, "Halakhah, Economics, and Ideology in the Beit Medrash of the Rosh in Toledo," *Zion* 72:4 (2007) pp. 387-419 (Hebrew).

This is already somewhat of a slim reed upon which to base an interpretation of the word *lishmah* which is radically different from every other place where it is mentioned, including with regard to Torah (as in *Berachot* 17a cited above). But to make things even more tenuous, there are several other textual variants of this passage in the Talmud, in which there is no contrast presented between deeds being done for the sake of Heaven and Torah being studied for its own sake.[29] And there is evidence from other Tannaic texts that even the version of the text used by the Rosh should be vocalized differently and would not lead to the inference drawn by the Rosh.[30]

Nevertheless, it is of great importance to R. Chaim to rely upon this interpretation of the Rosh's explanation of a particular variant of the Talmudic text, notwithstanding its going against the standard meaning of *lishmah*, as well as the explanation of *lishmah* given elsewhere in the Talmud and by other authorities. It enabled him to argue against the Hassidic approach that learning Torah was to be justified in terms of generating *devekut*, which led people to negate the less inspirational parts of the Talmud. But in order to justify the importance of studying Torah for its own sake, it required the construction of a mystical edifice in which the study of Torah has enormous metaphysical cosmic significance. This notion proved tremendously attractive, and R. Chaim's novel explanation of Torah *lishmah* gained widespread acceptance, to the point that many people do not even realize that the term classically meant something very different.

Talmud Torah K'neged Kulam

There is another prominent example of a phrase that has been given a radically different interpretation than its classical meaning. This is the phrase *talmud Torah k'neged kulam*, "the study of Torah is equal to everything," which is well known from its daily recital in the morning prayers:

---

[29] See R. Norman Lamm, *Torah Lishmah*, note 20 on pp. 247-8.
[30] Ibid.

These are the things which man performs and enjoys their fruits in this world, while the principal remains for him in the World to Come: honoring one's parents, bestowing kindness, arriving at the study hall early in the morning and evening, welcoming guests, visiting the sick, assisting a bride, escorting the dead, contemplation of prayer, and making peace between man and his fellow. And the study of the Torah is equal to them all. (Siddur)

While this is popularly taken to mean that the study of Torah is equal to all other *mitzvot*, it should be noted that this is all referring to things which man performs and enjoys their fruits in this world, while the principal remains for him in the World to Come. Accordingly, it is simply stating that the study of Torah brings benefits in this world equal to the benefits brought by the other *mitzvot* listed. For example, if one honors his parents, his children will see this and may ultimately emulate this and honor him when he is old; if a person is kind to others, then someday, when he is in need, others will be kind to him. Thus, the statement "And the study of the Torah is equal to them all" simply means that the extra benefits that are reaped in this world by studying Torah is as great as the extra benefits that are derived from all of the others combined.

Still, this passage has been taken as meaning that the mitzvah of studying Torah is altogether equal to all other *mitzvot*. While the idea that Torah is equal in value to all other *mitzvot* put together is not necessarily related to the mystical outlook, it does dovetail with it. After all, from a rationalist perspective, while Torah is extremely important in terms of its instructional and educational value, it is difficult to see why it would be equal in value to all other *mitzvot* put together. Whereas if learning Torah is of mystical significance, then this can easily be proposed to be equal to all other *mitzvot* combined, in terms of the supernatural, metaphysical effects that it creates.

Yet in practice, nobody, and certainly not Chazal, ever took *Talmud Torah k'neged kulam* to mean that any given moment of Torah study is equal in value to all other *mitzvot* combined. If they did, then there would never be grounds to do an optional mitzvah, much less to institute any kind of non-critical act, religious or otherwise, that could take people away from a moment of Torah study.

Furthermore, it is important to note that there are several *mitzvot* about which Chazal say that they are equal to all other *mitzvot* together:

> Shabbat is equal to all the *mitzvot* of the Torah. (Yerushalmi, *Berachot* 9a)

> Great is circumcision, for it is equal to all the *mitzvot* of the Torah. (Yerushalmi, *Nedarim* 12b)

> The mitzvah of *tzitzit* is equal to all the *mitzvot* of the Torah (Nedarim 25a, *Menachot* 43b)

> Charity and bestowing kindness are equal to all the *mitzvot* of the Torah (Yerushalmi, *Pe'ah* 3a)

> Settling the land of Israel is equal to all the *mitzvot* of the Torah (Tosefta, *Avodah Zarah* 5)

Now, it is logically impossible for all these things to be equal to all other *mitzvot*! Thus, the phrase *k'neged kulam* cannot be interpreted literally to mean that they are equal to all other *mitzvot*.

Most significantly, the version that we say in the *Shacharit* prayers, which has a long list of *mitzvot* regarding which it is said that *Talmud Torah k'neged kulam*, is not the original text. Rather, it is an expansion of the original text,[31] which is a Mishnah in *Pe'ah*. That Mishnah lists three *mitzvot*, and then says *Talmud Torah k'neged kulam*:

> These are the things which man performs and enjoys their fruits in this world, while the principal remains for him in the World to Come: honoring one's parents, bestowing kindness, and making peace between man and his fellow. And the study of the Torah is equal to them all. (Mishnah, *Pe'ah* 1:1)

Now, the significance of realizing that this is the underlying source for *Talmud Torah k'neged kulam* is that this text also has a corresponding text regarding sins, which states as follows:

> And correspondingly, these are the things for which a person is punished in this world, while the principal remains for him in the World to Come:

---

[31] See Talmud *Shabbat* 127b, which contains most of the additions, and explains them to be elaborations of the three *mitzvot* specified in the Mishnah. The two additions that are not found in the Talmud are explained by Maharshal to likewise be elaborations of the three that are specified in the Mishnah.

Idolatry, forbidden relationships and murder. And *lashon hara* (evil speech) is equal to them all. (Yerushalmi, *Pe'ah* 4a; Tosefta, *Pe'ah* 1:2)

What are we to make of this? *Lashon hara* is very bad, but it is certainly not worse than idolatry, adultery and murder! Clearly, the point is to emphasize the severity of *lashon hara*, which can be far-reaching in its effects.

Thus, when Chazal say that *lashon hara* is equal to idolatry, adultery and murder, this is not meant to be understood literally. Likewise, when Chazal say *in the corresponding text* that Talmud Torah is equal to all other *mitzvot*, it is likewise not meant to be understood literally.

Having said all that, what does *Talmud Torah k'neged kulam* actually mean? It means that it is of foundational significance vis-à-vis *mitzvot*, just as *lashon hara* is of foundational significance vis-à-vis sin. It is the same as the discussion in *Kiddushin* 40b that we discussed earlier, where the consensus is that study is greater than action—and the reason given is that study leads to action. Rambam explicitly explains *Talmud Torah k'neged kulam* this way:

> And when you investigate this matter, you will find that Talmud Torah is weighed as equivalent to everything, because through Talmud Torah a person merits all these [*mitzvot* in the list], just as we explained at the beginning—that study leads to action. (Rambam, *Commentary on the Mishnah*, *Pe'ah* 1:1)

There are "regular" *mitzvot*, like blowing *shofar*, *shiluach hakein*, building a sukkah, etc. And there are especially significant *mitzvot*, described by Chazal as being "equal to all others," such as circumcision, Shabbos, charity, and settling the land of Israel. Of the especially significant *mitzvot*, learning Torah is unique. But this is (primarily) because, as Chazal say, "study leads to action."

The Unique Nature of Talmud Torah

There are many passages in the Talmud that describe learning Torah in a way which, at first glance, does not seem to fit the rationalist perspective:

> Rav Yosef said: Talmud Torah is greater than saving lives. (*Megillah* 16b)

> Rav said: Talmud Torah is greater than building the Beit HaMikdash. (*Megillah* 16b)

> [God said to David:] One day that you sit and busy yourself with Torah is better to me than a thousand offerings that your son Solomon will bring on the altar. (*Shabbat* 30a)

> Rabbi Berakhya and Rabbi Hiyya of Kfar Dehumin [disagreed]. One said: Even the [wealth of the] entire world does not equal a single word of the Torah. And the other one said: Even all the *mitzvot* of the Torah do not equal a single word of the Torah. (Yerushalmi, *Pe'ah* 1:1)

However, there are also other passages which contain similar descriptions about other *mitzvot*:

> Charity is greater than all the sacrifices. (*Sukkah* 49b)

> Charity and acts of kindness are the equivalent of all the *mitzvot* of the Torah. (Jerusalem Talmud, *Pe'ah* 1:1)

Thus, all these statements about the importance of learning Torah are no different than the phrase *talmud Torah k'neged kulam*, which has its counterpart in several other statements about other *mitzvot* being *k'neged kulam*. They are a combination of exaggerations, aggadic prose, and a result of the fact that learning Torah is of foundational importance because it enables one to do the other *mitzvot*.

There is one passage in the Talmud which explicitly states that man was created to toil in Torah.

> Rabbi Elazar said: Every man was created in order to toil, as it is written, "For man is born to toil" (Job 5:7). I still do not know, however, if he was created for the toil of the mouth or for the toil of work; but when the verse says, "[The toiling soul...] his mouth compels him," this tells me that he was created for the toil of the mouth. I still do not know, however, if he was created for the toil of Torah or for the toil of speech; when the verse says, "This book of Torah should not depart from your mouth," this tells me that he was created for the toil of Torah. (Sanhedrin 99b)

This seems to conclusively prove that learning Torah is the ultimate human endeavor. Yet the Talmud derives this from a protracted and very subtle exegesis, from a book that is not even part of the Torah or Prophets.

If learning Torah was really and truly the goal of our existence, wouldn't there be something a little more explicit?!

Rather, the statement in Sanhedrin is a *drush*, a homiletical exegesis. An obscure exegesis can hardly be taken as the foundational directive for human existence. Furthermore, even this passage is not unequivocal. Maharsha suggests that it is actually referring to teaching rather than studying Torah, and further seems to understand Rabbi Elazar more in terms of saying that toil in this world is inevitable, and it is better to fulfill this by way of Torah.

The only clear source for Chazal's position on this topic is the passage where they explicitly, *en masse*, set out to discuss it. This is the dispute in the Talmud that we discussed in the beginning of our discussion, about which is greater, study or practice. And their conclusion was that study is greater; but the explanation of this was given in rationalist terms, that it leads to practice.

Daat Torah

- *See too Volume II, "Sod Hashem Liyreyav—the Expansion of a Useful Concept"*

The contemporary concept of "Daat Torah" is very different from traditional ideas about the wisdom and authority of rabbis. To be sure, traditionally, leading Torah scholars were consulted on numerous issues. But, for most of history, political and communal leadership was in the hands of positions such as kings, exilarchs, and *parnassim*, rather than the leading rabbinic authorities. Furthermore, it was generally the case that, even for rabbis, wisdom in non-Torah-specific areas was understood to be commensurate with experience in those areas. Torah was understood to be a form of wisdom that enhances knowledge and experience gained from other areas, along with a person's innate wisdom.[32]

---

[32] Thus, there was the possibility that a person simply lacks innate wisdom, which cannot be helped no matter how much Torah he learns. This is seen in the statement in the Midrash (Vayikra Rabbah 1) that "Any Torah scholars who lacks wisdom is worse than a putrid animal carcass." See Rabbi Aharon Lichtenstein, "If There Is No Da'at, How

Daat Torah, however, presented the opposite notion: that the ultimate guidance on *all* areas of life—even social and political decisions with no obvious connection to Torah—is provided precisely by those who are the *most* cloistered from the world and have only been immersed in Torah. Daat Torah also presented itself not as advice, but as obligatory commands that must be followed. A further significant characteristic is that in contrast to the time-honored approach of rabbinic responsa, Daat Torah presents its conclusions without any explanations, halachic or otherwise.

There are numerous historical forces involved in the evolution of the contemporary notion of Daat Torah.[33] However, here we shall just focus on the aspect which relates to the mystical vs. rationalist divide.

From the rationalist viewpoint, Torah is a guide to leading an ethically and intellectually enriching life, given to the descendants of Avraham Avinu with its focus on their particular historical context. Accordingly, while it is a source of wisdom, supplementary knowledge and experience is also useful. Thus, for example, Yitro was able to provide useful insight of which none other than Moshe Rabbeinu was unaware. Likewise, rabbinic wisdom does not emerge solely from studying Torah, but also from knowledge gained in other ways, including other fields of study and other life experience, along with a person's inherent mental character. And the wisdom of rabbinic pronouncements can be evaluated and potentially proved incorrect.

According to the mystical approach, on the other hand, Torah is the mystical blueprint of all creation. It contains all knowledge and the wisdom to know how to act in every situation. While no Torah scholar today is able to access all the mystically-based knowledge, they are able to extract some of it:

> There are principles of Torah hashkafa that can serve as guidelines to all
> situations in life. However, a person giving an opinion must be certain

Can We Have Leadership?" at http://www.zootorah.com/RationalistJudaism/Daat-TorahLichtenstein.pdf

[33] See my monograph "The Making of Haredim," available for download at www.RationalistJudaism.com

that his opinion is based on pure Torah concepts. This can only be someone whose entire thought process are the result of Torah knowledge… Therefore, daas Torah is a *talmid chacham* who was never influenced by anything other than Torah.

…The Torah indeed has answers to all problems, both physical and psychological. The Zohar says that Hashem used the Torah as the blueprint for creating the world, so that everything in the world is contained in the Torah. Inasmuch as the Torah is the wisdom of Hashem, it is perfect and complete in every way.

The problem is that we do not know how to derive the information from the Torah. For example, the Shelah Hakadosh says that anyone who would fully understand the first *passuk* in *perek* 2 of *Bereishis* would know the entire science of physiognomy (knowing everything about a person by studying his face) and palmistry (being able to interpret the hand) But who can say he achieved such knowledge?

…Of course *gedolim* have more access to the Torah's secrets than ordinary people. We know that there were instances where the Chazon Ish gave surgeons directions on how to operate.[34] (Rabbi Dr. Abraham Twerski, *HaModia*, May 3rd and 10th 2007)

Accordingly, the more that people are immersed in Torah, and the less corrupted they are by other forms of knowledge and other life experiences, then the more knowledgeable they are about all existence, and the more they are supernaturally attuned to making the right decisions. Such attunement precludes lesser people evaluating these decisions, and obviously requires absolute fealty.

What is the Mechanism via which Torah Protects?

Another example of the difference between how the rationalist and mystical schools of thought relate to Torah study is with regard to the protection that it provides. There is undeniably a traditional concept in

---

[34] For the record, many years ago I asked Rabbi Gedalyah Nadel, one of the foremost disciples of the Chazon Ish, about the Chazon Ish's medical knowledge. Rabbi Nadel told me that the Chazon Ish did not know that much, and that what he did know was gleaned from reading German medical journals.

Judaism that Torah can potentially provide protection from harm.[35] This is found in several passages in the Talmud. Rabbi Yochanan states that "the words of Torah are effective at providing refuge" (*Makkot* 10a). According to one understanding presented by the Talmud, this means that if a Torah scholar accidentally kills someone and is vulnerable to being killed by the victim's relative, he is nevertheless safe while he is studying Torah, because it will protect him. (According to another understanding presented in the Talmud, his Torah only protects him death via divine agency, not from death via human hand.) Elsewhere, the Talmud rules that Torah scholars are exempt from the expense of building protective walls for the city, since they are protected by virtue of the Torah that they learn.[36]

We find accounts of Torah study not only protecting those engaged in it, but even those who enable others to engage in it:

> Rabbi Yehoshua ben Levi said: What is that which is written, "Our legs were standing in your gates, Jerusalem" (Ps. 122:2)? Who caused our legs to stand in war? The gates of Jerusalem, where they were occupied with Torah" (*Makkot* 10a).

In the same vein, the Talmud (*Sanhedrin* 49a) says that if not for Yoav, David would not have been able to find time to learn Torah,[37] and were it not for David's Torah study, Yoav would not have succeeded in war.

Another reference to the protective power of Torah for those who enable its study is found in a discussion about the protection that it affords to the *sotah*, if she has enabled her husbands and sons to study Torah:

> "There is a merit that delays the *sotah*'s punishment for three years" (Mishnah) …the merit of Torah… the Torah is compared to light in

---

[35] This is believed by some to be one of the reasons why the charedi community is largely opposed to yeshivah students serving in the IDF. In truth, it is not actually one of the reasons, but that is a discussion for elsewhere.

[36] Bava Metzia 108a and Bava Batra 7b.

[37] See Maharsha ad loc., who comments that the verse brought as a source refers to David acting justly to the entire people, and thus indicates that he learned Torah, which enabled him to know how to act justly. The significance of his Torah study is thus that he was able to act justly.

order to say to you: Just as the light of the sun protects forever, so too, the Torah protects one forever. (Sotah 21a)

As I have discussed at length elsewhere,[38] the extent and parameters of this protection are classically (and logically and practically) understood very differently from how certain contemporary figures explain it. For example, regarding the Talmud's statement that the rabbis do not need protection, Radvaz greatly restricts the extent of the Gemara's ruling, including stating that it does not apply in cases where the rabbis consider themselves in need of protection;[39] and Chatam Sofer says that it only refers to exemptions from city taxes that are placed upon Jews in exile, not for defense against genuine military threats. But here, let us discuss a different angle: the very mechanism understood to lie behind this protection.

According the rationalist approach, learning Torah imparts valuable knowledge, improves our character, and teaches us how to improve society. With the rise of mysticism, on the other hand, came a new and primary function of Torah study. As expressed by R. Chaim of Volozhin in *Nefesh HaChaim*, the primary function of Torah study was now seen as being to create spiritual energies and thereby metaphysically influence the universe.

The notion of Torah providing protection is interpreted by mystically-inclined people in line with this. Learning Torah creates metaphysical protection around one's city, similar to that created by mezuzah around one's home. The more Torah that is learned, the more powerful the protection. As one Beit Shemesh rabbi said during Operation Cast Lead, when the Grodno Yeshivah relocated from Ashdod to Beit Shemesh, "the yeshivah is providing an 'Iron Dome' for Beit Shemesh."[40] (Of course, this raises the question as to why the yeshivah didn't remain in Ashdod and provide the protection where it was actually needed; soldiers don't go where it is safe, but rather where their services are needed.)

---

[38] See the numerous posts at www.RationalistJudaism.com, which I plan to one day compile and publish in book form.

[39] Radvaz 2:752.

[40] As reported in the local Beit Shemesh newspaper *Chadash*.

Both the classical approach and the medieval rationalist approach to the notion of Torah providing protection would be very different. According to the classical approach, it related to the personal merit of the person studying (or enabling the study of) the Torah, rather than a metaphysical protection provided by the act of Torah study itself.

This is similar to the concept of benefiting someone who has passed away. According to the mystical approach, you can benefit anyone who has passed away, via learning Torah in their name and transferring "spiritual currency." According to the classical/rationalist approach, on the other hand, there is simply no mechanism for such a thing. Instead, only the descendants and disciples of the dead can benefit them, via creating a merit for them.

Note that the Talmud's presentation of this concept is usually not phrased as "Torah study protects" but rather as "Torah scholars are protected." It refers to the person who has performed the act rather than the act itself. Just as Sodom could have been saved in the merit of righteous people, so too righteous people can create a merit which leads to the machinations of enemy forces being divinely repressed. Likewise, in the discussion of the *sotah*, it speaks about the *zechut*, the merit, of Torah and of the *sotah* enabling her family's Torah study.

One may wonder if there are any practical ramifications to this difference, since according to either understanding, the person receives protection. In fact, the ramifications are very significant. Consider the following criticism of a plan to limit the number of yeshivah students receiving a full exemption from the IDF draft: "I cannot understand how any believing Jew could ever think that we have enough Torah learning, and all the more so in the present security situation in which six million Jews in Eretz Yisrael find themselves."[41] This reflects the mystical approach in which Torah study provides metaphysical protective energy, and thus the more Torah that is studied, the more protection is provided. With this perspective, it makes little difference as to whether the person

---

[41] Jonathan Rosenblum, "Enough Torah?" *Mishpacha* Magazine, July 12, 2013.

should ideally be learning Torah or doing something else; the starting point is that Torah provides metaphysical protective energy.

According to the classical/rationalist approach, on the other hand, protection is earned not by Torah study itself, but rather as a consequence of the merit of the person learning it. Accordingly, the first question to consider is whether it is indeed meritorious, i.e. whether it is indeed appropriate for the person to be learning Torah. If he is supposed to be doing something else instead—such as supporting his family, or serving in the army—then his Torah study will not necessarily be a source of merit, and thus does not provide any protective benefits.

It should be noted that there are medieval rationalist interpretations of the Torah's protection which circumscribe it even further. One such explanation is given in a brief comment by R. Menachem Meiri: "Torah protects the world—i.e., that the Torah scholar influences others, and his wisdom enables society to endure."[42] While Meiri elsewhere writes about Torah study providing a source of merit which results in military victory,[43] here he makes no mention of any supernatural components. In his view, the meaning of the statement that Torah protects the world is simply that Torah scholars, with their wisdom, influence society for the better, thereby enabling it to thrive.

Can the World Survive Without Torah?

There is a widely-held belief that if Torah study were to entirely cease worldwide, even for a moment, the entire universe would cease to exist. Accordingly, in the famous Volozhin Yeshivah, study shifts were arranged so that there was at least one student learning Torah at every moment of every day and night.[44]

> Even more radically, R. Hayyim concludes from the supernal origins he assigns to Torah that is priority is to be taken also in a dynamic-metaphorical sense. Since Torah issues from the realms beyond the emanations of the worlds, their continued existence is conditional upon

---

[42] Meiri, Commentary to Sotah 21a.

[43] See his comments to the passage cited above from Makkot 10a.

[44] See Rabbi Norman Lamm, *Torah Lishmah*, p. 125 n. 33.

Torah… The sustenance of existence by Torah is achieved by Israel's study of Torah… In words often repeated by R. Hayyim, and what may be considered the *locus classicus* of Lithuanian talmudic scholarship: "The undoubted truth is that if all the world, from one end to the other, were—Heaven forbid—void even for one moment of our study of and medication on Torah, the immediately all the upper and lower worlds would be destroyed and revert to chaos and nothingness."[45] (R. Lamm, *Torah Lishmah*, pp. 105-107)

It is further widely believed that this is a normative, unequivocal, traditional Jewish belief, that is sourced in the Talmud itself. Now, there is no reason why this should be the case in a rationalist framework—what difference does it make to God whether Torah is learned at a particular minute? Thus, this is presumed to necessarily lend credence to the mystical view of Torah study; that it creates the spiritual energy necessary for the world to function.

However, careful study reveals that, yet again, we have a situation where a relatively mild view was strengthened over time, infused with mystical meaning, and then read back into earlier sources. Let us analyze each of the sources one by one, paying careful attention to exactly what they say, and what they do *not* say.

One source, cited by R. Haim of Volozhin,[46] is the tenth-century Midrash of *Tanna Devei Eliyahu*:

> The sages said: Whenever people neglect the Torah, the Holy One seeks to destroy the world. (*Tanna Devei Eliyahu Rabba* 2)

First, let us note that it does not say that if people cease studying Torah then the world will be destroyed. Rather, it is a somewhat milder statement that *when* people neglect Torah (implying something that actually happens from time to time), God *seeks* to destroy the world (but does not actually do so).

Second, it says that they neglect the Torah, not that they neglect *the study of* Torah, and so it might refer to neglecting the *observance* of Torah.

---

[45] *Nefesh HaChaim* 1:16, 4:11, 4:25, *Ruach Chaim* 1:2.

[46] *Nefesh HaChaim* 4:25.

If we look at the full text of the Midrash, we see that this does indeed seem to be the reference. The context is a discussion of the severity of the punishment for the trivial sins of the righteous, naming Moses, Aaron, Nadav and Avihu (which were not sins of neglecting Torah study), which segues into a discussion of the Deluge (which was likewise not a punishment for the sin of neglecting Torah study). It says:

> And why is there all this (punishment)? Because of [their transgression against] "The Torah of God which is perfect, restoring the soul; the testimony of God which is sure, making the simple wise; the precepts of God which are right, making the heart rejoice; the instruction of God is lucid, making the eyes light up; the fear of God is pure, abiding forever; the judgments of God are true, altogether righteous; more desirable than gold, than much fine gold; sweeter than honey, than drippings of the comb" (Ps. 19:8-11). From here we see, the sages said, that whenever people neglect the Torah, the Holy One seeks to destroy the world, as it says, "Give praise to God, you divine beings," (Ps. 29:1, which concludes with a reference to the Deluge), and the divine beings are the ministering angels. The Holy One said: I multiplied men (at the time of the Deluge) like the birds of the heaven and the fish of the sea, and they did not fulfill My will, therefore I hid My face from them. (*Tanna Devei Eliyahu Rabba* 2)

The entire discussion here is about people neglecting the *observance* of Torah, not the *study* of Torah.

Nevertheless, there are indeed sources about the existence of the world relating to the study of Torah, albeit from a later period. One such source cited by R. Chaim is the tenth-century Midrashic work *Tanna Devei Eliyahu Zuta*:

> Every day, angels of destruction depart from before the Holy One, to destroy the entire world, and were it not for the synagogues and study halls where Torah scholars are sitting and busying themselves with words of Torah, they would immediately destroy the entire world. (*Tanna Devei Eliyahu Zuta* 5)

This is the section that R. Chaim quotes, but, again, if we look at the entire source, the picture seems to be different. It is talking about the protection that is provided by the personal merit of people rather than the metaphysical power of Torah. The context is an exposition of a verse (I Sam. 2:8) referring to the "pillars of the earth," which the Midrash expounds as referring to Torah scholars. The Midrash proceeds to compare the importance of Torah scholars to a vineyard, in which the purpose of farming it is for the grapes, not for the weeds, which are often destroyed in order to make room for the vines. The Midrash concludes by saying "And likewise, all the righteous people, when they stand in the world, they are like the vines which stand in the vineyard, and all the world relies upon them." The reference to "righteous people" further demonstrates that it is talking about personal merit, not the inherent power of Torah.

R. Chaim further argues his case by explaining how a single person, if he were to be the only person in the world studying Torah at a particular moment, would be responsible for the continued existence of the universe. He attempts to prove this from the Talmud:

> Anyone who studies Torah *lishmah*… protects the entire world… and the entire world is justified for his sake… (*Sanhedrin* 99b)

Again, though, a careful analysis reveals that this passage does not seem to prove R. Chaim's claim. The first part of the statement, that anyone who studies Torah *lishmah* protects the entire world—whatever the exact meaning of "protects" is—simply means that any such person provides additional protection for the world. It does not mean that if there was only one such person, they would be the sole reason for the world to exist.

The second part of the statement, that "the entire world is justified for his sake," simply means that such a person is doing something of such value that it would justify the *creation* of the world. It does not mean that it is the only thing that justifies the ongoing *existence* of the world (and note that the Mishnah states that the world stands on *three* things: Torah, divine service, and acts of kindness). Nor does it mean that the world would cease to exist if there was nobody doing that at a given moment in time.

In this vein, let us examine another passage in the Talmud which is commonly brought to prove that if there was a moment in which nobody was studying Torah, the world would cease to exist:

> Rabbi Eleazar said: "Great is Torah, for without it, heaven and earth would not have come into existence (*nitkayma*), as it is stated [*Yirmiyahu* 33:25], 'Have I not established the covenant with day and night, the laws of heaven and earth' (Isaiah 33:25)!" (*Nedarim* 32a)

Rabbi Eleazar's statement is thought to necessarily imply a supernatural, mystical force to Torah study.[47] However, there are two critical points to clarify. One is that as other instances of the word *nitkayma* in the Talmud demonstrate,[48] it means "come into existence," not "exist." Indeed, the verse cited by the Talmud itself indicates that it is talking about creation, not the continued existence of the universe.

Furthermore, the Talmud's statement follows another statement which is worded identically, except that it is said with regard to circumcision.[49] Now, this clearly does not mean that if there is a moment in the world in which there is no circumcision taking place, then the world would cease to exist!

Thus, the Talmud is not saying that without constant Torah study, the world would cease to exist. Rather, it is saying that without Torah, the world could not have *come into existence*. From the rationalist perspective, this simply means that God would not have brought the world into existence were there not a way for mankind to perfect itself. This, too, is the explanation of a similar passage elsewhere in the Talmud:

> The Holy One stipulated with the Works of Creation and said to them: If Israel accepts the Torah, you shall endure; but if not, I will turn you back into emptiness and formlessness. (*Shabbos* 88a)

The Talmud is saying that the purpose of the world is justified in terms of people seeking to lead a good life via the Torah. It is not saying that Torah metaphysically sustains the world.

---

[47] The Talmud does not talk about Torah study; instead it just says "Torah." However, it does appear that this refers to the study of Torah, since the rationale of the exegesis is that the "covenant with day and night" alludes to the study of Torah, about which it is said "and you shall contemplate it day and night" (Josh. 1) (See Rashi to *Pesachim* 68b).

[48] *Berachot* 55b, *Sanhedrin* 48b, *Bava Metzia* 48b, *Nazir* 32b.

[49] Maharsha, ad loc., understands this to be disputing the previous view, that the world exists for Torah.

It should further be noted that the description of how, if Israel were not to have accepted the Torah, then the world would be destroyed, does not necessarily refer to the physical annihilation of the universe. It may simply mean that without the societal influence of Torah, the world would have descended into anarchy and chaos. In the previous section, we saw that Meiri gave precisely such an explanation for the Talmud's statement that Torah protects the world.

A similar misconception occurs with another oft-cited passage in the Talmud:

> Who is referred to as an *apikores*? Rav Yosef said: For example, those who say, "Of what benefit are the Rabbis to us? They read for themselves, and they study for themselves." Abaye said to him: But this too is a case of acting impudently against the Torah, as it is written, "But for My covenant [studied] day and night, I had not appointed the ordinances of heaven and earth." Rav Nachman b. Isaac said: It is also deduced from the verse, "Then I will spare all the place for their sakes." (*Sanhedrin* 99b)

This passage is often cited as a condemnation of those who question whether society should be funding perpetual Talmud students, as well as being presented as a demonstration of the mystical value of Torah. But a careful reading of the passage reveals that its meaning is quite different. First, it is referring to rabbis, not students! Second, the reference to the verse stating that God will "spare all the place for their sakes" again demonstrates that this passage is referring to the value of Torah study being based on the merit of the person, not the metaphysical effects of the Torah study itself.

Does Torah Study Contribute to Society?

As we have seen, the mystical view of the nature of Torah study results in it being of greater significance than with the rationalist view. Yet even according to the rationalist view, learning Torah is of profound and fundamental importance. So is there any real difference between the two approaches?

The answer is that yes, there are very significant practical ramifications of the different views. These relate to whether adults, who already know enough Torah to live their lives as observant Jews, are contributing to society by continuing to learn Torah in kollel. Of course, if they are studying to become rabbis, judges, teachers, and so on, then this is the necessary preparation to serve the community. But if their studies are not with such a goal in mind (which is the case for most people in kollel today), then does their learning benefit society, such that society should financially support them to this end?

According to the mystical perspective, learning Torah most certainly benefits society, in a very profound way. As we have seen, according to R. Chaim of Volozhin, it creates metaphysical energies which sustain the very universe. R. Aharon Kotler, the pioneering founder of the modern kollel system, stated that learning Torah is accordingly the ultimate form of kindness, since it benefits the entire world.[50]

However, with the rationalist perspective of the Rishonim, there is no room for such a view. They describe the goals and benefits of Torah study in terms of its instructional and educational value. They make no mention of mystical energies created by Torah study.

Thus, it is no surprise that we find the Rishonim to be opposed to the notion of financial support for people studying Torah.[51] In Ashkenaz, financing Torah study was unheard of; virtually all Torah scholars were self-supporting, and financing even teachers of Torah was only reluctantly permitted by some. In Sefarad, on the other hand, it was acceptable and normative to provide communal as well as private financial support for Torah scholars. Still, many of the Rishonim in these lands limited this license to Torah scholars who were serving in a professional capacity for the benefit of the community, with some extending it to Torah scholars

---

[50] *Mishnas Rabbi Aharon* vol. 1 p. 59, first ed. Also cited by Rabbi Zev Leff, in *Outlooks and Insights*: "Rabbi Aharon Kotler, *zt"l*, explains that Torah learning is the ultimate *chesed*. When we say, "Talmud Torah is equal to them all," it is other acts of *chesed* to which we are referring. For all other kindnesses are specific and limited, but Torah study is the source of existence. If not for constant Torah study the world would cease to exist. How profound and all-encompassing is the concern and kindness of the one who immerses himself in the study of Torah, thereby preserving the entire universe."

[51] For a full discussion, see my article "The Economics of Torah Scholarship in Medieval Jewish Thought and Practice," available at http://www.rationalistjudaism.com/2012/-06/economics-of-torah-scholarship-in.html.

training for such a role. None expressed any justification for supporting Torah students on the grounds that they are metaphysically supporting the world with their Torah.

There is a common misconception that Rambam wrote that anyone who dedicates themselves to learning Torah is considered as though he was from the tribe of Levi—with the corollary that he should therefore be supported by the community, just as the Levites were supported by the rest of the nation. Yet this is a severe misunderstanding of Rambam's position. According to Rambam, the tribe of Levi were not sitting and learning. Instead, they were *teaching*. As Rambam says:

> Why did the tribe of Levi not acquire a share in the Land of Israel and in its spoils together with their brothers? Because this tribe was set apart to serve God and to minister to Him, to teach His straight ways and righteous ordinances to the multitudes, as it is written: "They shall teach Jacob Your ordinances and Israel Your Law" (Deut. 33:10). (*Mishneh Torah, Hilchot Shemittah V'Yovel* 13:12)

In light of the rationalist reasons for learning Torah, Rambam's statement is eminently understandable. Learning Torah is immensely important because it teaches theology, improves character, and perfects society. But it does not provide any mystical energies or anything like that. Accordingly, only teaching Torah provides benefit to society, such that the Levites are supported by the rest of Israel. Learning Torah is wonderful for individuals; but they are not providing any benefit or service to society. According to Rambam—and most other Rishonim—this does not justify communal support.

(It should be noted that Rambam's description of the role of Levi is just one of many references to Torah in classical and traditional texts which are widely assumed today to be referring to *learning* Torah, whereas they are actually referring to *teaching* Torah. Indeed as R. Dr. Yehudah Levi notes in his classic book *Torah Study*, the very phrase Talmud Torah, properly translated, seems to refer to *teaching* Torah rather than learning Torah. This is also implied by the Gemara, which derives the mitzvah of Talmud Torah from the verse of *veshinantam levanecha*, "you shall teach it to your sons." Rambam's halachic definition of the mitzvah also includes both studying and teaching one's sons.[52] Certainly, later authorities took the phrase Talmud Torah to mean studying Torah. But it is not clear that Chazal meant it that way, at least not in every instance. And it certainly seems to be the case that even learning Torah was, as far as Chazal and the Rishonim were concerned, primarily about knowing how to observe halachah and how to teach others to observe halachah.)

Conclusion

As we have seen, while learning Torah is of foundational importance in Judaism, the rationalist and mystical views of this mitzvah are universes apart. In the Talmud and Rishonim, the value of learning Torah is described in terms of its instructional and educational role, and there are descriptions of the resultant merits for people who study, practice and teach it. With the rise of mysticism, on the other hand, and in particular as a result of the innovative teachings of R. Chaim of Volozhin, the value of learning Torah was presented in terms of mystical energies that it creates. This led to a number of ancient statements about the importance of Torah being given a greater meaning than they originally conveyed. It also led to a blurring of the distinction between the value of learning Torah and the greater value of teaching Torah. The societal consequences are highly significant.

---

[52] *Mishneh Torah, Hilchot Talmud Torah*, ch.1.

Afterword

How Modernity Forces Tension

Rationalism is doomed to fight a difficult battle. It is inevitable that over time, texts become canonized. And while the mystically-inclined sayings of Talmudic Sages are often ambiguous enough to be reinterpreted, the same cannot be said for the extensive, explicit writings of the Rishonim and Acharonim. When a figure of tremendous stature such as the Vilna Gaon endorses the Zohar, it becomes very difficult to maintain a non-Zoharic approach to Judaism.

But there are also opposing forces to the canonization process. Modern science presents evidence that various statements in sacred texts cannot be interpreted in the traditional manner, that they are not to be attributed to the authors to which they are traditionally attributed, or that they are actually incorrect. As time goes on, this tension inevitably becomes ever greater, as the traditionalists canonize more and more texts and as scientific investigation reveals problems with ever more of these canonized texts.

Another historical force challenging mysticism is the power and spread of the scientific process. It used to be easy to attribute all kinds of occurrences to mystical forces, but as the scientific mindset spreads, everyone is more inclined to attribute phenomena to naturalistic forces. As noted earlier, nobody is really afraid of demons anymore.

Then there is the challenge of the information age, with the free flow of information on the internet. This raises more awareness of challenges from critical thought, as well as more awareness of the rationalist approaches in Judaism. Perhaps most significantly, there is far more autonomy of thought in the modern era.

Ultimately, all this forces a split. Some accept science, realize how the canonization process works, and reject the authority of certain texts. Others fear how much science threatens traditionalism, and reject science—and rationalism—as dangerous. This tension is reflected in much heated rhetoric that takes place.

In many Orthodox Jewish communities today, there is simply no place for the rationalist approach. Such is the case in most Sefardic, Chassidic, and Charedi Lithuanian communities, both in Israel and the diaspora. There may be isolated individuals, or extremely segregated communities, with rationalist leanings. But in general, in these communities, the mystical approach has become canonized.

On the other hand, the rationalist approach is championed in Modern Orthodox communities, where it is considered to be the preferred approach, although many people are unaware of its full significance. There is also space for the rationalist approach in centrist Orthodox communities outside Israel and national-religious communities in Israel. In these communities, while there are many who adhere to the mystical approach, there is a general tolerance towards the rationalist approach.

The Problems with Rationalism

While this work seeks to give voice to the rationalist approach, as a rebuttal to those trying to extinguish it, it cannot be denied that those who oppose the rationalist approach have legitimate reasons for doing so. There are several dangers and problems which exist with the rationalist approach.

One danger is that explaining the reasons for *mitzvot* and halachot as being non-mystical can lead people to think that if they don't agree with the reason, or if the reason is not relevant, then they don't need to observe the halachah. However, there are several adequate responses to this concern. Even if a given reason for a halacha would seem not to apply, there may be additional reasons of which a person is unaware. Furthermore, there is a matter of the authority of God and the system of rabbinic law. It is important to adhere to the legal system even if, in a given situation, the reason for a law does not apply, because this is part of maintaining the authority of the system and one's consistent loyalty to it.

A more serious problem with rationalism is that it isn't a fully worked-out system. The rationalist approach is a Pandora's Box. Explaining the Torah's laws and Jewish history in a way that maximizes the naturalistic and rules out the mystical is relatively easy in terms of famous conflicts such as the development of the universe, but it is much more challenging with other parts of the Torah. And in the long run, rationalism can have disastrous consequences. As Paul Johnson notes in *A History of the Jews*, Rambam "laid dangerous eggs which hatched later… he brought a confidence in the compatibility of faith and reason which fitted his own calm and majestic mind but which was in due course to carry Spinoza outside Judaism completely."

Thus, there are clear problems and dangers with the rationalist approach. Nevertheless, it has a long and rich heritage in Judaism, and it deserves to continue. Furthermore, it is an approach which, for many people, is the only approach to Judaism which makes sense and which keeps them attached to Torah with a positive connection. And it is not as though the mystical approach is free of problems, as we shall now explore.

The Problems with Mysticism

From a rationalist standpoint there are just as many theological problems with mysticism as there are problems with rationalism from a mystical standpoint. But sometimes the dangers with mysticism are even apparent to many people who follow the mystical approach.

While the rationalist approach has its problems and dangers, the same is also true of the mystical approach. For example, just as the rationalist approach of explaining the functions of *mitzvot* risks leading people to rationalize their neglect of them, there is also a parallel danger with the mystical approach. When it is believed that the primary function of *mitzvot* is to effect certain metaphysical consequences, the risk is run that these *mitzvot* will be contravened by people who claim to be able effect the desired metaphysical results in other ways. In other words, just as R. Chaim of Volozhin says that Yaakov could marry two sisters because he perceived that the metaphysical results would be appropriate, so too there have all too often been influential rabbis who claim that they engage in what appears to be sinful behavior, because they can perceive that there are important metaphysical results. From Shabbtai Tzvi declaring that he could eat pork, or Rabbi Eliezer Berland in our day declaring that there are mystical reasons why he should be with various women, this has been a serious problem.

In fact, in general, the mystical approach presents a great danger of enabling predatory behavior by cult personalities who claim metaphysical powers. It is no coincidence that in a published list of the wealthiest rabbis in the world, all of them were aligned with a mystical approach. When the masses are taught a mystical approach, they are all too ready to give away their money for blessings from people who profess special powers. And even in less extreme cases, it is not necessarily in people's best interests for them to surrender their decision-making to those that they believe to have mystical insight.

Mysticism also provides opportunities to make money via selling mystical services and items, from pouring lead to silver rings. Unlike the rationalist approach, in which holiness and spirituality are states of mind and action, the mystical approach "materializes" holiness and spirituality into objects, setting the stage for commercialization. Sometimes even well-meaning charities which offer blessings to donors end up bankrupting people who are desperate for salvation.

Even aside from predatory behavior or financial transactions, the very nature of mysticism, in which people and objects are believed to be invested with special powers, can infringe upon pure monotheism. Sometimes, the mystical approach verges upon idolatry.

Can One Be Both Rationalist and Mystic?

Can one be both rationalist and mystic? There are certain select figures who seem to strongly express both aspects; Rav Avraham Yitzchak Kook comes to mind.

However, ultimately, there are many areas where the approaches are radically opposed. If a person has a developed approach in these areas, it will be one or the other; it cannot be both. It is either preferable for God to work through nature, or through miracles. The mitzvah of *shiluach hakein*, in a situation where one does not want the eggs, either does apply or it doesn't. More broadly, *mitzvot* either function solely to improve our minds and souls and society, or they also have metaphysical effects.

Theoretically it would be possible to be a rationalist in one area and a mystic in another area—for example, to prefer explaining Biblical events miraculously, but seeing the function of *mitzvot* in rationalist terms. However, it would be difficult to root these conflicting approaches in an underlying consistent theology.

Nevertheless, it should be realized that, in practice, the difference between rationalists and mystics is not black and white. People are rarely entirely rationalist or entirely mystic in orientation (though this may be because they do not have a fully thought-out and consistent approach). Certainly, this writer does not self-identify as fully rationalist!

Rather, rationalism and mysticism represent two poles on a spectrum, and people gravitate towards one or the other, to varying degrees. And even with regard to the poles themselves, there are disputes as to how far apart they are. The extent of Rambam's rationalism, for example, has been hotly debated.

An example of the non-uniform nature of rationalism is with Rambam and Rav Samson Raphael Hirsch. Rav Hirsch harshly criticized Rambam for having synthesized Judaism with Greco-Muslim philosophy. However, Rav Hirsch also followed Rambam's rationalism in many ways, such as in being open to God creating animals and man via a process of evolution, in rating Chazal as possessing no special expertise in science, and in negating kabbalistic purposes for *mitzvot*.[1]

Another example of this is with Rambam and Rav Yosef Ber Soloveitchik. Rav Soloveitchik was firmly in the rationalist camp—interpreting Creation non-historically, naturalizing the miracles of the Exodus, rating the sanctity of the Land of Israel as historically-contingent

---

[1] See *The Nineteen Letters*.

rather than intrinsic. But he did not hesitate to disagree with Rambam's strident opposition to *piyyutim*:

> Halakhic man never accepted the ruling of Maimonides opposing the recital of *piyyutim*, the liturgical poems and songs of praise. Go forth and learn what the *Guide* sought to do to the *piyyutim* of Israel… Nevertheless, on the High Holidays the community of Israel, singing the hymns of unity and glory, reaches out to its Creator… and we disregard the strictures of the philosophical Midrash… (*Halakhic Man* pp. 58-59)

It is even largely possible to be neither rationalist nor mystic.

> Who dares thrust his head between the two great mountains, the Rambam and the Ramban, whose views on this subject have split the worlds… It follows, therefore, that an intelligent person may have in such matters either point of view, without detracting from the other, or—and in my opinion this is the correct way—he may acknowledge ignorance in such matters… What practical difference does it make whether Rambam or Ramban is correct about magic and related matters? … God did not establish His covenant with us on the basis of concealed things but set our task to observe and guard the revealed things of the Torah. He assured us that to perform these we need not possess knowledge of things which transcend our world. We have but to perform those things which are accessible to us. (Rabbi Samson Raphael Hirsch, "Letter to R. Hile Wechsler," published by Mordechai Breuer in *HaMa'ayan* 16:2, Tevet 5736/1976)

Co-Existence and Separation

Co-existence between rationalists and mystics is difficult. There is an unfortunate tendency amongst some mystics to brand rationalists as heretics, and there is an unfortunate tendency amongst some rationalists to brand mystics as idiots.

But perhaps each can at least see that the other side has a long legacy, and that there are people for whom it is uniquely suited. It's a case of different strokes for different folks.

Furthermore, fortunately Judaism is largely a religion of deed rather than creed. There are relatively few practical ramifications, on a daily basis, between rationalists and mystics. I sometimes daven at a tiny *shteeble* that contains diehard rationalists and staunch mystics, and everyone gets along just fine, at least until someone delivers a Torah lecture.

On the other hand, while rationalists and mystics can co-exist, it is important for each to be aware of the distinct nature of their worldview. This reduces the tension discussed earlier. The enormous distress caused to many thousands of people by the ban over my own works was due to many of these people (including myself) not realizing that they were part of a different tradition than the rabbinic authorities who pronounced the ban.

While it is obvious to all that traditional Judaism encompasses many different approaches—Ashkenazim and Sephardim, Chassidim and Mitnagdim, Modern and Ultra-Orthodox, Zionist and non-Zionist—it is not often as well appreciated that these differing worldviews can result in differing approaches to many issues, including halachic issues. Good fences make good neighbors, and one way to reduce the friction between rationalism and mysticism is to be aware of the vast differences between the two schools of thought, the long history of each of them, and the futility of trying to bridge the gap.

I have implemented this philosophy in my own work. After my books presenting the rationalist approach to various Torah-science issues were banned, I republished them in a different format, packaging and presenting the material in such a way as to make it clear that these books were aimed solely at people operating within a rationalist framework. Meanwhile, in the museum that I founded, the Biblical Museum of Natural History, which caters to the full spectrum of society, there is no mention of any Torah-science topics in which there is a conflict between rationalist and mystical approaches—thus, there are no exhibits on dinosaurs or evolution. One must always be sensitive to one's audience.

Preserving Rationalist Judaism

A person should always pose his questions to someone operating from within his worldview. A religious Zionist Israeli with a question about whether to attend Hesder or a different army program would not and should not be asking his question to a Satmar *posek* from Williamsburg.

Likewise, the differences between the rationalist and mystical (or non-rationalist) schools of thought can be greatly relevant to rabbinic teachings, including all kinds of halachic and societal rulings. A person should follow rulings from rabbis who operate within his worldview, not from those who follow a different worldview.

But aside from rabbinic rulings, there is a person's entire Jewish education to take into account. The ramifications of the differences between the rationalist and mystical schools of thought are profound and far-reaching, extending beyond Torah-science conflicts to such things as the authority of various rabbinic leaders, the ability to challenge rabbinic or scientific authority on various issues, the goal of *mitzvot*, the value of material endeavor, and the function of long-term Torah study. Educational institutions must have teachers who are grounded in this school of thought. That is the only way for the rationalist approach to survive, to thrive, and to be available for those who need it.

PART TWO:

Studies in Rationalism vs. Mysticism

ONE

Sod Hashem Liyreyav: Does God Reveal Scientific Secrets?

Introduction

In popular discussions concerning the knowledge of the natural world possessed by the Sages of the Talmud, the concept of *sod Hashem liyreyav*, "God's secret is for those who fear Him," is often cited. The source of this phrase is a verse in Psalms:

סוֹד ה' לִירֵאָיו וּבְרִיתוֹ לְהוֹדִיעָם: (סֵפֶר תהילים כה יד)

> The counsel (or "secret") of the Lord is for those who fear Him; to them He makes known His covenant. (Psalms 25:14, JPS translation)

Simply speaking, this verse serves to restrict certain knowledge, of an esoteric nature, to the God-fearing. However, in the Talmud, this verse is cited to refer to the concept of knowledge about the natural world being divinely revealed to Torah scholars. This is often described in terms such as the following:

> Many times the Sages describe natural phenomena with which they could not possibly have had a personal acquaintance. The Talmud explains their amazing knowledge with this verse, 'The secret of Hashem is for [i.e. revealed to] those who fear Him' (see *Sotah* 4b, *Sanhedrin* 48b, *Niddah* 20b). (R. Avrohom Chaim Feuer, *Tehillim* (ArtScroll/Mesorah 1977) vol. I p. 313)

Despite this concept being well-known and utilized by many subsequent Torah scholars, there has not yet been any study of its nature and the parameters of its usage. This chapter engages in such a study, and also examines how the principle was utilized subsequent to the Talmudic era.

In the Talmud

The phrase *sod Hashem liyreyav* appears only a few times in the Mishnah and Talmud, and the cases can be divided into three general categories. Not all of these relate to the concept of divine revelation, and we shall proceed from the least relevant to the most relevant.

I. Turbans and Torah Scholars

A curious appearance of *sod Hashem liyreyav* in the Talmud is as an explanation of the etymology of the word *sudra*, "turban":[1]

> R. Zeira asked: …[What is the significance of the word] *sudra* (turban)? God's secret is for those that fear Him (*sod Hashem liyrevav*). (*Shabbat* 77b)

This is presenting a linguistic allusion to the notion that a turban is a head covering worn by those that fear God. The same linkage to a turban is found elsewhere:

> How should one who enters a bathhouse act? He should say, "May it be Your will, God my Lord, that You bring me inside in peace…" before he enters, then he should remove his shirt, open his belt and remove his hat… we see from here (that he can loosen his belt before removing his hat) that a hat does not possess sanctity, and this is only with regard to a hat, but not a *sudra*, as it is written "*sod Hashem liyreyav*." (Masechet *Kallah* 10)

Possibly along similar lines, we elsewhere find the Talmud referring to R. Papa as a *sudani*.[2] Some understand this term as being identical to *sudna*, which is explained elsewhere in the Talmud to refer to a beer-brewer.[3] Others relate it to the word to *sadeh* ("field") and render it as "countryman."[4] But Rashi and *Aruch* explain it to be based on the word *sod*, "secret." They relate it to *sod Hashem liyreyav* and therefore

---

[1] Translation following Michael Sokoloff, *A Dictionary of Jewish Babylonian Aramaic of the Talmudic and Geonic Periods.*

[2] *Berachot* 44b; *Menachot* 71a; *Niddah* 12b.

[3] Alternate view cited by Rashi to *Menachot* 71a, referring to *Pesachim* 113a.

[4] *Otzar HaGeonim*, cited in Aharon Maggid, *Beit Aharon* p. 467; Sokoloff, *A Dictionary of Jewish Babylonian Aramaic*, offers this as a tentative suggestion, noting that the etymology of the word is unknown.

understand *sudani* as a title for Torah scholars to whom these secrets are revealed.

II. Reaching the Right Conclusions

One context in which *sod Hashem liyreyav* is employed is as a proclamation in response to people reaching a halachic conclusion that, unbeknownst to them, was received as a tradition from Sinai. There is one case in which this is used:

> ...When R. Yosi ben Durmaskit came before R. Eliezer in Lod, R. Eliezer said to him, What is new in the Beit HaMidrash today? R. Yosi replied, They counted votes and concluded that Ammon and Moab must give the poor man's tithe in the Sabbatical year. R. Eliezer wept and proclaimed, "God's secret is for those that fear Him, and He has made his covenant known to them"; Go and tell them, Do not be concerned about your tally, I have received a tradition from R. Yochanan ben Zakai, who heard from his teacher, and his teacher from his teacher until it was a law transmitted to Moses at Sinai, that Ammon and Moab must give the poor man's tithe in the Sabbatical year. (Mishnah, *Yadayim* 4:3[5])

Does R. Eliezer mean that they could only possibly have reached this conclusion with divine guidance? This would seem to be too strong a claim; there could be any number of ways in which this conclusion was reached. It would seem more reasonable for him to be merely citing the verse to praise them for reaching the correct conclusion. However, in the corollary of this case, *sod Hashem liyreyav* is employed very literally. The corollary of the above case is a passage discussing Do'eg and Achitophel, where the Talmud states that they did *not* reach the correct halachic conclusions, and relates this to their *lack* of fear of Heaven:

> Rav Mesharshiya said: Do'eg and Achitophel could not understand *halachot*. Mar Zutra objected: This is one about whom it is written, "Where is one who could count? Where is one who could weigh? Where is one who could count [all these] towers?" (Isaiah 33:18), and you say that they could not understand *halachot*?! Rather, it is that they could not

---

[5] The story also appears with minor variations in *Tosefta Yadayim* 2:7 and Babylonian Talmud, Chagigah 3b.

derive the [correct] *halachot* from their studies, as it is written, "God's secret is for those who fear Him." (Talmud, *Sanhedrin* 106b)

Is Mar Zutra saying that their lack of fear of God actually impeded them from reaching the correct conclusion, or is this merely a way of deriding their inability to evaluate the *halachot* correctly? Since Mar Zutra's point is that their intellectual abilities were unrivalled, it seems that he is claiming that their lack of fear of God actually interfered with their intellectual abilities. Only someone possessing fear of God will reach the correct conclusions in their halachic studies. However, while Mar Zutra is broadly employing *sod Hashem liyreyav* as an ingredient that is constantly present in Torah study, it does not appear to necessarily involve supernatural revelation; rather it means that their judgment was clouded by their inappropriate interests.

III. Knowing Physical Facts via Supernatural Means

There are three instances in the Talmud where *sod Hashem liyreyav* is used to refer to knowledge about the physical world being obtained via supernatural assistance. The first is in the context of a discussion in the Talmud regarding the minimum duration of seclusion that can render a woman as a *sotah*. The duration is determined to be that required for the first stage of cohabitation to take place. Various Tannaim give different definitions of this amount of time, including Ben Azzai. The Talmud comments as follows:

> Rav Yitzchak bar Rav Yosef said in the name of Rabbi Yochanan: Each one evaluated it based on himself. But surely there was Ben Azzai, who was not married? If you want, I can say that he married and separated; and if you want, I can say that he heard it from his teacher; and if you want, I can say "God's secret is for those who fear Him." (*Sotah* 4b; similarly in Jerusalem Talmud, *Sotah* 4a)

What is the meaning of the word "secret" in this context? Does it mean that the duration named by Ben Azzai was the correct amount, which was unknown to the others? This would be difficult, as there is no indication that the matter is thereby decided in favor of Ben Azzai. It thus appears that the word "secret" is used in that the information could not otherwise be known by Ben Azzai. It was unobtainable and unknown via ordinary means, but since Ben Azzai was God-fearing, it was divinely revealed to him.

The second case where *sod Hashem liyreyav* is used to refer to knowledge about the physical world being obtained via divine assistance further confirms this interpretation of the word "secret":

> Mar Zutra son of Rav Nachman asked Rav Nachman: "What is podagra[6] (inflammation of the toe joint) like?" He replied: "Like a needle in living flesh." How did he know this? Some say: He himself suffered from it. And some say: He heard it from his teacher. And some say: "God's secret is for those who fear Him, to them He makes His covenant known." (*Sotah* 10a, also *Sanhedrin* 48b)

It is not much of a secret that podagra feels like a needle in living flesh; that is known to everyone who suffers from it. But it ought to have been a secret to someone who does not suffer from it. The Talmud is suggesting that it may have been known to him via some form of divine revelation.

(Interestingly, modern microscopy reveals that one of the primary causes of podagra, gout, occurs when *needle*-shaped crystals are formed in joints by excess uric acid. However, since one of the Talmud's explanations is that Rav Nachman derived his knowledge about it from his own suffering, this indicates that he was speaking about the sensations experienced rather than the physical shape of the cause of podagra; and the sensation is that of having needles driven into the flesh.)

The third and final case in the Talmud where *sod Hashem liyreyav* is used to account for knowledge of physical facts is as follows:

> Why was Rabbi Elazar called the authority of the Land of Israel? As there was a case of a woman who came before Rabbi Elazar, and Rabbi Ami was sitting before him. R. Elazar smelled her, and said to her, "That is the blood of desire." After she left, Rabbi Ami investigated, and she said to him, "My husband was on the way, and I desired him." R. Ami proclaimed on Rabbi Elazar, "God's secret is for those who fear Him." (*Niddah* 20b)

---

[6] The English word "podagra" is identical to the Talmudic term פדגרא, both taken from the Greek ποδάγρα; see Samuel Krauss, *Griechische und Lateinische Lehnwörter im Talmud, Midrasch, und Targum*, p. 422, s.v. פודגרא.

It is difficult to understand why R. Ami would have concluded that R. Elazar must have obtained this information via divine revelation. For, just as in the previous cases there were other options as to how the information was obtained, the same is surely true here; R. Elazar may have examined earlier such cases, and therefore learned to correlate the smell with the cause. Perhaps R. Ami was merely employing this verse in praise of the extraordinary feat of expertise that R. Elazar displayed, regardless of how he obtained this knowledge.

Analysis: A Limited Concept

When one considers the cases in which *sod Hashem liyreyav* is used to refer to knowledge about the physical world being obtained via divine assistance, several interesting observations can be made.

First of all, when one surveys the Talmud as a whole, the instances where *sod Hashem liyreyav* is raised are revealed to be strangely few. There are scores of cases in the Talmud where the Sages require knowledge of the natural world, and the vast majority of them make no mention of *sod Hashem liyreyav*. It is only invoked on three occasions! Furthermore, we see clearly on several occasions that the Sages did *not* consider themselves to have such a source of information. For example, the Talmud states that the rabbis learned agricultural information from the descendants of Seir.[7] Rav relates that he spent eighteen months with a shepherd in order to learn about the blemishes that affect sheep.[8] R. Shimon ben Chalafta is described as having performed experiments to discover information.[9] Rabbi Zeira stated that his lack of knowledge of the natural sciences rendered him incapable of rendering rulings regarding menstrual blood.[10] We also find that Rebbi considered that the sages were proven wrong in astronomy by the gentile scholars, which demonstrates that he did not consider their information to have been divinely inspired.[11]

---

[7] Shabbat 85a.

[8] Sanhedrin 5b.

[9] Chullin 57b.

[10] Niddah 20b.

[11] Pesachim 94b.

Second, in the first two cases, *sod Hashem liyreyav* is only presented as one option among three, and its position in third place may indicate that it is rated as a last resort; and in the third case, it is unclear that there is an acknowledgment of divine revelation being demonstrated.

Third, in no case does the person who possessed the information claim to have obtained it via *sod Hashem liyreyav*. One could counter that modesty would prevent this, but it is still worthy of note.

Putting these three observations together, it is clear that *sod Hashem liyreyav* is, at best, of very limited application. The Talmud is open to the possibility of the Sages receiving knowledge via divine revelation, but only in a handful of cases that are otherwise difficult to explain, and even in those cases it does not present *sod Hashem liyreyav* as the certain basis for the knowledge. Contrary to the description of this phenomenon that we cited in the introduction, which referred to it occurring "many times," the three citations are the only instances where it appears. And contrary to it being the explanation for something "with which they could not possibly have had a personal acquaintance," in each case there are alternate explanations of how they might indeed have had access to the knowledge via ordinary means.

Nevuah, Ruach HaKodesh, and *Halachah*

The concept of *sod Hashem liyreyav* appears similar to a number of other concepts in Jewish thought. It appears to be a form of prophecy, a supernatural process of revelation whereby God discloses information. R. Avraham Yitzchak Kook explicitly identifies *sod Hashem liyreyav* as a form of prophecy.[12]

Although the era of the Prophets finished long before the Talmudic era, and many have assumed that prophecy itself likewise ceased, this is not the case. The Talmud states that while prophecy was removed from the prophets following the destruction of the Temple, it was not removed

---

[12] R. Kook, *Mishpat Kohen* 96 p. 208.

from Torah scholars.[13] Others have shown that prophecy, albeit in a scaled-down version, was believed to have continued throughout the Talmudic era.[14] Some contend that such quasi-prophecy was even considered extant in the medieval period.[15] None of these scholars make any mention of *sod Hashem liyreyav*, and have apparently overlooked it, but it nevertheless appears to be of the same category.

Other similar concepts include *bat kol*, messages in dreams,[16] and *ruach hakodesh*.[17] The Talmud states that *ruach hakodesh* departed with the deaths of Chaggai, Zechariah and Malachi.[18] On the other hand, it also relates that Rabban Gamliel knew someone's name via *ruach ha-kodesh*.[19] It thus seems that *ruach hakodesh* was considered to have continued, but in a reduced form.

But since *sod Hashem liyreyav* involves supernatural revelation, this raises a problem. R. Tzvi Hirsch Chayes raises the question of how, if information is obtained via *sod Hashem liyreyav*, it can be used in the halachic process, since there is a principle of *lo baShamayim hi*—the Torah is not in Heaven, and supernatural revelation may not interfere with the halachic process.[20] Several rabbinic scholars answer this question by noting that *sod Hashem liyreyav* is not used for revelations of halachah per se, but

---

[13] *Bava Batra* 12a. For a discussion of the views of the Rishonim on this passage, see Rabbi Aaron Cohen, "The Parameters of Rabbinic Authority: A Study of Three Sources," pp. 109-112 and especially note 48.

[14] Ephraim Urbach, "When Did Prophecy Cease?" (Hebrew); *The Sages – Their Concepts and Beliefs*, pp 564-567, 577-579; Frederick E. Greenspahn, "Why Prophecy Ceased," p. 44; Benjamin D. Sommer, "Did Prophecy Cease," pp. 39-40, 44-45.

[15] Abraham J. Heschel, "On the Holy Spirit in the Middle Ages" (Hebrew).

[16] The Talmud (*Chullin* 133a) relates how Rav Safra learned information via a dream.

[17] Ramban to *Bava Batra* 12a states that the prophecy which was maintained amongst Torah scholars after the era of prophets was *ruach hakodesh*, a different version of prophecy which occurs by way of wisdom, without visions. For a discussion of the relationship between prophecy and *ruach ha-kodesh*, see Herbert Parzen, "The Ruah Hakodesh in Tannaitic Literature."

[18] *Sanhedrin* 11a.

[19] *Eruvin* 64b, Tosefta *Pesachim* 2:9 and Yerushalmi *Avodah Zarah* 7b.

[20] Maharatz Chayes to *Sotah* 4b.

rather for revelations of scientific facts that have ramifications for halachah.[21] R. Avraham Yitzchak Kook also provides an alternate answer, that it is only prohibited to receive new *halachot* via supernatural means, but resolving questions of doubt may be done this way. Some contemporary Torah scholars suggest that *sod Hashem liyreyav* does not refer to any form of supernatural revelation via *ruach hakodesh*, but rather to divine assistance in ascertaining facts which they identify as being part of the *da'at Torah* that all great Torah scholars possess;[22] however, it is difficult to see how this solves the problem of *lo baShamayim hi*.

While the popular view is that principles such as *lo baShamayim hi* show that supernatural sources of information are never allowed to interfere with the halachic process, the truth is much more complex. There is extensive scholarly literature on the interaction between halachah and supernatural sources of information.[23] Urbach concludes that there were differences of opinion among the sages as to whether such sources of information were admissible.[24]

In the Rishonim: Expansion and Appropriation

The Talmud relates a story in which R. Shimon son of Rebbi took offense at a student of his who did not stand in respect when he passed by. R. Shimon protested to his father that he taught this person much Torah; how could he not stand up for him? Rebbi responded, "Perhaps he was sitting and thinking about them (i.e. the Torah that he learned from him, and therefore there is no loss of respect implied)." Tosafot focuses on why Rebbi said that this person was specifically thinking about

---

[21] Chida, *Shem HaGedolim*, "R. Yaakov HaChassid" and *Birkei Yosef, Orach Chaim* 32:4; R. Avraham Yitzchak Kook, *Mishpat Kohen* 96 pp. 207-208. See too *Mishneh LeMelech, Hilchot Ishut* 9:6, end. Oddly, R. Tzvi Hirsch Chayes himself employs similar reasoning in his commentary to *Yoma* 75a.

[22] Reuven Noach Cohen, *Imri Reuven* to Sotah 4b, Tzvi Kreizer, cited in Avraham Noach Klein, *Daf al haDaf* to *Sotah* 4b.

[23] Albert I. Baumgarten, "Miracles and Halakhah in Rabbinic Judaism"; Ephraim Urbach, "Halachah and Prophecy" (Hebrew); Alexander Guttmann, "The Significance of Miracles for Talmudic Judaism."

[24] Urbach, "Halachah and Prophecy," p. 19.

the Torah that he had learned from R. Shimon, noting that whatever part of Torah he had been thinking about would have excused him from standing up. He concludes that Rebbi had divined via *sod Hashem liyreyav* that the person was specifically thinking about the Torah that he had learned from R. Shimon.[25]

Tosafot' explanation raises two questions. First of all, if Rebbi had really divined what this person was thinking, why would he say that only "perhaps" the person was thinking this? Second, there is a much simpler explanation for why he specified that the person was thinking about the Torah he had learned from R. Shimon—he was attempting to assuage R. Shimon's anger in the best way. The fact that Tosafot is ready to use this explanation notwithstanding this alternative indicates that Tosafot perceived *sod Hashem liyreyav* as something that was widely in use and therefore readily applicable. Yet our own analysis of the Talmud indicates that its usage was very rare.

Rambam makes use of *sod Hashem liyreyav* in a very mild way, without involving any idea of supernatural inspiration, citing it merely in reference to the fact that certain matters—Creation and the account of the Divine Chariot—ought to be kept secret and restricted to those for whom they are appropriate.[26] But Raavad personally invokes *sod Hashem liyreyav* in a way that initially appears similar to the prophetic sense in which it used in the Talmud. In his introduction to his commentary on *Eduyot*, Raavad takes all responsibility for any errors in his work, while he attributes all that is correct to his being in possession of the "secret, as per *sod Hashem liyreyav*." In one gloss on the *Mishneh Torah*, after stating his view, he adds, "and thus was revealed to me by way of *sod Hashem liyreyav*."[27] On another occasion, he concludes his gloss with the words, "Blessed is God Who has revealed His secrets to the one who fears Him."[28] Along similar

---

[25] Tosafot to *Kiddushin* 33a, s.v. *Shema bahen.*

[26] *Guide for the Perplexed*, introduction.

[27] Raavad to *Hilchot Beit HaBechirah* 6:14.

[28] Raavad to *Hilchot Metamei Mishkav Umoshav* 7:7.

lines, elsewhere he states that "for many years *ruach hakodesh* has been present in our *bet midrash*."[29]

R. Moshe Sofer and R. Avraham Kook write that Raavad's usage of the phrase *sod Hashem liyreyav* was intended to refer to special divine revelation, the same as when it occurs in the Talmud.[30] Heschel reaches the same conclusion.[31] Others claim that it is merely a figure of speech;[32] some specify that it was an acknowledgment of the divine source of his intellectual capabilities in general.[33] R. Meir Mazuz says that Raavad means that whatever he writes that is good *is as though* it came from heaven; he points out that Raavad himself, in his introduction to his commentary on Eduyot, writes that "whatever is found [in my commentary] to be good and correct, is known to be from *sod*, just as it says "*sod Hashem liyreyav*."[34] Twerski reviews the literature on this topic, and after showing that other such phrases speaking of knowledge being revealed from Heaven were commonly used in the medieval period in cases where there was clearly no mystical meaning, concludes that it is merely a literary device referring to his conviction in the truth of his statements.[35] (Note that this is not a viable explanation of the usage of the phrase in the Talmud.)

In the Acharonim: Further Expansion

In the Acharonim, we find that the concept of *sod Hashem liyreyav* is both extended to the post-Talmudic period and also expanded laterally to be posited as a basis for other statements in the Talmud (beyond those that the Talmud itself suggests were made via *sod Hashem liyreyav*).

---

[29] *Hilchot Lulav* 8:5.

[30] R. Moshe Sofer, Responsa *Chatam Sofer, Orach Chaim* 208; R. Avraham Yitzchak Kook, *Mishpat Kohen* 96 p. 208.

[31] Heschel, "On the Holy Spirit in the Middle Ages," p. 193.

[32] R. Moshe Ibn Chaviv, *Kappos Temarim, Sukkah* 33b.

[33] R. Avraham Gurwitz, *Ohr Avraham, Chagigah* 13, p. 288.

[34] R. Meir Mazuz, *Bayit Ne'eman* 222 (8/8/20).

[35] Isadore Twersky, *Rabad of Posquieres: A Twelfth Century Talmudist*, pp. 292-300.

There is a dispute amongst the Rishonim regarding which blood found in eggs is considered to be part of a forming chick and renders the egg non-kosher. R. Chizkiya da Silva notes that R. Yosef Karo sides with one group, and writes that he "pronounces upon him *sod Hashem liyreyav*, for the scientists have written the same."[36] It is difficult to determine whether this is intended literally to refer to divine guidance, or if it is merely an expression of praise and approval.[37]

A much more dramatic expansion of *sod Hashem liyreyav* occurs with R. Moshe Sofer. As we have seen, he was of the view that *sod Hashem liyreyav*, in the sense of divine revelation, was even available to Ra'avad. But he also expands it to be underlying many Torah rulings. He writes that despite the gentiles' extensive experiments and empirical investigations, their knowledge of anatomy and physiology is still eclipsed by that of the Sages, which he states is "entirely due to *sod Hashem liyreyav*."[38]

But by far the most radical expansion of *sod Hashem liyreyav* occurs with the kabbalist Rabbi Shlomo Elyashiv (1841-1925). He not only expands *sod Hashem liyreyav* to cover every single statement made by the Sages of the Talmud, but even makes this a mandatory belief:

---

[36] *Pri Chadash, Yoreh De'ah* 66:5.

[37] Da Silva himself did not ascribe scientific omniscience to the Sages of the Talmud, as others were wont to do; on another occasion he notes that R. Dosa, whose view was adopted by R. Yosef Karo, has been since proven to have made a scientific error (*Pri Chadash, Yoreh De'ah* 80:2, regarding whether there are non-kosher animals with horns). While this does not rule out his accepting supernatural inspiration in select cases, it perhaps makes it less likely.

[38] *Chatam Sofer al HaTorah*, Leviticus 20:25. Cf. *Torat Moshe* to *parashat Shemot*. Yekutiel Kamelhar, *HaTalmud VeMadai Tevel* p. 11, similarly cites *sod Hashem liyreyav* in support of the notion that information discovered by modern science was already known by the Sages. A similar statement is made by Rabbi Menashe Klein, Responsa *Mishneh Halachot*, 13:217. However, we see that R. Moshe Sofer did not apply *sod Hashem liyreyav* in a similarly broad way to the Rishonim; in his novellae to *Niddah* 18a he states that Rambam's medical training enabled him to be more accurate in his statements about anatomy than Rashi and Tosafos. This is especially interesting in light of the fact that, as we saw earlier, R. Sofer did take Raavad literally when he claimed to have been the beneficiary of *sod Hashem liyreyav*.

The main thing is: everyone who is called a Jew is obligated to believe with complete faith that everything found in the words of the Sages, whether in halachos or aggados of the Talmud or in the Midrashim, are all the words of the Living God, for everything which they said is with the spirit of God which spoke within them, and "the secret of God is given to those who fear Him." This is just as we find in *Sanhedrin* 48b that even regarding something which has no application to Halacha and practical behavior, the Talmud asks regarding [the Sage] Rav Nachman, "How did he know this?" and the reply given is [that he knew this because] "The secret from God is given to those who fear him...." (*Leshem Shevo Ve-achlama, Sefer HaDe'ah*, Sec. II, *Derush* 4, *Anaf* 19, *Siman* 6 p. 161)

R. Elyashiv's usage of *sod Hashem liyreyav* is also extraordinary in that he also applies it to halachic statements of the Sages, raising the problem of *lo baShamayim hi* that others solved only by stating that *sod Hashem liyreyav* does *not* apply to raw halachic statements. Michael Berger details further numerous problems and contradictions which arise with postulating that all the Sages' pronouncements in halachah were divinely inspired.[39] Nevertheless, it appears that R. Elyashiv's position is also held by many ultra-Orthodox Jews today.

Aside from *sod Hashem liyreyav* being expanded laterally to encompass every statement in the Talmud, it is also extended so as to apply not only to the Sages of the Talmud and the Rishonim, but even to the Torah scholars of today. Thus, in an introduction to a collection of biographical sketches of recent Torah scholars, we are told that *sod Hashem liyreyav* grants them (quasi?)-prophetic ability to divine solutions to the questions that are presented to them:

This exceptional capacity to apply knowledge culled from ancient texts to modern-day problems is more than the simple sum of its parts: the endless hours of study and thought, and the brilliance of mind and intensity of concentration. Somehow, it must also encompass the special gift of "*sod Hashem l'yireav*," the Divine secrets that G-d imparts to those who fear Him. This, too, is part of the makeup of a *gadol beTorah* and guides him in ways that cannot be reduced to scholarship *per se*. This very same factor guides the *gadol* in dealing with problems that appear to be extra-halachic

---

[39] Michael Berger, *Rabbinic Authority*, pp. 86-96.

in nature, appearing to belong to other disciplines, such as politics, sociology, or psychology. (Nisson Wolpin, *The Torah Personality*, p. 15)

Conclusion

Sod Hashem liyreyav has two distinct meanings in the Talmud. One is that reaching correct halachic conclusions is seen as being correlated with fear of God. The other is that God sometimes reveals information about the physical world to select people.

The Talmud rarely invokes this latter concept, mentioning it only on three occasions, and even in those three cases, not as a definitive interpretation of events but rather only as one possible explanation as to how something was known. In most cases where scientific information was needed, it was *not* obtained via *sod Hashem liyreyav*, even though this sometimes means that the Sages were forced to admit error.

In the medieval period, the usage of *sod Hashem liyreyav* becomes more liberal. Tosafos is already much more willing to see the Sages as having made use of such sources of knowledge, and according to some, Ra'avad saw himself as able to make use of it.

With the *acharonim*, we begin to see a dramatic expansion of *sod Hashem liyreyav*. It becomes widely employed, to the extent of it allegedly accounting for *every* scientific statement of the Sages. While most consider it problematic to apply it to halachic statements, some even apply it in this area. And it is expanded not only to other statements in the Talmud, but also as the definitive explanation for contemporary Torah scholars being equipped to deal with extra-halachic matters.

Why was the application of *sod Hashem liyreyav* expanded so much? One reason is that with the spread of kabbalah, the idea of receiving knowledge via prophetic or quasi-prophetic inspiration became widely accepted, and it would seem natural for the sages of the Talmud to possess it to an even greater extent. Another possible reason is that the concept of the decline of generations, itself part of enhancing the prestige and authority of the sacred texts, requires that the statements of the ancients must be granted greater credibility than statements of people today. There are two basic ways of accomplishing this; the ancients can be claimed to have been wiser, or to have been divinely inspired. *Sod Hashem liyreyav* is an easy way to enhance the authority of ancient texts, as well as the revered Torah scholars of medieval and modern times. This process can be done without any appearance of innovation, since the principle appears in the Talmud itself. However, as we have seen, it has been expanded far beyond its original Talmudic usage.

In the chapter on *The Sun's Path At Night*, I demonstrate how the fact of the Sages sometimes possessing incorrect beliefs about the natural world was widely acknowledged by the Rishonim, and yet this view gradually became less accepted to the extent that today there are some people who are in denial that any rabbinic authority ever subscribed to such a view. In this study, we see the other side of the same coin. The opposite belief, of the Sages possessing supernatural knowledge of the natural world, was dramatically expanded, from its original appearance in the Talmud as a rare possibility to its *definitively* accounting for *every* statement made by Chazal in both halachic and non-halachic contexts. This is yet another example of how the rationalist and rational approach to the Talmud has steadily declined in traditional circles to the extent that it has sometimes been written out of existence.

TWO

Messianic Wonders and Skeptical Rationalists

Three Who Expounded Upon Messianic Wonders

It is often not appreciated how vast are the differences between the rationalist and non-rationalist schools of thought within Judaism. Likewise, it is often not appreciated that both are rooted in hundreds of years of interpretation. The enormity of these differences, and yet their prominent pedigree, comes to light in several passages from the Talmud and Midrash which deal with the topic of rationalism itself, in the context of rationalist approaches to wonders that are stated to occur in the Messianic Era.[1]

One account in the Talmud describes a student of Rabbi Yochanan who is apparently berated for taking a rationalist approach:

> *"And I will make your windows of rubies, and your gates of beryl, and all your borders of precious stones"* (Isaiah 54:12)—It is as Rabbi Yochanan sat and expounded, The Holy One is destined to bring precious stones and pearls that are thirty by thirty (cubits) and hollow out of them an area ten by twenty and stand them at the gates of Jerusalem. A certain student scoffed at him: "Now that we do not even find such things in the size of a small dove's egg, can ones of such size be found?!" After some time, he set out to sea in a ship, and saw ministering angels that were sitting and carving precious stones and pearls that were thirty by thirty and hollowing out ten by twenty. He said to them, "Who are these for?" They said to him, "The

---

[1] See too Ephraim Kanarfogel, "Medieval Rabbinic Conceptions of the Messianic Age: The View of the Tosafists," in Carmi Horwitz ed., *Meah Shearim: Studies in Medieval Jewish Spiritual Life in Memory of Isadore Twersky* (Jerusalem: Magnes Press 2001) pp. 147-169.

Holy One is destined to stand them at the gates of Jerusalem." He came before Rabbi Yochanan and said to him, "Expound, my rebbe, it is fitting for you to expound; just as you said, thus I saw." Rabbi Yochanan replied: "Empty one! If you hadn't seen it, then would you not have believed it?! You are a scoffer at the words of the sages!" He gave him a look and he became a heap of bones. (Talmud, *Bava Batra* 75a)

Elsewhere in the Talmud, Rabbi Zeira presents this story as an example of how Rabbi Yochanan would define an *apikores*.[2] At first glance, this account seems to be a powerful condemnation of rationalism, which is indeed, as we shall see, how many invoke it.

But matters are not so simple. In another account, concerning a student of Rabban Gamliel, the rationalist student is likewise deemed incorrect, but instead of being castigated, he is re-educated:

Rabban Gamliel sat and expounded: [In the Messianic Era] women are destined to give birth every day,[3] as it states, "Pregnant and bearing young together" (Jer. 31:7). A certain student mocked him, saying. "There is nothing new under the sun!" Rabban Gamliel said to him, Come and I will show you an example in this world, and he went and showed him a chicken.

…Rabban Gamliel further sat and expounded: [In the Messianic Era] the Land of Israel is destined to grow fresh bread and garments of fine wool, as it states, "May there be an abundance of grain in the land" (Ps. 72:16).[4] A certain student mocked him, saying. "There is nothing new under the sun!" Rabban Gamliel said to him, Come and I will show you an example in this world, and he went and showed him mushrooms and truffles (as an example of instant bread-like food); and regarding the garments of fine wool, he showed him the fibrous growth around young palm-shoots. (Talmud, *Shabbat* 30b)

---

[2] *Sanhedrin* 100a.

[3] Rashi explains that this does not mean that a child is conceived and born on the same day, but rather that women will conceive multiple times in succession, such that when the pregnancies reach their term, the woman ends up giving birth on successive days. See Maharsha.

[4] See Rashi for an explanation of how Rabban Gamliel derives this from the verse.

Finally, in a little-known third account, the rationalist approach is neither condemned nor corrected, but rather presented as the appropriate scathing response to unrealistic predictions of such wonders:

> Rabbi Meir sat and expounded: The wolf is destined (in the Messianic Era) to have a fleece of fine wool, and the dog will have the coat of ermine (to make clothing for the righteous). They said to him, "Enough, Rabbi Meir! There is nothing new under the sun." (*Midrash Kohelet Rabbah* 1:28)

This account is especially odd in that the Messianic wonders described by Rabbi Meir are far less unrealistic than those described by Rabbi Yochanan and Rabban Gamliel; wolves in northern countries actually do grow a thick undercoat of soft fur during the winter. Yet while the Talmud presents the predictions of Rabbi Yochanan and Rabban Gamliel as being correct, the prediction of Rabbi Meir is dismissed by the other rabbis.

Clearly, these accounts require much explanation. We will make some initial observations regarding the first case, then explore it in detail, and then examine all the cases together.

Rabbi Yochanan and his Student

The story of Rabbi Yochanan and his student is challenging. Some throw up their hands in perplexity in trying to account for the student's crime:

> Could it be that this student, who questioned it in his heart, should be rated as a heretic? And afterwards, when he saw the ministering angels, he intended to proclaim the greatness of Rabbi Yochanan's words, not to challenge him, Heaven forbid. Why was he turned into a heap of bones? The bottom line is that the explanation of this passage eludes me. And that which is beyond you, do not expound upon. (Rabbi Yehudah HaLevi Epstein, *Minchat Yehudah* [Warsaw 1877], to *Bava Batra* 75b)

Later, we shall explore whether Rabbi Yochanan was speaking literally or metaphorically in his reference to giant gemstones and pearls. For now, let us assume that he was speaking literally. Before analyzing what the student's crime actually was, there are some other questions that need exploring.

One issue to clarify regarding Rabbi Yochanan's prediction is whether he was talking of God supernaturally creating these stones, or of God using gemstones and pearls that exist via natural processes. While not unequivocal, the intent does seem to be the latter. Rabbi Yochanan speaks of God "bringing" these gemstones, not "creating" them. Additionally, the student saw the angels already working on them in his own day (although the meaning of that statement itself requires discussion). It therefore seems that Rabbi Yochanan was talking about giant gemstones that are naturally found in the ground, and giant pearls from naturally existing giant oysters.[5]

A second issue to clarify is the source of Rabbi Yochanan's exegesis. Was he saying it based on a tradition, or based on his interpretation of the verse? Rambam was apparently of the view that all such eschatological predictions were based on the Sages' own interpretations of verses.[6] Rashbam,[7] Maharsha[8] and Ben Yehoyada[9] present different approaches as to how it is derived from nuances in the wording of the verse. On the other hand, Ran, as we shall see, apparently understands it to have been a tradition.

A third issue to clarify is whether Rabbi Yochanan heard the student's initial denial. While, as we shall see, some claim that he did, others point out that Rabbi Yochanan apparently did not hear the student's initial denial, deriving this from Rabbi Yochanan's statement, "If you wouldn't have seen it, then would you not have believed it?!"[10] Furthermore, had Rabbi Yochanan heard his initial statement, he would presumably have "given him a look" immediately. But we need not posit that the student's

---

[5] An opposing claim could perhaps be made on the grounds that Rabbi Yochanan, as we shall later see, specifically spoke about supernatural wonders in the Messianic Era.

[6] "Regarding all these and suchlike matters – nobody knows how they will be, to the extent that they were concealed from the prophets, and even the Sages have no tradition in these matters, resorting instead to weighing up the verses, and therefore there are disputes in these matters" (*Mishneh Torah, Hilchot Melachim* 12:4).

[7] In *Ein Yaakov* to *Bava Batra* 75a.

[8] To *Bava Batra* 75a.

[9] To *Sanhedrin* 100a.

[10] Rabbi Yehudah HaLevi Epstein, *Minchat Yehudah* ad loc.

disbelief was a private thought, as the aforementioned Rabbi Epstein does; perhaps even if Rabbi Yochanan did not hear him, others did.

The Obligation to Believe the Sages

Rabbi Yechezkel Levenstein explains that Rabbi Yochanan's student was liable for the death penalty as retribution for the heresy of disbelieving Rabbi Yochanan:

> Anyone who does not have absolute faith in everything from the Sages' words is a heretic and [this student] was therefore punished with death. (*Ohr Yechezkel* p. 207)

In the fifteenth century, Rabbi Yitzchak Abouhav brought the story of Rabbi Yochanan to prove that one must believe every single statement made by the Sages:

> We are obligated to believe everything that they, of blessed memory, said of the *midrashot* and the *haggadot*, just as with our belief in the Torah of Moshe Rabbeinu. If we find something that appears to be an exaggeration or scientifically impossible, we must attribute the deficiency [in comprehension] to our grasp, not to their statement. Someone who derides anything that they said is punished. (Rabbi Yitzchak Abouhav, *Menorat HaMaor*, 2:1:2:2[11])

In the previous century, Ran (Rabbi Nissim ben Reuven of Gerona) also used this story in a way that initially sounds the same as Rabbi Yitzchak Abouhav:

> And just as we are commanded to follow their consensus in the laws of the Torah, we are also commanded to follow everything that they say to us by way of tradition with opinions (*deyot*) and elucidations of verses, whether or not the saying is with regard to a commandment. (Ran proceeds to cite the story of Rabbi Yochanan and his student) …Behold, that which Rabbi Yochanan said here was not a law or ordinance from the laws of the Torah, and nevertheless it arises here that the student was saying words of heresy, that he scorns the word of God, in that he does

---

[11] In his introduction, Rabbi Abouhav does acknowledge that Rav Sherira Gaon did not see Aggadot as binding, but he claims that this was meant to be limited to certain categories of Aggada.

not believe the one whom he is commanded to believe. (Rabbi Nissim ben Reuven, *Derashot HaRan* 5)

Although this is sometimes invoked in support of the principle that one must believe everything in the Talmud, a close reading reveals that Ran's position is more limited in scope. He states that there is an obligation to believe everything that the Sages say *with regard to Deyot and exegeses of Scripture* and which they say *al tzad hakabbalah*—from received tradition. These important qualifying phrases are often overlooked. (Note too that Ran elsewhere writes that we must follow the Sages in halachah *even when they are wrong*,[12] which would mean that when he writes here that we are commanded to follow their consensus in the laws of the Torah, it does not mean that they must be right, merely that we must follow their view.[13]) It means that Ran is acknowledging that some statements of the Sages concerning opinions and/or exegeses of Scripture were *not* said via Sinaitic tradition, and it is not forbidden to dispute them. Ran's citation of Rabbi Yochanan's student must therefore mean that he considered Rabbi Yochanan's statement to have been presented *al tzad hakabbalah*—from received tradition, apparently differing from the views of Rambam, Rashbam, Maharsha and Ben Yehoyada.

It should be noted that the position of Rabbi Yitzchak Abouhav, and possibly that of Ran too, is highly innovative. Among the Geonim and Rishonim, we overwhelmingly find that they (a) considered the Sages' scientific assessments to be no superior to those of anyone else,[14] and (b) rated Aggadic statements as non-binding.[15]

---

[12] See *Derush* 3, pages 86 and 112 in the Feldman edition.

[13] For an important discussion of how our allegiance to the authority of the Sages does not presume their infallibility in halachah, see Rabbi Shlomo Fisher, *Derashot Beit Yishai* 15.

[14] See http://torahandscience.blogspot.com for an extensive list of sources and full citations.

[15] See Rabbi Chaim Eisen, "Maharal's *Be'er ha-Golah* and His Revolution in Aggadic Scholarship — in Their Context and on His Terms," *Hakirah* vol. 4, for an extensive list of sources.

Still, the fact remains that according to both Rabbi Yitzchak Abouhav and Ran, exegeses such as those of Rabbi Yochanan must be accepted. However, it is not clear whether these authorities interpreted Rabbi Yochanan's prediction literally or non-literally. This, as we shall, turns out to be a critical issue.

The Traditionalist Approach

Several authorities take the account concerning Rabbi Yochanan's student at face value, understanding Rabbi Yochanan as speaking of actual gemstones and pearls that are fifty feet in size. Maharsha states that Rabbi Yochanan's student's crime was in not accepting the literal truth of his prediction, and notes that "it is the way of heretics to remove words from their literal meaning."[16] Rabbi Shlomo Wolbe even writes that nobody has the right to adopt a non-literal interpretation of Rabbi Yochanan's words:

> There is no basis whatsoever to interpret this passage in a non-literal manner, for neither Maharsha nor Maharal strayed from the simple meaning of the matter, and we live from their mouths in how we explain Aggadata. (*Alei Shur* vol. II, p. 294)[17]

With the parallel discussion of Rabban Gamliel's expositions concerning the Land of Israel growing bread and garments of fine wool, Rabbi Yekusiel Aryeh Kamelhar even brings further present-day examples to support a literal understanding.[18] The breadfruit tree (*Artocarpus altilis*), as its name suggests, produces a large fruit which, when cooked, has a taste similar to fresh baked bread. (Rabbi Kamelhar claims that these trees from Southeast Asia and the Pacific islands were known to Rabban Gamliel, but he opted instead to tell his student about phenomena that were accessible to be verified.) Regarding the garments of fine wool, Rabbi Kamelhar mentions the paper mulberry tree (*Broussonetia papyrifera*), in

---

[16] Maharsha to *Sanhedrin* 100a, a.v. *Nachal mibeit Kadshei haKadashim*.

[17] I find this statement greatly perplexing; as we shall see, many authorities interpret these passages non-literally, and I do not know what binds us to Maharal and Maharsha.

[18] *HaTalmud U'Mada'ei HaTevel*, ch. 5, *Shaar Ha-Emunah*, pp. 95-96.

which the inner bark can be cleaned and beaten to produce a non-woven fabric known as Polynesian Tapa cloth.

Tosafos brings the story of Rabbi Yochanan's student to show that seeking empirical confirmation for a statement of the Sages is forbidden.[19] Rabbi Zvi Elimelech Shapiro of Dynov (1783-1841) invokes the story of Rabbi Yochanan and his student as part of a lecture against the evils of rationalism and empiricism.[20] He rejects the notion that rationalists such as Rav Saadia Gaon and Rambam present a contradiction to his thesis, on the grounds that there were mystical reasons which made their writings necessary for their generation. Rabbi Mordechai Gifter of Telz presents the story of Rabbi Yochanan's student as a powerful lesson of how it is forbidden for a person's belief in any of the Sages' words to be so weak as to require empirical confirmation:

> He saw that the student believed his rebbe's words due to his sense of sight, from experiencing it. This is not only a lack of faith—there is ridicule of the words of the Sages. Faith does not require confirmation from the senses; it is self-justifying, in the depths of the heart's wisdom, whereas sensory confirmation brings the concept into the material world and removes it from Torah. (Rabbi Mordechai Gifter, *Pirkei Emunah: Shiurei Daat*, p. 98)

A slightly more limited approach is presented by Rabbi Moshe Shapiro. He claims that Rabbi Yochanan heard the student's initial denial of his statement, but did not hold him accountable as a scoffer since the student may have genuinely considered the existence of such gemstones and pearls to be utterly impossible, which would have been legitimate. However, if so, then when the student traveled on the ship and saw such stones, he should have refused to believe his eyes. Since he did accept the evidence in front of him and changed his mind, this shows that he rated the physical

---

[19] Tosafos to *Chullin* 57b s.v. *Eizel v'achzi*. He raises this point to query the Talmud's account of how Rabbi Shimon ben Chalafta performed an experiment to confirm a statement of King Solomon about ants. Tosafos answers that he was merely seeking to clarify *how* Solomon knew it, not *whether* Solomon knew it. In contrast to this, Rabbi Yaakov Gesundheit, in *Tiferet Yaakov*, observes (in surprise) that Rashi states that Rabbi Shimon ben Chalafta was not willing to rely on Solomon's authority.

[20] *B'nei Yissachar, ma'amarei Sivan, ma'amar* 5:19.

evidence that he saw as having more credibility than Rabbi Yochanan's exegesis. This is heresy that classifies him as a scoffer of the words of the sages:

> ...At first, when he ridiculed it, it was possible that his view was that such a thing is truly impossible to exist in this world. And for such an attitude, he does not yet become a scoffer on the words of the sages. But if he was truly secure in the view that such a phenomenon is impossible, then when he saw the angels he should have concluded that in truth he did not see anything, and it was only a dream or illusion. Since after he saw it with his own eyes he concluded that such a thing is possible, then it turns out that in his view, that which he sees with his own eyes creates a strength of belief with a power that requires one to believe the fact of its existence more than that which the exegeses of Chazal require. (Rabbi Moshe Shapiro as cited by Reuven Schmelczer, *Afikei Mayim* p. 16)[21]

A problem with this approach is that the student's initial rejection of Rabbi Yochanan's statement was not due to some sort of philosophical conviction in the impossibility of large gemstones (itself difficult to justify), but rather for the empirical reason that all gemstones and pearls known to exist are vastly smaller. His subsequent reversal was due to new empirical evidence. If he is not accountable for rejecting Rabbi Yochanan's position due to empirical evidence, why would he be accountable for accepting it on those grounds?

In an apparent variation on this approach, Rabbi Chaim Shmulevitz considers that the reason why the student was not accountable at first is that he simply couldn't visualize it. The problem was that once he *was* able to visualize it, he should have accepted that the evidence for it was that Rabbi Yochanan had described it rather than that he himself had seen it:

---

[21] Rabbi Shapiro concludes by citing Ramban's condemnation of the Greek materialists who deny the validity of everything that they cannot sense or explain. However Ramban also relies upon Greek science to reject traditional understandings of the rainbow (see Gen. 9:12) and to present a viable alternative to the Sages' understanding of human conception (Lev. 12:2). In footnote 54 on p. 39 of *Afikei Mayim*, Rabbi Shapiro claims that Ramban in the latter discussion is referring to two different dimensions of Torah; many will find this explanation overly contrived.

In the beginning, Rabbi Yochanan did not punish him, for the student was not capable of believing in the possibility of gemstones measuring thirty by thirty, and it was for this reason that he did not believe it, but after he saw such things with his eyes, and then said, "Just as you said, thus I saw," he was now believing it on the grounds that he saw it… If the matter is entirely dependent upon his understanding and sensory perception, he is no servant at all, and that is heresy; he scorns the words of the Sages in and of themselves, and does not believe them unless he sees it with his own eyes. (Rabbi Chaim Shmulevitz, *Sichot Mussar*, 5731, *ma'amar* 11: "The Servant of God")

Nevertheless, in contrast to the approach of Rabbi Moshe Shapiro and Rabbi Chaim Shmulevitz, Rashi states that the student's heresy was in his initial skepticism.[22] As noted earlier, others point out that Rabbi Yochanan apparently did not originally hear the student's skepticism, deriving this from Rabbi Yochanan's statement, "If you wouldn't have seen it, then would you not have believed it?!" It was only later that Rabbi Yochanan was able to deduce that the student had originally been skeptical.

According to all these approaches, the account of Rabbi Yochanan's student is a powerful condemnation of rationalism. Even if one of the Sages' statements goes against everything we know about the natural world, we may not reject it for empirical reasons. (It should be noted, though, that the student's position was not that he refused to accept *anything* unless he saw it with his own eyes; rather, it was that if he was told something that seemed extraordinarily unlikely, he wouldn't accept it unless he saw it with his own eyes.)

All the above views, however, run counter to the many authorities who did not consider there to be any obligation to believe all the words of the Sages. As we noted earlier, many Geonim and Rishonim did not consider Aggadic statements or scientific assessments as binding. Furthermore, as we shall later discuss in more detail, the rabbis' dismissal of Rabbi Meir's prediction of wolf-wool indicates that they believed Rabban Gamliel's exegesis to be mistaken, as well as that of Rabbi Yochanan. We must

---

[22] Rashi to *Sanhedrin* 100a.

therefore seek to understand how these rationalist Geonim and Rishonim understood the story with Rabbi Yochanan—both with regard to why the student was condemned for his rejection, and with regard to what it means that there will be such extraordinary gemstones and pearls.

Different Fates: Different Disbelievers

The first question to address is why Rabbi Yochanan's student is castigated, whereas Rabban Gamliel's student is re-educated. To put it another way, whereas Rabbi Yochanan condemns his student for requiring empirical evidence to overcome his skepticism, Rabban Gamliel assuages his student's skepticism by providing empirical evidence!

The answer given by some is that since Rabban Gamliel's student cited a Scriptural basis for his skepticism (that "there is nothing new under the sun") this showed that he still had respect for the Torah and was basing himself on a Torah viewpoint. Rabbi Yochanan's student, on the other hand, did not base himself on any Torah source.[23] As a slight variation of this, one might wish to explain that with Rabban Gamliel, there was a prediction of a supernatural creation, which the student rejected based on a theological position that "there is nothing new under the sun." With Rabbi Yochanan, on the other hand, there was an account of a naturally-occurring but hitherto undiscovered phenomenon. The rejection of this was not due to the theological opposition of "there is nothing new under the sun" but instead based on skepticism as to the legitimacy of making unusual claims based on Scriptural exegesis.

However, rationalists will find difficulty with such explanations. While it is true that Rabbi Yochanan's student did not express his disbelief in theological terms, Rabbi Yochanan himself did not hear the original expression of disbelief (according to most authorities). From his perspective, how did he know that it was not theologically based? The giant gemstones of which Rabbi Yochanan spoke are so far beyond the norm that, even if not technically impossible, they might be legitimately

---

[23] Rabbi Yekusiel Aryeh Kamalher, *HaTalmud U'Mada'ei HaTevel*, ch. 5, *Shaar Ha-Emunah*, pp. 95-96.

considered beyond the natural order.[24] The giant pearls are probably even theoretically scientifically impossible, due to biological constraints on the maximum size of oysters. Rambam and others followed the principle that, wherever possible, one should always seek to interpret events naturalistically rather than posit the existence of phenomena beyond the natural order. The student's disbelief was therefore not necessarily a matter of simple cynicism, or of his following the skeptics' principle that "extraordinary claims require extraordinary proof." Rather, it could have been an opposition to the idea of positing the existence of something far beyond the natural order, which is also a theological stance, just as with Rabban Gamliel's student. In fact, we see a similar position taken by Rabbi Meir Abulafia, himself far from an extreme rationalist.[25] The Talmud cites Rava as exegetically deriving from Scripture that in the Messianic Era, there will be eighteen thousand righteous people standing before God. Rashi explains this as referring to "the celestial Jerusalem," to which Rabbi Meir Abulafia responds:

> …But we, in our poverty of understanding, do not know where this celestial Jerusalem, discussed in the Talmud, is, or where it is destined to be. If it is in the Heavens (i.e. a spiritual location)—is there building in the Heavens? And if it is the name of an elevation in the sky called Jerusalem, then it means that the future sitting of the righteous will be in the sky, and this is astonishing: How can these bodies sit in the sky, with it not being by way of a miracle? And it is difficult in my eyes to rely on [positing the] the work of miracles, in matters for which there is not a clear proof from Scripture nor a widespread acceptance amongst the words of the Sages.[26] But we have already discharged the obligation of truth, to clarify our doubts and the perplexity in which we are confused, and

---

[24] Cf. Maharal, *Be'er HaGolah*, *Be'er* 5, regarding why Moses could not have literally been ten cubits tall. For a discussion of this topic see my book *Sacred Monsters*.

[25] See Bernard Septimus, *Hispano-Jewish Culture in Transition: The Career and Controversies of Ramah* (Cambridge, Mass., 1982).

[26] "*Kabbalah peshutah b'divrei chachamim.*" See too *Yad Ramah* to *Sanhedrin* 90a. The translation of this phrase follows Septimus, loc. cit. See Rambam, *Mishneh Torah*, *Hilchot Tefillah* 2:19, 4:6, 5:15, 13:1; *Hilchot Ishut* 16:1; and numerous other places.

perhaps God will illuminate out eyes from Heaven to explain the simple meaning of this passage. (*Yad Ramah, Sanhedrin* 97b)

Rabbi Meir Abulafia is reluctant to accept that the Messianic Era will involve a miraculous event, in the absence of a clear proof from Scripture or a widespread acceptance among the words of the Sages. The more committed rationalists would all the more be opposed to this, and would not see there being any obligation to accept it on Rabbi Yochanan's say-so. From the rationalist perspective we are therefore still faced with the question of why Rabbi Yochanan's student was condemned rather than re-educated as with Rabban Gamliel's student.

Different Fates: Different Rabbis

There is another possible way of explaining the different responses of Rabbi Yochanan and that of Rabban Gamliel. Perhaps it does not reflect a difference between the students in each case, but rather a difference between Rabbi Yochanan and Rabban Gamliel. There are several instances in which we find that Rabbi Yochanan acted harshly towards someone that he understood as slighting him, with grave consequences.

The Talmud[27] records that when Resh Lakish once gave an opinion regarding the halachic status of certain weapons, Rabbi Yochanan commented that Resh Lakish, as a former bandit, would know about such things.[28] Resh Lakish responded: "And what good did it do me? Before I was called a master, and now I am called a master." Rabbi Yochanan took offense and retorted that he had done him good by bringing him back to Torah. As a result of Rabbi Yochanan taking offense, Resh Lakish fell sick, and when Rabbi Yochanan refused the request of his sister (to whom Resh Lakish was married) to pray for him, Resh Lakish died.[29]

---

[27] *Bava Metzia* 84a.

[28] Rabbi Chanoch Geberhard, *Shiurim B'Haggadot Chazal*, stresses that Rabbi Yochanan meant no offense with this comment; however, it perhaps comes as no great surprise that offense was taken.

[29] Maharsha explains that "master" means a master of Torah; Resh Lakish meant that before he was a bandit, he was a Torah scholar, and it was from those days that his knowledge of this law came, not from his days as a bandit. However, Rabbi Yochanan wrongly assumed that "master" meant a master of banditry, and Resh Lakish was saying

The Talmud records another instance[30] where Rabbi Yochanan was taken aback at the powerful questions of his new student Rav Kahana. He looked at Rav Kahana, and due to Rav Kahana having a cut on the side of his mouth, he thought that Rav Kahana was laughing at him. Rabbi Yochanan took offense, and Rav Kahana died as a result, for which Rabbi Yochanan later had to seek forgiveness. In yet another account,[31] Rabbi Yochanan was angry with his student Rabbi Elazar, who related one of his teachings without reporting it in Rabbi Yochanan's name. Others pointed out that he should not be angry, noting that Rabbi Elazar himself was rebuked for growing angry in a dispute with a peer. But at this, Rabbi Yochanan grew even angrier, retorting that while it was obviously inappropriate for Rabbi Elazar and his peer (who was his equal) to grow angry with each other, he is entitled to be angry at his student. He was only appeased when others pointed out that in any case, people know that Rabbi Elazar is reporting Rabbi Yochanan's teachings. While the Talmud proceeds to explain why Rabbi Yochanan legitimately wanted his teachings to be related in his name, it may be no coincidence that, of all people, it is Rabbi Yochanan who is involved in this case.

In all these stories, we see Rabbi Yochanan taking offense at what he inaccurately perceived as a slight to his honor, sometimes with disastrous results. In the case of Rav Kahana, we see that Rabbi Yochanan even brought about his death, despite the fact that he was mistaken in thinking that Rav Kahana had committed a wrong against him. Accordingly, the fate of Rabbi Yochanan's student in our story might not reflect so much on the student as it does on Rabbi Yochanan. Perhaps the student had legitimate reason not to believe his teacher, but Rabbi Yochanan was offended at the student not taking his word for it.

---

that it did him no good that Rabbi Yochanan brought him to Torah, since he is still described as a master bandit. Rashi has a different explanation of this story, in which Rabbi Yochanan correctly assessed that Resh Lakish had said something inappropriately cynical.

[30] *Bava Kama* 117a.

[31] Yevamot 96b.

However, this is not an entirely satisfactory explanation. Whereas these stories are cases in which Rabbi Yochanan misunderstood the situation, in our story he did not misunderstand the student; he was correct to infer that the student would not have believed him without seeing it. Furthermore, Rabbi Zeira presents the story of the skeptical student as a demonstration of who would be classified as a heretic according to Rabbi Yochanan, and apparently endorses it as a valid view. Thus, even if Rabbi Yochanan had a tendency towards harsh reactions, which would account for why this student suffered different consequences to Rabban Gamliel's student, it is still understood that this is genuinely rated as heresy, at least according to Rabbi Yochanan. We therefore still need to understand how the rationalist school of thought understands this story (if not by taking the simple approach of saying that Rabbi Yochanan was a non-rationalist).

Problems Other than the Student's Rationalism

One might wish to suggest that the crime of Rabbi Yochanan's student was not so much in his disbelieving Rabbi Yochanan's prediction, but rather in his expressing this disbelief in a scornful manner. The student in this story is described as scoffing rather than respectfully disagreeing, and it is for this attitude that he was culpable.

Yet this explanation is difficult. True, the term used is *lagleg*, which is variously translated as "scoff," "mock," "ridicule," etc. However this need not mean that he used such a tone; it may be in reference to the mere fact of his disagreement. The latter seems more likely, in light of the fact that Rabbi Yochanan did not condemn the student until the student came to him praising him for his words, at which point he was speaking with respect. Rabbi Yochanan calls him a scoffer based on his final statement in which he conditioned his acceptance on his empirical verification, not based on the way in which he expressed his initial disbelief.

Rabbi Moshe Tzuriel points to a different problem. He notes that while with Rabbi Yochanan's other expositions, it says "Rabbi Yochanan *said*...," here it says "Rabbi Yochanan *expounded*" i.e. in public. The student's critique therefore could harm the public's faith.[32] Still, this alone does not seem to explain Rabbi Yochanan's condemnation.

Could it be that there was a pre-existing problem with the student, and his skepticism of Rabbi Yochanan's words was merely the final straw? Several authorities note that the Talmud does not speak of "*talmid echad*" ("one student") but rather of "*oto talmid*" ("a certain student"). This term is frequently understood to refer to a particular subject whose name ought not to be mentioned.

Rabbi Menachem Tzvi Teksin suggests that the "certain student" in Rabban Gamliel's story is the student who "spoiled his dish" in public i.e. Jesus (see *Sanhedrin* 103a).[33] Maharatz Chajes cites a view that the "certain student" in this story is the apostle Paul, but disputes this as Paul learned from Rabban Gamliel the Elder, whereas the Rabban Gamliel of this passage is Rabban Gamliel of Yavneh.[34] However Rabbi Yaakov Brill states that this *was* Rabban Gamliel the Elder and thus the unnamed student was Paul.[35] Rabbi Nosson Nota Leiter cites several academics who are of the same view.[36]

The student in the story with Rabbi Yochanan must have been a different person, in light of the fact that Rabbi Yochanan lived much later. But if the phrase "a certain student" in the story with Rabban Gamliel referred to a problematic individual, the phrase in the story with Rabbi Yochanan may likewise refer to a similar such person. The Midrash[37] presents a slightly different version of the story of Rabbi Yochanan's student, in which instead of a reference to "a certain student" it states instead that "there was an *apikores* there" who challenged it. This might be because the Talmud (in *Sanhedrin*) states that what he said to Rabbi Yochanan appears as heresy, or it might mean that he was already an *apikores*. If this was such a person, we cannot necessarily extrapolate from

---

[32] *Otzros Ha-Aggadah: Biurei Aggados* (1990).

[33] *Orach Yesharim* (Peuterkov 1907) vol. I p. 66.

[34] Maharatz Chajes, *Kuntrus Acharon, Avodas HaMikdash* ch. 4.

[35] *Ben Zekunim* (Galicia 1889) p. 92.

[36] Responsa *Tziyon LeNefesh Chayah* 59.

[37] *Midrash Yalkut Shimoni*, Yeshayah 56, *remez* 478.

Rabbi Yochanan's condemnation that it would be unthinkable for anyone to doubt his statement.

However, again, since Rabbi Zeira presents this story as an example of that which Rabbi Yochanan would rate as heresy, it seems that there was a problem with his specific conduct in this case, not with his prior history.

The Rationalist Approach

The key to the rationalist approach to this story, to understanding why the student was condemned apparently for the crime of rationalism itself, is to realize that the rationalists' approach to Rabbi Yochanan's exegesis is very different. So far, all the authorities that we have cited interpret the statements of Rabbi Yochanan and Rabban Gamliel literally, as referring to wondrous physical phenomena that will appear in the Messianic Era. But there are others who interpret these accounts entirely differently. Another explanation of Rabbi Yochanan's words is given by Rabbi David HaKochavi of Avignon, France (c. 1260-1330):

> ...We have already noted that we are citing many passages without explaining them, and we have noted the reasons. Accordingly, we have cited this passage, but with a little contemplation it will be seen that there is hidden meaning... it alludes to the merit of the intellect when it penetrates the entrances of true opinions... (*Sefer HaBatim* I, 6:4, pp. 185)

Rabbi Yochanan was *not* making a statement about the physical world. The student interpreted it as a reference to the physical world and thus mocked it; he was castigated because, had he not been shown otherwise, he would not have appreciated that Rabbi Yochanan was speaking allegorically.

With regard to the parallel story of Rabban Gamliel's statements, Rambam writes that these were not intended to be interpreted literally as referring to the physical reality:

> There will be no difference between this world and the Messianic Era except regarding the subjugation to kingdoms... but in those days, it will be very easy for people to obtain sustenance, to the point that with minimal effort a person will reap great benefits, and this is what is meant when they said that the Land of Israel is destined to grow fresh bread and

garments of fine wool ... and therefore this sage, who stated this to his student, became angry when his student did not understand his words and thought that he was speaking literally. (Rambam, *Commentary on the Mishnah*, Introduction to *Perek Chelek*[38])

The student erred in interpreting Rabban Gamliel's statements in this way, and Rabban Gamliel, following the maxim of "answer the fool according to his folly," responded by giving him an illustration of how such things could be physically possible. But this did not reflect the true meaning of his original statement.

Rambam's son makes some sharp comments about Rabbi Shlomo ben Avraham of Montpellier, who had attacked Rambam for taking an allegorical approach to various wonders of the Messianic Era:

In his letter, he also anxiously complained and moaned about [the rationalist approach regarding] the feast of Leviathan, the wine that has been preserved in the grape [since creation], fresh bread of the finest quality, and garments of fine wool. He was raised from his youth and studied day and night with all his might and all his soul to receive these as his rewards to fill his stomach with the flesh of the Leviathan and the fresh bread of finest quality and his mind was in the wine that has been kept preserved in the grape, and to wear some of those garments of fine wool. It is certain that our Sages only cited these Midrashim and their like to engage his interest and others like him, just as we engage the interest of children in studying Torah in school all week by distributing sweets and nuts to them on Shabbat and dressing them in pressed cloths on the festivals... (Rabbeinu Avraham ben HaRambam, *Milchamot Hashem*)

A similar non-literal explanation is found in Riaz (Rabbi Yeshayah of Trani II, 1235-1300), who explains Rabban Gamliel's exegesis about the land being destined to grow fresh bread to mean that sustenance will be plentiful. Riaz also makes a fascinating statement:

---

[38] Cf. R. Yedaiah (En Bonet) ben Avraham Bedersi (c. 1270 – c. 1340), *Iggeret Hitnatzlut* to Rashba, who states that Rabban Gamliel's statement should be accepted on face value, as an example of the wonders of the redemption, were it not for the fact that there is a statement that there is no difference between this world and the Messianic Era aside from the subjugation to nations.

And they further said in the Talmud of the Land of Israel, in Chapter Seven of *Nazir*: "But are *midrashos* a matter of *emunah*? Rather, expound and receive reward." Thus it is made clear that the Sages did not say Midrashim by way of dogma and fundamentals, but rather to increase insights into Scripture, and to expound them in every way, and *perhaps* (emphasis added) they contain an allusion. (Introduction to *Perek Chelek* of *Sanhedrin*)

Rabbi Shem Tov ibn Shaprut (14th century) writes similarly:

Know that these sayings are not to be understood literally—for if the literal interpretation were true, then Scripture would state it. And even when (the Sages) say it, we will not believe that these could be true according to their literal meaning. For what advantage would there be in such things, save for those lacking in intellect who think that the goal of man is to eat and drink and enjoy this world. Rather, the intent of their saying that women will give birth every day is that God will strengthen the natural forces such that women will not miscarry, and that there will not be infant deaths (i.e. giving birth will be an "everyday occurrence" with no risk of tragedy)... And because that student did not devote himself to understanding this, but rather took the words at face value in order to mock the words of Chazal, his rebbe grew angry at him... (*Pardes Rimonim, Seder Moed*, pp. 45-46)

And we also find a non-literal interpretation in *Ein Yaakov*:

Here we learn that the truth of these expositions is not in accordance with their simple meaning, as the student thought. And that which Rabban Gamliel answered him according to his way of thinking, was by way of "Answer a fool according to his folly." But the true intent of these and similar sayings is that in the Messianic Era, success will be in abundance, and great outpouring, and it will be easy to obtain food to eat and clothing to wear, to the point that it will appear as though the earth is producing ready-baked bread to eat and clothes of fine wool to wear, and a person will be able to obtain all of them with little effort. It does not mean that the order of creation will change from its normal status, but rather that a person will be able to obtain his needs with ease, and he will not need the great effort that is required in times such as ours. (Rabbi Yaakov Ibn Chaviv, *HaKoteiv, Ein Yaakov* to *Shabbat* 30b)

In a detailed explanation of Rabbi Yochanan's allegory, Rabbi Avraham Stein explains that the gemstones symbolically represent the precious Torah sages, whose insights are dazzling and illuminating.[39] He states that it specifically alludes to the account:

> The Rabbis taught: Hillel the Elder had seventy students. Thirty of them were worthy of having the Divine Presence rest upon them, like Moshe Rabbeinu, thirty were worthy of having the sun stand still for them, like Yehoshua ben Nun, and twenty were intermediate. (Talmud, *Bava Basra* 133)

The gemstones and pearls, thirty by thirty, are the two groups of thirty students. The more precious gemstones represented the top thirty, and the less valuable pearls represented the lower tier. The twenty intermediate students are represented by the twenty cubits carved in the middle. Such was Rabbi Yochanan's intent; however, his student assumed that he was referring literally to gemstones and pearls, and therefore ridiculed his words. But when the student set sail—which metaphorically refers to his sailing in the sea of the Talmud[40]—he came across this account of Hillel's students and realized that Rabbi Yochanan was alluding to this account rather than speaking about physical gemstones.

Thus, the rationalist approach to Rabbi Yochanan's story is that the student was not castigated for being a rationalist, but rather for rejecting Rabbi Yochanan's words based on a foolish misinterpretation of them. He was rebuked for thinking that Rabbi Yochanan had said something irrational!

(It should also be noted that Rambam expressly states that any claims about the Messianic era made by the Sages are simply theories, based upon their various interpretations of verses, and that none of them are based on Sinaitic tradition.[41])

---

[39] Rabbi Avraham Stein, *Avnei Miluim* (Warsaw 1900), pp. 36-40.

[40] Cf. *HaKoteiv* in *Ein Yaakov*: "that he immersed himself deep in wisdom, and grasped the matter."

[41] *Mishneh Torah, Hilchot Melachim* 12:2.

Two Distinct Approaches

There is another approach to this entire topic which does not rest upon a commitment to either the rationalist or traditionalist interpretation. Let us recall the third case, buried in *Midrash Kohelet Rabbah*, which appears to have escaped the attention of those who compared and discussed the first two cases:

> Rabbi Meir sat and expounded: The wolf is destined (in the Messianic Era) to have a fleece of fine wool, and the dog will have the coat of ermine (to make clothing for the righteous). They said to him, "Enough, Rabbi Meir! There is nothing new under the sun." (*Midrash Kohelet Rabbah* 1:28)

Here, too, there is the same potential for dispute as to whether the prediction was intended literally. *Etz Yosef* explains Rabbi Meir's view as allegorically alluding to the subjugation of nature to man's will. But regardless of whether it was meant literally or allegorically, the Midrash presents Rabbi Meir's prediction as being firmly rejected by his colleagues. Maharzav, in his commentary on the Midrash, relates this to a well-known dispute elsewhere:

> Rabbi Chiyya bar Abba said: Rabbi Yochanan said that all the prophecies of the prophets (concerning the wondrous events of the future salvation) were only with regard to the Messianic Era, but in the World to Come, "The eye has not seen, O God, except for You [what He will do for he that awaits Him]" (Isaiah 64:3) (and we have no image of how it will be). And he argues with Shmuel, for Shmuel said, There is no difference between this world and the Messianic Era aside from the subjugation to empires alone, as it says, "For the poor shall not cease from amidst the land" (Deut. 15:11). (Talmud, *Berachot* 34b; cf. *Sanhedrin* 99a and *Shabbat* 63a)

Maharzav explains that the Rabbis who scorned Rabbi Meir's view were of the same opinion as Shmuel, that there is no difference between this era and the Messianic era aside from the Jewish People's subjugation to other nations. Now, these Rabbis and Shmuel would presumably equally oppose the prediction of Rabbi Yochanan.[42] Accordingly, while Rabbi Yochanan condemned the student for rejecting his view, there is an accepted body of authorities who would have likewise rejected it, although possibly in a different manner (and it may be more acceptable for established authorities, rather than students, to dispute Rabbi Yochanan). There is a fundamental dispute between these authorities regarding whether the usual natural order will continue into the Messianic Era.

The Riddle of Rambam

The above resolution, however, presents us with a question. We saw earlier that Rambam and several others reinterpreted Rabban Gamliel's prediction according to a naturalistic perspective. But we can now ask why they did this when in any case, of the two parallel accounts, one (Rabbi Meir's prediction) is rejected precisely because it is not a naturalistic perspective, and the other (Rabbi Yochanan's prediction) is from someone who is disputed by Shmuel precisely because it is not a naturalistic perspective! Why did they not simply state that Rabbi Yochanan and Rabban Gamliel were of the non-naturalistic school of thought, whereas they follow the rationalist school of thought?

The answer to this question may emerge from a consideration of another difficulty with Rambam's approach to this topic. Many, beginning with *Kesef Mishnah* and *Lechem Mishneh*, have questioned that Rambam appears to be siding with both sides of the dispute between Rabbi Yochanan and Shmuel. At first, he presents Rabbi Yochanan's opinion, that the wondrous benefits promised by prophets will take place in the Messianic Era:

> The early Sages already informed us that it is not within the power of man to properly grasp the pleasures of the World-to-Come; there is nobody who knows its greatness, beauty and strength apart from the Holy One

---

[42] This is certainly true with regard to the literal meaning of his prediction, and possibly even with regard to an allegorical meaning, if there was one (assuming that they understood Rabbi Meir to have had an allegorical meaning and nevertheless rejected his view). Whether they would also have opposed Rabban Gamliel's prediction is debatable; he seemed to be from their school of thought, since he saw fit to demonstrate that his prediction did *not* contravene the concept that there is nothing new under the sun.

alone, and all the benefits that the prophets prophesied for Israel were only with regard to material matters that Israel will enjoy in the Messianic Era when rulership will return to Israel. But the pleasure of the life of the World-to-Come have no value or comparison, and the prophets did not give it any analogy, so as not to degrade it with the analogy. That is what Isaiah said, "The eye has not seen, O God, except for You [what He will do for he that awaits Him]." (*Hilchot Teshuvah* 8:7)

Yet Rambam immediately proceeds to cite Shmuel's view that the Messianic Era will not include any departures from the norm, aside from Israel being released from its subjugation to other nations:

> ...but the days of the Messiah are in this world, and the world will proceed as usual, except that kingship will return to Israel. And the early Sages already said, There is no difference between this world and the Messianic Era apart from the subjugation to empires. (*Hilchot Teshuvah* 9:2)

In a different context, Rambam likewise sides with Shmuel and mentions no other view:

> Do not think for a moment that in the Messianic Era, something from the worldly norms will be annulled, or that there will be an innovation in the works of Creation. Rather, the world will function as usual... (He proceeds to explain the prophecies about predators living in peace with their prey as speaking metaphorically about the enemies of Israel.) The Sages said: There is no difference between this world and the Messianic Era apart from the subjugation to empires. (*Hilchot Melachim* 12:1-2)

How can Rambam side with both positions of a dispute—both with the view that the Messianic Era will include wonders, and with the view that it will generally be no different from today? One suggestion is that since, as Rambam notes, it is impossible to know the future with any certainty, Rambam did not take sides in this dispute and cited both views.[43] But this seems difficult; Rambam did not withhold his firm predictions about the Messianic Era. Another suggestion is that Shmuel was referring to the era of Mashiach ben Yosef, while Rabbi Yochanan was

---

[43] *Arba'ah Turei Even* to *Hilchot Teshuvah* ch. 8.

referring to the era of Mashiach ben David.[44] But there is no hint of this in the Talmud, and it states that Shmuel is arguing with Rabbi Yochanan's view.

Many answer that while Rabbi Yochanan and Shmuel were in disagreement, the aspects of the views of Rabbi Yochanan and Shmuel cited by Rambam are not contradictory. Rambam was siding with Shmuel, and was only citing the words of Rabbi Yochanan insofar as they support Shmuel's position. Shmuel also agrees that the wondrous prophecies were said with regard to the Messianic Era (not to the World-to-Come), but he interprets them allegorically, whereas Rabbi Yochanan interpreted them literally. Accordingly, Rambam cited the verse brought by Rabbi Yochanan, which indicates that the prophecies refer to the Messianic Era, in that respect alone, and not with regard to Rabbi Yochanan's view that the prophecies are to be interpreted literally.[45]

In a similar yet inverse approach, *Lechem Mishneh* and *Markevet HaMishneh* explain that Rambam was siding with Rabbi Yochanan, and was only citing the words of Shmuel insofar as they support Rabbi Yochanan's position. In Rambam's view, Rabbi Yochanan himself did not believe that the prophecies of wonders in the Messianic Era were speaking of supernatural events, but rather of naturalistic developments. Shmuel, on the other hand, did not believe that even naturalistic changes will occur, other than Israel being released from subjugation. But Rambam

---

[44] Ben Aryeh to Rambam, *Hilchot Teshuvah* 8:7, also discussed by Rabbi Hillel Rotenberg, *Mefa'arei Lev* (Jerusalem 2006) pp. 52-53.

[45] Rabbi Yedidyah Shmuel Tarika, *Ben Yedid* (Salonika 1806) to *Hilchot Teshuvah* 8:7; *Maase Rokeach* to *Hilchot Teshuvah* loc cit.; *Mishneh Kesef* to *Hilchot Teshuvah* loc cit.; *Be'eros HaMayim* to *Hilchot Teshuvah* loc cit.; Rabbi Yosef Kappach, *Kesavim*, vol. II, *shaar revii.* Cf. Chida, *Responsa Chaim Sho'el* 98, Rabbi Shlomo Algazi, *Gufei Halachos* (Izmir 1675), *Klalei Ha-Alef* 35, and Dror Fixler, "*HaBitui Chachamim/Chassidim Rishonim beMishneh Torah LeRambam,*" *Sinai* (1992) vol. 109 pp. 75-79. Rabbi Chaim Nethanzen in *Avodah Tamah* (Altona 1872) *Neilas Shearim* similarly states that Rambam adopted Shmuel's view and reinterpreted the position of Rabbi Yochanan so that he could present it in a way that would not conflict with this. Rabbi Ben-Tzion Sternfeld in *Shaarei Tziyon* (Pieterkov 1903), vol. III, *Biyur Ma'amar Temuha*, also seems to be presenting this approach.

only quoted Shmuel's statement insofar as it as a good way of expressing the idea that nature itself will not change.

Others, however, take an entirely different view, and claim that in Rambam's view, there was no dispute between Rabbi Yochanan and Shmuel. Both were of the view that the prophecies were intended allegorically (and in regard to the Messianic Era). Why, then, did the Talmud present them as being in dispute? Radvaz suggests that this was done because the masses will not be motivated to aspire to the Messianic Era if it does not include supernatural wonders. The Talmud therefore presented it as a dispute between Rabbi Yochanan and Shmuel, such that the masses will believe that according to Rabbi Yochanan, there are supernatural wonders to await.[46]

Among the above answers, we see that according to *Lechem Mishneh*, *Markevet HaMishnah* and Radvaz, Rambam did not believe that any of the Sages believed in supernatural events in the Messianic Era. Accordingly, that is why he interpreted Rabban Gamliel's predictions in a deeper manner, and he would even do the same with Rabbi Yochanan's predictions.

While this explains why Rambam explained Rabban Gamliel's predictions in this way, it does seem that in light of the Midrash concerning Rabbi Meir, which may not have been available to Rambam, there were Sages who were understood by their contemporaries as being literal in their predictions of supernatural Messianic wonders.

Another Debate over Rationalism

Earlier, we cited the account of Rabbi Yochanan's bitter exchange with Resh Lakish in the context of a halachic dispute about weapons. Rabbi Shmuel Dvir relates this to a dispute between Rabbi Yochanan and Resh Lakish about rationalism, and connects this to Rabbi Yochanan's attitude to his disbelieving student, as follows:[47]

---

[46] Responsa Radvaz from manuscript, vol. VIII #71.

[47] Cited by Rabbi Moshe Tzuriel, *Biurei Aggadot* to *Bava Matzia* 84a.

Rabbi Yochanan rated tradition as the primary source of knowledge, and rejected empirical observations as a worthy alternative. It was for this reason that he reacted harshly to his student's rejection of his statement about gemstones. Resh Lakish, on the other hand, considered empirical experiences to be a legitimate source of knowledge, and disputed Rabbi Yochanan's halachic rulings concerning weapons based on his own experiences. Rabbi Yochanan derided the notion of accepting the knowledge of a bandit, but Resh Lakish responded that just as his mastery of Torah gives him authority, so did his mastery of banditry give him expertise in these weapons. Rabbi Yochanan retorted that by bringing him to Torah, he attached Resh Lakish to a higher source of knowledge, and took offense at Resh Lakish's position that there is another legitimate way to acquire knowledge.

Rabbi Dvir accordingly sees Rabbi Yochanan as standing for the principle that traditional sources of knowledge are to be utilized, and fought against empiricism. He notes that it was for this reason that Rabbi Yochanan reacted harshly to his student's rejection of his statement about gemstones.

Summary and Conclusion

We began by noting that the story of Rabbi Yochanan's student appears to be a powerful condemnation of rationalism, and it is indeed interpreted that way by several authorities. But our investigation has shown that matters are far from unequivocal. There is a long-standing dispute regarding whether Rabbi Yochanan was speaking literally. If he was speaking literally, then while he had his own reasons for condemning the student's naturalistic view, the student's essential position is held by Shmuel, Rambam, and others. If Rabbi Yochanan was not speaking literally, then this account is not at all a condemnation of rationalism, but rather a condemnation of those who do not interpret the Sages in a rationalist way.

We therefore have an extraordinary situation which sets rationalists and traditionalists at polar extremes. In explaining Rabbi Yochanan's definition of a heretic, rationalists and traditionalists each see the other as the focus of Rabbi Yochanan's condemnation! The traditionalists see

Rabbi Yochanan as castigating his student for being a rationalist, while the rationalists see Rabbi Yochanan as castigating his student for not realizing that he himself was a rationalist.[48] This story demonstrates how the difference between rationalists and traditionalists can have enormous consequences. Yet, at the same time, we see that both rationalists and traditionalists of today can each point to a long history of authorities whose approach they are following.

---

[48] However, Rabbeinu Avraham ben HaRambam writes that while the literalist interpretation is wrong, it does no harm provided that one does not reject the interpretation as a result. Rambam, on the other hand, writes that literalist interpretations make a mockery of the Sages.

THREE

Rambam's Naturalization of Miracles

Introduction

One of the many difficulties that faced Rambam in harmonizing the Aristotelian worldview with Judaism was the interpretation of Biblical miracles. In the philosophical understanding, the constancy and even inviolability of natural law was fundamentally linked to God's perfection. Any change or intervention in these laws would amount to a deficiency in them and a change in God's mind. How, then, are miracles— interventions into, and violations of, natural law—to be understood?

Rambam dealt with the question of miracles directly in six different places among four different works, along with scattered insights elsewhere in the context of addressing specific miracles. However, as with many other topics, there are apparent contradictions between the various statements presented by Rambam. In addition, given Rambam's explicit warning that he will be employing contradictions to hint at esoteric levels of meaning, this complicates matters even further.

Over the last few decades, several studies on this topic have appeared, which fall into two general categories of approach.[1] In this chapter, I shall

---

[1] Joseph Heller, "Maimonides' Theory of Miracles," in A. Altmann (ed.), *Between East and West - Essays Dedicated to the Memory of Bela Horovitz* (London: East and West Library 1958) 112-127; Hannah Kasher, "Biblical Miracles and the Universality of Natural Laws: Maimonides' Three Methods of Harmonization," *The Journal of Jewish Thought and Philosophy* Vol. 8 (1998) pp. 25-52.; Haim Kreisel, "Miracles in Medieval Jewish Philosophy," *Jewish Quarterly Review*, 75 (1984) 99-133.; Y. Tzvi Langermann, "Maimonides and Miracles: The Growth of a (Dis)Belief," *Jewish History* 18:2-3 (2004); Alvin J. Reines, "Maimonides' Concept of Miracles" *HUCA* 45 (1974) 243-85; Michael

survey these studies and elaborate upon them, and I shall further suggest a third potential approach to this problem. First, let us review the six places in Rambam's writings where he presents general principles concerning miracles and the specific interpretations that he gives to various miracles.

Rambam's Conflicting Writings

1. *Commentary on the Mishnah*—Miracles are Preprogrammed

Rambam's first discussion of miracles occurs in the context of arguing against the Kalaam view that God's will is continually activated:

> ...I have heard it said that God's Will is [initiated] in everything, moment after moment, constantly. But we shall not believe this. Rather, God's Will is that from the six days of Creation everything should continue constantly on the basis of natural law, as is stated: "What was, will be, and what has happened, will happen, and there is nothing new under the sun" (Ecclesiastes 1:9). Because of this our Sages had to state that the miracles that are outside of nature—those that have happened as well as those that will happen due to Scripture promising them—all of them were preceded by the Will in the six days of Creation, and it was then placed in the nature of these things that these innovations would take place. And when this innovation takes places, at the time of need, the observer thinks that something has been innovated now, but it is not so. And this matter has already been greatly expanded upon in the Midrash of Ecclesiastes and elsewhere, and their saying in this matter was that "the world functions according to its custom" (*Avodah Zarah* 54b). (Rambam, *Commentary on the Mishnah, Shemona Perakim* 8)

Rambam takes the approach that all miracles are pre-programmed into the nature of the world. Later,[2] Rambam explains that the ten miracles listed in the Mishnah as being created on the eve of the primal Shabbat were not the only miracles to have been designated during creation; rather,

---

Tzvi Nahorai, "The Problem of Miracles for Maimonides," (Hebrew) in Moshe Idel, Warren Zev Harvey, and Eliezer Schweid, eds., *Shlomo Pines Jubilee Volume*, part II (Jerusalem, 1990), 1–18.

[2] Commentary to Mishnah, *Avot* 5:6.

they were the only ones to have been designated at the *end* of the Creation week, whereas all other miracles were instilled in the nature of their objects at the time that they were created.

2. *Guide for the Perplexed*—Miracles are Supernatural Interventions

In the *Guide for the Perplexed*, Rambam introduces the topic of miracles by stressing that one reason why Aristotle's eternal universe conflicts with Judaism is that it would force us to deny the existence of miracles:

> If we were to accept the Eternity of the Universe as taught by Aristotle, that everything in the Universe is the result of fixed laws, that Nature does not change, and that there is nothing supernatural, we should necessarily be in opposition to the foundation of our religion (i.e. Sinai), we should disbelieve all miracles and signs, and certainly reject all hopes and fears derived from Scripture (i.e. providence, and/or the final redemption), unless the miracles are also explained figuratively. The Allegorists amongst the Mohammedans have done this, and have thereby arrived at absurd conclusions. (*Guide* II:25)

Rambam continues to note that rejecting Aristotle's view leaves two options: Plato's view or the traditional creationist view. Either one has the valuable function of enabling the possibility of revelation and miracles:

> If, however, we accepted the Eternity of the Universe in accordance with the second of the theories which we have expounded above, and assumed, with Plato, that the heavens are likewise transient, we should not be in opposition to the fundamental principles of our religion; this theory would not imply the rejection of miracles, but, on the contrary, would admit them as possible. The Scriptural text might have been explained accordingly, and many expressions might have been found in the Bible and in other writings that would confirm and support this theory. But there is no necessity for this expedient, so long as the theory has not been proved. As there is no proof sufficient to convince us, this theory need not be taken into consideration, nor the other one at all; we take Scripture literally, and say that the Torah teaches us a truth which we cannot prove;

and the miracles are evidence for the correctness of our view.[3] And know that by accepting the Creation, all miracles are possible, and the [revelation of] Torah is possible, and that every difficulty in this question is removed. (Ibid.)

Thus far, Rambam has presented a very different view of miracles than that which he presented in the *Commentary on the Mishnah*. Here, miracles are not built into nature, but rather are independent innovations by a Creator who stands outside of the universe. The benefit of rejecting Aristotle is that *all* miracles become possible.

Four chapters later in the *Guide*, Rambam returns to the topic of miracles, addressing the principles of there being "nothing new under the sun" and "the world functions according to its normal routine." These very same principles that he quoted in the *Commentary on the Mishnah* as meaning that miracles are *not* supernatural innovations, he now explains as meaning that these occurrences, which *are* supernatural innovations, are always only temporary:

> Our opinion, in support of which we have quoted these passages, is clearly established, namely, that no prophet or sage has ever announced the destruction of the Universe, or a change of its present condition, or a permanent change of any of its properties… The words, "There is nothing new under the sun" (Eccles. 1:9), in the sense that no new creation takes place in any way and under any circumstances, express the general opinion of our Sages, and include a principle which every one of the Sages of the Mishnah and the Talmud makes use of… And do not think that this contradicts that which I explained; but rather it is possible that their intent was that these assured states—the nature which defines them—exists from when they were created in the Six Days of Creation, due to concern for miracles (i.e. that if nothing is stable, then nothing is miraculous). For although the rod was turned into a serpent, the water into blood, the pure and noble hand into a leprous one, without the existence of any natural cause that could effect these or similar phenomena, these changes were not permanent; they have not become a physical property. On the

---

[3] I have not managed to understand the meaning of this statement, since Rambam previously stated that the Platonic approach would render miracles as being possible.

contrary, the Universe since continues its regular course. This is my opinion; this should be our belief. (*Guide* II:29)

3. *Guide for the Perplexed,* cont.—Attribution of Naturalistic View to Sages

Rambam follows this by citing the view that miracles are naturalistic, although he makes no mention of that the fact that he himself presented this view in his *Commentary on the Mishnah*:

> However there were Sages that said very extraordinary (*gharib*) things regarding miracles: they are found in *Bereshit Rabbah*, and in *Midrash Kohelet*, namely, that the miracles are to some extent also natural: for they say, when God created the Universe with its present physical properties, He made it part of these properties, that they should produce certain miracles at certain times, and the sign of a prophet consisted in the fact that God told him to declare when a certain thing will take place, but the thing itself was effected according to the fixed laws of Nature. If this is really the meaning of the passage referred to, it testifies to the greatness of the author, and shows that he held it to be impossible that there should be a change in the laws of Nature, or a change in the will of God [as regards the physical properties of things] after they have once been established. He therefore assumes, e.g., that God gave the waters the property of joining together, and of flowing in a downward direction, and of separating only at the time when the Egyptians were drowned, and only in a particular place… The same is the case with the rest of the miracles. (Ibid.)

What is Rambam's opinion of this view that he attributes to the Sages? He introduces it by describing it with the Arabic word *gharib*, which is usually translated as "strange," and some take this as an indication that he was not in favor of it. However, in an extensive study of Rambam's usage of this word, Nuriel has shown that the Arabic word *gharib* need not carry a negative connotation.[4] It sometimes means "wondrous" and sometimes means "strange"—thus, I have used the neutral translation of

---

[4] Avraham Nuriel, "The Use of the Word *Gharib* in the *Guide for the Perplexed*: A Note on the Esoteric Method in the *Guide for the Perplexed*" (Hebrew) Sefonot 5(20) 1991 137-143. Reprinted in "*The Revealed and the Hidden in Medieval Jewish Philosophy*" (Hebrew) (Jerusalem: Magnes Press).

"extraordinary." Furthermore, later in this paragraph, Rambam states that this view attests to the greatness of the Sages that hold it. Yet this raises the obvious question: If this view of the Sages is praiseworthy, why does Rambam reject it? Rambam does not openly address this question; we shall return to it later.

4. *Treatise on Resurrection*—Miracles Should Be Naturalized Wherever Possible

Thus far we have seen two views presented in Rambam: the view that miracles are entirely naturalistic, and the view that God freely innovates supernatural miracles. In Rambam's other writings, he complicates matters further by introducing a third approach: that we are to accept the existence of supernatural miracles, but only to the least extent possible:

> …Our efforts, and the efforts of select individuals, are in contrast to the efforts of the masses. For with the masses who are people of the Torah, that which is beloved to them and tasty to their folly is that they should place Torah and rational thinking as two opposite extremes, and will derive everything impossible as distinct from that which is reasonable, and they say that it is a miracle, and they flee from something being in accordance with natural law, whether with something recounted from past events, with something that is in the present, or with something which is said to happen in the future. But we shall endeavor to integrate the Torah with rational thought, leading events according to the natural order wherever possible; only with something that is clarified to be a miracle and cannot be otherwise explained at all will we say that it is a miracle. (*Treatise Concerning the Resurrection of the Dead*)

It is not clear why Rambam believes that miracles should be minimized, in light of his statement in the *Guide* that with the belief in Creation, "all miracles are possible."

5. *Treatise,* cont.—Two Types of Miracles

Elsewhere in this treatise, Rambam systematically classifies miracles in two categories: those that are supernatural, and those that are naturalistic but are nevertheless considered miraculous:

> Miracles are sometimes by way of things that are supernatural, such as the staff changing into a snake, and the sinking of the ground with the congregation of Korach, and the splitting of the sea. And sometimes, they are by way of things that are possible within nature, such as the locust, hail and pestilence in Egypt, for such events do happen on rare occasions in some places. However, such naturally viable events are miracles if one or more of the following conditions are met: One, if this event occurs exactly when forecast by a prophet... Two, if it is exceedingly unusual in nature... Three, if this event perpetuates. (Ibid.)

The last section seems to reflect a conflict in defining a naturally viable event as miraculous—if the event does not perpetuate, then it is a fluke and not a miracle; but if it happens with frequency, then it is an ordinary, albeit rare, event. The resolution of this is that it depends upon which type of event is being discussed. Some events are extraordinary by nature, such as the particularly intense plague of hail, and are further defined as miraculous by their one-time occurrence. Other events are not extraordinary, and are defined by miraculous only by their perpetuation in response to certain conditions, as we shall later suggest to be Rambam's understanding of *tzara'at*.

6. *Epistle Against Galen*—Supernatural Miracles are Modifications of the Natural

The final chapter of Rambam's medical work *Fusul Musa* (translated into Hebrew as *Pirkei Moshe*) is a critique of Galen's philosophical views and is often found published separately under the title *Epistle Against Galen*. In this text, Rambam claims that Galen mistakenly attributed three positions to the Torah, but was correct in attributing the position that God can instantaneously transform dust into an ox or horse. Rambam further refines his explanation of even the supernatural miracles that he delineated in the *Treatise on Resurrection*. He states that they fall into two categories. This first type of supernatural miracle involves accelerations of natural processes:

> Something which usually comes into existence via specific stages and always under particular conditions, instead comes into existence without those usual conditions, for its nature has been changed, such as the staff

changing into a snake, dust into lice, water into blood, air into hail,[5] and the holy and honorable hand (i.e. Moses') turning white as snow, and this all happening suddenly and abruptly.

In order to understand how Rambam can describe these as accelerations of natural processes, we must recall that Rambam's concept of nature was quite different from our own. For example, Rambam believed in the regular spontaneous generation of insects from dirt.[6] And although he was skeptical of reports about mice being generated from dirt as a regular occurrence, he did not dismiss them entirely.[7] The Islamic philosopher al-Ghazālī presents this explanation in detail to account for how the staff changed into a snake, and how the dead shall be resurrected. Plants grow from earth; they are eaten by animals, which change their matter into blood and then into sperm, which is placed in a womb and produces a new animal. The instantaneous transformation of a staff into a snake is therefore merely an acceleration of an existent natural process.[8]

Rambam then describes the second type of supernatural miracle as being the acquisition of new properties:

> Something is innovated which is not in the nature of the present reality to come into existence, such as the entire innovation of the manna, which had the property of being hard and could be ground to make bread, but when the sun shone upon it, it became soft and melted. And likewise all other such Biblical accounts of the miracles.

The manna itself was not supernatural; what was supernatural was that it was a hard substance that turned into a liquid under sunlight. This is, to say the least, an unexpected aspect of the manna to highlight as being miraculous. In the *Guide*, Rambam describes the survival of the Israelites

---

[5] Strangely, in the *Treatise on Resurrection*, Rambam categorized the plague of hail as one of the naturalistic miracles. This discrepancy may point towards the evolution of Rambam's views.

[6] *Guide For The Perplexed* 1:72. In *Sefer HaMitzvot*, Negative Commandment 179, he dismisses those who disbelieve such phenomena as fools.

[7] *Commentary on the Mishnah, Chullin* 9:6.

[8] Abu Hamid al-Ghazali, *Tahafut al-Falasifa* (*Incoherence of the Philosophers*), translated into English by Sabih Ahmad Kamali (Pakistan Philosophical Congress 1963), Problem XVII.

in the wilderness via the manna as one of the greatest of all miracles, stressing that it is not a normally occurring substance.[9]

7. The Miracles of the Bible

With regard to miracles and other events in the Bible and Midrash that are inconsistent with a naturalistic understanding of the world, Rambam frequently reinterprets them in such a way as to avoid such conflicts. Balaam's donkey did not talk except in Balaam's own prophetic vision.[10] Og was only around eight feet tall, despite Scriptural and Talmudic statements that led many to believe otherwise.[11] The description of the sun standing still during Joshua's battle was apparently a subjective impression of the participants, not an actual physical reality.[12] The youth that Elijah restored to life was not actually dead to begin with, only unconscious.[13] The Messianic redemption will not involve any supernatural miracles, and all prophecies and predictions to that effect are to be interpreted allegorically.[14] The extraordinary events involving Adam and Eve stated by the Sages to have occurred on the sixth day are to be interpreted allegorically.[15] Rambam also issues a general statement that many of the wonders in the Bible are spoken of using hyperbolic or allegorical descriptions.[16]

In striking contrast to the rest of the *Guide* is one instance where Rambam appears to clearly categorize two phenomena as supernatural

---

[9] *Guide* III:50.

[10] *Guide* II:42.

[11] *Guide* II:47. For further discussion, see my book *Sacred Monsters*, p. 119.

[12] *Guide* II:35.

[13] *Guide* II:42.

[14] *Commentary on the Mishnah*, Introduction to *Perek Chelek; Mishneh Torah*, Laws of Kings 12:1.

[15] *Guide* II:29, as explained by *Akeidat Yitzchak, Bereishis, Shaar* 3; Abarbanel, Commentary to Genesis, p. 10; Shem Tov ben Joseph, *Shem Tov* 2:30:9; Moses Narvoni, Commentary to *The Guide of the Perplexed* 1:67; Sara Klein-Braslavy, *Maimonides' Interpretation of the Story of Creation* (Jerusalem 1978), chapter 14.

[16] *Guide* II:47.

miracles. One is leprosy,[17] and the other is the bitter waters of the suspected adulteress:

> All agree that leprosy is a punishment for slander. The disease begins in the walls of the houses. If the sinner repents, the objective is attained: if he remains in his disobedience, the disease affects his bed and house furniture: if he still continues to sin, the leprosy attacks his own garments, and then his body. This is a miracle received in our nation by tradition, in the same manner as the effect of the trial of a faithless wife. (*Guide* III:47)

This passage stands in sharp contrast to the rest of the *Guide*, which minimizes, naturalizes, or allegorizes miracles. Later, we shall explore this case further.

How are we to understand the contradiction between the *Commentary on the Mishnah*, where Rambam states that all miracles are pre-programmed into nature, and the *Guide*, where Rambam states that miracles are supernatural contraventions of natural laws? Several approaches have been suggested.

Approach #1: Preferring the Supernatural

Kasher and Nehorai take the approach that in the *Commentary*, Rambam was merely explaining the view of the Sages (as he perceived it), which he also quoted in the *Guide* as an alternate viewpoint. Rambam's own view, however, was that miracles are indeed supernatural.[18] In a variation on this, Heller and Langermann argue that while Rambam was agreeing with the Sages' view in the *Commentary on the Mishnah*, he later changed his mind and decided that miracles were supernatural

---

[17] I am using this translation of *tzara'at* for convenience. However it is clear that the *tzara'at* of the Bible is not leprosy, otherwise known as Hansen's disease, which probably only reached the Middle East in the last two thousand years. See Joseph Zias, "Lust and Leprosy: Confusion or Correlation?" *Bulletin of the American Schools of Oriental Research*, No. 275 (Aug. 1989) 27-31. The "leprosy" of the Bible might be more accurately translated as a form of mold—specifically, *Stachybotrys* sp. See Richard M. Heller, Toni W. Heller, and Jack M. Sasson, "Mold: "Tsara'at," Leviticus, and the History of a Confusion," *Perspectives in Biology and Medicine* 46:4 (2003) 588-591.

[18] Kasher, Nehorai, loc. cit.

interventions.[19] While the young Rambam saw no difficulty in relegating all miracles to being implanted in nature, he later began to struggle with the issue of how to correlate miracles with the necessary belief in the supernatural creation of the world. Rambam subsequently decided that belief in God as the Creator of the Universe is inextricably linked to the acceptance of supernatural miracles.

Yet if Rambam perceived the naturalistic approach as problematic, why did he praise it by saying that it testifies to the greatness of the one who holds this view? Even if he still saw some value in this approach, surely he ought to spell out the difficulties that led to his own rejection of it, or else he is misleading his reader into thinking that it is an acceptable or even preferable approach—which, as we shall see, is precisely the inference that some have drawn! Perhaps one could say that he has already hinted to the problems in this view, by connecting it with the Aristotelian eternal universe. Alternatively, Kasher suggests that Rambam had a policy of noting alternate legitimate approaches for people who would be dissatisfied with his.

A further difficulty is that if Rambam believed that the supernatural creation of the world necessarily allows for free supernatural interaction by the Creator, why does Rambam minimize the supernatural aspect of so many Biblical miracles? Heller argues that Rambam found the specific form of certain miracles to be problematic, in their being permanent, too far-reaching or too fundamental. The innovation of Written Tablets of Law would mean the supernatural creation of a permanent entity; the sun standing still would mean a change in the entire course of nature, and the physical manifestation of angels and the creation of a talking donkey would be an intrinsic change in their nature. But Heller does not explain why in the *Treatise* Rambam sets out a general principle of minimizing the supernatural, nor why he pursued this approach in the *Guide* with so many Biblical miracles.

Nehorai claims that since Rambam stresses that God never acts purposelessly or trivially, but rather always out of wisdom,[20] supernatural

---

[19] Heller, Langerman, loc. cit.

[20] *Guide* III:25.

intervention likewise only occurs as a deliberate decree of Divine wisdom; but since the human mind cannot grasp this wisdom, one should not posit that a Biblical event involves supernatural intervention unless there is an unequivocal tradition of interpreting it in this way.[21] However, Nehorai's justification would not seem to adequate to account for the great lengths to which Rambam went in naturalizing miracles, often in marked contrast to traditional approaches.

I would like to suggest a different explanation for why Rambam, if we understand him as allowing for miracles being supernatural, would nevertheless seek to avoid this wherever possible. Supernatural intervention means that nature itself is not producing the required result. Ralbag and others take the position that because God's creation of natural law should be seen as a superb feat of engineering, one should not posit that He had to interfere with it except in special circumstances.[22] Yet like the other solutions above, this is not without its difficulties; if this was Rambam's reason, we would expect him to mention it somewhere.

Approach #2: Esoterically Naturalistic

Many others take the approach that Rambam's own, preferred view was in line with the second approach that he brings in the *Guide*, and which he attributes to the Sages and praises: that no miracles are supernatural.[23] As to why he claims in the *Guide* that his own view is that miracles do involve supernatural acts, it is argued that this is simply another instance of Rambam concealing his true views from the masses.[24] It is pointed out that the word *gharib* (strange/extraordinary), which Rambam uses to describe the naturalistic view, is used by Rambam elsewhere to describe positions that he considered correct but appropriate

---

[21] Nehorai, loc cit., pp. 14-15.

[22] Gersonides, Commentary to Genesis 6:9, *HaTo'elet HaShevi'i*; R. Bachya ben Asher, commentary to Exodus 17:13.

[23] Ibn Kaspi cited by Kasher; Narvoni pp. 37-38; Abarbanel, *Nachalat Avot*, pp. 326-327.

[24] Reines, loc. cit., pp. 279-285. Kreisel also leans towards this interpretation.

to conceal and pretend that he was not espousing.[25] Rambam also defines prophecy in terms of its ability to forecast miracles, and since he held prophecy to be the full understanding of the nature of the physical world,[26] this would mean that the miracle foreseen by the prophet is an anomaly of nature, along the lines of a tsunami, that he is able to predict with his superior understanding of the laws of nature.[27]

But what about Rambam rating supernatural miracles as an indispensable part of religious belief? Let us consider again his reasons for rejecting the Aristotelian view of existence: "we should necessarily be in opposition to the foundation of our religion (i.e. the Sinaitic revelation), we should disbelieve all miracles and signs, and certainly reject all hopes and fears (providence, the Messianic redemption) derived from Scripture." Now, as Reines points out, while Rambam did not reject the Sinaitic revelation, providence, or the Messianic redemption, elsewhere he does suggest the possibility of radically redefining them. It seems that Rambam did not believe that providence involved supernatural intervention,[28] and he also allows for this belief regarding the Sinaitic revelation.[29] The same can therefore be true of miracles.

There is, however, a difficulty in proposing that Rambam held the non-supernatural approach to miracles to be an esoteric secret that was too radical for the masses. In his *Commentary on the Mishnah*, which was certainly written for a broad audience, Rambam was explicit about miracles being pre-programmed natural events! Furthermore, how unsuitably radical for the unsophisticated masses can Rambam consider it to be, if he presents it as being the view of the Sages?

---

[25] Nuriel, loc cit., p. 142.

[26] *Guide* II:32,36.

[27] Reines, loc. cit., pp. 266-267. This does, however, raise a question: Rambam states that God can interfere to prevent a person attaining this knowledge, and he states that this is a miraculous interference just like all miracles, thereby implying that miracles themselves are supernatural interferences.

[28] Alvin Reines, "Maimonides Concept of Providence and Theodicy," *HUCA* 43 (1973) 169-206.

[29] *Guide* I:21.

Perhaps we can adapt Langerman's suggestion that Rambam modified his position between writing the *Commentary* and the *Guide*. When Rambam wrote the *Commentary*, he may have not seen the notion of miracles being built into nature as being at all problematic; he was focused on it being a perfect rejoinder to the Kalaam claim of God constantly renewing His will. But subsequent to writing the *Commentary*, perhaps Rambam realized that this approach has difficulties in its implementation and/or ramifications that will not be easily accepted by all. Positing that miracles are wired into nature sounds acceptable in theory, but how does it actually work? As Abarbanel points out, in the context of a host of objections to Rambam's approach, it would appear impossible for certain miracles (such as Moshe's hand changing to being leprous and back again) to be pre-programmed into nature; what characteristics could the physical entities have that would be activated at such a time?![30]

Thus, perhaps when writing the *Guide*, Rambam came to realize that only certain kinds of miracles can be built into nature, and the others will have to be reinterpreted—by toning down their effects, or simply allegorizing them away. In the *Guide*, Balaam's talking donkey does not appear as a miracle, as it does in *Pirkei Avot*; instead, it only appears in a prophetic vision. Rambam would also have been forced to reject the countless additional miracles that tradition stated to have occurred at the Splitting of the Red Sea. Perhaps in light of these problems, Rambam could not bring himself to explicitly endorse this approach as the correct one.

Yet with miracles such as Moses' hand becoming leprous, and water changing into blood, it is even less easy to dismiss them as having taken place in a prophetic vision or some other such non-literal interpretation.

---

[30] Abarbanel, *Nachalat Avot*. Abarbanel also objects that many miraculous events in the Torah are preconditioned upon free will; however, Rambam's position was that God is aware of all contingencies (*Guide* III:20). Another objection presented by Abarbanel, of how miracles can be used to validate someone's standing as a prophet if they are natural occurrences, would be of no difficulty for Rambam, since in his view the understanding of nature is precisely the function of prophesy. But a particularly difficult objection that he raises is how God can ask Ahaz to request a sign (Isaiah 7:11); if miracles must be pre-programmed, how would it be possible to fulfill the challenge?

Reines implies that Rambam likewise did not believe in the literal meaning of these events. If this is the case, then it is certainly understandable that Rambam could not openly identify with this approach. An alternate possibility is that Rambam was unsure how to resolve such cases, which is why although praising the Sages' approach, he could not fully commit to it.

Approach #3: Unnatural, Not Supernatural

I would like to tentatively posit a third approach to understanding Rambam's view of miracles. To my mind, claiming that Rambam held all miracles to be naturalistic, pre-programmed anomalies is unsatisfactory, in light of his efforts in the *Epistle Against Galen* to categorize different types of supernatural miracles and detail their mechanism. Furthermore, he strongly correlates belief in supernatural miracles with belief in creation, in opposition to Aristotle's eternal universe. Of course, there are those who believe that Rambam secretly believed in Aristotle's eternal universe, but I share Davidson's view that this approach would "transform the *Guide for the Perplexed* into one of the most grotesque books ever written."[31] On the other hand, Rambam praises the naturalistic view, and he certainly avoids supernatural interpretations of many Scriptural miracles.

Therefore, what I would like to suggest is that Rambam differentiated between two types of miracles, which I shall label the unnatural and the supernatural. Rambam was of the view that miracles are flexible adaptations of nature, not wholly impossible supernatural interventions. In the *Epistle Against Galen* Rambam seems at first glance to be legitimizing supernatural miracles, but in fact he is severely circumscribing them. Rambam endorses Galen's understanding of Biblical theology as allowing for the possibility of God creating a horse from dirt; this would presumably not be the case with creating a horse from thin air, for which

---

[31] Herbert Davidson, *Moses Maimonides: The Man And His Works* (New York: Oxford University Press 2005) pp. 401-402.

there is no conceivable acceleration of a natural process.[32] Rambam is not merely denying God the ability to perform the logically impossible; he is also denying His ability to perform the absolutely scientifically impossible. Fortunately for Rambam, according to his understanding of the original creation process, creating a horse from dirt is not absolutely scientifically impossible, merely unnatural in its acceleration.

Likewise with the manna. Rambam certainly did not believe that this was a substance created *ex nihilo*, and apparently did not even believe that there was anything supernatural about its formation *per se*. He seems to have shared the view found in certain Yemenite Midrashic texts, that manna is essentially a naturally-occurring substance.[33] It was miraculous in it occurring with unnatural properties and with constantly fortuitous timing.

Certain other phenomena are, however, utterly impossible. In the *Guide*, Rambam describes the idea that God could grant prophecy to a non-intellectual as being as absurd as granting prophecy to a frog or ass.[34] It would appear that Rambam would consider all these to be categorically impossible. One cannot help but wonder if Rambam's mention of an ass is a reference to Balaam's ass, which Rambam elsewhere states did not talk except in a vision. God can turn a stick into a snake, but He does not, and perhaps cannot, turn a donkey into a prophet.

Does this mean that miracles are all preprogrammed into nature, as per Rambam's understanding of the Sages' view? To some extent, they are natural; but it is not clear that they have causation, such that someone who fully understood the natural world could predict their occurrence.

---

[32] One may ask: If God can create the universe *ex nihilo*, why can He not create a horse *ex nihilo*? The answer may relate to the difference between creation outside of time and creation within time, or it may relate to the limitations that God has created for Himself with the creation of the universe.

[33] Rabbi Nataniel ben Yeshayah, *Nûr al-Zalâm*, written in 1329, extract published in Y. Tzvi Langermann, *Yemenite Midrash: Philosophical Commentaries on the Torah* (New York 1997), pp. 216-217. See too Ibn Ezra to Exodus 16:13.

[34] *Guide* II:32.

Conclusion

Rambam's various discussions of miracles can be summarized as follows:

Commentary on the Mishnah	Miracles are all preprogrammed into nature since creation
Guide for the Perplexed	1. Rambam professes own view: Miracles are supernatural, and all are possible, as an essential parallel to creation
	2. Praises sages' view that miracles are built into nature
	3. Extensively reinterprets many Biblical events so as to remove supernatural aspects
Treatise on Resurrection	1. Presents policy of only accepting supernatural as last resort
	2. Categorizes some miracles as supernatural and others as natural
Epistle Against Galen	Explains supernatural miracles as being relatively minor modifications of nature

It is exceedingly difficult to synthesize Rambam's various statements concerning miracles, and radically different conclusions have been drawn by different investigators. Rambam, at least exoterically, considered belief in supernatural miracles to be a necessary corollary to belief in creation. At the same time, Rambam made extensive attempts to minimize the supernatural component of Biblical miracles. Even the miracles of Moses' staff changing into a snake and his hand turning leprous, which are presented by Rambam in some places as the archetypical supernatural miracles, and the manna, which is described in the *Guide* as being the greatest of all miracles, are greatly constrained in their supernatural aspects to the extent that it is not clear if they can even be called supernatural. Our struggle to understand Rambam's approach to this topic may reflect Rambam's own struggle; trying to find a way to accept the divinely unnatural, without interfering with the divinely natural.

Appendix: Naturalizing the Sotah and Leprosy

We noted above that while in general Rambam follows a pattern of interpreting Biblical events to avoid a divergence from the natural order, he seems to take a different approach with leprosy and the suspected adulteress, freely referring to them as miraculous. How are we to understand this, if we are to take the approach that Rambam was always opposed to the notion of God having to supernaturally intervene? Indeed, some have viewed these cases as proof positive that Rambam *did* accept supernatural miraculous events.[35]

The claim has been made that Rambam perhaps saw the death of the adulteress as being psychologically induced, in much the same way as tribal witch-doctors are able to kill people.[36] Still, this seems far-fetched, and there is no parallel explanation for *tzara'at*. But there are alternate possibilities. Leprosy and abdominal maladies are not, in and of themselves, supernatural phenomena; they take place all the time.[37]

I would like to propose a different possibility. Maybe, in Rambam's view, the miracle was not in the event *per se*, but in it always happening at the appropriate time. In the Kapach translation, it is not called a *nes*, but

---

[35] Yitzchak Twersky, "Halachah and Science" (Hebrew), *Shanaton HaMishpat Ha-Ivri*, vol. 14-15, p. 149.

[36] Yehudah Nachshoni, *Hagot BeParashiyot HaTorah*, p. 579, who also cites Moshe Chefetz, *Meleches Machsheves* pp. 226-227. However, Nachshoni seems to have misunderstood Chefetz, who only refers to the psychological effect on the taste of the water, not on its effects.

[37] As a point of interest, modern scholarship suggests that the fate of the adulteress is actually a prolapsed uterus, resulting in sterility. Note that the Bible itself makes no mention of death. See Tikva Frymer-Kensky, "The Strange Case of the Suspected *Sotah* (Numbers V 11-31)" *Vetus Testamentum*, Vol. 34, Fasc. 1 (Jan. 1984) pp. 11-26 and Fred Rosner, *Medicine in the Bible and Talmud* (New York: Yeshiva University Press 1997), pp. 239-247.

an *ot ve'pele,* "a sign and wonder." This is consistent with Rambam's description of it in the *Mishneh Torah*:

> This change which is spoken of in clothing and houses, which the Torah calls *tzara'at* by way of borrowed terminology, is not from the way of the world, but is a sign and wonder amongst Israel, to warn them against slander. (*Mishneh Torah*, Laws of Leprosy 16:10)

This certainly sounds somewhat less than supernatural. It is not "*davar hanimna be'ha'teva,*" something scientifically impossible (the appellation used in the *Treatise* to describe supernatural as opposed to naturalistic miracles), only "*aino miminhago shel olam,*" not the way of the world. While Twersky is convinced that this term refers to a supernatural event, this may not necessarily be the case. The term "way of the world" appears in several places in the *Mishneh Torah* simply in reference to ordinary norms. Rambam condemns mourners who divert from the "way of the world" in displaying excessive grief,[38] but they are not engaged in a supernatural activity! Rambam describes it as being the "way of the world" that the Egyptians were sent to oppress the Israelites, noting that any individual Egyptian had the choice not to do so,[39] but he is not suggesting that such an Egyptian would have been acting supernaturally. And when speaking about the Messianic Era, Rambam states that there will be no change in the "way of the world" or a change in creation.[40] While this may sound as though such a change would be supernatural (since Rambam does accept drastic changes in the social order), the fact it is followed by the alternative of "a change in creation" indicates that a change in the "way of the world" is something less than that.

In the new Hebrew translation of the *Guide* by Schwartz, it states that *tzara'at* is a miracle that was *perpetuated* in the nation. This itself might be the basis for classifying it as a miracle, in line with Rambam's view in the *Treatise Concerning the Resurrection of the Dead* that a natural event is rated as a miracle if it perpetuates and especially if it occurs at a significant time. Mold and fungus do occur; here they are occurring in conjunction

---

[38] Laws of Mourning 13:11.

[39] Laws of Repentance 6:5.

[40] Laws of Kings 12:1.

with a skin disease, and after the person has engaged in evil talk. Leprosy and abdominal maladies are not supernatural events, but when they consistently happen to people who have sinned, they are revealed to be miraculous—that is to say, providentially ordained.

I would also like to propose another much more radical possibility. This is perhaps hinted at by Rambam's stress in both cases about how the fear of the result was extraordinarily intense and would prevent people from ever putting themselves in such a situation:

> The advantage in this belief is clear. Furthermore, leprosy is contagious, and all people flee from it; this is virtually in their nature. (*Guide For The Perplexed* 3:47)

The benefit is in the effect of the *belief* about the punishment, more than in the effect of the punishment itself. Rambam stresses how people are in such fear of this contagious disease that it is "virtually natural" for them to avoid it. Likewise with the adulteress, Rambam stresses how the fear of the punishment and its associated procedure was so great that women would go to any lengths to avoid it:

> This Scriptural passage forced every married woman to extensively guard herself, and to be cautious to the maximum extent possible, lest her husband grow suspicious of her, out of fear of the waters of the *sotah*. For even if she was innocent of sin and confident of herself, most people would give everything they own to avoid the procedure that would have to be done. In fact, people would prefer death over that great shame; the uncovering of her head, the loosening of her hair, the tearing of her clothing until her chest was exposed, and being paraded around the entire Temple in front of the public, both women and men, and in the presence of the Great Bet Din. This fear prevented great diseases that ruin the order of so many homes. (*Guide* 3:49)

Rambam even hints that a woman would do anything, even kill herself, to avoid the shame of the test; hence the claim of its miraculous effects would never be open to corroboration. Perhaps, then, Rambam is relegating these wondrous events to the same category as Biblical accounts of God becoming angry: necessary beliefs to promote social order, but not factually true beliefs.[41] This is not at all straightforward—does it mean that Rambam believed that no cases ever occurred with a guilty woman?—but it cannot be ruled out.

---

[41] See *Guide* III:27-28. Yair Lorberbaum argues as such in *Bikoret Ha-Aggdah BeMoreh HaNevuchim*, p. 216; see note 66 there. See too James Diamond, "Maimonides on Leprosy: Illness as Contemplative Metaphor," *Jewish Quarterly Review*, Volume 96, Number 1, Winter 2006, pp. 95-122 and "Maimonides on Leprosy: From Idle Gossip to Heresy," (Hebrew) *Maimonides: Conservatism, Originality, Revolution,* ed., Aviezer Ravitzky, (Zalman Shazar Center for Jewish History: Jerusalem, 2008), vol.2, pp.375-394

FOUR

Arguing with God: When May Students Dispute Teachers?

Introduction

As discussed in part one of this work, the rationalist/mystical divide, at least in its contemporary manifestation, often relates to issues of authority. May one disagree with one's teachers, or with the greatest Torah scholars of the generation? Historically, this was not necessarily related to the rationalist-mystic divide. The recent emphasis upon being *mevatel* one's *da'at*—negating one's own thoughts and conclusions in favor of those of respected authorities—has more to do with sociology. The modern era's emphasis on personal autonomy caused a reactionary movement in the Hassidic world, and this spread to the Lithuanian community in the early twentieth century. Still, the contemporary arguments in each direction certainly relate to the rationalist/mystic divide, and are similar to those regarding disputing the Sages' statements about the natural world.

To what extent is it permissible for a student to disagree with his teacher? May he do so privately, in his own mind, or should he be "*mevatel* his *da'at*," annul his own thoughts to his teacher's way of thinking? May he air his disagreement to the teacher's face? May he do so publicly? May he actually issue contrary rulings?

Then, to the extent that it is not permissible for a student to disagree with his teacher, what is the reason for this? There are a number of possibilities. It could be that there is no reason to think that he is correct, due to the principle of "the decline of generations." It could be that we are concerned for the honor of the teacher. Alternately, it could be due to it being an inappropriate mode of behavior for the student. A final possibility is that it is due to it harming the status of the teacher-disciple relationship in society. Which of these (and it could be more than one) is/are the reason?

This chapter discusses how classical Judaism has dealt with these questions. To some extent, they are intertwined with general questions of rabbinic authority. However, here we focus on these questions in cases where they are unaffected by broader considerations of rabbinic authority. In other words, questions such as the extent to which one must listen to rabbinic authority "even if they tell you that right is left and left is right"[1] relate to authoritative bodies of rabbinic authority. This chapter, on the other hand, focuses solely on the individual teacher-disciple relationship.

In the Talmud

In the Talmud, there are two types of sources for dealing with these questions: Principles that the Talmud itself sets out, and stories from which principles can be derived. Let us first explore the principles that the Talmud explicitly presents:

> Rav Chisda said: Anyone who disputes his teacher, is as one who disputes the Divine Presence, as it says (regarding Korach's rebellion), "When they quarreled with God" (Numbers 26:9).
>
> Rabbi Chama son of Rabbi Chanina said: Anyone who makes a quarrel with his teacher, it is as though he is making it with the Divine Presence, as it says, "They are the waters of strife which the Children of Israel quarreled with God" (Ibid. 20:13).
>
> Rabbi Chanina bar Papa said: Anyone who complains about his teacher, is as one who complains about the Divine Presence, as it says, "Your complaint is not upon us, but rather upon God" (Exodus 16:8).
>
> Rabbi Avahu said: Anyone who thinks negatively about his teacher, is as one who thinks negatively about the Divine Presence, as it says, "And the people spoke against God and Moses" (Numbers 21:5) (Talmud, *Sanhedrin* 110a).

---

[1] See Rashi to Deuteronomy 17:11, citing Midrash *Sifri*.

Here, the Talmud stresses the great severity of disputing one's teacher, comparing it arguing with God. However, it does not elaborate upon the definition of "disputing," which could be interpreted in all kinds of ways.

Yet there are numerous accounts in the Talmud of disciples disagreeing with their teachers, which raise questions for the principles cited above. Rebbe disagreed with Rabban Shimon ben Gamliel who, aside from being his father, was also his teacher (*Bava Metzia* 7a; in *Eruvin* 32a he states that "my words appear more correct than those of my father"). Rabbi Shimon ben Elazar argues with his teacher Rabbi Akiva (*Bava Metzia* 4b);[2] Rava disputed his teachers Rabbah and Shmuel (*Gittin* 2a-b and *Bava Batra* 7b); Ravina disputed his teacher Rav Pappa (*Bava Metzia* 7b); Rav Yosef disputed his teacher Rav Nachman (*Bava Batra* 6a); Rav Nachman disputed his teachers Rabbah bar Avuha and Shmuel (*Bava Batra* 6a-b); and Resh Lakish had 24 refutations for everything his teacher Rabbi Yochanan said (*Bava Metzia* 84a). We have another important account which implicitly shows that students were expected to be disagreeing with their teachers:

> Rava said to Rav Papa and Rav Huna b. Rav Yehoshua: "When a legal ruling of mine arrives before you, and you see a difficulty with it, do not tear it up until you have come before me. If I have an explanation, I will tell you, and if not, I will retract. After my death, do not tear it up, and do not learn from it either. Do not tear it up, for if I was there, maybe I would be able to explain it to you; and do not learn from it, for a judge has nothing other than what his eyes see" (*Bava Batra* 130b).[3]

At least on a superficial level, there is a clear disparity between the various principles cited, and the accounts in the Talmud of what actually happened. This requires some form of reconciliation.

---

[2] See Tosafot to *Bava Metzia* 4b, *s.v. "ain,"* who notes that R. Shimon b. Elazar was a disciple of R. Akiva and nevertheless argued with him, as did Rebbi with his father R. Shimon b. Gamliel.

[3] For an analysis of this passage and its ramifications for our topic, see Jeffrey Woolf, "The Parameters of Precedent in *Pesak Halachah*," *Tradition* 27:4 (1993) pp. 41-42.

In the Halachic Codes: Reinterpretation

Rambam repeats the Talmud's statement that disputing one's teacher is like disputing God, and then adds an explanation of who exactly falls into this category:

> Who is he that disputes his teacher? This refers to one who established a study hall, and sits and expounds and teaches without the permission of his teacher, while his teacher is still alive, and even if his teacher is in a different country… (*Mishneh Torah, Hilchot Talmud Torah* 5:2)

The person who disputes his teacher and earns the Talmud's condemnation has now become not someone who commits an act of intellectual disagreement or even someone who consistently maintains such intellectual disagreements. Rather, it refers to someone who might not even be disagreeing with the positions of his teacher at all, but who strikes out on his own to establish himself as an authority without the dispensation of his teacher. Tur gives the same explanation, and a similar view may be seen in Rashi, who defines the person who disputes his teacher as one who disputes "his yeshivah."[4] Rabbi Yoel ben Shmuel Sirkis (the "Bach," 1561-1640) explains that establishing a study hall is disputing the *authority* of his teacher. As Rabbi Alfred Cohen notes, "the intention here is not that he disagrees with his teacher's theses but rather that he tries to usurp his power or degrade his status."[5]

What is the basis for this qualification of the Talmud's principle—effectively a fundamental reinterpretation? The commentaries to the *Mishneh Torah* bring various sources from the Talmud which prohibit a student from striking out on his own, but these sources do not define this prohibition as disputing one's rabbi. Bach suggests that Rambam was seeking to draw the parallel with Korach more closely, where Korach was trying to usurp the authority of Moses and break off into a new group. But perhaps the basis is that it is simply impossible to understand the Talmud as placing a blanket prohibition on intellectual disagreements

---

[4] Bach suggests that Rashi was forced to distinguish this category from the category of quarrelling with one's teacher and therefore defined it in this way.

[5] Rabbi Alfred Cohen, "Daat Torah," *The Journal of Halacha and Contemporary Society* (Spring 2003) p. 101.

with one's teacher; Rambam himself on one occasion states explicitly that he is disagreeing with the views of his teachers.[6]

When R. Yosef Karo repeats Rambam's exact formulation in the *Shulchan Aruch*, R. Moshe Isserlis adds an explanatory gloss:

> But it is permitted for the student to disagree with him concerning some ruling or teaching if he has evidence and proofs that his position is correct. (Rema, *Yoreh Deah* 242:3)

This significant qualification, apparently simply the consequences of Rambam's interpretation, is taken from Rabbi Yisrael Isserlin ben Petachiah (*Terumat HaDeshen*, Germany 1390 - Austria 1460) who notes that "this has been the way of Torah since the days of the Tannaim."[7] R. Yissacher Ber Eilenberg (1570-1623) adds that "his words do not need reinforcing, since the Gemara is full to the brim with students arguing with their teachers in all circumstances; whether in front of him or not, whether the student is alone or has others arguing with his teacher, whether it is in his seniority or his youth…" and proceeds to give many examples not just from the Talmud, but also from the Rishonim.[8] The Gra makes a similar observation;[9] it should be noted that he himself felt free to argue with earlier authorities (he did not have a teacher per se), and preferred to base his rulings directly on the Talmud.[10] However, it is not entirely clear if Rema means to only permit disputes in rare, isolated instances (as *Levush* understands it), or if he is emphasizing that the prohibition is only upon establishing his own yeshivah and has no bearing on intellectual disputes.

In the Halachic Responsa: Emasculation

In the halachic responsa literature, we find a different way of removing the force of the Talmud's prohibition. In the course of a lengthy responsum dealing with various aspects of rabbinic authority, R. Yosef

---

[6] *Mishneh Torah, Hilchot Ishut* 5:15.

[7] *Terumat HaDeshen* 238.

[8] *Be'er Sheva* to *Sanhedrin* 110a.

[9] *Bi'ur HaGra* to *Shulchan Aruch, Yoreh De'ah* 242:6.

[10] See R. Norman Lamm, *Torah LiShmah* (Hoboken, NJ: Ktav 1989), p. 36 note 31.

Colon ben Solomon Trabotto (Maharik, France 1420- Padua 1480) finds ramifications for our topic.[11] He states the prohibition is only applicable to the case where the teacher is *rabbo muvhak*—where the student is dependent upon him for his knowledge. But in a case where the student has attained the rank of *talmid-chaver*—student-colleague, having reached a comparable level of scholarship as the teacher—he may dispute his teacher's rulings. Maharik observes that since the prohibition of disputing one's teacher is learned from a case involving a dispute with Moses, it must be only referring to a case comparable to Moses i.e. involving a teacher upon whom one is dependent for knowledge.[12] Although Maharik has thereby greatly restricted the scope of the prohibition, he is at least maintaining its simple meaning, namely, referring to a disagreement with the teacher's actual positions, as opposed to Rambam, who explained it in a different way entirely.

Based on Maharik, R. Shabbatai ben Meir ha-Kohen ("Shach," Vilna 1621 - Czechoslovakia 1662) challenges the aforementioned position of *Terumat HaDeshen*.[13] *Terumat HaDeshen* gave blanket permission for intellectual disagreements, but Maharik maintained the simple under-standing of the prohibition against disputes for a student-disciple. Shach argues that all the cases of people arguing with their teachers in the Talmud (which *Terumat HaDeshen* used to reject the simple understanding of the prohibition) may be cases where they received permission, or after the teacher had already died.[14] We see that while, from one perspective, Maharik greatly restricted the scope of the prohibition, from another perspective he increased it, in applying it to disputes about Torah instead of only to usurping authority.

R. David ben Zimra ("Radvaz," 1480-1573), the chief rabbi of Egypt, has a responsum specifically on this topic. He explains its parameters as follows:

---

[11] *Responsa Maharik* 169.

[12] *Responsa Maharik* p. 188.

[13] *Siftei Cohen* to *Shulchan Aruch, Yoreh De'ah* 242:3.

[14] I do not know why Shach does not simply say that those cases could be referring to student-colleagues.

You asked of me that I make my opinion known to you, regarding that which they said that a disciple may not argue with his teacher, and why should he not argue with him in a case where he has clear proofs, for surely we find that the early ones, of blessed memory, argued with their teachers.

The answer is that it is indeed true that the early ones had such disputes, for Rabbeinu HaKadosh argued with his father and his teacher on numerous occasions. We likewise find with the Amoraim that Rava would disagree with Rabbah bar Nachmani on several occasions, and likewise Rashba with Ramban, the Rosh with Ramah, and likewise in every generation. And he can argue with him in his lifetime with proofs, by way of debate, but he should not establish himself to expound in public or to establish a yeshivah. And thus wrote Rambam in *Hilchot Talmud Torah* ch. 5… And it is obvious that if a matter came to a vote, that he should not vote against his teacher with the disputants. Included in this is that he should not argue with his teacher in the way of those who argue in order to defeat their teacher, but rather he should state his proofs before him, and if they are correct in his eyes, good, and if not, he should be silent. And he should not say to him, "Thus it appears to me," and included in this is that he should not say to others, "My teacher permits it but I prohibit it," and so too the reverse, and likewise with all such similar matters. It is permitted for him to write his proofs for himself, even against his teacher, but it is prohibited for him to write a ruling, or to teach others, against that of his teacher in his lifetime. It is permissible to disagree with him after his death, and to issue rulings and teachings according to his [own] proofs, and to act on their basis, even though they are in opposition to his teacher, and to establish a study hall and to expound his arguments in public without naming [his teacher], but not to say, "My teacher would say this, and I say otherwise." For this, aside from disagreeing with his teacher, is publicly deriding him. But to write his teachers positions and proofs together with his own positions and proofs in a book, even if he is disputing the positions of his teacher, is permitted. So did all the early ones, and there is no derision involved in this whatsoever, for whoever comes after will choose which he sees as being correct and appropriate. And with everything, his words should be for the sake of Heaven. Thus I have written, as it appears to me. (*Responsa Radvaz* 1:495)

The responsum of Radvaz is presented in a confusing manner, but it can be reorganized and simplified as follows:

	Permissible	Forbidden
Between them	Arguing with his teacher with proofs, by way of debate. Silently maintaining his position after his teacher has rejected it.	Arguing with his teacher in an overly-forceful or disrespectful manner. Vocally maintaining his position after his teacher has not accepted it.
In public	Presenting his teacher's positions and proofs together with his own positions and counter-proofs.	Writing a ruling, or teaching others, against the rulings or teachings of his teacher.
Post-humously	Issuing rulings and teachings against those of his teacher. without naming him.	Stating, "My teacher would say this, and I say otherwise."

Radvaz does not present any earlier sources as a basis for his conclusions here. It seems that he was acting simply out of his own sensibilities and sensitivities. He agrees with Rambam's position that it is prohibiting establishing a study hall without authorization but, unlike Rambam, he does not limit it to that (which is really very far from the plain meaning of the prohibition). But, although he does incorporate the plain meaning of the prohibition, he cannot ignore the numerous instances in the Talmud where people do dispute their teachers. Radvaz's approach is to illustrate a number of situations in which he can distinguish between appropriate and inappropriate forms of dispute. In contrast to Rambam, there is a clear emphasis on the student's relationship to the teacher and the restrictions that this places on their interaction. But despite the numerous restrictions that Radvaz places upon the student, he does not intellectually constrain him in any way; even if the teacher rejects the student's arguments, the student can still silently maintain it (and apparently can also posthumously issue it as a ruling) and is not expected to be "*mevatel* his *da'at*."

Unlike Maharik, Radvaz makes no mention of any distinction between student-disciple and student-colleague. It is odd that Radvaz does not mention it, and it is unlikely that he intended to refer to both categories, since the distinction is surely significant. It may well be that he took it for granted that only the category of the student-colleague is being discussed.

R. Yaakov Emden, in an extremely lengthy responsum,[15] takes an approach which combines elements of Rambam, Maharik and Radvaz. His conclusions can be summarized as follows:

	Student-Disciple	Student-Colleague
Arguing for the sake of one-upmanship	Forbidden	?
Arguing for the sake of truth	Permitted in some cases (see below)	Permitted
Arguing about something with no halachic consequences	Forbidden	?
Arguing about something with halachic consequences[16]	Obligatory	Obligatory
Acting differently	Forbidden	Permitted
Ruling differently in the teacher's jurisdiction	Forbidden	Forbidden
Ruling differently elsewhere (even after the teacher's death)	Forbidden	Permitted

---

[15] *Responsa Yaavetz* 1:5.

[16] R. Emden is certain that with consequences *d'Oraita* this is so, and says that he is "near-certain" that it is also the case with something that has consequences *d'Rabbanan*, but only where the student is absolutely sure that he is correct.

Like Maharik, R. Emden draws an important distinction between a student-disciple and a student-colleague, giving the latter the all-important license to act against his teacher's opinion and to rule against it, but giving the former no such permission. Like Rambam, R. Emden sees an important role in preserving the authority of the teacher, not allowing even the student-colleague to rule against the teacher in the teacher's area of jurisdiction. And like Radvaz, R. Emden places an emphasis on the relationship between the two, stating that a student may not dispute his teacher by way of combativeness and one-upmanship, but he may dispute him if the goal is solely to reach the truth. An interesting twist in Emden's response is his distinction between different areas of Torah, noting that if it is something with halachic ramifications, whether for stringency or leniency, it is a mitzvah and obligation for the student to speak his mind and show his proofs, as the honor of the Torah is more important than that of his teacher, whereas in cases with no halachic ramifications the student-disciple may not air his disagreement.

Further Emasculation: The Aggadic Exemption

R. Chaim Joseph David Azulai (Chida, 1724 –1807) questions Radvaz, citing a Talmudic discussion in which Rabbi Shimon rejects four teachings of Rabbi Akiva and which does not fall into the permitted categories established by Radvaz.[17] R. Mordechai Fogelman disputes the question, understanding that Rema allows such isolated disagreements.[18] But Chida answers that this passage in the Talmud is referring to a dispute concerning Aggadah, which is different from halachah. In such areas, states Chida, there is nothing wrong with a student disputing his teacher.

Chida provides no rationale for this distinction. It stands in marked contrast to the approach of R. Yaakov Emden, for whom disputes in matters of no practical consequence are more severe than disputes in areas of halachah. But it is consistent with the general approach of attributing

---

[17] *Birkei Yosef, Yoreh De'ah* 242:3, citing *Rosh HaShanah* 18b.
[18] *Responsa Beit Mordechai* 60 p. 126.

less authority to aggadic statements than halachic statements, which was broadly prevalent until relatively recently.[19]

Rabbi Shlomo Fisher (b. 1932, dean of Itri Yeshivah) discusses a similar such distinction between halachah and aggadah. In seeking an explanation as to why we do not dispute the halachic rulings of the Talmud, R. Fisher builds upon R. Yosef Karo's discussion of a national acceptance of the Talmud's canonical status. But he notes that this acceptance did not take place with regard to statements concerning Aggadah, which may therefore be disputed.[20]

Personality Differences

In considering the views of various rabbis regarding the legitimacy of disputing teachers, the personality of the rabbi under discussion should also be taken into consideration. For example, Rabbi Chaim of Volozhin writes that not only is a student permitted to disagree with his teacher, he is obligated to do so if he cannot accept what the teacher is saying:

> It is forbidden for a student to accept the words of his teacher when he has difficulties with them. And sometimes, the truth will lie with the student. This is just as a small branch can ignite a larger one. (*Ruach Chaim* to *Avot* 1:4)

R. Chaim does not consider it impossible that the student will turn out to be correct, and obligates him to hold his ground. R. Chaim himself, despite his great reverence for his teacher the Vilna Gaon, did not follow the Gaon in various aspects of his opposition to Hasidism.[21] But instead of perceiving this as a result of intellectual independence—viewing him

---

[19] See Rabbi Chaim Eisen, "Maharal's *Be'er ha-Golah* and his Revolution in Aggadic Scholarship," *Hakirah* 4 (Winter 2007) pp. 137-194.

[20] Rabbi Shlomo Fisher, *Derashot Beit Yishai*, p. 113. For further discussion of differences between halachah and aggadah vis-à-vis rabbinic authority, see Shalom Rosenberg, "Emunat Hakhamim," in Isadore Twersky and Bernard Septimus, eds., *Jewish Thought in the Seventeenth Century* (Cambridge, Mass.: Harvard University Press, 1987) pp. 285-341; Simhah Friedman, "Emunat Hakhamim: Faith in the Sages," *Tradition* 27:4 (Summer 1993) pp. 10-34; and Nahum Rabinovitch, "What is Emunat Hakhamim," *Hakirah* 5 (Fall 2007) pp. 35-45.

[21] Rabbi Norman Lamm, *Torah LiShmah*, pp. 12, 70.

from the perspective of being a student—it might be preferable to consider him from the perspective of being a teacher. Rabbi Norman Lamm suggests that R. Chaim's openness to students disputing their teacher is "basically a reflection of R. Hayyim's goodness and meekness."[22]

Rabbi Moshe Feinstein (1895-1986) also encouraged people to form their own opinions and stick to them, even if this meant disagreeing with their teachers.[23] And he himself was likewise known to be a very humble and amenable person; he once commented that he was not at all perturbed by criticisms of his rulings and was happy to see that "there are people full of spirit, who are not afraid or embarrassed to criticize."[24]

By the same token, but on the other side of the coin, Rabbi Yochanan's opposite stance towards the student who doubted his words, which we discussed earlier, may reflect his own personality. There are several instances in which we find that Rabbi Yochanan acted harshly toward someone that he understood as slighting him, with grave consequences. In one case, he understood Resh Lakish as insulting him, and refused to pray for him when he fell sick as a result.[25] In another instance[26] Rabbi Yochanan took offense at a (mistakenly) perceived insult by his student Rav Kahana, who died as a result, for which Rabbi Yochanan later had to seek forgiveness. In yet another account,[27] Rabbi Yochanan was angry with his student Rabbi Elazar, who related one of his teachings without reporting it in Rabbi Yochanan's name. Others pointed out that he should not be angry, noting that Rabbi Elazar himself was rebuked for growing angry in a dispute with a peer. But at this, Rabbi Yochanan grew even

---

[22] Ibid. p. 30.

[23] *Iggrot Moshe, Yoreh De'ah* III:88. The subject of the responsum is regarding the propriety of a rabbi in Bnei Brak disputing the Chazon Ish, and Feinstein notes that based on Rava's instructions to his students (cited earlier), it is permitted to disagree even with one's teacher; all the more so with a rabbi who is not one's teacher. See also *Iggrot Moshe* vol. 2, *Yoreh De'ah* I:101, p. 186, where he permits disputing Rishonim.

[24] *Iggerot Moshe* vol. 4, *Even HaEzer* II:11.

[25] *Bava Metzia* 84a. According to Rashi, Rabbi Yochanan correctly understood Resh Lakish; according to Maharsha, he misunderstood him.

[26] *Bava Kama* 117a.

[27] *Yevamot* 96b.

angrier, retorting that while it was obviously inappropriate for Rabbi Elazar and his peer (who was his equal) to grow angry with each other, he is entitled to be angry at his student. He was only appeased when others pointed out that in any case, people know that Rabbi Elazar is reporting Rabbi Yochanan's teachings. While the Talmud proceeds to explain why Rabbi Yochanan legitimately wanted his teachings to be related in his name, it may be no coincidence that, of all people, it is Rabbi Yochanan who is involved in this case.

In all these stories, we see Rabbi Yochanan taking offense at what he inaccurately perceived as a slight to his honor, sometimes with disastrous results. In the case of Rav Kahana, we see that Rabbi Yochanan even brought about his death, despite the fact that he was mistaken in thinking that Rav Kahana had committed a wrong against him. Accordingly, the fate of Rabbi Yochanan's student in our story might not reflect so much on the student as it does on Rabbi Yochanan. Even though the problem with the student may relate to the particular nature of his disagreement or the manner in which he expressed it,[28] Rabbi Yochanan's harsh response may be attributable, to some extent, to his own personality. Yet, notwithstanding all this, Rabbi Yochanan ends up being greatly disappointed when Resh Lakish, who always challenged his teachings, died, and he complained when someone responded to his teachings by offering arguments to reinforce them.[29]

Conclusion

In his book *Rational Rabbis*, Menachem Fisch argues that the Babylonian Talmud seeks to transmit an approach to Torah whereby one learns how to diverge from the rulings of earlier authorities (even those considered canonical) without actually appearing to do so. One speaks in reverential tones about the greats of a previous era, but under the guise of merely fixing errors in the transmission of their words, one actually modifies them as appropriate. Whether or not this is true, it is interesting

---

[28] See the earlier chapter "Messianic Wonders and Skeptical Rationalists."

[29] *Bava Metzia* 84a. See the analysis of Menachem Fisch, "*Rational Rabbis: Science and Talmudic Culture* (Indianapolis: Indiana University Press 1997), pp. 189-191.

that the Talmud warns how one must not dispute one's teachers, while being full of cases of rabbis doing exactly that.

The Talmud's objection to disputing one's teacher is very severe. Yet, taken at face value, it is contradicted by numerous such disputes in the Talmud. Subsequent generations of halachic authorities removed its force greatly by either redefining it altogether, to refer to usurping authority instead of intellectually disagreeing, or by greatly restricting its scope.

The truth is that if we consider the heinous crime to which disputing one's teacher is likened—disputing God—we see that that case, too, turns out not to be as unthinkable as one might assume. Let us consider the famous story of dispute regarding the laws of ritual impurity applying to a certain oven called the Achinai oven:

> On that day, Rabbi Eliezer brought forward every argument in the world, but the Rabbis did not accept them. He said to them: If the halachah agrees with me, let this carob-tree prove it! And the carob-tree was torn a hundred cubits out of its place—and some say, four hundred cubits. But they said to him: One cannot bring a proof from a carob-tree. So he said to them: If the halachah agrees with me, let this stream of water prove it! And the stream of water started to flow uphill. But they said to him: One cannot bring a proof from a stream of water. Se he said to them: If the halachah agrees with me, let the walls of the study-house prove it! The walls started to lean and fall, but Rabbi Yehoshua rebuked them, saying: When Torah scholars are engaged in a halachic dispute, you have no right to interfere! So they did not fall, in honor of Rabbi Yehoshua, and nor did they return upright, in honor of Rabbi Eliezer; and they are still standing at an angle. So Rabbi Eliezer said to them: If the halachah agrees with me, let it be proved from Heaven! Whereupon a Heavenly Voice cried out: Why are you arguing with Rabbi Eliezer, seeing as the halachah always agrees with him! But Rabbi Yehoshua got up on his feet and said: "[The Torah] is not in Heaven!" What did he mean by "It is not in Heaven"? Rabbi Yirmiyah said: The Torah was already given to us at Mount Sinai, and we therefore do not pay attention to a Heavenly Voice, because God already wrote in the Torah, "Incline after the majority." Rabbi Natan found Eliyahu, and said to him, What was the Holy One doing at that moment? He replied, He was laughing, and saying, You have defeated Me, My son, You have defeated Me! (Talmud, *Bava Metzia* 59b)

Why might it be unthinkable to dispute God? It could be because it is impossible for God to be wrong. It could be because it is disrespectful. Or it could be because it undermines His authority.

The first reason is not applicable. True, it is impossible for God to be wrong. However, man's goal is not necessarily to reach objective truth; rather, it is to reach truth to the best of his ability. Indeed, many see this as the very point of the story of the oven of Achnai.[30] This story likewise refutes the idea that it is necessarily disrespectful to argue with God. When one does so by following the Torah's own protocol, and for the right reasons, it is seen as ingenious rather than disrespectful. The same is true with regard to undermining God's authority; God has enabled, via the Torah, for people to dispute His view—within certain parameters— without undermining His authority. Korach exceeded the correct parameters of dispute and, perhaps more fundamentally, he did so for the wrong reasons.

Translating all this back to the case of disputing one's teacher, we can understand why the prohibition is so limited. Even if there is more reason to believe that the teacher is correct, this does not mean that the student should not be reaching his own conclusions. There may not be any disrespect, depending on how the disagreement takes place, and it likewise may not be undermining the teacher's authority—depending on how one defines the parameters of that authority.

It is also clear that even to the extent that it is forbidden for the student to dispute his teacher, it is not the case that a student is supposed to literally be *mevatel* his *da'at* and force himself to think differently, but rather not to challenge his teacher's authority. Much like the *zaken mamre*, the rebellious elder, the problem is not holding a different view, but rather translating that view into action in such a way as to undermine the stability of the system of authority. Various authorities voice concern for

---

[30] See, for example, Rabbi Moshe Feinstein in his introduction to *Iggrot Moshe*. But cf. Rabbi Jonathan Sacks, *Creativity and Innovation in Halakhah*," in Moshe Z. Sokol, ed., *Rabbinic Authority and Personal Autonomy* (Northvale, New Jersey; 1992) pp. 129-130, who notes that this story does not serve the purposes of those who argue for halachic liberty, since it places ultimate authority in the consensus of the halachic authorities.

the honor of the teacher, the appropriate form of behavior for the student, but most of all for the status of the student-teacher relationship. In seeking to determine the parameters for when a student may dispute his teacher, one must draw a difficult balance between the importance of intellectual independence and the preservation of authority.

Returning to the rationalist/mystical divide, in its contemporary manifestation, we see that it is the rationalist approach which is consistent with the classical views on this topic. In the rationalist approach, one may well submit to authority in terms of halachah and practical action, for a variety of reasons such as those discussed above. However, one does not submit one's intellect. Much like the *zaken mamre*, the rebellious elder, the problem is not holding a different view, but rather translating that view into action in such a way as to undermine the stability of the system of authority. As long as there is no undermining the system of authority in the practical realm, one is free to form one's own conclusions—and one should indeed do so.

In non-rationalist circles, on the other hand, people are discouraged from ever disagreeing with Torah scholars of renown. It is often argued that one is obligated to "brainwash" oneself into rejecting one's own conclusions in favor of the thought processes of people who are believed to be greater Torah scholars. The only logical justification for such a position would be if the Torah sage is presumed to possess greater supernatural input to his positions. But as seen in this chapter, this does not accord with classical rabbinic thought on this matter, which certainly permits intellectual disagreements.

FIVE

The Evolution of the Olive

Introduction

R. Moshe Sofer (Chatam Sofer, 1762-1839) notes that today, when there is no Temple, there is only one Biblically-ordained mitzvah involving eating: that of eating matzah on the first night of Pesach.[1] Accordingly, he stresses that one must be careful to be punctilious in the fulfillment of this mitzvah. Aside from the mitzvah requiring a certain type of food, there is also a requirement of a sufficient minimum quantity to qualify as "eating." This quantity is defined in the Midrash:

> There is no "eating" with less than a *kezayit* (equivalent to an olive). (*Toras Kohanim*, *Acharei* 12:2; *Emor* 4:16)

How much is this quantity? R. Chaim of Volozhin (1749-1821) is widely revered as the father of the yeshivah world. Less known and certainly less popular in the yeshivah world is his view as to the size of the matzah that one is obligated to eat on Pesach. R. Chaim was of the view that this *kezayit* is actually the size of an olive—around three or four cubic centimeters.[2] This results in a piece of matzah about half the size of a credit card.

Yet this is in sharp contrast to common custom today. The widespread policy is to quantify a *kezayit* as 28.8 cubic centimeters. The *Mishnah Berurah* states that one should eat a volume equal to an egg, which is about 55cc. And there are boxes of machine matzot which state on the packaging that one whole matzah equals a *kezayit!* The greatest irony is that, in the

---

[1] Responsa Chatam Sofer, *Choshen Mishpat* 196.

[2] R. Yisrael Yaakov Kanievsky, *Kehillat Yaakov, Pesachim* 38. See too A. Z. Katzenallenbogen, *Shaarei Rachamim* (Vilna 1871) p. 19, #165 note 3.

effort to perform the mitzvah as scrupulously as possible, some might engage in *achilah gasah* (gorging oneself), which surely could not be the intent of the mitzvah and which might prevent a person from fulfilling his obligation.

Recently, there have been efforts by some individuals to prove that the *kezayit* should be scaled down, but they have met with little success and much opposition.[3] In this study, while proving that the *kezayit* is the size of a regular olive, the focus will be on exploring how it happened that so many authorities ruled it to be far bigger, and why it is difficult to overcome this view.

Logically, in order to reach the conclusion that a *kezayit* is much larger than olives are today, two separate positions must both be taken: First, that olives of ancient times were much larger, and second, that we are obligated to follow the size of ancient olives rather than the olives of today. Neither one of these positions on their own is sufficient to require a larger measurement; they must both be adopted. Let us begin by evaluating both of these positions in turn.

Were Olives Bigger in Ancient Times?

Were olives of the Biblical or Talmudic era larger than those of today? From the standpoint of archeology, there is clear evidence the olives of ancient times were *not* any bigger than those of today. Many olive pits from ancient times have been discovered, including a huge number in the remains of the settlement at Masada and in caves in the Judean Desert dating from the Bar-Kochba revolt. These pits were mostly from the Nabali strain of olives, but also included the local Suri and Melisi varieties, as well as the large Shami and Tohaffi olives that were imported as luxuries from other countries. All these pits are not significantly different in size from the pits of those olive strains today.[4] One could claim that the flesh-

---

[3] A recent excellent work is Rabbi Hadar Margolin's *Hiddurei HaMiddot* (2015), freely available for download at http://www.zootorah.com/RationalistJudaism/Hadar-MargolinHiddureiHaMiddos.pdf

[4] Mordechai Kislev, "*Kezayit* – The Fruit of the Olive as a Measure of Volume" (Hebrew), *Techumin* 10 pp. 427-437; "Everything is According to the Opinion of the

to-pit ratio used to be greater, but this is unlikely, and should not be accepted without good reason.[5]

Furthermore, there are dozens of olive trees alive today of the Suri variety, in Israel and elsewhere, which are thought to be thousands of years old.[6] These trees even still produce fruit, which are no different in size from the fruit produced by young olive trees.[7] One could claim that they used to produce larger fruit, but this is exceedingly unlikely from a botanical perspective.

All the empirical evidence, then, indicates that in Talmudic and even Biblical times, olives were no larger than those found today. The Mishnah specifies which of the various strains is intended when the olive is given as a halachic measurement:

> The *kezayit* of which they spoke is neither a large one nor a small one, but rather a medium-sized one, which is the *egori*. (Mishnah, *Keilim* 17:8)

The large olive mentioned in the Mishnah would correlate with the Shami, which measures around 12-13cc, and the small olive would correlate with the Melisi, which measures around 0.5-1cc. The medium-sized olive would be the prevalent Suri and/or the slightly larger Nabali strains. The Suri ranges from 2.5-3.5cc, while the Nabali ranges from 4-6cc.[8] The *kezayit* of the Talmud, which would be the same as the *kezayit* of today, would range from 2.5-6cc with an average of around 4cc.

Observer – A New Evaluation of the Measurement of a *Kezayit*," (Hebrew) *BDD* vol. 16 pp. 77-90.

[5] The Talmud (*Sotah* 48a) does state that since the destruction of the Temple, the *shuman* of olives was reduced. However, this is never brought up by any Rishon in their halachic discussions; perhaps it refers to the nutritional benefit rather than the size of the flesh,

[6] Calculating the age of olive trees is, however, complicated, and there is dispute as to the legitimacy of the methods used. Yael Ehrlich, Lior Regev and Elisabetta Boaretto, "Radiocarbon Dating of an Olive Tree Cross-Section: New Insights on Growth Patterns and Implications for Age Estimation of Olive Trees," *Frontiers in Plant Science* 8 (2017).

[7] M. Kislev, Y. Tabak & O. Simhoni, Identifying the Names of Fruits in Ancient Rabbinic Literature, (Hebrew) *Leshonenu*, vol. 69, p.279.

[8] Kislev, ibid.

There is also evidence from the Mishnah itself that the *kezayit* was no larger than the olive of today:

> A pure cloak of which a three-by-three [finger-breadths] piece entered an impure house becomes impure. If it was an impure cloak, if he extended **even** the volume of an olive of it into a pure house, it makes the house impure. (Mishnah, *Nega'im* 13:8)

This Mishnah states that a piece of a cloak which is the volume of an olive is less than three-by-three finger-breadths. Three by three finger-breadths is approximately three inches square, or a little less. To translate that into a popular frame of reference—matzah—the fabric of a cloak is approximately the thickness of matzah, or less. Unless one is going to say that people back then were much bigger (which indeed some people do say, albeit against all evidence), then we see from the Mishnah that a *kezayit* of matzah is less than three inches square.[9]

There is additional powerful evidence in the Talmud that the *kezayit* was no larger than the olive of today. The Talmud (*Menachos* 26b) discusses the laws of *kometz* (the slightly-less-than-a-fistful of flour that the kohen takes). It establishes that the norm for the *kometz* is that it encompasses the volume of two *kezaysim*. This is physically impossible if a *kezayit* is substantially larger than the size of the olive. Aside from positing that people used to be enormous (as indeed some do in explaining this passage[10]), the conclusion is that a *kezayit* was always the size of an olive.

There are further passages in the Talmud with inferences regarding the size of an olive. The Talmud says that one may use stones to clean oneself after attending to one's needs on Shabbat, and lists three sizes one can use: the size of an olive, a walnut, and an egg.[11] It is accepted that the Talmud's

---

[9] For further demonstrations from the Talmud that olives in that period were no larger than those of today, see R. Aharon Avichai Amos Cohen, *Kuntrus Shiur Kezayit* (Yeshivat Mercaz HaRav 5772).

[10] See R. Yisrael Yaakov Kanievsky, cited in the Schottenstein Talmud.

[11] Talmud, *Shabbat* 81a. See Rashi ad loc. s.v. *kehechreia* and *Beit Yosef* Orach Chaim 312:1.

lists start from the smallest novelty to the biggest, which means that the olive is the smallest size of the three, smaller than a walnut.

Elsewhere, the Talmud describes a piece of food the size of a *kezayit* with the term *peirur*, which means *crumb* in Aramaic.[12] And in another place, the Talmud states that an olive is size of nine ants.[13] Both these sources indicate that the *kezayit* of the Talmud was very small.

The Geonim: Following the Observer

Already, then, we see that there appears to be no reason to ever assume that an olive was any larger than olives today. But what if, for whatever reason, someone were to believe that perhaps olives of ancient times were larger—would they be obligated to replicate that quantity? The Geonim rule that this is not the case. Around 130 years ago, three responsa on this topic from the Geonic period were discovered. The first is from Rav Sherira Gaon (Babylonia, c.900-c.1000):

> You asked me to explain if there is a weight given for the fig, olive, date and other measurements, in the weight of Arabic coins, and you explained that Rav Hilai Gaon clarified that the weight of an egg is 16 2/3 silver pieces. [You wondered,] if the others do not have an ascribed weight, why is the egg given one?
>
> It is known that these other measurements are not given any equivalent weight in silver, not in the Mishnah nor the Talmud. If [the Sages] had wished to give a measurement in terms of the weight in *dinarim*, they would have done so originally. Rather, they give the measurements in terms of grains and fruit, which are always available, and one is not to say that they have changed.
>
> ...We practice according to the Mishnah: Everything goes according to the observer... And likewise with regard to the olive and date, it is explained in this Mishnah that it is not referring to a large one, or a small one, but rather an average one—and it is also according to the view of the observer. The reason why some rabbis gave their view as the size of an egg, and did not do the same with an olive, date or fig, is that there are many

---

[12] *Berachot* 52b.

[13] *Makkot* 16b.

things that are dependent upon the size of an egg—the *kab*, the *sa'ah*, the *efoh*, the *omer*; all are evaluated in terms of eggs, and therefore they estimated it according to their views, but these other measurements are left to the opinion of the observer... (Cited in *Sefer Ha-Eshkol* (Albeck ed.) vol. II, *Hilchot Challah* 13 p. 52)

The intent may be that since the *kab*, *sa'ah* etc. are multiples of eggs (a *kab* is 24 eggs, a *sa'ah* is 144 eggs), it is difficult to visualize this in terms of eggs, and it is easier to visualize it in terms of silver.[14] However, with measurements given as a *kezayit*, there is no reason or basis for giving an alternate measurement.

Rav Sherira Gaon's son, Rav Hai Gaon (Babylonia 939-1038), writes as follows:

...And therefore the Torah gave measurements in terms of eggs and fruits—for *divrei sofrim* were given at Sinai...—because eggs and fruit are found in every place. For it is known and revealed before the One Who spoke and brought the universe into existence, that Israel is destined to be scattered amongst the nations, and that the weights and measures that were in the days of Moses and that which were added to in the Land of Israel would not be preserved, and that the measurements change in different times and places... Therefore the Sages related the quantities to fruit and eggs, which always exist and never change. They made the quantity of an egg depend upon the view of the observer. (Ibid. pp. 56-57)

A final responsum, from an unknown Geonic author, states:

And that which you wrote regarding the size of a large fig and a medium fig, and likewise a large olive and a small and medium olive—surely these are *shiurim*, and how can there be a *shiur* for a *shiur*? And should you say that it is [a matter of ascribing] a weight—our rabbis did not specify a weight, and the Holy One was not particular with us regarding the weight. Every person, in acting according to his own assessment, has fulfilled his obligation, and there is no need to learn the quantity from another... (*Teshuvos HaGeonim* 268, Harkavey ed.)

---

[14] R. Chaim Beinish, *Midot VeShiurei Torah*, pp. 522-523.

In all these responsa, we see that the *kezayit* is intended to be assessed, very simply, by each person looking at an olive. Even if one were to believe that the olives of the Talmudic era were larger than those of today, there would be no need to attempt to replicate that quantity.[15] With the Geonim, we see a presumption that the size of olives does not change, and that in any case each person is supposed to follow his own assessment of an olive.[16] This was seen to be the underlying rationale of the Torah prescribing quantities in terms of familiar fruit rather than by some independent system of measurement.

The Rishonim of Sefarad

Let us now turn to the era of the Rishonim, and we shall begin with the Rishonim of Spain and comparable regions. Rambam (Spain/Egypt 1135-1204) makes no statement regarding the size of a *kezayit*. But an inference regarding its maximum size can be drawn from his statement

---

[15] There is a statement in the Talmud which might seem to show that we are supposed to replicate the measurements of the Talmud rather than to use the measurements of our own era: "Rabbi Elazar said: One who eats *chelev* nowadays must record for himself the quantity, in case a future Beis Din will increase the measurements (for which one is liable)" (Talmud, *Yoma* 80a). A similar ruling is found in the Yerushalmi: "Rabbi Hoshea said: One who eats a forbidden food in our day must record the quantity, in case a later Beis Din will arise and change the quantity (for which one is liable), and he will know how much he ate" (Yerushalmi, *Pe'ah* 2a). This sounds like there is an absolute measurement of a *kezayit*, valid for all times and places. Each Beis Din does its best to assess what this measurement is, but because it is possible that they are mistaken, one must record the amount eaten in case a future Beis Din assesses matters more correctly. Accordingly, it seems that the objective is to figure out the quantity used in the Talmud, not to follow the size of olives in one's own era! However, further analysis shows that this could not be the intent of the Talmud. How is the person going to be recording the amount that he ate? There was no possibility of a person recording it in terms of cubic centimeters or some other such absolute unchanging standard; and if such a standard had existed, surely the Sages would have used it for their measurements! Instead, the intent of the Talmud is that he is recording whether, for example, he ate the volume of a big olive, a medium olive, or a small olive. The concern is not that the size of olives will change, but rather that the quantity for which one is liable will change – is one liable for a big olive, a medium olive or a small olive. See *Sdei Chemed, Ma'areches HaAlef*, 34, s.v. *velashon*.

[16] These responsa are also cited by R. Eliezer Waldenberg in *Tzitz Eliezer* vol 13, 76:3.

that a dried fig is 1/3 of an egg.[17] Since the Talmud notes that a *kezayit* is smaller than a dried fig,[18] this would result in a *kezayit* being less than 1/3 of an egg.[19]

It is important to note that our inference of Rambam's view regarding olives does not tell us anything as to the absolute size of a *kezayit*, only that it must be less than 1/3 of an egg (which is, of course, true of a regular olive). However, this inference was later apparently later interpreted to mean that Rambam was of the view that a *kezayit* is actually *equal* to *slightly less than* 1/3 of an egg, and then to mean that he was of the view

---

[17] *Mishneh Torah, Hilchot Eruvin* 1:9.

[18] Talmud, *Shabbat* 91a.

[19] There is a potential difficulty with this inference, in reconciling it with an inference from two statements in the Talmud. As we shall see later, the Talmud in one place states that a person can swallow food up to the size of two olives, while elsewhere it states that a person can swallow food up to the size of an egg. These passages indicate that an olive is half the size of an egg. How can this be reconciled with our inference that Rambam's position is that an olive is less than 1/3 of an egg? The Vilna Gaon (1720-1797) claims that the inference in the Talmud that an olive is half the size of an egg is referring to a person swallowing an egg without its shell, but an egg with its shell is three times the size of an olive (*Biyur HaGra* to *Orach Chaim* 486:1). This does not necessarily mean that a shell changes an egg from being twice the size of an olive to being more than three times its size (which is clearly not the case!). Rather, the point is that a hard-boiled egg without the shell is sufficiently pliable that a person can swallow a whole one, just as a person can swallow two olives. But the olive is less than a third the size of an egg with its shell. R. Chizkiya ben David DiSilva (1659-1698, author of *Pri Chadash*) writes that the Talmud's statement that the throat cannot hold more than two olives is imprecisely written, and actually refers to an olive and a date (*Pri Chadash, Orach Chaim* 486:1). R. Yaakov Orenstein (author of *Yeshuas Yaakov*) states that Rambam simply considers the Talmud's statement to be disputed by the other statement about the throat being able to hold an egg, and Rambam does not follow that view (*Yeshuas Yaakov, Orach Chaim* 301). According to both these approaches, Rambam is indeed of the view that a *kezayit* is less than 1/3 of an egg. R. Avraham Gombiner (c.1633-c.1683, author of *Magen Avraham*) suggests that according to Rambam, when the Talmud rated an olive as being smaller than a dried fig, it was only referring to a small olive, but an average olive is larger than a dried fig. It seems that R. Gombiner interpreted Rambam's view as being than an average olive is equal to half an egg. However, it does not seem that anyone else adopted this understanding of Rambam.

that a *kezayit* is *equal* to *about* 1/3 of an egg.[20] One can propose how this happened; since it was not known how much less than 1/3 of an egg it was,[21] nor is it convenient to quantify "less than 1/3 of an egg," the upper limit was taken as the bottom line and simplified to 1/3 of an egg. The problem with this result is that when the process itself is forgotten, it is assumed that Rambam's position *opposes* the idea that a *kezayit* is much smaller than 1/3 of an egg,[22] whereas the truth is that he does not oppose it at all.

Furthermore, from the fact that Rambam does not specify the size of a *kezayit*—whereas he does specify the size of other quantities[23]—one can presumably infer that his position was that a *kezayit* is the size of an ordinary olive, and/or that it is up to each person to assess it on their own, rather than to attempt to calculate the size of a Talmudic olive.[24]

Rambam was not the only prominent authority with which we can see that a *kezayit* is less than 1/3 of an egg. Both Rif and Rosh likewise state that a fig is a third of an egg, and since a *kezayit* is less than a fig, this means that a *kezayit* is less than a third of an egg.[25]

---

[20] See *Mishnah Berurah* 486:1 and R. Pinchas Bodner, *The Halachos of K'zayis* p. 25 note 27. R. Yaakov Yisrael Kanievsky, in *Shiurin Shel Torah* 11 p. 70 notes that Rambam should not be misinterpreted in this regard.

[21] R. Yosef Kotkovski argues that an olive must be significantly smaller than a dried fig; see *Darkei HaChaim* (Petrikow 1884), *Hilchot Borei Minei Mezonos* 4, *Chelki b'Chaim* 3. However, R. Chaim Na'eh, *Shiruin Shel Torah* p. 190 n. 24 disagrees.

[22] See Rabbi Moshe Petrover, "The Size of the *Kezayit* for Eating Matzah: A Clarification of the View of the Chazon Ish" (Hebrew), *Moriah* 5754, p. 106.

[23] *Commentary on the Mishnah, Eduyos* 1:2, *Keilim* 2:2; *Mishneh Torah, Eruvin* 1:12.

[24] R. Hadar Margolin, "A Clarification of the View of the Chazon Ish," (Hebrew) *Moriah* 3-4 (5753) p. 100.

[25] R. Yishmael HaKohen (18th century; Italy), in his work *Shevach Pesach* (sec. 8, p. 16-18), thereby observes that all three pillars of the *Shulchan Aruch*—Rif, Rambam and Rosh—held that the *kezayit* is less than 1/3 of an egg. R. Yishmael does state that one should only rely on Rif, Rambam, and Rosh in a time of need, presumably in deference to the *Shulchan Aruch's* "yesh omrim" in *Orach Chaim* 486. He also asserts (baselessly) that when we infer that the *kezayit* is less than a third of an egg, "it is only a little less than a third," and then says that since "we don't know how much less it is, one cannot eat less than a third." R. Ovadia Yosef, in *Yechaveh Daat* 1:16, agrees with *Shevach*

Recently, two very significant further sources from Sefarad came to light. Rashba (R. Shlomo ben Aderes, Spain, 1235-1310), in discussing a different topic, mentions that fifteen eggs are "much" more than sixty olives; hence, an olive is *much* less than ¼ the size of an egg.[26] Ritva (R. Yom Tov ben Avraham Asevilli, Spain, 1250-1330), in a newly published manuscript, states that a dried fig is the volume of "several" olives.[27] Since he is also of the view that a dried fig is 1/3 the size of an egg, this means that an olive is around 1/9 the size of an egg.

It is important to note that none of these authorities set out to specify the size of an olive, or grappled with statements concerning its size (as we shall see to have been the case with the Rishonim of Ashkenaz). Our knowledge of their position regarding the size of an olive, or the upper limit of the size of an olive, is inferred from statements of theirs made in a different context. The clear implication is that they took it for granted that a *kezayit* is the size of an ordinary olive.

By the same token, the fact that most authorities of this period did not make any statement relating to the size of an olive does not mean that we have no idea as to what their view was. For someone for whom a *kezayit* is obviously an olive, there is no need to make any comment about it. One can assume that the reason why they did not comment on the size of a *kezayit* is that it was obvious to them that a *kezayit* is *kezayit*.

The Rishonim of Ashkenaz

It is in Ashkenaz that we find the olive beginning to evolve with the statements of the Rishonim themselves (as opposed to with later mistaken inferences regarding the Rishonim). The Rishonim of Ashkenaz translated the size of an olive into a proportion of an egg, but they gave different

---

Pesach, but instead of accurately citing *Shevach Pesach* to say Rif, Rambam, and Rosh held that the *kezayit* is less than a third of an egg, he writes that all three hold that a *kezayit* **is the size** of a third of an egg, which even R. Yishmael doesn't claim. But he, like R. Yishmael, says that one can only rely on this in time of need ("for a sick or elderly person"), again because of *Shulchan Aruch*'s "*yesh omrim.*" My thanks to Boruch Fuzailov for bringing these sources to my attention.

[26] Rashba, *Mishmeret HaBayit* 4:1.

[27] Ritva to *Shabbat* 76b; printed at the back of the Mossad HaRav Kook edition.

quantities. This was based on differing resolutions of various passages in the Talmud. In one place, the Talmud states that a person can swallow food up to the size of two olives:

> The Sages evaluated that the throat cannot hold more than two olives. (*Kritut* 14a)

Elsewhere, the Talmud states that a person can swallow food up to the size of an egg:

> The Sages evaluated that the throat cannot hold more than a chicken's egg. (*Yoma* 80a)

These passages indicate that an olive is half the size of an egg. However, in a third place, a different conclusion emerges. The Talmud (*Eruvin* 82b) discusses the amount of food required for an *eruv*. Two of the views cited express their opinion in terms of *kabin*, which in turn can be expressed in quantities of eggs (since 1 *kav* is 24 eggs):

- Rabbi Shimon: Two meals are 2/9 of a *kav*, which is 5 1/3 eggs.
- Rabbi Yochanan ben Beruka: Two meals are ¼ of a *kav*, which is 6 eggs.

Elsewhere, the Talmud states that two meals are equal to 18 dried figs.[28] Now, as we saw earlier, an olive is known to be smaller than a dried fig.[29] This results in the following calculation:

- Rabbi Shimon: Two meals = 5 1/3 eggs = 18 dried figs; thus 1 olive is less than 3/10 of an egg
- Rabbi Yochanan ben Beruka: Two meals = 6 eggs = 18 dried figs; thus 1 olive is less than 1/3 of an egg

How are all these sources to be reconciled?

Ri (R. Yitzchak ben Shmuel the Elder of Dampierre, 12th century) concludes from the passages concerning swallowing that an olive is half

---

[28] *Eruvin* 80b.

[29] *Shabbat* 91a.

the size of an egg.[30] As for the passage in *Eruvin*, he states that we do not follow the views of either Rabbi Shimon or Rabbi Yochanan ben Beruka; thus that discussion has no inferences for the size of an olive. Ri's view that an olive is half the size of an egg was adopted by R. Mordechai b. Hillel (Germany, 1240-1298),[31] R. Alexander Zusslein HaKohen (France/Germany, d. 1348)[32] and R. Yaakov Weil (Germany, 15th century).[33]

Rabbeinu Tam (Yaakov ben Meir Tam, France, c. 1100–c. 1171), on the other hand, states that we rule in accordance with Rabbi Shimon, an olive must be less than 3/10 of an egg (although he does not propose how much less). Regarding the statements concerning swallowing which indicate that an olive is half the size of an egg, Rabbeinu Tam suggests that the foods are in different states, which affects the volume that can be swallowed. An egg is much easier to swallow than an equivalent volume of olives. Because olives are hard and contain pits, only two can be swallowed at a time, even though they are much smaller than a single whole egg, which can be swallowed in one gulp.

In a variant of this approach, *Tosafot Yeshanim* reconciles it by suggesting that they are descriptions of different types of swallowing. When the Talmud spoke of a person being able to swallow two olives, it was referring to what a person can swallow in the course of ordinary eating. However, when it spoke of a person being able to swallow a whole egg, it was referring to the maximum that a person can force themselves to swallow.

Rabbeinu Tam's approach does not draw any conclusions as to the absolute size of an olive, only that it must be less than 3/10 of an egg (which is, of course, true). However, this view was later apparently interpreted to mean that it *equals* slightly less than 3/10 of an egg. (The

---

[30] Tosafot to *Yoma* 80a s.v. *Veshiaru*. (The same inference is apparently made by *Sefer HaChinnuch*, mitzvah 313.) R. Chaim Na'eh argues that Ri must mean that an olive is slightly less than half the size of an egg; see *Shiurei Torah*, p. 192.

[31] Mordechai, end of *Pesachim, Seder Leil Pesach*.

[32] *Sefer Ha-Agudah, Eruvin* 82b.

[33] Mahari Weil 193.

ratio of 3/10 was later slightly expanded to 1/3, for reasons that are unclear; perhaps as it is a simpler quantity to assess.)

Reasons for the Ashkenazi Expansion

Why did the Ashkenazi authorities relate the size of an olive to the size of an egg, especially since, according to Ri, this results in the error of considering an olive to be half the size of an egg? Why did they not follow the position of the Sephardic authorities, that a *kezayit* is the size of an olive?

The simple answer is given by Rabbi Akiva Yosef Schlesinger (1835-1922). He writes:

> The measurement of an egg is not found in the Torah; rather, it says, "a land of… olives" etc., that all its measurements are like olives, and this olive was only rated by the measurement of an egg for those who did not have olives. But not for us, who see the olive in front of us—there is no need to push aside the *ikkar* for the *tafel*. (*Tel Talpiot*, Shevat 5661 p. 103)

The medieval Ashkenazic authorities never saw an olive. Olives do not grow that far north; they only grow in the Mediterranean region. In medieval Europe, transporting commodities was expensive, and was only done with foodstuffs for which there was high demand. Many food items were simply unknown in some regions. In an early 15th century Bavarian translation of an Arabic pharmacopoeia, the German translator has to explain to his readers what various foodstuffs (such as sesame seeds and pistachio nuts) actually are.[34] In northern Europe, unlike with the Mediterranean region, olives were not part of the menu and they were virtually unheard of.[35] Only olive oil was imported, and even that was very expensive and only used by the wealthy. In the oldest German cookbook

---

[34] Prof. Melitta Weiss Adamson of the University of Western Ontario, personal communication.

[35] Melitta Weiss Adamson, *Food in Medieval Times* (Greenwood Press 2004), pp. 29-30; John Ayto, *The Glutton's Glossary: A Dictionary of Food and Drink Terms* (Routledge 1991), p. 198.

entered in a parchment codex in Wuerzburg around 1350, no olives are mentioned, and oil (which may not even be olive oil) appears only once.[36]

Thus, the Rishonim of Ashkenaz were simply unfamiliar with olives. They could only attempt to calculate the olive's size based on deductions from various statements in the Talmud. As a consequence, they greatly increased the size of a *kezayit*.[37]

The same explanation is mentioned by others, such as R. Chaim Beinish in *Midot veShiurei Torah*.[38] R. Meir Mazuz also mentions this and provides further evidence, noting that Tosafos[39] interpreted a Talmudic statement about the olive being bitter to refer to the olive tree; R. Mazuz notes that Tosafos mistakenly presumed that olives are sweet (like other fruit) because the Baalei Tosafos never encountered olives.[40]

R. Eliezer b. Yoel HaLevi (Germany, c.1140-c.1225) explicitly acknowledges that his community in Ashkenaz knew that they were missing direct observation, and that they therefore decided to err on the side of caution:

> And wherever a *kezayit* is required, the food should be measured generously, since we are not familiar with the measurement of an olive, and so that the blessing should not be in vain. (Ravyah, *Berachot* 107)

Another revealing statement comes from one of the Rishonim from the generation of the Rosh. He was addressing a question that arises from

---

[36] Melitta Weiss Adamson, personal communication.

[37] It is also possible that even if the Rishonim of Ashkenaz would have had access to olives, they would still have ignored empirical investigation in favor of Talmudic analysis. R. Menachem Meiri (Catalonia/Provence 1249 – c. 1310) also calculates that an olive is half the size of an egg, based solely on an internal analysis of the Talmud, even though olives did exist in his region (*Beit HaBechirah* to *Eruvin* 80b). In medieval Europe, empirical investigation was not valued as highly as it is today. Furthermore, as we shall soon discuss, Ri and Rabbeinu Tam did not deliberate over the size of a *kezayit* in the context of issuing a practical ruling, but rather as part of an attempt to resolve a conflict in the Talmud.

[38] Bnei Brak 5760.

[39] *Eruvin* 18b s.v. *merurin*, *Pesachim* 37a s.v. *mah*.

[40] From his weekly Torah leaflet, *Bayit Neeman*, 7 Kislev 5778. My thanks to Marc Shapiro for calling my attention to this.

Hillel having eaten a *kezayit* each of matzah, *maror* and *charoses* simultaneously, which was problematic for those who believed that two olives was the maximum that the throat can hold. This rabbi pointed out that based on what he had seen on his travels to Israel, there is no difficulty in this:

> To me there is no difficulty, for I saw olives in Israel and Jerusalem, and even six were not as large as an egg. (*Piskei Rabboseinu SheBeAshkenaz, Moriah* 2:3)

We thus see that the Rishonim of Ashkenaz themselves acknowledged that, living in Ashkenaz, they had not seen olives. Note that no Rishon claimed to have measured the olive and seen that it is equal to half or third of an egg. They all used indirect textual arguments to try to determine the size of the olive. The aforementioned Rishon is the only Rishon who describes using observation, and he says that an olive is less than a sixth of an egg.

This in turn answers the following question. Even given the view of Ri that the Talmud dictates that an olive is half the size of an egg, why assume that this means that olives back then were larger? Why not explain instead that eggs back then were smaller? This question is especially potent since the fundamental measurement for the *mitzvot* of eating is in terms of olives, not in term of eggs.[41] So why pick a different unit of measurement as the barometer?

As R. Chaim Beinish explains, the answer is that for Ri, and many others after him, there was no first-hand experience with olives. On the other hand, they were familiar with eggs. Since the olive was the food whose size they didn't know and were trying to determine, it was natural to assume that the egg of the Talmud was the same as their egg, and the olive was half that size.[42] There was no reason to assume otherwise. Today, however, when we know that olives are not and were not that big, and we also know that eggs were formerly smaller (as we shall later discuss), there is no reason why, even if we are reconciling the Talmudic statements

---

[41] See Moshe Koppel, "*The Sages Evaluated*" (Hebrew), *Higayon* 5 pp. 55-62 for a valuable discussion of the concept of primary and secondary units of measurement.

[42] R. Chaim Beinish, *Midot veShiurei Torah*, p. 526.

about olives and eggs, this should lead us to the conclusion that olives must have been bigger.

There is a further point to consider in evaluating the adoption of the view of the Rishonim of Ashkenaz. Ri and Rabbeinu Tam did not deliberate over the size of a *kezayit* in the context of issuing a practical ruling, but rather as part of an attempt to resolve a conflict in the Talmud. It is far from clear that they were of the view that for one's own obligation, one always needs to replicate the size of a Talmudic olive. They may well have adopted the view of the Geonim, that if one has access to olives, one should follow the size of an olive in one's own time and place. Perhaps initially the rulings of the Ashkenazi Rishonim were adopted because nobody had anything better to go with. And even later when people did have alternatives, the statements of these authorities had already been accepted as formal rulings regarding what size a *kezayit* should be.

The *Shulchan Aruch*'s Ambiguous Ruling

In the *Shulchan Aruch* of R. Yosef Karo (Spain/Israel, 1488-1575), the chapter concerning the size of a *kezayit* contains only one section, and it is probably the shortest chapter in the entire work. Its wording is intriguing:

> The amount of a *kezayit*—some say that it is around half of an egg. (*Shulchan Aruch, Orach Chaim* 486:1)

This ruling is surprising in that R. Karo does not rule what a *kezayit* is; he just notes what "some say" it is. This is widely understood to mean that he is citing this view as a stringency, but that he himself is of the view that it is smaller.[43] But how much smaller? An inference can be drawn from a ruling elsewhere,[44] where in discussing the quantity of two meals for an *eruv*, he follows the ruling of Rabbi Yochanan ben Beruka in quantifying this as being the size of six eggs, and equates this with 18 dried figs. The

---

[43] Responsa *Vayomer Yitzchak, Orach Chaim* 8. See too *Ner Mitzvah* 17 and Benish, *Middos VeShiurei Torah* p. 254 note 111 and p.527.

[44] *Orach Chaim*, 368:3; 409:7.

inference is that a *kezayit*, which is smaller than a dried fig, must be less than 1/3 of an egg.

Many therefore state that while the *Shulchan Aruch* records the stringent view of a *kezayit* being ½ an egg, it rules a *kezayit* to be slightly less than 1/3 of an egg. However, a careful analysis shows that this is not the case. All we can derive from the discussion regarding *eruv* is that the *maximum* size must be somewhat less than 1/3 of an egg; we still have no inference as to how *much* less it is. In theory it is still entirely possible that the view of R. Yosef Karo was that a *kezayit* is the size of a regular olive. One might claim that since he quotes the view of Ri, this indicates that he was working within the Ashkenazi approach, which therefore makes it unlikely that he himself viewed it as being a much smaller quantity. But on the other hand, the fact that he does not specify what he considers to be the normative view (only quoting what "some say" it to be) could indicate that he considered the normative view to be obvious—namely, that a *kezayit* is the size of an olive. This is especially likely in light of the fact that R. Yosef Karo himself, unlike Ri and Rabbeinu Tam, would have been familiar with olives.

Whichever way one understands R. Karo, it seems that the *Shulchan Aruch* denotes a critical point of transition; in recording the explicit view of the Ashkenazi Rishonim and being silent about the silent Sefardic Rishonim, it thereby strengthens the impression that Ri was the mainstream view and Rabbeinu Tam, interpreted maximally, was the alternative.

Reasons for the Ashkenazi Adoption

When later authorities who were familiar with normal olives nevertheless followed the positions of the Ashkenazi Rishonim, they were implicitly adopting the notion that olives of ancient times were larger. Some were explicit about this. For example, in adopting the view of Ri that an olive is half the size of an egg, Rabbi Shlomo Luria (Poland, 1510-1574) writes as follows:

> It is a received tradition in our hands from the Tosafists that an olive is half the size of an egg. And even though in our time we see with our eyes that the size of an olive is much smaller than half of an egg, this is not

surprising, for in the days of the Sages the fruit of the Seven Species were unusual in their size, and they have since changed. (*Yam Shel Shlomo, Chullin* 3:86, also cited in Taz, *Yoreh De'ah* 44:12)

R. Yaakov Yisrael Kanievsky (1899-1985) similarly writes that although the strain of olives found today is the same as that mentioned in the Mishnah, "it has become weak and the fruit have become smaller"[45] (however, as we shall see, he was not of the view that the earlier larger size is to be replicated).

We have seen that the botanical and archeological evidence shows that olives were always the same size as they are today. But the belief that they used to be larger was consistent with a general worldview of the "decline of generations"—that the world used to have a golden age in which people, animals and plants were superior in every way to those of today. The most radical application of this concept to the size of the *kezayit* was that of R. Yechezkel Landau, which we shall now explore.

The Alleged Egg Shrinkage

R. Yechezkel Landau (Poland/Bohemia, author of *Noda B'Yehudah*, 1713-1793) created a famous revolution in the determination of halachic quantities.

> Since a mitzvah performed at a designated time is precious, and on this night we are required to eat a *kezayit* of matzah and *maror* and to drink a Torah-determined *revi'is* of the four cups, I need to clarify my view concerning the size of a *kezayit* and a *revi'is*, which I concluded by way of proofs is not in accordance with the words of the *Shulchan Aruch*. For in truth it is clear in the *Shulchan Aruch*, chapter 486, that the size of a *kezayit* is half the size of an egg. However, it is clear to me by way of measurement that with the eggs that we have in our day, a whole egg of our day is only half the size of an egg that was used for the Torah quantities... (*Tzlach, Pesachim* 120a)

R. Landau proceeds to describe his measurements which resulted in a ratio of thumbs to eggs that differed from the ratio that results from the Talmud. He continues:

---

[45] *Shiurin Shel Torah* p. 8.

And against our will we see that things have changed in our time; either thumbs have grown, and they are bigger than the thumbs of the days of the Tannaim, or the eggs have shrunk and in our day they are smaller than the eggs of the era of the Tannaim. And it is known that the generations progressively decline, and it is therefore impossible that our thumbs should be larger than the thumbs in the day of the Sages of the Mishnah. (Ibid.)

R. Landau therefore concludes that the eggs mentioned in the Talmud were larger, and his calculations enable him to conclude that they were twice as large:

It is therefore necessarily the case that the eggs of our day are smaller… and since it has become clear that our eggs are smaller by half, therefore the size of a *kezayit*, which is (originally) half an egg, is as the size of a whole egg of today. And thus I evaluate the eating of matzah and *maror*… (Ibid.)

Many authorities adopted the view of R. Landau.[46] In some cases, they only did so vis-à-vis measurements dependent on thumbs, such as *challah* and *revi'is*, but not vis-à-vis measurements dependent on eggs, such as a *kezayit*.[47] But others adopted it for eggs (and calculated the volume of today's eggs as being 50cc and that of eggs in ancient times as being 100cc) and thus for the *kezayit* too, such as R. Yisrael Meir Kagan (Poland, 1838-1933) in the *Mishnah Berurah*:

…And with regard to the ruling, with a Biblical mitzvah, such as the positive commandment of eating matzah, one should be stringent and eat at least the volume of half an egg… and know that what the *Shulchan Aruch* wrote about a *kezayit* being half an egg is not a final statement in our day, for some of the Acharonim proved that the eggs found in our day are much smaller, as much as half, of the eggs that were in ancient times, with which the Sages gave their measurements. Accordingly, wherever the required quantity is half an egg, one needs to measure this as a whole egg

---

[46] Vilna Gaon, *Maaseh Rav* 105; R. Akiva Eiger, *Teshuvot R. Akiva Eiger HaChadashot* 39; *Beit Ephraim, Rosh Ephraim, Kuntrus HaTeshuvot* 16.

[47] Chatam Sofer, *Responsa Chatam Sofer Orach Chaim* 127, 181; *Responsa Gidulei Taharah* 1; R. Chaim of Volozhin, as per *Shaarei Rachamim* 165 and at the end in *Minhagei HaGraCh* 51.

of our day.... According to this, in our day a person is obligated to eat matzah of the size of an egg... (*Mishnah Berurah*, 486:1)

Note the three steps taken in the *Mishnah Berurah* which result in this gigantic measurement of 50-60cc for a *kezayit*.[48] First is that, again, we have a presumption that the obligation is to consume the presumed size of an olive of ancient times, not an olive of today—which is in contrast to the view of the Geonim. Second is that he states that one should follow the stringent view that a *kezayit* is half an egg—which we have seen to based on the Ashkenazi Rishonim not being familiar with olives. Third is that he claims that the Acharonim *proved* that eggs have shrunk—which we shall now demonstrate to be incorrect.

Evaluating the Alleged Egg Shrinkage

From a rationalist perspective, Rabbi Landau's claim that the relative sizes of thumbs and eggs has changed, and that it must be that eggs have shrunk rather than that thumbs have grown, is problematic on several counts. First, we know that thumbs have indeed grown; second, we know that eggs have not shrunk. As for his difficulty regarding the apparently changed ratio, there are other solutions. Let us explore these three points in turn.

R. Landau's belief that people could not have grown larger was based on his understanding of the decline of generations. The concept of a "decline of generations" sets traditionalists squarely against rationalists, depending on how it is defined.[49] But even if one accepts the notion of a general spiritual and/or intellectual decline, R. Landau's extrapolation to a *physical* decline is quite a leap. Furthermore, evidence from archeology shows that between the Talmudic era and the era of R. Landau, mankind

---

[48] The range of 50-60cc is due to the different assessments of the volume of a contemporary egg.

[49] Menachem Kellner, in *Maimonides on the Decline of Generations*, argues that Maimonides did not subscribe to this doctrine as a general pattern.

did not become any shorter; in fact, beginning in the 18th century, people began to grow taller.[50]

With regard to R. Landau's claim that eggs have become smaller, R. Eliezer Waldenberg points to the aforementioned responsa of the Geonim, which state that halachic measurements are given in terms of eggs because they remain constant in size.[51] In fact, empirical research shows that eggs in ancient times, far from being twice the size of today's eggs (which measure 50-60cc), were actually smaller than those of today. There are several independent lines of evidence for this.

One argument, concerning the size of eggs in Rambam's era, is based on his relating the size of an egg to certain Arab coins. R. Chaim Na'eh (1890-1954) used this technique to calculate the size of eggs in Rambam's day as being 57.6cc.[52] However, R. Chaim Beinish states that the coin of Rambam's era was of a different weight than that known to R. Chaim Na'eh, and it results in an egg size of 49cc.[53] The fact is that the size of Arab coins varied tremendously in different places and eras, which makes any such calculation questionable,[54] but there are many other more reliable forms of evidence.

The Talmud records that R. Yehudah HaNasi measured a vessel called the *modia* or *modius* as containing the volume of 217 eggs.[55] We know

---

[50] R. Elazar Fleckeles, a disciple of R. Landau, is recorded as having claimed that R. Landau reached his conclusion due to his own thumb being unusually large, reflecting his tall stature. See David Katz, "A Case Study in the Formation of a Super-Rabbi: The Early Years of Rabbi Ezekiel Landau, 1713-1754," (PhD dissertation, University of Maryland, 2004)

[51] R. Eliezer Waldenberg, *Tzitz Eliezer* vol 13, 76:3.

[52] *Shiurei Torah* (Jerusalem 1947) pp. 111-120.

[53] *Middot VeShiurei Torah* 13:7 and 30:6.

[54] See, for example, Stefan Heidemann, "The Merger of Two Currency Zones in Early Islam. The Byzantine and Sasanian Impact on the Circulation in Former Byzantine Syria and Northern Mesopotamia," *Iran* 36 (1998) pp.95-112.

[55] *Eruvin* 83a. The Talmud further states that R. Yehudah HaNasi had a tradition that this vessel held the volume of 207 eggs of the size that existed at the time of the Revelation at Sinai, and attributed the slight difference of about 5% to the natural change in egg size over so many years.

that the *modius* was one-third the size of a standard Roman measuring vessel called the amphora, and we are able to measure extant amphoras at one cubic Roman foot, which equals 25.79 liters.[56] This means that the eggs of R. Yehuda HaNasi's era measured 39.6cc.[57]

Professor Yehudah Feliks examined eggs that were preserved whole in the volcanic destruction of Pompeii two thousand years ago, and states that they were "around the size of the small Arab eggs of our time," which he defines as 41.4cc.[58]

My own research indicates that the eggs of ancient times were considerably smaller than those of today. Domestic fowl have been selectively bred for larger eggs, which would mean that eggs used to be smaller. Furthermore, we know that the domestic chicken was domesticated from the red junglefowl several thousand years ago, and its eggs are very small, only 32.1cc.[59] Assuming a gradual increase to the size of today's eggs, this would indicate that two thousand years ago, eggs were around 40cc. In addition, records show that the chickens used in Roman Italy were able to incubate twice as many eggs at a time than chickens of today are able to do, which shows that their eggs were much smaller.[60]

We thus see that, contrary to R. Landau's assertions, neither thumbs nor eggs are smaller than those of ancient times. As for R. Landau's

---

[56] Lesley Adkins, Roy A. Adkins, *Handbook to Life in Ancient Rome* (Oxford Uni. Press 1998), p. 314.

[57] There is some dispute regarding the precise size of the *modius*. Greenfield, "Has the Egg Volume Really Decreased in the Thousands of Years since Matan Torah?" (Hebrew) *BDD* 16 pp. 91-94 concludes that the egg had a volume of 43cc.

[58] Feliks, *Kelai Zera'im VeHarkavah*, p. 184 note 5.

[59] Gardiner Bump, *Special Scientific Report 62: Red Junglefowl and Kalij Pheasants* (Washington DC: U.S. Fish & Wildlife 1962), gives the dimensions of the egg as 4.53x3.44cm (compare large chicken eggs at around 5.7x4.4cm). Using the calculation $V = (0.6057-0.0018B)LB^2$ in which L is the egg length, and B is the egg maximum breadth, the volume is 32.14cc. The calculation is from V.G. Narushin, "Egg Geometry Calculation Using the Measurements of Length and Breadth," *Poultry Science* 84:3 (March 2005) pp. 482-484.

[60] George Jennison, *Animals for Show and Pleasure in Ancient Rome* (Manchester University Press 1937), p. 106, citing Pliny, Varro and Columella.

question regarding the apparently changed ratio of eggs to thumbs, other solutions have been presented.[61] In fact, the eggs of ancient times were slightly smaller than those of today; according to my research, around 40cc. This may also assist in solving the difficulty in the olive-egg ratio implied by the Talmud's statement regarding a person being able to swallow a whole egg or two olives.

Recent and Contemporary Poskim

The *Mishnah Berurah*, as noted above, rules that for Biblically-ordained *mitzvot* one should follow R. Landau's conclusion that the eggs of ancient times were twice the size of today's eggs. But most authorities rejected the notion that one should double the size of the measurements. R. Elchanan Wasserman (1875-1941) noted that based on the words of R. Hai Gaon (that we cited early in this study), the size of eggs and olives does not change.[62] R. Chaim Na'eh, a prominent rabbinic authority in Jerusalem, compiled an extensive study of halachic weights and measures. As noted above, he concluded that R. Landau had erred about eggs in ancient times being larger than those of today. On the other hand, R. Avraham Yeshayah Karelitz (the "Chazon Ish," 1878-1953) wrote that regardless of whether it is factually true that eggs have halved in size, since this was the assessment of R. Landau and others, and it has become widely accepted, it is as though it has been established by a Beis Din for all Israel and is binding.[63]

Putting aside the issue of whether one assumes that eggs used to be twice the size, what proportion of an egg is a *kezayit*? R. Avraham Danzig (*Chayei Adam*, 1748–1820)[64] rules that a *kezayit* is half an egg, as does R. Yechiel Michel Epstein (*Aruch HaShulchan*, 1829-1908).[65] R. Yisrael Meir

---

[61] Avraham Greenfeld, "*Middah Kenegged Middah*,' *Moriah* 10 (5742). This provoked heated responses; see, for example, R. Kalman Kahana, "*Lo Zu HaMiddah*," *Moriah* 11 (5743) 11-12 pp. 67-76.

[62] *Kobetz Shiurim* 2:46.

[63] Chazon Ish, *Kuntrus HaShiurim* 39:6. However, as we shall soon see, this was far from R. Karelitz's last word on the topic.

[64] *Chayei Adam* 50:12

[65] *Aruch HaShulchan* 202:5 and 486:1.

Kagan (*Mishnah Berurah*, 1838-1933) rules that when following the stringent view (e.g. for Biblically-ordained *mitzvot* such as eating matzah at the *seder*) one should follow the stringent view of Ri cited in the *Shulchan Aruch* that a *kezayit* is half an egg. R. Chaim Na'eh also states that for such *mitzvot* one should follow the view that a *kezayit* is half an egg and specifies this as being 28.8cc.[66]

Partly because R. Chaim Na'eh was the first to address the topic comprehensively, and partly due to his stature, many of his conclusions became widely accepted. Thus, the most widespread view today concerning a *kezayit* is that it measures 28.8cc. This is based on following the stringent view of Ri along with the egg calculation of R. Chaim Na'eh. This view has been advanced by authorities such as R. Shlomo Zalman Auerbach[67] (1910-1995) and R. Yosef Shalom Elyashiv.[68] It is also the standard adopted for R. Pinchas Bodner's popular work *The Halachos of Kezayit*.

A less widespread view is that a *kezayit* is 17cc. This is based on following what is presumed to be the *Shulchan Aruch*'s own view, following Rabbeinu Tam and Rambam, that a *kezayit* is slightly less than 1/3 of an egg. The aforementioned recent and contemporary authorities also propose that one may rely on this "leniency" for rabbinically-mandated requirements, especially when it is difficult to rely on the larger quantity, such as when eating *maror* at the *seder*.

Yet even in recent times there were still those who maintained that a *kezayit* is the size of an ordinary olive. As noted at the beginning of this study, R. Chaim of Volozhin is one such example. When the manuscripts of the Geonim came to light around 130 years ago, revealing their view that one is to follow the size of the fruit of one's own era, some adopted this position. As noted earlier, Rabbi Akiva Yosef Schlesinger (1835-1922) writes:

> The measurement of an egg is not found in the Torah; rather, it says, "a land of... olives" etc., that all its measurements are like olives, and this

[66] See R. Chaim Na'eh, *Shiurei Torah*, 3:12 p. 193.

[67] *Halichot Shlomo* vol. II p. 90.

[68] *Kobetz Teshuvot* II:30.

olive was only rated by the measurement of an egg for those who did not have olives. But not for us, who see the olive in front of us—there is no need to push aside the *ikkar* for the *tafel*. (*Tel Talpiot*, Shevat 5661 p. 103)

R. Yitzchak Elchanan Spektor (1817-1896) likewise stated that the Geonic view is the fundamentally correct approach.[69] Apparently following the same approach, R. Avraham Bornstein (1838-1910, author of *Avnei Nezer*) maintained that the *kezayit* is the size of an ordinary olive and did not see any basis for expanding it to half the size of an egg, even as a stringency.[70] R. Yaakov Yisrael Kanievsky (1899-1985) states that we follow the size of today's olives regardless of the presumed greater size of olives in ancient times.[71]

The same was stated by R. Avraham Yeshayah Karelitz (the "Chazon Ish," 1878-1953), but there is much confusion and dispute with regard to his ultimate ruling. At one extreme, in some editions of his chart for the measurements of *shiurim*, he gives a measurement of 50cc for a *kezayit*. This view reflects his acceptance of R. Landau's radical expansion of the *kezayit*, based on the assumption that eggs have halved in size. Elsewhere he states that if one wishes to be stringent, one can follow the view of the Ri that a *kezayit* is half the volume of an egg.[72] The combination of these positions results in a *kezayit* measuring 50cc—half the presumed volume of an egg in ancient times. But at the other extreme, Chazon Ish writes that the essential concept of *kezayit* is that one follows the dimensions of olives that one observes and one does not need to concern oneself with calculating if olives in an earlier era were larger.[73] An intermediate position emerges from an account by R. Chaim Kanievsky that at the *seder* of the Chazon Ish, he allocated portions that were 17cc in size.[74] Reconciling all

---

[69] Quoted by R. Dov Aryeh Ritter, *Tel Talpiot*, 5661 p. 71.

[70] Testimony recorded in *Middos VeShiurei Torah*, p. 510 note 111.

[71] *Shiurin Shel Torah* 11 p. 71. Puzzlingly, however, he rates the size of a contemporary *kezayit* as being slightly less than a third of the size of an egg (17-19cc).

[72] Ibid. 39:17.

[73] Chazon Ish, *Shiurin Shel Torah* 11; Letters, 194.

[74] Related by R. Hadar Margolin, "A Clarification of the View of the Chazon Ish," *Moriah* 3-4 (5753) p. 102.

these conflicting statements and accounts is difficult, and varying conclusions have been drawn.[75] Suffice it to say that while it is "common knowledge" that a "Chazon Ish *shiur*" is the largest measurement for a *kezayit*, the truth is far more complex and it seems that he acknowledged that fundamentally a *kezayit* is the size of an ordinary olive.

The Canonization and Conservatism of Halacha

Given the botanical/archeological evidence and the discovery of the Geonic manuscripts, both of which independently show that there is no reason to exceed the size of a contemporary olive, why is it that there are so many who rule otherwise? Of course, in non-rationalist communities, it is common to treat scientific evidence with suspicion. But there is another reason why many adopt the position that a *kezayit* is much larger than olives are today: the nature of the halachic process in general. The question of whether halachic practice should be changed in light of new empirical data or newly discovered manuscripts is complex. There is a strong case to make for saying that halachah follows its own protocols and should not be re-evaluated in light of new data, even if it seems clear that the halachah is in opposition to objective facts.[76] A fundamental value in halachah is creating and preserving stability. If a halachah has become canonized, then it ought not to be changed.

However, this case has two factors that make it easier to rely on the new data if one wishes to do so. One is that upon closer inspection, the halachah is not at all canonized in the way that it is commonly assumed. The primary authorities who are assumed to have ruled that a *kezayit* is 1/3 of an egg, Rambam and Rabbeinu Tam, in fact did not say any such

---

[75] See R. Hadar Margolin, "A Clarification of the View of the Chazon Ish," *Moriah* 3-4 (5753) pp. 99-103 and R. Moshe Petrover, "The Volume of a *Kezayit* for Eating Matzah – A Clarification of the View of the Chazon Ish," *Moriah* 7-9 (5754) pp. 106-109. See too Menachem Friedman, "The Lost Kiddush Cup: Changes in Ashkenazi Haredi Culture - A Tradition in Crisis," in Jack Wertheimer, ed., *The Uses of Tradition: Jewish Continuity in the Modern Era*, (New York: JTS/Harvard University Press 1992), pp. 175-186.

[76] See my book *Sacred Monsters*, pp. 362-367.

thing; it is only the upper limit of a *kezayit* that can be inferred from them. The same may well also be true of the *Shulchan Aruch*.

The second factor is that this is not a case where the halachah was ruled unequivocally in one direction. There have always been those, such as Rabbi Chaim of Volozhin, the *Avnei Nezer* and others who maintained that the *kezayit* is the size of an ordinary olive. Even the Chazon Ish acknowledged that this is the fundamentally correct position. It is thus an established halachic view, which is merely being given greater weight in light of new discoveries of manuscripts and new data concerning olives and eggs.

Yet while this justifies someone who wishes to evaluate a *kezayit* as being the size of a regular olive, we can still understand why others do not take this approach. Even if a halachah has not been unequivocally canonized, it can still be sufficiently entrenched that it becomes problematic to change. Orthodox Judaism is a traditionalist way of life, and traditionalist religions are inherently and necessarily conservative.

Further Growth—Weight Replaces Volume

Another factor that is sometimes involved in the expansion of the *kezayit* is the change from measuring volume to measuring weight. There is no doubt that the *kezayit* is supposed to be a measure of volume, and there are several independent lines of evidence for this. First is a Mishnah which appears in a chapter discussing how to evaluate the quantity of a food:

> An airy loaf is evaluated as it is. If there is a hollow inside, it is compressed. (*Uktzin* 2:8)

The Mishnah tells us that an airy loaf, which is much less dense than other foods, is nevertheless evaluated as it is, and not compressed into a density comparable to other foods. Only if there is actually a distinct large single pocket of air is it to be removed from the equation. This clearly means that it is volume being measured rather than weight. This position, emerging from this Mishnah, is found in a number of halachic authorities.[77]

We also have an explicit statement from the Geonim that *kezayit* is a measure of volume rather than weight:

> And that which you asked regarding the measure of… a *kezayit* etc., surely these are *shiurim* (designated quantities), and how can there be a designated quantity for a designated quantity? And if you suggest to give a weight, our rabbis did not explain things in terms of their weight, and the Holy One does not exact with us in weight. (*Teshuvos HaGeonim* 268)

Finally, the discussions of Rabbeinu Tam, Ri and others regarding the calculation of a *kezayit*, which were based on reconciling various statements in the Talmud concerning how much a person can hold in his throat, only make sense if the discussion is regarding volume. Yet we do find several later halachic authorities stating a weight measure for an egg, a *kezayit*, and so on. R. Yaakov Chaim Sofer (1870-1939) cites several such authorities, and affirms that this is widespread custom among all God-fearing Jews.[78] He concludes that since an egg weighs 18 *drahms* and a *kezayit* should be half an egg, a *kezayit* is 9 *drahms*. But how are we to understand these halachic authorities in light of the clear positions in the Mishnah, Geonim and Rishonim that we cited above?

There are two reasons why we nevertheless find some halachic authorities prescribing measures of weight rather than volume. One is that it is sometimes more convenient to prescribe quantities in terms of weight, especially since it is less likely to cause measuring errors. For this reason, some halachic authorities converted measures of volume to measures of weight. But this does not mean that they considered the halachic requirement to be essentially one of weight. In fact, it is pointed out that R. Yaakov Chaim Sofer, as well as all the halachic authorities that he cites,

---

[77] Rama, *Orach Chaim* 486:1; *Magen Avraham* 486:1; Chida, *Machzik Berachah* 486:2; *Mishnah Berurah* 486:3. See too *Shulchan Aruch, Orach Chaim* 456:1; Chazon Ish, *Orach Chaim* 39:17.

[78] *Kaf HaChaim* 168:46, citing *Bnei David*, and *Pesach HaDvir*, who in turns cites several others.

themselves make it clear elsewhere that halachic measures are all volume rather than weight.[79]

The second reason why some convert the measurement to weight is that, as we have seen in the Mishnah, large air pockets are not to be included in the calculation. However it is difficult to draw the line between a large air pocket and a small one. R. Chaim Na'eh therefore rules that *any* visible air pocket is not to be included in a volume measurement.[80] Since it is difficult to calculate the volume of a food item without any air pockets, a weight measure was sometimes substituted. It should be stressed, though, that R. Chaim Na'eh himself explicitly stated that the essential definition is one of volume, and that he was only converting it to weight due to this uncertainty and subsequent stringency.[81]

However, R. Chaim Na'eh's stringency in this regard was widely rejected. Contemporary halachic authorities are emphatic that the *kezayit* is to be measured by volume, not weight.[82] Nevertheless, in popular discourse, a *kezayit* is often defined in terms of weight—specifically, 30 grams. It is this that leads to the greatest quantity of matzah designated as a *kezayit*: the labeling on certain machine-made matzah stating that one whole matzah equals a *kezayit*.

Conclusion

At the beginning of this study, it was noted that logically, in order to reach the conclusion that a *kezayit* is much larger than olives are today, two separate positions must both be taken: First, that olives of ancient

---

[79] R. Eliyahu Topik, *Responsa Kol Eliyahu, Orach Chaim* 30, p. 137, pointing to *Kaf HaChaim* 456:10, *Pesach DaDvir, Kisei D'Chayay* 196a, and others; Chida, *Machzik Berachah* 486:2. A similar point is made by R. Chaim Na'eh, in *Shiurei Torah* 1:1, pp. 71-72.

[80] *Shiurei Torah* pp. 182-184.

[81] *Shiurei Torah*, 1:1, pp. 71-72. In a subsequent work, *Shiurei Tziyon* p. 18, he himself expressed reservations about his innovation.

[82] R. Avraham Yeshaya Karelitz, *Chazon Ish, Orach Chaim* 39:17; R. Tzvi Pesach Frank, *Chag Ha-Asif* p. 316; R. BenZion Abba-Shaul, Responsa *Ohr LeTziyon* p. 124; R. Ovadiah Yosef, *Chazon Ovadiah*, vol. II p. 518.

times were much larger, and second, that we are obligated to follow the size of ancient olives rather than the olives of today.

The first is refuted by empirical evidence. We have living trees from the Talmudic era, which produce olives that are exactly the same size as olives from the trees of our own era, and we have olive pits from ancient times that are similar to those of today. Furthermore, there is no testimony otherwise in any source in the Talmud or Rishonim (contrary to popular belief). In fact, there is testimony from some of the Rishonim that olives were the same size as those of today. Alleged indications from inferences regarding eggs having been larger are likewise disproved by evidence that eggs of ancient times were actually smaller.

The second position, that we are obligated to follow the size of ancient olives, was assumed by many authorities, but it is explicit in the Geonim, implicit amongst many Rishonim and acknowledged by several recent authorities that there is no such obligation.

An olive measures 4-6cc. How did it arise that virtually all halachic authorities are ruling that a *kezayit* is at the very least 17cc, and most are ruling that it is in the region of 28cc or even 50cc and more? We have seen that a combination of seven factors was involved:

- As some of them explicitly admit, the Rishonim of Ashkenaz were working with the basic disability of not being familiar with olives. In one case this led to interpreting the Talmud to mean that an olive is half the size of an egg, and in another case, it led to only being able to calculate an upper limit for an olive's possible size.

- The Rishonim of Sefarad, who were familiar with olives, never saw a need to discuss their size. Their silence on the matter led to a fundamentally misleading situation: from the discussion in the period of the Rishonim, the impression arises that there is a divide between those who rate it as measuring 1/3 of an egg and those who rate it as ½ an egg. Thus it was those who were not familiar with olives, and thereby increased its size, who formed the framework for subsequent halachic discussion.

- The view that an olive must be *less than* 1/3 of an egg, which was explicit in Rabbeinu Tam and inferred from Rambam, was simplified/misunderstood to mean that an olive is *equal to* slightly less than 1/3 of an egg.

- Difficulties with resolving various questions led to the belief that eggs and/or olives of ancient times were vastly larger than those of today. Given the lack of scientific knowledge, the understanding of the decline of generations from a golden age, as well as the intellectual climate that was pervasive at the time, this was seen as a reasonable position.

- The manuscripts from the Geonim stating that one need only follow the size of olives of one's era were only discovered and published relatively recently, as was also the case with the statements of Rashba and Ritva that olives are very small.

- The substitution of measuring by weight rather than volume, initially instituted for convenience, led some to believe that matzah ought to be measured this way. Since matzah is very lightweight, this resulted in a huge increase in volume.

- Finally, the process of halachic tradition, with its canonization and conservatism, meant that even when the above factors came to light, it was too late; the rulings had already become entrenched.

Those who have attempted to prove that a *kezayit* is the size of a regular olive have encountered strong opposition. Understanding how the alternate views arose is the key to both understanding the cause of this opposition and to overcoming it.

Postscript: Why On Earth Would Anyone Eat A *Kezayit*?

The reaction of many people to my conclusions about the *kezayit* is one of shock, followed by the question: "So do you yourself really eat such a small portion of matzah and *maror*?" Yet this is a very strange question. It sheds light on the problems caused by the evolution of the large *kezayit* measurement.

Why on earth would anyone only eat an olive-sized portion of matzah? The mitzvah comes late at night, after a really long day, when people haven't eaten for hours. Any normal person will eat much more than an olive-sized portion!

The *kezayit* is a *minimum*. The halachah says that eating anything less than a *kezayit* is simply not called an act of eating. But any ordinary act of eating is obviously more than the bare minimum! Does anyone build a sukkah ten *tefachim* high?!

So why do so many wonder if people like me will be eating an olive-sized portion? This is probably because the evolution of the large *kezayit*, along with the change from traditional *maror* (wild lettuce, sowthistle, etc.) to horseradish, has made eating a *kezayit* such a tricky and stomach-challenging ordeal that this is all that people aim for. The *Mishnah Berurah* states[83] that ideally, one should swallow the *kezayit* in a single gulp (after chewing it), which is extraordinarily difficult with enlarged sizes. Many are lenient to chew and swallow it *toch k'dei achilas pras*, "within the amount of time required to eat half a loaf of bread," which is the maximum time permitted for it to still be defined as a proper act of eating; yet even this presents a challenge with a jumbo-sized *kezayit*. Thus, people struggle to eat the *minimum* amount of food within the *maximum* time allowance!

Kezayit becomes not the minimum, less than which is simply not an act of eating, but rather the challenge, the goal. And people become so focused on eating the right quantity that this becomes the main thing that they think about—the quantity, rather than the mitzvah itself. But when you eat traditional matzah, and traditional *maror* (which was the normal *hors d'oeuvre* in antiquity), and a *kezayit* is a *kezayit*, nobody would only eat a *kezayit*. And instead of focusing on the quantity of what they are eating, they focus on its significance.

-

---

[83] *Mishnah Berurah* 475:9.

SIX

The Sages vs. Science: The Sun's Path at Night

This is a very long and intricate chapter. However, there is no other topic which better demonstrates the vast gulf between traditional approaches to Torah/science topics and contemporary non-rationalist approaches.

Introduction

The clash between reason and authority has many manifestations. But it comes to the fore with the issue of statements by the Sages of the Talmud concerning the natural world that are subsequently contradicted by science. In traditionalist circles, arguments about this topic have become especially heated in recent years, with many ultra-Orthodox authorities claiming that to attribute such error to the Sages was never a traditional view and is actually heresy.

Typically, arguments about this topic range far and wide, covering many different statements in the Talmud and Midrash. But there is one short passage in the Talmud—a mere five lines in length—which crystallizes the entire issue. Dealing with an aspect of cosmology that is outdated and obscure from a modern perspective, most students of the Talmud today gloss over it with little comprehension; indeed, the very word "cosmology" (which refers to the structure of the universe) is unfamiliar to many people. Yet when clarified, and the views of rabbinic scholars throughout the centuries on this passage are surveyed, it powerfully illustrates the radical transformation that has taken place over the ages with regard to how Jews view the Sages of the Talmud.

The Talmud describes a dispute between Jewish and gentile scholars relating to aspects of cosmology, and concludes with R. Yehuda HaNasi conceding that the gentile scholars appear to be correct:

> The Sages of Israel say, During the day, the sun travels below the firmament, and at night, above the firmament. And the scholars of the nations say, During the day the sun travels below the firmament, and at night below the ground. Rebbi said: Their words seem more correct than ours, for during the day the wellsprings are cool and at night they steam (due to being heated by the sun passing beneath them—Rashi). (*Pesachim* 94b)

When the views of rabbinic scholars throughout the centuries on this passage are surveyed, and placed in context, it powerfully illustrates the radical transformation that has taken place over the ages with regard to how Jews view the Sages of the Talmud.

Babylonian Vs. Ptolemaic Cosmology

When thinking of revolutions in astronomy, it is usually the Copernican revolution that comes to mind, and that was indeed a topic of concern to many rabbis of the early modern period. But that was not the first revolution in astronomy. Many centuries earlier there was another dramatic transformation, in which the Babylonian cosmology, to which many of the Talmudic sages subscribed, was replaced by the Ptolemaic system.[1]

The Talmud consecutively relates two disputes between Jewish and gentile scholars concerning matters of astronomy. The first is with regard to the celestial sphere which encompasses the earth, and the constellations:

> The Rabbis taught: The Sages of Israel say that the sphere is fixed and the constellations revolve [within it], and the scholars of the nations say that

---

[1] Whether this can be termed a "revolution" is debatable; see Nicholas Campion, "Was There a Ptolemaic Revolution in Ancient Egyptian Astronomy? Souls, Stars & Cosmology," *Journal of Cosmology* 13 (Feb.-Mar. 2011): 4174-86; Thomas S. Kuhn, *The Copernican Revolution: Planetary Astronomy in the Development of Western Thought* (Cambridge, MA, 1957) 108-10; and H. Floris Cohen, *The Scientific Revolution: A Historiographical Enquiry* (Chicago, IL, 1994), 21-22.

the sphere revolves [around the earth] and the constellations are fixed [within it]. (*Pesachim* 94b)

As we shall later demonstrate from both general history as well as the interpretations of the medieval rabbinic scholars, the view of the Sages of Israel was that of ancient Babylonian cosmology.[2] They believed that the earth is a roughly flat disc,[3] and the rest of the universe is a hemispherical solid dome fixed above it. The stars move around the surface of this dome; hence, "the [hemi]sphere is fixed and the constellations revolve [within it]."

The opposing view, of the gentile astronomers, was that presented by Aristotle and refined by Ptolemy in his *Almagest*. In this view, the earth is a perfect sphere, and the rest of the universe is a larger sphere[4] which encompasses it and revolves around it. The stars are permanently embedded in the surface of the larger sphere, and move along with it; hence, "the sphere revolves and the constellations are fixed."

The Talmud then cites a debate involving Rebbi (R. Yehuda HaNasi) and Rav Acha bar Yaakov:

> Rebbi said: A response to their words is that we have never found the Great Bear constellation in the south and the Scorpion constellation in the north. Rav Acha bar Yaakov objected: But perhaps it is like the axle of a millstone, or the hinges of a door socket. (*Pesachim* 94b)

Rebbi argues that if the universe was a celestial sphere revolving around the earth, in which the constellations are embedded, then the constellations should move all over the place, and yet some constellations are always found in the north, and others always in the south. But Rav

---

[2] See Wolfgang Heimpel, "The Sun at Night and the Doors of Heaven in Babylonian Texts," *Journal of Cuneiform Studies* 38 (1986): 127-51, and Moshe Simon-Shoshan, "The Heavens Proclaim the Glory of God—A Study in Rabbinic Cosmology," *Bekhol Derakheka Daehu* 20 (2008): 67-96.

[3] More precisely, they believed it to be slightly raised at the center, with the Land of Israel at the apex, and Jerusalem at the very center of the apex (Babylonian Talmud, *Kiddushin* 69a and *Sanhedrin* 87a; Midrash *Sifri*, *Ekev* 1). See too the statement of the Babylonian Talmud, *Shabbat* 65b, regarding rainfall in the Land of Israel resulting in a rise in the Euphrates (and see the comments of Rashi and Tosafot ad loc.).

[4] In fact, the model involved a series of larger spheres.

Acha bar Yaakov voices a counter-argument that the sphere could have a north-south axis around which the rotation takes place.

While some attempt to interpret this passage differently, there is evidence that the correct explanation is the straightforward one that we presented. A near-identical set of arguments is found in the writings of Cosmas Indicopleustes of Alexandria, a sixth-century monk. Cosmas, in a polemic against those who believed in a spherical earth,[5] presents the same argument used by R. Yehuda HaNasi and echoes Rav Acha bar Yaakov's counter-argument:

> But you will most effectually rebuke them if you say: Why does that [celestial] sphere of yours not revolve from the north to the south, or from some other quarter to its opposite? ...But if, again, it rolls and rotates always in the same spot without moving from place to place, then it must be upheld by supports like a turner's lathe, or an artificial globe, or on an axle like a machine or a wagon. And if so, then we must again inquire by what the supports and axles are themselves upheld, and so on *ad infinitum*... When these problems then concerning the nature of things are discussed, there remains the conclusion, as we said before, that the heaven is fixed and does not revolve. (*Christian Topography*, part I, pp. 119-120[6])

Cosmas Indicopleustes uses the same terminology as the Talmud. Like R. Yehuda HaNasi, he argues that if the universe was a celestial sphere revolving around the earth, in which the constellations are embedded, then the constellations should move all over the place, and yet some constellations are always found in the north, and others always in the south. He notes that there is a counter-argument—in the Talmud, voiced by Rav Acha bar Yaakov—that the sphere has a north-south axis around which the rotation takes place, but argues that this axis itself would require support. With identical arguments being used, we can see that the context

---

[5] Cosmas was not the only figure to engage in such battles. In the fourth century, Lactantius, a Christian advisor to Emperor Constantine, included in his *Divine Institutes* a chapter ridiculing the notion of a spherical earth (Book III Chapter XXIV).

[6] Page numbers from Montfaucon's edition, *Nova Collectio Patrum et Scriptorum Graecorum*, reprinted in the 88th volume of the *Patrologia Graeca*, ed. J.P. Migne, (Paris, 1864). Translation by J. W. McCrindle, (London, 1897).

of the dispute between the Jewish and gentile scholars was a broader dispute between the ancient Babylonian cosmology and the newer Ptolemaic model.

The Talmud immediately continues to relate another difference of opinion between the Sages and the gentile astronomers, which is the aforementioned focal point of this chapter:

> The Sages of Israel say, During the day, the sun travels below the firmament, and at night, above the firmament. And the scholars of the nations say, During the day the sun travels below the firmament, and at night below the ground. Rebbi said: Their words seem more correct than ours, for during the day the wellsprings are cool and at night they steam (due to being heated by the sun passing beneath them—Rashi). (Talmud, ibid.)

This is a corollary of the first dispute. Consistent with the ancient Babylonian cosmology, the Sages believed that when the sun sets, it cannot continue downwards, and it must instead change direction. First it turns to enter the firmament horizontally, and then after passing through the firmament, it changes direction again, rising up to pass behind the firmament back to the east.

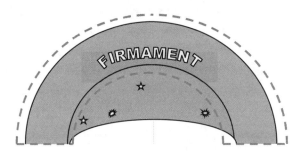

The dotted line depicts the path of the sun, according to the view of the Jewish sages.

The gentile astronomers, on the other hand, knew that the world is spherical and that the universe (or "celestial sphere," in their model) surrounds it on all sides, and thus the sun can make a full orbit around the earth. This time, instead of disputing the view of the astronomers, R. Yehuda HaNasi acknowledges that their description appears correct, since it would account for the mist rising up in the morning from natural bodies of water; he believed this mist to be steam caused by the sun heating the water from beneath. (Note that while he conceded that the sun travels on the far side of the earth at night, he did not necessarily concede that the earth is spherical.)

There are some variations in this text between different manuscripts of the Talmud, some of which we shall later discuss.[7] However, these need not concern us here; in any case, the text in our version of the Talmud is consistent with the arguments appearing in non-Jewish works of the period, as well as being more coherent than the variant texts, and thus appears to be the most accurate. By conceding to the astronomers, R. Yehuda HaNasi was accepting a significant aspect of the Ptolemaic system, which, while in error concerning geocentricity, was vastly closer to reality than the Babylonian system. His intellectual honesty is all the more striking in light of the fact that in the first dispute, he presented an argument to bolster the Babylonian cosmology.

The ancient Babylonian cosmology held by the Sages appears in many places in the Talmud,[8] such as in the following discussion:

> It was taught in a Beraita: Rabbi Eliezer says, the world is like an exedra, and the northern side is not enclosed, and when the sun reaches the north-western corner, it bends back and rises above the firmament. And Rabbi Yehoshua says, the world is like a tent, and the northern side is enclosed, and when the sun reaches the north-western corner, it circles around and returns on the other side of the dome, as it says, "traveling to the south, and circling to the north…" (Eccl. 1:6)—traveling to the south by day,

---

[7] R. Menachem Kasher discusses the variant texts in "The Form of the Earth and its Relationship to the Sun in the Works of Chazal and the Rishonim" (Hebrew) *Talpiyot* 1-2 (Sivan 5705): 155-76. We shall later discuss Kasher's conclusions.

[8] See Azariah de Rossi, *Me'or Einayim, Imrei Binah* 1:11 (Mantua, 1573-75) pp. 55b-57b; Menahem Kasher, "*Shabbat Bereshit VeShabbat Har Sinai*," *Talpiyot* 3-4: 636-39; Gad ben-Ami Tzarfati, "Talmudic Cosmography," (Hebrew) *Tarbitz* 35 (1966): 137-48, and Moshe Simon-Shoshan, "The Heavens Proclaim the Glory of God—A Study in Rabbinic Cosmology." There are also certain statements in the Talmud and Midrashim, such as Jerusalem Talmud, *Avodah Zarah* 18b, regarding Alexander rising above the world and seeing it as a ball, that *may* indicate that *some* Sages realized the earth to be spherical, but the correct interpretation of such texts is unclear.

and circling to the north by night—"it continually passes around, and the wind returns again to its circuits" (ibid.)—this refers to the eastern and western sides, which the sun sometimes passes around and sometimes traverses. (*Bava Batra* 25a-b)

Rabbi Eliezer is presenting the view attributed in *Pesachim* to the Sages of Israel,[9] in which the sun rises up behind the sky at night, while Rabbi Yehoshua is presenting a variant in which at night the sun moves horizontally along the northern edge of the celestial dome.[10] This is consistent with how others present this ancient cosmology. Severianus, Bishop of Gabala (d. 408), wrote that the earth is flat and the sun does not pass under it in the night, but travels through the northern parts "as if hidden by a wall."[11] The same view is stated by Cosmas Indicopleustes, who brings the same verse to support this position that Rabbi Yehoshua did:

> These things being so we shall say, agreeably to what we find in divine scripture, that the sun issuing from the east traverses the sky in the south and ascends northwards, and becomes visible to the whole of the inhabited world. But as the northern and western summit intervenes it produces night in the ocean beyond this earth of ours, and also in the earth beyond the ocean; then afterwards when the sun is in the west, where it is hidden by the highest portion of the earth, and runs its course over the ocean through the northern parts, its presence there makes it night for us, until in describing its orbit it comes again to the east, and again ascending the southern sky illumines the inhabited world, as the divine scripture says through the divine Solomon: "The sun rises and the sun goes down and hastens to its own place. Rising there, it goes to the south, and turns in its circuit, and the wind turns round to its circuits." (*Christian Topography*, part II, p. 134)

---

[9] As Azariah de Rossi (loc. cit.) points out, this is also consistent with numerous statements of his in *Pirkei d'Rebbi Eliezer*.

[10] Gad ben-Ami Tzarfati, "Three Notes on the Words of the Tanna'im," p. 141. Cf. Samuel Edeles (Maharsha) to *Bava Batra* 25b and also to *Bava Batra* 74b, s.v. "*Amar leih ma'or gadol ra'iti*," who writes that Rabbi Eliezer follows the Sages of Israel and Rabbi Joshua follows the gentiles.

[11] Reference from John L. Dreyer, *A History of Planetary Systems* (Cambridge, MA, 1906) p. 211.

In the Midrash, the dispute appears with some of the Sages following the Babylonian cosmology with regard to the path of the sun, others having adopted the Ptolemaic cosmology, and still others believing that the sun changes its path at different times of the year:

> How do the orbs of the sun and moon set? R. Yehudah b. R. Ila'i and the rabbis [disagree]. R. Yehudah says, behind the dome and above it. The rabbis say, behind the dome and below it. R. Yonatan said: The words of R. Yehudah b. R. Ila'i appear [correct] in the summer, when the entire world is hot and the wellsprings are cool, and the words of the rabbis, that it sets below the dome in the winter, when the whole world is cold and the wellsprings are warm. R. Shimon b. Yochai said: We do not know if they fly up in the air, if they scrape the firmament, or if they travel as usual; the matter is exceedingly difficult and it is impossible for humans to determine. (*Midrash Bereshit Rabbah* 6:8)

The Jerusalem Talmud also mentions 365 different windows in the firmament through which the sun enters the sky.[12] This view is reflected in the *siddur*, where it describes God as "piercing windows in the firmament, taking the sun out from its place."[13]

The Medieval Rationalist Approach

The first reference to this topic is found in an anonymous responsum from the Geonic period.

> [With regard to the dispute regarding the stars and spheres], this matter is not part of the laws relating to property, nor to capital offenses, and nor to ritual purity and impurity, such that a ruling would have to be determined. Nevertheless, it seems that even though Rebbi said that a response to their words is that we have never found the Great Bear constellation in the south and the Scorpion constellation in the north, and thus the sphere is fixed and the constellations revolve—it is apparent that Rabbah (in our text: Rav Aha bar Jacob) refuted Rebbi... And it is an established principle that the law is always in accordance with the later

---

[12] Jerusalem Talmud, *Rosh HaShanah* 2:5 (58a). See Daniel Sperber, *Magic and Folklore in Rabbinic Literature* (Tel Aviv, 1994), 206.

[13] *Siddur Rinat Yisrael* (Jerusalem, 2008), Shabbat morning prayers, 250.

view. And furthermore, the Talmud in *HaMokher Et HaSefinah*[14] supports Rabbah... And likewise, the gentile scholars say that during the day, the sun travels below the firmament etc., and in that case, the law follows the gentile scholars, as Rebbi said, "Their words appear more correct than ours, for by days the wells are cool, and at night they steam,"—and nobody disputes Rebbi in this. And furthermore, we ourselves see that the wells are just as Rebbi described. (*Otzar HaGeonim* (Jerusalem 1931) *Pesachim*, p. 88)

The Geonic author sees the resolution of the dispute as being of little importance, due to the lack of *halakhic* ramifications. Nevertheless, he points to a range of reasons to believe that the gentile scholars were correct, and does not evince any distress at this.[15] Rav Sherira Gaon and Rav Hai Gaon are likewise cited in later texts as stating that the view about the sun travelling through the firmament is incorrect and must be rejected.[16]

Rambam was not only unconcerned with the Sages being incorrect; he valued this passage as setting a useful precedent for other cases:

One of the ancient opinions that are widespread among the philosophers and the general run of people consists in the belief that the motion of the spheres produces very fearful and mighty sounds... This opinion also is generally known in our religious community. Do you not see that the Sages describe the might of the sound produced by the sun when it every day proceeds on its way in the sphere?... Aristotle, however, does not accept this and makes it clear that the heavenly bodies produce no sound... You should not find it blameworthy that the opinion of Aristotle disagrees with that of the Sages, may their memory be blessed, as to this point. For this opinion, I mean to say the one according to which the heavenly bodies produce sounds, is consequent upon the belief in a fixed sphere and in stars that return. You know, on the other hand, that in these astronomical matters they preferred the opinion of the sages of the nations of the world to their own. For they explicitly say: The sages of the nations of the world have vanquished. And this is correct. For everyone who

---

[14] *Bava Batra* 74a, which refers to the sphere moving.

[15] Y. Tzvi Langermann, "Hebrew Astronomy: Deep Soundings from a Rich Tradition," in *Astronomy Across Cultures: the History of Non-Western Astronomy*, ed. Helaine Selin, (Dordrecht, 2000), 557.

[16] See Moses Alashkar, *Responsa* (Sabbionetta, 1554), #96, pp. 155a-157a.

argues in speculative matters does this according to the conclusions to which he was led by his speculation. Hence the conclusion whose demonstration is correct is believed. (*Guide for the Perplexed* 2:8)

In Rambam's reference to the Talmud, there are two apparent points of divergence from our version of the Talmud. The first is that Rambam claims that the text explicitly states that the gentiles "vanquished" (*nitzhu*) them. In our text, however, R. Yehuda HaNasi only says that *venir'in divrehen midvarenu*, "their words appear more [correct] than ours."[17] One suggestion is that Rambam was paraphrasing the text according to his understanding of it (or from memory).[18] However, as we shall see, Rabbeinu Tam quoted the same version as Rambam, and thus it appears that there was a legitimate alternate text of the Talmud in circulation at that time.[19]

The second point of divergence is that Rambam apparently cites R. Yehuda HaNasi's verdict in reference to the first dispute in the Talmud, concerning the sphere and the constellations, instead of with regard to the second dispute, concerning sun's path at night. In our text, R. Yehuda HaNasi did not endorse the gentile scholars' position in the first dispute; instead, he challenged it. As we shall see, a number of other authorities also recorded the gentiles as having triumphed in the first dispute, concerning the spheres and constellations.[20]

---

[17] As we shall see, there were later rabbinic figures such as R. Yosef Ashkenazi who interpreted the word "appear" to mean that R. Yehuda HaNasi only accepted that the gentile scholars had presented superior arguments for their position, but not that they were ultimately correct. Ironically, however, Rabbeinu Tam, who (like Ashkenazi) also believed that the Sages of Israel were actually correct and that the gentile astronomers had only presented superior arguments, quoted the Talmud with the same terminology as did Maimonides.

[18] Azariah de Rossi, *Me'or Einayim, Imrei Binah* 1:11.

[19] Sid Z. Leiman, cited by Joanna Weinberg, *The Light of the Eyes* (New Haven, CT, 2001), 204-5, note 20.

[20] R. Shmuel Ibn Tibbon was the first to raise this difficulty; see *Ma'amar Yikavu Ha-Mayim* (Pressburg, 1837), p. 52; see Carlos Fraenkel, *From Rambam to Samuel ibn Tibbon: The Transformation of the Dalalat al Ha'irin into the Moreh ha-Nevukhim* (Jerusalem, 2007), 220-22.

Some suggest that Rambam was working with a different text of the Talmud, in which R. Yehudah HaNasi conceded to the gentile scholars in the first dispute.[21] However, this approach is not confirmed by any manuscript evidence.

Another approach is possible. A careful reading shows that Rambam refers to the gentiles being correct in "such matters" of astronomy. Rambam may have meant that in the same way as R. Yehudah HaNasi concedes that the gentiles were correct with regard to the sun's path at night, it has likewise since become clear that they were correct in the former dispute, too.

Yet another possibility emerges from the discussion by Rambam's son Rabbeinu Avraham (1186-1237). He notes, as we did, that the view of the Jewish scholars that the sun passes behind the firmament at night is linked to the view that the sphere is fixed and the constellations revolve in it—both being aspects of the ancient Babylonian cosmology. Accordingly, when R. Yehudah HaNasi conceded that the gentiles were correct regarding the sun's path at night, this meant that they also must have been correct regarding the sphere revolving and the stars being fixed in it.

Rambam was the paradigmatic rationalist, and his approach to this topic is consistent with rationalism. His son R. Avraham famously cites this story to prove that the Sages of the Talmud did not possess a Divine source of knowledge for their statements about the natural world, and cites R. Yehudah HaNasi's concession to the non-Jewish scholars as an example of intellectual honesty.[22] Rambam's disciple R. Shmuel Ibn Tibbon notes that the Sages' error is unsurprising in light of the fact that astronomy in the Talmudic era was greatly deficient, and adds that even in his day there are many unresolved questions in astronomy.[23] The thirteenth-century Provencal rationalist R. Yitzchak b. Yedaiah notes that unlike the sages of the Land of Israel, who were flawless experts in

---

[21] Moses Maimonides, *The Guide for the Perplexed*, ed. Solomon Munk (Paris, 1856), vol. II p. 79 note 1.

[22] Rabbeinu Avraham ben HaRambam, *Ma'amar Al Derashot Hazal, Milhamot Hashem*, ed. R. Margaliot (Jerusalem, 1953): 83-84.

[23] *Yikavu HaMayim* (Pressburg, 1837), 52.

astronomy and knew full well that the stars are embedded in the sphere(!), the Jewish sages of Babylon accepted that they were deficient in this knowledge and thus engaged in discussion and debate with the gentiles, unashamed to be vanquished.[24] Both R. Bachya b. Asher (d. 1340)[25] and R. Menachem b. Aharon ibn Zerah (Spain, d. 1385)[26] note that the Sages conceded to the gentiles that the stars are fixed in the spheres.

But it is not only Spanish rationalists who accepted that R. Yehudah HaNasi rejected the view of the Sages. This acceptance was widespread, for two reasons. One was that it was the clear and straightforward meaning of the Talmud. Another was that for medieval scholars of Islamic lands, educated in astronomy, Ptolemaic cosmology was considered established fact; it was thus self-evident that the Sages had been mistaken in thinking that the sphere was fixed and the sun passes behind the firmament at night.

We thus find many medieval scholars mentioning that the Sages' views had been rejected. The Tosafist R. Eliezer b. Samuel of Metz (1115-1198) suggests that the reason why one must knead matzah dough only with water that had sat the night after being drawn is to prevent it from being heated during the night by the sun, which is passing beneath the earth at that time. He notes that this follows the view of the gentile scholars, which R. Yehudah HaNasi had concluded to appear correct.[27] R. Eliezer b. Samuel's view is quoted, endorsed and further explained by R. Asher ben Yechiel ("Rosh," 1250-1328),[28] notwithstanding his position that the critical speculations of secular wisdoms have no place within tradition-

---

[24] See Marc Saperstein, *Decoding the Rabbis: A Thirteenth-Century Commentary on the Aggadah* (Cambridge, MA, 1980), 23-24.

[25] Commentary to the Torah (Warsaw, 1879), Genesis 1:14, p. 12.

[26] *Tzedah la-Derekh* (Warsaw, 1880), part I, ch. 25, p. 17a.

[27] R. Eliezer of Metz, *Sefer Yere'im* (Warsaw, 1931), vol. I, section 2 - *akhilot*, #52, p. 22. See R. Avraham Abba's commentary *To'afot Re'em* for an important correction to the text of *Sefer Yere'im*. On the other hand, in section 7, *Mehalelei Shabbat* #274 (numbered in some editions as #102), p. 302, he does adopt the view that the luminaries pass behind the firmament.

[28] Rosh, Pesachim 2:30 and *Responsa*, (Jerusalem, 1994), *Kelal* 14, #2, p. 71.

based Judaism, as well as by R. Yerucham b. Meshullam (1280-1350),[29] R. Moshe b. Yaakov (13th century),[30] and R. Yom Tov b. Avraham Asevilli ("Ritva," 1250-1330).[31] R. Manoach b. Yaakov (13th-14th century) likewise states that one must use drawn water that has stood overnight because of R. Yehudah HaNasi's concession that the sun passes beneath the world at night.[32]

R. Todros ben Joseph Abulafia (ca.1225-ca.1285) was a rabbinic leader in Castille and a kabbalist. In arguing how the esoteric knowledge traditionally known as *sod ha-ibbur* (lit. "the secret of intercalation") could not refer to astronomy, he points out that gentile astronomers were more accomplished in this field than the Sages, as evinced by their triumphing over the Sages with regard to the spheres and constellations. In a particularly sharp comment, R. Abulafia adds that "anyone who has tasted even a little knowledge knows that there is not a fool in the world [today] who believes that the sphere is stationary."[33] R. Yeshaya di Trani (1180-1250) observes that the view of the gentile scholars is the main ("*ikkar*") view.[34]

We see that it was widely accepted that this topic demonstrated the Sages of the Talmud to be fallible regarding the natural sciences. But it should be noted that the fact of scholars in Ashkenaz acknowledging that

---

[29] *Toldot Adam Ve-Havah* (Istanbul, 1516), *Netiv* 5, Part 3, p. 41b. However, in *Netiv* 12, Part 1, p. 65a, he approvingly cites Rabbeinu Tam's view that the Sages were actually correct.

[30] *Sefer Mitzvot Ha-Gadol* (Venice 1547), *Mitzvot Lo Ta'aseh* #79, p. 31a. Note that in *Mitzvot Asei* #32 he endorses the view of Rabbeinu Tam, which, as we shall later note, relates to the position that the Sages were actually correct. However, it seems that that connection was not made by R. Moshe b. Yaakov.

[31] Commentary on the Haggadah, s.v. *Matzah zo she'anu okhlim* (Warsaw, 1876), p. 25b.

[32] *Sefer Ha-Menuha* (Pressburg, 1879), Laws of *Hametz* and *Matzah* 5:11, s.v. *Ela bemayim shelanu*, p. 23b.

[33] *Sefer HaKavod* to *Ketubot* 111a, printed in Leon A. Feldman, "*Otzar HaKavod HaShalem lemasekhet Ketubot leRabbeinu Todrus HaLevi Abulafia miTolitula*," *Sefer HaYovel leKavod Shalom Baron*, vol. 3 (Jerusalem, 1984), 309-10.

[34] *Tosafot Rid*, ed. Moses Reinhold (Levov, 1862), *Shabbat* 34b, s.v. *Eizehu* (no page numbers printed).

the Sages were in error does not necessarily indicate that they had rationalistic leanings away from the idea of the superiority of the ancients, or a grasp and acceptance of Ptolemaic cosmology. Rather, it may well have more to do with their reverence for the Talmud in its straightforward meaning. It is the simple, straightforward meaning of the Talmud that there was a dispute regarding the physical reality and that R. Yehudah HaNasi preferred the view of the non-Jewish scholars. The Ashkenaz scholars may well have reasoned that if the great R. Yehudah HaNasi said that the Sages of Israel were incorrect, who are they to disagree? Still, if they would have considered it entirely unthinkable for any of the Sages to have been in error, no doubt they would have found a way to say so, as indeed did many later figures.

Rabbeinu Tam's Radical Approach

There was one medieval scholar who did find a way to say that the Sages of Israel were actually correct. In contrast to all the other medieval scholars, R. Yaakov b. Meir ("Rabbeinu Tam," c. 1100–c. 1171) is cited as follows:

> And likewise I have heard in the name of Rabbeinu Tam, of blessed memory, that he would say regarding that which is said in the chapter *Mi Shehaya Tamei* that the Sages of Israel said that the sphere is fixed and the constellations revolve within it… and it is said there, "R. Yehudah HaNasi said, A response to their words etc…" And Rabbeinu Tam said, that even though the gentile scholars were victorious over the Sages of Israel, that is a victory in arguments, but the truth is in accordance with the Sages of Israel, and that is what we say in prayer, "Who pierces the windows of the firmament" (*Shitah Mekubetzet* to *Ketuvot* 13b, s.v. *mai ka-amar lehu*, p. 126)

In Rabbeinu Tam's writings elsewhere, this view relates to a contradiction between two statements in the Talmud which give differing definitions of the duration from sunset to nightfall. Rabbeinu Tam resolves this contradiction by explaining that there are two stages of sunset. The first takes place when the sun stops moving downwards and instead moves horizontally to enter the firmament via a window. The second occurs when it has completed its journey through the four-*mil* thickness of the firmament and begins to move up and around behind it.[35] This view has important *halakhic* consequences for the time at which the Sabbath is considered to depart.

It may seem remarkable that as late as the twelfth century, Rabbeinu Tam was still maintaining a view of the sun passing behind the sky at night, which suggests that he fully subscribed to Babylonian cosmology, including a flat earth. This attests to the lack of schooling in science by the Jews of northern France, who were evidently unaware of the Ptolemaic model that was standard elsewhere. This was not a uniquely Jewish phenomenon; Christian Europe itself was only just beginning to absorb the new astronomy from Islamic scholars.[36] Discoveries take time to be accepted, and obsolete theories can survive in the face of overwhelming evidence to the contrary; Ptolemaic cosmology would in turn be taught in the universities long after it had been discredited.

More surprising is that even Ramban (Nachmanides) approvingly cites Rabbeinu Tam's view.[37] The wonder of this is only partially mitigated by noting that, despite his rationalistic leanings and studies of philosophy, Ramban's formative education was under the Tosafists, and he had no training in the sciences.[38] But this would not account for how R. Nissim of Gerona, who was not only educated in Spain but was even an astronomer, also adopts Rabbeinu Tam's model.[39] It is true that a number

---

[35] *Tosafot* to *Pesachim* 94a, s.v. Rabbi Yehudah; Rabbeinu Tam, *Sefer HaYashar*, ed. S. Schlesinger (Jerusalem, 1959), *Helek Ha-Hiddushim* #221, *Shabbat* 34b, p. 139. See too Rashba's discussion of Rabbeinu Tam's view in *Hidushei HaRashba, Shabbat* 34b, and also R. Avraham de Boton, *Lehem Mishneh*, in Maimonides, *Mishneh Torah*, Vol. II - *Zemanim* (Warsaw 1882), Laws of Sabbath 5:4, p. 22.

[36] Frank Durham and Robert D. Purrington, *Frame of the Universe: A History of Physical Cosmology* (New York, NY, 1983), 77-78.

[37] *Kitvei HaRamban*, ed. C. Chavel (Jerusalem, 1963), vol. II, *Torat Ha-Adam*, p. 251. Cf. his commentary to Gen. 1:5 (ed. M. Chavel, Jerusalem, 1959), p. 18, where he demonstrates awareness of the Ptolemaic model.

[38] Y. Tzvi Langermann, "Torah and Science: Five Approaches from Medieval Spain," in José Luiz Goldfarb & Márcia M. H. Ferraz, eds., *Anais do VII Seminário Nacional de História da Ciência e da Tecnologia* (São Paulo, 2000), 36.

[39] *Chiddushei HaRan* to Alfasi, Shabbat 34b.

of medieval and later authorities adopted Rabbeinu Tam's view regarding the existence of two stages of sunset, and many early modern scholars noted that this did not mean that they believed the Sages to have been correct regarding the sun's path at night.[40] However, it is more difficult to say this with authorities such as Ramban and R. Nissim of Gerona, who explicitly described Rabbeinu Tam's view as involving the sun passing behind the firmament. Yet, as we shall later see, these were not the only ones to take this view; we find such positions lasting through to the eighteenth century!

But the question to be addressed is what motivated Rabbeinu Tam to adopt this approach. Many contemporary non-rationalist advocates of Rabbeinu Tam's approach base themselves on the position that the Sages of the Talmud must be right, since they were spiritual and intellectual giants who possessed Divine inspiration and who knew all the metaphysical secrets of the universe. They therefore cannot accept the notion that the gentile scholars were right and the Jewish sages wrong, and they adopt Rabbeinu Tam's view that the Jewish sages were actually correct. But this was apparently not the basis for the position of Rabbeinu Tam himself. For if Rabbeinu Tam was of the view that the Sages were such divinely-inspired geniuses, then how could it be proposed that they were not able to provide adequate arguments for their position, especially since (according to Rabbeinu Tam) they had physical reality on their side!

One might suggest that what motivated Rabbeinu Tam was simply harmonizing disparate texts (regarding differing definitions of the duration from sunset to nightfall), in the standard manner of Tosafists.[41]

---

[40] See, for example, R. David ben Solomon ibn Zimra, *She'eilot U'Teshuvot Radbaz* (Jerusalem, 1882), Part IV, #282, p. 150; R. Chizkiyah da Silva, *Kuntrus Binah Ve'Da'at* (also known as *Kuntrus D'vei Shamsha*, Krakow, 1927), p. 5b-6a; R. Avraham Cohen Pimentel, *Minhat Kohen* (Amsterdam, 1668), *Sefer Mevo HaShemesh* 1:4, pp. 10b-12a.

[41] Y. Tzvi Langermann, "Hebrew Astronomy: Deep Soundings from a Rich Tradition," in *Astronomy Across Cultures: The History of Non-Western Astronomy*, ed. Helaine Selin, (Dordrecht, 2000), 565. For discussion of the general approach of the Tosafists in harmonizing disparate texts, see Israel M. Ta-Shma, *Creativity and Tradition: Studies in Medieval Rabbinic Scholarship, Literature and Thought* (Cambridge, MA, 2006), p. 88.

However, it does not seem plausible that he could have done so had he been aware of the power of the Ptolemaic model.

It seems that Rabbeinu Tam believed the Sages to have been correct in their statement due to his understanding of cosmology—that is to say, that he still maintained the ancient Babylonian view of the universe and had never been taught the Ptolemaic model.[42] Accordingly, in Rabbeinu Tam's view, it is not that the Sages *must* have been correct in their dispute with the gentiles, but rather that they *happened* to have been correct, even though they were not able to prove their case.

The same certainly appears true for Ramban. Ramban was not averse to saying that the Sages of the Talmud may have been mistaken in their scientific beliefs.[43] Thus, his apparent belief that they were correct in their description of the sun's path at night presumably stems from his believing that the reality demonstrates them to have actually been correct, rather than an *a priori* assumption that they *must* have been correct.

To sum up: In general, the Geonim and medieval rabbinic scholars followed the straightforward reading of the Talmud, according to which R. Yehudah HaNasi conceded that the view of the gentile astronomers appeared to be correct. A notable exception was Rabbeinu Tam, who argued that the concession was only with regard to gentiles being able to better argue their position, but that the Babylonian cosmology of the Sages was nevertheless correct. However, it seems that Rabbeinu Tam was motivated by considerations other than a refusal to accept any shortcomings on the part of the Sages.

Continuations of the Rationalist Approach

R. Moshe ben Yitzchak Alashkar ("Maharam Alashkar," 1456-1542), discusses the view of Rabbeinu Tam concerning there being two parts of sunset (which we shall soon explore), which is based on the belief that the

---

[42] Incidentally, as R. David Yehudah Leib Silverstein points out in *Shevilei David* (Jerusalem, 1862), *Orah Haim* no. 455, p. 96b, Rabbeinu Tam's grandfather Rashi also appears to have maintained the Babylonian cosmology; see Rashi's comments to *Ta'anit* 25b, s.v. *Bein Tehoma*, and to *Eruvin* 56b, s.v. *Zehu Pnei Tzafon*.

[43] See his commentary to Leviticus 12:2.

Sages were actually correct in saying that the sun passes behind the sky at night. He observes that the Geonim, Rambam and numerous other medieval scholars accepted the view of the gentiles, as did R. Yehudah HaNasi himself, and he brings further scientific proofs for its veracity.[44] R. David ben Shlomo ibn Zimra ("Radbaz," 1479-1573) describes the Sages as having recanted and conceded to the gentiles.[45] R. Eliyahu Mizrachi (1450-1526), in arguing that it is permissible to teach science to non-Jews, brings evidence for his position from the dispute between the Sages and the gentile astronomers regarding the sun's path at night, which indicates that there was a discussion between them on such matters; and he notes in passing that R. Yehudah HaNasi decided that the view of the gentiles appears more correct.[46] Even such a dedicated kabbalist as Rabbi Moshe Cordovero ("Ramak," 1522-1570), describes the Sages as having recanted and conceded to the gentile astronomers.[47]

R. Avraham ben Moshe de Boton ("*Lechem Mishneh*," 1545-1585), in referring to the dispute concerning the sun's path at night, also describes the non-Jewish scholars as having triumphed (*nitzchu*) over the Jewish sages, using the stronger terminology that appears in Rambam's *Guide*.[48] He also notes that the view of the non-Jewish scholars is confirmed (*sevara beduka*) and points out (following R. Eliezer of Metz) that the Jewish sages themselves ended up establishing the laws of *mayim shelanu* based on the view of the non-Jewish scholars. Like Maharam Alashkar, *Lechem Mishneh* concludes that the view of Rabbeinu Tam, which is based on the belief that the Sages of Israel were actually correct, is problematic.

Still more positive towards this passage of the Talmud was R. Azariah de Rossi (1513-1578). Citing Rambam and elaborating further, he utilized this passage as a foundation for his position that the Sages were fallible in such matters of science; de Rossi describes at length how many

---

[44] *Shailot u'Teshuvot Maharam Alashkar* (Sabbionetta, 1554), #96, pp. 155a-157a.

[45] *Shailot u'Teshuvot Radbaz* (Jerusalem, 1882), Part IV, #282, pp. 148-9.

[46] *Shailot u'Teshuvot R. Eliyahu Mizrachi*, (Jerusalem, 1938) #57, pp. 177-8.

[47] *Pardes Rimonim* (Karetz, 1780) 6:3, p. 30. He takes it in reference to the dispute concerning whether the sphere or the constellations are fixed.

[48] *Lechem Mishneh* to *Mishneh Torah, Hilchot Shabbat* 5:4.

passages in the Talmud and Midrash reflect an obsolete cosmology, as well as other empirical errors.[49] De Rossi's writings aroused the severe ire of Maharal, as we shall later discuss.

Rabbi Avraham Menachem Rapoport (1520-1596) interprets the Scriptural account of God placing the luminaries in the firmament as being consistent with the view of the gentiles that the stars are fixed in the spheres, and he notes that the Jewish sages conceded to the gentiles regarding this point.[50] R. Shmuel Eliezer Edels ("Maharsha," 1555-1631) also describes the Jewish sages as having conceded to the non-Jewish scholars regarding the sun's path at night.[51] R. Avraham Cohen Pimentel (*Minchat Cohen*, d. 1697), points out that the view that sun goes behind the sky at night is simply not true and can be proven false.[52]

R. Chaim Bachrach ("*Chavot Ya'ir*," 1638-1702) was a towering halachist who also studied astronomy. A descendant of Maharal, his approach to this topic is certainly not one of which his ancestor would approve. While, as we shall later note, he was uncertain as to whether the gentile scholars were ultimately correct, he accepts that this may well be the case and that Rambam saw it that way:

> The blemish of one who errs in the study of Kabbalah is greater than that of one who errs in astronomy... albeit the common denominator [of Kabbalah and astronomy] is that [such errors reflect] mistaken understanding of the reality. And [in astronomy, unlike Kabbalah] almost nothing is entirely agreed upon and not subject to dispute, as per the dispute between the Jewish and gentile sages regarding whether the sphere is fixed and the constellations revolve, or the sphere moves and the constellations are fixed in it. And see *The Guide for the Perplexed* Part II, the end of Chapter 8 and Chapter 9, (where Rambam cites the dispute

---

[49] *Me'or Einayim* (Mantua, 1573-75), *Imrei Binah* 1:11 pp. 55b-57b.

[50] *Mincha Belula* (Verona, 1594), Bereshit 1:17, p. 3b.

[51] *Chidushei Aggadot* to *Bava Basra* 25b, s.v. *Rabi Eliezer omer.* Note that in *Ta'anit* 9b he describes a dispute between the sages regarding the source of rain, for which each side brings Scriptural proofs, as "hinging on the views of the scientists, according to the opinions of the philosophers."

[52] *Minchat Kohen, Sefer Mevo HaShemesh* 1:4, discussing how Rabbeinu Tam's view concerning sunset is not viable from a scientific perspective.

and says that the non-Jewish scholars were correct); and the Tannaim dispute whether the sun travels above the covering of the sky at night or below the earth... (*Responsa Chavot Ya'ir* #210; see too #219)

R. Chizkiya da Silva (1659-1698), author of the important *Pri Chadash* commentary to the *Shulchan Aruch*, notes that the opinion of the Sages of Israel regarding the sun's path at night was mistaken.[53] He adds that this incorrect view seems to have been the opinion of all the Tanna'im and Amora'im.

R. Yitzchak Lampronti (1679-1756) had a complex, even contradictory attitude towards disputes between the Sages and science. On some occasions, he writes that the Sages knew all wisdom and that objections for scientists should be rejected.[54] But on another occasion, he states that the Sages seem to have erred in stating that lice spontaneously generate, and cites the dispute concerning the spheres and constellations as an example of the Sages themselves conceding that they were in error.[55]

It is perhaps surprising that Rabbi Moshe Schick ("Maharam Schick," 1805-1879), despite being a student of the famously conservative R. Moshe Sofer,[56] did not insist on the infallibility of the Talmudic sages. While he notes that our version of the Talmud does not state, as Rambam has it, that the Talmudic sages were definitively proven wrong, he does accept that R. Yehudah HaNasi judges them to be likely mistaken, and notes that their position on this matter was not based on divine sources of knowledge:

---

[53] *Kuntrus Binah Ve'Da'at* (also known as *Kuntrus D'vei Shamsha*), (Krakow 1927), p. 5b.

[54] *Pachad Yitzchak*, vol. 6, *erech nikkur*, p. 85a.

[55] *Pachad Yitzchak, erech tzeidah*. In *Pachad Yitzchak*, vol. 4 p. 72b, *erech klayos yoatzos,* he notes that he sometimes maintains that the Sages had divine sources of knowledge for their statements and sometimes does not. For a discussion of Lampronti's approach, see David Malkiel, "Empiricism in Isaac Lampronti's *Pahad Yishaq," Materia Giudaica* 10 (2005) pp. 341-351.

[56] Although even R. Moshe Sofer ("Chassam Sofer") was not so conservative in these issues; discussing an anatomical issue in the Mishnah, he dismisses the explanation of Rashi and Tosafos as being not in accordance with the physical reality (Commentary to *Niddah* 18a).

Regarding the question concerning what is written in Tosafot, *Berachot* 2b, s.v. "*dilma*," in Rashi, *Pesachim* 93b, s.v. "*mei'alot hashachar*," and in several other places, that the sun enters into the thickness of the firmament [at night]—which contradicts the conclusion of the Gemara on *Pesachim* 94b, where Rebbi says, "Their view (that the sun travels beneath the earth at night) appears more correct (*nir'in*) than our own"; and where the word *nir'in* is used, Tosafot on *Eruvin* 46b, s.v. "Rabbi Eliezer etc." writes that we rule accordingly, and the Rosh, in Chapter *Kol Sha'ah*, and the Tur and *Beit Yosef* (*Orach Chaim* 455) concur, as they quote from Rabbi Eliezer of Metz that the sun travels beneath the earth at night, and we therefore knead matzah dough only with water that has sat at least one night since being drawn. Even more perplexing (than Rashi and Tosafot's contradiction to the Gemara's conclusion) is the statement established in the Shabbat prayers: "He who opens daily the doors of the gates of the east and breaches the windows of the sky; He brings the sun out from its place, and the moon from its resting-place, and illuminates the world"— which implicitly concurs with the view that the sun enters the thickness of the firmament at night.

It seems to me that matters that were not received by the Sages as *halachah leMoshe miSinai*, but rather which they said according to their own reasoning—and with something that is not received [from Sinai] and has no root in our Torah, but rather comes from investigation and experience, it is difficult to determine [that it is true]. And there are many occasions when the sages determined, according to their own intellects, that a matter was a certain way, and the subsequent generation analyzed the matter further and disputed the earlier view. Any conclusion drawn from experimentation can only be considered probable, [not certain]. Indeed, in the dispute on *Pesachim* 94b, Rebbi said that the gentile sages' view *appeared* more correct, but he did not express certainty; for a matter like this, which is investigated only by finding evidence [of one view or the other], cannot be resolved with certainty. In truth, according to the reading of the Gemara found in *The Guide for the Perplexed*, the Jewish sages recanted their position; but according to our reading, Rebbi said only that the gentile sages' view *appears* more correct... (Responsa Maharam Schick, *Even ha-Ezer*, Responsum #7)

Maharam Schick further states that while Rebbi was only able to say that the view of the gentiles appears more likely to be correct, in his time scientific experimentation has shown it to be clearly the case:

> Regarding the fundamental issue: the text of the [Shabbat] prayer quoted above has already been questioned in *Sefer HaBrit, ma'amar 4—Shnei Me'orot*, Chap. 20, where he explains that it is the poetic style to describe things based on how they appear to the human observer [as opposed to how they really happen]. Regardless, in our Gemara it is not decided one way or the other, and we must therefore observe the stringencies resultant from each view. Therefore with regard to water passing the night we implement the stringency resulting from the gentile scholars' view; while Rashi and Tosafot described the sun's movement according to the Jewish sages of the time of the dispute in the Talmud. Although scientists now agree—and it is apparent to the eye and by experimentation—that the sun travels below the earth at night, the Shabbat prayer describes it based on how it appears to us... (Ibid.)

Another disciple of Chatam Sofer, R. Eliezer Lipman Neusatz of Magendorf (c. 1797-1858), observes that the Sages were mistaken in their belief about the sun's path at night, and that they accepted the opinion of the gentiles, just as "one accepts the truth from whoever says it."[57] He notes that this was not the only instance of their making statements about the universe which are now known to be incorrect, and explains that the Sages were simply putting forward their own beliefs, which they occasionally attached to Scriptural verses by way of *asmachta*.

A contemporary and correspondent of Maharam Schick, R. David Yehudah Leib Silberstein (d. 1884), was a prominent Hungarian rabbi who likewise noted that R. Yehudah HaNasi had conceded that the Sages of Israel were mistaken in their view that the sun slips under the firmament at night to pass behind it (and points out that Rashi in several places seems to have followed this incorrect view).[58] He adds "and so too is indeed the case [that the Sages of Israel were mistaken], for the sphere of the earth is in the center of space, with the sun making a circuit around

---

[57] *Mei Menuchot* (Pressburg 1884), pp. 36a-39a. Chatam Sofer referred to R. Neusatz as his "son, pupil and bracelet" in his 1839 approbation to his book *Betzir Eli'ezer*.

[58] *Shevilei David, Orach Chaim* (Jerusalem 1862) no. 455, p. 96b.

it…" R. Silberstein also notes that while R. Yehudah HaNasi was correct to concede to the view of the gentile scholars, his reasons for doing so (regarding bodies of water being heated by the sun passing below the earth) were incorrect and were based on his not knowing about the existence of continents on the other side of the world. He also adds that some of the Talmud's earlier discussions of the cosmos are also based upon their original, mistaken view of the firmament. Later, R. Silberstein presents a defense against those who would ask how the Sages of Israel could have thought that the sun passes behind the sky at night, in light of the fact that at the North Pole, there is daylight for half the year; he responds that since the Land of Israel is the designated homeland for the Jewish People, the Sages never sought to investigate matters in distant countries. Apparently uncomfortable with this extensive analysis of the Sages' mistaken beliefs, he concludes his discussion by noting that the real wisdom to be sought after and cherished is the esoteric wisdom of the Upper World, and that there is no reason to busy oneself with knowledge of the physical universe, which is of no importance.

It is not only among Mitnagdim that we find authorities who conceded that this passage in the Talmud reveals the Sages of Israel to have erred in their understanding of the cosmos. In the Hassidic world, Rabbi Yisrael Friedman of Ruzhin (1797-1850) also admits this, saying that because the gentiles dedicated themselves to lower forms of wisdom such as the natural sciences, they were able to attain greater proficiency in them than the Jews, who dedicate themselves to higher forms of wisdom.[59]

While Rabbi Samson Raphael Hirsch (1808-1888) condemned Rambam as having been unduly influenced by Greek philosophy, he does follow the same approach as Rambam with regard to the scientific knowledge of the Sages. In a letter written to Rabbi Pinchos Wechsler,[60] he stresses that the Sages' statements about the natural world were not based on Sinaitic tradition or prophetic inspiration. He writes that the Sages themselves "respected the opinion of the gentile scholars, admitting

---

[59] Cited by Rabbi Menachem Nachum Friedman in *Masechet Avos Im Perush Man*, p. 8.

[60] Published by Rabbi Dr. Mordechai Breuer in *Hama'ayan* 16:2 (Tevet 5736/1976) pp. 1-16.

when the opinion of the latter seemed more correct than their own," citing the dispute concerning the sun's path at night as clear proof for this.

But perhaps the most surprising endorsement of the straightforward approach to this topic is that of the kabbalist Chacham Yosef Chaim (Ben Ish Chai, 1832-1909). In his early writings, which we shall later cite, he insists that the Sages of Israel must have actually been correct. But in his later writings, he echoes Rambam's approach when discussing the statements of R. Eliezer and R. Yehoshua regarding the sun passing behind the firmament at night:

> Know that regarding what R. Eliezer and R. Yehoshua say here regarding the motion of the sun, was said according to their intellectual assessment, according to whatever seemed true to them in the science of astronomy. And they did not determine these things and establish them as true; rather, each went according to whatever appeared to him in accordance with his principles of astronomy; they did not say these things as a tradition from their teachers. And therefore, nowadays, when the principles of astronomy are widespread, and they have devised observational tools for the stars and constellations and the globe and the elevations of the sun, they have seen and know many things that can be genuinely determined and universally agreed upon, [such as that] the sun travels below the earth at night on the other side of the globe… And if the Sages of Israel said this from their tradition, how could it be said that the words of the non-Jewish scholars seem more correct? And how could one bring a proof from the argument regarding steaming waters to contradict matters that were received via tradition, Heaven forbid? Rather, it is certain that the Sages of Israel did not determine these things to establish them as true; rather, they said that their intellectual assessment suggests it according to the science of astronomy that they possessed in their era, and they only suggested it as a possibility… (Chacham Yosef Chaim, *Benayahu*, *Bava Batra* 25b)

We see that even some staunch traditionalists, Chassidim and mystics nevertheless accepted that this topic demonstrated the Sages of the Talmud to be fallible regarding the natural sciences. This was because the Talmud clearly and unambiguously stated as such. Nevertheless, this did not prevent others from interpreting it differently, as we shall now see.

Sixteenth-Century Revolutions

As we have seen, there is a long tradition of those who accepted the straightforward reading of the Talmud, without showing any signs of concern. But it was in the sixteenth century[61] that we first find those who are greatly uncomfortable with this passage in the Talmud. Five distinct novel categories of response emerge in this period:

(I)   Reluctant acceptance of the Talmud in its plain meaning, with apologetic explanations of how the Sages could have been incorrect and/or suggestions that the matter has not been definitively resolved;

(II)   Reinterpretation of certain terms such that the Sages were not saying anything inaccurate;

(III)   Reframing the entire discussion as referring to mystical concepts rather than astronomy;

(IV)   Ignoring the general errors in the cosmology of the Sages and focusing upon one aspect in which they were vindicated;

(V)   Flat-out denying that the Sages could have been mistaken.

We shall explore these categories in turn, showing how various figures adopted each of these approaches, and how these were followed in later centuries.

I. Apologetic Acceptance: R. Yitzchak Arama and Abarbanel

R. Yitzchak Arama (*Akeidat Yitzchak*, 1420-1494) describes the non-Jewish scholars as having triumphed (*nitzhu*) over the Jewish sages, using the stronger terminology that appears in Rambam's *Guide*, and also refers to the Jewish sages as having conceded to the non-Jewish scholars. While understanding R. Yehuda HaNasi's statement as referring to the first dispute regarding whether the sphere or the constellations are fixed, he makes some important comments about why he believes the non-Jews to be superior in their knowledge of astronomy:

---

[61] Note that, borrowing a well-accepted idea first proposed by Fernand Braudel, I am referring here to the "long" sixteenth century, beginning with Isaac Arama (1420-1494) and Isaac Abarbanel (1437-1508), and concluding with Joseph Delmedigo (1591-1655).

This truth was discovered first by the gentile scholars and their kingdoms because of their immense efforts in pursuing this study [of astronomy], which they concentrated on in order to serve [the heavenly bodies]... in the foreign ways of their religions, which the Torah forbade; while the Jewish sages did not need to know [all this astronomy]—except as it related to the intercalation of months and the timing of the seasons and the new moons, necessary for the Torah and [its] commandments.... The rest they considered foreign and a waste of time—foreign matters that they were never permitted to study.... (*Akeidat Yitzhak, Parashat Bo,* Chap. 37, p. 46a)

R. Arama accepts that the Sages had an incorrect view, but in contrast to all his predecessors, he provides an explanation for this error that serves to prevent the Sages from being cast in a negative light in any way. His explanation even serves to elevate the Sages, arguing that their error was the result of such studies being beneath them.

R. Yitzchak Abarbanel (Portugal 1437-1508) was influenced by a wide range of cultures, and his attitude to this topic is far from absolute.[62] He cites Rambam's conclusion that the gentiles disproved the Sages' view that the constellations possess independent motion. Abarbanel presents an explanation as to how the Sages took their position due to a particular astronomical theory of Pliny and Plotinus that was prevalent in their day, so as to avoid people thinking that the Sages arrived at their view due to intellectual shortcomings.[63] (Note that by positing that the Sages could be excused in light of the information at their disposal, Abarbanel demonstrates his Renaissance humanist awareness of the significance of historical context.)

Initially it appears that Abarbanel is not disagreeing with Rambam's conclusion that the Sages were wrong in this belief. But later he states that, although he personally prefers the Ptolemaic view and is adopting it in his commentary, the matter is still not definitively resolved; he quotes Simeon b. Jochai from the Midrash that the Sages themselves knew that such

---

[62] See Eric Lawee, *Isaac Abarbanel's Stance toward Tradition* (Albany, NY, 2001).

[63] Commentary to Genesis, (Jerusalem, 1964) p. 57. For discussion, see Andre Neher, *Jewish Thought and the Scientific Revolution of the Sixteenth Century: David Gans (1541-1613) and His Times* (New York, NY, 1986), 220-22.

questions are impossible to answer with certainty. This reveals Abarbanel's discomfort in attributing error to the Sages, as does his explanation as to how, if indeed their view was incorrect, they arrived at it due to following Pliny and Plotinus. His approach here is consistent with his lengthy apologetic discussion elsewhere regarding how to relate to statements by the Sages which appear to be contradicted by science. In that discussion, Abarbanel invokes the notions of their being divinely inspired, and of nature having changed; and he adds that we should not attribute seeming scientific errors to any deficiency on their part, but rather we should realize that if we were to have known their premises, we would see how their conclusions follow correctly.[64]

All this clearly reveals Abarbanel's discomfort with the idea of the Sages being in error. Abarbanel's fidelity to the past "was notably self-conscious"[65]; he was only too aware of the vast challenges raised to traditional views, and saw himself as a defender of that tradition. As such, whereas earlier figures were not overly concerned with the Sages conceding victory to the gentile astronomers, Abarbanel had to rein in that concession and limit its significance.

As we have seen, in the seventeenth and eighteenth centuries, there were still those who acknowledged that the Sages were mistaken in their cosmological worldview. This was presumably because the Talmud clearly and unambiguously stated as such, as the medieval rabbis had near-universally acknowledged. But those advocating this view in the early modern and modern period were proportionately far fewer in number, and were vastly more uneasy about this than were the rabbis of the medieval period.

---

[64] *Yeshu'ot Meshiho* (Karlsruhe, 1828), part II, introduction, p. 9b.

[65] Lawee, loc cit., p. 206.

II. Textual Reinterpretation: R. Moshe Isserles and R. Menachem Azariah da Fano

R. Moshe Isserles ("Rema," 1520-1572) studied astronomy extensively,[66] although his sources of information were restricted to Hebrew translations of scientific works and he showed no awareness of recent developments such as Copernican theory. Rema discusses the topic of the Sages' alleged astronomical errors in his *Torat Ha-Olah*, an explanation of how the Temple and its artifacts correspond to structures in divine and natural philosophy. He maintains that the Sages of Israel, in their view regarding the constellation and spheres, were actually correct. But unlike our explanation regarding Rabbeinu Tam, R. Isserles takes the position that they did not merely *happen* to be correct; rather, they *must* have been correct.

Early in this work,[67] he describes how the seven parts of the Temple correlate to the "seven climates" (a Greek division of the inhabited part of the earth into seven longitudinal bands, each of which covers an area in which all parts share the same feature, such as the weather or the length of a summer day[68]). Through a complex calculation involving numerology which converts linear distances into words, he argues that the eight-cubit area between the northernmost wall of the Temple courtyard and the butchering area symbolizes the "power of God" in "closing the world" at its northern edge. At this point, Rema says that he will diverge to discussing statements by the Sages that the world is open on its northern side (via which the sun exits).

As noted earlier, the Talmud (*Bava Batra* 25a) presents the view of Rabbi Eliezer that the world (lit. *olam*, and thus referring to the surface of

---

[66] David E. Fishman, "Rabbi Moshe Isserles and the Study of Science Among Polish Rabbis," *Science in Context* 10:4 (December 1997), 571-88.

[67] *Torat Ha-Olah* (Prague, 1570), 1:2, p. 6b.

[68] See Shlomo Sela, *Abraham Ibn Ezra and the Rise of Medieval Hebrew Science* (Leiden, 2003), 107.

the universe, i.e. the firmament[69]) is open on the northern side. The sun exits through this opening when it sets, in order to travel above the firmament back to the east:

> It was taught in a Beraita: Rabbi Eliezer says, the world is like an exedra, and the northern side is not enclosed, and when the sun reaches the north-western corner, it bends back and rises above the firmament. And Rabbi Yehoshua says, the world is like a tent, and the northern side is enclosed, and when the sun reaches the north-western corner, it circles around and returns on the other side of the dome, as it says, "traveling to the south, and circling to the north..." (Eccl. 1:6)—traveling to the south by day, and circling to the north by night—"it continually passes around, and the wind returns again to its circuits" (ibid.)—this refers to the eastern and western sides, which the sun sometimes passes around and sometimes traverses. (*Bava Batra* 25a-b)

Rema also cites various other Talmudic and Midrashic allusions to the world being open on one side. These sources present a great difficulty: Rema objects that it is known and uncontested that the world is surrounded on all sides by the spheres, so how could the Talmud state that it is open on one side? (The real answer is that the Talmud is operating within the Babylonian cosmology, but Rema does not countenance that possibility.) He continues to note that even Rabbi Yehoshua, who he (mistakenly) understands as presenting the correct Ptolemaic model in which the spheres are solid and unbroken, describes the sun as travelling in the south by day and in the north at night, which is contrary to the reality of it travelling from east to west. Rema concludes the question and introduces his solution with the following:

> And should someone say that the words of the Sages, of blessed memory, are an accepted tradition—and it is possible that such is the case—I shall not dispute him, for if they are an accepted tradition, we shall accept them, even though they are far from the intellect. But if it is up for evaluation, there is a rejoinder; and if there is any possibility of explaining the words of the Sages, may their memory be for a blessing, in such a way that they

---

[69] The word *olam* is sometimes translated as "world" and sometimes as "universe," but in the Babylonian cosmology, in which all celestial bodies were contained in a dome over a flat earth, they were identical.

do not differ from that which is well known, and to bring them in line with the intellect, how good and pleasant would that be.

Rema proceeds to argue that the Talmud's description of the world being open on its northern side is referring to the line tracing the sun's path around the earth, which would be invisible, i.e. "open," on the northern side (since the line passes below the horizon at that part). His justification for claiming that the word *olam* refers to the orbital path of the sun (in the Talmud's statement that the world is open on its northern side) is that the existence of the world fundamentally depends on the existence of the sun! He also notes that according to all this, Rabbi Eliezer and Rabbi Yehoshua are not arguing at all; rather, one is describing the visible portion of the sun's orbital path, while the other is describing the entire orbital path. As regards Rabbi Eliezer's statement that the sun rises above the firmament at night, Rema refers us to his later discussion, where he explains that the word *rakia* can refer to the land, which is spread out (*roka*) over the water, and thus Rabbi Eliezer is simply referring to the sun still being above the earth in places beyond the horizon.[70] Returning to his original launching point for this discussion, about the power of God being displayed in the "closing of the world" at its northern edge, Rema explains that the "closing of the world" refers to the continuation of this path beneath the horizon, and it demonstrates God's power in that it shows how He forces the sun to set.

After these extraordinarily forced apologetics, Rema explains what led him to reinterpret the passages in this way:

> And behold, I say that the words of our Sages, may their memories be for a blessing, are all built upon the true wisdom, and their words contain nothing perverse or crooked—even though sometimes, at first thought, it seems that they do not accord with the words of the scholars which are developed via proofs, especially in the field of astronomy. And some scholars (in disputing the Sages) support themselves with that which they said that "the gentile scholars triumphed over the Sages of Israel"; this is also with the words of the Master, the Guide, who wrote that "the science

---

[70] See *Torat Ha-Olah* 3:27, p. 94a, where Isserles insists that the *rakia* of Genesis 1:6 refers to the earth while that mentioned in other verses refers to the heavens.

of astronomy was not fully developed in the days of the prophets and the early sages." But one who investigates this will be shocked to say that the Sages, may their memories be for a blessing, did not know these matters! A person who is concerned for the honor of his Creator and the honor of the Sages of the Torah will not think thus, but rather will be meticulous with their words.

As a final demonstration of the scientific wisdom of the Sages, Rema cites the Midrash that we mentioned earlier:

> How do the orbs of the sun and moon set? Rabbi Yehudah b. R. Ila'i and the rabbis [disagree]. Rabbi Yehudah says, behind the dome and above it. The rabbis say, behind the dome and below it. Rabbi Yonatan said: The words of Rabbi Yehudah b. R. Ila'i appear [correct] in the summer, when the entire world is hot and the wellsprings are cool, and the words of the rabbis, that it sets below the dome in the winter, when the whole world is cold and the wellsprings are warm. Rabbi Shimon b. Yochai said: We do not know if they fly up in the air, if they scrape the firmament, or if they travel as usual; the matter is exceedingly difficult and it is impossible for humans to determine. (*Midrash Bereshit Rabbah* 6:8)

Rema presents yet another forced explanation, via which Rabbi Yehudah, the Rabbis, and Rabbi Yonatan are all agreeing and presenting a correct scientific view about the path of the sun which has nothing to do with it travelling above the firmament. He concludes by noting that Rabbi Shimon b. Yochai is describing an intractable problem in astronomy, which is a conflict between three models of the universe: that of Ptolemy, in which the stars are fixed in the spheres; that of the Sages, in which the spheres are fixed and the stars move; and another model proposed by al-Bitruji and described by Isaac Israeli in *Yesod Olam*.[71] But in order to argue that the Sages' model remains a viable possibility despite their concession to the gentile scholars, Rema has to explain that this concession was not as it appears:

> Know that there are three views in astronomy. The first is the view of astronomy that has been made famous in the *Almagest*, after which all the astronomers were drawn from the time that this book was published. And

---

[71] See Bernard Goldstein, *Al-Bitruji: On the Principles of Astronomy* (New Haven, CT, 1971).

it is built upon the opinion of the gentile scholars who said that the constellations are fixed and the sphere revolves.

The second is the view of the Sages of Israel, who said that the constellations revolve and the sphere is fixed. And even though they said that "the gentile scholars were victorious etc.", I have already written in my commentary to the Megillah[72] and *Sefer Aggadot* that they did not mean to say that the Sages of Israel retracted, but rather that due to the reasons of exile, they forgot that approach, and they did not know how to calculate all the ways of astronomy via that system, and they were forced to study via the gentiles' astronomical system. And this is the concept of their "concession," just as I have proved with clear proofs in the aforementioned works. (*Torat Ha-Olah* 1:2)

In his commentary to the Megillah, entitled *Mechir Yayin*, Rema rates the Sages' view that the sphere is fixed and the constellations revolve as being a position originally espoused by the prophet Ezekiel.[73] This is based on Rambam in *Guide* II:8, where the idea of the spheres producing sounds is explained to be predicated upon the belief that the stars move around the spheres, making noise as they bore through them.[74] Accordingly, Rema expresses astonishment that not only the Sages, but even a prophet, could express a scientific belief that has been disproved. His solution is to point out that Rambam himself notes that the science of astronomy does not seek to present models that accurately reflect reality, but rather models that are mathematically simple. Since the Sages forgot how to present their knowledge of the actual reality in a way that was mathematically straightforward, it was the Ptolemaic model that triumphed. Nevertheless, Rema assures his readers, the Sages' position that the sphere is fixed and

---

[72] *Mechir Yayin*, Esther 2:5. Rema there claims that the view of the Sages of Israel can be traced back to the Prophets.

[73] The myth that all true scientific knowledge originated with the Jewish prophets is discussed by Abraham Melamed, *Al Kifei Anakim*, p. 34.

[74] According to Maimonides later in the *Guide*, this means that Ezekiel 1:24 is speaking of such a phenomenon. The commentators to the *Guide* thus observe that Maimonides himself was thus of the view that Ezekiel's prophecy was packaged in a mistaken scientific worldview. Isserles strongly disagrees; in *Torat Ha-Olah* 1:5, he references his discussion in *Mechir Yayin* and stresses that since the description of the spheres producing sounds was given by Ezekiel, it must be true, and the view of the philosophers is to be rejected.

the constellations revolve is necessarily factually correct, since it was known via prophecy, "which is superior to philosophical speculation."[75]

In considering Rema's discussion, there are a number of observations to be made. First is that his apologetics are remarkably strained, as his contemporaries observed. Azariah de Rossi writes that he was initially excited to read a work which purported to reconcile the statements of the Sages with contemporary science, but upon reaching Rema's conclusions, he observed that Rema "was interpreting the passages in a far-fetched manner... He covered them with plaster, such that one could not believe that our Sages' statements could be described in the manner he suggested, and if they had intended to say that which he claims, they undoubtedly would never have used those words... it is certainly the best course to be silent rather than to justify the righteous with arguments that are not correct."[76] It is remarkable that Rema went to such lengths, at the time unprecedented, rather than following the medieval authorities and simply acknowledging that the Sages were incorrect in their cosmological model.

The second observation to make is that Rema never addresses the dispute between the Jewish and gentile scholars regarding the sun's path at night.[77] In light of all his rhetoric concerning the status of the Sages' pronouncements and his apologetics to uphold them, he surely could not have accepted that the Jewish scholars were in error regarding the sun's path at night. But it is difficult to see how he could possibly have explained away their words, and the consequences regarding water in wells, even with his view that the word *rakia* refers to the earth rather than to the firmament.

---

[75] Herbert Davidson discusses Rema's position in "Medieval Jewish Philosophy in the Sixteenth Century," in *Jewish Thought in the Sixteenth Century*, ed. Bernard Cooperman, (Cambridge, MA, 1983) 132-36; however, it seems to me that he inaccurately portrays Isserles' view of the Sages' position as being less certain than he actually was. See too Y. Tzvi Langermann's analysis in "The Astronomy of Rabbi Moses Isserles."

[76] *Me'or Enayim* (Mantua, 1573-75), *Imrei Binah* 1:11 p. 56b (pp. 237-238 in Weinberg edition).

[77] Note that he has the gentile scholars' victory over the Jewish scholars as being with reference to the stars and spheres, in contrast to our version of the Talmud.

But most puzzling of all is a statement by Rema much later in *Torat Ha-Olah*. He presents a novel astronomical model in which the stars, rather than being unchanging and incorruptible, periodically cast off their forms and attain new and different ones. This serves to solve certain problems in astronomy. Rema notes that this approach has far-ranging explanatory power, and yet he abandons it as a general model, retaining it only for the eighth sphere:

> In truth, in this manner we could account for all aspects of astronomy. However, this would be in accordance with the view of the sages who said that the sphere is fixed and the stars revolve, and they already said that the gentile scholars triumphed regarding that. (*Torat Ha-Olah* 3:49)

This is an extremely perplexing turnaround. As we saw, earlier in *Torat Ha-Olah*, Rema says that the gentiles only triumphed with regard to making a better case, but the view of the Sages remains valid. And in *Mechir Yayin*, Rema rated the view of the Sages as being based on the prophets and thus necessarily correct. He also continued to follow the Sages' view, rejecting that of the Ptolemaic astronomers, in other places in *Torat Ha-Olah*.[78] Why, then, does he abandon it here, where it would "account for all aspects of astronomy"? Perhaps he is taking his cue from the Sages as he understood them—even though he is certain that the Jewish view is correct, he does not see it as being fruitful to pursue that, in light of the gentile view being dominant in the world of science.

What are we to make of Rema' strained apologetics to maintain the Sages' views about the constellations and sun? If we examine the reason as to why he wrote about astronomy in the first place, we may find the answer.

R. Yosef Shlomo Delmedigo (1591-1655, also known as *Yashar MiCandia*), speaks disparagingly of the Polish Jews for their opposition to the sciences.[79] But while they may not have matched the openness of an Italian-educated scholar such as Delmedigo, or that of Jews in Moslem

---

[78] See *Torat Ha-Olah* 1:5, discussed in footnote 23 above, and 2:38.

[79] *Ma'ayan Ganim* (Odessa 1865), introduction, p. 129. For more on Delmedigo, see Isaac Barzilay, *Yoseph Shlomo Delmedigo (Yashar of Candia): His Life, Works and Times* (Leiden, 1974).

lands, they were certainly very, very different from Ashkenazi Jews before the sixteen century, who did not engage in any branch of science in any way at all. The 16th century Polish chronicler Maciej Miechowicz writes that in Lithuania, "the Jews use Hebrew books and study sciences and arts, astronomy and medicine,"[80] and the cardinal Lemendone describes them as devoting time to the study of "literature and science, in particular astronomy and medicine."[81] Fishman notes that close to a dozen Hebrew works on astronomy were composed in Poland between 1550 and 1648.[82] These include a number of sixteenth-century Hebrew translations and commentaries to Georg Peurbach's 1456 book *Novae Theoricae Planetarum*, which was a popular text for teaching astronomy.[83] (In one anonymous such commentary, there is an off-handed reference to how the gentile scholars triumphed over the Sages of the Talmud with their view that the constellations are embedded in revolving spheres.[84])

What was the reason for this new interest in astronomy? There was a certain influence from Italian and Spanish Jewry, as well as a revival of interest in Maimonidean rationalism and philosophy.[85] But perhaps most relevant to our topic is the environment in which the Jews lived. Cracow was home to Copernicus and to a university which, beginning in the mid-15th century, became the world's greatest center for astronomy.[86] It is reasonable to propose that in such an environment, where gentile wisdom was so prominent, the Jews would likely either absorb the interest in this wisdom, or feel the need to catch up.

---

[80] *Tractatus de duabus Sarmatiis* (1517), II:1,3, cited by H. H. Ben-Sasson in "Poland," *Encyclopedia Judaica*, vol. 13 (Jerusalem, 1972), 721.

[81] Cited by Ben-Sasson, ibid.

[82] David E. Fishman, "Rabbi Moshe Isserles and the Study of Science Among Polish Rabbis," *Science in Context* 10:4 (December 1997), 574.

[83] Y. Tzvi Langermann, "Peurbach in the Hebrew Tradition," *Journal for the History of Astronomy* 29 (1998), 137-50.

[84] MS. Paris, BN heb1097, p. 1b.

[85] See Davis, "Ashkenazi Rationalism," 607-8.

[86] Eugeniusz Rybka, *Historia Astronomii w Polsce* (History of Astronomy in Poland), vol. 1 (Wroclaw, Poland, 1975).

Returning to Rema, perhaps the question of why he strained himself with apologetics can now be answered. Ruderman notes that it is unclear to what extent Rema pursued his astronomical studies simply as a way to understand various Talmudic concepts, and to what extent it reflects a genuine interest in the sciences, or at least an accommodation to the fact of astronomy holding a privileged place in the larger environment of Cracow.[87] Davidson argues that Rema was simply involved in harmonizing disparate texts rather than displaying any genuine interest in science for its own sake,[88] while Fishman considers that Rema perceived a religious value in studying the laws of God's creation. Langermann, while essentially agreeing with Davidson, observes that Rema's goal with these textual harmonizations was to address serious doctrinal problems such as Aristotle's eternal universe.[89] Consistent with this understanding of Rema seeing science and natural philosophy as a threat to the faith that must be countered, we see that with the topic of the Sages' potential fallibility in astronomical matters, Rema is very much on the defensive. As Fishman observes, this suggests that Rema was aware of the prestigious accomplishments by gentiles in astronomy taking place in his city, and sought to reaffirm the validity of Talmudic teachings and the superiority of the sages.

Other Adherents of Alternate Astronomical Approaches

Among the followers of Rema's approach was R. Yonatan Eibeschütz (1690-1764). He cites Delmedigo's astonishment at the Sages, whose position was based on traditions from the prophets, apparently conceding their error (with regard to the constellations and spheres) to the gentile

---

[87] David B. Ruderman, Jewish Thought and Scientific Discovery in Early Modern Europe (Detroit, MI 1995), 69-76.

[88] Herbert Davidson, "Medieval Jewish Philosophy in the Sixteenth Century," in *Jewish Thought in the Sixteenth Century* , ed. Bernard Cooperman, (Cambridge, MA, 1983) 132-36.

[89] Y. Tzvi Langermann, "The Astronomy of Rabbi Moses Isserles," in *Physics, Cosmology, and Astronomy, 1300-1700*, ed. Sabetai Unguru, (Netherlands, 1991), 83-98, reprinted in Y. Tzvi Langermann, *The Jews and the Sciences in the Middle Ages* (Aldershot, 1999), ch. 7.

scholars, whose opinions are "entirely based on fallible reasoning." R. Eibeschütz answers that there was no error and there was no concession. He presents a lengthy explanation as to how the Sages and the gentile scholars were both correct, with each having a different frame of astronomical reference. R. Eibeschütz presents a novel explanation of the statements that the Sages conceded (*hodu*) to the gentiles; he claims that *hodu* does not mean "acknowledged" in the sense of "conceded," but rather in the sense of "praised" (as in, "*hodu l'Hashem ki tov*"). The Sages were not admitting that they were wrong; rather, they were praising the gentile scholars for being correct with regard to the astronomical frame of reference that they were discussing.[90]

A different way of reinterpreting the Talmud passages was implemented by R. Menachem Azariah da Fano (Fano-Mantua 1548-1620). He interprets the Talmud as referring to the metaphysical causes of the celestial motions, leading off from a discussion of the Midrashic account of the moon arguing with God:

> And [the notion of] the argument (of the moon with God), which assigns wisdom and rebuke to the moon, can be justified; whether the celestial causes are live intelligences, or whether their operators (i.e. angels), who work on their behalf and are named after them, are the ones speaking. Establishing them as intelligent beings is the matter which was validated by the Sages of Israel in chapter *Mi Shehayah Tamei*, in their saying that "the sphere is fixed and the constellations revolve." And this means that the constellation is the uniquely intelligent aspect of the sphere, just as the brain in a man, which guides his body with intelligence, and desires and cleaves and becomes a throne of glory to the soul. So, too, is the situation with the constellation, which intelligently guides the sphere with its wisdom, and desires and cleaves and becomes a throne of glory to an angel. If so, the sphere is a possessor of an animate spirit, "fixed" in its perfection which exists in a man, and its intellect is the constellation which "revolves" to contemplate the will of its Creator, and arouses the appropriate movement in its sphere, and the soul which provides its intelligence is the angel, for otherwise it cannot fulfill its desire of contemplating the Divine Presence, just as the brain in a person cannot recognize its Creator with

---

[90] *Ya'arot Devash* (Yozifov, 1866) 1:4, p. 31a.

perfection without a soul. And the one who said that the constellation is fixed and the sphere revolves [also] spoke the truth, for it is the feet that transport the head... and the commentator who said that the Sages of Israel retracted and conceded to the one who said this, was out of line, for the passage is not in accordance with his words, leaving it as being that they were silent... Behold, in their wisdom, they did not wish to reveal their rejoinder and their reasoning. (*Asarah Ma'amarot* (Amsterdam 1649), *Em Kol Hai* 1:12, pp. 96b-97a)

According to da Fano, when the Sages stated that the sphere is fixed and the constellations revolve, they were not disputing the Ptolemaic model. Rather, they were explaining that the sphere does not move of its own accord; instead, its movement is caused by the constellations, due to their (or their controlling angels) being intelligent, animate entities.

Another figure who insisted that the Jewish Sages were correct was R. Meyer Leibush (Malbim, 1809-1879). He claimed that the correct understanding of the Jewish Sages' view is that the sun passes beneath the watery depths on the other side of the world at night, and the dispute was regarding whether there was land on the other side of the planet or not.[91] Thus, while the Jewish Sages were in error in not knowing about the existence of the Americas, their error was much less than believing in a flat earth and a domed universe. Another such reinterpretation was performed by R. Meir Chanoch Henoch Yeshayavitch.[92] R. Menachem Kasher (1895-1983) claimed that while this cannot be the interpretation of the Talmudic text as we have it, there are variant texts that support such an approach.[93] However, his conclusion, that the Jewish sages actually said

---

[91] Malbim, *Artzot HaChaim* (Warsaw 1837), *Orach Chaim* 1, p. 3b. Note that in his commentary to Gen. 1:6, Malbim rejects the view (which he attributes to all the Rishonim, but not to Chazal) that the *rakia* is a solid firmament, arguing (problematically) that it refers to the atmosphere. He claims that the Sages were also of the view that there are no solid spheres, citing R. Shimon bar Yochai as saying that the stars move through the air; however, Malbim apparently had a corrupted text, since our version of *Bereishit Rabbah* 6:8 (cited earlier) reads quite differently.

[92] *Me'or Chadash* (Warsaw 1882) pp. 16-18.

[93] "The Form of the Earth and its Relationship to the Sun in the Works of Chazal and the Rishonim" (Hebrew) *Talpiyot* Year One Vols. 1-2 (Sivan 5705) pp. 155-176.

that the sun travels beneath the watery depths at night, is not consistent with the other statements in the Talmud, and is clearly influenced by his explicit wish to restore honor to the Talmudic Sages by minimizing their error.[94]

III. The Metaphysical Approach: Maharal

R. Yehuda Landa of Prague ("Maharal," 1529-1609), in the sixth part of *Be'er HaGolah*, uses a different technique to argue against the rationalist approach to this topic.[95] Maharal begins by citing the relevant section of the Talmud, but with some interesting variations:

> "The Sages of Israel say, During the day, the sun travels below the firmament, and at night, above the firmament. And the scholars of the nations say: During the day the sun travels above the firmament, and at night below the firmament. Rebbi said: Their words seem more correct than ours, for during the day the wellsprings are cool and at night they steam."[96]

Maharal's citation of the Talmud, in which the gentile scholars have the sun traveling *above* the firmament by day and *below* it at night, is found in certain manuscripts.[97] However this version is not that which is found in other manuscripts and which was adopted by all other commentators, in which the gentiles had it traveling *below* the firmament by day, and below the *earth*, not the firmament, at night; and furthermore, it is not coherent. Later, we shall see that this is of considerable significance.

Maharal continues:

> They understand that the intent of the Sages was to say that the sun passes through the sphere, and that this is what was said by, "at night it travels above the firmament"; and if so, this would mean that the firmament was

---

[94] See p. 156.

[95] Maharal, *Be'er Ha-Golah*, ed. Y. Hartman (Jerusalem, 1997) *Be'er HaShishi*, section 3, p. 177ff.

[96] For discussion of Maharal's view regarding the spheres and the constellations, see Herbert Davidson, "Medieval Jewish Philosophy in the Sixteenth Century," 136-39.

[97] New York, Jewish Theological Seminary, Rab. 1623.

being temporarily pierced as the sun passes into the sphere. And this is impossible; it is also contradicted by the senses, for the sun only sets from the horizon; it does not set [at that time] for those that have a different horizon. And this cannot be contradicted by any intelligent person.

Maharal's rejection of the straightforward understanding of the Talmud, on the grounds that it is "clearly impossible," is based upon an anachronistic view. The truth is that something which appears "obviously" false in one era does not necessarily appear false to people in another era. There were many intelligent people, over a long period, who believed that the world is flat, even though to later generations there appeared to be very obvious proofs that this is not the case.

Maharal continues further:

> And these people want to consider the words of the Sages, yet they have not grasped their meaning at all. For if the opinion of the Sages was that the sun passes through the sphere at night and travels above the sphere, they would not have said that "the sun travels above the firmament," but rather that it travels above the sphere, just as they said previously, that the sphere is fixed and the constellations revolve.

It is indeed interesting that the Talmud uses the word "firmament" instead of "sphere," but this would not appear to be sufficient grounds to depart from the plain meaning of the text. Note that Rambam considers the two terms to be basically synonymous.[98] The Talmud probably used the term "sphere" simply to match the previous discussion, concerning whether the constellations or the sphere move.

Maharal proceeds to explain that the firmament, rather than being a physical, solid dome over the earth, is the name for the separation between the material and spiritual realms:

> Rather, the concept of the sphere and the concept of the firmament are distinct from each other. The "firmament" refers to that which is the firmament for the lower regions, and this is called "firmament" in the words of the Sages, and that is the firmament which is mentioned in the Torah; for the word "firmament" is never used for the sphere. And now, the opinion of the Sages who said that during the day it travels below the

---

[98] Rambam, *Mishneh Torah*, Vol. I – *Mada*, Laws of the Foundations of Torah 3:1, p. 6.

firmament, and at night it travels above the firmament, means that during the day, the sun is found in the world, and the firmament is the beginning of the lower region, and the sun travels below the firmament during the day, together with the lower regions. But at night, the sun is separated from the world, and it is with regard to this that it says that the sun travels above the firmament—meaning, the firmament which is the beginning of the lower regions. And then it is said that the firmament separates between the sun and the lower regions, for the sun is not found with the lower regions, and there is no doubt that the lower regions have their own border and this border is the firmament, and this explanation is well explained. And because they thought that the words of the Sages were in reference to the firmament which is the sphere, they thought it was something strange.

But you should know, that the sages were not speaking about this, except insofar as that their intent was that God, who separated between those that are on the earth below and those that are not on the earth and are above, and the firmament separates between them, and therefore the sun that God gave to the day to illuminate the earth travels below the firmament, and the firmament does not separate between the sun and the lower regions. But at night, when He did not give the sun to illuminate the earth, therefore the firmament, which God gave to separate between the upper and lower regions, separates the sun from the earth.

Maharal is stating that *because* God did not want the sun to illuminate the earth by night, *therefore* its spiritual essence is removed from the earth at that time (traveling above the firmament), which *results* in the sun disappearing from view—by passing below the horizon. Only during the day, when God wanted it to illuminate the earth, did He permit its spiritual essence to be exposed and for it to travel below the firmament.

And the scholars of the nations say that it is the opposite of this; that during the day, the sun travels above the firmament, as the firmament separates between the sun and the lower regions, and that such is appropriate, for otherwise the sun would be too effective in the lower regions, and they would not be able to exist, and therefore when the sun is on the earth, it travels above the firmament, and when it is nighttime and it is separated from the earth, there is no separation of the firmament.

According to the gentile scholars—with the version of the text that Loew had—the spiritual essence of the sun has to be restricted by day, so as not to overpower the earth, and it therefore travels *above* the firmament. Only at night, when the sun is in any case physically removed from the earth, can its spiritual essence be allowed to express itself unchecked, and it can travel *below* the firmament.

> And this is what Rebbi replied with "their words appear more correct than ours, for during the day the wellsprings are cold, and at night they steam," for from this you see that at night the sun is not separated from the lower regions, and therefore the wellsprings steam, but by day the wellsprings do not steam as they do at night, for God placed the firmament, which separates between the upper and lower regions, to separate between them, and therefore the wellsprings are cold by day. And according to our position, that we say that the sun travels above the firmament at night, the firmament separates between the sun, and it cannot operate upon the wellsprings.

According to Maharal, Rebbi conceded that since the wellsprings are warmer by night than by day, this means that the sun travels below the firmament at night, as the gentile scholars maintained.

> And this is true, for the waters themselves are suited to steam at night in that the sun travels opposite the sea and rules over the element of water, and during the day it is the opposite. This is the truth of the firmament, for Scripture states, "Let there be a firmament in the midst of the waters, and it will separate between the waters." And it further states, "And God separated between the waters that were below the firmament and the waters that were above the firmament."

Maharal appears to be saying here that the real reason why the wellsprings steam at night is not because the sun is passing below the firmament, but rather because the sun has power over the spiritual element of water at night. He does not explain why the Talmud omits this important explanation as to why the Jewish Sages were actually correct.[99] Instead, he simply concludes by putting down those who interpret this account literally:

---

[99] Rabbi Yehoshua Hartman, in his annotated edition of *Be'er HaGolah* (Jerusalem, 1997), invokes Rabbeinu Tam, claiming that his explanation sheds light on Maharal's explanation, but this is difficult, as Rabbeinu Tam (barring apologetics) was referring to the physical universe.

And all these things were concealed from them and they knew nothing of this, for those people only have a portion in that which is revealed and can be detected, and if so, how can they respond to matters that are concealed and hidden, for they do not know what the concept of the firmament is. And this is not the place to explain the concept of the firmament further; we shall yet explain it.

I must admit that Maharal's approach is incomprehensible to me, especially in terms of correlating it with the fact that the earth is inhabited on all sides.[100] Maharal's approach even seems to be apparently incomprehensible to dedicated students of Maharal's works, who fail to explicate his view.[101]

Whatever the nuances of Maharal's view, it was radically different than anything preceding it. His approach of interpreting Talmudic statements as referring to a metaphysical reality is a creative novelty when applied to aggadic legends in the Talmud, but to apply it to this discussion is another matter entirely. Maharal was the first to claim that the Talmud is not actually describing a dispute regarding astronomy. His argument that nobody could have ever believed that the sun goes behind the sky at night is not only anachronistic from a modern perspective; his predecessors never thought to make such an argument in order to discard the plain meaning of the discussion.

Maharal's explanation goes against every previous interpretation. This does not necessarily mean that it is incorrect from a historical perspective, but it certainly points in that direction. If the authors of the Talmud did

---

[100] Although Maharal writes at length, he either does not provide sufficient words that actually explain his interpretation, or his explanation is simply incompatible with the fact of the earth being inhabited on all sides.

[101] Rabbi Yitzhak Adlerstein, in his English adaptation of select portions of *Be'er HaGolah* (New York, 2000), omits this section entirely, and Rabbi Yehoshua Hartman, in his annotated edition of *Be'er HaGolah* (Jerusalem, 1997), provides very little in the way of actual explanation. For some further discussion of Maharal's approach to this topic, see Andre Neher, *Jewish Thought and Scientific Revolution of the Sixteenth Century*, 206, 210 and 246. The only comprehensive discussion of Maharal's exceedingly cryptic words that I have been able to find is that of the French Algerian philosopher Henri Atlan, in *Enlightenment to Enlightenment* (Albany, NY, 1993), pp. 266-7; unfortunately, his elaboration is scarcely less cryptic.

mean what Maharal thought them to mean, they excelled at misleading their readers! One must wonder whether Maharal realized that his approach went against that of all the Rishonim, and how he accounted for this. Did he think that he had rediscovered the true meaning of the Talmud, that all the Rishonim had somehow missed? Or did he think that their words, too, require some sort of deeper explanation? It is impossible to know.

It is not unusual for a conflict to be resolved by positing that one side is referring to a different plane of existence; such a technique was used in the sixteenth century to harmonize different kabbalistic systems. But to apply this approach to a straightforward Talmud text is revolutionary. The idea that the Sages were not even discussing the science of astronomy goes against the plain meaning of the Talmud, as well as going against the full spectrum of previous interpretations. But the appeal of such an approach is obvious; it allows one to maintain belief in the infallible knowledge of the Jewish sages, and the superior level of discourse at which they operated.

Other Adherents of the Mystical Approach

Maharal was the first to adopt a mystical interpretation of this topic, but it subsequently proved very popular. R. Menachem Azariah da Fano ("Rema MiPano," Fano-Mantua 1548-1620) interprets the Talmud as being a metaphor for esoteric concepts rather than an account of a dispute regarding astronomy.[102] R. Moshe Chaim Luzzatto (1707-1746) likewise explains (referencing *Bava Batra* 25b and *Sanhedrin* 91b) that when the Sages spoke of the sun passing behind the firmament at night, they were referring to the spiritual root of the sun.[103]

Rabbi Pinchas Eliyahu Hurwitz of Vilna (d. 1821), in *Sefer HaBris*, writes that references to the sun passing through windows refers to the upper spiritual worlds, where there truly are windows in the path of the spiritual sun. He notes that this was the view of all the Sages, being mentioned in *Eruvin*, *Bava Batra*, the Talmud Yerushalmi and *Pirkei*

---

[102] *Asarah Ma'amaros, Em Kol Chai* 1:12.

[103] *Adir BeMarom*, part I, *B'Shaata DiTzlota DeMincha DeShabbata* p 66b.

d'Rebbi Eliezer, as well as in *Pesachim*. R. Hurwitz therefore expresses surprise at Rabbi Yehudah HaNasi's apparent acquiescence to the gentile scholars and rejection of the all aforementioned Talmudic Sages—"surely they are all holy, and God is in the midst of them," since Scripture also makes reference to the doors,[104] gates[105] and windows[106] of Heaven. He also objects that Rabbi Yehudah HaNasi brings "reason and experiment," i.e. empirical evidence, to support the view of the gentile scholars, "and the Sage is not like the experimenter." R. Hurwitz resolves this by saying that "these and those are the words of the Living God"—Rabbi Yehudah HaNasi was referring to the physical reality, whereas the aforementioned Sages were referring to the spiritual reality.[107]

R. Naftali Tzvi Yehudah Berlin ("Netziv," 1816-1893), in the context of distinguishing between the physical sun and the spiritual force of the *mazal* of the sun, states that the Sages of Israel, in their dispute with the gentile scholars concerning the sun's path at night, were referring to the spiritual sun, "but they did not reveal their intent, as was their way in matters of sanctity."[108] Interestingly, Netziv was not averse to the rationalist approach and even cites de Rossi on several occasions.

Although earlier we cited Chacham Yosef Chaim as taking the straightforward, rationalist approach to this topic, in his own earlier writings he took a very different approach.[109] Like Netziv, he claims that the Sages of Israel were referring to the spiritual "soul" of the sun, which at night returns to the spiritual heavens, resulting in the physical sun's power being diminished. He compares this to the human soul leaving the body at night, while the body sleeps and operates at a lower level. (This explanation does not appear to square with the fact of the earth being round; the sun operates with equal power at all times, but in different parts of the world.)

---

[104] Psalms 78:23.

[105] Genesis 28:17.

[106] Genesis 7:11.

[107] *Sefer HaBrit* 1:4 *Shnei HaMe'orot* 10.

[108] *Ha'amek Davar* to Deuteronomy 4:19.

[109] *Ben Yehoyada* to *Pesachim* 94b.

> Whatever the explanation, you must know with truth and faith that the words of the Sages of Israel in every place are living and enduring, for they are truth and their words are truth. And aside from the secret meaning to which they intended to allude with their words, sometimes you find that even in the *peshat* approach they had a deep intent. And it is because we are lacking many preparations even in the way of *peshat*, we cannot understand their true meaning, even according to the *peshat* of their words…

The motivation behind the mystical approach, as Hurwitz makes clear, was to ensure that the revered Sages of the Talmud should not have committed a scientific error. As the centuries progressed, this consideration was also extended to the Rishonim, and it became difficult for some to accept that Rabbeinu Tam believed in a flat earth with a dome-shaped firmament. Thus, R. David Luria (Lithuania, 1797-1855) claimed that Rabbeinu Tam, too, was referring to a spiritual mystical reality rather than physical facts.[110]

IV. Scientific Vindication: R. David Gans, R. Yom Tov Lippman Heller, and R. Yosef Delmedigo

R. David Gans (1541-1613) was an unusual figure.[111] A disciple of both Rema and Maharal, he was a diligent student of science, and grappled with many issues raised by the discovery of the New World and the revolutions in the field of astronomy. Gans notes that the Sages conceded to the gentiles regarding the constellations being embedded in

---

[110] See his note at the end of his introduction to *Pirkei De-Rabbi Eliezer*.

[111] For a full (albeit bordering on hagiographic) study, see Andre Neher, *Jewish Thought and the Scientific Revolution of the Sixteenth Century: David Gans (1541-1613) and his Times*; but see the extremely critical review of Neher's work by Yaakov Elbaum, *Tarbitz* 55:1 (1986), 145-59. See too David Ruderman, *Jewish Thought and Scientific Discovery in Early Modern Europe*, 82-86. For more on Gans see Yaakov Reifman, "A Biography of Rabbi David Gans (author of *Tzemach David*) and his Literary Activities" (Hebrew) *HaMagid* 14, and the response by Mattityahu Strashun, *Mivhar Ketavim* (Jerusalem, 1969), 234-42; Mordecai Breuer, "Modernism and Traditionalism in 16th Century Jewish Historiography: A Study of David Gans' Tzemah David," in *Jewish Thought in the Sixteenth Century*, edited by Bernard Cooperman (Cambridge, MA, 1983); and Yaakov Elbaum, *Petihut VeHisgarut*, 250-52.

the spheres rather than having independent movement.[112] However, he reports that the famous astronomer Tycho Brahe told him that the Sages were actually correct and that the stars do possess independent motion; he adds that he heard the same astronomical fact from Johannes Kepler.[113] He concludes by citing Abarbanel's mention of how such questions were in doubt amongst the Sages, apparently in order to show that it had already been pointed out that the Sages' concession was not absolute.

In presenting Brahe as having vindicated the Sages, Gans apparently failed to realize that the view of the Sages was part of a Babylonian cosmology, in which the stars move around a dome above a flat earth. Whereas the Sages had believed that the stars move and the sphere is fixed, Brahe had shown that there is no sphere at all, only space.

Gans describes the Ptolemaic, Copernican and Tychonic cosmological systems, praising them all. He does not attempt to evaluate which was ultimately correct, which would have been beyond the goals of producing an introductory text, too technical for his readers, and which was in any case impossible to resolve definitively at that time.[114] Yet he makes no mention of the ancient Babylonian system. Could he really have been unaware of all the passages in the Talmud and Midrash which indicated that the Sages believed in an entirely obsolete cosmological model? Even as he was delighted that Tycho Brahe had apparently justified the Sages' statement that the stars move independently of the sphere, did he not notice that the Sages had described the sun as passing behind the firmament at night? This does not seem possible, especially since Gans was familiar with de Rossi's work, which dwells on this topic at length.

It seems that Gans would have been embarrassed by the Sages not having subscribed to any of three cosmological models that were currently considered viable. Living in Prague, alongside Kepler and Brahe, the

---

[112] *Nehmad Ve-Na'im* (Jesnitz, 1743) 1:25, p. 15b.

[113] For extensive discussion of this passage in *Nehmad Ve-Na'im*, see Noah J. Efron and Menachem Fisch, "Astronomical Exegesis: An Early Modern Jewish Interpretation of the Heavens," *Osiris*, 2nd Series, Vol. 16 (2001), 72-87; Andre Neher, *Jewish Thought and the Scientific Revolution of the Sixteenth Century*, 216-28.

[114] Efron and Fisch, "Astronomical Exegesis," 80-81.

Talmudic views on cosmology would have appeared especially primitive. As Efron and Fisch note, Gans feared that Jews appeared ignorant in the eyes of the Christian intelligentsia, and sought to rehabilitate their image. In the introduction to his works, he describes the goals of his writings as being to reassert the expertise of Jews in these topics vis-à-vis the gentiles. In his introduction to *Tzemah David*, he writes:

> Since we are foreign residents [*gerim ve-toshavim*] among the gentiles, and when they tell or ask us of the first days of ancient dynasties we put our hands to our mouths and we do not know what to answer, and we seem to them like beasts who do not know their left from their right, and it is as if we were all born yesterday. But with this book, the respondent can answer and say a tiny bit about every epoch, and through this we will appeal to and impress them.[115]

And in the introduction to *Nehmad Ve-Na'im*:

> When the Gentiles see that we are devoid of this wisdom, they wonder about us and they taunt and curse us [Isa. 37.23], and they say, "Is this the great nation about which Scripture said 'This great nation [comprises] only wise and understanding people?'" [Deut. 4.6] And what will we do on the day that the wise men of the nations speak to us and ask us the reasons behind the foundation of our intercalation, and for them the fact that we received [this wisdom] will not suffice. Is it proper for us to put our hands before us and appear as a mute who cannot open his mouth? Is this [to] our honor, or the honor of our creator?[116]

Given this background to his enterprise, it comes as no surprise that he seized upon an instance where the latest science appeared to confirm a Talmudic position and show it have been mistakenly rejected, and ignored those instances where the Talmudic view of cosmology had clearly been proven false.

An important contemporary of David Gans was R. Yom Tov Lipmann Heller ("Tosafot Yom Tov," 1578-1654), a prominent rabbi who lived in

---

[115] *Tsemah David*, ed. Mordecai Breuer (Jerusalem, 1983), 166-7. Translation from Efron and Fisch, "Astronomical Exegesis."
[116] *Nehmad Ve-Na'im*, p. 10a. Translation from Efron and Fisch, "Astronomical Exegesis."

Prague and various communities in Poland. R. Heller first addresses the dispute between the Jewish and gentile scholars in the context of a discussion regarding comets. Although some of the ancient Greeks considered comets to be planets,[117] Aristotle believed comets, along with shooting stars, to be atmospheric phenomena—a flash of light caused by interactions between elements rising from the earth.[118] This view continued throughout the medieval and Islamic era,[119] and was thus adopted by Rambam.[120] In 1614, R. Heller cited Rambam's view, and explained it as being consistent with a statement in the Talmud by Shmuel of Nehardea, who admitted (in Heller's interpretation) that he could not account for the way in which comets, unlike stars, appear and disappear. But fourteen years later, R. Heller returned to the topic of comets, and this time he also refers to the view of Rashi. In contrast to Rambam, Rashi describes comets as "stars that shoot like arrows."[121] Heller suggests that the dispute between Rashi and Rambam correlates with the dispute between the Jewish and gentile scholars regarding whether the constellations move or are fixed in the spheres, with Rashi's view following that of the Jewish sages, and Rambam's view correlating with that of the gentile scholars.[122] Yet he does not take sides as to which is correct.

A few years later, however, R. Heller returned to this topic again. This time, he rates the view of the Sages as being supported by Scripture itself:

> There is a well-known dispute from the time of the ancient rabbis, of blessed memory, whether the stars move and the sphere is fixed, or whether the sphere moves and the stars are fixed. The view of our sages, of blessed memory, is that the stars move and the sphere is fixed... And Scripture supports them, for after it is written, "God made the two

---

[117] Tofigh Heidarzadeh, *A History of Physical Theories of Comets, From Aristotle to Whipple* (Secaucus, NJ, 2008), 10.

[118] Ibid., 4-15.

[119] Ibid., 23-30.

[120] Maimonides, *Commentary on the Mishnah, Berakhot* 9:2.

[121] Rashi to Talmud, *Berakhot* 58b, s.v. *kokhva d'shavit*.

[122] In correlating Rashi's view with that of the Jewish sages, he may be quite correct; as noted above, Rashi and Rabbeinu Tam apparently maintained belief in the ancient Babylonian cosmology of the Sages of the Talmud.

luminaries" (Gen. 1:16), Scripture explains that "He placed them in the firmament" (v. 17). It may be seen from this that the luminaries are distinct entities rather than being [made] out of the firmament itself. This correlates with the view that the luminaries are that which moves and that the sphere is that which is fixed. The luminary is an entity that is separate from the firmament and it moves in an orbit around the firmament.

He does, however, continue to note that the verses can be explained differently, in which the description of the luminaries being "placed" refers to their having a special designation rather than describing a physical process. Nevertheless, it seems that he prefers to see Scripture as supporting the view of the Sages. At this point, much of the manuscript is missing, but Joseph Davis ingeniously argues that Heller apparently followed Gans in presenting Tycho Brahe's vindication of the Sages' position.[123]

It is clear that, like Gans, R. Heller was concerned that the Jewish People should demonstrate their tradition's expertise in astronomical matters. In striking contrast to Jews who lived in these lands in previous centuries, R. Heller writes about how every Jew, beginning in his youth, has an obligation to study astronomy.[124] He also wrote a greatly enthusiastic approbation to David Gans' *Magen David*, noting that such works restore the Jewish Peoples' wisdom in the eyes of the nations.[125]

R. Yosef Shlomo Delmedigo (1591-1655) wrote extensively on the topic of astronomy, in a work that would be the only comprehensive Jewish book on this topic for a long time.[126] While generally working within the framework of Ptolemaic astronomy, he was ahead of it in

---

[123] Joseph Davis, "Ashkenazic Rationalism and Midrashic Natural History: Responses to the New Science in the Works of Rabbi Yom Tov Lipmann Heller (1678-1654)," *Science in Context* 10 (1997): 619-21; *Yom-Tov Lipmann Heller: Portrait of a Seventeenth-Century Rabbi* (Oxford 2004), 166-68.

[124] MS. Oxford-Bodleian 2271, fol. 23a-b. See Davis, "Ashkenazic Rationalism and Midrashic Natural History," 606.

[125] On the approbation, see Neher, *Jewish Thought and the Scientific Revolution*.

[126] For general discussion about Delmedigo's writings on astronomy, see Isaac Barzilay, *Yoseph Shlomo Delmedigo (Yashar of Candia): His Life, Works and Times* (Leiden, 1974), 150-66.

several ways, such as in his enthusiastic acceptance of heliocentrism as well as the potential for the existence of other inhabited planets.[127]

R. Delmedigo first mentions the dispute between the Jewish and gentile scholars as part of a general discussion about how the clash between Judaism and Greek philosophy that has existed for centuries was not only with regard to the conflict between an eternal universe and one that was created, but also with regard to other topics:

> And similarly, there are many opinions or beliefs amongst us that are a heritage from our ancestors, and the philosophers mock us and bring proofs against them that are victorious, [albeit] not proven; and nevertheless we do not listen to their voice, and our hearts cling to our Torah, "as Mount Zion that shall never move."[128] And, by the life of my head—the Sages of Israel did not act appropriately, when they abandoned their opinion with regard to the sphere being fixed and the constellations revolving, and accepted the opinion of the gentiles. For in our time, most scholars have disqualified that which they accepted, and have adopted that which they negated... (*Sefer Elim* (Odessa 1867) p. 87)

He returns to this theme in a later volume, in the context of a specific discussion about whether the stars possess independent movement or are embedded in spheres:

> And others believe that the stars move in orbits without spheres. And in their view, the Sages of Israel did not act correctly in acknowledging to the gentile scholars that the constellations are fixed and the spheres revolve. For perhaps their original opinion was transmitted from the prophets; and they should not have abandoned those who had access to the Source in favor of those who provide explanations and reasons, as long as they do not establish their position with clear proofs. (*Sefer Elim*, part 4, *Gevurot Hashem, madregah* 5, p. 299)

Yet for all his passion for the validity of the Sages' view, and the suggestions that it was based on tradition from the prophets, R. Delmedigo would not have *fully* endorsed the Sages' position that the stars

---

[127] *Sefer Elim*, part 4, *Gevurot Hashem*, pp. 292-3. The idea of an infinite number of solar systems had been proposed by the ill-fated Giordano Bruno.

[128] Psalms 125:1.

move and the sphere is fixed, since elsewhere he stresses how the ancient belief in spheres is without foundation, and all that exists in space is ether.[129] Like Rema, Gans, and R. Heller, he makes no reference to the Sages' position regarding the sun's path at night, but much later he acknowledges that the Sages' general model of the universe was incorrect, both in their belief that the earth floats on water, and in their belief that the sun penetrates the firmament:

> And regarding the suspension of the earth on nothingness, it seems that your question stems from your discomfort with the words of the psalmist who wrote, "To He that spread out [le-roqa] the land upon the waters," because the support needs a support, and on what are the waters spread out? He thus has ignored the main miracle in favor of a secondary aspect! If [the psalmist] believed, like Thales the Milesian, that the land floats on the water—which is unnatural, [for it requires] the heavier substance to float on the lighter one—he would have believed that the waters are infinitely deep. But that view, with all its ideas, is incorrect, since it has been proven empirically that [the earth] is spherical. Thus the expression established [by the sages] in the first blessing of Sabbath morning, "and [God] splits the windows of the firmament," is in accordance with their belief, which is mentioned in the Talmud. One should not be astonished if they strayed from the truth when they spoke of matters outside of their occupation and expertise, and regarding which they had no tradition; for the Greek experts erred in them, and their successors perpetuated those errors. (Sefer Elim, Ma'ayan Hatum #67, p. 438)

But, like Gans and R. Heller, R. Delmedigo wishes to focus on the Sages' technically correct belief in the stars possessing independent motion, as a vital part of his wider presentation about how Jews should be confident in their ancient traditions and not abandon them under pressure from alien ideologies which have not adequately proven their case. Yet this sentiment, which he expressed on several occasions,[130] is somewhat ironic in light of the fact that few were as progressive as R.

---

[129] Sefer Elim, p. 61. See Isaac Barzilay, Yoseph Shlomo Delmedigo (Yashar of Candia): His Life, Works and Times, 156, 159-160.

[130] See too p. 61, where Delmedigo disdains modern science in favor of ancient Jewish traditions.

Delmedigo in accepting so many aspects of the new astronomy. But perhaps it was precisely his realization that so much of the new astronomy was correct, and so different from ancient views, that sensitized him to the need to "save face" for the Sages in any way possible.

There were many authorities who followed in the footsteps of Gans, R. Lippman-Heller and R. Delmedigo in claiming that the new astronomy had vindicated the Sages. R. Yehuda Briel of Mantua (1643-1722), when addressed with a question concerning scientific error in the Talmud with regard to spontaneous generation, responds that the Sages of the Talmud are more reliable than scientists; and as an example of the superior wisdom of the Sages, he argues that they have been vindicated in their belief that the sphere is fixed and the constellations revolve within it.[131] Tuvia Cohen (Poland-Italy-Jerusalem, 1652–1729), in a work that explicitly had as its goal to prove that Jews were just as enlightened and educated as non-Jews, makes the same point.[132] R. Aviad Sar-Shalom Basilea (Italy, c. 1680-1743), while reluctantly acknowledging that a person's faith is not compromised if he disputes some of the Sages on something that they said based upon their own reasoning, is at pains to stress that their intellects were greater than ours, and that those who attribute error to them often turn out to be mistaken; as an example, he cites the Sages' position that the sphere is fixed and the stars revolve.[133]

V. Complete Rejection of Science: R. Yosef Ashkenazi

R. Yosef Ashkenazi (Poznan-Livorno-Safed, c. 1529-before 1582) was a staunch anti-rationalist who fought against the study of philosophy and the adoption of the philosophical approach.[134] Included in this battle was a polemic against the entire Ptolemaic cosmology, in which he marshals Scripture and Talmud as well as scientific arguments against the notion of

---

[131] Cited in R. Yitzchak Lampronti, *Pahad Yitzhak*, s.v. *Tzedah Asurah*, p. 21a.

[132] *Ma'aseh Tuviah* (Lvov, 1867) vol. 1, *Olam ha-galgalim*, ch. 3, n.p.

[133] *Emunat Hakhamim* (Warsaw, 1888), ch. 5, p. 15a.

[134] For more on Ashkenazi and his opposition to philosophy, see Elchanan Reiner, "The Attitude of Ashkenazi Society to the New Science in the Sixteenth Century," *Science in Context* 10:4 (December 1997), 589-603.

a spherical earth surrounded on all sides by the heavens.[135] As part of this, R. Ashkenazi insists that the Sages' declaration, that the position of the gentile scholars "appears" correct, only meant that it superficially *appears* correct; they were not conceding that the gentile scholars were actually correct. He argues that the Sages themselves would not have thought that a Ptolemaic sun would have heated up the waters from its passage on the other side of the world, since, in that model, it is even more distant from them than during the day.

Unlike the figures discussed earlier, it appears that what motivated R. Ashkenazi was actually not an insecurity vis-à-vis advances in science, nor a traditionalist desire to boost the authority of the Sages. Rather, it appears that his insistence on the Sages being correct stems from a desire to discredit Ptolemaic cosmology, which in turn stems from a desire to undermine Greek philosophy in general.

Now, R. Ashkenazi was not the first figure from Ashkenaz to oppose Greek philosophy. Most notable of his predecessors in this was R. Moshe Taku, a thirteenth-century Tosafist, who also wrote against certain aspects of Ptolemaic cosmology; he argues that the earth is suspended directly by God, rather than through the force exerted on all sides by the heavenly sphere.[136] Yet Taku does not deny that there exists a sphere which encompasses the earth on all sides, which is the most fundamental component of Ptolemaic cosmology vis-à-vis Babylonian cosmology. True, he later regards it as offensive to posit that angelic entities are below the earth as well as above, and he seems fairly committed to the idea of the celestial heavens being vertically above the earth rather than surrounding them on all sides.[137] Nevertheless, while he argues that it is overly presumptuous of the philosophers to be certain that the sun and stars must be embedded in spheres, and that the Sages knew of their

---

[135] Portions of this were published by Gershom Scholem, "*Yediyot Hadashot al R. Yosef Ashkenazi*," *Tarbiz* 28 (1959), 218-20, who identified Ashkenazi as the author of this manuscript.

[136] *Ketav Tamim*, ed. R. Kirchheim, *Ozar Nehmad* 3 (Vienna, 1860), p. 82.

[137] Ibid., 84.

limitations regarding such determinations, he does not go so far as to argue that the philosophers must be incorrect.

Why, then, did R. Ashkenazi feel the need to go so much further than his predecessor and to discredit Ptolemaic cosmology in its entirety? Perhaps the question should instead be as to why R. Taku did not go as far as Ashkenazi. Facing a threatening alternate system of knowledge, both R. Taku and R. Ashkenazi desired to discredit it as much as possible. But R. Taku was unwilling to go against the plain meaning of the Talmud itself, which had the Sages conceding to the gentiles in at least some aspects of Ptolemaic cosmology; for following the straightforward reading of the Talmud formed the basis of much of his arguments for God's corporeal nature. R. Ashkenazi, on the other hand, lived in an era when reinterpreting difficult passages of the Talmud, from corporeal descriptions of God to otherwise challenging sections of the Aggadah, was the accepted norm. He was not as constrained by the plain meaning of the Talmud, and so could reject the notion that there had ever been any concession to Ptolemaic cosmology.

Amazingly, even through to the eighteenth century, there were still those who followed R. Ashkenazi in maintaining that the Sages were actually correct.[138] R. Yair Chaim Bahrakh ("*Chavot Ya'ir*," Germany, 1638-1702), a towering halakhist who also studied science extensively, accepted that it is possible that the Sages may well have been in error, but was uncertain whether the gentile scholars were ultimately correct, and argued that such matters are in any case rarely ever resolved.[139] R. Yaakov Reischer (1661-1733), author of *Shevut Yaakov*, derided the science of his day on the grounds that it opposes the Talmud's position that the earth is flat.[140] R. Eliyahu Kramer, the "Vilna Gaon" (1720-1797), makes some

---

[138] See the sources cited by Kasher, "*Shabbat Bereshit ve-Shabbat Sinai*," pp. 647-48 n. 16.

[139] *Responsa Chavot Ya'ir* (Lvov, 1896) #210, p. 111a; see too #219, p. 113b, where he describes how he destroyed his own writings on astronomy in a fire. Davis ("Ashkenazi Rationalism," 607) points to this as an interesting contrast to Moses Rivkes, a scholar of the previous generation, who, when forced to flee his home, took only his *tefillin* and an astronomical table.

[140] *Responsa Shevut Yaakov* (Metz, 1789) 3:20, p. 8b.

cryptic comments about how the Ptolemaic astronomers developed their model of stars embedded in spheres and rejected the Sages' model due to various astronomical objections, which he claims it is possible to resolve.[141] He in turn is cited by R. Tzadok HaKohen Rabinowitz (Kreisburg-Lublin, 1823-1900), who heaps scorn on the way that astronomers constantly change their minds, and states that we are therefore only to rely upon the Sages, who possessed divine inspiration.[142]

Conclusion

The Talmud's discussion concerning the Sages' views of cosmology struck people over the centuries as being quite extraordinary. First there is the matter of the Jewish sages holding a view of the universe that is startlingly inaccurate; then there is R. Yehudah HaNasi deciding that the gentiles are correct and the revered Jewish sages are in error. Isadore Twersky observed that "the passage has a long history of interpretation, reflecting various moods: embarrassment, perplexity, satisfaction, with some attempts at harmonization or reinterpretation or restricting the significance of the report."[143]

But the *pattern* of this long history of interpretation is significant. For the rabbis of the medieval period, there was absolutely no doubt that the Talmud was discussing a dispute about astronomy, and for the overwhelming majority of them, it was to be straightforwardly understood as attesting to the Sages having been in error. Most reported this in a matter-of-fact way, apparently not seeing it as any cause for concern, while for some it was positive testimony of the Sages' intellectual honesty. The dissenting voice of that time, Rabbeinu Tam, was not necessarily motivated by any consideration other than the desire to reconcile conflicting statements in the Talmud, coupled with the fact that he genuinely believed that the sun does indeed travel behind the sky at night.

---

[141] *Sefer Yetzirah* with commentary (Jerusalem, 1965), 6:1, p. 39.

[142] *Tiferet Tzvi* (Lublin 1909) 92, *Yoreh De'ah*, paragraph 8, and *Kuntrus Meishiv HaTa'anah LeHaRav Tzaddok HaKohen*, printed at the end of *Sefer HaZichronot* (Tel Aviv 1956) p. 196.

[143] "Joseph Ibn Kaspi: Portrait of a Medieval Jewish Intellectual," p. 256 note 52.

Beginning in the mid-sixteenth century, this all changed. R. Yitzchak Arama and Abarbanel still accepted that the Sages were likely in error, but found it necessary to apologize for them and explain how this error came about. Rema and R. Menachem Azariah da Fano reinterpreted Talmudic texts and insisted that the Jewish Sages *must* have been correct. Maharal innovated an entirely new method of ensuring that the Sages remained infallible, by attributing an entirely different meaning to their words, according to which it was beneath the dignity of the Sages to be speaking about physical cosmology. David Gans, R. Tom Tov Lippman Heller and R. Yosef Delmedigo focused on those statements of the Sages which appeared to have been vindicated by modern astronomy. And R. Yosef Ashkenazi insisted that the Sages were entirely correct all along. As the centuries passed, even while there were still those who could not ignore the straightforward and traditional meaning of the text, such reinterpretations and apologetics became increasingly desirable. In traditionalist circles today, on the rare occasions when this passage in the Talmud is discussed, the *only* approaches to be cited on this topic are those of Rabbeinu Tam[144] and/or Maharal[145]—while the approach of virtually all the Geonim and Rishonim is often deemed heretical![146]

This topic reveals a clear divide between the medieval period and the early modern period. What was the reason for this radical transformation in the attitude towards the Sages' obsolete cosmological worldview? One could propose that it relates to a wider context of Talmudic authority. Those who became known as the *Aharonim*—and probably even perceived themselves as launching a new era—now had to justify and

---

[144] This is sometimes proffered by people who apparently see no difficulty in saying that the sun really does go behind the sky at night, while at other times Rabbeinu Tam's view is itself re-interpreted to be talking about the Sages being correct in a mystical sense.

[145] See, for example, *Mishpachah* magazine's supplement *Kolmus: The Journal of Torah and Jewish Thought* 14 (Kislev 5771): 13. An interestingly self-contradictory approach is seen in the Schottenstein Talmud; it introduces the discussions of cosmology in *Pesachim* by assuring the reader that they all conceal a deeper meaning (i.e. only validating Maharal-type approaches), but then later cites R. Avraham ben HaRambam that R. Yehudah HaNasi's statement attests to the Sages' intellectual honesty!

[146] This was one of the core issues involved in the 2004 ban on some of my own books.

uphold the authority of post-Talmudic authority figures, and this in turn would mean that the Sages themselves would, *a fortiori*, have to be elevated to an even greater stature.

But it appears to me that there may be a more specific reason why the sixteenth century saw such dedicated innovations aimed at avoiding the notion that the Sages erred in this area. Jews in Europe, feeling intellectually put to shame by the scientific advances of Christendom in general, and the achievements in astronomy of Prague and Cracow in particular, could not accept that the Sages of the Talmud had been so grossly mistaken in these matters. Jews in Moslem lands in the medieval period had also been exposed to non-Jews making magnificent accomplishments in science, but the Jews at that time felt a part of a grand universal enterprise of scientific discovery and were already accustomed to accepting Greek philosophy. In contrast to this, Jews in Christian Europe had more of a competitive or adversarial relationship with gentiles and their knowledge, as well as being greatly behind them in their scientific knowledge. The ensuing sense of insecurity meant that concessions to gentile knowledge that had hitherto been acceptable now had to be reinterpreted.

R. Yehudah HaNasi had no difficulties in accepting that the gentile astronomers were victorious over the Sages of Israel. But as the centuries passed, it became more and more difficult for rabbinic scholars to share his openness. Unsurprisingly, it was also difficult for them to accept the Copernican revolution that was taking place.[147] The transition from Babylonian cosmology to Ptolemaic cosmology was actually much easier at the time than the later transition from Ptolemaic cosmology to Copernican cosmology was later to be, but it was just as difficult for later generations to look back upon. A new era of insecurity about rabbinic

---

[147] Hillel Levine, "Paradise Not Surrendered: Jewish Reactions to Copernicus and the Growth of Modern Science," in Robert S. Cohen and Marx W. Wartofsky, eds. *Epistemology, Methodology and the Social Sciences* (Holland, 1983), 203-225; Michael E. Panitz, "New Heavens and New Earth: Seventeenth to Nineteenth Century Jewish Responses to the New Astronomy," *Conservative Judaism*, vol. XL (1987-88), n. 2, pp. 28-42; and especially Jeremy Brown, *New Heavens and a New Earth: The Jewish Reception of Copernican Thought* (Oxford University Press 2013).

inferiority in scientific matters, to a degree that could not tolerate even the most explicit and hitherto acceptable of such cases, had begun.

SEVEN

Maharal's Multiple Revolutions in Aggadic Scholarship

Introduction

Several years ago, Rabbi Chaim Eisen published a seminal article in *Hakirah* entitled "Maharal's *Be'er ha-Golah* and His Revolution in Aggadic Scholarship — in Their Context and on His Terms."[1] A major focus of the article was to exhaustively document that whereas the Geonim and Rishonim saw Aggadata as being on a lower level than other sections of the Gemara and open to dispute, Maharal elevated Aggadata to the level of dogma. But there are other crucially important ways in which Maharal's approach to aggadah was revolutionary. In this chapter I shall briefly review R. Eisen's discussion of one aspect of Maharal's revolution and add some points, after which I shall discuss the other aspects. With each aspect, I shall describe Maharal's revolution and then give one or more examples. I shall conclude the chapter with exploring the ramifications of Maharal's revolutionary approach.

I. The Elevation to Dogma

Maharal's Revolution

R. Eisen has a superbly detailed discussion of how Maharal stood in sharp contrast to his predecessors with his elevation of aggadah to dogma. As R. Eisen notes, Maharal was not actually the first to insist on the binding authority of aggadah—much earlier figures in Ashkenaz had insisted on the literal truth of all aggadot, which by inference, means that

---

[1] *Hakirah* vol. 4, Winter 2007.

one may not dispute the authority of the aggadot. However, by the time Maharal arrived on the scene, such views had long faded into obscurity. R. Eisen provides a long list of Geonim and Rishonim who did not see all aggadot as binding.

One could also add the even longer list of Rishonim who held that Chazal's statements about the natural world were not all correct.[2] True, Maharal does not explicitly categorically reject the idea that Chazal could ever have been mistaken in their statements about the natural world. However, from his repeated insistence that Chazal were always speaking about metaphysical rather than physical phenomena, that knowledge obtained from Torah is much more reliable than that obtained via the scientific method, and from his reinterpretations of passages in the Talmud that seem to explicitly impart such errors to Chazal, it seems clear that he held such a possibility to be unthinkable.

There is also another aspect to add to a discussion of Maharal's elevation of Aggadah. Maharal did not only make polemical statements about Aggadic material being sacrosanct. He also gave explanations which showed, at least in some cases, why he believed them to be of such status. In at least some cases, it was not merely a statement that Chazal's statements were unarguable, but also that they were of divine authority.[3] Maharal specifically claimed that various homiletic exegeses of Scriptural verses were not the Sages' own ideas, as Rambam claimed, but rather are God's intent.[4]

Example: The Peg Exegesis

One such example is his explanation of the nature of the Sages' *derashos* as applied to the commandment that soldiers should pack a peg (*yated*) in their gear. Rambam explains this as follows:

---

[2] An extremely comprehensive list of citations can be found at http://torahand-science.blogspot.com/2006/04/sources-indicating-that-chazal-did-not.html.

[3] On the other hand, in *Chiddushei Aggados* to *Shabbat* 31a, Maharal writes that those who reject the Oral Torah are not classified as heretics.

[4] Elbaum, *Petichut VeHistagrut* pp. 112-113.

The Sages use the text of the Bible only as a kind of poetical language [for their own ideas], and do not intend thereby to give an interpretation of the text. As to the value of these Midrashic interpretations, we meet with two different opinions. For some think that the Midrash contains the real explanation of the text, whilst others, finding that it cannot be reconciled with the words quoted, reject and ridicule it. The former struggle and fight to prove and to confirm such interpretations according to their opinion, and to keep them as the real meaning of the text; they consider them in the same light as traditional laws. Neither of the two classes understood it, that our Sages employ biblical texts merely as poetical expressions, the meaning of which is clear to every reasonable reader. This style was general in ancient days; all adopted it in the same way as poets. Our Sages say, in reference to the words, "you shall have a peg (*yated*) upon your weapons" [*azenecha*, Deut. 23:14]: Do not read *azenecha*, "your weapon," but *oznecha*, "your ear." You are thus told, that if you hear a person uttering something disgraceful, put your fingers into your ears. Now, I wonder whether those ignorant persons believe that the author of this saying gave it as the true interpretation of the text quoted, and as the meaning of this precept: that in truth *yated*, "peg," is used for "finger," and *azenecha* denotes "your ear." I cannot think that any person whose intellect is sound can admit this. The author employed the text as a beautiful poetical phrase, in teaching an excellent moral lesson, namely this: It is as bad to listen to bad language as it is to use it. This lesson is poetically connected with the above text. (*Guide for the Perplexed* 3:43)

Rambam scorns those who believe that the Sages' homiletic discourse represents the literal, straightforward interpretation of the verse. Instead, he states, the Sages simply used the verse as a hook on which to hang their interpretation. Maharal, on the other hand, introduces an intermediate position: that the homiletic discourse is indeed the intent of the Torah, but as a secondary meaning that is deliberately alluded to in the text, not the primary, straightforward meaning.

...When you investigate their words, you will find that all their words are wisdom... it is written, "and you shall have a peg on your weapons"—but why does it write it this way, it could have just written, "and you shall have a peg," and we would certainly know that it is stuck in something? However, it comes to teach you that a person needs a cover for that which receives, namely, the ear, that no evil matter should penetrate it... and this matter is clear it is not far-fetched but appropriate and acceptable; there is no doubt that the Torah alluded to this, with hints in its terminology…. (*Be'er HaGolah, Be'er HaShlishi*)

In so doing, Maharal effectively converted something of human origin to being of divine origin. That which is of human origin can be disputed; that which is of divine origin is sacrosanct and inviolable.

II. The Nature of the Non-Straightforward Meaning

Maharal's Revolution

It is not just with regard to the status accorded to aggadah that Maharal was revolutionary. Maharal also innovated an entirely new approach to understanding the very nature of aggadah. True, Maharal was certainly far from the first to state that aggadah should not be interpreted in accordance with its straightforward meaning. But the *type* of interpretation that he ascribed to it was completely novel.

The Rishonim who took the approach that aggadah should not be interpreted in accordance with its straightforward meaning instead interpreted aggadah in a non-literal manner. They saw aggadah as being metaphor and parable. Maharal, on the other hand, saw aggadah as speaking of the spiritual inner "essence" of existence. According to Maharal, aggadah is neither a literal account of a physical reality nor a non-literal metaphor; rather, it is a *literal* account of a *meta*physical reality.

Is there any precedent for Maharal's method of interpretation? While kabbalah introduced the idea of spiritual worlds, and of a metaphysical dimension to *mitzvot*, as far as I know it did not yet, by Maharal's time, apply this concept to the physical world as mentioned in the Talmud.

R. Eisen writes that Maharal followed "in the footsteps of Rambam" (p. 180) and claims that:

…Maharal, not only in his propensity to cast apparently historical aggadic tales as abstractions, is manifestly beholden to Rambam for much more than a general *weltanschauung*. More than any other classic of Jewish thought, Rambam's *Moreh ha-Nevukhim* established the centrality of symbolism and metaphor in explicating not only *aggadot* but also the prophet's parables and even certain aspects of Torah. (p. 186)

In a footnote, however, R. Eisen notes that "a facile comparison between Maharal's allegorical abstractions and Maimonidean parables is misleading."[5] I think that this is somewhat of an understatement. It is true that Rambam was a trailblazer in non-literal interpretations, but Maharal's method of non-literal interpretation is so fundamentally different from that of Rambam that I do not think he can be rated as following in Rambam's footsteps.

Example: The Height of Moses

The Talmud (*Berachot* 54a, *Nedarim* 38a) states that Moses was ten cubits tall, which is approximately fifteen feet. Some, such as R. Nissim ben Reuven of Gerona (1290-1375), accepted this as being literally true.[6] But for more dedicated rationalists such as Rambam, this was impossible to accept. Rambam does not directly address the topic of Moses, but when discussing the height of the giant Og, he brings Og's height down to about six cubits by explaining that although Scripture describes his bed as being nine cubits long, people are only two-thirds the length of their beds.[7] Rambam stresses that while a six-cubit height "is undoubtedly rare in the human race, it is in no way impossible." The notion that Moses, who is not rated in Scripture as being a giant, to have been nearly twice as tall Og, would certainly be unacceptable to Rambam.

How, then, would Rambam have understood the Talmud's account of Moses being ten cubits tall? He would undoubtedly have interpreted it similarly to Rabbi Yitzchak Arama, who insisted that it was not literal, but rather was an allegory for spiritual greatness.[8] Moses was a giant in his spiritual stature. This great height is quantified as ten cubits due to the symbolic significance of that number; either because ten, as the base unit of the numerical system, signifies completeness, or because of some achievement of Moses involving the number ten, such as his involvement

---

[5] P. 188 n. 92.

[6] *Derashot haRan* 5.

[7] *Guide for the Perplexed* 2:47.

[8] Rabbi Yitzchak Arama, *Akeidat Yitzchak*, Bamidbar 81 (p. 107 in 1868 edition).

in brining the ten plagues, receiving the ten commandments, or building the ten-cubit tall Mishkan.

In sharp contrast to this approach is that of Maharal. Maharal agrees that the Talmud's statement cannot be true in the simple, literal sense, but he explains that such seemingly impossible accounts of people's height are describing the metaphysical rather than physical reality:

> Every person has two aspects: One, his physical form, which is common to the entire species... but every person also has a personal (inner metaphysical) form... Sometimes, the Sages said that so-and-so was such-and-such a height, and they attributed huge dimensions to him. This, too, is from the perspective of his inner form, even though it is cannot be actualized [in the physical world] because of the general form [of human beings], since every person is created within the framework of the laws of nature, and these dictate that a person cannot be so small or so big. (Maharal, *Be'er HaGolah, Be'er* 5)

Maharal explains that when the Sages described Moses as being ten cubits in height, this was not referring to his physical size but rather his inner spiritual dimensions:[9]

> Know that size is [stated] according to the [spiritual] level of the thing; and therefore, you will find that the earlier generations, who had a greater spiritual level, are described as being of greater size. And in tractate Shabbat, it states that Moses was ten cubits tall; and this does not mean from the perspective of his physical body being so big... Do not under any circumstances say at all that the measurement given here is one that is empirically detectable; rather, this is as we have explained on many occasions, divorced from the physical reality, just as one finds [many] measurements that are not detectable to the senses and are only conceptual. For this itself, that the height of Moses was ten cubits, is not a physical measurement; rather, that he was suited to ten cubits' worth of perfection and spiritual elevation. (*Chiddushei Aggados* to *Bava Metzia* 84a s.v. *ve-ka'asher teida*)

---

[9] Maharal in *Gevurot Hashem* 18 explains why Moses was ten cubits tall in a way that sounds as though he is interpreting it literally, but at the end he states that for the meaning of the concept of someone being tall, one should refer to *Be'er HaGolah* – where he explains it metaphysically.

According to Maharal, there is a metaphysical spiritual reality which is the source of the reality in this world. In this plane of existence, Moses really was ten cubits tall. Because the laws of nature do not permit a human to be so tall, when this spiritual genetic code was actualized in this world, Moses could not be ten physical cubits in height.

In this case, we have a way in which the difference between Maharal's approach of "literal description of metaphysical reality," and those who simply interpret statements symbolically, is brought sharply to light. Maharal adds that it would be appropriate if the physical world perfectly expressed the spiritual, but such is not the case; however, the physical world does express the spiritual world to the extent possible, and therefore Moses would have been very tall, within that which is ordinarily possible:

> It states that Moses was ten cubits tall; and this does not mean from the perspective of his physical body being so big. Rather, it is due to that in accordance with the spiritual level and qualities that someone has, his body will be synchronized accordingly... If such an amount was not to be found, it was due to the deficiencies of the body (which cannot attain such a size), but nevertheless he possessed as great a [physical] size as is possible. (Ibid.[10])

According to Maharal, then, Moses was not fifteen feet tall, but he would have been extremely tall—the tallest man in the world, within the realm of the physically possible. Those who simply interpret the Talmud's statement non-literally, as a metaphor alluding to Moses' greatness, would have no need and no place for such an explanation.

III. The Extended Definition of Aggadah

Maharal's Revolution

R. Shmuel HaNaggid defined aggadah as "anything that is not halachah." However, this definition is too broad for our purposes. The fact is that when scholars such as Rambam spoke about, and applied, their

---

[10] Maharal states similarly in *Be'er HaGolah* 5: "And likewise, when someone has a great measurement from the point of view of his inner form, even though it is impossible that he can be so big from the point of view of the general [physical] form [of human beings], he does possess whatever increase is possible due to his inner form."

methodology of interpreting aggadah against its straightforward meaning, they had a particular group of statements in mind: homiletic discourses, and usually specifically those homiletic discourses that sound extremely strange if interpreted as being literally true. But for Maharal, his approach of interpreting statements as literal descriptions of a metaphysical reality was applied, and was applicable, to a much broader category of statements; indeed, there was virtually no part of the Talmud to which this could *not* theoretically be applied.[11]

Example #1: Discussions about Astronomy

In several places, the Talmud recounts discussions concerning astronomy; let us focus on the discussion concerning the path of the sun.

> The Sages of Israel say, During the day, the sun travels below the firmament, and at night, above the firmament. And the scholars of the nations say, During the day the sun travels below the firmament, and at night below the ground. Rebbi said: Their words seem more correct than ours... (Talmud, *Pesachim* 94a)

As discussed at length in the previous chapter, most of the Geonim and Rishonim understood this passage in accordance with its straightforward meaning, that Rebbi concluded that the gentile scholars were correct and the Jewish scholars were mistaken. Rabbeinu Tam interprets it to mean that the arguments of the gentile scholars were more convincing, but that the truth nevertheless lay with the Jewish sages. However, all of the Geonim and Rishonim, *without any exceptions whatsoever,* interpreted this passage as relating a dispute about astronomy. Maharal, on the other hand, interpreted it as referring to a dispute about metaphysical matters, in which the "firmament" represents the division between the physical and spiritual world:

> The "firmament" refers to that which is the firmament for the lower regions... And now, the opinion of the Sages who said that during the day it travels below the firmament, and at night it travels above the firmament,

---

[11] An exception is that Maharal states that when the Talmud gives specific historic details, this signifies that the event is literally true; see the fourth *Be'er* of *Be'er HaGolah*. Ironically, this is a case where Rambam would *not* necessarily see it as being literally true; see his comments regarding the Book of Iyov in *The Guide for the Perplexed* 3:22.

means that during the day, the sun is found in the world, and the firmament is the beginning of the lower region, and the sun travels below the firmament during the day, together with the lower regions. But at night, the sun is separated from the world, and it is with regard to this that it says that the sun travels above the firmament—meaning, the firmament which is the beginning of the lower regions. (*Be'er HaGolah, Be'er Shishi*[12])

There is no indication in the Talmud that this is anything other than a discussion about astronomy.[13] Nobody before Maharal interpreted is as being anything other than this. It can perhaps be considered aggadah in the sense of not being halachah, but it is not aggadah in the sense of being a homily, parable or suchlike. But Maharal, by explaining the subject of the dispute as referring to a metaphysical reality, was able to do away with the plain meaning of the text, extending his approach that he applies to other types of aggadah.

Example #2: Halachic Discussions

Perhaps the strongest demonstration of how Maharal's unique approach can be extended is that it can even be applied to halachic matters. We find a passage in the Talmud discussing the height of Moses and other Levites which, at first glance, seems impossible to interpret as anything other than a reference to the physical reality. It begins by discussing the practical law that carrying items on Shabbat is prohibited even when done high above the ground (without putting it down):

> Rabbi Elazar said: One who transfers a load [from one domain to another] at a height of more than ten handbreadths above the ground, is liable (for violating Shabbat), for thus was the carrying done by the sons of Kehath... And how do we know that this was the way in which the sons of Kehath

---

[12] In the Machon Yerushalayim/Hartman edition, Maharal's discussion of this topic can be found in the third section of *Be'er HaShishi*, beginning on p. 177.

[13] Maharal rejects the straightforward understanding of the Sages' view on the grounds that it is clearly scientifically absurd, but this is anachronistic. That which appears obviously false in one era does not necessarily appear false to people in another era. There were many intelligent people, over a long period, who believed that the world is flat, even though to later generations there appeared to be very obvious proofs that this is not the case.

carried? As it is written, "…surrounding the Tabernacle and the Altar" (Numbers 3:26), comparing the Altar to the Tabernacle; just as the Tabernacle was ten cubits tall, so too the Altar was ten cubits tall… and it is written, "He spread the Tent over the Tabernacle," and Rav said: "Our teacher Moses spread it out"—from here you learn that the height of the Levites was ten cubits. There is a tradition that any load that is carried with poles has one third above [the carriers' shoulders] and two thirds below. We thus find that it was [carried] well above [ten handbreadths]. (Talmud, *Shabbat* 92a)

The Talmud thereby establishes that the Altar was carried at least ten handbreadths above the ground from the fact that the Levites carrying it were ten cubits tall. There does not appear to be any way to interpret this other than as a factual statement about the height of the Levites. And indeed, many Torah scholars over history clearly understood the Talmud in this way.[14]

How would rationalists have dealt with this Gemara? The Talmud's account of the Levites' great height, while based on an extrapolation from Moses to the rest of the tribe, was linked with the view that the bronze Altar was ten cubits tall, which necessitated that the Levites must have been of great height for them to carry it. Yet as it turns out, while it is Rabbi Yosi's view that the altar was ten cubits tall, Rav Yehudah's view is that the bronze Altar was only three cubits tall, and thus the Levites would not have needed to be any taller than the average person in order to carry it. Yet Rambam would not have had this way out; he states that the altar was ten cubits high (*Hilchot Beis HaBechirah* 2:5). Perhaps he would have simply rejected this method of deriving the law concerning carrying on Shabbat.

---

[14] See, for example, *Moshav Zekeinim* to Exodus 26:1, who wonders how Aharon managed to fit inside the Tabernacle when he was wearing his turban. Bnei Yissacher, cited in R. Yisrael Berger, *Eser Tzachtzachos* (Pieterkov 1910) 8:23, states that unlike Moshe, Aharon was of regular height, which can be deduced from the requirement that there be three steps leading up to the menorah, as recorded in the Gemara (*Menachos* 29a) and Sifri (*Beha'alotecha* 8:3). On the other hand, Maharil Diskin, Commentary to the Torah, *parashas Beha'alosecha*, states that the steps were for future generations, and Aharon himself did not require them.

But what of Maharal? Since Maharal understands that the Levites were, metaphysically speaking, ten cubits high, is this approach transferable to this case? According to Rabbi Moshe Shapiro, probably the most famous exponent of Maharal's approach in recent times, it is.[15] The halachah regarding carrying on Shabbat ten handbreadths above the ground is learned from a calculation involving the metaphysical height of the Levites.

Conclusion

Some see Maharal's revolutionary approach to Aggadah as being a boon to the advancement of science in the Jewish world:

> ...Maharal's most important clarification was to disentangle natural philosophy from the assumptions and restraints of Jewish theology and Aristotelian metaphysics, and in so doing to provide an autonomous realm in which scientific pursuit could legitimately flourish. (David Ruderman, *Jewish Thought and Scientific Discovery*, p. 77)

Similarly, André Neher compares Maharal to Galileo, in the latter's famous *Letter to the Grand Duchess Christina*.[16] Galileo drew a distinction between Scripture, which teaches theological truth, and science, which teaches physical truths. Likewise, Maharal viewed Torah and science as operating in different and separate domains.

In this vein, I would like to recount what the late Rabbi Aryeh Carmell told me about a conversation that he had with Rabbi Yitzchak Hutner, the primary expositor of Maharal's thought in his generation. Rabbi Carmell had asked him what to do about all the scientific evidence that there was no global Deluge. Rabbi Hutner replied, "Explain it with the approach of Maharal." In other words, the point of the Torah's story of the Deluge is the inner message, not the historical account. It is difficult to imagine any other traditionalist Rosh Yeshivah in the *haredi* world being so liberal. But R. Hutner's dedication to Maharal allowed him to focus on what he considered to be the essence of the Torah's account.

---

[15] Based on a conversation with Rabbi Mordecai Kornfeld, who asked Rabbi Shapiro this question at my request.

[16] *Jewish Thought and the Scientific Revolution of the Sixteenth Century*, p. 209.

Yet is it true that Maharal's approach rendered Torah as being completely detached from the physical world? As noted, Maharal held that Moshe was as tall as humanly possible. Maharal did claim that the metaphysical reality would be expressed in the physical world to the extent possible. The metaphysical reality is the source of physical phenomena. And not only does this mean that it is expressed in the physical world to some degree; it also means that those who are learned in metaphysical knowledge possess authority when making statements about the physical world.

Neher claims that, according to Maharal, "to be contemptuous of science and to make the Torah into an infallible scientific authority is to display a childish obscurantism."[17] But Maharal *was* contemptuous of science. He describes astronomy as a valuable study, but qualifies this by insisting that only when based on Jewish tradition and wisdom can one hope to attain truth.[18] He gives that as the explanation of the verse "for it is your wisdom and understanding in the eyes of the nations" (Deut. 4:6), emphasizing that without Torah, it is impossible to reach conclusions in astronomy with certainty or precision.

Neher further claims that Maharal had a positive view of Copernicus.[19] Yet in describing Copernicus, Maharal relates that he overturned the work of all his predecessors, but notes that this astronomer himself admits that he is unable to resolve everything. Maharal does not express any theological objections toward heliocentrism per se; rather, he is disparaging towards Copernicus just as he was to all secular science. In my view Neher distorts Maharal's position, presenting him as describing science as the noble march of human thought with its ups and downs, whereas in fact Maharal's goal is to dismiss such secular endeavors as lacking any credibility.[20] Maharal may have provided an "autonomous

---

[17] *Ibid.*

[18] *Netivot Olam, Netiv HaTorah* 14.

[19] *Jewish Thought and the Scientific Revolution of the Sixteenth Century*, pp. 208-10, and *Copernicus in the Hebrew Literature* p. 213.

[20] Neher brings the Maharal's discussion of Copernicus and astronomy in which, according to Neher's translation, Maharal describes the "magnificent achievements" of

realm in which scientific pursuit could legitimately flourish," but any true disciples of Maharal would not assign credibility to such scientific pursuits.

Furthermore, even if Maharal's approach grants free reign to the study of the natural sciences, it asphyxiates rational thought when applied to the study of Talmud. I cannot agree with R. Eisen's assessment that Maharal's analyses "resonate with a palpable authenticity."[21] When considering Maharal's interpretation of various passages, such as those dealing with astronomy, it often strains credulity to imagine that the Talmud actually means what Maharal claims it to mean. There is no hint of Maharal's approach in the words of the Talmud, and not one of his predecessors interpreted it in that way.

In addition, Maharal's approach virtually forces irrational conclusions when applied to the study of Talmudic interpretation over the ages. The result of Maharal's elevation of aggadata to dogma is that the approach of most of the Rishonim and many Acharonim becomes invalid, even heretical. What, then, is one to do with all these Rishonim? For traditionalists, rating these Rishonim and Acharonim as heretics is not an option. The result can be seen in the contemporary polemical work by Rabbi Reuven Schmelczer, *Chaim B'Emunatam*, which advocates Maharal's approach and endorses Maharal's claim that any other approach is unacceptable. The author is thus forced to ignore other authorities, perform extremely contrived reinterpretations of their positions, or denounce them as forgeries.[22] Maharal thus forces one of the greatest revolutions in Jewish intellectual history of all time.

---

non-Jewish scientists, whereas in fact the word "magnificent" does not appear in Maharal and is Neher's insertion.

[21] "Maharal's *Be'er ha-Golah* and His Revolution in *Aggadic* Scholarship," p. 192.

[22] See my critique "Rewriting Jewish Intellectual History," available online at www.zootorah.com/controversy/ChaimBEmunasam.pdf.

EIGHT

The Question of the Kidneys' Counsel

Introduction

The kidneys (*kelayot*) are mentioned in Scripture in two contexts. On several occasions they are listed among the organs of an animal that are offered on the altar.[1] But on over a dozen other occasions they are described as organs with functions relating to cognition (which itself may be the reason why they play a role in sacrificial rites, due to the animals' kidneys representing the parallel organ in man[2]); specifically, functioning as the mind, conscience, or the source of counsel/free will:

> You are present in their mouths, but far from their kidneys. (Jer. 12:2)

> I bless God, Who has counseled me; my kidneys admonish me at night. (Ps. 16:7)

On several occasions, the kidneys are mentioned in this context together with the heart:

> God of Hosts, just Judge, Who examines the kidneys and heart... (Jer. 11:20)

> I, God, probe the heart, and examine the kidneys, and repay each man according to his ways, with the fruit of his deeds. (Jer. 17:10)

> God of Hosts, Who tests the righteous, looking at the heart and kidneys... (Jer. 20:12)

> ...the Lord, the righteous, examines the hearts and kidneys. (Ps. 7:10)

---

[1] Exodus 29:13; 29:22; Leviticus 3:4; 3:10; 3:15; 4:9; 7:4; 8:16; 8:25; 9:10 and 9:19.

[2] As per the comments of Ramban and Rabbeinu Bechaya to Leviticus 1:9, and Tashbetz, *Magen Avot* 3:4.

> My son, if your heart is wise, my heart also rejoices. My kidneys rejoice,
> when your lips speak with uprightness. (Prov. 23:15-16)

Indeed, the heart itself is described as being the source of the mind and its thoughts:

> "And God saw that the evils of man were great, and that all the drives of
> the thoughts of his heart were only evil all day long." (Gen. 6:5)

The King James Bible, when translating *kelayot* in its non-sacrificial context, uses the word "reins" rather than kidneys. While the two terms are essentially synonymous, the differentiation was probably done out of a desire to indicate an allegorical use of the term. The JPS translation uses "mind" or "conscience."

But did the authors of Scripture mean the term metaphorically? Or did they indeed intend that the kidneys are the seat of part of the mind, a role that we would assign today to the brain? This is a question that has been discussed extensively in several articles,[3] with the general conclusion being that it does indeed reflect a belief that the kidneys actually possess such functions. In this chapter, however, I shall focus on how various medieval and later rabbinic authorities differed in their understanding of this topic.

The Kidneys in the Talmud and Midrash

It is clear that the Sages of the Talmud understood the Scriptural references to the kidneys literally. This is evident from the following passage:

> The Rabbis taught: The kidneys advise, the heart considers, the tongue
> articulates, the mouth finishes, the esophagus brings in all kinds of food,
> the windpipe gives sound, the lungs absorb all kinds of fluids, the liver
> causes anger, the gallbladder secretes a drop into it and calms it, the spleen
> laughs, the gizzard grinds, the stomach [causes] sleep, the nose [causes]
> wakefulness. (*Berachot* 61a; similarly in Midrash *Vayikra Rabbah* 4:4)

---

[3] Garabed Eknoyan, "The Kidneys in the Bible: What Happened?" *Journal of the American Society of Nephrology* 16:12 (2005) pp. 3464-3471; Giovanni Maio, "The Metaphorical and Mythical Use of the Kidney in Antiquity," *American Journal of Nephrology* (1999) 19:2 pp. 101-6.

This is not an aggadic legend intended to be understood metaphorically. The descriptions of the functions of the tongue, mouth, esophagus, windpipe, lungs, stomach and nose are all clearly scientific descriptions intended to be interpreted literally. The account of the liver causing anger is also consistent with standard belief in the ancient world.[4] Thus, the account of the function of the kidneys and heart are thus also clearly intended to be literal descriptions. This, too, is consistent with standard belief in the ancient world, which placed the mind in the heart and nearby organs.[5]

The immediately preceding statement in the Talmud relates that the two kidneys have two distinct roles:

> The Rabbis taught: A person has two kidneys, one of which counsels him to do good, and the other counsels him to do evil. And it is reasonable that the good one is on his right and the evil one on his left, as it is written, "The heart of the wise man is to his right, and the heart of a fool is to his left." (Talmud ibid.)

Due to its juxtaposition with the other passage, there is every reason to believe that this was likewise intended literally as an account of the two kidneys' respective functions.

---

[4] See too *Midrash Shemot Rabbah* 7 and *Midrash Lekach Tov* on the verse "*kaveid lev Pharaoh.*"

[5] For an extensive discussion of ancient views concerning whether the mind is housed in the brain or the heart, see Julius Rocca, *Galen on the Brain: Anatomical Knowledge and Physiological Speculation in the Second Century AD*, pp. 17-47. While Galen knew the brain to have a cognitive function, Aristotle believed that the brain only serves to cool the blood. Along with other ancient cultures, he believed the mind to be housed in the heart. The Rabbinic word for "brain," *moach*, only appears in Scripture in one instance (Job 21:24) where it refers to the marrow inside bone. It does appear that some of the Sages of the Talmud may have adopted aspects of Galen's view, since we find R. Yehudah HaNasi disputing people with the statement, "It appears that he does not have a brain in his head;" see too Midrash Mishlei 1. However, the fact of some of the Sages attributing *some* cognitive function to the brain, does not mean that they ruled out the heart and kidneys serving to make moral decisions. In general, the Sages of the Babylonian Talmud followed Akkadian and ancient Babylonian understandings of physiology and medicine; see Mark J. Geller, "Akkadian Healing Therapies in the Babylonian Talmud," (Berlin: Max-Planck-Institut für Wissenschaftsgeschichte 2004).

Another source in the Talmud, to which we will later return, discusses how we know where to cut the spinal cord of a sheep that has been brought as a sacrifice. The Talmud answers that the Torah instructs it to be cut "opposite the *atzeh*" (Lev. 3:9). The word *atzeh* does not appear anywhere else in Scripture, and is usually translated as "spine." But the Talmud expounds it to mean, "the place of the kidneys, which give counsel ('*etzah*,' vocalizing the word differently)."[6]

Elsewhere, there is a description of how man is a microcosm of everything in the universe, with a description of how each of his bodily parts corresponds to something in the world; in this list, it describes his kidneys as corresponding to advisors.[7] In another place, the Talmud states that God placed wisdom (*chachmah*) in the kidneys.[8]

A Midrash also relates that Abraham was taught the Torah by his kidneys,[9] while another Midrash elaborates upon the Scriptural accounts of God examining the kidneys and heart, explaining that out of all the limbs and organs in the body, it is these that are directly responsible for determining a person's actions.[10] Note that this Midrash entirely excludes any role for the brain in this process.

Finally, in the *Nishmat kol chai* prayer, of uncertain authorship and origins, it is made clear that it is the heart and kidneys, not the brain, that house a person's consciousness:

> For every mouth is in acknowledgment to You, and every tongue swears to You, and every knee bows to You, and every erect spine prostrates itself to You, and all hearts fear You, and all innards and kidneys praise Your Name, as it is written, "All my bones say, Who is like You, O God."

Medieval France/ Germany: No Difficulties

Rashi (1040-1105), in all his commentaries on all the verses and Talmudic statements about the kidneys, does not make any comment

---

[6] *Chullin* 11a.

[7] *Avot d'Rabbi Natan* 31:3. This probably dates to somewhat after the Talmudic period.

[8] *Rosh HaShanah* 26a.

[9] Midrash *Bereishit Rabbah* 61:1; similarly in Midrash Tanhuma, *parashat Vayigash*.

[10] Midrash Tehillim 14.

about their being a metaphor. While it is true that in general Rashi does not do anything other than explain the simple meaning of the text, he does see fit to explain where a word is a metaphor. We see this specifically in the context of anatomy. On the verse, "and you shall circumcise the foreskin of your hearts" (Deut. 10:16), Rashi (along with the other commentaries) stresses that the word "foreskin" is a metaphor—but not the word "hearts"! Furthermore, in his commentary to the Talmudic account of the kidneys giving counsel, Rashi elaborates that the kidneys advise the heart on what to do, bringing Scripture as a source for this. From all this, we see that Rashi believed that the kidneys actually do provide counsel. There is no reason why he would not have unquestioningly accepted this. Living in France and Germany, Rashi's education was limited to Jewish studies alone; he would not have been exposed to the scientific and medical texts that would lead one to question whether the kidneys really do have such a function.

Somewhat strangely, on the word *atzeh* (Lev. 3:9), Rashi explains that it refers to the kidneys, which give counsel—thus citing the Talmudic interpretation. However, the Talmudic interpretation would appear to be an exegesis (*derash*), rather than the straightforward translation (*peshat*). Yet Rashi presents it as the *peshat*. Whatever the reason for this perhaps unexpected approach, it accentuates the fact that Rashi genuinely believed the kidneys to be the source of counsel.

I have not been able to locate any source in the literature of French-German rabbinic authorities which, either explicitly or implicitly, demonstrates any awareness of the scientific difficulties with the Scriptural and Talmudic descriptions of the kidneys' function.

Medieval Spain: Grappling with the Challenge

In sharp contrast to Rashi, **R. Judah HaLevi** (c. 1075–1141) expresses awareness at the scientific objections to the kidneys being the source of counsel, and offers a scientific quasi-defense:

> Now, with that which is said about the function of the following organs— the kidneys give counsel, the spleen laughs, the liver causes anger and the stomach causes sleep—there is room for doubt. However, it is not surprising that the kidneys would have an effect upon the nature of

thoughts. Surely we see something similar in the function of the testicles; for eunuchs are weak of intellect, even more than women. (*Kuzari* 4:25)

While he ends up with the same position as Rashi, that the Talmud is to be accepted literally, his approach could not be more different. For Rashi, there was no reason to question the Talmudic account. But for HaLevi, who was educated in Arabic literature, science and philosophy, the Talmud was not studied in a vacuum. In particular, his training as a physician is doubtless responsible for his being sensitive to the problem raised by the Talmud's accounts of the functions of these organs. Still, given the limited development of the medical sciences in his era, his decision to nevertheless maintain belief in the Talmud's statement is not unreasonable; although it was probably fuelled by his general goal of defending traditional Jewish teachings against external threats. R. Yehudah HaLevi's approach was to form the basis for many later authorities in their approach to this topic, but they would not emulate his hesitancy. He admits that there is room for doubt as to the correctness of the Talmud's statement, and his proposed solution seems somewhat tentative.

Abraham Ibn Ezra (1089-c.1164) takes a different approach and explains the Scriptural references to kidneys as a metaphor.[11] The kidneys are hidden deep within the body, and thereby represent man's innermost self. Furthermore, Ibn Ezra elsewhere explains the function of kidneys as relating to the generation of sperm.[12] He thus did not believe them to be the source of counsel, and therefore explained the verses metaphorically.[13]

---

[11] See his commentary to Psalms 7:10, 16:7, and 139:13.

[12] Long Commentary to Ex. 23:25. See Shlomo Sela, *Abraham Ibn Ezra and the Rise of Medieval Hebrew Science*, pp. 130-137, for a discussion of this passage.

[13] In his commentary to Psalms 139:13, "It was You who created my kidneys, You formed me in my mother's womb," as an alternative to explaining the term metaphorically, he suggests that they are invoked due to their being the seat of desire. As we shall see, there those who used this belief to explain the Talmudic notion of the kidneys counseling man. However, in the context of this verse, the kidneys are not necessarily mentioned as being sources of counsel, and thus there is no reason to believe that Ibn Ezra's mention of their being the seat of desire represents any sort of effort to accommodate the Talmud's statement.

Additionally, in his comment to Lev. 3:9, regarding the word *atzeh*, Ibn Ezra states that the word is not related to any other in Scripture—clearly rejecting the aforementioned Talmudic exegesis which relates it to the word *etzah* and sees the verse as referring to the kidneys.

Ibn Ezra "received his secular education in the best tradition of the Arabic-Andalusian science."[14] His scientific interests are most prominently in the fields of mathematics, astronomy and astrology, rather than physiology or medicine. Still, as can be seen from his discussion of the function of the kidneys, he certainly studied physiology also, and it is presumably for this reason that he was perturbed by the Scriptural description and the Talmudic elaboration.[15] While he had no difficulties simply rejecting the Talmudic statement—and in so doing, acted consistently with the standard approach to Aggadata among the Geonim and Sephardic Rishonim[16]—he could not do that with the Scriptural verses, and therefore chose to interpret them allegorically instead.

Ramban (Gerona, 1194—Land of Israel, 1270) accepts that the kidneys truly are the sources of counsel. He explains that the reason why with sacrifices, the animal's kidneys are burned, is that they are the instruments of thought and desire, and thereby remind man that it was these with which he sinned.[17] He makes no mention here of the scientific issues involved. Yet Ramban, having medical training in thirteenth century Spain, was aware that the brain is the seat of the mind.[18] But while there is no open reference to the problem, there is perhaps an implicit reference, which emerges when we contrast the commentary of Ramban

---

[14] Sela, p. 8.

[15] Note that in his commentary to Exodus 23:25, Ibn Ezra writes that the soul, which is the intellect, is housed in the brain, and the *ruach* is housed in the heart.

[16] See Chaim Eisen, "Maharal's *Be'er ha-Golah* and His Revolution in *Aggadic* Scholarship — in Their Context and on His Terms." *Hakirah* vol. 4 (Winter 2007) pp. 137-194.

[17] Commentary to Leviticus 1:9.

[18] In *Torat Hashem Temimah* (*Kitvei HaRamban*, vol 1. p. 150), Ramban notes that the purpose of the *tefillin* of the head is to be facing the brain, which is the "chariot of the soul." Note, however, that in his commentary to Ex. 13:16, he writes that the seat of thought is in the brain *and* the heart.

with that of Rabbeinu Bachya, who often expresses similar ideas. Both correlate the act of bringing the sacrifice with atoning for sinning with deed, speech and thought. But whereas Rabbeinu Bachya simply describes the innards and kidneys as "instruments of counsel and thought," Ramban says that these are the instruments of "thought *and desire*." The latter appears to be an accommodation with the scientific view of the time that the kidneys are linked to the sexual organs. Yet, unlike Ibn Ezra, this does not mean that Ramban saw that function as existing in exclusion to the kidneys functioning as a source of counsel; it seems that he may have considered this to be part of their role as a source of counsel, as advocating sexual desire (and perhaps general counsel too). This is an approach that, as we shall later see, others presented explicitly.

As noted, **Rabbeinu Bachya b. Asher** (mid-thirteenth century - 1340), a disciple of Rashba, also notes that the kidneys of an offering correlate with the organs in man which give counsel to the heart and lead him to sin.[19] Yet he was also aware that the brain has a cognitive function. In order to reconcile this with the Scriptural and Talmudic accounts of the role of the heart and kidneys, he proposed that thoughts are conceived in the head, but need to descend to the heart and kidneys in order to be actualized and transmitted as directions to the body.[20] **R. Yehoshua Ibn Shuib** (Spain, early 14th century), another disciple of Rashba, cites and endorses the view of R. Yehudah HaLevi that the Talmud's statement is correct and scientifically defensible. He also claims further evidence in support of the Talmud's statement, noting that there was a case of a person who had his kidneys injured and as a result had his mental faculties harmed.[21] Yet another disciple of Rashba, **R. Yaakov b. Chananel Skili**

---

[19] See commentary to Leviticus 1:9, 3:9 and 9:9.

[20] See his commentary to Genesis 1:27 and Genesis 6:6. A similar view of the role of the kidneys can be found in the thirteenth-century work *Sefer Ma'arechet Elokut*, chapter 10 and in R. Yitzchak Caro, *Toldot Yitzchak* to Genesis 6:6. Note that in Rabbeinu Bachya's presentation, there is a conspicuous absence of any specification that it is sexual desire that the kidneys provide; this, in conjunction with his general description of the role of the kidneys and heart, shows that unlike Ramban, he saw the kidneys as responsible for all counsel, not specifically sexual desire.

[21] *Drashot Ibn Shuib* to *parashat Emor*, p. 284.

(Spain-Israel-Iraq, 14th century), similarly defends the position that the kidneys genuinely do provide counsel. He cites verses and statements from the Talmud that the kidneys contain knowledge and provide guidance. R. Jacob explains the reason why he is citing these verses at length:

> It was necessary for me to bring all these because I heard that there are some of my people, small of faith, who challenge our Sages for saying that the kidneys give counsel, and they say that the kidneys have no power to understand and to give counsel, but rather are just like the lower intestines. But behold, we have learned from the words of the prophets, and from the words of Solomon... who was wise in the natural sciences... and from God's response to Job... that the kidneys are an organ of wisdom, just like the heart. (*Torat HaMincha* (Jerusalem: Ahavat Shalom Publications 2000), Discourse 74 for *parashat Ki Tavo*, p. 665)

Note, however, the difference between the approach of R. Yaakov b. Chananel and that of R. Yehudah HaLevi and R. Yehoshua ibn Shuib. They both saw it as necessary to include some sort of scientific justification for their position, whereas for R. Yaakov b. Chananel, the authority of the prophets and King Shlomo alone is enough.

R. Shimon b. Tzemach Duran ("Tashbatz," Majorca-Algiers 1361-1444) studied philosophy and science extensively, focusing in particular on medicine, which he practiced for many years at Majorca. In his work *Magen Avot* he provides a scientific basis for the Talmud's description of the kidneys' function.[22] He argues that since the kidneys are located close to the sex organs and are related to sexual desire, and the sex organs differ with men and women, and counsel is only found with men (!), thus the kidneys are seen to be the source of counsel. As further evidence for this, he points out that eunuchs lack counsel and wisdom. R. Duran states that R. Yehudah HaLevi is his basis for this. But in fact HaLevi's claim was milder, being only that since the testicles are observed to be linked to cognitive functions, it is not far-fetched to suppose that there is also some sort of link between the kidneys and cognitive functions. R. Duran's son **R. Shlomo** ("Rashbash," Algiers 1400-1467) cites and further elaborates

---

[22] *Magen Avot* 3:4.

upon the explanation given by his father as well as that given by R. Yehoshua ibn Shuib.[23]

Early Modern Italy

The discussion about the kidneys flared up again in sixteenth century Italy. This was a place where many Jews received an extensive secular education, especially in medicine. The first person to weigh in on the issue was **R. Moshe ben Avraham Provençal** (Italy 1503-1576), a halachist and Chief Rabbi of Mantua. Among his responsa is a question that was posed about the Talmud's description of the kidneys giving counsel, since scientists and physicians had concluded that the brain is the seat of counsel. R. Moshe responds that the opinion of scientists and physicians is irrelevant vis-à-vis the tradition of the Sages. He points out that the concept of the kidneys giving counsel is also stated by the Prophets and is even found in the Torah itself, citing the verse from Lev. 3:9 that the spinal cord be cut "opposite the *atzeh*."[24]

His disciple and later successor R. **Yehudah Moscato** (Italy c.1530-c.1593), on the other hand, while still defending the Talmudic position, sought to reconcile it with science. R. Moscato had also studied with R. Azariah de Rossi and, as a product of the Renaissance, he was well read and respected modern knowledge, which meant that he could not simply dismiss medical opinion.[25] In his commentary on the *Kuzari*, he offers some brief comments in elaboration of R. Yehudah HaLevi's pointing out that the reproductive organs are likewise connected to the cognitive faculties.[26] But in his collection of sermons, he has a lengthy explanation

---

[23] Responsa Rashbash 309-310 (Jerusalem: Machon Yerushalayim 1998).

[24] *She'elot u'Teshuvot Rabbeinu Moshe Provençal* (Jerusalem 1989), also cited in *Pachad Yitzchak, erech Kilyaot Yoazot.*

[25] According to one study, R. Moscato was "deeply affected by Renaissance culture and it left a noticeable imprint on the essential character of his thought." See Moshe Idel, "Judah Moscato, a late Renaissance Jewish Preacher," in *Preachers of the Italian Ghetto* (1992) pp. 41-66.

[26] *Kol Yehudah* (Venice, 1594) to *Kuzari* 4:25.

of his own to justify the Talmud's statement.[27] This is based on the ancient ideas of the bodily humors, with the medieval modification of how these produce vapors which affect the brain. R. Moscato explains that the spleen filters black bile from the blood, and the gallbladder filters yellow bile. The kidneys, he states, remove the "watery elements" from the blood, which are released as urine. Since the result of this is that the blood is cleansed, and it is clean blood that produces clear and pure vapors, which in turn means that the forces that power the intellect will produce elevated and perfected thoughts, R. Moscato argues that it is correct for the kidneys to be described as the source of wisdom, understanding and counsel. His explanation for why the spleen and gallbladder are not also described in this way is that their role in filtering the blood is not as obvious and prominent as that of the kidneys. But aside from the outdated physiological views of R. Moscato, his explanation does not even suffice for his own time period, since he does not address the fact that the Talmud describes one of the kidneys as providing *harmful* counsel.

R. Yitzchak Lampronti (Italy, 1679-1756) studied with the prominent rabbinic scholar and physician Yitzchak Cantarini, and completed his medical studies at the University of Padua. He continued to practice medicine even while working as rabbi and Rosh Yeshivah.[28] In his Talmudic encyclopedia *Pachad Yitzchak*, he has an extensive entry on the topic of the kidneys giving counsel.[29] Due to his extensive medical background, he must have considered this an obviously and deeply problematic statement that required addressing at length.

After citing the relevant portions from the Talmud, R. Lampronti begins by noting that while the natural philosophers have discovered many wondrous things, they have not penetrated the true nature of things. Our sages, on the other hand, were privy to divine secrets regarding

---

[27] *Nefutzot Yehudah* (Venice, 1588; Lemberg, 1859), *derush* 9. He also cites *Derech Emunah, shaar bet,* but I have been unable to determine to which of the numerous works by this title he refers.

[28] David Ruderman, "Contemporary Science and Jewish law in the Eyes of Isaac Lampronti of Ferrara and Some of his Contemporaries," *Jewish History* 6:1-2, *The Frank Talmage Memorial Volume* (1992), pp. 211-212.

[29] *Pachad Yitzchak, erech Kilyaot Yoazot.*

creation. However, R. Lampronti proceeds to note that when faced with a conflict between the Sages and science, he chooses between two approaches: one being that the Sages' received knowledge enabled them to reach truths that secular scientists cannot attain, and the other being that the Sages did not speak from tradition and were mistaken in their view. The latter is an approach that he applies in the case of the Talmudic statement that lice spontaneously generate, yet in the case of the kidneys, R. Lampronti adopts the approach that the Sages were correct (and later cites R. Moshe Provencal's insistence on this). Ruderman claims that R. Lampronti is simply inconsistent and self-contradictory.[30] However, I do not believe that to be the case. R. Lampronti explains why he is taking the approach here that the Sages were correct: because Scripture itself attributes such a role to the kidneys.

R. Lampronti proceeds to give a scientific explanation for why the Talmudic account of the function of the kidneys is correct. Like R. Yehudah HaLevi, Ibn Shuib and Tashbatz, R. Lampronti begins with the notion that the kidneys are involved with generating sperm for the testicles. He explains the concept of "one for good, one for evil" as meaning that there are both good and evil manifestations of the sexual urge. As for the Talmud's calculation that the good kidney is on the right and the evil on the left, he interprets this allegorically, to mean that the wise person will use his sexual urge for the "right"—i.e. for the good—namely, for the purpose of procreation, whereas the evil person will use his heart for the "left"—for evil purposes of lust.

But R. Lampronti's interpretation of the Talmud is problematic on several counts (aside from the fact that the actual connection between the kidneys and sperm is minimal). First is that he interprets one statement of the Talmud (concerning the function of the kidneys) literally, and the adjacent statement (concerning the placement of the kidneys) allegorically, which is unreasonable. Second is that if "right" means good and "left" means evil, then it does not make sense for the Talmud to say that the good kidney is on the right and the evil kidney is on the left; this means that it is saying that the good aspect of kidneys is good and the evil

---

[30] Ruderman, p. 219.

aspect is evil! Third is that restricting the notion of the kidneys giving counsel to referring only to the sexual urge hardly seems consistent with the verses and Midrash Tehillim, which imply that all of man's inner struggles are dictated by the kidneys.

Although R. **Chaim Yosef David Azulai** ("Chida," 1724-1807) spent several years in Italy, he was essentially a product of Jerusalem, dedicated to Talmud and Kabbalah. Nevertheless, he had broad interests, which come to light in his defense of the Talmud's statement about the kidneys. Chida claims that the microscope[31] reveals connections between the kidneys and the brain.[32] His reference is apparently to vascular microcirculation and macrocirculation which connects the heart, kidneys and brain.[33] Chida thereby sees evidence that the kidneys are transmitting information to the brain, apparently relying on the ancient belief that blood is a vehicle of the mind.

The Modern Period: Literalists, Allegorists and Rationalists

In the modern era, many still insisted on the literal truth of the kidneys providing counsel. Rabbi **Eliezer Waldenberg** (1915-2006), who was the rabbi of the Shaarei Zedek Medical Center, uses the Talmud as reason for warning against kidney transplants, since one risks the donor's kidneys counseling the recipient in a harmful manner.[34] The prominent Sephardic authority Rabbi **Ovadia Yosef** (b. 1920) recommends that Jews receiving kidney transplants choose, wherever possible, to receive the organ from a Jewish donor, due to the Talmudic account of the kidneys providing counsel.[35] Rabbi **Yitzchak Silberstein** recommends that a kidney donor give the left rather than the right kidney, due to the role given to the right kidney by the Talmud.[36] These authorities probably were simply unaware

---

[31] Chida actually uses the term telescope ("*tel iskopio*"), but presumably intended to refer to the microscope.

[32] *Pesach Einayim*, Berachos 60a, and *Midbar Kadmus, Kaf*.

[33] My thanks to Rabbi Dr. Edward Reichman for explaining this to me.

[34] Responsa *Tzitz Eliezer* 13:91:4. See too 17:66:7

[35] Responsa *Yabia Omer* vol. 8 *Choshen Mishpat* 11.

[36] Cited in *VeHaarev Na*.

and/or unconcerned with modern scientific views as to the function of the kidneys. But Rabbi **Chaim Elazar Spira** (the Munkacher Rebbe, 1871-1937) claims that medical science provides support for the Talmud's statement, albeit somewhat reinterpreted to be referring to nineteenth-century beliefs concerning the pathophysiology of kidney stones.[37] He explains that renal colic results from an inability to digest calcium properly, which in turn results from psychological stress and anxiety—which he describes as "the inability to provide counsel to the soul." R. Spira thereby sees medical science as justifying the Sages' statement that the kidneys provide counsel; although he seems not to have noticed that even with this very loose interpretation of "providing counsel," it is the heart affecting the kidneys, rather than the other way around, as described in the Talmud. In a similar manner, many traditionalists today claim scientific support for the Talmud's account,[38] citing papers attesting to a (very minor) connection between the brain and kidneys.[39] These people ignore the fact that the Talmud is not speaking of a potential minor negative impact of kidney disease on the cognitive function of the brain, but rather of the kidneys providing counsel and being the organ that God inspects in order to judge a person, with the brain playing no role whatsoever.

Other traditionalists, who accept the modern scientific view regarding the kidneys, interpret the Scriptural and Talmudic accounts allegorically. In the non-Jewish world, Reverend **J. G Lansing** develops a lengthy argument to prove that the kidneys in the Bible are a metaphor for a specific component of man's spiritual/mental self, namely, his

---

[37] *Divrei Torah* 6 p. 880. My thanks to Rabbi Chaim Rapoport for referring me to this source, and to Rabbi Dr. Edward Reichman for explaining R. Spira's discussion.

[38] See, for example, Abigail Atlas, "'The Kidneys Give Advice,' Revisited," *Derech HaTeva* vol. 10 (2005-6) pp. 9-10.

[39] E.g. Anne M. Murray, "The brain and the kidney connection. A model of accelerated vascular cognitive impairment," *Neurology* 1331819 (August 19, 2009); Raymond Vanholder, Peter Paul De Deyn, et al., "Marconi Revisited: From Kidney to Brain—Two Organ Systems Communicating at Long Distance." *Journal of the American Society of Nephrology* (2008) 19 pp. 1253-1255.

conscience.[40] Following from the premise that the kidneys in Scripture are allegorical, **Frank Chamberlin Porter** (1859-1946), Professor of Biblical Theology at the Yale Divinity School, claims that the same is true with the Talmud. Referring to the passage in *Berachot*, he writes as follows:

> Here we have, of course, not a literal identification of the impulses with the two kidneys. The word reins (*kelayot*) is used in the Old Testament prevailingly, as the word heart is used almost exclusively, not of the physical organ, but of the inner man, the inmost self. In the saying before us, the two kidneys in the physical man suggest the two impulses in man as a moral being. (Frank C. Porter, "The Yeçer Hara: A Study in the Jewish Doctrine of Sin," in *Biblical and Semitic Studies: Yale Historical and Critical Contributions to Biblical Science* p. 102)

The physician Dr. **Yehudah Leib Katzenelson** (1846-1917) insists that the Talmud's account of the kidneys providing counsel must be a metaphor, since the sages "surely knew" that the brain is the seat of the intellect and counsel.[41] In a lengthy discussion, Rabbi **Yekutiel Aryeh Kamelhar** (1871-1937) claims that the Talmud is allegorically referring to the spiritual counterpart of the kidneys, which are so named because just as the actual kidneys provide "good counsel" by filtering urine, so too these spiritual organs provide good counsel.[42] Rabbi **Chaim Friedlander** of the Ponovezh Yeshivah (1923-1986) similarly insists that the Scriptural and Talmudic references must be to "metaphysical kidneys" which cleanse the soul of evil, paralleling the function of the physical kidneys which cleanse the body of waste.[43] None of these authorities explain how the Talmud's account of the kidneys also providing harmful counsel occurs with the spiritual counterparts to the kidneys; nor do they provide any

---

[40] Lansing J. G. "The Reins." *The Old Testament Student* 3:6 (Feb. 1884), pp. 191-196.

[41] *HaTalmud VeChachmat HaRefuah* (Berlin 1925), p. 106. For further discussion of the Talmud's statement about kidneys, see R. Meyer Lebush Malbim, *Chiddushi HaMalbim Al HaShas, Berachot* 60b; R. Eliyahu Eliezer Dessler, *Michtav MeEliyahu* vol. 5 p. 26.

[42] *HaTalmud U'Mada'ei HaTevel* (Levov 1928) 3:1. pp. 17-20.

[43] *Sifsei Chaim, Emunah u'Bechirah* II, p. 316. My thanks to Rabbi Chaim Rapoport for this source.

justification for reading the various Talmudic statements in this light (beyond the general claim of the Sages' supernatural wisdom).[44]

For Orthodox Jews of a more rationalist persuasion, on the other hand, it is relatively easy to accept that the Talmud's views on the kidneys were simply mistaken. More challenging, however, are the descriptions of the kidneys found in Scripture. Some take the approach that the Scriptural verses to this effect are allegorical, and were misunderstood by the Sages and Rishonim.[45] But others are able to accept that they are literal and mistaken without this harming their faith, by adopting a variant of the principle of *dibra Torah k'lashon bnei adam*, "the Torah speaks like the language of men."[46] This phrase appears in numerous places throughout the Talmud and Midrash, in the rabbinic works of the medieval period, and in the writings of recent scholars. However, the concept is utilized in very different ways.[47]

In the Talmud and Midrash, the phrase *dibra Torah k'lashon bnei adam* means that pleonasms (excesses in language) are used as a rhetorical flourish in the Torah, just as people speak, and are not intended to provide a basis for an additional exegesis. In the writings of the Geonim and Rishonim, on the other hand, we find them employing this principle to account for Scriptural anthropomorphisms.[48] But according to Rambam,

---

[44] They also do not address the account in *Avot d'Rabbi Natan* that man's hair, innards, nostrils, nasal mucous, tears, teeth, saliva, neck, arms, fingers, head, stomach, kidneys, spleen, navel, blood, legs and other bodily parts all correspond with something in the physical world (e.g. with his hair corresponding to forests). It is difficult to imagine that they could argue that this is actually referring not to physical organs, but to man's "spiritual" hair, innards, nostrils, nasal mucous, tears, teeth, saliva, neck, arms, fingers, head, stomach, spleen, navel, blood, legs and other bodily parts.

[45] They do not explain why Scripture never makes any mention of the brain.

[46] See Avraham Korman, *Ha-Adam Ve-Tiv'o* (Tel Aviv, 1986, reprinted edition 2003), pp. 289-290.

[47] See Zion Ukshi, "The Torah Speaks Like the Language of Men—The Development of the Expression and its Nature" (Hebrew), *Derech Efrata* 9-10 (5761) pp. 39-59.

[48] *Otzar HaGeonim, Berachos, Chelek HaPerushim* 271 pp. 91-94; R. Bachya Ibn Pakuda, *Chovos HaLevavos, Sha'ar HaYichud* 10; R. Yehudah HaLevi, *Kuzari* 5:27; R. Avraham Ibn Daud, *Ha-Emunah HaRamah*, introduction, p. 2; Ibn Ezra, Commentary to Genesis 6:6, Long Commentary to Exodus 4:8, Commentary to Daniel 10:21; Rambam, *Guide*

this does not mean that the Torah uses anthropomorphic descriptions of God simply because this is the way that people *speak* about God; rather, it is because this is the way that many people *think* of God. The corporeal description of God given in the Torah is based upon the intellectual framework of the masses.[49]

Rambam further explains that various laws in the Torah are based upon false but prevalent beliefs; the punishment for cursing someone, for example, is based upon the popular but false belief that cursing someone actually has an effect.[50] In addition, according to the standard interpretation of the *Guide*, Rambam believed that Ezekiel's vision included the mistaken notion that the spheres make sounds, since prophetic insights are received by a prophet within the framework of his worldview, regardless of the scientific accuracy of this worldview.[51] Ralbag takes the same approach.[52] According to this approach, since in antiquity people believed that the mind was housed in the heart and kidneys, the Torah packaged its messages within this framework.

R. **Yosef Ibn Kaspi** (1280-1340) likewise extends "the Torah speaks in accordance with the language of men" beyond descriptions of God to a

---

for the Perplexed 1:26. See Avraham Nuriel, "*Dibra Torah K'Lashon Bnei Adam* in the *Guide for the Perplexed*" (Hebrew), in *Galuy VeSamuy BePhilosophia HaYehudit BiYemei HaBeinayim* (Jerusalem 5760) pp. 93-99.

[49] *Guide to the Perplexed* 1:26 and 1:33. Note Rambam's definition in 1:26: "But in accordance with 'the language of men,' that is to say, the imagination of the multitude..." As Rabbi Dr. Isadore Twersky describes it: "In its Maimonidean adaptation, the rabbinic dictum may then be paraphrased as follows: 'The Torah speaks in conformity with the imagination (and frequently crude perception) of the multitude' and therefore uses anthropomorphic imagery when speaking of divine attributes" ("Joseph ibn Kaspi: Portrait of a Medieval Jewish Intellectual," p. 239).

[50] *Sefer HaMitzvot* 317 and *Guide for the Perplexed* 3:41. See Twersky, loc cit., pp. 240-241.

[51] See *Guide for the Perplexed* 2:8 and 3:3, with the commentaries of Efodi, Shem Tov, Narvoni, and Abarbanel in *Ta'anos*, 4, and Rabbi Shlomo Fisher, *Derashos Beis Yishai*, *Ma'amar Hamo'ach Vehalev*, fn. 4. For further discussion, see Warren Zev Harvey, "How to Begin to Study *Moreh Nevuchim*," (Hebrew) *Da'at* 21 (1988) pp. 21-23.

[52] Ralbag, commentary to Gen. 15:4, and commentary to Job, end of ch. 39. I am indebted to Dr. Marc Shapiro for this reference.

broad range of additional phenomena. Rabbi Dr. Isadore (Yitzchak) Twersky (1930-1997) explains Ibn Kaspi's approach at length:

> Kaspi frequently operates with the following exegetical premise: not every Scriptural statement is true in the absolute sense. A statement may be purposely erroneous, reflecting an erroneous view of the masses. We are not dealing merely with an unsophisticated or unrationalized view, but an intentionally, patently false view espoused by the masses and enshrined in Scripture. The view or statement need not be allegorized, merely recognized for what it is... The key factor is Kaspi's use of the well-known rabbinic dictum: *dibrah Torah bileshon bene adam*, "The Torah speaks in the language of men," famous for its medieval use in the realm of anthropomorphism... Many scriptural statements, covered by this plastic rubric, are seen as errors, superstitions, popular conceptions, local mores, folk beliefs, and customs (*minhag bene 'adam*), statements which reflect the assumptions or projections or behavioral patterns of the people involved rather than an abstract truth. In its Kaspian adaptation, the rabbinic dictum may then be paraphrased as follows: "The Torah expressed things as they were believed or perceived or practiced by the multitude and not as they were in actuality." (Rabbi Dr. Isadore Twersky, "Joseph ibn Kaspi: Portrait of a Medieval Jewish Intellectual," pp. 239-242[53])

R. **Samson Raphael Hirsch** (1808-1888) writes about scientific inaccuracies in Scripture as follows:

> Jewish scholarship has never regarded the Bible as a textbook for physical or even abstract doctrines. In its view the main emphasis of the Bible is always on the ethical and social structure and development of life on earth; that is, on the observance of laws through which the momentous events of our nation's history are converted from abstract truths into concrete convictions. That is why Jewish scholarship regards the Bible as speaking consistently in "human language;" the Bible does not describe things in terms of objective truths known only to God, but in terms of human understanding, which is, after all, the basis for human language and

---

[53] The cases of *dibra Torah* that I have so far located in Ibn Kaspi are not the same as that of the kidneys. However it is a natural extension of those cases, and perhaps even proceeds *a fortiori* from them.

expression. (Rabbi Samson Raphael Hirsch, *Collected Writings* vol. 7 p. 57[54])

Similarly, Rabbi Hirsch notes that although there is no actual solid layer surrounding the earth that could be called a firmament, Scripture nevertheless uses that term because that is how the sky appears to man; as a dome over and around the earth.[55]

Rabbi **Avraham Yitzchak Kook** (1865-1935) also invokes the concept of "the Torah speaks in the language of men" to explain why there is no reason to seek scientific accuracy in the Torah:

> Every intelligent person knows that there is no relevance to our faith… with regard to the state of astronomical or geological knowledge… it makes no difference with regard to the words of the Torah… It is already adequately known that prophecy takes its metaphors to guide mankind according to that which was then well-known in the language of men at that time, to direct the ear according to that which it is able to hear in its time…[56] The intellectual truths of the depths of Torah are elevated and exalted far beyond these; the human illustrations—whatever they may be— with regard to the nature of existence, certainly also have a particular path in the ethical development of mankind… in each generation, according to his way of framing things, which constantly changes. (R. Avraham Yitzchak Kook, *Eder HaYekar*, pp. 37-38)

---

[54] Rabbi Hirsch is discussing the Scriptural usage of the Ptolemaic description of the universe rather than the Copernican model. There are two ways of employing the approach of "the Torah speaks in the language of men" for this case. One is that just as we today speak of sunrise even though we know that it is the earth moving, so too the Torah uses such figures of speech and they were not intended to be understood by its audience as actually describing the sun moving. Another is that the Torah is speaking in accordance with how people actually understood the universe. Rabbi Hirsch seems to be following the latter approach, with his mention of the Torah speaking in terms of human *understanding*.

[55] Commentary to Genesis 1:6. Cf. Rabbi Akiva Eiger, note to the phrase *u'vokeya chalonei rakia* in *Siddur Otzar HaTefillos* p. 672. See too Maharzav to *Midrash Bereishis Rabbah* 6:8.

[56] Rabbi Kook proceeds to refer to the opinion of Rambam in the *Guide for the Perplexed* 3:7, and the Jerusalem Talmud at the end of *Taanis* (4:5) regarding the corruption in the calculation of the ninth of Tammuz.

Accordingly, Orthodox Jews can accept that Scripture speaks of the kidneys as actually providing counsel, and also accept that the kidneys do not in fact do this. Furthermore, this approach has many applications beyond the question of the kidneys' counsel. Aside from the astronomical and cosmological issues discussed by Rambam, Ralbag, Rav Hirsch and Rav Kook, there are a number of instances where the Scriptures, according to traditional and scholarly interpretation, conflict with modern science.[57] While traditionalists struggle to reinterpret these verses and fit them into modern science, the principle of "the Torah speaks in the language of men" as utilized by the aforementioned authorities, while not without its own difficulties, renders these reinterpretations unnecessary.

Conclusion

The topic of the kidneys' function well illustrates the differing education that Jews received in different times and places. Already in the early medieval period, science had recognized that cognitive functions occur in the brain, with the kidneys serving as filtering organs. But for Jews in northern France and Germany, these discoveries had not entered their intellectual horizons, and the Scriptural and Talmudic accounts posed no difficulties. Not so for Jews in Spain, whose broad education caused them to realize that there was a problem here. Depending on whether they were more traditionalist or rationalist in orientation, they either justified the Talmud's statement or rejected it, but either way, they grappled with the problem. A similar phenomenon occurred much later in Italy, where Jews likewise had a broad education in general and with physiology in particular.

Today, one can find both Orthodox Jews who maintain their belief in the Talmud's account and those who reject it, but few are they who can

---

[57] Thus, as well as the inconsistency between the Genesis account of the age and development of the universe, the geocentric description of the universe, and the description of the firmament being a flat, firm structure, there is also the description of dew descending from the heavens and the descriptions of the hare and hyrax as ruminants.

be oblivious to the challenge that it poses. Yet even Orthodox Jews who adopt a rationalist approach to the Talmudic and Midrashic accounts are often reluctant to accept that the Scriptural accounts pose a similar challenge. However, in light of the growing awareness of similar such challenges in Scripture, the approach of "the Torah speaks in the language of men," as implemented by Rambam, Ibn Kaspi, Rav Hirsch and Rav Kook, is likely to become more widely accepted.

NINE

Brain Death and Organ Donation

In this chapter I will argue that according to the rationalist approach to Judaism, the conventional method of resolving halachic questions—which involves finding precedents and drawing halachic inferences from the Gemara, Rishonim and Acharonim—simply cannot be used to resolve the question of brain death, for two reasons. I will then propose alternate methodologies for determining the status of brain death, and for resolving the related question of organ donation.

How Different Worldviews Affect Judaism

There are several characteristics of the medieval rationalist school of thought, such as its preference for a natural rather than supernatural order of events, and its perception of the primary function of *mitzvot* as serving to refine human nature and society rather than as manipulating a metaphysical reality. But the aspect of the rationalist approach that is particularly relevant to determining the status of brain death is the principle expressed by Rambam and dozens of other authorities throughout the ages:[1] that the statements of Chazal regarding scientific matters, and all the more so those of subsequent Torah scholars, were not based on Sinaitic tradition or divine inspiration, but were instead the human and fallible assessments of that period. This is explicitly stated with regard to medical matters by Rav Sherira Gaon, by Rambam's son Rabbeinu Avraham, and by Rabbi Samson Raphael Hirsch:

> Our Sages were not physicians, and what they said was based on their experience with the diseases of their time. Therefore, there is no

---

[1] For a comprehensive list, see www.torahandscience.blogspot.com.

commandment to listen to the sages [regarding medical advice]. (Rav Sherira Gaon, *Teshuvot HaGeonim* 394)

We are not obligated to accept the views of the sages of the Talmud on matters concerning medicine, natural science or astronomy, simply because of their greatness and authority, as we are concerning their explanations of the Torah. (Rabbeinu Avraham ben HaRambam, *Ma'amar Al Aggadot Chazal*)

In my opinion, the first principle that every student of Chazal's statements must keep before his eyes is the following: Chazal were the sages of God's law—the receivers, transmitters and teachers of His *toros*, His *mitzvot*, and His interpersonal laws. They did not especially master the natural sciences, geometry, astronomy, or medicine—except insofar as they needed them for knowing, observing and fulfilling the Torah. We do not find that this knowledge was transmitted to them from Sinai. (Rabbi Samson Raphael Hirsch, Letter to R. Pinchos Wechsler)

While there are halachic authorities today who will claim to agree with this, many of them are not aware of the ramifications of this notion for the topic of brain death, and have not incorporated it into their evaluation.

The Impossibility of Precedent

Halachic questions are usually resolved by looking at the Talmud, and at the commentaries and responsa literature from Rishonim and Acharonim (the Torah scholars of the medieval and modern period). If a case is not discussed directly, then inferences are deduced from cases that are discussed. Yet many apply this methodology to brain death in a problematic manner.

Rabbi Shlomo Zalman Auerbach was widely respected as one of the greatest halachic decisors of the late twentieth century. For a long time, Rabbi Auerbach categorically rejected the notion that brain death constitutes death.[2] His reasoning was based on the Gemara which states that if a pregnant woman dies, there is no chance of survival for the fetus.[3]

---

[2] *Shulchan Shlomo*, vol. II p. 24.

[3] *Erechin* 6a.

With a pregnant woman who suffers brain death, on the other hand, the fetus can survive. Hence, Rav Auerbach deduced, brain death is not death.

Yet Rav Auerbach, in a powerful demonstration of intellectual honesty, eventually admitted that his inference was incorrect. This was after being presented with the report of an experiment in which a pregnant sheep was decapitated and its heartbeat maintained via the use of a ventilator;[4] the baby lamb was successfully delivered via C-section. Every halachic authority agrees that a decapitated sheep is dead,[5] and yet in this experiment, its lamb survived. Rav Auerbach therefore noted that today, when we have the ability to maintain certain bodily systems even in the absence of others, Chazal's criteria no longer apply.

Rav Auerbach's ultimate conclusions regarding the halakhic position vis-à-vis brain death are not relevant to our current discussion, and they are analyzed elsewhere. For our discussion the important point is R. Shlomo Zalman's acknowledgment that he had been mistaken in thinking that the Gemara about a pregnant woman's death could be used to resolve the contemporary question of brain death.[6]

---

[4] Avraham Steinberg and M. Hersch, "Decapitation of a Pregnant Sheep: A Contribution to the Brain Death Controversy," *Transplantation Proceedings* 27:2 (1995) pp. 1886-1887.

[5] Mishnah, *Ohalot* 1:6.

[6] Note that the Bush Document (2010), authored by Rabbi Asher Bush upon request by the Rabbinical Council of America, stresses that there was no retraction by Rav Auerbach on the halachah of brain death, just a withdrawal of one of the arguments that he formerly presented. Yet this does not seem to be the case. In *Shulchan Shlomo*, it is recorded that this argument alone was originally used repeatedly by Rav Auerbach to conclusively rule against brain death, and it states that as a result of the sheep experiment, he modified his view from categorical rejection of brain death to fundamental acceptance of brain-death (restricted by the concern that current brain-stem death diagnosis is not a sufficient measure of brain death, and thus he required proof that every cell of the brain has died). Furthermore—and most significantly—the Bush document suggests that due to various reasons, the sheep experiment is not analogous to the Gemara's case, and that cases where pregnancy continues despite brain death caused by stroke or cancer are analogous and do indeed demonstrate that brain death is not death. But this is exactly the same type of mistake that Rav Shlomo Zalman Auerbach admitted to making. The Gemara is not talking about a case of a person who is brain dead and has their heartbeat maintained artificially via a ventilator—such a situation was beyond the imagination of

The explanation of Rav Auerbach's retraction is clear. When the Gemara says that a dead woman cannot deliver a live baby, this was a perfectly correct description of the reality of 1500 years ago; Chazal did not have in mind the modern situation of brain death, in which life-supporting systems can be artificially maintained, and thus this statement has no bearing on the question of whether brain death is death. Rav Shlomo Zalman's revised position regarding brain death conforms to his reported position on cloning, that there are no precedents in the Gemara for drawing halachic conclusions about it.[7]

Just as the Gemara's statement that a dead woman cannot deliver a live baby cannot be applied to the modern situation of brain death, so too it is problematic to draw inferences from another ruling in the Gemara that is commonly cited to resolve the case of brain death. This is the Gemara's ruling regarding a person found under a collapsed building on Shabbat, where the presence of respiration is ruled to determine that he is still alive and one may transgress Shabbat in order to rescue him. This only tells us (and correctly so) that when a person was found under a collapsed building 1500 years ago, the presence of respiration indicated that he might return to full health. But this Gemara does not tell us anything at all about whether the presence of respiration via a ventilator is sufficient to classify someone as being alive. (It would likewise seem that even those that accept brain death as death are not correct to base it on the Gemara that requires spontaneous respiration as a sign of life—since many people with spinal injuries cannot spontaneously respirate, and yet are very clearly alive.[8] Just as Chazal never addressed the situation of a decapitated sheep delivering a lamb while being maintained on a ventilator, Chazal never addressed the situation of a person breathing via a ventilator.

---

anyone 1500 years ago, and no inference can be brought from the Gemara for such a case. One can make a reasonable argument that, given the fact that a brain-dead woman can grow a baby within her womb, this indicates that brain death is not death—but one cannot draw this conclusion as a halachic inference from the Gemara.

[7] As reported by Dr. A. S. Abraham and Rabbi Nachman Cohen to this author.

[8] Those that consider that *Yoma* 85a does indicate a brain-dead person to be halachically dead argue that in addition to lack of respiration, the person is not moving or showing signs of consciousness.

A similar consideration may be raised with regard to the Mishnah's ruling in *Ohalot* (1:6) that a decapitated animal is considered dead even if its limbs twitch. One cannot draw any direct inferences to brain death, which is not the same. A person can judge that it is sufficiently analogous. The Gemara does not address the situation of brain death at all—and it *cannot* address it. In order to do so, it would have to conceive of the human organism as comprising circulatory, respiratory and neurological systems capable in some circumstances of functioning independently, and then to determine which of these systems is significant. But 1500 years ago, this was not a medical possibility, and nobody conceived of such a thing. Human life, as the functioning of different organs and systems, was indivisible; if one system or basic organ failed, all other systems would fail at approximately the same time. Inasmuch as Chazal were unaware of the possibility of one system functioning *in the absence* of other systems functioning, no statements in the Gemara could reveal what they would have regarded as indicating death in such a situation. Hence no inferences about brain death—either way—could possibly be drawn from Talmudic rulings.

This is not to say that the Gemara can never be used to resolve modern questions. While it is impossible to draw direct inferences from cases in the Gemara, it may be possible to perceive analogies. This is a route that we shall later discuss. For now, we are merely establishing the logical flaws of drawing direct inferences from the Gemara. This is because the question that needs resolving is the significance of respiration or cardiac activity *vis-à-vis* neurological activity—a differentiation that no ancient text could possibly discuss.

The same is true with those attempting to support their ruling from the Rishonim and Acharonim. Rashi states that cessation of respiration is a conclusive indicator of death only when the person is entirely lacking in movement.[9] This leads to a dispute about whether the action of the heart in a brain-dead person counts as movement. But Rashi was addressing the case of a person who may return to ordinary functioning, not a situation of brain death.

---

[9] Rashi to *Yoma* 85a.

Similarly, there are those who point to the Chacham Tzvi's position[10] that the heart is the fundamental organ of life, and use this to argue that a brain-dead person is not dead as long as his heart is beating. But Chacham Tzvi was not addressing a situation of a brain-dead person whose respiration and heartbeat are being maintained via artificial means. Rather, he was addressing a question regarding a slaughtered chicken whose heart could not be located. The question was as to whether the heart had fallen out and been misplaced (in which case the chicken would be kosher), or if the chicken had lacked a heart. Chacham Tzvi proves, and correctly so, that the presence of a heart is required for an animal to be alive. He is arguing for it as a *necessary* condition, not a *sufficient* condition. The modern situation of a person whose heart is beating via artificial help, with neurological activity having irreversibly ceased, was inconceivable to him. Thus, no inference can be drawn from his discussion to the situation of brain death; we have no idea if he would rate a beating heart alone as sufficient to determine that the brain-dead person is alive.

Another source often invoked by contemporary halachic authorities, on both sides of the brain-death debate, is the famous responsum of R. Moses Schreiber, the Chatam Sofer.[11] In the eighteenth century, there was widespread fear that people were being buried alive due to doctors mistakenly diagnosing them as dead. Moses Mendelssohn agreed to take these concerns into account, as did R. Tzvi Hirsch Chajes, and recommended that even in the absence of respiration the families should wait several days before burying the dead, until the onset of putrefaction. Chatam Sofer, on the other hand, firmly opposed the idea that a person who was not breathing could be considered even doubtfully alive. He famously wrote that "even if all the winds in the world were to blow against us," we would not move from the determination of death established by Chazal in the aforementioned case of the collapsed building. There is some debate about whether Chatam Sofer also required the absence of a pulse. But, aside from the inherent problems in Chatam

---

[10] *She'elot u'Teshuvot Chacham Tzvi #77.*
[11] *She'elot u'Teshuvot Chatam Sofer, Yoreh De'ah #338.*

Sofer's responsum that we shall later discuss, it cannot possibly be used to resolve the question of brain death in either direction. Chatam Sofer's point was that the *absence* of respiration (and possibly pulse) are sufficient to establish that the person is lifeless. He was not saying anything about whether the *presence* of respiration (and/or a pulse), in the absence of brain function, is *sufficient* to rate a person as being alive.

There are several reasons that halakhic authorities have generally based their discussions of brain stem death on Talmudic sources, despite the fact that these sources do not relate to the situation that we have today. Some *poskim* adopt the mystical approach that all knowledge is to be found in the Gemara, in accordance with a broad interpretation of the Mishnah: "*Hafoch bah v'hafoch bah, d'kulah bah*—Delve into it again and again, for everything is in it."[12] However, this statement does not necessarily refer to *all* knowledge! Seforno explains it to simply refer to correct religious philosophy. And Ramban notes that the Torah, as a finite document, cannot possibly provide rulings for all questions of interpersonal laws, for which we only have general moral principles.[13]

But even among those who do not formally subscribe to the approach that all knowledge is in the Gemara, there is a strong tendency to attempt to derive the status of brain death from the Gemara, and from Rishonim and Acharonim. One reason for this is that halachic authorities are accustomed to operating in this way; halachah is ordinarily determined simply by referring to the canonical text of the Gemara and its interpretations and applications by the Rishonim and Acharonim. Yet these people simply do not realize that Talmudic sources could never differentiate between neurological activity and cardiac or respiratory function, because there was never a scenario that divided them. Rav Auerbach was not the only one to make the mistake of trying to infer the status of brain death from a case in the Gemara that was not actually relevant; he was just the only one who realized that it was a mistake.

---

[12] Avot 5:6.

[13] Commentary to Deuteronomy 6:18.

Chazal's Beliefs about Physiology

There is a second reason why it is impossible to derive modern halachah from earlier halachic sources in the case of brain death. Even if Chazal, the Rishonim or the Acharonim would have differentiated between the status of different bodily systems, their understanding of the *role* of the organs involved in these systems has been disproved by modern science.

Is the determination of the end of a person's life a halachic or a scientific issue? Some claim that it is a halachic issue which is entirely independent of science, just like the determination of the beginning of life.[14] It is true that while something may be considered alive according to a scientific definition, it may not be considered alive according to a halachic definition—for example, bacteria are not considered to be "alive" in halachah. And it is true that science cannot determine at which point a developing fetus is considered "alive" from a halachic standpoint. But halachah cannot provide an appropriate determination if it is *significantly misinformed* about the physical reality. For example, if one mistakenly believes that human sperm contains a fully developed but miniature human being—as one relatively recent authority believed[15]—then halachic rulings based upon this belief are clearly problematic.

Similarly, any halachic determination as to whether respiration, cardiac activity or neurological activity determines life should reflect a correct understanding of the role of these systems and the organs that provide them. It is therefore highly problematic to base halakhic discussions regarding definition of life and death on Talmudic sources, given that at least some of Chazal—and probably most or all—believed that the heart and kidneys are the seat of the mind and personality:

> The Rabbis taught: The kidneys advise, the heart considers, the tongue articulates, the mouth finishes, the esophagus brings in all kinds of food, the windpipe gives sound, the lungs absorb all kinds of fluids, the liver

---

[14] Rabbi J. David Bleich, *Judaism and Healing: Halakhic Perspectives* (Ktav 2002), pp. 186-187.

[15] R. Yechiel Epstein, *Aruch HaShulchan, Even Ha-Ezer* 23:1, based on Antonie van Leeuwenhoek's mistaken belief that he saw a homunculus in a microscope.

causes anger, the gallbladder secretes a drop into it and calms it, the spleen laughs, the gizzard grinds, the stomach [causes] sleep, the nose [causes] wakefulness. (*Berachot* 61a; similarly in *Midrash Vayikra Rabbah* 4:4)

As discussed in the previous chapter, this is not an aggadic legend intended to be understood metaphorically. There is no reason to assume that the descriptions of the functions of the tongue, mouth, esophagus, windpipe, lungs, stomach and nose are anything but scientific descriptions intended to be interpreted literally. The account of the liver causing anger is also consistent with standard belief in the ancient world. The account of the function of the kidneys and heart are thus also clearly intended to be literal descriptions. This, too, is consistent with standard Aristotelian belief in the ancient world.[16] The Rishonim and Acharonim agree that Chazal were speaking literally.[17] Elsewhere, the Gemara discusses the laws pertaining to the kidneys of animal offerings and relates them to the kidneys' function in man of providing counsel. Other Midrashim likewise echo this understanding of the role of the various organs:

> " 'And God said to Moshe: Pharaoh's heart has become heavy (*kaveid*)' — He was angry. Just as the liver is angry, so too the heart of this one became a liver (*kaveid*), without understanding, as a fool." (*Midrash Shemot Rabbah* 9:8)

> "That is to say, the heart of Pharaoh was turned into a liver (*kaveid*)—just as a liver has no understanding to understand and comprehend, so too there was no understanding in his heart to understand and comprehend. Therefore, his heart was hardened and was stubborn for him." (*Midrash Lekach Tov*)

Note that in all these sources no important role is ascribed to the brain. There are sources demonstrating that *some* of Chazal attributed at least

---

[16] For an extensive discussion of ancient views concerning whether the mind is housed in the brain or the heart, see Julius Rocca, *Galen on the Brain: Anatomical Knowledge and Physiological Speculation in the Second Century AD*, pp. 17-47. While Galen knew the brain to have a cognitive function, Aristotle believed that the brain only serves to cool the blood. Along with other ancient cultures, he believed the mind to be housed in the heart.

[17] See the extensive sources cited in the previous chapter, "The Question of the Kidneys' Counsel."

some cognitive functions to the brain.[18] However, such sources do not prove that these members of Chazal did not attach any mind-role to the heart; and they certainly do not undermine the aforementioned sources which demonstrate that some or many of Chazal clearly believed that the mind is housed in the heart.

Scriptural references to the heart are interpreted by most people today metaphorically, as actually referring to the mind and thus the brain. But in accordance with standard beliefs in the ancient world, Chazal interpreted all such references literally. Scriptural descriptions of the heart having various emotional states, of its housing wisdom and cognition, and of God judging a person based on examining his heart and kidneys, were all taken literally by Chazal.[19]

Thus, even if it were somehow possible to determine that Chazal would have ruled that a brain-dead person is alive provided that his heart was beating, this would not resolve the modern question. Chazal believed that fundamental components of a person's mind are housed in his heart. Anyone with such a mistaken belief would consequently judge a person as being alive for as long as his heart is beating.

---

[18] We find certain figures rejecting opinions with the statement, "It appears that he does not have a brain in his head" (Talmud, *Yevamot* 9a and *Menachot* 80b). Note that the Rabbinic word for "brain," *moach*, only appears in Scripture in one instance (Job 21:24) where it refers to the marrow inside bone. In general, the Sages of the Babylonian Talmud followed Akkadian and ancient Babylonian understandings of physiology and medicine; see Mark J. Geller, "Akkadian Healing Therapies in the Babylonian Talmud," (Berlin: Max-Planck-Institut für Wissenschaftsgeschichte 2004).

[19] Since many people will be reluctant to posit that Chazal's interpretation of a verse is incorrect, it should be pointed out that Chazal also interpreted Scriptural references to the "firmament" to be describing a solid layer above the earth (*Midrash Bereishis Rabbah* 4:2; Talmud Yerushalmi, *Berachot* 1:1). In all these cases, we must either differ from Chazal and posit that the Torah was not speaking literally, or agree with Chazal that the Torah was speaking literally, but posit that *dibra Torah k'lashon bnei adam*, "the Torah was speaking in the language of men," which, according to several authorities, means that the Torah worked within the scientific worldview of ancient times; see the extensive discussion in the previous chapter.

When Halachah is Based Upon Obsolete Science

To the extent that a statement utilized in resolving a scientific-halachic issue is based upon a relevant misunderstanding of the physical reality, this undermines the innate validity of the halachic conclusions. For example, the issue of using electricity on Shabbat or Yom Tov is a scientific-halachic issue. If someone were to make a ruling on this topic based upon a misunderstanding of what electricity is, this would undermine the ruling (to the extent that the misunderstanding is relevant).

Does this mean that, in such cases, the halachah should be changed? There are Acharonim and contemporary halachic authorities who do indeed believe that halachah should change in response to our greater scientific knowledge. One notable example is with the Gemara's ruling that it is permitted to kill lice on Shabbat because they spontaneously generate; when that reason was discovered untrue, there were authorities such as Rav Yitzchak Lampronti who forbade it, as did Rav Zalman Nechemiah Goldberg.[20] Similarly, many halachic authorities today forbid eating worms found in fish, against the Gemara which explicitly and without qualification permits it.

On the other hand, there are those who take the position that in general, our greater scientific knowledge does not warrant changing halachah. Even in cases where Chazal's rulings are based upon mistaken beliefs about the natural world, there can be other reasons to uphold their rulings. Rav Moshe Shmuel Glasner explains (based on earlier sources) that due to the authority of Chazal and the canonization of the Gemara, the rulings of the Gemara are binding even if based upon mistaken scientific beliefs.[21] Thus, he, and others such as Rav Herzog, maintain that we still follow the Talmud's ruling about killing lice on Shabbat, even though it is based upon a scientific error.

However, even for those who maintain such an approach, this would not apply to rulings about brain death that are based on inferences from

---

[20] Personal conversation.

[21] Rabbi Moshe Shmuel Glasner, *Dor Revi'i* to *Chullin*, introduction. See the final chapter of my book *Sacred Monsters* for an extensive discussion of this approach.

the Talmud which are in turn based on obsolete views of physiology. There are two reasons for this.

First of all, brain death is not comparable to cases such as killing lice on Shabbat. There is no canonized ruling in the Gemara (or indeed any form of ruling) about brain death. Rather, it is other material in the Gemara which is potentially being (mistakenly) used to create a modern halachic conclusion. It is only Talmudic rulings that are canonized, not Talmudic concepts that being used later.

Second is that in cases of potential *pikuach nefesh*, where human life is at stake, *all* halachic authorities override the rulings of Chazal, Rishonim and Acharonim in favor of modern medicine. This point cannot be overstated. All modern *poskim* overrule Chazal in situations of *pikuach nefesh* if Chazal's comments were based on mistaken medical information. One notable example is with Chazal's ruling that one does not transgress Shabbat to save the life of a fetus born after a gestation of eight months, because they believed it not to be viable, unlike a fetus born after seven months.[22] No contemporary halachic authority follows this ruling, whether because they recognize that Chazal followed now-discredited scientific theories, or because they assume that "nature has changed." Another example is with the Gemara's ruling that if no respiration is detected at a person's nostrils, he is judged to be dead, and Shabbat may not be desecrated by clearing away the rubble from the rest of his body. While this may have been a valid judgment given the limitations of that era, no halachic authority today would issue such a ruling, now that we know how to perform CPR.

Indeed, Rav Shlomo Zalman Auerbach points out that despite Chatam Sofer's famous declaration that "all the winds in the world will not sway us" from following Chazal's ruling that a person who is not detectably breathing is considered dead, new techniques in restoring respiration

---

[22] For discussion of this belief, see Samuel S. Kottek, "Embryology in Talmudic and Midrashic Literature," *Journal of the History of Biology*, vol. 14, no. 2 (Fall 1981), pp. 299-315, and Rosemary E. Reiss and Avner D. Ash, "The Eighth-Month Fetus: Classical Sources for a Modern Superstition," *Obstetrics & Gynecology* 71 (1988) pp. 270-273 (available at HODS.org).

result in it now taking longer to determine that respiration has irreversibly ceased, and thus the determination of death has certainly *effectively* changed since the times of Chazal:

> With regard to the fundamental words of Chatam Sofer, in my humble opinion it appears that just as with regard to the law that an eight-month fetus is like a stone and one does not transgress Shabbat on its behalf, certainly the rule has changed in our time, and forfend to rule in that way (of the Gemara)... and one is forced to say that only in the times of Chazal was the fetus given the status of a stone, because at that time they did not know how to enable it to survive, unlike in our time... So, too, in my humble opinion it appears clear that in our time, it is impossible to decide that someone as already died except via the latest techniques which establish the boundaries between life and death. And forfend to rely in our time just on the signs of breathing and suchlike, more than other checks, and to rule with someone under a collapsed building on Shabbat that if his breathing has stopped, and his heart has stopped beating, that he should be left under the rubble and Shabbat not be transgressed on his behalf... (*Shulchan Shlomo*, vol. II, pp. 34-35[23])

Even the idea of determining death based upon respiration having *irreversibly* stopped is a change from Chazal's definition; Chazal's view was that once respiration has stopped, it is *ipso facto* irreversible. Furthermore, we depart from the Gemara's definition of absence of respiration even today; in cases of people who have overdosed on certain medications and then suffered exposure to extreme cold, respiration cannot be detected even if they are still alive, and so physicians attempt to gradually restore bodily functions—and it seems unlikely that any halachic authority would object.

Thus, even if there were positions of Chazal, Rishonim or Acharonim which would indicate that a brain-dead person is considered alive, these would not and should not be utilized for halachic decisions today if they were based upon incorrect understandings of physiology. For this reason,

---

[23] Rav Auerbach adds that "this does not, forfend, contradict that which our Sages of blessed memory learned from the Scriptural exegesis, that [life] depends solely upon breathing." Yet, as we shall later discuss, Chatam Sofer himself was not convinced that Chazal derived this from a Scriptural exegesis.

it is important to not only fully understand modern science, but also to understand the history of science, which assists us in interpreting statements made by Chazal, Rishonim and Acharonim. As an example, a statement in Rashi about the movement of the heart, which appears to be a reference to a pulse and consequently to circulation of blood, is actually—taken in its historical context—a reference to respiration.[24] Chazal also in turn believed the heart to be directly maintained via respiration; the heart's role in blood circulation was not discovered until the seventeenth century. More significantly, as we have seen, Chazal believed that fundamental components of the mind are housed in the heart. As such, even if it were to be possible to infer from Chazal that a brain-dead person is alive since he has a pulse, this would be based upon mistaken beliefs about physiology and could not be used to make halachic rulings that lead to the death of others.

In this context, it should be pointed out that while we have already noted that the Chatam Sofer's responsum regarding delayed burial should be irrelevant to this topic, there is another reason why it is problematic for halachic authorities to rely upon it in formulating their decision regarding brain death. It is far from clear that Chatam Sofer was actually correct in dismissing the concerns about people being buried prematurely, or just fortunate. As it happens, the eighteenth-century physicians were mistaken in their concerns; they were misled into believing that a large proportion of people were being buried prematurely.[25] Our modern knowledge that there is no need for such concerns leads us to assume that Chatam Sofer was likewise correct to dismiss them. But, back then, there was no way back then to be sure of that, and there were very reasonable grounds for people to be concerned. Note that R. Avraham Portaleone (d. 1612),

---

[24] See Edward Reichman, "The Halakhic Definition of Death in Light of Medical History," pp. 155-156. In light of the fact that Rashi's physiological understanding was counter-factual, the statement on p. 87 of the Bush document that "according to all standard interpretations... to exclude the straightforward reading of the words of רש"י from a serious analysis of the גמרא is simply not an acceptable option," reflects an approach that is decidedly non-rationalist.

[25] See Jan Bondeson, *Buried Alive* (New York: Norton 2001) for an extensive historical and medical discussion.

author of *Shiltei Gibborim*, requested that his corpse be watched for three days before burial, and freely admitted that this was following a different approach than that of his ancestors. The primary concern is to preserve human life.

The question thus remains as to why Chatam Sofer saw fit to ignore the concerns of physicians, against the general practice of halachic authorities. This question is especially potent in light of the fact that, as we shall later discuss, Chatam Sofer himself suggests that Chazal relied upon the gentile physicians of *their* day for the method of determining death. Perhaps he was suspicious of the reports of premature burial; not all physicians agreed that such a problem existed. Alternately, perhaps light can be shed on this from a follow-up letter by Chatam Sofer, not published in the standard collection of responsa, in which he explicitly admits that he is inflating the importance of same-day burial in response to this topic having become part of the general arsenal of Jews who sought to weaken tradition and embrace modernity.[26] From this we see that his ruling was based at least in part on meta-halachic concerns relating to the circumstances of his era, giving us even more cause to be cautious about using his responsum to derive a halachic ruling for brain death.

Alternate Methodologies for Resolving the Question

As we have seen, it is highly problematic to rule on brain death based on direct inferences from Talmudic sources. This is true regardless of one's position regarding the impact of changes in scientific knowledge on traditional halakhic rulings. Even if earlier generations were correct in their understanding of the role of the different organs in the human body, they simply never addressed a situation relevant to brain death. But if we cannot infer the halachah on this issue via halachic inferences from traditional texts, how is to be resolved?

One possible approach is that we simply cannot resolve the question. Some might say that since the Gemara does not discuss anything about

---

[26] The letter is printed in R. Tzvi Hirsch Chajes, *Darchei Ha-Hora'a*, *siman* 6, p. 19b. See Moshe Samet, "Early Burial: The History of the Controversy on Determining Time of Death,"' *Asufot* 3 (1988), (Hebrew)

brain-death, we have no valid basis for rendering any kind of halakhic ruling. And while the lives of organ recipients are at stake, it is also a matter of potentially murdering the brain-dead patient. Given our inability to rule halakhically that disconnecting life support from such a patient is not murder, we have no choice but to treat the matter as *safek* (doubt), and follow the principle of *shev v'al ta'aseh*—do nothing rather than do the wrong thing.

Yet this, too, is an approach which reflects a non-rationalist worldview. In certain Orthodox circles, there is a sentiment that with every passing generation, our halachic capabilities have declined, and we are no longer able to make various halachic judgments. To give an extreme example, some say that even though Chazal decreed that one pronounces a *berachah* upon seeing a mountain, we don't know exactly which type of mountain they had in mind—and therefore we don't pronounce the *berachah* at all. One who adopts the approach that halakhic capabilities have declined and current halakhists have neither the wisdom nor the authority to create new halakhot will be unable to resolve any issue for which he cannot find clear Talmudic precedent (though adherents of this worldview will often not agree that such cases could exist; which will lead them to stretch Talmudic rulings to situations for which they were not designed).

But others, usually of a more rationalist persuasion, are of the view that current halakhic authorities are charged with the responsibility, and accordingly endowed with the ability, to address and find appropriate halakhic responses for all situations. According to this view, statements such as *Lo baShamayim hi* (the Torah is not in Heaven) and *Lo nitna Torah lemalachei hashareit* (the Torah was not given to angels) indicate that we have the responsibility, authority, and capability to resolve halachic questions.[27]

---

[27] Cf. Rav Soloveitchik's fourteenth "article of faith"" "I believe with perfect faith that the Torah can be observed, practiced, and fully implemented in all places and at all times, in all social, economic, and cultural contexts, in all technological circumstances, and under all political conditions." *Five Expositions* [Hebrew], (Jerusalem: Machon Tal Orot, 1974), p. 112.

Indeed, it is important to consider the following question: How is the question of brain-death potentially to be resolved? Does it require some sort of knowledge about spiritual or metaphysical realities involving the soul? If so, then even a Sanhedrin could not resolve it, without prophetic input. If not, then it should be theoretically possible to resolve it.

How might this be done? We will explore several alternatives.

The Trend of Aggadic Thought

One option follows a line of thought suggested by Rabbi Ezra Bick regarding cases of donor IVF, with regard to the question of whether it is the egg donor or the birth mother who is halachically considered to be the parent.[28] As with determining the status of brain death, there are those who seek to deduce the answer from various statements in the Gemara. And just as with determining the status of brain death, Rabbi Bick demonstrates that such inferences are unwarranted, and that the Gemara really does not contain any halachos from which we can resolve this novel, modern situation. He further points out that any attempt to derive the halachah from Chazal is hindered by the problem that Chazal did not realize that a woman produces an ovum, from which the fetus develops— instead, they thought that it develops from a man's sperm in conjunction with a woman's blood.[29] Instead, Rabbi Bick proposes, we need to draw guidance for a halachic conclusion from the general trend of non-halachic statements in Chazal:

> What then do we do if there is no Talmudic halakha relevant to the assumptions needed for a decision in our question? It appears to me that we are justified in trying to determine the Talmudic assumptions, the base conceptions of the Talmudic world-view, from other sources. This is not the same as the oft-rejected aggadic source for halakhic conclusions. To derive a halakha from a single aggadic source is misleading, as we cannot

---

[28] Rabbi Ezra Bick, "Ovum Donations: A Rabbinic Conceptual Model of Maternity," *Tradition* 28:1 (1993) pp. 28-45.

[29] For further discussion, including regarding how Chazal's views on embryology developed and are related to the passage in *Yoma* discussing where life begins and ends in the body, see Samuel S. Kottek, "Embryology in Talmudic and Midrashic Literature," *Journal of the History of Biology*, vol. 14, no. 2 (Fall 1981), pp. 299-315.

be sure what the intent or precise factual meaning of the aggada is. To use the aggada to determine a general approach of the Sages to a question, in order to determine what halakha must necessarily arise from that approach, is, although risky and lacking the certitude we are accustomed to expect in halakhic discourse, in principle as valid as what the Sages would have done in the first place had they faced the question we are facing today. Were there to exist absolutely no Talmudic guidance for our question, neither in halakhic or aggadic sources, in principle we would have to formulate for ourselves the proper way to understand the necessary concepts, in the same way that the Talmudic scholars did. I cannot imagine any serious Torah scholar being happy with such a situation; we depend upon direct Talmudic sources as a fish depends on water. Nonetheless, I believe it is a valid way to derive halakha; indeed, it is one of the bases for Talmudic halakha itself.

In fact, even those who do attempt to resolve the halachic status of brain-death via conventional methodologies often incorporate non-halachic sources. The responsum of Chacham Tzvi regarding the necessity of the heart for life is itself replete with non-halachic sources about the role of the heart. Perhaps, then, we can make use of non-halachic material in order to resolve the question.[30]

If we are to look at the underlying concept of life in traditional Jewish sources, we see that it is broken down into three aspects. Plants are considered to have a "vegetative soul"—the most basic form of life, sufficient only to keep the organism alive and growing. Animals have an "animate soul," which is related to their capacity for willful movement. And man is defined as the being with a "rational soul"—which Ramban and other Rishonim define not in some abstract mystical manner, but rather as his rational faculties.[31] The Rishonim further debate whether a human being possesses a single soul which combines the vegetative growth force, the animate life force, and the rational faculty, or whether he

---

[30] See too Alan Jotkowitz, "Chimeras and the Limits of Casuistry in Jewish Bioethics," in *Hakirah* 11 (Spring 2011), for a discussion of how modern biological and medical science raises halachic questions that cannot be resolved via traditional halachic methodology.

[31] See Ramban to Genesis 1:26 and 2:7, as well as Rabbeinu Bachya and Seforno.

possesses these three aspects as distinct components. Ramban takes the latter view, which he further argues as being Chazal's view. In making his case, Ramban states that the human body can contain some of these components, without others; specifically, he explains that the first man possessed an animate soul before he acquired rational faculties, and he argues that a golem is a human without rational faculties.

This discussion about whether the soul is divisible is itself an ancient dispute between Plato and Aristotle, and one could argue that it is now just as outmoded and irrelevant as Greek medicine. However, the point is that Ramban accepted that a human body which is breathing is not necessarily considered to possess the life of a human being. This is a value judgment, independent of scientific beliefs, and it is one which is very relevant to brain-death. A person who has suffered brain-stem death has irreversibly lost his capacity for any form of neurological activity; furthermore, he has no capacity for willful movement. According to Ramban and other Rishonim, he no longer possesses either a rational soul or an animate soul; he is no longer alive as a human being.[32]

However, it may be problematic to develop an approach along these lines. It is difficult (although perhaps not impossible) to make an approach involving the notion of a distinct "rational soul" which is consistent with our knowledge of fetal and infant mental development. Likewise, it is difficult to make this approach consistent with our treatment of people with severely diminished mental capacity, versus animals such as dolphins and apes with extremely high mental capacities. Let us examine alternate ways of resolving our question.

Seeking Analogies

Where there is no possibility of drawing a direct inference from the Gemara to a modern circumstance, another option exists. That is to seek a case in the Gemara which is sufficiently analogous to the case that we seek to resolve. Very often, the principles and rulings discussed in the

---

[32] Note that Rabbi Yaakov Emden (*Responsa Yaavetz* 2:82), citing *Chessed L'Avraham*, deduces from Rabbi Zeira's destruction of the golem that it is permissible to kill it, and explains that this must be because it only has an animal soul, but not a human soul.

Gemara can be found to contain underlying similarities to modern situations. Of course, here is where the question arises of what degree of similarity is sufficient to consider cases analogous. Not everyone will agree to the resultant determinations.

For example, using electricity on Shabbat is not discussed in the Gemara. Yet some argue that constructing a circuit is sufficiently analogous to various forbidden activities mentioned in halacha. On the other hand, Rabbi Shlomo Zalman Auerbach felt that there is no precedent that is sufficiently analogous to electricity, and thus ruled that completing electrical circuits is only prohibited as a safeguard against people turning on electric lights.[33]

The obvious case which is potentially analogous to brain death is the ruling of the Mishnah in *Ohalot* that a decapitation is equivalent to death even if the limbs twitch. We noted earlier that one cannot draw any *direct inferences* to brain death, which is not exactly the same as a decapitated person. However, there may be a way to decide whether brain death is sufficiently analogous to this situation such that it can fit into the same halachic category. We shall now explore one such possibility.

Science, Logic and Torah: Man is in the Mind

Perhaps we can use a thorough understanding of contemporary medical science to determine that brain death is sufficiently similar to the case of the beheaded person. This may sound startling, yet no less a figure than Chatam Sofer himself proposed that medical science may contain the answer to the question of how to determine death. When discussing his view on the determination of death—the definition about which he claimed "all the winds in the world will not sway us"—he presents three possible sources for this definition. One is that this was derived from a Scriptural exegesis via Chazal; another is that it was received as a tradition from Moses. But the first, primary suggestion of Chatam Sofer is that it was learned by Chazal from ancient non-Jewish physicians!

> Let us see: Behold, there is no doubt that when the Torah said, "When a man commits a sin punishable by death, and is executed… his corpse

---

[33] *Minchat Shlomo* 74, 84.

should not be left hanging overnight... you shall surely bury him," and one who transgresses this with any dead person has transgressed a positive and negative commandment—it must be that the definition of death was then transmitted. Perhaps there was a tradition from the first scientists, even though it was subsequently forgotten from the physicians of our era, and the Sages relied upon them in many matters relating to Torah, as is explained in Chapter "Rabbi Akiva" 85a, and relied upon the verse, "Do not encroach upon the boundaries that were established by the first ones" (Deut. 19:14). Alternately, if they did not have a tradition from the scientists, it must be that Moshe Rabbeinu accepted the definition as "A Law to Moses at Sinai"; alternatively, the Sages relied upon the verse of "everything with the spirit of life in its nose," that everything depends upon respiration at the nostrils, as explained in *Yoma* 85a, and as ruled by Rambam, *Tur* and *Shulchan Aruch*. (Responsa *Chatam Sofer, Yoreh De'ah* #338)

If Chatam Sofer believed that the determination of death could have been adopted from the gentile physicians of antiquity (and even considered this to be the most likely possibility), then we have a powerful case for saying that this is a matter to be determined on the basis of medical science.

Now, Chatam Sofer himself was of the view that, if Chazal had indeed taken their determination of death from gentile physicians, this possesses absolute authority. It is for this reason that he ignored the physicians of his era who, out of fear that people were being prematurely diagnosed as dead, were recommending that burial be delayed until death could be more conclusively recognized. However, it is unclear why the science of the period of Chazal should carry greater weight than that of contemporary science,[34] and as we noted earlier, Chatam Sofer's

---

[34] Chatam Sofer writes that Chazal often relied on gentile scientists, relying on the verse of "Do not encroach upon the boundaries that were established by the first ones" (Deut. 19:14). In its plain meaning, this refers to laws of property; however, Chazal (*Shabbat* 85a) expound it to also refer to not encroaching upon the minimum distance that one may plant one species from another in order to avoid *kilayim*, which was designated by Chazal in their reliance on ancient gentile farmers (the "first ones"). But it is far from clear how this could be extended as a Scriptural mandate to give absolute authority to specifically ancient gentile physicians with regard to matters of life and death.

reluctance to rely on contemporary doctors appears to have been motivated by meta-halachic concerns relating to the fact that this cause had been adopted by the anti-Orthodox. We today would certainly say that the modern sciences of physiology and medicine are vastly more advanced than those of antiquity. They are not infallible, and they are constantly being further refined, but they are certainly light-years ahead of science in earlier eras. Indeed, as noted earlier, all halachic authorities today rely upon the judgments of modern medical science, even where it means overruling Chazal. If Chazal could have relied upon the physicians of antiquity in order to determine when death could be assumed to have occurred, surely we are in a much better position to rely upon our own physicians.

It is true, however, that there is a difference between the reliance upon doctors posited by Chatam Sofer, and the contemporary situation of brain-death. Both at the time of Chazal and the time of the Chatam Sofer, when the irreversible failure of one vital function inevitably brought about the swift failure of all others, the determination of death depended entirely on the question of whether a person lacking certain vital signs could return to normal functioning. This is a factual question, which can indeed be based solely on scientific knowledge. But in the current reality, where vital functions can be artificially maintained, sometimes indefinitely, new questions have arisen to which science alone cannot provide an answer. Today, when one or another vital function has failed and is being maintained artificially, the question is moral, legal, and halakhic: whether the remaining activity of the body can be considered "human life." However, while this is not solely a scientific question, our knowledge of modern science may provide us with the information and the tools to resolve it.

Even if one argues that the soul is a metaphysical entity that cannot be measured by scientific techniques, its interaction with the body can be determined. Medical science shows that respiration and circulation of blood are not particularly significant, even from a spiritual perspective. For we have learned that they can be artificially produced in a corpse! And even in ordinary cases of (heart-lung) death, we have discovered that there are still metabolic processes taking place in some cells, as well as growth of hair and fingernails. Thus, these other organs, and/or the presence of a body that is breathing and has blood circulating, cannot define the presence of a living person.

At the same time, modern procedures of organ transplantation and artificial limbs, as well as cases of congenital abnormalities, shed much light on the question of the interaction of the soul with the body. Many organs can be replaced with artificial devices, without there being any halachic consequences of murder or of harming the soul—but not the brain. Many organs can be maintained outside of a body, without any notion of their being considered a "human life" —but not the brain. Many organs can be transplanted into other people without anyone proposing that personal identity has been transferred—but not the brain.[35]

The neurological activity of the brain creates the presence of a person. When babies are born with extra appendages or organs, they are not considered to be two persons. It is only when they have two heads that they are considered to be two persons.[36] Full head transplants have been successfully performed in monkeys and dogs, and are certainly possible with humans; surely all logic dictates that if a person's head would be transplanted onto another body, the personhood and life would entirely transfer with the head.

---

[35] Although there are claims that people who received a heart transplant suddenly begin to like the food that the organ donor had liked, these are nothing more than urban myths.

[36] Note that with the view of Chazal that a person's identity is located in his trunk rather than his head (due to their view regarding the mind being located in the heart and kidneys), such dicephalus twins—conjoined twins with a single trunk and one head—were regarded as a single person. The Talmud (*Menachot* 37a) discusses the question of upon *which* head such a person (described in the singular!) should place *tefillin*; whereas we today would say that these are two different people, *both* of whom are obligated to wear *tefillin*. A Midrash also describes King Solomon as performing a test to determine if such twins are one person or two; when he discovers that one blindfolded head can sense heat applied to the skin of the other head, he concludes that they are a single person. In fact, in all cases of dicephalus twins (and there are many), there are two brains and thus two separate nervous systems; one head would never be able to sense what is happening to the other head. For further discussion of dicephalus twins, see *Sacred Monsters* by this author.

It is true that there are still developments and changes in the science of neurology. But this is irrelevant, because science typically moves in the direction of refining and further clarifying reality. The situation is similar to how science progressed with regard to the shape of the earth. In antiquity, it was thought that the earth is flat. Then it was thought to be spherical. Later, this was changed to it being roughly spherical, but flattened slightly. And now we know it to be roughly spherical and flattened slightly, but more so at one end than at the other. With the exception of the first transition, it wasn't that the earlier position was entirely discarded; rather, it was continually refined. So, too, with brain science: we are going to further refine our knowledge regarding which *part* of the brain is essential to personhood, but we are not going to suddenly realize that personhood and the soul is housed in the appendix, kidneys, or heart.

Thus, the presence of a human being can be logically and empirically demonstrated to be located in the brain, and in the brain alone.[37] Any other view results in contradictions, inconsistencies and impossibilities. And for those who wish to speak about the soul, it is certainly housed in the mind and/or interfaces with the body via the mind. All the tasks of the soul—exercising free will, forging relationships with God and man, studying Torah—take place in the brain. By the process of elimination (literally), we can rule out the soul being housed in any other part of the body. Accordingly, the irreversible loss of the brain's fundamental functions means that the person has died. It is functionally identical to the case of the decapitated person discussed in the Mishnah.

The Noble Sacrifice of Lesser Life

The above discussion of why brain-death is death should and would suffice for many people. But there may also be a halachic mechanism which can be used either in conjunction with the aforementioned

---

[37] See Dr. Noam Stadlan's excellent article, "Conceptual and Logical Problems Arising from Defining Life and Death by the Presence or Absence of Circulation," *Me'orot* 8 (September 2010, Tishrei 5771), freely available online at http://www.hods.org/-pdf/Problems-Defining-Life-and-Death-by-Circulation.pdf.

arguments, or as stand-alone approach for someone willing to become an organ donor in the eventuality of his becoming brain-dead. In such a case, even if brain-death is not considered to be death, and all the more so if it is of uncertain status, several contemporary rabbinic scholars have argued that there is a halachic option of "noble sacrifice."[38]

Ordinarily, halachah absolutely prohibits saving one person's life at the expense of the life of another person: "Who says that this person's blood is redder?" We cannot judge whose life is more valuable. R. Yisrael Lipschitz, however, permits it if the person being sacrificed is already in the process of dying.[39] He argues that one can sacrifice a person's *chayey sha'ah*, temporary life, for the *chayey olam*, full life, of another person. Similarly, there are authorities who state that one is permitted to hand over a *terefah* (someone with a mortal injury) to be killed, in order to save the lives of healthy people.[40]

Admittedly, this is a far-reaching view, not generally followed by mainstream halakhah. But even if we reject it regarding the cases mentioned above, we might accept this reasoning regarding the case of brain-death. First, the life of a brain-dead person, even if it is considered to be human life, is much less of a human life than that of a *chayey sha'ah*, a *terefah*, or even a *goses*. The reason usually advanced as to why even a few moments of a suffering or dying person's life are precious is that "a single moment of repentance and good deeds in this world is worth more than

---

[38] Rabbi Yehudah Dik, "*Terumat Eivarim Mi-Goses LeHatzalat Chayey Adam*," *Assia* vol. 53-54 (Elul 5754/ August 1994) pp. 48-58; Rabbi Naftali Bar-Ilan, "*BeInyan Mi SheTorem Lev O Kaveid LeHashtalah*," *Assia* 47-48 (Kislev 5750), pp. 131-141; "*Terumat Lev HeHashtalah*," *Assia* 83-84 (5769) pp. 108-118; Rabbi Dr. Michoel Avraham, "*Terumat Evarim*," in *Techumin* (5769) 29 pp. 329-339; Rabbi Shmuel Eliyahu, Chief Rabbi of Tzfat, at the HODS Rabbis & Physicians Seminar, Albert Einstein College of Medicine (video available at HODS.org). For an analysis of the philosophical framework behind such determinations, see Rabbi Dr. David Shatz, "As Thyself: The Limits of Altruism in Jewish Ethics" and "Concepts of Autonomy in Jewish Medical Ethics," in *Jewish Thought in Dialogue* (Brighton, MA: Academic Studies Press 2009) pp. 326-384.

[39] *Tiferet Yisrael* to Mishnah *Yoma* 8:6.

[40] *Me'iri, Sanhedrin* 72a, and *Minchat Chinuch*, no. 296.

all the life of the World-to-Come."[41] But the brain-dead person is not even capable of a single moment of repentance and good deeds—he cannot take any actions, speak any words, or think any thoughts. His life is certainly worth less than the lives of those waiting for his organs, by any measure.

Even more pertinent is another difference with organ donation. There is a distinction drawn by many classical authorities between taking someone *else's* life and volunteering one's *own* life. This is based upon the Talmud itself, which records how the Roman authorities once threatened the entire Jewish community of Lod with annihilation if they did not hand over the murderers of the emperor's daughter. Normally, halachah does not permit the community to choose someone to hand over; yet when Papus and Lulianus chose to sacrifice themselves in order to save the others, they were praised for their martyrdom.[42] This shows that we have more autonomy over our own lives than we do over the lives of others. A person voluntarily signing an organ donor card indicating his or her desire to donate organs upon brain death would be similarly praiseworthy.

A person is never *obligated* to sacrifice his own life in order to save that of another; as Rabbi Akiva famously ruled, if there are two travelers in the desert and only one of them has sufficient water to survive, he is not obligated to give it to the other person. But may a person *choose* to do so? May a person choose to sacrifice his life in order to save the life of another person? This is a matter of dispute between halachic authorities. Some, such as R. Moshe Feinstein,[43] forbid it; others, such as R. Chaim b. Moshe Attar (the *Ohr HaChaim*),[44] permit it; and some, such as R. Yechiel Yaakov Weinberg,[45] not only permit it but also consider it praiseworthy. Those in the latter two categories would surely also permit someone to

---

[41] Mishnah, *Avot* 4:17.

[42] *Ta'anit* 18b; *Pesachim* 50a.

[43] *Igrot Moshe, Yoreh De'ah* II:174:4.

[44] *Rishon Letziyon* (Istanbul 1750), *Yoreh De'ah* 247:1 (p. 103a). For further sources, see the articles cited in footnote 38 above.

[45] *Seridei Aish* II:34, comments 12 and 17.

donate his organs in order to save lives in the eventuality of his suffering brain-death.

Choosing to sacrifice oneself in order to save the lives of others is also encouraged by some authorities in cases where the other person's life is more valuable. R. Yehudah HaChassid states that it is praiseworthy for an *am ha'aretz* to choose to sacrifice his life in order to save the life of a Torah scholar who is needed by the community.[46]

Thus, we have authorities who permit taking the life of a dying person in order to save the life of a healthy person, even against his will; and we have authorities who permit a healthy person to voluntarily sacrifice his life in order to save another. And so in a case where both factors are present—a *dying* person *voluntarily* sacrifices his quasi-life of no human consciousness—there are vastly more grounds for permitting and even encouraging it.[47]

Even with regard to those who forbid the traveler to give his water to the other person, the case of organ donation is vastly different. The traveler would be sacrificing a regular life of inestimable value. But in the case of organ donation, it is a matter of one person choosing to sacrifice a few days of a brain-dead state, during which he will not take any actions, speak any words, or think any thoughts, in order to save the lives of several people who will, as a result, lead full lives. Even if one were to consider this to be the sacrifice of a life, it is barely human life, and there is thus a firm basis to judge it to be an appropriate and praiseworthy act of self-sacrifice.

Conclusion

Halachic authorities who attempt to resolve the status of brain-death using a traditional Chazal-based halachic methodology, whichever conclusions they reach, are using a decidedly anti-rationalist approach. They are either taking the position that all knowledge, even of future

---

[46] *Sefer Chassidim* 698.

[47] The question of how, even if it is permissible for a person to sacrifice his life in this case, the doctor is permitted to take his life, is addressed by Rabbi Dr. Michoel Avraham, "*Terumat Evarim,*" in *Techumin* (5769) 29 pp. 329-339.

scenarios, is found in the Torah and Talmud—or they effectively analyze the topic as though that were the case. Understandably, many people are uncomfortable with the idea that such an approach is inadequate. But, from a rationalist perspective, it is clear that there can be no precedent for addressing the modern situation of brain-death, which only came about in in the late 1950s with the invention of a ventilator. Chazal, the Rishonim and the Acharonim had no reason to ever differentiate and isolate the role of the brain and that of the heart and lungs in maintaining life. And even if they were to have differentiated between the role of these independent organs and systems, their conclusions would have been marred by their obsolete and incorrect understanding of the functions of these organs and systems, as based on the medicine and science of their day.

Yet it is our responsibility to resolve halachic questions, especially when lives are at stake—and it can be done, even in this case. While the Mishnah and Talmud does not discuss the case of brain-death, it does discuss the case of an animal that has been beheaded, and we can determine that the two cases are analogous. Whether one approaches the topic from the Rishonim's view of the essence of human life as relating to the mind, or from logical and empirical analyses based upon science (suggested by Chatam Sofer as being the basis for Chazal's determinations) which reveal a person's presence and soul to be located in neurological activity, these approaches converge to the same result. If a person is brain-dead, he is no longer present as a person; he has died. And one can further incorporate the entirely different method of evaluating the option of heroic sacrifice. For a person to choose in advance that in a situation of brain death— when he is not going to be able to have any meaningful existence—then his body should be used to save the lives of others, this is a noble and entirely appropriate choice.

Many important authorities have accepted brain death as death based on classic halakhic argumentation from Talmudic sources (while many others rule differently). Hence, even those who insist that halakha can be grounded only on Talmudic precedent have authorities on which to rely in order to accept brain death as death and to rule that the organs of a brain-dead person should be used to save the lives of other people. But from a rationalist outlook, this conclusion is reached via a different methodology.

TEN

The Sages' Powers of Life and Death

The Talmudic Accounts

In the *Amidah* prayer, we describe God as *memit u'mechayah*, the One Who has the ability to cause death and bring back to life—with these powers implicitly presented as being unique to God. Yet in the Talmud, there are stories which seem to describe the sages as possessing these same abilities.

There are numerous accounts from the Talmud and Midrash concerning the rabbis killing or hurting people by gazing at them.[1] A principle found in several places in the Talmud is that "whenever the Sages gave someone a look (lit. "set their eyes"), the result was either death or poverty."[2] The Talmud relates that when Rabbi Shimon ben Yochai and his son emerged from the cave where they had been hiding, and saw people toiling in agriculture, they exclaimed, "They are deserting eternal life and busying themselves with temporary life!"; the story continues that "whatever they set their eyes upon was instantly burned up."[3] An even more graphic description of this ability occurs in another story:

> "...Rabbi Yochanan sat and expounded, The Holy One is destined to bring precious stones and pearls that are thirty by thirty (cubits) and hollow out of them an area ten by twenty and stand them at the gates of Jerusalem. A certain student scoffed at him: "Now that we do not even find such things in the size of a small dove's egg, can ones of such size be found?!" After some time, he set out to sea in a ship, and saw ministering

---

[1] For a comprehensive list of citations, see Rivka Ulmer, *The Evil Eye in the Bible and in Rabbinic Literature* (Hoboken, NJ: Ktav, 1994), pp. 83-104.

[2] *Moed Katan* 17b, *Chagigah* 5b, *Nedarim* 7b, *Sotah* 46b.

[3] *Shabbat* 33b.

angels that were sitting and carving precious stones and pearls that were thirty by thirty and hollowing out ten by twenty. He said to them, "Who are these for?" They said to him, "The Holy One is destined to stand them at the gates of Jerusalem." He came before Rabbi Yochanan and said to him, "Expound, my rebbe, it is fitting for you to expound; just as you said, thus I saw." Rabbi Yochanan replied: "Empty one! If you hadn't seen it, then would you not have believed it?! You are a scoffer at the words of the sages!" He gave him a look and he became a heap of bones. (*Bava Batra* 75a)

R. Shimon ben Yochai is likewise said to have set his eyes upon someone and thereby bringing about his death, and then he sets his eyes upon another person who turns into a heap of bones.[4] The Talmud also relates that Rav was bothered by a man who sought to marry his daughter and refused to leave, whereupon Rav set his eyes upon him and he died.[5]

The opposite phenomenon, of people bringing the dead back to life, first appears in Scripture, where Eliyahu and Elisha are both described as having accomplished this feat.[6] In the Talmud, Rabbi Yochanan is described as having caused the death of Rav Kahana, as a consequence of Rav Kahana having inadvertently causing him embarrassment; subsequently, Rabbi Yochanan prayed for mercy on behalf of Rav Kahana, and he was restored to life.[7] Perhaps the most famous of such accounts concerns Rabbah:

> Rabbah and Rabbi Zeira held a Purim feast together. They became intoxicated, and Rabbah arose and slaughtered Rabbi Zeira. The next day, he asked for mercy and Rabbi Zeira was revived. The following year, Rabbah said to him: "Let the master come and we will make a Purim feast together." R. Zeira answered: "A miracle does not happen every time." (*Megillah* 7b)

The Talmud also relates a story of how the Roman emperor Antoninus would visit Rabbi Yehudah HaNasi. He kept his visits secret, killing the

---

[4] *Shabbat* 34a.

[5] *Yevamot* 45a.

[6] I Kings 17 and II Kings 4.

[7] *Bava Kama* 117a.

servants that accompanied him. On one such visit, he found Rabbi Yehudah's student R. Chanina bar Chama sitting with him. Antoninus reminded R. Yehudah that no person was supposed to know about these visits, whereupon R. Yehudah responded that R. Chanina is no ordinary human being. To test this, Antoninus asked R. Chanina to "wake up" the servant that he had just killed. R. Chanina prayed for mercy, and the man was resurrected. Antoninus acknowledged to R. Yehudah that "the least among you can resurrect the dead."[8]

The Literalist-Scientific Approach

In a comprehensive study of this topic, Sinai Turan argues that the phenomenon described in these cases is not the same as the "evil eye."[9] The evil eye refers to unfortunate feelings of jealousy, whereas "giving the eye," on the other hand, is a conscious act of causing harm. Still, as we shall see, the mechanism involved in both cases appears similar, and the concepts are undoubtedly related, even though not identical.

The formulation in several of these cases is that the Torah sage "set his eyes upon him, and he became a heap of bones."[10] The extreme literalist, traditionalist interpretation would be that the student (a) died, (b) instantly, (c) by way of unnatural disintegration of his flesh and organs, and that all this was (d) as a result of a special power that the sage possessed.

The first three aspects are found with Rashi (1040-1105), who writes that the phrase refers to a person "whose flesh has rotten away, and it is as though he has fallen long ago."[11] Maharal (1520-1609) likewise explains that the phrase refers to sudden death, although he does not take a literal

---

[8] *Avodah Zarah* 10b.

[9] Sinai Turan, "'Wherever the Sages Set Their Eyes, there is Either Death or Poverty' - On the History, Terminology and Imagery of the Talmudic Traditions about the Devastating Gaze of the Sages," *Sidra* 23, pp. 168-170.

[10] This expression also appears on *Berachot* 58a and *Shabbat* 34a.

[11] This is the comment of Rashi to the phrase in *Shabbat* 34a.

approach to the description of the student turning into a heap of bones.[12] R. Shmuel Eliezer Eidels (Maharsha, 1555–1631) follows Rashi's view, and, noting the problem that Rav Sheshet (who is one of the Sages described as having given such a look) was blind, suggests that his sight was miraculously restored in order for him to accomplish this feat.[13]

It should be noted that from ancient times through the medieval period, the idea that people can inflict damage with their eyes was considered perfectly normal, and even to have a scientific basis.[14] Whereas modern science reveals that the eye only absorbs radiation, in antiquity the eye was thought to emit radiation—a kind of "fire."[15] Plato wrote about how this fire emerges from the eyes and combines with daylight to form a homogenous entity, through which images are conducted back into the eye.[16] When coupled with harmful intent on behalf of the viewer, this radiation was thought to become especially dangerous. Abarbanel explains the scientific mechanism for this:

> The damage that comes from the evil eye is well known amongst people. It is just as the Philosopher wrote; that extraneous vapors are pushed out of the body, from a person with an evil, jealous spirit. And due to the toxicity of these vapors, they have effects on things that are prone to

[12] *Chiddushei Aggados* to *Shabbat* 34a. He writes that it was "a sudden death... *as though he was burned and became a heap of bones.*"

[13] To *Berachot* 58a, s.v. *Natan einav bo.* He also suggests an alternative answer, that it refers to the sage cursing the person to turn into a heap of bones. R. Chaim Chizkiyah HaLevi Medini (1833-1885), raising the difficulty with Rav Sheshes, explains the term "set his eyes upon him" allegorically; see *Sdei Chemed, klal* 35, *Natan einav bo.* In *Shiurim B'Haggadot Chazal* (*Sanhedrin* 100a), the author points out that (a) the same phrase is used with Rav Sheshes who was blind, (b) it is forbidden to look at the face of a wicked person, and (c) Rabbi Yochanan is said to have almost never looked up from his studies. He thus explains the term allegorically to mean that he "looked into the depths of his soul."

[14] See Matthew W. Dickie, "Heliodorus and Plutarch on the Evil Eye," *Classical Philology*, Vol. 86, No. 1 (Jan. 1991), pp. 17-29.

[15] Charles G. Gross, "The Fire That Comes from the Eye," *The Neuroscientist* (1999) 5:1, pp. 58-64.

[16] Plato, *Timeaus*, translated by Benjamin Jowett (Rockville, MD: Serenity Publishers 2009), p. 24.

absorbing these effects, to the point that it is possible to kill someone by looking at them. (Abarbanel, Commentary to Deuteronomy, *parashat Ki Tisa*, p. 293)

Rabbi Pinchas Eliyahu Hurwitz of Vilna (1765-1821) in *Sefer ha-Brit* 1:14:5 (Brünn, 1797) describes how ostrich incubates eggs by staring at them, and sees in this a lesson as to the dangers of staring at forbidden sights. He further adds that the Sages of the Talmud, who were careful never to look at forbidden sights, thus had exceptional power in their vision and could kill people by looking at them. Rabbi Eliyahu b. Shlomo ha-Cohen of eighteenth-century Turkey bemoans those who scoff at the accounts of sages killing with their vision, and notes that there are animals and birds with this power, which prove it to be possible.[17] At the end of the nineteenth century, R. Chaim Schwartz noted that there are those who scoff at the possibility of killing someone by looking at them, and therefore cites German encyclopedias and journals reporting that "there are great non-Jewish scholars who attested to the ability of some to accomplish marvelous feats with their eyes and who even themselves were able to kill vermin by looking at them."[18]

It is important to appreciate the relevance of this worldview to the significance of these stories in the Talmud. According to this perspective, the stories of sages killing people by looking at them were not considered to be "miracle" stories. Instead, they were merely noting that the Sages' visual powers were more potent than those of ordinary people. There is nothing remarkable about ending someone's life; it can be done with the sword. The novelty of these stories is in the method used, but according to the understanding of nature held in antiquity, this method is not supernatural.

But what about the stories with the Sages bringing the dead back to life? There is no ancient scientific explanation for this phenomenon. However, it must be noted that there is a crucial difference between the

---

[17] *Midrash Talpiot, Anaf Chayot*, pp. 251-252.

[18] Rabbi Chaim Schwartz, *Orach Chaim* (Frankfurt 1892) pp. 24-25. He refers the reader to Gottlieb Tobias Wilhelm's *Unterhaltungen aus der Naturgeschichte* ("*Discourse of Natural History*," 1795), chapter 68, and other sources.

two cases. Whereas the Sages are described as killing people, they are not described as themselves bringing people back to life; instead, they are described as praying to God for His mercy and *Him* bringing them back to life. Furthermore, in the case of R. Zeira, he was revived by way of a miracle, which R. Zeira notes cannot be relied upon. The clear inference is that R. Zeira was resurrected via a fortunate act of God, not via the power of Rabbah. Thus, these stories are likewise not "miracle" stories about the Sages.

The Literalist-Metaphysical Approach

Others explained the phenomenon of the "death stare" without recourse to scientific explanations. R. Chaim ben Moshe ibn Attar (1696-1743), seeking to understand how a righteous person can be the cause of death, resolves the problem with a metaphysical rationalization of the phenomenon. He explains that wicked people derive the ability to live from a spark of good within them; when sages "set their eyes upon them," this spark is drawn to the life-force of the sage, like a piece of iron being attracted to a magnet, resulting in the death of the wicked person.[19] Chacham Yosef Chaim (1834-1909) has a similar explanation of how Rabbah killed R. Zeira; rather than being an intentional act of murder, Rabbah was teaching such exalted secrets of Torah that R. Zeira's soul flew out of his material body in attraction to the spiritual dimension.[20]

In modern times, when the notion of a scientific basis for damaging looks is entirely abandoned, this metaphysical approach became the only option for those traditionalists who take a literalist approach to such stories about the Sages. Rabbi Yosef Yehudah Leib Bloch of Telz (1860-1930), taking the view that Rabbi Yochanan himself was able to accomplish this "death stare," explains the mechanism via which he accomplished it:

> Their *shiur komah* (metaphysical dimensions) was exceedingly great, reaching to other worlds that are far distant and immeasurably higher than our lowly world, and so their words and thoughts, which began from a

---

[19] *Ohr HaChaim* to Exodus 11:5.
[20] *Ben Yehoyada* to *Megillah* 7b.

very high place—from a world where the root of their soul is found and lives—flood down with great force and immense power, descending from above to below, to the extent that they are powerful enough to kill... thus we find in tractate *Bava Basra*... "He gave him a look and he became a heap of bones." Such were their powers! Their words and thoughts were so powerful, that when he gave him a look, he immediately became a heap of bones. May dust fill the mouths of those who say that they were men like us... (*Shiurei Daat* vol. II p. 177)

On the other hand, we find other recent traditionalists arguing that it was not R. Yochanan's innate powers that accomplished it. Rabbi Yisrael Yaakov Kanievsky (the "Steipler Gaon," 1899–1985) raises the question of why Rabbi Yochanan was not liable for murder, and among his suggested answers are that Rabbi Yochanan prayed for it to happen, or that he issued a halachic ruling that the student deserved death, and Heaven concurred and executed instant, supernatural judgment.[21] However, it should be noted that R. Kanievsky is not arguing with the notion that R. Yochanan would have such power; only with the idea that it would be legitimate for him to use it in such a way.

With regard to the accounts of the Sages resurrecting the dead, as we noted earlier, the Talmud does not actually state that they performed this via their own innate power, but rather that they prayed to God and He did so. It is true that not everyone's prayers are that efficacious, so in a sense it can be attributed to the sages' special natures. But one does receive the impression from contemporary traditionalists, who talk about "Chazal's ability to resurrect the dead," that they are presenting this feat as being caused by the sages' own powers. This is despite the fact that the Talmud itself, even if it rates the Sages as being able to bring about the resurrection of the dead, does not consider all their words to be sacrosanct; on other occasions it points to them being unaware, misinformed, or simply mistaken. For dedicated traditionalists today, who wish to counter such a view and establish the absolute superiority and hence authority of the Sages, there is no better or more popular way to do so than to point to their ability to resurrect the dead.

---

[21] *Kehillat Yaakov, Bava Kama* 45.

...If the Gemara tells us a *metziyus*, it's *emes veyatziv*. There's nothing to think about. Anything we see with our eyes is less of a reality than something we see in the Gemara. That's the *emunah* that a *yid* has to have... *Chazal HaKedoshim—hakatan shebetalmidei Rabbeinu haKadosh mechayeh meisim* (With the holy sages, the least of Rabbi Yehudah's disciples were able to resurrect the dead)! ...Our *emunah* has to be, and will continue to be, that every word of *Chazal haKedoshim* is *emes le'amitoh!* (Rabbi Uren Reich, Address at Agudath Israel of America's 82nd National Convention)

The Traditionalist-Rationalist Approach

Marc Saperstein describes three classes of people who respond to a new world view which appears to be in radical conflict with sacred texts.[22] One group steadfastly remains committed to tradition; at the other extreme are those who are committed to the new way of looking at things and ignore or explicitly repudiate the authority of the ancient text; and in the middle are those who try to discover new meaning in the text in order to resolve the tension. Traditionalists of the rationalist persuasion, in a world that no longer subscribes to the idea of the eye emitting radiation, consider it obvious that the accounts of the "death stare" cannot be literal. Aside from the scientific impossibility, if the righteous were able to kill sinners by simply looking at them the wrong way, most of ancient Jewish history doesn't make much sense; why couldn't the Jews simply kill their enemies by looking at them, and why did nobody else, even such complimentary historians as Josephus, ever mention this phenomenon? They thus resort to non-literal interpretations.

Although not usually considered a rationalist, an early non-literal interpretation of these accounts is found in the writings of Rabbi Nachman of Breslov (1772-1810). He explains that a sinner usually blinds himself to the effects of his crime. The sage "sets his eyes" and sees the effects, then reveals (*megaleh=gal*) to the sinner that to which he had closed (*otzem=atzamot*) his eyes. R. Nachman concludes by noting that the

---

[22] *Decoding the Rabbis: A Thirteenth-Century Commentary on the Aggadah* (Cambridge, MA: Harvard University Press 1980) pp. 11-12.

greatest punishment for a person is for him to see the damage that he has caused.[23]

R. Avraham Stein, a nineteenth century rabbinic scholar with clear maskilic leanings, explains the Talmud's phrase as follows:

> ...when the student realized that he had caught himself out with his words, his bones trembled, for fear had befallen him, and he stood shaken and silent. And this is what is intended with the words "he became a heap of bones." (*Avnei Miluim* [Warsaw 1900] pp. 39-40)

It is similar to how one would say, "He gave him a withering look," which, in contemporary English, does not literally mean that the person withered away—although this English expression may well be historically derived from the belief in the power of the evil eye. In a footnote, Stein adds a suggestion that if a person gained the disapproval of the rabbis, people would make his life miserable, effectively destroying him and making him into a "heap of bones."

R. Avraham Korman (1917-2002) takes a similar approach, insisting that it is impossible that the sages would commit murder, and further noting that one should always avoid explaining events supernaturally if possible. He thus explains these stories as referring to the Sages growing angry, and the subjects of their anger feeling like they had been made into a heap of bones.[24]

With regard to the accounts of the sages resurrecting the dead, such as that of Rabbah resurrecting Rabbi Zeira, some point to Maharsha as a precedent for a rationalist approach. Maharsha explains that the wild merriment led to a situation in which R. Zeira drank too much and became seriously ill, whereupon Rabbah prayed for him and he was restored to health. However, it would be a mistake to interpret this as Maharsha expressing a rationalistic tendency, and that his reluctance to accept a supernatural story forced him to a non-literal interpretation. With the story of Rabbi Yochanan's student, Maharsha says that the student's crime was in not accepting the literal truth of his prediction, and

---

[23] *Likkutei Moharan* 1:98.

[24] *Ha-Aggadah veMehuta* (Tel Aviv 2001) pp. 251-252.

notes that "it is the way of heretics to remove words from their literal meaning."[25] With Rabbah and R. Zeira, Maharsha is thus presumably not perturbed by the scientific problem of Rabbah bringing a dead person back to life—instead, he is bothered by the moral issue of his killing him in the first place!

If we want to find rabbinic authorities refusing to take such stories at face value due to rationalist considerations, we need to begin much earlier in the medieval period. According to Rambam, the youth that Eliyahu restored to life was not actually dead to begin with, only unconscious.[26] R. Avraham ben HaRambam (1186-1237), discussing a category of Aggadata that he considers exaggerations, includes the story of Rabbah and R. Zeira. He explains that Rabbah struck R. Zeira a damaging blow, then helped him recover. R. Avraham insists that all such stories about the Sages resurrecting people should be interpreted similarly.[27] A similar approach is found with R. Menachem Meiri (1249—c. 1310), a rationalist who generally avoided interpreting the Talmud as referring to supernatural matters.[28] He explains it to mean that Rabbah "squeezed" R. Zeira (apparently into a loss of consciousness), and then revived him.[29]

Although not specifically mentioning the cases in our discussion, R. Samson Raphael Hirsch, in a letter discussing how to approach Aggadata, cites various views from the Geonim and Rishonim about how it does not need to be interpreted literally. Discussing miraculous stories involving the Sages, R. Hirsch writes as follows:

> I tend to think it not at all farfetched that even in Talmudic times, the Holy One performed miracles—in special circumstances—for the greatest and most pious of Chazal... But if one of our contemporary rabbinical scholars should say to me, "Brother, I believe wholeheartedly like you that the Holy One has the power and the ability to change nature at His will... But my feeling is that the Holy One changes nature only for some great

---

[25] Maharsha to *Sanhedrin* 100a, a.v. *Nachal mibeit Kadshei haKadashim*.

[26] *Guide* II:42.

[27] R. Avraham ben HaRambam, *Ma'amar al Aggadat Chazal*.

[28] See Louis Jacobs, "Demythologizing the Rabbinic Aggadah: Menahem Meiri."

[29] Meiri to *Megillah* 7b.

need or to publicize some lofty matter, for the order of nature is His will, which was ordained and is maintained by Him. So if I know for sure that Chazal intended the miracle stories related in their aggados to be taken literally, God forbid that I should doubt their veracity, and I would believe as you do that these incidents really took place. But I wonder: Are we to understand these stories as having really taken place or are they analogies or parables? I personally tend to accept the opinion of those who say that aggadic miracle stories are not to be taken literally," —may I push this person away? May I grow angry at him? May I consider myself a greater believer than he? Both of us are equally firmly rooted in the principles of Jewish faith. (Letter to R. Hile Wechsler, published by Mordechai Breuer in *HaMa'ayan* 16:2 (Tevet 5736/1976) p. 7)

In modern times, an interesting approach to this topic, albeit somewhat cryptic, is found in the writings of R. Aryeh Carmell (1917-2006):

We see [the Sages of the Talmud] in the midst of life, suffering and enjoying, being annoyed and asking pardon, nodding off to sleep and waking up with a jerk, buying meat in the market place and shipping barrels of beer down the river—and always, always, learning, discussing, arguing, centering their lives round Torah and Mitzvot, molding their actions and their character on ethics of Torah, while living life to the full. We are told that every sage in the Talmud has the power to bring the dead back to life. I say they still retain that power if we are prepared to open ethically dead hearts of our pupils to their life-giving influence. (Rabbi Aryeh Carmell, "Is There An Ethical Aim To Education?")

While R. Carmell is not absolutely clear here as to how he is interpreting the accounts in the Talmud, based on my own numerous discussions with him it appears to me that he is understanding such stories metaphorically.

It may even be that there was no conscious intent to create a metaphor. Rather, stories were created without concern as to whether they were factually true or not. This does not mean that the creators of such stories acted in bad faith or were dishonest. It simply means that we have very different ideas as to the nature of recording history than did the writers of old. To quote a work on medieval literature:

...To ask why medieval writers claimed that what appears to us obviously "invented" material was "true" is another reminder of the incommensurability of our cultures... "Historical"...might be thought of as an exemplary narrative based upon events which had occurred at some point in the past, told in order to move and persuade its audience to imitate the good and eschew the evil, a "true tale about the past" which included a vast range of what modern readers would regard as invented material... In the different conceptual space of the Middle Ages, "true" might mean "in the main" or "for the most part" true, or even, "it could have happened like this."[30]

The Rationalist-Academic Approach

For rationalists who are less traditionalist in their orientation, although they do not accept that the Sages killed with their vision and brought about the resurrection of the dead, they are willing to accept that the Talmud did indeed mean to describe such phenomena as actually occurring. "Natural human admiration for a charismatic figure and widespread belief in such an individual's supernatural abilities to ease the daily travails of the faithful, account for the preponderance of the biographical legend in Talmudic literature."[31]

As noted earlier, the ancients all believed in the ability of the eye to emit harmful radiation, as well as in the existence of animals that kill people by looking at them; hence, there is every reason to think that the legends of the sages killing people by looking at them evolved over time and were generally thought of as being literally true.[32] The story about Antoninus remarking to R. Yehudah HaNasi that the least of his students can resurrect the dead, one of many stories in which Antoninus marvels at the Jews, is rated as based on Hellenistic literature in which a foreign

---

[30] Ruth Morse, *Truth and Convention in the Middle Ages: Rhetoric, Representation and Reality* (Cambridge University Press 1990) pp. 2-6. My attention was drawn to this by Marc Shapiro, *Changing the Immutable: How Orthodox Judaism Rewrites Its History* (Oxford: The Littman Library of Jewish Civilization 2015), which includes many examples of this phenomenon.

[31] Eli Yassif, *The Hebrew Folktale: History, Genre, Meaning* (Indiana University Press 1999) p. 106.

[32] Sinai Turan, idem., pp. 176-177.

ruler asks questions of a sage and is amazed at his wisdom.[33] Such accounts are not so different from the Talmud account of how Rava "made a man," who could not speak; as Idel comments, "The pietists, or the righteous, are endowed indeed with extraordinary powers… those editors who included the story in the Talmud were living in a society which assumed that wonderful powers were the prerogative of the very few, who are capable of imitating the acts of the divine…"[34]

One need not assume that this approach is only to be found within contemporary academia. Several of the Geonim and Rishonim made statements about aggadah not being dogma[35] and about how one may reject aggadic statements that do not conform to reason; and it is clear that Rambam and others did indeed reject many aggadic statements entirely (rather than interpreting them non-literally). Thus, even if the stories about the Sages killing people and resurrecting the dead were thought to be factual by those who wrote them in the Talmud, this does not mean that one is obligated to accept them as factual.

Conclusion

The Sages' power to kill with a look was not especially supernatural according to ancient and medieval understandings of the world. Yet this understanding disappeared entirely. While from an academic perspective it is simply myth, amongst traditionalists it was either promoted to an extraordinarily supernatural power of the sages, or demoted to allegory.

A similar history occurs with the accounts of the Sages' power to restore life. This was originally seen as God's work that was granted in response to the sages' prayers. Yet it was later either demoted to a non-literal

---

[33] Luitpold Wallach, "The Colloquy of Marcus Aurelius With the Patriarch Judah I," *JQR* 31 (1940-41) pp. 259-86.

[34] Moshe Idel, *Golem: Jewish Magical and Mystical Traditions on the Artificial Anthropoid*, pp. 28, 47.

[35] For an exhaustive list, see R. Chaim Eisen, "Maharal's *Be'er ha-Golah* and His Revolution in *Aggadic* Scholarship — in Their Context and on His Terms." *Hakirah* vol. 4 (Winter 2007) pp. 137-194.

resurrection, or was elevated and presented as effectively being caused by the actual power of the Sages.

In these cases, we see how stories are forced to change their meaning and significance over time, depending upon the worldview of those that read them. That which appears miraculous in one culture may appear entirely normal to another. That which represents a factual account of extraordinary events to some is interpreted allegorically by others. The meaning of such stories is not provided by those who tell them; it is created by those who hear them.

ELEVEN

Wrestling with Demons:
A History of Rabbinic Attitudes to Demons

Introduction

From Scripture to Talmud and Midrash through medieval Jewish
writings, we find mention of dangerous and evil beings. Scripture refers
to them as Azazel and *se'irim*; later writings refer to them as *sheidim, ruchot*
and *mazikim*. All these are different varieties (or different names) of
demons.

Belief in demons (and the associated belief in witches, magic and occult
phenomena) was widespread in the ancient world, and the terror that it
caused is unimaginable to us.[1] But in the civilized world today there is
virtually nobody who still believes in them. The transition from a global
approach of belief to one of disbelief began with Aristotle, gained a little
more traction in the early medieval period, and finally concretized in the
eighteenth century.

Perhaps surprisingly, there has not been any comprehensive review of
Jewish attitudes to demons over the ages. In this study I shall attempt such
a review. When beginning this project, I decided to divide the list between
those who did believe in demons, and those who rejected their existence.
In the conclusion, however, I will explain why this division is seen to be
ultimately unsatisfactory.

---

[1] See Joshua Trachtenberg, *Jewish Magic and Superstition*, p. 44.

The Talmud's Demonology

There are numerous references to demons in the Babylonian Talmud.[2] With regard to their formation, there is a view that demons were created on the eve of the first Shabbat of creation,[3] another statement about bats turning into demons,[4] and another account of how demons of various types were generated from Adam's wasted seminal emissions.[5] Another passage, later to become very important to those discussing demonology, specifies the nature of demons:

> The Rabbis taught: Six things were said about demons; three in which they resemble ministering angels, and three in which they resemble human beings. The three in which they resemble ministering angels are that they have wings, they fly from one end of the earth to the other, and they know the future... And the three in which they resemble humans are that they eat and drink, reproduce, and die. (*Chagigah* 16a; *Avot D'Rabbi Natan* 37)

Demons played a role in halachic discussions, such as whether a voice uttering a declaration of halachic significance, heard from a person who cannot be found, is suspected as having been uttered by a demon,[6] and whether a warning to a criminal given by a demon counts as a warning such as to render him liable for subsequently sinning.[7] The Talmud also warns about many situations in which there is danger from demons, such as in the shade of various trees and touching their stumps,[8] in ruined buildings,[9] in graveyards,[10] in a house in which one is sleeping alone,[11]

---

[2] A comprehensive collection of Talmudic, Midrashic and medieval statements about demons can be found in Ronald H. Isaacs, *Ascending Jacob's Ladder: Jewish Views of Angels, Demons, and Evil Spirits* (Rowman & Littlefield, 1997) pp. 91-118.

[3] Mishnah, *Avot* 5:6; Talmud, *Pesachim* 54a.

[4] *Bava Kama* 16a.

[5] *Eruvin* 18b.

[6] *Yevamot* 122a; *Gittin* 66a.

[7] *Makkot* 6b.

[8] *Pesachim* 111a-b.

[9] *Berachot* 3a-b.

[10] *Chagigah* 3b.

[11] *Shabbat* 151b.

when having things in pairs,[12] and when drinking from rivers or lakes at night.[13] There is also a demon by the name of Yosef who gave one of the Sages information about the nature of demonic activities,[14] as well as being suggested to have possibly taught the Sages various teachings.[15] Another demon, which haunted the study hall of Abaye, appeared to Rav Acha bar Yaakov as a seven-headed snake and was killed by him.[16] The Talmud also tells of how King Solomon trapped the demon Ashmodai and forced him to reveal secrets to him.[17] Another passage speaks of the great prevalence of demons, as well as giving instructions on how to detect them:

> It has been taught: Abba Benjamin says, If the eye had the power to see the demons, no creature could endure them. Abaye says: They are more numerous than we are and they surround us like the ridge round a field. R. Huna says: Every one among us has a thousand on his left and ten thousand on his right. Rava says: They are responsible for the crushing in the Kallah lectures, fatigue in the knees, the wearing out of the clothes of the scholars from rubbing against them, and the bruising of the feet. If one wants to discover them, let him take sifted ashes and sprinkle around his bed, and in the morning he will see something like the footprints of a cock. If one wishes to see them, let him take the afterbirth of a black she-cat which is the offspring of a black she-cat, the firstborn of a firstborn, roast it in fire and grind it to powder, and then let him put some into his eye, and he will see them. Let him also pour it into an iron tube and seal it with an iron signet that they should not steal it from him, and let him also close his mouth, so that he should not come to harm. R. Bibi b. Abaye did so, saw them and came to harm. The sages, however, prayed for him and he recovered. (*Berachot* 6a-b)

---

[12] *Pesachim* 110b.

[13] *Pesachim* 112a. For discussion, see Bar-Ilan, Meir, "Exorcism by Rabbis: Talmudic Sages and Magic," *Da`at* 34 (1995), pp. 17-31.

[14] *Pesachim* 110a.

[15] *Eruvin* 43a.

[16] *Kiddushin* 29b.

[17] *Gittin* 68a-b.

References to demons in the Jerusalem Talmud are much less common.[18] In fact, there is a reference in the Babylonian Talmud to a certain verse which was translated in Babylon as referring to male and female demons, but which in the west (i.e. in the Land of Israel) was translated as referring to carriages.[19] The Babylonian Talmud further notes that the demonic risk involved in pairs, which was a subject of great concern in Babylon, was not an issue for their counterparts in the Land of Israel:

> In the West, they are not cautious about having things in pairs... The rule of the matter is that for those who take note of the pairs, the pairs take note of them; those who do not take note of the pairs are not bothered by them. Nonetheless, it is good to show a modicum of concern. (*Pesachim* 110b)

Medieval Deniers of Demons

It is the general consensus of the academic community that **Rambam** denied the existence of demons. Among traditional scholars, those who accepted that Rambam denied the existence of demons include the Gerona kabbalist R. Shlomo b. Meshullam da Piera,[20] R. Yosef b. Shem Tov,[21] R. Yosef Shlomo Delmedigo,[22] R. Aviad Sar-Shalom Basilea,[23]

---

[18] Louis Ginzberg, *The Palestinian Talmud* (New York, 1941), pp. xxxiii-xxxvi: "Palestinian authors of the Talmud excluded, almost entirely, the popular fancies about angels and demons, while in Babylonia angelology and demonology gained scholastic recognition and with it entrance into the Talmud... A similar observation can be made in regard to the difference in the attitudes of the two Talmuds toward sorcery, magic, astrology, and other kinds of superstitions." For examples of references in the Jerusalem Talmud, see *Shabbat* 1:3, 3b and *Gittin* 6:6, 48b.

[19] Talmud, *Gittin* 68a.

[20] In Chaim Brody, "Poems of Meshullam ben Shlomo da Piera," *Yediyot HaMachon LeCheker HaShirah HaIvrit* 4 (1938) pp. 33, 55. This and the following sources are taken from Marc Shapiro, *Studies in Maimonides and his Interpreters* (University of Scranton Press 2008), pp. 105-108.

[21] His comment is printed in his translation of Crescas' *Bittul Ikkarei HaNotzrim* p. 93.

[22] *Eilim* (Amsterdam 1628) p. 83.

[23] *Emunat Chachamim* (Warsaw 1888) p. 8a.

Abarbanel,[24] the Vilna Gaon,[25] R. Yosef Ergas,[26] R. Yosef Shaul Nathanson,[27] R. Menashe ben Yisrael,[28] R. Eliezer Neusatz,[29] R. Eliezer Simcha Rabinowitz,[30] *Nofet Tzufim*,[31] and R. Yosef Kapach.[32]

However, there is a long list of traditionalists who did not (perhaps one should say: could not[33]) accept that Rambam denied the existence of demons, and claimed that he believed in their existence.[34] This list

---

[24] Commentary to Deuteronomy 18:9, p. 173.

[25] *Bi'ur ha-Gra, Yoreh De'ah,* 179:6 note 13. Traditionalists are often disturbed by the Gra's declaration that Rambam was "led astray by the accursed philosophy" to deny the existence of demons and other such phenomena. See, for example, Reuven Schmeltzer, *Chaim B'Emunasam*, pp. 290-291. They claim that the Vilna Gaon did not mean to denigrate Rambam himself, and report an account of how the Vilna Gaon spoke highly of the Rambam and wished to share his portion in the World-to-Come; however, this story appears to be nothing more than a folktale, with no authentic basis. See Jacob I DiEnstag, "Was the Gra Opposed to the Philosophical Approach of the Rambam?" [Hebrew], *Talpiot* 4:1-2 (Tammuz 5709) p. 254.

[26] *Shomer Emunim* (Amsterdam 1736) p. 11.

[27] Responsa *Shoel U'Meishiv* (Lvov 1865) 4:87.

[28] *Nishmat Chaim* (Amsterdam 1652) 3:12.

[29] *Mei Menuchot* (Pressburg 1884), pp. 43b.

[30] *She'elot uTeshuvot ve-Chiddushei Rabbi Eliezer Simchah* (Jerusalem 1998), no. 11.

[31] Cited by R. Avraham Noah Klein, et al., *Daf al ha-Daf* (Jerusalem 2006), *Pesachim* 110a.

[32] *Ketavim* (Jerusalem, 1989), vol. 2, pp. 600-601.

[33] I think it would be accurate to say that all those who do not believe that Rambam denied the existence of demons, are themselves people who believe in the existence of demons and who greatly revere Rambam.

[34] Many sources are cited by Marc Shapiro, *Studies in Maimonides and his Interpreters* (University of Scranton Press 2008), pp. 106-111.

including recent figures such as R. Tzefanyah Arusi,[35] R. Zvi Yehudah Kook[36] and R. Shlomo Aviner.[37]

Rambam's most explicit denial of the existence of demons would seem to be found in his *Commentary on the Mishnah*:

> Amongst that which you should know is that the perfected philosophers do not believe in *tzelamim*, by which I mean talismanery, but scoff at them and at those who think that they possess efficacy... and I say this because I know that most people are seduced by this with great folly, and with similar things, and think that they are real—which is not so... and these are things that have received great publicity amongst the pagans, especially amongst the nation which is called the Sabians... and they wrote works dealings with the stars, and witchcraft... and demons, and soothsaying... (*Commentary on the Mishnah, Avodah Zarah* 4:7)

Some claim that this text is only rejecting conversing with demons, rather than rejecting the actual existence of demons per se. However, a careful reading does seem to make it clear that Rambam is saying that demons are not real.[38]

Other evidence for Rambam's denial of demons emerges from his discussion in the *Guide* of the prohibition against eating an animal's blood was due to the belief that doing so has the effect of summoning demons who then become of assistance. In the course of this discussion, he writes as follows:

---

[35] R. Tzefanyah Arusi, "*Lo ba-Shamayim Hi' be-Mishnat ha-Rambam*," *Mesorah le-Yosef* 6 (2009), p. 396, objects to Gra's condemnation of Rambam, asking how he knows that Rambam denied their existence.

[36] *Sichot haRav Tzvi Yehudah: Bereishit*, ed. Aviner (Jerusalem, 1993), pp. 295-297, 310-312.

[37] Letter to Marc Shapiro, at http://seforim.blogspot.com/2009/10/some-assorted-comments-and-selection.html, also published in Marc Shapiro, *Iggerot Malchei Rabbanan*.

[38] Marc Shapiro (ibid.) relates that Dr. Dror Fixler from Yeshivat Birkat Moshe in Maaleh Adumim, who is an expert on Arabic and is working on a new edition of the *Commentary on the Mishnah*, asserts that there is no doubt whatsoever that Maimonides *is* denying the existence of demons here.

> Know that this belief was widespread in the era of our teacher Moses. Many conducted themselves in accordance with it, and people were seduced by it. You find this written in the song of *Ha'azinu*: "They sacrificed to demons, not to God; to gods that they had never known."[39] The Sages explained the significance of the phrase "not to God," when they said that the people not only worshipped actual beings but even imaginary ones. (*Guide* 3:46)

Further evidence for Rambam's denial of the existence of demons comes from the fact that Rambam consistently either ignore the Talmudic references to demons or reinterprets the statements in such a way as to avoid accepting that demons exist. For example, the Talmud (*Makkot* 6b) refers to the possibility of someone being warned against a crime by a demon (which renders him liable for punishment if he nevertheless continues). But Rambam records this as a person hearing someone warning him but not having seen them.[40] The Talmud (*Berachot* 3a) gives one reason why a person should not enter a ruined building as being due to danger from demons, but Rambam does not record any reason.[41] The Talmud speaks of Adam giving birth to demons, but Rambam presents this as him giving birth to people who did not refine their intellects.[42] There are countless other such examples.[43]

Other rationalists are likewise seen not to accept the existence of demons. **R. Nissim Gaon** (990-1062), citing R. Sherira Gaon, and commenting on the Midrashic account about Adam giving birth to "spirits, demons and liliths," describes these as deformed humans.[44] Rambam's son **R. Avraham** (1186-1237) writes that stories about demons in the Talmud are accounts of events in dreams rather than being intended as descriptions of actual entities, and only a fool would take them in that

---

[39] Deut. 32:17.

[40] *Mishneh Torah, Hilchot Sanhedrin* 12:2.

[41] *Hilchot Tefillah* 5:6 and *Hilchot Rotzeach* 12:6.

[42] *Guide to the Perplexed* 1:7.

[43] See Shapiro, *Studies in Maimonides and his Interpreters*, pp. 111-134.

[44] R. Nissim Gaon, ed. Shraga Abramson (Jerusalem: Mekiz Nirdamim 1965) p. 112. See José Faur, *Homo Mysticus: A Guide to Maimonides' Guide for the Perplexed*, p. 127 and p. 231 n. 7.

way.[45] **R. Yaakov b. Abba Mari Anatoli** (c. 1194-1256), the son-in-law of Shmuel Ibn Tibbon and devoted follower of Rambam, denied the existence of demons and lamented the fact that the majority of Jews, including famous scholars, had their faith corrupted by their belief in such "nonsense."[46] **R. Levi b. Gershon** (Ralbag, 1288–1344) describes satyrs (*se'irim*) as "demons, which are the false images that bring people to believe that something not divine is divine."[47] Later, he describes the existence of demons as being illusory,[48] and finds support for this in the statement of the Sages that "with one person, a demon may be seen and cause harm, with two it is seen but does not cause harm, and with three it is not seen at all."[49] Likewise, in his commentary to Averroes' *Epitome of Parva Naturalia*, Ralbag flatly denies the existence of demons.[50] **R. Avraham Bibago** (c. 1446-c. 1489) argued that all references to demons can be interpreted as referring to figments of peoples' imagination.[51]

A particularly interesting discussion is found in the writings of **R. Levi ben Avraham ben Chaim** of Villefranche (ca. 1245 - ca. 1315), a Provencal rationalist whose allegorical interpretations of the Torah earned

---

[45] R. Avraham b. HaRambam, *Ma'amar al Derashot Chazal*.

[46] *Malmad HaTalmidim* (Lek 1866) p. 184a. For a full discussion of R. Yaakov b. Abba Mari Anatoli's rationalist views, see Isaac Barzilay, *Between Reason and Faith*, pp. 28-32.

[47] Commentary on the Torah, to Leviticus 17:1-7, 158a in Venice 1759 ed. Avraham b. Chananiah Yagel's understanding of Ralbag's view is discussed by David Ruderman, *Kabbalah, Magic, and Science: The Cultural Universe of a Sixteenth-Century Jewish Physician*, pp. 46-47.

[48] Ibid., p. 242b, in *parashat Ha'azinu*.

[49] Talmud, *Berachot* 43b.

[50] Alexander Altmann, "Gersonides' Commentary on Averroes' *Epitome of Parva Naturalia*," II. 3 Annotated Critical Edition, *Proceedings of the American Academy for Jewish Research*, Vol. 46, Jubilee Volume (1928-29 / 1978-79) [Part 1] (1979 - 1980), p. 10. Averroes himself denied demons, but only implicitly. See Seymour Feldman, *Levi ben Gershom: Wars of the Lord*, vol. II, p. 8, and Moritz Steinschneider, *Die Hebräischen Übersetzungen des Mittelalters und die-Juden als Dolmetscher, etc.* (Berlin, 1893), p. 155, note 353b.

[51] In *Derech Emunah* 2:2, as referenced by Menashe b. Yisrael in *Nishmat Chaim*.

the ire of Rashba.[52] He writes that one of the reasons for the Jewish People's forty-year sojourn in the wilderness was to impress upon them that demons, the alleged inhabitants of the wilderness, do not exist.[53] Demons are merely delusions, to which depressed or anxious people are particularly susceptible. Levi b. Avraham concludes as follows:

> An enlightened person should not believe everything he is told, even if the person telling it is a scholar and pious person... one should only believe that which can be sensed, that which can be comprehended, and that which is accepted from our prophets and sages. (Levi Ben Avraham, *Eichut HaNevuah VeSodot HaTorah: Livyat Chen,* p. 769; a similar formulation is found in Rambam's *Letter to the Sages of Montpellier*)

We have here an initial outline of a rationalist approach ("one should only believe that which can be sensed"), followed by an acceptance of a dogmatist approach ("and that which is accepted from our prophets and sages"). However, matters are a little more complicated, since demons were certainly an accepted tradition from the Sages, and yet Levi b. Avraham reinterpreted the Sages' words so as not to accept their existence. Of course Levi b. Avraham thought that he was presenting the true meaning of the Sages' words, and one can only speculate what he would have said if he would have realized that the Sages did indeed believe in demons—would he have then accepted their existence, or would he have decided that the Sages were mistaken? We shall discuss this further in the conclusion.

---

[52] For more on Levi b. Avraham, his approach, and its reception, see *Eichut HaNevuah VeSodot HaTorah: Livyat Chen* (ed. Chaim Kreisel, Jerusalem: World Union of Jewish Studies 2004), introduction; Abraham S. Halkin, "Why Was Levi ben Hayyim Hounded?" in *Proceedings of the American Academy for Jewish Research* 34 (1966), pp. 65-76; Warren Harvey, "Levi ben Abraham of Villefranche's Controversial Encyclopedia," *The Medieval Hebrew Encyclopedias of Science and Philosophy*, ed. Steven Harvey (Dordrecht 2000) pp. 171-188; Howard Kreisel, "Reasons for the Commandments in Maimonides Guide for the Perplexed and in Provencal Jewish Philosophy," *Maimonidean Studies*, vol. 5, pp. 159-188.

[53] Levi Ben Avraham, *Eichut HaNevuah VeSodot HaTorah: Livyat Chen* (Ed. Chaim Kreisel, Jerusalem: World Union of Jewish Studies 2004) pp. 764-770.

R. Menachem Meiri (1249–c.1310) does not categorically deny the existence of demons. Yet, commenting on the verse, "The fool believes everything" (Prov. 14:15), he states that the question of the existence of demons is to be determined by investigation rather than acceptance based on authority.[54] And following the approach of Rambam, he interprets Talmudic discussions about demons in a way that avoids them being understood as actual entities.[55] Meiri explains the Talmudic statements about demonic harm with even numbers as being aimed at helping with psychosomatic problems rather than addressing an objective reality.[56] He interprets the account of how reciting the bedtime *Shema* wards off demons as referring to the driving away of false and evil thoughts.[57] And in discussing the Mishnah's account of how *mazikim* were created at the eve of the first Shabbat, he first explains them as "things that are not found naturally," and later gives his own preferred explanation that it refers to the evil inclination.[58] He also refers to "those who believe in the existence of demons," implying that he himself was not one of them.[59]

The position of **Avraham Ibn Ezra** (1089-1164) with regard to demons is difficult to determine, and has been the subject of dispute:

- The tosafist R. Moshe Taku reports Ibn Ezra as writing that "there are certainly no demons in this world."[60] He continues to claim that Ibn Ezra erred greatly, and recounts that Ibn Ezra ironically died in London as a result of demons, in the guise of black dogs, which stared at him and caused him to fall sick. However, aside

---

[54] *Sefer HaMiddot LeHaMeiri* (ed. Menachem Mendel Meshi-Zahav, Jerusalem 1966), p. 100.

[55] See Louis Jacobs, "Demythologizing the Rabbinic Aggadah: Menahem Meiri," online at https://seforimblog.com/2014/06/demythologising-rabbinic-aggada/. For discussion of Meiri's general stance regarding magic and superstitions, see Shapiro, *Studies in Maimonides and his Interpreters*, pp. 147-148.

[56] Commentary to *Pesachim* 109b.

[57] Commentary to *Berachot* 4b.

[58] Commentary to *Avot* 5:8.

[59] Commentary to *Sanhedrin* 101a, s.v. *Sheratzim*.

[60] R. Moshe Taku, *Ketav Tamim*, p. 97.

from there being no such known record of this fate befalling Ibn Ezra, the text that R. Taku quotes from is also unknown.

- R. Levi b. Avraham explains that the Torah prohibits belief in demons and related matters due to their being fraudulent,[61] and notes that Ibn Ezra likewise writes regarding necromancy that "the Torah does not prohibit truth, only falsehood."[62]

- R. Avraham b. Chananiah Yagel, on the other hand, claims that Ibn Ezra accepted the existence of demons.[63] As his first evidence, he cites *Sefer Ha-Azamim*, which was attributed to Ibn Ezra. This work gives an unusual definition of demons, describing them as being formed when emanations from the constellations collide with vapor and smoke ascending from earth, and enter people with melancholic and fearful dispositions. However, while *Sefer Ha-Azamim* was formerly attributed to Ibn Ezra, and was the cause of several Jewish philosophers deciding to accept the existence of demons according to its description,[64] its authorship is actually unknown. Yagel also cites Ibn Ezra's commentary to Job 1:6, which refers to the Satan and angels as autonomous beings, but this is inconclusive.

Other evidence regarding Ibn Ezra's position relates to the goat that is sent to Azazel.[65] In his commentary on this topic, Ibn Ezra writes as follows:

> Now if you can understand the secret of the word after Azazel, you will know its secret and the secret of its name, since it has parallels in the

---

[61] Levi Ben Avraham, *Eichut HaNevuah VeSodot HaTorah: Livyat Chen* (ed. Chaim Kreisel, Jerusalem: World Union of Jewish Studies 2004) pp. 767-768.

[62] Ibn Ezra to Leviticus 19:31. Ramban (*Derashot Torat HaShem Temimah*) criticizes Ibn Ezra for this.

[63] See David Ruderman, *Kabbalah, Magic, and Science: The Cultural Universe of a Sixteenth-Century Jewish Physician*, p. 47.

[64] See Dov Schwartz, *Astrologia u-Magia beHagut HaYehudim* (Astral Magic in Medieval Jewish Thought), pp. 196-199.

[65] For extensive discussion, see Aron Pinker, "A Goat to go to Azazel," *Journal of Hebrew Scriptures* (2007) vol. 7 pp. 2-25.

Scriptures. And I will reveal to you part of the secret by hint: when you will be thirty-three, you will know it. (Commentary to Lev. 16:10)

The hint tells us to count 33 verses from this verse, bringing us to Leviticus 17:7: "they may offer their sacrifices no more to the *se'irim*." Ramban, who explains this to mean that Ibn Ezra considered Azazel to be a demon, notes that this is not an especially concealed secret, since Chazal state this in a number of places. However, this is still not clear proof that Ibn Ezra understood Azazel or the *se'irim* to be actual demons. Furthermore, Abarbanel refers to a different version of Ibn Ezra's commentary in which he defines Azazel as a heavenly constellation.[66] If we look at Ibn Ezra's commentary to the verse that is 33 verses later, matters are still complicated:

> *To se'irim*: They are the demons (*sheidim*) and are called this because the body which sees them trembles (*yishta'er*). And a close [second explanation] is that the crazy people see them in the form of goats... *After whom they go astray:* For anyone who seeks them out, and believes in them, he is straying from after his God, that he thinks that there is one who can make things good or bad aside from the Honored and Awesome God. (Commentary to Leviticus 17:7)

Ibn Ezra might mean here that demons are only a delusion of crazy people, and that is why someone who "seeks them out and believing them" is going astray.[67] On the other hand, he might be saying that demons are real, albeit not possessing any power independent of God, and that they are perceived by crazy people as looking goat-like, even though that is not their true appearance (or perhaps only crazy people can actually

---

[66] See Abarbanel's seventh question in his commentary on the Torah.

[67] Possibly Ibn Ezra was referring to the followers of Muhammed, who was known in medieval Jewish literature from Islamic lands as "the crazy one," and who saw djinns (demons) as monstrous, hairy creatures that lived in ruins and desert places (the *Jewish Encyclopedia* notes that "the association of monstrous beings with ruins and desert places is still a prevalent element in the folklore of Arabia and Syria; and the Arabian jinn also are represented as having monstrous hairy forms").

see them).[68] In conclusion, then, it is difficult to determine what Ibn Ezra believed about demons.

Medieval and Early Modern Believers in Demons

There is no point in citing all those in Jewish history who accepted the existence of demons; since the Talmud speaks of demons, obviously there are countless Jews who likewise believed that they exist.[69] This led to various authorities discussing questions such as the status with regard to a person who has intercourse with a demon,[70] and the permissibility of appeasing demons.[71] What is relevant to our investigation is to cite those who gave an extensive presentation of demonology, and especially to cite those who saw fit to *justify* their belief in the existence of demons—who were aware that some denied their existence, and sought to explain why this view was wrong.

The first person to acknowledge those who denied the existence of demons was **R. Yehudah HaLevi** (c.1075–1141):

> The Rabbi: I feared that you would be deceived, and acquiesce in the views (of the philosophers). Because they furnish mathematical and logical proofs, people accept everything they say concerning physics and

---

[68] It has also been claimed that Ibn Ezra interpreted the word Meriri, which appears in Deuteronomy 32:24 and Iyov 3:5, as being the name of a demon; see Scott B. Noegel, "Job iii 5 in the Light of Mesopotamian Demons of Time," *Vetus Testanzentum* 57 (2007), p. 561. However, while Rashi interpreted Meriri in this way, I have not been able to find this being stated by Ibn Ezra.

[69] A survey of medieval demonology can be found in Dan Ben-Amos, "On Demons," in *Creation and Re-Creation in Jewish Thought*, ed. Rachel Elior and Peter Schäfer (Tübingen, 2005), pp. 27–37.

[70] R. Yitzchak of Vienna (1200-1270), *Ohr Zarua*; *Beit Shmuel* to *Shulhan Aruch, Even haEzer* 6:17; R. Benzion Uziel, *Mishpetei Uziel, Mahadurah Tinyana, Even ha-Ezer* 11. See Hannah Sprecher, "Diabolus Ex-Machina: An Unusual Case of Yuhasin" in *Jewish Law Association Studies VIII: The Jerusalem Conference Volume*, pp. 183-204; and J. H. Chajes, *Between Worlds: Dybbuks, Exorcists, and Early Modern Judaism* (Philadephia: University of Pennsylvania Press 2003).

[71] R. Menashe Stathon, *Knessiah Leshem Shamaim* (Jerusalem 1874). The entire work discusses (and condemns) a prevalent procedure of appeasing demons on behalf of a sick or childless person.

metaphysics, taking every word as evidence… Why is it difficult for you to accept… the accounts of the Sages regarding demons, and the aggadot regarding events to be expected during the Messianic era, the resurrection of the dead and the world to come? Why do we need to bring philosophical arguments for the continued existence of the soul after the destruction of the body, seeing as it has already been verified by our tradition… If you would attempt to confirm or refute these views logically, it would take a lifetime and you would not reach a conclusion. (*Kuzari* 5:14)

While HaLevi fought against the philosophical approach, he himself was educated in it and used the tools of philosophy to combat it. But in arguing against those who do not accept the existence of demons, he had little to say other than insisting upon the reliability of tradition and the futility of philosophical speculation.

A similar discussion is found in *Ketav Tamim* by the thirteenth century tosafist **R. Moshe Taku.** He condemns those who do not believe in demons as part of a general polemic against the philosophic approach, and insists that we should rely upon the Sages of the Talmud, who clearly believed in their existence.[72] As mentioned earlier, R. Taku claims that Ibn Ezra denied demons and was killed by demonic dogs.

Ramban (1194-1270) discusses demons in numerous places. He considers the term *sheidim* to be synonymous with *ruchot*,[73] *mazikim*,[74] and the Scriptural term *se'irim*.[75] He describes them as being produced by witchcraft and possessing bodies composed of air that cannot be detected,[76] along with the element of fire.[77] Since they are composed of these light elements, they are able to fly,[78] and since they travel in the sky, they are able to learn about future events from the angels of the

---

[72] *Ketav Tamim* p. 97.

[73] Commentary to Exodus 20:3

[74] Commentary to Leviticus 16:8.

[75] Ibid. and Commentary to Leviticus 17:7.

[76] Commentary to Exodus 7:11.

[77] Commentary to Leviticus 17:7.

[78] Ibid.

constellations.[79] Ramban also explains Chazal's statement about demons eating like people[80] to mean that they also subsist on food—although theirs consists of evaporated moisture and smoke from fires.[81] Ramban notes that some demons are assigned to various nations, "as is known from the wisdom of necromancy."[82]

Most significantly, Ramban views the denial of the existence of demons as signifying a general heretical worldview. He proclaims that the miracles attested to in Scripture, whether performed by God or by Pharaoh's magicians, oppose Aristotle's concept of the eternal universe, in which nothing in the natural order can ever change. But he expands the concept of the supernatural to include demons:

> And from here you see the cruelty of the head of the philosophers and his obstinacy, may his name be erased! For he denies several things that many people have seen, and the truth of which we have seen, and which have been publicized in the world. And in the earlier times, such as in the days of our master Moses, these were known to all, for the wisdom in that generation was all with regard to spiritual matters, such as matters involving demons and witches... but when the Greeks arose, a new nation that did not inherit wisdom... that man arose and did not believe anything that could not be detected, and sought after empirical sciences, and denied the realm of the spiritual. And he said that demons and witchcraft are emptiness, and that there are only natural forces in the world.[83] But it is

---

[79] Commentary to Leviticus 17:7.

[80] Talmud, *Chagigah* 16a.

[81] Commentary to Leviticus 17:7.

[82] Commentary to Exodus 20:3.

[83] In fact, Aristotle's position regarding demons is unclear, and historically there has been much dispute about it. In 1580, the Aristotelian philosopher Andrea Cesalpino published *An Aristotelian Investigation of Demons* in which he sought to argue that Aristotle did indeed accept their existence. Aristotle describes a class of beings that live in fire, which are interpreted by some as demons; he also writes that dreams emanate from the demonic realm (see Arthur Hilary Armstrong, *The Cambridge History of Later Greek and Early Medieval Philosophy*, p. 34 note 1). On the other hand, the Aristotelian philosopher Pietro Pomponazzi (d. 1525) presented cogent arguments that Aristotle did not believe in the existence of demons, Thomas Aquinas had already noted with regret that Aristotelian philosophy did not admit the existence of demons, and Agostino Steuco (d. 1548) likewise accepted that Aristotle denied the existence of demons, even though

known and publicized that this is not so... (*Derashat Torat Hashem Temimah*, in *Kitvei Ramban*, ed. H. D. Chavel, vol. I, pp. 147, 149)

Ramban was not averse to admitting that the Sages may have on occasion been mistaken about the natural world.[84] However, the denial of demons was part of an Aristotelian worldview that was fundamentally incompatible with Judaism. In the words of Jose Faur, "By denying belief in demons and the realm of the spiritistic (*ruchniyos*), the Maimonideans were in fact rejecting the grounds of religion. This is why their teaching represents the rankest of all heresies."[85] Yet, even given the fundamental religious nature of the necessity of believing in the occult, Ramban did not solely justify it on religious grounds; he also repeatedly stressed that there is eyewitness testimony for it.[86] Unlike R. Yehudah HaLevi and R. Moshe Taku, Ramban thus invoked rationalist considerations for his mystical conclusions.

Ramban's disciple, **R. Shlomo b. Aderet** (Rashba, 1235-1310) is usually presented as someone who was sharply opposed to the rationalist approach of the philosophers. But a study of his long responsum discussing supernatural remedies (and the supernatural in general) reveals that this description is far too simplistic.[87] True, he insists on the reality of magic and demons. But he does not simply invoke the authority of the Sages for this. Rashba argues that it is undeniable that not all phenomena in the universe are part of the scientific order that can be grasped by man. He presents the magnet as an example of such a phenomenon which is not part of the ordinary natural order and yet clearly exists, following its own rules. Unlike his teacher Ramban, he does not simply argue that supernatural phenomena are empirically proven; he also seeks to incorporate them into a scientific classification of the universe as a class

---

he criticized him for it (see Walter Stephens, *Demon Lovers: Witchcraft, Sex, and the Crisis of Belief*, pp. 76-80).

[84] Commentary to Leviticus 12:2.

[85] Faur, "Anti-Maimonidean Demons" p 47.

[86] See also Ramban's Commentary to Deuteronomy 18:9.

[87] *Responsa HaRashba* 413.

called *teva ha-mesugal*, which is intermediate between the fully natural and the utterly supernatural (acts of God).[88]

A disciple of Rashba, **R. Bachya b. Asher** (d. 1340) quotes the Sages as identifying Tuval Kain's wife Na'amah as the mother of Ashmodai and other demons, along with Lilith, Igroth, and Machalat.[89] He points out that Adam HaRishon likewise fathered demons, and notes that it is part of man's special and elevated nature that he is capable of such things.[90] Quoting the Midrash that demons had to be saved along with the animals in Noah's Ark,[91] he describes demons as animate beings, found in the atmosphere, that move by flying.[92] Elsewhere, he divides demons into three categories—those that live in the atmosphere and cause nightmares, those that live among people and cause sin, and, following the Midrash, those that are restrained in the depths of the oceans.[93] Following Ramban's lead, he also states that, as creatures that are formed from fire and air and live in the atmosphere, demons are able to learn about future events from the angels of the constellations, just as birds do, and they subsist on evaporated moisture and smoke from fires.[94] But unlike Ramban or Rashba, R. Bachya sees no reason to ever justify his belief in the existence of demons, and makes no claims about eyewitness testimony to their existence. In contrast to R. Bachya's lack of concern with opposing views is **Meir b. Yitzchak Aldabi**, a 14th century writer, who goes into some detail regarding the nature of demons, and explains that he is doing this because some of the nation, who were engaged in philosophy, denied the existence of demons.[95]

---

[88] See *Rashba's Ma'amar al Yishmael shechibber ha-Datot*, in *R. Salomo b. Abraham b. Adereth: Sein Leben und seine Schriften* (Schletter, 1863), p. 11 in the Hebrew section, and the discussion by David Horwitz, "Rashba's Attitude to Science and its Limits," *The Torah u-Madda Journal* vol. 3 (1991-92) pp. 59-60 and 76-77.

[89] To Genesis 4:22.

[90] Ibid.

[91] Midrash Bereishit Rabbah 31:13.

[92] To Genesis 6:19.

[93] To Exodus 20:4, based on *Mechilta, Yisro*.

[94] To Leviticus 17:7.

[95] *Shevilei Emunah, Netiv haTishi*, p. 178

Among the Jewish philosophers, we find only two figures who believed in the existence of demons. In the beginning of a chapter dedicated to demons,[96] **R. Chasdai Crescas** (1340-1410) argues that their existence is made clear in Scripture and in the words of the Sages, as well as experientially demonstrated. He notes that they possess four characteristics: knowledge of the future, the desire for people to serve them in exchange for granting wishes, the desire for evil, and the ability to suddenly take on human form. After discussing these aspects in some detail, he concludes by noting that "these matters are hidden, and the gates of investigation are virtually locked; therefore we should not depart from the tradition of the Sages, who said that they have certain aspects in which they are similar to ministering angels and certain aspects in which they are similar to people."

The second philosopher to believe in demons was Crescas' student **R. Yosef Albo** (c. 1380–1444). He notes that the heathens worship them in order to find out about their future, and states that this is forbidden due to it emanating from the side of impurity—not due to its lack of efficacy. He adds that non-Jews resort to this because they think that there is no way for a human being to attain knowledge of the future, yet God promised prophets for the Jewish People who can accomplish this.[97]

Shem Tov ibn Shem Tov (Spain, c. 1390-c. 1440), a kabbalist who fiercely opposed rationalistic philosophy, introduces one chapter of his work with the announcement that it will serve to strengthen belief in the simple meaning of Scriptural verses and the words of the Sages with regard to the existence of demons and sorcery. His method of doing so, however, is to emphasize how Scripture and the Sages attest to their reality.[98]

R. Yitzchak Abarbanel (Lisbon, 1437-Venice, 1508), in his commentary to the verses dealing with sorcery records the dispute between Rambam and Ramban, and argues that Rambam's denial of the reality of such things is decisively disproved in several ways—by the Torah's description of people worshipping demons, and by the tradition of the

---

[96] *Ohr Hashem* (Pirara 1555) 3:3:6.

[97] *Sefer HaIkkarim* 3:8.

[98] *Sefer Ha-Emunot* (Ferrara 1556) 5:1.

Sages who accepted their reality.[99] Of course, Rambam himself held that the Torah is not attesting to demons being actual entities, and that the Sages were simply mistaken—which are points that Abarbanel does not address.

On the other hand, in his commentary to the Haggadah, Abarbanel is critical of the explanation (which he attributes to the Sages "by way of *derush*") that *Ha lachma anya* is recited in Aramaic in order that the demons should not hear the invitation to come and eat. Abarbanel states that

> this explanation is questionable on numerous levels—first with regard to the very existence of demons, second that they would understand Hebrew but not Aramaic, and third that even if we acknowledge the existence of demons, which is difficult, and a heavy burden of belief... surely those involved in a mitzvah cannot be harmed. (*Seder Haggadah shel Pesach - Zevach Pesach Shvilei haLeket* (Lodz, 1936) p. 26)

This is not an absolute denial of the existence of demons, but it is demonstrative of skepticism and of the strain involved for a worldly figure such as Abarbanel, intimately familiar with the philosophical approach of Rambam, to accept their existence. Furthermore, in his commentary to *Avot*, Abarbanel seems to give a metaphorical explanation of the demons that are said to have been created in the first week of Creation and from Adam's seed, apparently explaining them to be harmful sins rather than entities.[100] This also demonstrates his reluctance to accept their reality, notwithstanding his professed subservience to the Sages having done so.

This kind of difficulty involved in accepting the existence of demons is found among others in the sixteenth century. **R. Eliezer Ashkenazi** (1513-1586) admits that he is somewhat skeptical regarding the existence of demons, which cannot be detected by the senses. However, he acknowledges that the sages believed in their existence, and is very much taken by accounts of demonic possession. He therefore suggests a "scientific" way of explaining their existence—they consist of a fine substance that formerly existed within the bodies of evil people that died,

---

[99] Commentary to Deuteronomy, *parashat Shoftim* 18:9, pp. 173 — 174.

[100] *Nachalat Avot* (New York 1953), commentary to *Avot* 5:6 (p. 332).

and which can subsequently take on the form of both people and animals.[101]

Avraham b. Chananiah Yagel (Italy 1553-1623), a kabbalist, physician and naturalist, likewise grappled with the question of the existence of demons, acknowledging that some of the great philosophers did not believe in any such occult matters and argued that there is no rational explanation for them. But, Yagel claims, there is such overwhelming eyewitness testimony for these phenomena, as well as a vast range of authorities—rabbinic, kabbalistic, and non-Jewish—who attest to their existence, that the only reasonable conclusion is that demons must indeed exist. He even attempts to offer a "scientific" explanation of their existence, based—ironically—upon Aristotelian causes.[102] This kind of investigation into their nature had been performed a century earlier in Italy by **R. Ovadiah Seforno** (1475-1550), who was somewhat involved in philosophy and opposed to mysticism, but nevertheless considered demons to be real entities. He writes that it is appropriate to contemplate their nature, and argues that since they are invisible and yet eat, their food must be of a very fine nature. He concludes that they eat the "vapor" of blood.[103]

R. Yosef Shlomo Delmedigo (1591-1655, also known as *Yashar MiCandia*), possessed a strong rationalist tendency, accepting Copernicus' revolutionary understanding of the cosmos and demonstrating a sharp skepticism of many popular beliefs. Taking a similar position to R. Eliezer Ashkenazi, while he did not affirm the existence of demons, he did not rule it out either:

> With regard to the wondrous properties attributed to minerals, herbs and creatures, few are genuine. Who can believe that the remora, a small fish

---

[101] *Maasei Hashem* (Venice 1583) p. 5a. For discussion, see Ruderman, *Kabbalah, Magic and Science*, p. 55, and Jeffrey Howard Chajes, *Between Worlds: Dybbuks, Exorcists, and Early Modern Judaism*, pp. 11-12.

[102] For a lengthy discussion, see David Ruderman, *Kabbalah, Magic and Science: The Cultural Universe of a Sixteenth-Century Jewish Physician*, pp. 43-55.

[103] Seforno to Leviticus 17:7.

of a handspan in length, can stop a boat from moving?[104] Or that a diamond can neutralize a magnet's attraction of iron? And there are books full of many such nonsensical things. I have heard so many of them, and have witnessed so few to be true, that I decided not to validate and mention anything other than that which I have examined and tested several times. But that which I have not examined, or which I have not witnessed, I shall neither validate nor deny, and I shall not mention it at all; for example, magic, sorcery, demons and suchlike, which I have not seen from Egypt to here—and there (in Egypt) they say that they are found in the extreme north, and here they say that they are found in Egypt and Babylon—and therefore I shall not deal with them. It is true that from the words of the Torah, there is no determination; for those who deny them say that the verse, "they slaughter to the demons, not to gods" (Deut. 32:17) means to say that they can neither harm nor help, since they are nothing and emptiness, and that which it states, "that they did not know" (ibid.) means that they did not know of them from seeing or sensing them, only from hearsay... and as I mentioned, I have never seen them, even though I have seen many countries and have travelled through wilderness and forest. But nevertheless, I shall not conclude that since I have not seen them, there is no such thing; for there are many thousands more things that are concealed from us than that are known to us. All the more so is it fitting to pay respect to the Sages of the Talmud, the kabbalists and the Platonists, who tell many stories of them. And I do not say this in order to curry favor with those who believe in them... for these things are not of the fundamentals of faith, and if it was clear to me that they do not exist, I would publicize it. (*Sefer Elim* p. 83)

While some have claimed that Delmedigo was speaking somewhat sarcastically, and that he completely rejected the existence of demons,[105] others point out that there is no reason not to take him at face value, especially in light of similar statements from people such as R. Avraham

---

[104] This capability was widely attributed to the remora in antiquity. See Eugene W. Gudger, "The Myth of the Ship-holder: Studies in Echeneis or Remora I," *Annals and Magazine of Natural History* 9:2 pp. 271-307, and Brian P. Copenhaver, "A Tale of Two Fishes: Magical Objects in Natural History from Antiquity through the Scientific Revolution," *Journal of the History of Ideas* 52:3 (July-September 1991) pp. 373-9.

[105] Isaac Barzilay, *Yoseph Shlomo Delmedigo, Yashar of Candia: His Life, Works and Times*, pp. 260-262.

Yagel.[106] In seventeenth century Europe, there was little reason not to believe in demons; it is perfectly understandable for Delmedigo to temper his skeptical inclination with an acknowledgment that demons may well exist and that respected sages attest to their existence.

R. Menashe ben Yisrael (Portugal/Netherlands/Brazil 1604-1657), writes that since many prohibitions in the Torah are based on the existence of demons, he will prove their existence in three ways—by way of tradition, the intellect, and the senses.[107] He begins with a lengthy list of citations from Scripture, Talmud, Midrash, and Zohar, as well as from many Rishonim, all affirming the existence of demons. He admits that Rambam was opposed to their existence, but dismisses him as having been negatively influenced by Aristotle's philosophy. R. Menashe then moves to intellectual arguments for the existence of demons.[108] Observing that the elements of earth and water produce life (animals and fish), he argues that the elements of fire and air, which are closer to the all-important spheres of the heavens, should certainly generate life. Finally, moving to the lack of empirical detection of demons, he first points out that God is also not detectable by the senses, yet is known to exist from His actions; he also notes that the wind, too, is not visible. Then he moves to a lengthy listing of six categories of empirical evidence for demons: stories of demonic possession, demons teaching people knowledge that they could not otherwise have known, demons causing infants to speak shortly after birth, demons having intercourse with women, oracles foretelling the future by way of demons, and demons preventing grooms from consummating their union with their brides.[109]

---

[106] David Ruderman, *Jewish Thought and Scientific Discovery in Early Modern Europe*, pp. 142-143.

[107] *Nishmat Chaim* 3:12. For an extensive discussion of Menashe b. Yisrael's views, see Jeffrey Howard Chajes, *Between Worlds: Dybbuks, Exorcists, and Early Modern Judaism*, pp. 126-140.

[108] *Nishmat Chaim* 3:13.

[109] *Nishmat Chaim* 3:14-18,

The kabbalist **R. Avraham b. Mordechai Azulai** (Fez-Hebron 1570 - 1643) presents an extensive discussion of many aspects of demonology.[110] But unlike his contemporaries from Italy and such places, he makes no reference whatsoever to those who deny the existence of demons, nor does he display any urge to demonstrate their reality. **R. Moshe Chaim Luzzatto** (Ramchal, Italy-Amsterdam-Acre 1707-1746) likewise discusses the nature of demons without any arguments to prove their existence.[111]

As noted earlier, **R. Eliyahu of Vilna** (1720-1797) condemned Rambam for being "led astray by the accursed philosophy" to deny the reality of magic, spells, amulets and demons.[112] The Vilna Gaon rejects this viewpoint on the grounds that the Talmud extensively discusses such things, and argues that it cannot be interpreted allegorically. He also notes that "everyone" who came after the Rambam disagreed with him. His rebuttal of Rambam thus consists of an appeal to the authority of the Talmud and the rabbinic tradition.

Modern Discomfort with Demons

In the wider world, belief in demons and witches had largely died out by the early eighteenth century. This was probably largely due to the acceptance of Newton's mechanical universe, in which natural causes explained all the diverse phenomena in the world.[113] In the Jewish world, this put all but the most insulated of rabbinic scholars in a difficult position. **R. Solomon Judah Löb Rapoport** (Galicia-Prague 1790—1867), one of the founders of the *Wissenschaft des Judentums* movement, evinced great discomfort with Talmudic discussions of occult phenomena. He claimed that Aggadot describing these were later insertions, pointing to the scarcity of such material in the Jerusalem Talmud as evidence that

---

[110] *Chesed le-Avraham,* (Amsterdam 1685, reprint Lvov 1860), *Ma'ayan Shishi, Ein Ganim, Nahar* 1, pp. 42a in Lvov edition; *Maayan Shevii, Ein Gedi, Nahar* 14-25, 46b-49b in Lvov edition.

[111] *Derech Hashem, Maamar Ha-Ikarim* 2.

[112] *Bi'ur ha-Gra, Yoreh De'ah,* 179:6 note 13.

[113] Darren Oldridge, *Strange Histories,* p. 93.

the Sages did not subscribe to such beliefs.[114] With regard to demons, he claimed that there were people with evil natures, and others who were skilled at illusions, who were metaphorically described as demons and were subsequently believed by many to actually be demons.[115]

R. Zvi Hirsch Chajes (Galicia 1805-1855), who was familiar with R. Rapoport's work, took an approach that was more rational in terms of an honest reading of what the Talmud intended, but less rationalistic in terms of apparently accepting demons as real entities:

> Concerning the subject of demons, the evil eye, and the evil spirits referred to in the Talmud, there can be no doubt that the Rabbis believed in their existence, and consequently we should not attempt to offer other interpretations which will explain them in a sense remote from the literal... We do, however, observe a substantial difference in regard to this matter between the Babylonian and the Palestinian sages, although both believed in the existence of these beings and both tell us of conversations which they held with them, and of the marvelous things which these demons sometimes performed... Yet these Palestinian sages did not elaborate these tales at such inordinate length as is done in the Babylonian Talmud, where they are told with great detail. (Zvi Hirsch Chajes, *Mevo HaTalmud: The Students Guide through the Talmud*, translated by Jacob Shachter, Ch. 31, p. 233)

While R. Chajes does not explicitly affirm that demons must therefore exist, this seems to be the inference.[116] However, he makes no attempt to rationalize this belief. **R. Samson Raphael Hirsch** (Germany, 1808-1888), on the other hand, basing himself on the Rishonim rather than the Talmud, claims that the question of the existence of demons is a long-standing dispute with which one can take whichever side one chooses:

> A related topic is the question of the nature of magic, astrology, demons, and suchlike... Who dares get involved in a dispute between Rambam and Ramban, following whom the camp of Israel is split in two on such matters? ...And if so, every intelligent person is entitled to adopt either

---

[114] *Erech Milin* (Prague 1852), *Aggadah*, p. 10.

[115] Ibid., *Ashmodai*, pp. 242-251.

[116] See Bruria Hutner David, "The Dual Role of Rabbi Zvi Hirsch Chajes: Traditionalist and Maskil." Ph.D. dissertation, Columbia University (1971) pp. 218-221.

view in the absence of either being ruled out. Alternatively—and in my view, this is the more correct approach—he can admit that he has no clarity in the matters.

And I will admit without shame that I have never bothered to investigate and analyze the nature of these things, just as I have never been curious to investigate and inquire as to the nature of the World-to-Come, the world of the resurrection, and so on. For the truth of these things is concealed from everyone, and it is impossible to attain clarity on these things with decisive proofs... What difference does it make if with regard to matters of witchcraft and suchlike, the truth lies with Rambam or Ramban? Either way, we have to distance ourselves from such things, whether they are genuine or nonsensical. (Letter to R. Hile Wechsler, published by Mordechai Breuer in *Hama'ayan* 16:2 (Tevet 5736/1976) p. 6)

Many (on both sides of the issue) would dispute R. Hirsch's claim that there is no way to determine whether Rambam or Ramban was correct. Traditionalists would point to testimony, or the body of rabbinic authority, to rule in favor of Ramban, while rationalists would argue that our increased knowledge of the world renders belief in demons unnecessary, and our understanding of how beliefs are formed accounts for all those who did believe in demons. (Interestingly, R. Hirsch does not take such a non-committal approach with regard to the question of the Sages' knowledge of science; in the same letter, he is content to definitively state that the Sages did not possess any special knowledge of natural phenomena, and to accept that the science of his day appeared to have proven them incorrect on various matters.) Furthermore, the question of whether Rambam or Ramban was correct is indeed of significance, in light of the numerous laws and practices which are based on the presupposition of the reality of such things.

An extensive and intricate discussion regarding the supernatural in general, and demons in particular, is to be found in *Mei Menuchot* by **R. Eliezer Lipman Neusatz** of Magendorf (c. 1797-1858), a disciple of Chatam Sofer.[117] He begins by adopting and elaborating upon Rambam's

---

[117] *Mei Menuchot* (Pressburg 1884), pp. 39a-46b. Chatam Sofer referred to R. Neusatz as his "son, pupil and bracelet" in his 1839 approbation to his book *Betzir Eli'ezer*; Ketav Sofer called him "the one of a kind and unique" of Chatam Sofer's disciples.

view, stressing at length that magic, demons and so on have no objective reality and are all figments of people's imagination. He admits that Ramban countered that one cannot deny all the eyewitness testimony, but humbly points out that people can easily be deceived by illusionists. R. Neusatz then goes further, insisting that Chazal must also have known that these phenomena are not real. This raises obvious questions regarding countless statements of Chazal which appear to accept the existence of such phenomena, to which R. Neusatz proposes several possible solutions. His preferred solution to the majority of cases is that Chazal were simply catering to the superstitious beliefs of the masses, explaining that there may have been positive benefits to such beliefs. He also suggests that some of Chazal did actually believe in the reality of such supernatural phenomena. Another argument that he makes is that many aggados dealing with these phenomena are likely to be later, non-authoritative additions from the post-Talmudic period.[118] Finally, several pages later, R. Neusatz backtracks somewhat; he states that there are real demons, formed from the lighter elements of fire and air and intermediate between man and angels, which were occasionally miraculously revealed to the Sages.

Although it does not appear that **R. Avraham Yitzchak Kook** (1865–1935) ever explicitly stated his view regarding whether or not demons exist, in numerous places he explains references to demons (such as Azazel of Scripture as well as Talmudic references) as speaking about evil and wild aspects of human nature.[119] This would indicate that he did not consider them to be real entities. However it remains unclear as to whether he thought that the Torah and the sages likewise did not consider them to be real entities, or if he was consciously providing a new interpretation of ancient practices and beliefs.

---

[118] In this context, he notes that Chatam Sofer told many of his disciples that the vast majority of the Zohar was not authored by R. Shimon bar Yochai and was added by later writers. Chatam Sofer himself wrote an oblique but unequivocal statement to that effect in *Responsa Chatam Sofer* 6:59, s.v. *U'ma SheKatav SheHaRav*.

[119] *Olat Re'iyah* vol. II p. 357; *Shemonah Kevatzim* IV:91, V:193; *Orot HaKodesh* vol. I, p. 226; *Ein Eyah* vol. II, p. 279. See R. Yitzchak Blau, "Demons in the Talmud," at http://www.vbm-torah.org/archive/aggada/18aggada.htm.

R. Aharon Soloveitchik (1917-2001) claimed that all references to demons in the Talmud actually refer to invisible forces such as germs and mental delusions.[120] He further claims that this in accordance with Rambam's view. But whereas Rambam indeed explained many passages of the Talmud in this way, he does not appear to be of the view that the Sages themselves had this view, whereas R. Soloveitchik claims that the Sages themselves did not actually believe in demons as supernatural entities.

There are some devout *charedim* today who insist upon the reality of demons, and engage in revisionist scholarship in order to show that even Rambam believed in them.[121] At the other end of the spectrum, there are those who are dogmatic about the rationalist approach and claim that no great Rabbinic scholars ever believed in the existence of demons.[122] But most traditionalists take a different approach; they simply ignore the entire topic, as Haym Soloveitchik observes:

> Mention of demons evokes nowadays unease in most religious circles, including *haredi* ones. For the contemporary Ashkenazi community is acculturated, and one of its hallmarks... is its basic acceptance of the mechanistic universe of modern science with its disallowance of ghosts and demons. The simple fact, however, is that demons are part of both the Talmudic and kabbalistic cosmology, and equally, if not more so, of the traditional, East European one. Only one major halakhic figure, Maimonides, influenced by the no less mechanistic universe of Aristotle, denied their existence. For this, he was roundly castigated by the GRA, who equally pinpointed the source of Maimonides' skepticism on the matter *(Bi'ur ha-Gra, Yoreh De'ah,* 179:13). Despite the enormous influence of the GRA today, his words on this issue have fallen on deaf ears, or rather, consigned to oblivion. Significantly, demons and ghosts are still part of the popular Israeli Sefaredi cosmology, and is reflected in the preachings available on cassettes in Israel. (Haym Soloveitchik,

---

[120] *Logic of the Heart, Logic of the Mind,* pp. 50-52.

[121] See e.g. Reuven Schmeltzer, *Chaim B'emunatam,* pp. 290-291.

[122] R. Moshe ben Chaim, a product of Rabbi Yisroel Chait's Yeshivah Bnei Torah, claims that not only did the Sages not believe in demons (http://www.mesora.org/-shadim.html), but neither did Ramban or any of the other Rishonim (http://www.mesoraforum.org/archive/index.php/t-39.html).

"Rupture and Reconstruction: The Transformation of Contemporary Orthodoxy")

The approach of the Schottenstein (Artscroll) edition of the Talmud to demons is also revealing. Although written by traditionalists for traditionalists, they are aware of many contemporary challenges, and seek to address them wherever they can do so without upsetting traditionalist sensibilities. Thus, when the Talmud incorrectly describes bats as laying eggs, the Schottenstein edition notes that some mammals do lay eggs, implying that the Talmud may indeed be correct. When the Talmud makes various statements about planet Earth and the cosmos that are clearly since disproven, the Schottenstein edition insists that the Talmud is not speaking literally. But with demons, where it is not possible to get away with insisting that they exist or that the Talmud does not mean to describe such things, the Schottenstein commentary simply notes the dispute between Rambam and others. And when the Talmud writes at length about the demonic dangers involved in having things in pairs, the Schottenstein commentary notes the (convenient) approach of Chacham Yosef Chaim (the "Ben Ish Chai," Baghdad-Jerusalem 1832-1909) that this is no longer a concern, since the power of demons to harm via pairs has disappeared.[123]

Analysis and Conclusion

One usually imagines a disagreement about the existence of demons to be a dispute between superstition and reason, between loyalty to authority and devotion to rational investigation. This was indeed the case with some rabbinic scholars. Figures such as R. Moshe Taku did not care for rational investigation; it was only received tradition that counted. At the other extreme, R. Yaakov b. Abba Mari Anatoli fully acknowledged that great Sages had believed in the existence of demons, but nevertheless was emphatic that they did not exist and lamented the errors of the greats.

Yet we see very little difference between some of those who believed in demons and some of those who denied their existence. Compare, for example, Chasdai Crescas and Levi b. Avraham. Both state that one

---

[123] *Ben Yehoyada* to *Pesachim* 110b s.v. *Lo yochal.*

should accept that which is a received tradition from prophets and Sages, and that which is experientially demonstrated. Crescas determines that demons are indeed a received tradition from prophets and Sages, and have been experientially demonstrated, whereas Levi considers that they have not been experientially demonstrated and are not a received tradition from prophets and Sages. Likewise, figures such as Ramban and Avraham Yagel justified their belief in such things on the grounds of (alleged) empirical evidence. In principle, the methodology is the same; the difference in application and results simply reflects a difference between the intellectual climates in which the different figures lived.

Or maybe not. It can be argued that while all proclaim the same methodology, in fact they are different. For Crescas (and much more so with non-philosophers) it is received tradition that is dominant, whereas for Levi it is experiential demonstrations which are dominant, with the traditions being (subconsciously re-)interpreted in light of this. After all, at the end of the day, most of the rationalist philosophers did not accept the existence of demons. The reason why their intellectual climate did not include them is precisely because their focus was on that which can be experientially demonstrated and intellectually comprehended.

Perhaps both ways of looking at it have are partially true. It is clear that *some* of the authorities who believed in demons, especially in the earlier period, were nevertheless at least in principle much closer to the rationalist approach than those in recent times and today who believe in their existence for solely traditionalist reasons. And even many people today who do not believe in demons are themselves far from rationalistically inclined; they simply accept the beliefs of the society in which they live. Ramban and Levi b. Avraham, who believed in demons, were not only more rationalistically inclined than many of those who believe in demons today, but even more than many of those who do *not* believe in them.

It is important to realize that belief in demons is not inherently irrational. In the context of the ancient world, it was a perfectly reasonable belief; indeed, it can be argued that it was the *most* reasonable belief:

> Suppose a tree suddenly falls over in the forest. If others account for this
> by saying that somebody invisible pushed it, the explanation probably
> seems implausible. But consider *our* explanation: that an unimaginably

large number of unimaginably small and invisible particles, working in concert but without any cognitive capacities to coordinate their activities, *pulled* the tree down. Is that really easier to believe?—especially for someone who knows nothing of the complex theory of gravitational pull by atomic particles? Without thousands of years of recorded data fed through the geniuses who led to modern physics, the simplest explanation is that the tree fell either because it chose to or because someone willed it to do so-an analogy of cause, if you like, to daily life. But if we can't *see* anyone or anything making many of the observable things happen, then we must conclude that some possessors of will are invisible. Enter the deities and spirits: invisible possessors of will, who can make things happen out of nowhere... The question is now not "*What* made the tree fall? but "*Who* made it fall?" and to answer the latter, one's entire attention and data-collecting capacities are focused in a different direction. (Elizabeth Wayland Barber and Paul T. Barber, *When They Severed Earth From Sky: How the Human Mind Shapes Myth* (Princeton University Press 2004) p. 42)

As a result, what has been termed a "towering edifice of authority"[124] was built up to support demonic magic, supported by religion, classical literature, scientific writing, and popular belief. The belief in demons thus cannot be classified as an inherently irrational belief.

We do well to remember that the [pre-modern] world... was a rational world, in many ways more rational than our own. It is true that it was a world of witches and demons... But this was the given reality about which most of the decisions and actions of the age, throughout the entire western world, revolved. (David E. Stannard, *The Puritan Way of Death* (*Oxford University Press* 1977) p. 69)

However peculiar they now seem, the beliefs of pre-modern people were normally a rational response to the intellectual and social context in which they were expressed. (Darren Oldridge, *Strange Histories*, p. 3)

This was not only true of the early medieval period, but even of the seventeenth century:

---

[124] Sydney Anglo, "Melancholia and Witchcraft: The Debate between Wier, Bodin, and Scot," in *The Literature of Witchcraft*, Ed. Brian P. Levac (Routledge 1992) p. 110.

Delmedigo's *testimonia* for these beings are hardly ludicrous when judged by the sensibilities of seventeenth-century Jewish and Christian culture. Moreover, as I have discussed in the case of Abraham Yagel, demonology in this era was more than pseudo-science and superstition. At its best, it represented a rational attempt to explain the unknown and could often contribute to the scientific discourse of the sixteenth and seventeenth centuries. (David Ruderman, *Jewish Thought and Scientific Discovery in Early Modern Europe*, p. 143)

Thus, instead of categorizing the rabbinic authorities cited in this study as those who believed in demons and those who denied their existence, it would be more meaningful to categorize them as rationalists (which includes many who did believe in demons) versus dogmatists. We should further acknowledge that there is a spectrum of attitudes rather than a clear division between two extremes. The mere fact of someone ultimately accepting that demons exist does not at all mean that he is not a rationalist—it all depends upon the historical context.

TWELVE

Ayin Hara—Ocular Radiation or Heavenly Accounting?

Introduction

What is the "Evil Eye," known in Hebrew as *ayin hara*? Does it affect the person giving it (the person looking) or the person receiving it (the person being scrutinized)? Can it be given to inanimate objects, or only to people? Can you bring an *ayin hara* upon yourself? Does it require seeing something? Does the damage result from the eye, or from the mind? How exactly does it work? And is there a way to protect against it?

Let us consider two views. One is that the Evil Eye refers to harmful forces that are emitted from the eyes as a result of looking at something or someone with negative intentions. The other is that it refers to the effect of envying someone or praising their (or one's own) good fortune, which causes God to re-examine whether they are really deserving of such good fortune and perhaps reduce it. Which is the rationalist view and which is the mystical view? Most people would assume that the first view is mystical and the second is rationalist. But the truth is much more complex.[1]

Classical Sources

The earliest Jewish source for the concept of *ayin hara* is often claimed to be the Torah itself. In fact, this is not the case. There is no explicit or unequivocal reference to the Evil Eye in Scripture. Instead, there are passages which have been interpreted as referring to the Evil Eye, but which do not necessarily do so.

---

[1] An extensive review can be found in Rivka Ulmer, *The Evil Eye in the Bible and in Rabbinic Literature* (Ktav 1994).

In Exodus, God instructs Moses as follows:

> When you take a census of the Children of Israel according to their count, each shall pay ransom for himself to God on being enrolled, that no plague may come upon them through their being counted. (Exodus 30:12)

Many of the commentaries explain that all this was about avoiding an *ayin hara*. Rashi, for example, states that things that are counted are vulnerable to *ayin hara*.[2]

However, the verse itself states nothing about the reason involved.[3] Ultimately, the true explanation of the verse is unclear. Rambam rules that it is forbidden to count Jews but does not give a reason for the prohibition, and as we shall see later, his understanding of the reason was certainly not anything to do with the Evil Eye.[4]

There are numerous references to the Evil Eye in the Babylonian Talmud—though, as Maharatz Chajes notes, there are considerably fewer references in the Talmud Yerushalmi.[5] (It should be noted that such references are not unique to Judaism; similar concepts of the Evil Eye are found in virtually every ancient culture.)

For example, the Talmud discusses how Joshua was concerned about the effects of the Evil Eye, and thus urged the tribe of Joseph to settle inside the forests, where they would not be seen by others. They

---

[2] See too Rabbeinu Bechaya, Ralbag, Mizrachi, Abarbanel, and *Kli Yakar*.

[3] Rabbi Moshe Shamah, *Recalling the Covenant* (pp. 445-460) reviews a number of possibilities.

[4] *Mishneh Torah, Hilchot Temidin u-Musafim* 4:4.

[5] "Concerning the subject of demons, the evil eye, and the evil spirits referred to in the Talmud, there can be no doubt that the Rabbis believed in their existence, and consequently we should not attempt to offer other interpretations which will explain them in a sense remote from the literal... We do, however, observe a substantial difference in regard to this matter between the Babylonian and the Palestinian sages, although both believed in the existence of these beings and both tell us of conversations which they held with them, and of the marvelous things which these demons sometimes performed... Yet these Palestinian sages did not elaborate these tales at such inordinate length as is done in the Babylonian Talmud, where they are told with great detail." (R. Zvi Hirsch Chajes, *Mevo HaTalmud: The Students Guide through the Talmud*, translated by Jacob Shachter, chapter 31, page 233)

responded that, being descendants of Joseph, they need not be concerned about the effects of the Evil Eye:

> The verse includes the protest of Joseph's descendants in order to teach us a measure of good advice: That a person should be wary of the Evil Eye. And this is what Joshua said to them, as it is written: "And Joshua said unto them: If you be a great people, go up to the forest…" (Joshua 17:15). Joshua said to them: Go and conceal yourselves in the forests so that the Evil Eye will not have dominion over you. They replied: We are descendants of Joseph, upon whom the Evil Eye had no dominion, as it is written: "Joseph is a fruitful vine, a fruitful vine by a fountain [*alei ayin*]" (Genesis 49:22), and Rabbi Abahu states: Do not read it as "*alei ayin*," rather read it as "*olei ayin*" ("above the eye," i.e. transcending the influence of the Evil Eye). Rabbi Yosei, son of Rabbi Ḥanina, said that the proof (that Joseph is not vulnerable to the Evil Eye), is from here "[The angel who has redeemed me from all evil, bless the lads…] and let them multiply fishlike in the midst of the earth" (Genesis 48:16). Just as with the fish in the sea, water covers them and the eye has no dominion over them, so too, with the seed of Joseph, the eye has no dominion over them. (*Bava Batra* 118a-b; *Sotah* 36b)

Likewise, the Talmud states that Rabbi Yochanan, when displaying his beauty, was not afraid of the Evil Eye, because he was a descendant of Joseph, upon whom the Evil Eye held no sway.[6] (No explanation is give, however, of why or how Joseph was able to avoid the effects of the Evil Eye.)

The Evil Eye is something that is risked when things are looked at with desire, jealousy or resentment by others. This finds expression in a warning given elsewhere in the Talmud:

> The Sages taught: One who earns a living from selling cane or jugs will never see a sign of blessing from them. What is the reason for this? Since their volume is great, the evil eye dominates them. (*Pesachim* 50b)

Cane (large reeds) and jugs have a large size, and thus attract attention (out of proportion to their actual value). The immediately following

---

[6] *Berachot* 20a, *Bava Metzia* 84a.

passage, while not explicitly mentioning the Evil Eye, seems to refer to the same concept (and is explained thus by Rashi):

> The Sages taught: Merchants in an alleyway (where they are seen by all), and those who raise small livestock (which tend to damage other people's fields), and those who chop down good (fruit) trees, and those who direct their eyes to the fine portion (with the intention of taking it for themselves when dividing something with others), will never see a sign of blessing. What is the reason? Because people wonder about them. (Ibid.)

Rashi explains that people's attention and resultant resentment is drawn to these things, which causes the Evil Eye to exert influence. A corollary of this is found in the Talmud's statement that "blessing is only found in things that are concealed from the eye."[7]

The Talmud discusses the case of someone who finds a lost garment, and their responsibilities in looking after it until it can be returned to its owner.[8] The Talmud says it should not be spread over the bed when guests are in the house, and gives two reasons for this: in case it will be stolen, and in case "it will be burned by the eye" of the guests. It is the desire and perhaps jealousy of the guests that could harm the garment, and thus the finder must ensure that it is not spread out for their view.

Elsewhere, the Talmud discusses rules regarding fences that are built between people's property, and the concept of *hezek re'iyah*—"damage caused by looking." This could potentially refer to different kinds of damage, such as loss of privacy. But one ruling in this area, issued by Rav, is in a situation where there are no privacy concerns, and thus refers to damage caused by looking:

> Rav said: It is prohibited for a person to stand in another's field and look at his crop while the grain is standing. (*Bava Batra* 2b)

Rashi explains that this is to avoid damage being caused by *ayin hara*. Indeed, it appears that Rav is particularly sensitive to the concept of the Evil Eye:

---

[7] *Taanit* 8b.

[8] *Bava Metzia* 30a.

"And God will take all sickness away from you" (Deut. 7:15). Rav says: This refers to the evil eye. Rav follows his line of reasoning, as Rav went to a graveyard, and performed a method (of divination), and said: Ninety-nine of these died by the evil eye, and one by natural means. (*Bava Metzia* 107b)

There are also numerous accounts from the Talmud and Midrash concerning the rabbis killing or hurting people by gazing at them.[9] A principle found in several places in the Talmud is that "whenever the Sages gave someone a look (lit. "set their eyes"), the result was either death or poverty."[10] Some argue that such references are not related to the concept of the Evil Eye; the Evil Eye refers to unfortunate feelings of jealousy, whereas "giving the eye," on the other hand, is a conscious act of causing harm.[11] Still, as we saw in the chapter, "The Sages' Powers of Life and Death," the mechanism involved in both cases appears similar, and the concepts are undoubtedly related, even though not identical.

Protection and Counterforces

How does one protect oneself against the Evil Eye? Many contemporary popular measures are not found in classical Jewish sources and originate in ancient pagan cultures. The *hamsa*—an amulet in the shape of a hand, often with an eye in it—originates in Mesopotamian pagan cultures.[12] The red string is a widespread ancient amulet, found in ancient Greek, Egyptian and even Chinese mythology;[13] the Tosefta refers

---

[9] For a comprehensive list of citations, see Rivka Ulmer, *The Evil Eye in the Bible and in Rabbinic Literature*, pp. 83-104.

[10] *Moed Katan* 17b, *Chagigah* 5b, *Nedarim* 7b, *Sotah* 46b.

[11] Sinai Turan, "'Wherever the Sages Set Their Eyes, there is Either Death or Poverty' - On the History, Terminology and Imagery of the Talmudic Traditions about the Devastating Gaze of the Sages," *Sidra* 23, pp. 168-170.

[12] Daniel Sayani, "The Hamsa in Jewish Thought and Practice," at http://blogs.timesofisrael.com/the-hamsa-in-jewish-thought-and-practice/.

[13] See Ely Teman, "The Red String: A Cultural History of a Jewish Folk Symbol," in *Jewishness: Expression, Identity, and Representation*, Simon J. Bronner, ed. (Oxford: The Littman Library of Jewish Civilization 2008, pp. 29–57.)

to it as an idolatrous practice.[14] Sprigs of the ruta (rue) shrub, distributed in Israel today and described in various recent rabbinic texts as protection against the Evil Eye,[15] were widely used since Roman times, and in places as diverse as Italy, Persia, India, and Guatamala.

Pouring molten lead into cold water, known in Yiddish as *bleigiessen* and in English as molybdomancy, appears to have originated in Ancient Greece, and later became a popular custom in Germany, where one can still buy *bleigiessen* kits today—though authorities there have tried to discourage it, due to the dangers of lead poisoning, and *bleigiessen* kits that are sold in Germany today (including on Amazon.de, pictured here) contain tin rather than lead.

A contemporary exorcist of the *ayin hara* in the Orthodox Jewish community, Rebbetzin Aidel Miller, practices *bliegiessen*, along with vials of "holy water" from the Baal Shem Tov's well, and ruta sprigs.[16] Another contemporary practitioner of *bleigiessen*, Rabbi Doniel Hool of England, says that while tin is safer, it simply does not have the metaphysical qualities that lead possesses, and so he only uses lead.[17]

In the Talmud, as we have seen, one can avoid *ayin hara* by preventing oneself and one's property from being seen by others. But the Talmud also gives other recommendations as to how one can protect oneself from the evil eye—or from accidentally giving it to others:

> Whoever is about to enter a city and is afraid of the evil eye, should stick his right thumb in his left hand, and his left thumb in his right hand, and

---

[14] Tosefta, *Shabbat* 7.

[15] R. Eliezer Papo, *Pele Yoatz, Ayin Hara*; Chida, *Kikar L'Eden, Anaf Etz Avot* 2:16.

[16] See http://5tjt.com/pouring-away-ayin-hara-the-work-of-rebbetzin-aidel-miller/.

[17] Personal communication.

say: "I, so-and-so, son of so-and-so, am of the seed of Joseph, whom the evil eye may not touch" …and if he is concerned about his own Evil Eye, he should look at the side of his left nostril. (*Berachot* 55b)

Various such incantations were mentioned by medieval authorities. Today, many people resort to simply stating *bli ayin hara*, "without bringing on the evil eye."

Is there an opposite to *ayin hara*? There are several references in rabbinic literature to *ayin tov*,[18] a "good eye," but it appears to be a positive trait to possess for oneself (seeing the good in others), not something that actually helps others. As such, it does not seem to be an opposite to *ayin hara* in terms of its effect.

Heavenly Judgment

The Midrash, teaching about the virtues of modesty, notes that the first Tablets were given in public, and thus the Evil Eye ruled over them and they were broken, unlike with the second Tablets, with which it was said that "nobody should be seen at the mountain," meaning that they were given in private.[19] Rashi's disciple R. Simcha of Vitry explains this to mean that the first Tablets were given amid great fanfare, which caused the angels to be jealous, and Satan then brought about the sin that caused the Tablets to be smashed.[20] The second Tablets, on the other hand, were given privately, and thus endured. According to R. Simcha's explanation, while there is a visual component to the Evil Eye, the damage is not done by the ocular component itself, but rather as a result of the jealousy that it engenders, which in turn has consequences in the Heavenly realm.

In a somewhat similar vein, several medieval rabbinic authorities explain that drawing attention to someone leads God to examine their deeds more carefully and exactly, which makes it more likely for them to be found lacking and receive Divine punishment. Rabbenu Bechaye and Rav Ovadia Seforno take this approach in explaining the prohibition

---

[18] See e.g. Mishnah *Avot* 5:19 – "Those who possess an *ayin tova*, a lowly spirit, and a humble soul, are of the disciples of our forefather Abraham."
[19] Midrash Tanhuma, Ki Tisa 31.
[20] *Machzor Vitri* 508.

of counting the Jewish People.[21] Rabbenu Bechaya elsewhere describes *ayin hara* in cases where there is no visual contact involved, such as with Gechazi being incapable of reviving a child with Elisha's staff, since he had told others of his plan and thereby brought on an *ayin hara*.[22] Accordingly, *ayin hara* does not need to necessarily involve any ocular component, and refers to a divine accounting, which only happens to usually (but not always) be brought about by someone seeing something.

This sort of explanation of the Evil Eye is popular today, as we shall see later. Such contemporary explanations of the Evil Eye do not involve any ocular component. However, the rationalist Rishonim do not mention such an explanation, and probably would not have agreed with it. The notion that one person's feelings of envy can cause God to re-evaluate the merits of someone else does not really fit with the rationalist view of how God operates. Furthermore, and perhaps more significantly, it is difficult to claim that this is what the Gemara itself means in its discussions of the Evil Eye. For example, it is difficult (albeit not impossible) to claim that this is what the Gemara is referring to when it speaks about a found garment being burned by the eye of guests in the home of the finder; the emphasis appears to be on the garment, not on the owner awaiting its return.

The Physiological Approach

For many centuries, there was a fascinating custom of hanging ostrich eggs in synagogues. The original reasons for this are obscure,[23] but some suggest that it relates to the belief that the ostrich incubated its eggs by staring at them rather than by sitting upon them. R. Yaakov Emden

---

[21] See their commentaries to Exodus 30:12.

[22] Rabbeinu Bechaya, commentary to Gen. 30:38. Note that others explain the story with Gechazi differently; see Reuven Chaim Klein, "Gehazi and the Miracle Staff of Elisha," *Jewish Bible Quarterly* 45 (2017) 2:103-110.

[23] See Nile Green, "Ostrich Eggs and Peacock Feathers: Sacred Objects as Cultural Exchange between Christianity and Islam," *Al-Masaq: Islam and the Medieval Mediterranean* 18:1 (2006), 27-66.

explains that this in turn reminds people of the power of concentration, and is the reason why ostrich eggs were hung in synagogues.[24]

The ostrich's method of incubation was cited as an example of the power of vision by numerous kabbalists, including the Arizal,[25] R. Chaim Vital,[26] and *Rema MiPano*.[27] R. Tzvi Hirsch Kadinover discusses the ostrich hatching its eggs by starting at them and presents it as a lesson that one should stare at things and think about the relevant *mitzvot*, so as not be harmed by staring at forbidden things (apparently seeing the effects of staring as working in both directions).[28] R. Pinchas Eliyahu Hurwitz of Vilna likewise describes how the ostrich presents a lesson as to the dangers of staring at forbidden sights.[29] He further adds that the Sages of the Talmud, who were careful never to look at forbidden sights, thus had exceptional power in their vision and could kill people by looking at them.[30]

It was not only synagogues which displayed ostrich eggs; churches and mosques also displayed them. The belief that the ostrich incubates its eggs by staring at them was entirely normative in antiquity. The Physiologus, a 2nd-4th century bestiary, claimed that the ostrich lays its eggs in the sand, returns later, and hatches its eggs by staring at them.

From ancient times, the idea that animals and people can affect their surroundings with their eyes was considered perfectly normal, and even to have a scientific basis.[31] Whereas modern science reveals that the eye only absorbs radiation, in antiquity the eye was thought to emit radiation—a

---

[24] *Perush al Ma'amados, Yom Alef,* to Mishnah Keilim 17:14.

[25] Ari, *Otzros Chaim, Shaar HaNekudim* 1.

[26] *Otzros Chaim, Shaar HaNekudim* 1.

[27] Rema MiPano, *Ma'amar Me'ah Keshita* 71.

[28] *Kav hayashar* ch. 2.

[29] *Sefer ha-Berit* 1:14:5.

[30] For further discussion, see my essay "The Sages' Legendary Powers of Life and Death," in *Rationalist vs. Mystical Judaism*.

[31] See Matthew W. Dickie, "Heliodorus and Plutarch on the Evil Eye," *Classical Philology*, Vol. 86, No. 1 (Jan., 1991), pp. 17-29.

kind of "fire."[32] Plato wrote about how this fire emerges from the eyes and combines with daylight to form a homogenous entity, through which images are conducted back into the eye.[33] When coupled with harmful intent on behalf of the viewer, this radiation was thought to become especially dangerous. In the second century of the Common Era, Galen adopted this theory of vision, known as "extramission," and further developed it; his view was enormously influential.

The notion that the eye emits some sort of energy was perfectly reasonable. After all, many animals can see in the dark, which would indicate that their eyes are emitting some sort of light. And as noted by Pliny the Elder, the eyes of some animals such as cats actually seem to shine at night. Furthermore, it also accounted for why, as noted by Alcmaeon of Croton in the fifth century BCE, when you close your eyes and press your eyelids, you sometimes see flashes of light. In addition, many people think they can "feel" when someone is looking at them.

The extramission theory of vision was likewise adopted by scientifically-oriented Jewish scholars, and it was understood to be a scientific explanation of *ayin hara*. A particularly detailed discussion is given by Ralbag (Gersonides), in the context of explaining the problem with counting the Jewish People:

> And the cause of the damage which is found in it, according to what I think, is that certain excess vapors which nature expels [from the body] leave through the eye, to the extent that the Philosopher has related[34] that if a woman shall gaze into a new mirror while menstruating, there shall appear in it a blood-stain whose mark shall remain there for a perceptible period of time, and these vapors can possibly kill some people because they are toxic to them, and due to the ease of their becoming affected by them. And this is, according to what I think, the cause of the plague that is a consequence of the census, and therefore some of the counted men will die as opposed to others, due to a difference of nature between the

---

[32] Charles G. Gross, "The Fire That Comes from the Eye," *The Neuroscientist* (1999) 5:1, pp. 58-64.

[33] Plato, *Timeaus*, translated by Benjamin Jowett (Rockville, MD: Serenity Publishers 2009), p. 24.

[34] Aristotle, *De Insomniis*.

recipients who are affected by this. And it is clear that the eye is the organ that is most damaged from this poisonous gaze, and the damage comes via it to the brain due to its proximity to it. For this reason you will find that they were not concerned if the items that were counted were parts of the people, e.g., their fingers, for it is not the nature of those organs to be damaged by this action. You will find this in that which they would do when they cast lots [to determine] who would do each of the various services that were done in the Temple, according to that which is explained in *Yoma*, that each one would extend his finger, and they would count the fingers and did not worry about this, for the entire danger is when the gaze is upon the face, for in it are locations through which these vapors can pass easily, and be transported to the brain, e.g., the eyes, due to the ease with which they can be affected, and the nose and the ear since they are open to the brain, and since the Torah has said "that no plague may come upon them through their being enrolled," we have learned from this that it is not appropriate to count them directly, so that a plague shall not befall them. (Ralbag, Commentary to Exodus 30:12)[35]

Rabbeinu Yonah of Gerona (1180-1263) quotes the "scholars of nature" that a person's jealous thoughts can cause a certain vapor to arise and burn that which he is contemplating.[36] He adds, in explaining the Mishnah's statement that *ayin hara* removes a person from the world, that a consequence of this is shortness of breath, which shortens a person's life. Abarbanel likewise explains the scientific mechanism for this in terms of vapors:

> The damage that comes from the evil eye is well known amongst people. It is just as the Philosopher wrote; that extraneous vapors are pushed out of the body, from a person with an evil, jealous spirit. And due to the toxicity of these vapors, they have effects on things that are prone to absorbing these effects, to the point that it is possible to kill someone by looking at them. (Abarbanel, Commentary to Deuteronomy, *parashat Ki Tisa*, p. 293)

---

[35] See Yitzhak Grossman, "The Scholar Rabbi Levi"— A Study in Rationalistic Exegesis," in *Hakirah* 12 (Fall 2011) pp. 171-208, for a full discussion of this and Ralbag's rationalist worldview in general.

[36] Rabbeinu Yonah, Commentary to *Avot* 2:11.

Others, while also explaining it in naturalistic terms, used terminology relating to fire rather than vapors. Rabbi Yitzhak Arama (15th century, Spain), elaborately explain how eyes can emit certain sparks that can cause massive, even lethal, damage, and he notes that this is similar to the creature that kills with its gaze—apparently referring to the mythical basilisk.[37] Maharal similarly describes *ayin hara* as referring to the eye's ability to burn things in a manner similar to fire.[38]

The 15th century kabbalist R. Menachem Zioni of Speyer writes that there are animals and people that can kill with their stare.[39] He adds that Alexander of Macedonia once came to a place with such beasts and birds, and in order not to have his army destroyed, they placed mirrors in front of these creatures, and when they saw their reflection, they killed themselves.[40] R. Zioni's comments are approvingly cited by R. Betzalel b. Shlomo (1640-1691).[41] He explains the verse "*Bat ami l'achzar k'ya'enim bemidbar*—My people have become cruel, like ostriches in the wilderness" (Lamentations 4:3) to mean that when the cruel person (Titus) entered Jerusalem (*bat ami*), he saw its beauty and emitted an *ayin hara* that destroyed it, just as an ostrich in the wilderness has the power of its sight to affect its eggs.

Undoubtedly the most fascinating example of how the Evil Eye used to be understood is that which emerges from a responsum of R. Yosef Karo, author of the *Shulchan Aruch*.[42] He discusses the case of somebody who wishes to open up the wall of his home which will overlook the neighbor; however, he will place a "glass sunlight" (i.e. a glass window) called a *camaria*, in the opening. The question is presented as being whether the neighbor can object on the grounds of *hezek re'iyah*, visual damage, since glass often breaks. R. Karo responds that one need not be

---

[37] *Akeidat Yitzchak, Parashat Tazria* 61.

[38] *Netivot Olam, Netiv Ayin Tov.*

[39] *Sefer Tziyoni* (Crimona 1560), *parashas Balak.*

[40] This is a retelling of a story about Alexander and the basilisk, found in the 3rd century *Historia Alexandri Magni.*

[41] *Korban Shabbat* 19, pp. 45b in 1806 edition.

[42] *Responsa Avkat Rachel* 121.

concerned about it breaking, and the glass prevents the *hezek re'iyah*, and it "interrupts and partitions before the Evil Eye, provided that it is well sealed and there are no holes that would allow the *hezek re'iyah* to pass though."

Rabbi Avraham Tzvi Eisenstat (1812–1868) insists that the glass being spoken of is not clear glass, but rather clouded glass which lets light through but does not enable one to see through it.[43] Clear glass, he states, does not block *hezek re'iyah*. However, this does not seem to be the straightforward interpretation of R. Karo's words, which speak of holes that would allow the *hezek re'iyah* to pass through. Rabbi Dov Berish Weidenfeld (1881–1965), Chief Rabbi of Tshebin, Poland, understands R. Karo to mean that even though glass enables one to see, it does not allow the eye to exert influence.[44] Accordingly, he notes that wearing spectacles solves the problem of giving an *ayin hara*![45]

Rambam and the Evil Eye

As we saw earlier, the Talmud, discussing the fences that are built between properties, cites a ruling from Rav that "It is prohibited for a person to stand in another's field and look at his crop while the grain is standing." Rambam, on the other hand, rules that a fence that partitions one person's land from that of his neighbor need only be ten handbreadths high.[46] Such a fence is far too low to prevent a person seeing his neighbor's land. Raavad therefore objects to Rambam's ruling and states that a fence of four cubits in height is required. The sages of Lunel wrote to Rambam to ask him about this, and he replied that *hezek re'iyah*, which requires a wall of four cubits, is only with regard to a separation between living spaces, such that a person should have privacy as he goes about his daily

---

[43] *Pitchei Teshuvah, Choshen Mishpat* 154:9.

[44] Responsa *Dovev Meisharim* 1:124.

[45] *Gilyonot Dovev Meisharim Al Shulchan Aruch, Choshen Mishpat* 378. Printed in *Kovetz Moriah* 281. This view is approvingly cited and explained by a contemporary rabbi, R. Ziv Schtzilka, "*Hezek Ayin Hara Derech Mishkafayim,*" *Umka D'Parasha* (Modiin Ilit), Parashas Balak 5774, available online at beinenu.com/sites/default/files/alonim/-25_40_74.pdf.

[46] *Mishneh Torah, Hilchot Shechenim* 2:16.

business. Separations between plots of land, on the other hand, only require demarcation to avoid property infringement and theft. The *hezek re'iyah*, says Rambam, of seeing one's neighbor's crops, is only to avoid the Evil Eye rather than actual visual damage, and it is only *middat chassidut* (pious trait) to avoid this, not something that must be legally enforced with a tall fence.[47]

What does Rambam mean when he refers to the Evil Eye? He does not explain. But in light of the fact that he does not see it as something that substantially harms the neighbor, perhaps he is understanding it to refer to the loss of privacy that the neighbor experiences with his field. Alternately, perhaps he understands it to refer to jealousy, with the "victim" of *ayin hara* being the onlooker rather than the person they are looking at. A third possibility is that he understands it to refer to a mystical or allegedly scientific phenomena that he rejects the existence of, but instead of explicitly denying its validity, he prefers to downgrade it to being *middat chassidut.*

This is not the only case when Rambam negates the Talmud's view regarding the Evil Eye. As we saw earlier, the Talmud says that if one finds a garment, it should not be spread over the bed when guests are in the house, and gives two reasons for this: in case it will be stolen, and in case "it will be burned by the eye" of the guests. When Rambam cites this ruling, he gives only the first reason and omits the second.[48] Here, too, we see that Rambam does not believe that the Evil Eye is something that can harm other people or property.

But was this related to Rambam being a scientifically-oriented rationalist? As we have seen, throughout antiquity and until just a few centuries ago, normative scientific belief was that vision is based on emissions from the eye, lending credence to the effects of the Evil Eye. Thus, the question is not why rationalist scholars other than Rambam

---

[47] Rambam's view is discussed in Marc Shapiro, "Maimonidean Halakhah and Superstition," in *Studies in Maimonides and his Interpreters* pp. 128-129. Shapiro points out that Meiri defends Rambam's view without being aware of Rambam's letter to the sages of Lunel, and believing that Rambam accepts the existence of the Evil Eye.

[48] *Mishneh Torah, Hilchot Gezelah VeAvidah* 13:11.

believed in the Evil Eye. The question is, why didn't Rambam believe in it?

Perhaps the reason for Rambam's rejection of the Evil Eye is that he followed Aristotle's theory of vision rather than that of Plato and Galen. Aristotle disputed his teacher Plato in rejecting the extramission theory of vision. He wrote that "it is unreasonable to suppose that seeing occurs by something issuing from the eye," he declared. Instead, he posited that there is a certain medium connecting the eye with the visible object which causes the latter to be transmitted to the former.[49] This is an instance of a case where Aristotle's view was not widely accepted.

In fact, Aristotle's view of vision was not consistent. As noted above, Ralbag and Abarbanel quoted "the philosopher" to support their view of the Evil Eye as being scientifically-based. Aristotle even wrote that pigeons spit on their young three times to protect them from the Evil Eye. Still, it seems that Rambam followed Aristotle in his stances that rejected the extramission theory; he may also have followed certain Islamic thinkers such as Avicenna who likewise rejected the extramission theory.[50] But it is important to bear in mind that while Rambam rejected the classical notion of the Evil Eye due to his own scientific reasons, those who accepted its reality likewise did so due to scientific reasons.

The Evil Eye in the Modern Era

In the seventeenth century, the British physician Sir Thomas Browne expressed some doubts about the existence of the mythical basilisk. He challenged accounts of its deadly stare by pointing out that "sight is made by Reception, and not by Extramission; by receiving the rays of the object into the eye, and not by sending any out." Also in the 17th century, the German professor Georg Kaspar Kirchmayer wrote a treatise entitled *On*

---

[49] David C. Lindberg, *Theories of Vision from Al-kindi to Kepler* (University of Chicago Press 1996) pp. 6-9.

[50] For further discussion, see John Elliott, *Beware the Evil Eye, Volume 2: The Evil Eye in the Bible and the Ancient World—Greece and Rome* (Wipf and Stock 2016), pp. 18-20 and Berthold Hub, "Aristotle's 'Bloody Mirror' and Natural Science in Medieval and Early Modern Europe," in Nancy Frelick, ed., *The Mirror in Medieval and Early Modern Culture: Specular Reflections* (Brepols Publishers 2016) pp. 31-71.

The Basilisk in which he likewise rejects the power of the basilisk for the same reason.[51]

Yet it took a long time for the intromission understanding of vision, which precluded being able to exert harm via staring, penetrated into wider society. Controversy continued, and rabbinic scholars sided with the extramission theory, which fit with the Talmudic accounts. Several mystical figures endorsed the notion of the Evil Eye as referring to damage done with the vision of the physical eye. Rabbi Nachman of Breslav writes that vision has actual power to cause harm,[52] and Rabbi Simcha Bunim of Peshischa explains that Bilaam had to go and physically see the Jewish people in order to strike them with the Evil Eye.[53] It is unclear if they believed this to be a natural or supernatural phenomenon, but there were certainly many rabbinic scholars who believed it to be natural, scientifically supported phenomenon. Rabbi Eliyahu b. Shlomo ha-Cohen of eighteenth-century Turkey bemoans those who scoff at the accounts of sages killing with their vision, and argues that there are animals and birds with this power, which prove it to be possible.[54]

At the end of the nineteenth century, R. Chaim Schwartz noted that there are those who scoff at the possibility of killing someone by looking at them, and therefore cites German encyclopedias and journals reporting that "there are great non-Jewish scholars who attested to the ability of some to accomplish marvelous feats with their eyes and who even themselves were able to kill vermin by looking at them."[55] Malbim writes that "the Evil Eye is just as even the naturalists have explained; that when a jealous person looks at something, sparks of evil and noxious fumes

---

[51] *On the Basilisk* is translated in Edmund Goldsmid, *Un-Natural History, or Myths of Ancient Science* (Edinburgh 1886).

[52] *Sichot HaRan* 242.

[53] *Kol Simcha, parashat Balak.*

[54] *Midrash Talpiot, Anaf Chayot*, pp. 251-252. He adds, however, that it does not mean that it works by way of vision, noting that even blind sages possessed this ability.

[55] Rabbi Chaim Schwartz, *Orach Chaim* (Frankfurt 1892) pp. 24-25. He refers the reader to Gottlieb Tobias Wilhelm's *Unterhaltungen aus der Naturgeschichte* ("*Discourse of Natural History,*" 1795), chapter 68, and other sources.

emanate from his eyes… and they can even kill people, just as the viper (i.e. basilisk) kills with its gaze."[56]

Rabbi Baruch Halevi Epstein (1860–1941) writes that Balaam harmed the Jewish People with the Evil Eye. To prove the validity and power of this phenomenon, he cites an account from a local Russian paper, the *Ilustriravansk Mir* from 1881. It told of how the Russian government allowed the Academy of Science to perform an experiment on a convict sentenced to death. He was starved for three days while loaf of bread was placed on the other side of the cell door, such that he could see it but not reach it. At the end of the third day, the bread was examined and was found to contain a poisonous substance. R. Epstein explains how "the scholars decided that this must be the result of the gaze of this man, who, from his great pain and anger at the fact that he could not reach the bread, thrust into it half of his venom. From this these scholars arrived at the conclusion that there must be a poisonous power to the eye, just like there is a power of electricity, magnetism and hypnosis. Even though we cannot experience this power, there is no doubt as to its existence and potency."[57]

The story from the *Ilustriravansk Mir* itself proves nothing, of course—the bread probably spoiled as a result of being kept in a damp cell for three days. Still, the fact that the newspaper reported it, and that the experiment was apparently actually done, demonstrates that this belief was widely held. There are also other such accounts of this belief from the nineteenth century.[58]

Nevertheless, the modern era also saw some rabbinic authorities acknowledging that there did not appear to any longer be a danger posed by *ayin hara*. R. Chaim Yosef David Azulai (Chida, 1724-1806) writes that just as the change in location and time has caused such things as Talmudic remedies to be no longer efficacious, so too the Evil Eye no longer possesses any danger at all.[59]

---

[56] *Sefer HaCarmel, Erech Ayin Hara.*

[57] R. Baruch Epstein, *Tosefet Beracha*, Bamidbar 24:8.

[58] Alan Dundes, *The Evil Eye: A Casebook*, pp. 268-9.

[59] Chida, *Brit Olam* 477.

The 20ᵗʰ Century Downgrade

In the 20ᵗʰ century, we see a dramatic transformation in approaches to the Evil Eye. No longer did anyone attempt to provide scientific explanation of vapors or radiation being emitted from the eye. Perhaps the closest to such an approach was Chazon Ish, who writes that it is of the "secrets of Creation" that a person's thoughts, when triggered by looking at something successful, can activate hidden forces in the world, which can result in physical damage of material objects.[60]

Most, however, defined the Evil Eye as referring to damage caused due to jealousy and other such thoughts, without there being any ocular component. Rav Kook explains that the Evil Eye is a societal influence that one person has on another, and from which one protects oneself with self-confidence and a commitment to self-perfection.[61] Rav Dessler states that it refers to how a person can be punished for causing someone else to be jealous of him.[62]

But the 20ᵗʰ century did not only see a difference in the explanation of the mechanism of the evil eye. It also saw a dramatic downgrade in the power that people attributed to it. This, however, raised discomfort with the extensive concern given to *ayin hara* in classical rabbinic literature. One solution to this was to take the approach of Chida mentioned earlier, which was that the evil eye is just one of many supernatural phenomena which have been on the decline over history.[63] Another solution was to argue that *ayin hara* was only dangerous for those who acknowledged its power. This view finds expression in the writing of several rabbinic authorities, notably R. Moshe Feinstein, writing in the context of concerns with *ayin hara* for a young woman who became pregnant:

> One must certainly be concerned about the Evil Eye; however, one need not be greatly particular with it, because with such things there is the principle of "one who is not particular about it, it is not particular about

---

[60] Chazon Ish, Notes to *Bava Batra* 21.

[61] *Ain Ayah*, Ber. 20, p.120.

[62] *Michtav Me-Eliyahu* vol. III p. 314, col. IV pp. 5-6.

[63] See R. Yaakov Kaminetsky, *Emet LeYaakov*, Ex. 7:22, and R. Yosef Chaim, *Ben Yehoyada* to *Pesachim* 110b s.v. *Lo yochal*.

him," just as we find with regard to "pairs" in *Pesachim* 110... The Rambam and Meiri certainly do not dispute the Gemara with regard to matters with which one must be concerned about the Evil Eye, but one need not be all that particular; and also, one need only be concerned with regard to [doing] something unusual, and not with things that are commonly [done]. (R. Moshe Feinstein, *Igrot Moshe, Even Ha-Ezer* 3:26)

R. Feinstein is simultaneously issuing a castigation against the blanket dismissal of *ayin hara*, yet also discouraging people from being overly concerned with it. The Talmudic principle that he invokes, "one who is not particular about it, it is not particular about him," was originally stated with regard to the fears of demonic risk when doings things in pairs. This was a subject of great concern for the Sages of Babylon, but was far less of an issue for their counterparts in the Land of Israel:

In the West, they are not cautious about having things in pairs... The rule of the matter is that for those who take note of the pairs, the pairs take note of them; those who do not take note of the pairs are not bothered by them. Nonetheless, it is good to show a modicum of concern. (*Pesachim* 110b)

This approach is also taken by another authority, albeit not explicitly linking it to the passage about pairs. There is a longstanding practice that a father and son are not called up consecutively to read the Torah. While the reasons for this are disputed, some explain that it is due to *ayin hara*.[64] R. Yechiel Michel Epstein (1829–1908) says that while the reason for this practice is indeed due to *ayin hara*, someone who is unconcerned with *ayin hara* may do as he wishes.[65]

There are logical difficulties in applying the Talmudic principle of "one who is not particular about it, it is not particular about him," to the Evil Eye. Whatever the mechanism of the Evil Eye—whether radiation or provoking divine judgment—there would not seem to be any reason why this would be affected by whether the recipient believes in it. Furthermore, if the solution to suffering the effects of the Evil Eye is to deny its effects, then surely the Sages should have stated as such. Still, adopting this

---

[64] Tashbatz 190; Mordechai, *Hilchot ketanot* 968; *Shulchan Aruch, Orach Chaim* 141:6.
[65] *Aruch ha-Shulchan* 141:8.

principle seems to have presented a reassuring way of enabling the Talmud itself to provide an explanation of why the Evil Eye does not seem to pose a particular danger anymore.

Conclusion

In Orthodox circles today, it is widely believed that a "rational" view of *ayin hara* is that it means stirring up Divine judgment of others via jealousy, whereas a mystical, non-scientific view is that it involves some form of energy being emitted from the eye. In the medieval period, however, the situation was more-or-less the reverse. While Rambam denied the power of the Evil Eye, he was a lone figure in this regard. Other rabbinic scholars believed in its existence; not because they were any less rationalistically inclined, but rather because it was believed to be a natural phenomenon. This view persisted in some circles until as recently as the nineteenth century.

In the 20th century, fear of the Evil Eye declined dramatically. This is presumably because as people gained a more correct understanding of science, it became unreasonable to posit that eyes emit radiation, and with the increased mechanistic understanding of how the universe works, there was less room to attribute misfortune to supernatural causes. Still, belief in the Evil Eye has not declined to the same extent as belief in demons. This is probably due to the psychological factors involved in people feeling nervous about their good fortune. For such people, there is often concern about trying to prevent problems caused by the Evil Eye. Many will say "*bli ayin hara*," "with no Evil Eye," as a kind of preventative incantation.

For contemporary traditionalist rabbinic scholars, the Evil Eye presents something of a problem. They are unwilling to continue the medieval approach that it is a natural phenomenon. Some explain it instead a supernatural phenomenon, and still as powerful as ever, and there are people who are happy to pay hundreds of dollars to have their *ayin hara* removed via various superstitious techniques.

Most people today, however, seem to prefer to explain *ayin hara* as referring to causing divine judgment via jealousy, with no ocular component. Yet it is difficult for many people to believe in it as being any kind of significantly powerful force. But since classical and medieval authorities clearly saw it as a significant danger, the solution is to claim that it has been on the wane and may have even ceased to exist, or that it only exists if you believe in it. Such is the way that a more rationalist approach spreads in the Orthodox Jewish community, when few people are willing to simply adopt Rambam's approach and entirely deny the existence of *ayin hara* as a damaging force.

THIRTEEN

Shiluach HaKein: Compassion or Cruelty?

Introduction

> If you happen upon a bird's nest along the road, in any tree or on the
> ground, with fledglings or eggs, and the mother is crouching over the
> fledglings or on the eggs, do not take the mother together with the young.
> Send away the mother, and take the young for yourself, in order that it
> may be good for you, and your days shall be lengthened. (Deuteronomy
> 22:6-7)

The mitzvah of *shiluach hakein*[1] seems straightforward enough. It
presents itself as an innocent and charming mitzvah. Be kind to birds, and
God shall be kind to you.

Yet, tracing the exposition of this mitzvah through Midrash, Mishnah,
Talmud, Rishonim, and Acharonim, we encounter extraordinary
perspectives that turn the simple understanding upside-down. We shall
see it highlight the existence of radically different conceptions of what the
Torah's commandments are all about, the rationalist and mystic schools
of thought.

I. Rationalist Approaches

The Torah itself does not give any explanation as to the rationale for
the mitzvah of *shiluach hakein*. As we shall see, to some this meant that we
cannot claim to know any rationale. But others saw it as being no different
from other *mitzvot* such as honoring one's parents, which likewise have
no rationale given in the Torah, but for which the rationale is obvious.
This is very much consistent with the rationalist school of thought—that

---

[1] While in Scripture, the nest is called *kan*, that is because it has the word *tzippor*
appended to it. When not connected to that word, it is correctly vocalized as *kein*.

the Torah's commandments serve to improve one's intellect, personality, or to serve various goals of social improvement.[2]

In the Midrash

In the Midrash, the mitzvah of *shiluach hakein* was explained to stem from God's compassion for His creations:

> Why is an infant circumcised at eight days? Because the Holy One, had compassion on him, waiting until the child was strong. And just as the Holy One has compassion on human beings, so too He has compassion on animals. How do we know this? As it is said, "And from the eighth day on it shall be acceptable..." (Lev. 22:27). Furthermore, the Holy One said, "no animal ... shall be slaughtered on the same day with its young" (Lev. 22:28). And just as the Holy One extended His compassion over animals, so too He was filled with compassion for birds. How do we know this? As it is said, "If you happen upon a bird's nest along the road." (*Midrash Devarim Rabbah, parashat Ki Tetze* 6:1)

We also find a similar view elsewhere in the Midrash:

> Rabbi Berachyah said in the name of Rabbi Levi: It is written, "A righteous man knows the needs of his animal" (Prov. 12:10). "A righteous man"—this is the Holy One, for it is written in His Torah, "Do not take the mother together with her young" (Deut. 22:6). (*Midrash Vayikra Rabbah* 27:11)

Neither of these texts elaborate upon the nature of the compassion in the mitzvah, but it can easily be guessed; they are referring to the compassion in sparing the mother, and/or to the compassion in sending her away such that she does not witness the young being taken (birds are more distressed to see this than to return and find the nest empty). It may sound obvious that the mitzvah is related to compassion, but as we shall see later, some disagree.

---

[2] See Rambam, *Guide for the Perplexed* 3:31: "The truth is undoubtedly as we have said, that every one of the six hundred and thirteen precepts serves to inculcate some truth, to remove some erroneous opinion, to establish proper relations in society, to diminish evil, to train in good manners or to warn against bad habits."

In the Rishonim

In the period of the Rishonim, the mitzvah of *shiluach hakein* was widely explained to be related to compassion. Some focused on the rationale for the negative prohibition, of taking both mother and young, while others focused on the rationale for the positive commandment of sending away the mother bird before taking the young. Authorities in the former category sometimes explained that it is simply heartless to take both mother and young. This is the approach of Rashbam (c.1085-c.1158) and Chizkuni (13th century) who both state that it cruel and greedy to take both mother and young.[3] (Much later, Chatam Sofer added the nuance that taking both mother and young is only possible because the mother stays to protect her young, and taking advantage of her maternal instincts in this way is especially heartless.[4]) Others, such as Ramban (1194-1270), Ralbag (1288–1344) and Rabbeinu Bachya ben Asher (d. 1340), went further and spoke of such an act as conceptually being the extermination of the species, due it showing lack of regard for the bird's perpetuation.[5] In a similar vein, *Sefer HaChinnuch* (13th century) states that the mitzvah teaches about the value of providence vis-à-vis the perpetuation of species.[6]

Rambam (1135-1204) raises the idea that as well as the prohibition of taking the mother bird likely having the effect of leaving the entire nest untouched, the positive commandment of sending away the mother before taking away the young serves to minimize her distress of seeing her young being taken:

> He also forbade slaughtering an animal and its young on the same day, to take care to avoid slaughtering the young before its mother's eyes, for the distress caused thereby to animals is great; there is no difference between the distress felt by human beings and the distress of other creatures, for a

---

[3] Rashbam and Chizkuni to Deut. 22:6.

[4] Chatam Sofer to *Chullin* 139b. This is perhaps also implicit in Ramban, who speaks of taking the birds when they are free to fly away.

[5] Ramban, Ralbag and Rabbeinu Bachye to Deut. 22:6-7. In a similar but more utilitarian view, Abarbanel explains that one must enable the mother to produce further young, just as one harvests fruit but one may not cut down a fruit tree.

[6] *Sefer HaChinnuch*, mitzvah 545.

mother's love and compassion for the fruit of her womb is not guided by the intellect but by the power of imagination, which exists equally in most animals as in humans... This is also the reason for sending away the mother bird from the nest, for the eggs on which the mother nests and the fledglings that need their mother are not generally fit for food; and when a person sends off the mother and she goes away, she will not be distressed at seeing her young taken. And since that which would be taken in most instances is not fit to be eaten, for the most part there will be reason to leave everything. If the Torah takes pity on the suffering of animals and birds, all the more so on human beings! (Rambam, *Guide for the Perplexed* III:48)

All these rationalist explanations for the mitzvah revolve around the theme of compassion, which seems perfectly reasonable. However, the Mishnah issues a ruling which raises a difficulty with this, as we shall now explore.

II. The Mishnah: No Speaking Of Mercy

The Mishnah pronounces a perplexing ruling regarding someone who invokes the mitzvah of *shiluach hakein* in his prayers:

> If someone says, "Your mercy extends upon the nest of birds"... we silence him. (Mishnah, *Berachot* 5:3)

The Mishnah is presumed to mean that one may not ask that God extend His compassion upon man in the same way that He extends it upon birds. But why is it not legitimate to mention that this commandment demonstrates God's mercy upon the bird? Surely our prayers are full of references to God's compassion over the natural world, such as with the verse, "His mercy is upon all His works" (Psalms 145:9)!

Explanation #1: Anti-Christian Measures

It has recently been proposed that the Mishnah's ruling was directed against Christian influences on prayer, which was a particular threat during the period of the Mishnah in Israel.[7] This cannot be ascertained

---

[7] Zohar Amar, *Mesorat Ha-Ohf*, p. 223; Robert T. Herford, *Christianity in Talmud and Midrash*, p. 202; Ephraim Yitzhaki, "Of Birds and Heretics," Bar-Ilan University's Parashat Hashavua Study Center, *Parashat Ki Tetze* 5761/2001. For other examples of

with certainty, due to the fact that anything relating to Christianity has been censored out of the Talmud. But there are clues to this, especially from an analysis of the Mishnah as a whole, in an expanded version of the Mishnah that appears in *masechet Megillah*:

> If one says, "The good ones shall bless you," this is the way of heresy.[8] "Your mercy extends upon the nest of birds," "Your Name shall be remembered for the good," "We thank You, we thank You,"—we silence him. (Mishnah, *Megillah* 4:9)

The term used for heresy, *minnut*, is often a reference to Christianity. Saying "The good ones shall bless you," in the plural, may therefore be a reference to the trinity.[9] Repeating "We thank You, we thank You," may likewise be interpreted as a reference to more than one deity.

There are two suggestions as to how the ruling regarding *shiluach hakein* is to be understood as preventing Christian influence. According to the Unitarian theologian Robert Travers Herford (1860-1950) who carefully studied Talmudic attitudes to Christianity, it should be understood in light of the Pauline antithesis of Law and Grace.[10] In a different approach, Ephraim Yitzhaki of the Department of Talmud at Bar-Ilan points to the variant reading in the Talmud Yerushalmi:

> Rabbi Pinchas in the name of Rabbi Simon: Like one who cries foul on the attributes of the Holy One; Your mercy extends upon the bird's nest,

---

the Sages fighting against Christian influences, see *Berachot* 28b concerning the prayer against heretics in the Amidah prayer, and *Berachot* 12 concerning the removal of the Ten Commandments from the recitation of *Shema* (see Rashi ad loc. and *Machzor Vitri*, par. 16). See too Elijah Schochet, *Animal Life in Jewish Tradition*, p. 183.

[8] While this phrase is lacking in the parallel Mishnah in *Berachot*, it does appear in Rif and Rosh, as well as in the Talmud (*Berachot* 34a; see *mesoret haShas*).

[9] In a similar vein, the final Mishnah in *Berachot*, ruling that one should greet a friend with the Name of God, is likewise explained by R. Hai Gaon as countering a popular greeting that invoked the trinity. See José Faur, *The Horizontal Society*, vol. II, p. 96.

[10] R.T. Herford, *Christianity in Talmud and Midrash*, p. 202.

but Your mercy did not extend upon that man. (Yerushalmi, *Berachot* 40a[11])

"That man" is usually interpreted to refer to the person issuing the prayer.[12] But Yitzhaki proposes that, as with many other Talmudic usages of the phrase "that man," it refers to Jesus.[13] The Christians saw the Biblical account of *shiluach hakein* as an allegory for the sacrifice of Jesus: "Let the mother go, and only take the child, in order that it may be good for you." Thus Yitzhaki proposes that the prayer was prohibited due to its having a Christological allusion.[14]

However, for the purposes of our discussion, it is more important to consider the Talmud's explanation of this strange ruling of the Mishnah. The Talmud provides two rationales:

> What is the reason? Two Amoraim from the West, Rabbi Yosi bar Avin and Rabbi Yosi bar Zeveida, disagreed on this. One said, because he is placing jealousy among the creations. And one said: Because he is making the attributes of the Holy One into mercy, whereas they are nothing other than decrees. (Talmud, *Berachot* 33b)

Both of these reasons appear cryptic. We shall explore these two reasons in turn, showing that the second has been interpreted in radically different ways. Following this, we shall document another explanation that has been given for the Mishnah's ruling, which is particularly astonishing and leads into a discussion of a radically different approach to the entire mitzvah.

---

[11] For a comparison between the Jerusalem and Babylonian Talmud on this topic, see Zohar Amar, *Mesorat Ha-Ohf*, pp. 224-225; Ephraim Urbach, *Chazal – Pirkei Emunot VeDeyot*, pp. 335-336.

[12] Meiri ad loc.; Tzlach ad loc.; Jastrow, *Dictionary of the Talmud*, s.v. *tagar*.

[13] For a comprehensive study of Talmudic references to Jesus, see Jacob Z. Lauterbach, *Rabbinic Essays*, pp. 473-570. It should be noted, though, that the phrase "that man" is also used on plenty of occasions without it being a reference to Jesus.

[14] A difficulty with this is that the opinion in the Yerushalmi which uses the phrase "that man" is describing the problem in this as crying foul on the attributes of the Holy One, not as being Christian.

Explanation #2: Highlighting Inequalities

Rashi explains the Talmud's first reason—"that it places jealousy among the creations"—as meaning that drawing attention to God's compassion over the mother bird serves to highlight an inequality. This presumably refers to the fact that this mitzvah of compassion only applies to kosher birds, and there is no equivalent commandment for other members of the animal kingdom. Alternately, this reason might be identical to that mentioned in the Talmud Yerushalmi, that this prayer is intended to contrast God's mercy upon the bird with God's lack of mercy upon the one issuing the prayer.

It is important to note that according to this reason, the Mishnah's ruling is not negating compassion as the reason for the mitzvah; on the contrary, the mitzvah is very much based upon compassion, but it is inappropriate to publicly draw attention to that.[15]

Explanation #3: A Decree, Not God's Mercy

The Talmud's second view as to why we silence a petitioner from relating *shiluach hakein* to mercy is that it is a decree, not an expression of mercy. However, there are dramatically different explanations of this view.

3a. An Incomprehensible Statute

The first and more straightforward explanation is that the Talmud is saying that this commandment is a statute that has no explanation. This is the view presented by Rashi:

> "His attributes"—His *mitzvot*. But He did not act out of compassion; rather, to place the statutes of His decrees upon Israel, to make known that they are his servants, guardians of His commandments and the decrees of his statutes, even with matters where there is room for Satan and gentiles to respond and say "What need is there for this mitzvah?"

---

[15] In a different twist, Meiri (*Berachot* 33b) states that this refers to an error in thinking that birds receive individual divine providence, causing jealousy among the other creatures, which only receive divine providence over the species as a whole, not for individuals.

In fact, Rashi seems to be going even further and saying that it is precisely because *shiluach hakein* (and other *mitzvot*) have no reason that they were commanded—for the true sign of a servant is that he fulfills the wishes of his master even when there is no reason for them.

Maharsha explains this view of the Talmud to be saying that since the Torah did not ascribe a reason to *shiluach hakein*, we have no right to claim that it is based upon compassion, and we must simply accept it as a *chok*, a commandment with no reason that we can determine.[16]

Rambam, in his *Commentary on the Mishnah*, also explains this view in the Talmud to be rejecting any rationale for the mitzvah:

> The issue of saying, "Your mercy extends upon the nest of a bird," concerns the notion that just as God has compassion on the nest of a bird, instructing us not to take the mother with her young, so too, He should have compassion on us. One who says this is to be silenced, since he is saying that the reason for this commandment is the God's mercy on birds. But this is not so, for were it a matter of mercy, He would not have allowed slaughtering animals at all; rather, this is an accepted commandment without a reason being given. (*Commentary on the Mishnah*, *Berachot* 5:3)

Thus, Rambam understands this view in the Talmud as saying that there is no reason for *shiluach hakein* that man can grasp. He adopts a similar approach in the *Mishneh Torah*.[17] However, it is important to note that in the *Guide*, Rambam notes that he is not following this view:

> This is also the reason for sending away the mother bird from the nest... If the Torah takes pity on the suffering of animals and birds, all the more so on human beings! And you cannot challenge me by arguing, "as far as the nest of a bird does Your mercy reach," because that argument is based on one of the two views which we mentioned, i.e., the approach of those who believe there is no explanation for the commandments of the Torah other than the will of God alone; but we are inclined to follow the other view. (*Guide for the Perplexed* III:48)

---

[16] Maharsha to *Berachot* 33b.

[17] *Mishneh Torah*, Laws of Prayer 9:7.

Why does Rambam present the view in the *Commentary* and *Mishneh Torah* that the mitzvah is not related to compassion, if in the *Guide* he states that he does not follow that view? A variety of solutions have been suggested.[18] Among contemporary academic scholars, Jacob Levinger claims that Rambam's halachic works were geared to the masses, and Rambam considered it safer for them to consider that the *mitzvot* have no discernable reasons; only in the *Guide* could Rambam reveal his true views.[19] Roslyn Weiss specifies that Rambam had to pretend for the masses that it was not based on compassion, as otherwise they might think that eating meat is wrong.[20] Josef Stern explains that Rambam really means that the mitzvah serves to teach man compassion rather than being based on God's compassion, in line with the view of Ramban and others that we shall now explore.[21]

Rabbi Yom Tov Heller (1578-1654) softens this explanation of the Mishnah, stating that it is only in the context of prayer that it is forbidden to link this mitzvah with compassion, since one is thereby making an absolute statement regarding the ultimate reason for the mitzvah. However, he states, there is no problem in relating this mitzvah to compassion in the context of *peshat* or *derash*.[22] As we shall now see, others took an even stronger approach in avoiding the idea that this view is ruling out a theme of compassion for this mitzvah.

3b. Medieval Rationalist Interpretations

As we saw earlier, many medieval authorities understood the mitzvah of *shiluach hakein* as being clearly related to compassion. They were

---

[18] See Menachem Slae, *Chayto Aretz*, p. 89 for a survey of several different solutions.

[19] Levinger, *Darchei haMachshavah haHilchatit shel haRambam*, pp. 135-136; *Al ta'am hanezirut beMoreh Nevuchim*, p. 302. In sharp contrast to this is Rabbi Dror Fixler, "*Iyun beTaami Mitzvot Shiluach HaKein*," who claims that Rambam's true view was that *shiluach hakein* has no reason, and only in the *Guide* did he claim that it was related to compassion, so as to appeal to the philosophically-confused readership.

[20] Weiss, "Maimonides on Shilluah Ha-Qen," *Jewish Quarterly Review* 79 (1989) pp. 345-366.

[21] Stern, *Problems and Parables of Law* pp. 49-66.

[22] *Tosafot Yom Tov to Berachot* 5:3.

therefore challenged by this opinion in the Talmud which seemingly stated that the mitzvah is an incomprehensible *chok*, unrelated to compassion. Rambam simply stated that he does not follow that view, but others were unwilling to take that approach—either because they were too modest to openly dispute an Amora, or because it was inconceivable to them that someone could hold such a view. Instead, they reinterpreted the Talmud's statement to mean something very different: that God did not issue the mitzvah due to His concern for the bird's welfare, but rather in order to teach people to be compassionate. Ramban is one of those who presents this approach:

> ...These *aggadot* which presented difficulties for the Rav (Rambam), in my view have a different meaning. They mean to say that there is no benefit in the *mitzvot* to the Holy One himself, but rather the benefit is for man, to prevent him from being harmed, or from a false belief or a deplorable attribute... Similarly, that which they said, "Because he is making the attributes of the Holy One into mercy, whereas they are nothing other than decrees," means to say that God did not have compassion on the nest of bird, and His mercy did not extent to "the animal and its young," for His compassion does not extend to animals to prevent us from fulfilling our needs with them; for if so, He would have prohibited their slaughter. Rather, the reason for the prohibition is to teach *us* the trait of compassion. (Ramban, Commentary to Deut. 22:7)

According to this view, when the Talmud describes this mitzvah as a "decree," it does not mean it in the sense of *gezerat ha-katuv*—a decree with no discernable meaning. Instead, it means that it is not motivated by God's compassion, but rather to legislate compassion among people. The same explanation is presented by Meiri (1249–c.1310).[23] It appears that Rambam may have even taken this approach in his halachic work, notwithstanding his declaration that the mitzvah is not related to compassion.[24]

---

[23] Meiri to *Berachot* 33b. Cf. Maharal, *Tiferet Yisrael* 6.

[24] Rabbi Dr. Yosef Tabori, "*Shiluach HaKein:* On the Relationship between the Reason for the Mitzvah and its Laws" (Hebrew), p. 126, notes that in *Hilchot Shechitah* 13:7 Rambam issues a ruling based on the idea of not taking advantage of the mother's desire to protect her young.

Explanation #4: Cruelty, Not Mercy

Notwithstanding the two explanations given in the Talmud for the Mishnah's ruling, some of the Acharonim give an alternate explanation. It is not only remarkable that an entirely different explanation to those in the Talmud is proposed; the very nature of this explanation is bizarre.

Of the two explanations that we have seen so far, one maintains the idea that the mitzvah of *shiluach hakein* is related to compassion, and the other, which seems to oppose this—the view that the mitzvah is a decree—is reinterpreted by many medieval authorities so as to still be consistent with the idea that the mitzvah is related to compassion. In sharp contrast to all these views, is the view that the reason why we silence someone who utters this prayer is that he is wrong: instead of *shiluach hakein* reflecting God's compassion, it reflects cruelty. This is the view of the Vilna Gaon (1720-1797);[25] Rabbi Yonatan Eibeschutz (1690-1764)[26] and Rabbi Eliyahu Schick (19th century)[27] state similarly. This startling view reflects the kabbalistic approach to the mitzvah, which we shall now explore.

III. Mystical Approaches

Esoteric Reasons

In the medieval period, those who gave explanations for the mitzvah of *shiluach hakein* usually explained it in terms of reflecting compassion. However, there were those from the mystical school of thought who gave mystical explanations of the mitzvah. Ramban, who straddled both the rationalist and mystical schools of thought, stated that as well as the rationalist rationale of compassion, there are also mystical dimensions to this mitzvah, based on the *Sefer HaBahir*.[28] *Akeidat Yitzchak* and

---

[25] *Imrei No'am* to *Berachot* 33b.

[26] *Yaarot Devash* 6. He calls it a "decree," seemingly subsuming it under the Talmud's explanation in that vein, but he nevertheless cites the Zohar's explanation of cruelty to explain why the Mishnah rules against invoking this mitzvah as an example of compassion.

[27] Rabbi Eliyahu ben Binyamin Schick, *Ein Eliyahu* to *Berachot* 33a, p. 93.

[28] Ramban quotes the kabbalistic work *Sefer HaKannah* by Kanah ibn Gedor.

Abarbanel both mention that the mother bird symbolizes the human soul. Rashba writes that he is doubtful that anyone living in his generation is able to offer a valid reason for the mitzvah of *shiluach hakein*, as it contains many hidden secrets of the Torah.[29]

Benefits of Cruelty

The Zohar, in *Midrash HaNe'elam*,[30] introduced a very different view of the mitzvah, which was further elaborated upon in *Tikkunei Zohar*.

> There is an angel appointed over the birds… and when Israel performs this commandment, and the mother departs weeping and her children crying, he agonizes for his birds, and asks God: "Does it not say that 'His compassion is on all of His works (Psalms 145:9)'? Why did You decree on that bird to be exiled from her nest?" And what does the Holy One do? He gathers all of His other angels and says to them, "This angel is concerned for the welfare of a bird and is complaining of its suffering; is there none amongst you who will seek merit on My children Israel, and for the Shechinah which is in exile, and whose nest in Jerusalem has been destroyed, and whose children are in exile under the hand of harsh masters? Is there no-one who seeks compassion for them, and will attribute merit to them?" Then the Holy One issues a command and says, "For My sake I shall act, and I shall act for My sake," and compassion is thereby aroused upon the Shechinah and the children in exile. (*Tikkunei Zohar* 23a)

The approach of the Zohar is also cited by Rabbeinu Bachya ben Asher, with slightly different nuances.[31] However it is important to note that Rabbeinu Bachya presents this as a mystical alternative to the approach that it is an act of compassion (which he presents as being *al derech hasechel*). R. Yitzchak Caro likewise presents this view with the preface "Some say…" thereby acknowledging that it is not the straightforward understanding of the mitzvah.[32]

---

[29] Responsa *HaRashba* 1:94.

[30] *Zohar Chadah, Midrash Ruth, Ma'amar Kan Tzippor.*

[31] Rabbeinu Bachya, commentary to Deut. 22:7.

[32] Rabbi Yitzchak Caro, *Toldot Yitzchak,* Deut. 22:6.

The Cruel Engineering of Compassion

The idea of *shiluach hakein* as explained by the Zohar stands in sharp opposition to the normal understanding of how we encourage God to deal compassionately with us—which is that we should act with compassion. The Talmud itself states that being compassionate upon animals leads to His treating us with compassion, whereas being cruel to animals leads to God dealing harshly with man:

> It was taught: Rabban Gamliel bar Rebbi said: "And He shall give you compassion, and be compassionate to you and multiply you" (Deut. 13:18); Anyone who is compassionate to the creations, they have compassion on him in Heaven, and anyone who is not compassionate to the creations, they do not have compassion on him in Heaven. (Talmud, *Shabbat* 151b[33])

The Zohar's idea, on the other hand, is that one deliberately performs an act of cruelty in order to engineer a process that causes God to extend compassion upon the Jewish People. According to the Zohar, the bird's cries of distress have an automatic effect, via the protests of the angels, of arousing God's compassion; an effect that is more powerful than a Jew himself seeking God's compassion. Instead of directly entreating God for compassion, or acting with compassion in order to deserve it, a person is instead engineering a process (diametrically opposed to the normal method of receiving compassion) that will achieve this result more effectively. This certainly seems strange.

It might seem that there is precedent for such manipulation as being acceptable. A similar case appears in a different context—the repentance of the city of Nineveh.

> The tidings reached the king of Nineveh, and he arose from his throne, and laid his robe from him and covered it with sackcloth, and sat in ashes. And he caused it to be proclaimed and published through Nineveh by the decree of the king and his nobles saying, "Let neither man nor beast, herd nor flock, taste anything; let them not feed, nor drink water, but let them be covered with sackcloth, both man and beast; and let them cry mightily

---

[33] See too *Bava Metzia* 85a, where Rebbi's fate is determined by his compassion toward animals.

unto God. Let them turn every one from his evil way and from the violence that is in their hands. Who knows whether God will not turn and repent, and turn away from His fierce anger, that we shall not perish?" And God saw their works, that they turned from their evil way; and God repented of the evil, which He said He would do to them and He did not do it. (Jonah 3:6-10)

The Talmud elaborates upon the strategy that the King of Nineveh pursued with the animals:

[The King of Nineveh said,] "But let man and beast be covered with sackcloth. (Jonah 3:10)." What did they do? They tied the animals separately and the young separately. They said before Him: "Master of the Universe! If You do not have mercy on us, we will not have mercy on these!" (Ta'anit 16a)

This is slightly different from the case of *shiluach hakein*; in this case, they were threatening, even blackmailing God, via threatening hostages. We can therefore understand why the Talmud Yerushalmi[34] and Midrash[35] condemn this method of obtaining God's compassion, whereby it certainly does not provide precedent for legitimizing the Zohar's approach to *shiluach hakein*.[36] But what about the Babylonian Talmud, which was understood to be approving this form of repentance? Does this also serve to legitimize the Zohar's approach to *shiluach hakein*? If we study the commentaries, we see that they interpreted this case in such a way that avoids it being comparable in any way to the Zohar's explanation of *shiluach hakein*:

This was as if to say: "Just as You wish us to have mercy upon them, in keeping with the verse, 'For His mercy is upon all His works' (Psalms 145:9), so You should [set an example of this by having] mercy upon us" (Rashi, ad loc.).

---

[34] Yerushalmi, *Ta'anit* 8a.

[35] *Pesikta D'Rav Kahana* 24:11.

[36] Ephraim E. Auerbach explains that in Israel, where Christians used the repentance of Nineveh to mock the Jews, it was necessary to show that the repentance of Nineveh was deficient. "The Prophecy of Jonah: The Repentance of the Men of Nineveh and the Jewish-Christian Debate" (Hebrew), *Machanayim* 33 (5718).

As explained by Rashi, it is actually very different from the Zohar. Here was the idea that God wants us to be compassionate on animals, and the people of Nineveh wished to point out that God should likewise have mercy upon them. This is certainly not the straightforward understanding of the Talmud, but Rashi was probably forced into this interpretation in order to make their actions acceptable. Rabbi Yosef Dov Soloveitchik explains that they were saying that compassion is not a natural trait, and if God does not teach it to man by way of example, man will not know to practice it himself. This is likewise far from straightforward, but Rav Soloveitchik stresses that it is inconceivable that it is acceptable to threaten and to force God into acting compassionately.[37]

Thus, the case of Nineveh, as it was interpreted, does not provide a precedent for legitimizing the manipulation of God into being compassionate by being cruel to animals; if anything, it shows the opposite.

IV. Optional, Recommended or Obligatory?

Relating the Halachah and the Rationale

Thus far, we have seen diametrically opposed views regarding the nature of *shiluach hakein*—the view of the Midrash and the Rishonim that it is an act of compassion, and the view initiated by the Zohar that it is an act of cruelty. Our next task is to see how this relates to a halachic dispute regarding the fundamental status of the mitzvah of *shiluach hakein*. One approach is that the mitzvah is optional—only in a case where one wants the young is one obligated to send away the mother. The second approach is that even if one does not want the young, there is a mitzvah to send away the mother bird.

The Talmud's position on this matter is not absolutely clear; some Rishonim clearly take the position that it is optional; and debate regarding it begins with the Acharonim. Usually, such a halachic question would be resolved via legal reasoning and hermeneutics, entirely independent of any

---

[37] Quoted by Rabbi Hershel Schechter, "Gems from the Rav" (Hebrew), *Beit Yitzchak* '5756) 28, p. 34.

considerations as to the assumed rationale underlying the mitzvah. But with *shiluach hakein*, the assumed rationale often does play a role in resolving this halachic question, sometimes explicitly and sometimes implicitly. The reason why it is related is as follows: If the nature of the mitzvah is showing compassion (by not taking both mother and young, and by sending away the mother so that she does not see one taking the young), then clearly in a case when one does not want the young, there is no purpose in sending the mother away. But if the nature of the mitzvah is to arouse Divine mercy via a procedure involving causing suffering to the mother bird, then there is reason to perform the mitzvah even if one does not want the young.

It should be noted that the fact of something being a mitzvah does not necessarily mean that it is praiseworthy to seek a way to fulfill it. There is a mitzvah of *yefat toar* with a woman who is captured in war, but nobody would deem it praiseworthy to enlist in order to fall in love with such a woman; the Talmud explicitly notes that the mitzvah is a way to accommodate someone who has given in to his desires. There is a mitzvah of *eglah erufah* in the case of an unsolved murder, but it is absurd to suggest that one should go searching for corpses of murder victims. Many other such examples could be brought. The rationalist approach would place *shiluach hakein* in the same category: it is a way to act nobly in a situation where one wants to enjoy a free meal, not a situation that should be sought out in order to send away the mother bird. Those following the mystical approach, on the other hand, would see it differently.

Determining the Halachah

In evaluating the statements of the Rishonim and Acharonim, some are too quick to conclude there is evidence that they consider it obligatory. Statements such as that of the *Shulchan Aruch*, which determine that in various circumstances, "one is obligated to send away the mother bird," do not necessarily mean that one is obligated to do so even if one does not want the young.[38] First of all, it may simply be an abbreviation for saying that one is obligated to send away the mother bird in a case where one

---

[38] Rabbi Dan Schwarz, in *Kan Tzippor* p. 19, errs in this regard.

wants to take the young.[39] Second, it is important to note that ancient authorities considering *shiluach hakein* would likely take it for granted that a person would want to take the young. One must appreciate the enormous difference between the world of today and that of ancient times. Today, if a person were to come across a bird's nest, he would never have a desire to take the mother, and the only circumstances in which he would take the eggs would be if he was a professional egg collector. Nobody would take the eggs to eat, and certainly not the chicks. But in ancient times, when food was scarcer, people would ordinarily seize upon the opportunity for a free, nutritious and tasty meal.[40]

Another important point to note is that the mitzvah actually includes two distinct components: a negative prohibition (of taking both mother and young) and a positive commandment (of sending away the mother). There are two schools of thought as to the relationship between these two commandments. One is that the positive commandment is only applicable in a case where the negative prohibition has been transgressed, as a rectification of it. A person may not take both mother and young, but if he did so, he should then send away the mother in order to rectify this. (The halachic terminology for this structure is לאו הניתק לעשה.) The other approach is that the two commandments are independent of each other; a person may not take mother and young, and when taking the young, he is obligated to send away the mother bird first. (The halachic terminology for the commandment of sending away the mother bird in this structure is that it is a מצות עשה מעיקרא.) There is dispute regarding which of the Rishonim subscribed to each of these views;[41] however many are of the opinion that the former view, that the positive commandment only applies in a case where the negative prohibition was transgressed,

---

[39] It should be noted that the words *shiluach hakein* are themselves an abbreviation for *shiluach ha'eim min hakein* – one does not send away the nest, but rather one sends away the mother from the nest.

[40] See Zohar Amar, *Mesorat Ha-Ohf*, pp. 233-236 for extensive discussion of this point and its ramifications for the mitzvah.

[41] See Schwartz, *Kan Tzippor*, especially pp. 197-207.

necessarily means that the mitzvah is not obligatory i.e. that it does not apply in a case where one does not want the young.[42]

1. Optional - Only if one wants the young

Many Rishonim rule that when a person has no need for the young, he is not obligated to send away the mother bird. This is the explicit view of Rokeach (c.1176–1238),[43] Meiri (1249–c.1310),[44] Rabbeinu Bachya (d. 1340),[45] and Ran (1320–1380).[46] It is also widely understood to be the view of Tosafot[47] and Rambam.[48] Note too that in the *Guide*, Rambam saw the prohibition of taking the mother as serving in most cases to cause the entire nest being left untouched, since the young are often not fit to be eaten. Ralbag explicitly states that the goal of the mitzvah is to encourage the person to leave the nest entirely alone.[49] There is dispute regarding whether it is the view of Rashba that one is not obligated to perform the mitzvah if one has no need for the young.[50]

---

[42] Chatam Sofer and Rabbi Asher Weiss see this as being the case; see later note.

[43] Rokeach, Commentary to *Ki Teze*, p. 244.

[44] *Chiddushei HaMeiri* to Chullin 139b

[45] Rabbeinu Bechaye to Deuteronomy 22:7.

[46] *Chiddushei HaRan* to Chullin 139a.

[47] *Tosafot* to *Chullin* 140b, s.v. *Shnei*, as explained by Rabbi Yair Bachrach, *Chavot Yair* 67; *Tosafot* to *Kiddushin* 34a, s.v. *Maakeh*, as explained by Rabbi Shlomo Zalman Auerbach, cited in *Kan Tzipor* p. 159.

[48] *Megillat Sefer, Laavin* 150. Rabbi Asher Weiss in *Minchat Asher*, Devarim 40, p. 275 notes that according to Rambam, *shiluach hakein* is a case of *lav hanitak le'asei*, and is therefore clearly not obligatory. See too *Hilchot Shechitah* 13:5. Rabbi Yisrael Yaakov Fisher, in *Kan Tzippor* p. 202, disputes this, but does not address most of the sources cited by Rabbi Weiss.

[49] Ralbag, Commentary to Deuteronomy 22:7.

[50] R. Yaakov Tzvi Mecklenberg in *HaKetav VeHaKabbalah* to Deut. 22:6, R. Chaim Kanievsky (cited by Weinberger), and R. Asher Weiss in *Minchat Asher*, Devarim 40, p. 275, all understand Rashba in Responsa 18 as saying that the mitzvah does not apply if one does not want the young. Tabori states that Rashba's view is unclear, and R Yisrael Yaakov Fisher in *Even Yisrael, Hilchot Shechitah* claims that Rashba considers it obligatory.

Did these authorities reach this conclusion, that one is not obligated to perform the mitzvah when one has no need for the young, based on the understanding that the mitzvah is an act of compassion? It is impossible to determine this with certainty. However it is perhaps relevant to note that, unlike the Acharonim who reached this conclusion based on analyzing various statements in the Talmud, the Rishonim who took this position generally do not provide any such analysis and thus seem to have taken it for granted, which may reflect their having understood it as being the fundamental nature of the mitzvah.[51] I am therefore not convinced by the claim that this halachic conclusion is apparently entirely unrelated to their understanding of the mitzvah's rationale.[52]

There are those who apparently did not necessarily see a connection— Rabbeinu Bachya states that the mitzvah only applies in a case where one wants the young, even though he quotes the view of the Zohar as a valid rationale (albeit not the only one).[53] However there certainly are those who explicitly made this connection. Chatam Sofer (1762–1839) notes that since the purpose of the mitzvah is to inculcate in us the trait of compassion, then it is clear that we are not obligated to send away the mother bird when we have no need for the offspring, because doing so causes distress to the bird for no reason, and it would in fact be *forbidden* to do so.[54] While he acknowledges that the Zohar's explanation would lead to a different policy, and he admits that there is no problem of wanton cruelty if one is acting for the greater good of summoning mercy for the Jewish People, he nevertheless determines that the Zohar conflicts with the Talmud, and that in such cases "we have no business with esoterica." It should be noted that elsewhere Chatam Sofer expressed his disapproval even for someone wanting to follow the Zohar as a *halachic*

---

[51] The exception being the Meiri, that we shall later discuss.

[52] Tabori, "*Shiluach HaKein:* On the Relationship between the Reason for the Mitzvah and its Laws" (Hebrew), pp. 140-141.

[53] Rabbeinu Bachya to Deuteronomy 22:7.

[54] Responsa Chatam Sofer, *Orach Chaim* 100.

stringency,[55] as well as his belief that most of the Zohar was not written by Rabbi Shimon bar Yochai.[56]

Amongst more recent authorities, Rabbi Baruch HaLevi Epstein (1860-1941) is vehement about the connection (notwithstanding the fact that, as we shall see later, his father took the opposite view):

> ...In general, I am in astonishment. How could someone possibly think that the Torah commanded us to do this even against His will regarding the outcome? For it is clear and beyond all doubt, that of the foundational reasons in this mitzvah in general is that we should not be cruel and take the mother while she is sitting on her young; and it is only because, at the end of the day, the goal of all creatures is that they were created for man, just as slaughtering an animal [for food] is permitted, that the Torah permitted man to take the young in this way, via sending away the mother beforehand so that she should not see her young being taken. And if so, it is clear that the Torah is only granting an allowance with this, but with someone who does not all want to involve himself, it is certain that he is permitted to simply pass it by. In fact, he is making things even better for the mother and young by leaving them together. There is no argument at all that he should be obligated to break them apart, just as there is no argument that the mitzvah of "Do not slaughter an animal and its young on the same day" is a warning against slaughtering them both, but that it is a mitzvah and obligation to slaughter one of them. (*Torah Temimah* to Deut. 22:7)

Among contemporary halachic authorities, Rabbi Menashe Klein likewise explicitly states that since the mitzvah is rooted in compassion, it defeats the purpose to perform it when one has no desire for the young, which would be cruelty.[57] In a more cautious vein, Rabbi Asher Weiss

---

[55] Responsa Chatam Sofer, *Even HaEzer* II:85. See too Responsa Chatam Sofer, *Orach Chaim* 197 and Binyamin Hamburger, *Shorshei Minhag Ashkenaz* vol. I pp. 160-164.

[56] See the oblique but unequivocal statement in Responsa Chatam Sofer 6:59, s.v. *U'ma SheKatav SheHaRav*. R. Eliezer Lipmann Neusatz, one of Chatam Sofer's leading disciples, in *Mei Menuchot* (Pressburg 1884) p. 43b, attests that Chatam Sofer told his students that R. Shimon bar Yochai authored only a few pages from the Zohar.

[57] Responsa *Mishneh Halachot* 12:223.

rules that one should not perform the mitzvah without a pressing practical reason, and relates this to the cruelty involved.[58]

In fact, most Acharonim and contemporary halachic authorities rule that there is no obligation to send away the mother bird in a case where one has no desire for the young. This is the ruling of Rabbi Pinchas Horwitz (1730-1805),[59] Rabbi Yaakov Tzvi Mecklenburg (1785-1865),[60] Rabbi Naftali Tzvi Berlin (1817-1893),[61] Rabbi Avraham Bornsztain (1838-1910),[62] the Chafetz Chaim (1838-1933),[63] the Chazon Ish (1878-1953),[64] Rabbi Yechezkel Abramsky (1886-1976),[65] and Rabbi Yehuda Henkin (1945-present).[66] However, with these authorities it is impossible to know whether their ruling had any connection to their understanding of the rationale for the mitzvah.

Rabbi Moshe Shmuel Glasner rules that one should not send away the mother bird unless one wants the young, and while he bases this on the Talmud rather than on reasons of compassion, he rejects those who rule it to be obligatory due to the Zohar; Rabbi Glasner argues that kabbalistic reasons do not need to correlate to halachah.[67] As we shall now see, the approach that he disputes was (and remains) a popular position.

---

[58] *Minchat Asher*, Devarim 40, p. 276. He states that in a situation where one is any case going to remove the nest, such as a bird nesting in one's house, one should perform the mitzvah.

[59] *Sefer HaMakneh* to Kiddushin 41a.

[60] *HaKesav VeHaKabbalah* to Deut. 22:6.

[61] *Meromei Sadeh*, part 5, p. 104. His commentary on the Torah contains mixed messages; on the one hand, he explains the mitzvah in terms of compassion, but on the other hand he insists that it is a decree and a *chok* beyond human comprehension (*Ha-Amek Davar* to Deut. 22:6-7).

[62] *Avnei Nezer*, Orach Chaim 481:6.

[63] *Sefer HaMitzvot HaKatzer, Mitzvot Aseh* 74.

[64] Chazon Ish, *Yoreh De'ah* 175:2.

[65] *Chazon Yechezkel* to *Tosefta Chullin* 10, p. 39.

[66] Responsa *Bnei Banim* 3:5.

[67] Rabbi Moshe Shmuel Glasner, *Dor Revi'i*, Chullin, p. 168.

2. Obligatory, Recommended, or Praiseworthy

This linkage, between the reason for the mitzvah and the halachah of whether it is obligatory, also occurs in the other direction—that due to the explanation of the Zohar, the mitzvah is obligatory. One of the first authorities that ruled the mitzvah to be obligatory is Rabbi Mordechai Jaffe (1530-1612).[68] It is probably no coincidence that he had a reputation not only as a halachic authority, but also as a kabbalist. There are authorities who explicitly used the Zohar's explanation that the mitzvah is one of cruelty as a (partial) basis for the halachic determination that the mitzvah is obligatory. Rabbi Yair Bachrach (1638-1702) in *Chavot Ya'ir* concludes that one is obligated to send away the mother bird even if one does not want the young. He proves this in part via technical halachic reasoning, but supports it with the explanation of the mitzvah provided by the Zohar, that the cruelty to the bird results in Divine compassion.[69] Rabbi Tzvi Hirsch Eisenstadt (*Pitchei Teshuvah*, 1813-1863) cites this view and adds that if a person comes across a nest and does not perform the mitzvah, he will be punished in a time of Divine anger.[70] Rabbi Tzvi Hirsch ben Azriel of Vilna (circa 1800) clearly rules that the mitzvah is obligatory, and, along with Rabbi Yosef Molko (circa 1750) and Rabbi Yechiel Michel Epstein (1829-1908), takes the position that due to the Zohar's reason, a person must take the young even if he doesn't want them, so as to ensure that the mother will be distressed and the process described by the Zohar will be activated![71]

Rabbi David Luria likewise notes that the mitzvah is obligatory and that this is consistent with the Zohar's explanation.[72] Rabbi Chaim Vital goes even further and adds that one should go out of his way to find birds'

---

[68] Rabbi Mordechai Jaffe, *Levush Ateret Zahav* 292:1. It is, however, possible that he only intends to refer to someone who wants the young.

[69] *Chavot Yair* 67.

[70] *Pitchei Teshuvah, Yoreh De'ah* 292:1.

[71] Rabbi Tzvi Hirsch ben Azriel, *Beit Lechem Yehuda, Yoreh De'ah* 292:1; Rabbi Yosef Molko, *Shulchan Gavoa, Yoreh De'ah* 292:19; Rabbi Yechiel Michel Epstein, *Aruch HaShulchan, Yoreh De'ah* 292:2.

[72] *Chiddushei HaRadal, Midrash Devarim Rabbah* 6:3.

nests so that he can be obligated to fulfill the mitzvah.[73] Other authorities who likewise ruled the mitzvah to be obligatory, albeit without explicitly linking this to the Zohar, include Maharal (1525-1609),[74] Rabbi Zvi Ashkenazi (Chacham Tzvi, 1660-1718),[75] Rabbi Akiva Eiger (1761-1837),[76] Rabbi Shalom Mordechai Schwadron (Maharsham, 1835-1911),[77] and Rabbi Yisroel Yaakov Fisher (1928-2003).[78]

Several other authorities, although not necessarily stating it to be a halachic obligation, also stress that even if one has no need for the young, one should still make every effort to send away the mother bird, because of the Zohar's rationale. Authorities in this category include the Arizal (1534-1572)[79] and Rabbi Chaim Yosef David Azulai (Chida, 1724-1807).[80] (The Arizal also adds another mystical reason for striving to perform this mitzvah; that if one fails to do so, one will return to this world as a *gilgul*.[81]) Rabbi Yechiel Michel Epstein (1829-1908), while stating that the mitzvah is a decree with no revealed reason, simultaneously cites the Zohar's explanation in support of his ruling that choosing to simply leave the bird and nest alone is a failure to perform the mitzvah equivalent to finding a lost object and ignoring it instead of returning it to its owner.[82]

Likewise, although most recent and contemporary halachic authorities rule that there is no requirement to send away the mother in a case where one has no need for the young, many are of the view that even though one

---

[73] Rabbi Chaim Vital, *Sha'ar HaMitzvot*, Introduction.

[74] *Tiferet Yisrael*, end of chapter 61.

[75] Responsa *Chacham Tzvi* 83. This is the way that most understand him; however, Responsa *Avnei Nezer, Orach Chaim* 481:6 does not understand his view in this way.

[76] Rabbi Akiva Eiger to *Shulchan Aruch, Yoreh De'ah* 292:1.

[77] Maharsham 1:209.

[78] Rabbi Yisroel Yaakov Fisher, "*Biur Yesodi BeMitzvat Shiluach HaKein*," in Schwartz, *Kan Tzippor*, p. 208.

[79] As cited in Rabbi Aharon Azriel, Responsa *Kfi Aharon* 10 p. 40; Rabbi Yosef Molko, *Shulchan Gavoa, Yoreh De'ah* 292:8.

[80] Birkei Yosef, *Gilyon Shulchan Aruch, Yoreh De'ah* 292:8.

[81] Quoted by Rabbi Chaim Vital in his introduction to *Sha'ar ha-Mitzvot*.

[82] *Aruch HaShulchan, Yoreh De'ah* 292:1-2.

is not obligated to send away the mother bird in such a case, it is still praiseworthy to do so, for the reason given by the Zohar. Some state this explicitly, such as Rabbi Shlomo Zalman Auerbach (1910-1995),[83] and Rabbi Chaim Kanievsky (1928-present).[84] With many halachic authorities, although they may well rule that the mitzvah is optional, it is apparent that they view it as praiseworthy. This is evident from the fact that they have been photographed performing the mitzvah, even though in this day and age nobody has any desire for bird's eggs from a nest.[85]

A Mitzvah to Seek Out?

In the Talmud, we find a halachic discussion that has ramifications on this dispute. The Talmud is discussing whether one should travel the countryside seeking opportunities to fulfill the mitzvah of *shiluach hakein*. It proves from the words "*Ki yikarei*—when you happen upon"—that there is no such obligation:

> I might have thought that one should travel the mountains and hills in order to find a nest, therefore it tells us "When you happen across it"— only when it happens for you. (*Chullin* 139b)

It is this passage that is utilized by Rabbi Yair Bachrach—the primary proponent of the view that the mitzvah is obligatory—as a basis for his ruling. He reasons that the Talmud's question only makes sense if there is an obligation to send away the mother bird when one encounters a nest. If there is such a requirement, then it makes sense to ask whether one has to search for opportunities to fulfill this requirement, or whether it is only a requirement when the opportunity presents itself. He thus reads the Talmud as follows:

---

[83] *Minchat Shlomo* 2:5:4.

[84] Rabbi Chaim Kanievsky, *Siach Ha-Sadeh, Kuntrus HaLikkutim* 9. However in *Shalech Teshalach*, p. 79, Rabbi Kanievsky is quoted as stating that even if one only wishes to acquire the young in order to be obligated in the mitzvah, and not that one has any desire to actually eat them, this is still a perfectly acceptable way to fulfill the mitzvah.

[85] See Weinberger, *A Practical Guide to the Mitzvah of Shiluach Hakan*, pp. 252-269, where he displays pictures of 29 prominent rabbinic authorities from the *haredi* community performing the mitzvah.

> I might have thought that one should travel the mountains and hills in order to find a nest [and be obligated to send away the mother], therefore it tells us "When you happen across it"—only when one happens across it [is one obligated].

Initially, this appears convincing; if one takes the approach that the mitzvah is optional, it would seem to require reading this passage in the following, rather awkward, way:

> I might have thought that one should travel the mountains and hills in order to find a nest [and choose to fulfill the mitzvah if one wants the chicks], therefore it tells us "When you happen across it"—[one is only asked to fulfill the mitzvah] when one happens across it [and wants the chicks, and one is not required to look for opportunities to fulfill the mitzvah.]

However, several of those who take the approach that the mitzvah is optional address this passage and interpret it very differently. They focus less on the technical parsing of the Talmud's wording, and more on the essence of the exegesis—that the words "When one happens across" serve to rule out one having to actively seek to fulfill the mitzvah. Accordingly, this passage in the Talmud serves precisely to resolve the issue of whether the mitzvah is optional or obligatory. The Talmud is to be read as follows: "I might have thought that one has to actively pursue the mitzvah; thus the Torah teaches us that it is optional." The Talmud is thereby deriving that the mitzvah only applies if one actually wants the young.[86] This appears to be the way that Meiri understands it:

> The mitzvah of *shiluach hakein* is not a mitzvah that one is required to pursue—that is to say, that if one finds a nest, that one must take the young in order to fulfill the mitzvah of sending away the mother, or that one should travel the mountains and hills after this mitzvah. Rather, when

---

[86] Chatam Sofer; Rabbi Yechezkel Abramsky, *Chazon Yechezkel* to *Tosefta Chullin* 10; Rabbi Asher Weiss, *Minchat Asher*, Deuteronomy 40 p. 272. R. Weiss draws a parallel to similar cases: Talmud Yerushalmi, *Sotah* 9:1, regarding the statement that one is not obligated to search for a corpse of a murder victim in order to be obligated in the mitzvah of *eglah arufah* (see *Pnei Moshe* ad loc.), and *Sifrei*, *Re'ah* 40, regarding *Ir HaNidachat*. See too Rabbi Yehudah Henkin, Responsa *Bnei Banim* 3:5.

the opportunity presents itself, he can fulfill it, as it says, "When one happens across..." (Meiri to *Chullin* 139b)

Meiri sees the Talmud's exegesis as ruling out both that one would have to travel the hills in order to find an opportunity, and that one must send away the mother bird when one finds a nest. His view that the mitzvah is optional, while fitting well with his understanding of the rationale for the mitzvah as being one of compassion, is actually understood by him to be an explicit exegesis of the Talmud.

Reverting back to those who adopted the Zohar's approach, whether or not they saw the mitzvah as actually obligatory, they were led to understand this passage in the Talmud as saying that while one is not obligated to seek out opportunities for this mitzvah, it is nevertheless praiseworthy to do so. Earlier, we saw that Rabbi Chaim Vital states that one should go out of his way to find birds' nests so that he can be obligated to fulfill the mitzvah.[87] We also have the following testimony from the eighteenth century from Rabbi Yosef Molko:

> Pious men, and those of deeds, go around the mountains and hills of the villages, in the darkness of night, and put themselves in danger, in order to fulfill the mitzvah of *shiluach hakein*. (*Shulchan Gavoa, Yoreh De'ah* 292:8)[88]

Rabbi Yosef Chaim of Baghdad (Ben Ish Chai, 1835-1909) likewise attests to pious people who travel the countryside in order to perform the

---

[87] Rabbi Chaim Vital, *Sha'ar HaMitzvot*, Introduction.

[88] There is a much earlier statement in this regard, but it is a little ambiguous. Rabbi Aharon HaKohen of Lunel, one of the Provencal rabbis at the turn of the 14th century, wrote: "Someone who goes around the hills and forests seeking a bird's nest in order to fulfill the mitzvah of *shiluach hakein*, receives reward and is not considered a fool, even though he is exempt from searching after it" (*Orchot Chaim, Hilchot Shabbat, Hilchot Kiddush* 20). I am not convinced that this means that he saw a positive aspect in seeking to perform the mitzvah; rather than praising such an action, he merely notes that the person "receives reward and is not considered a fool." We must also note that it is possible that Rabbi Aharon HaKohen was referring to a case where the person will be eating the eggs as part of his nutrition, and would not sanction it in a case where the person would not be interested in the eggs.

mitzvah.[89] He himself considers that this is a contravention of the Talmud's ruling; yet on the other hand, he permits a person to recapture the mother bird after sending it away and eat it, and even states that this is a precious opportunity, "since a mitzvah was performed with it."[90] This is diametrically opposed to the rationalist approach that the prohibition of taking both mother and young serves to perpetuate the species.

Today, it is common for people to seek out opportunities to fulfill the mitzvah. As noted earlier, there are photographs of numerous prominent rabbis performing the mitzvah, even though they presumably did not "happen across" a nest. However, the reason for this zeal is not only due to the Zohar's explanation of the purpose of this mitzvah; it also relates to the rewards that are promised for it. The nature of these rewards is discussed in the next section.

V. Rewards and their Logic

Good Days and a Long Life

Shiluach hakein is virtually unique amongst mitzvot in terms of the rewards promised in the Torah; along with honoring one's parents, it is the only mitzvah for which the Torah describes the reward. *Shiluach hakein* also stands out from other mitzvot with regard to the list of rewards promised in the Midrash. Those of the mystical school saw the rewards as reason for one to make an effort to perform the mitzvah, even if one does not want the young. Those of a rationalist inclination saw the rationale behind the rewards in a way that made sense only if one actually wants the young.

The Torah promises a good, long life in reward for this mitzvah. The Mishnah elaborates upon the significance of this:

> And if for an easy mitzvah which [costs] about an *issar*, the Torah states, "So that it may be good for you and your days will be lengthened," all the more so for the more serious *mitzvot* in the Torah. (Mishnah, *Chullin* 12:5)

---

[89] Rabbi Yosef Chaim, Responsa *Torah Lishmah* 277.

[90] Responsa *Torah Lishmah* 276.

The medieval authorities explained the Biblical rewards as logical recompense for the compassion displayed. The promise of God being good to you was explained very straightforwardly to mean that He will be compassionate, in reward for the compassion displayed to the mother bird.[91] Obviously this only makes sense if the mitzvah is one of compassion, not cruelty, which in turn must mean that the person actually wants the young. The "lengthening of days" (i.e. extra life) was explained to be in reward for not taking the mother bird, hence enabling her to have further offspring (i.e. extra life).[92] This likewise only makes sense in the context of a person having to suppress his desire to take the bird for himself. Rabbi Yosef Bechor Shor (12th century) explains that such a reward is always promised for *mitzvot* that come at financial cost; accordingly, this likewise makes sense only if one would have wanted the bird to eat.

In fact, Chatam Sofer points out that this idea is inherent in the Mishnah itself, which speaks about the mitzvah costing an *issur*. The description of personal cost demonstrates that the mitzvah only applies in a case where one would have wanted to take the mother bird to eat.[93]

Midrashic Rewards

In addition to the rewards promised in Scripture, the Midrash adds several other promised rewards. One of these is the promise of children:

> There are *mitzvot* whose reward is wealth, and there are *mitzvot* whose reward is honor. And what is the reward for this mitzvah? That if you do not have children, I will grant you children. How do we know this? As it is stated, "Send away the mother," and what reward do you take? "You shall take the young." (*Midrash Devarim Rabbah* 6:6[94])

---

[91] Ibn Ezra, Rabbeinu Bachya. Chizkuni explained it to be a general promise that is described as referring to the lengthening of days.

[92] Ibn Ezra, Rabbeinu Bachya, Chizkuni, and Seforno. *Perush Baalei HaTosafos* states that the lengthening of days refers to one lengthening the days of the mother bird by leaving her alive.

[93] Responsa *Chatam Sofer, Orach Chaim* 100; *Chatam Sofer* to *Chullin* 142a.

[94] Similarly in *Yalkut Shimoni, Devarim* 930, and *Midrash Tanchuma, Ki Tetze.*

This reward fits well with the rationalist approach; even though one desires to eat the mother, one lets her go, thereby enabling her to have more children, and as a reward, one is blessed with children.[95] According to the mystical/obligatory approach, there is no obvious reason for this reward. One has not put oneself out and allowed her to have more children if one never would have stopped her from doing so in the first place without the mitzvah. (Some claim that this is not an independent reward at all, merely an implicit component of the blessing of having one's days lengthened.[96])

Another reward promised in the Midrash is that one will be able to build a new home:

> How do we know that one mitzvah drags along another? As it is written, "When you happen across a nest of birds… Send away the mother… That it should be good for you and your days shall be lengthened"; and what is written afterwards? "When you build a new house…"—you shall merit to build a new house. (*Midrash Tanchuma, Ki Tetze* 1[97])

This reward likewise makes perfect sense in light of the rationalist view of the mitzvah. The person desired the entire nest of birds, but he nevertheless let the mother bird go to produce a new nest. As a reward, he will likewise be blessed with a new home. But according to the mystical/obligatory approach, there is no obvious reason for this reward.[98]

The next reward promised in the Midrash is the hastening of the Messiah:

> Another explanation: What does it mean, "Send away the mother"? That if you fulfill this mitzvah, you will hasten the coming of the King Messiah, about whom it is written, "sending." How do we know? As it is written,

---

[95] *Likkutei Batar Likkutei*, citing Chatam Sofer. Ktav Sofer provides a different explanation for the reward, but one that is likewise connected to the mitzvah being one of compassion, not cruelty.

[96] Rabbi Yehudah Assad, *Dvire Mahari*, vol. II p. 62; Rabbi Avraham Shmuel Sofer, *Chashav Sofer al haTorah*, p. 219.

[97] Similarly in *Midrash Devarim Rabbah* 6:4.

[98] *Kli Yakar* suggests a connection relating to the mitzvah opposing the Aristotelian eternal universe and supporting belief in the creation of a new world, but this hardly seems straightforward.

"sending the ox and donkey" (Isaiah 32:20). (*Midrash Devarim Rabbah* 6:7)

This is the first reward for which there is no obvious connection to the rationalist approach that the mitzvah is one of compassion. Accordingly, it is stated that this reward fits with the explanation offered by the Zohar, whereby causing suffering to the mother bird sets a process into motion which results in God feeling pity for the Jews in exile.[99] However, this is by no means conclusive. Others relate the hastening of the Messiah to the building of a new Temple, which in turn is related to the reward of building a new home that we discussed above.[100] It may also be related to the following reward. The Midrash continues to state that another reward is that it will hasten the coming of Elijah the Prophet:

> Another explanation: Rabbi Tanchuma said: If you fulfill this mitzvah, you hasten the coming of Elijah the Prophet, about whom it is written "sending," as it is said, "Behold, I am sending Elijah the Prophet to you, and he shall come and console you" (Malachi 3). How do we know? As it is said, "And he shall restore the hearts of the fathers upon the sons" (ibid.) (Ibid.)

Here, while the reward fits with both approaches to the mitzvah, it seems to fit better with the rationalist approach. Rabbi David Luria explains that just as the mother bird is consoled by being spared to raise further children, so too Elijah consoles the Jewish People.

In summary: Of the various rewards for the mitzvah that are listed in the Midrash, some can be reconciled with both the rationalist and mystic approaches to the mitzvah, but others, when one considers the logic

---

[99] Rabbi Avraham Gombiner (c.1633-c.1683), *Zayit Ra'anan* to *Yalkut Shimoni* 530; Rabbi Alexander Susskind (d. 1794), *Yesod VeShoresh Ha-Avodah, Shaar Hakolel* 20; Rabbi Eiyahu Schlesinger, Responsa *Shoalin VeDorshin*, vol. 4 p. 542, based on Rabbi Yosef Meir Weiss (1838-1909), *Imrei Yosef* to Deut. 22:7.

[100] *Baal HaTurim* to Deut. 22:7; Rabbi Chanoch HaKohen, in R. Rosenbaum, *Sefer HaZikaron leRav Moshe Lifschitz*, p. 63. In a different explanation, Rabbi Hirsch Dachawitz in *Pri Shlomo* pp. 84-85 relates it to the verse speaking about sending out animals free; he explains that *shiluach hakein* involves the idea of letting everything be under the rule of God alone, which will be a feature of the Messianic Era.

behind them, clearly support the rationalist approach and oppose the mystical approach.

Highlighting Anti-Rationalism

The Vilna Gaon discusses the fact that *shiluach hakein* and honoring one's parents are the only *mitzvot* for which the Torah promises a good and long life.[101] While we have seen above how the rationalist approach easily accounts for this, the Vilna Gaon takes a very different approach in explaining why these two *mitzvot* are highlighted as receiving the same reward. He takes the position that while honoring one's parents is an act of kindness, sending away the mother bird is, following the Zohar's explanation, an act of cruelty. The Vilna Gaon explains that a spiritually complete person must contain both traits. If one is only performing *mitzvot* of compassion, this does not mean that one is a servant of God; one might simply be a compassionate person by nature. It is therefore necessary to also have *mitzvot* of cruelty, just as Abraham was commanded to slaughter his son, in order to demonstrate that one is acting out of allegiance to God rather than following one's character.

The idea that one might have to sometimes override one's natural compassion in order to demonstrate loyalty to God is not innately an anti-rationalist position. And surely all would agree that it is legitimate and sometimes essential to inflict suffering upon animals for the greater good of mankind.[102] However, the Vilna Gaon appears to be going further than that. While the rationalist camp understood that such a requirement may occur on a rare basis—such as with the *akeidah*—they apparently did not accept that it would be legislated into a normative mitzvah.[103] Any *mitzvot* that appeared to be cruel, such as slaughtering Amalek and so on, were always explained in such a way as to show how they were just. Furthermore, the Vilna Gaon does not make any mention of *shiluach hakein* being a rare aberration for a specific purpose, in contrast to the

---

[101] Commentary to Proverbs 30:17, and *Imrei No'am* to *Berachot* 33b.

[102] Such as experimenting upon animals in order to devise medical cures.

[103] Compare the Chatam Sofer with regard to this mitzvah: "Surely it is written. 'Its ways are ways of pleasantness;' it is inconceivable that God would command us to be cruel!"

mitzvot normally being ethical; instead, he presents matters simply as there being some *mitzvot* that are compassionate, and some that are cruel, with both being equally beneficial to the one that performs them. It seems that he has a negative view of someone who performs *mitzvot* due to their resonating with his sense of compassion. Thus, his presentation appears to be stating that the *mitzvot* as a whole are not to be interpreted as an ethical system, rather they are acts of obedience. If this analysis is correct, it is the ultimate antithesis to the rationalist view, and *shiluach hakein* is taken as the indicator of it.

Modern Anti-Rationalists

Modern followers of the mystical approach are enthusiastic about the rewards that are promised by the Midrash. They do not analyze the rationale behind the promise of rewards, which (as we have discussed) reveal that these generally make sense only in a case where one actually wants the birds. In corollary with the mystical belief that the fundamental purpose of the mitzvah is to engineer compassion for the Jewish People, the rewards add yet another reason to send away the mother bird even if one does not want the young. As a result, great efforts are made to fulfill the mitzvah. There are even advertisements for people to fulfill the mitzvah of *shiluach hakein,* publicized by community activists/ entrepreneurs who seek out suitable nests and charge up to $600 for the facilitation of the mitzvah.

Based on the wording of some of these advertisements, it seems that the reason why many are willing to pay such sums is not for the sake of serving God, and not even for the benefits to the Jewish People promised by the Zohar, but rather for the personal rewards that they anticipate. But since the promised rewards include obtaining a livelihood, finding a spouse, and conceiving children, those who are in unfortunate need for these blessings find such an opportunity to be tempting.

Above: Some *shiluach hakein* advertisements from New York

Conclusion

If we look back at the history of this mitzvah, both in its laws and explanations, we see a clear pattern. In the Midrash, *shiluach hakein* was seen as demonstrating compassion, and there were rewards to reflect that. For the rationalist Rishonim, it was so clearly a mitzvah of compassion that a Talmudic statement indicating otherwise had to be either rejected or reinterpreted. It likewise does not appear to be a coincidence that the Rishonim understood the mitzvah as only applying in a case where one actually wants the young.

With the rise of kabbalah, the mitzvah was transformed into an act of cruelty that engineers a process that causes God to help His people. Correspondingly, the view arose that the mitzvah is obligatory even if one does not want the young, or at least recommended. With the Vilna Gaon, *shiluach hakein* even became a flag bearer for anti-rationalism. The Zohar's view began to become the dominant approach.[104]

---

[104] One contemporary volume of the topic, *Kan Tzippor*, has the Zohar's words preceding the table of contents, as setting the tone for the entire work.

Most contemporary halachic authorities do rule that the mitzvah is optional, but this is merely due to the fact that they are operating via a purely halachic analysis, without factoring in the assumed rationale for the mitzvah. Nevertheless, the fact that many of them still consider it praiseworthy to perform the mitzvah, whereas the Rishonim would not have said this, means that they have radically transformed both the understanding *and* the application of the mitzvah.

The striking difference between the rationalist and mystical approaches to the mitzvah presents a difficulty for those who try to portray Jewish intellectual history as being monolithic. Accordingly, we find contemporary rabbinic authors engaging in feats of intellectual gymnastics in an attempt to harmonize the rationalist and mystical approaches.

Some attempt this by engaging in outright revisionism of the rationalist approach. In a popular contemporary work of the laws of *shiluach hakein*, which seeks to present a normative viewpoint, it opens with the following ruling:

> From the standpoint of the essential law, there is no obligation to travel around the hills after a nest, in order to fulfill the mitzvah of *shiluach hakein*; yet nevertheless one should certainly make an effort to fulfill it, and it is a great matter. (Weinberger, *Shalech Teshalach*, p. 27[105])

Another such work claims that even those who saw the mitzvah as optional, and who considered that it does not apply if one does not want the young, would still say that it is praiseworthy to perform it.[106] As we have seen, both these works are severely distorting the halachic picture.

With regard to whether the nature of the mitzvah is one of compassion or cruelty, outright revision of the rationalist approach was not an option, due to the statements of the Rishonim being explicit. Instead, what we find are highly implausible attempts to show how the mitzvah is

---

[105] In the English edition of this work, pp. 57-58, he writes that even according to the *poskim* who maintain that the mitzvah is not obligatory, it is "certainly commendable to pursue this mitzvah."

[106] Rabbi Dan Schwarz, *Kan Tzippor*, p. 140.

simultaneously compassionate and cruel.[107] While it is true that the act itself can involve aspects of both—the mother does suffer some distress upon being forcibly sent away, and there is compassion in not taking both mother and young—the presentation and focus of each explanation in the Midrash, Rishonim and Acharonim does not permit such reconciliations.

There is no intellectually honest way of avoiding Chatam Sofer's conclusion that the rationalist and mystic approaches to this mitzvah are irreconcilable. Menachem Kellner has compared the rationalist and mystic views of Judaism in general, with Rambam and the Zohar as paradigms of each model, and has shown that the difference between them is vast.[108] *Shiluach hakein* is a particularly striking example of this difference.

Martin Gordon has extensively documented the phenomenon of how with some *mitzvot*, the rise of mysticism caused a dramatic revolution in the understanding of the mitzvah.[109] For example, for the rationalist Rishonim, mezuzah serves only to remind one of one's duties to God; whereas with the rise of mysticism came the idea that it also serves as a metaphysical protective device for the home. For the rationalist Rishonim, the mitzvah of washing one's hands in the morning serves only hygienic and psychological purposes, whereas with the rise of mysticism came the idea that one is removing harmful spiritual forces. This sometimes even had halachic ramifications, notwithstanding the alleged independence of halachah from mystical explanations of its reasoning. In tracing the history of the mitzvah of *shiluach hakein*, from Scripture through Chazal through to the halachic authorities of today, we see a similar metamorphosis—

---

[107] Weinberger cites Rabbi Shaul Barzam (as quoted in *Zichron Shaul* vol. II p. 161) stating that the act as a whole is one of cruelty, but it is done in a relatively compassionate way. Rabbi Aharon Yehudah Grossman, in *VeDarashta VeChakarta* pp. 464-465, presents a similarly far-fetched reconciliation of the rationalist approach with the mystical approach; he even acknowledges that it is strained, but states that he is doing it so as to avoid the sharp conflict between them (in accordance with *haredi* protocol).

[108] Menachem Kellner, *Maimonides' Confrontation with Mysticism*; see especially p. 39 and p. 288. See too Yaakov Katz, "Tradition and Crisis" (Hebrew), p. 255.

[109] "*Netilat Yadayim Shel Shacharit*: Ritual of Crisis or Dedication?" *Gesher* vol. 8 (5741) pp. 36-72; "Mezuzah: Protective Amulet or Religious Symbol?" *Tradition* 16:4 (Summer 1977) pp. 7-40. Both these articles can be downloaded at www.rationalistjudaism.com.

from compassion to cruelty; from a mitzvah so clearly rationalistic that any statements otherwise must be reinterpreted, to a mitzvah that celebrates the anti-rationalist approach; and from a mitzvah that is preferably unnecessary to a mitzvah that one should actively pursue. Notwithstanding apologetic attempts to interpret matters otherwise, it is an absolute and striking transformation of a mitzvah.

FOURTEEN

What Can One Do For The Deceased?

Introduction

When it comes to losing a loved one, and dealing with that loss, we may wonder: What types of deeds can we do for them? Can anyone do something for them, or only certain people? And in which way can our deeds be of benefit?

Today, it is widely believed that one can provide an *aliyah* (spiritual elevation) for the *neshamah* (soul) of someone who has passed away. It is further widely believed that anyone can do this. And it is further popularly held that the best way to do this is to study Torah on behalf of the deceased, with an oral declaration that the Torah is being studied to that end.

However, if we analyze all the sources and practices in Jewish history, we see a very different picture. There are four distinct approaches with regard to doing something for someone who has passed away. They can be briefly described as follows:

1. *Aliyah*—an **elevation** of the person's soul in the afterlife, that anyone can enable via studying Torah or performing good deeds for their sake.

2. *Zecher*—creating a **remembrance** for the person in this world by honoring them.

3. *Kapparah*—providing **atonement** for the soul of the person in the afterlife, via prayer and/or charity. This is mentioned in the Midrash and in the Talmud, though there is a dispute as to the extent of its applicability.

4. *Zechus*—providing a **merit** for the person, by way of their descendants and disciples. This is mentioned in the Talmud, and has different permutations.

We shall now explore these different approaches in detail.

"An *Aliyah* for the *Neshamah*" - The Modern/Mystical Approach

The mystical approach essentially is of the view that when a person has passed away, the person continues to exist, albeit in Heaven rather than earth, but in a very real and present sense. Specifically, just as a living person exists under a continually changing set of circumstances, so too a person who has passed on is living under a continually changing set of circumstances. Just as you can help out a living person—give them a ride, host them for a meal—so too you can help out a person who has passed away.

How can one help them out? According to the mystical approach, *mitzvot* create spiritual rewards as discrete entities. These can be transferred to other people, just as one can transfer material goods to other people. This would apply to any mitzvah at all. By doing *mitzvot*, you can make someone's afterlife a more pleasant experience, by bringing them into a higher spiritual realm—one can "elevate their soul."

Furthermore, according to the mystical approach, the study of Torah creates the most "spiritual energy" of all *mitzvot*. Accordingly, it provides the greatest elevation for the soul.

Another aspect of this approach is that anyone in the world can provide this benefit to anyone that has passed away. All that is required is for them to make a declaration that the Torah study or mitzvah that they are performing is being done in order to elevate the soul of so-and-so. As long as this declaration is recited, the reward for their study and actions is directed appropriately.

Problems with the Modern/Mystical Approach

The modern/mystical approach is contrary to the position of the Geonim and Rishonim who weighed in on this topic. They state that ordinarily a person cannot do *mitzvot* to help the deceased (with the exceptions that we shall later discuss of a person's descendants or disciples), for two reasons.

One is that according to the rationalist approach, someone who has passed from this world is no longer under changing circumstances. Rambam makes it clear that the person who has passed away exists in a fixed and timeless relationship with God.[1] Maharam Chalavah, a prominent 14th century Torah scholar who was a disciple of Rashba, writes as follows:

> There is no doubt that what one person does for another after their passing is of no benefit or aid, for each person is judged according to what they are at the time of their death. In accordance with the person's level and attainments at the time that his soul departs from his body, so will he attain elevations and merit light with the Light of Life, and there is no additional elevation or benefit in that which others do afterwards to benefit him... (Maharam Chalavah, Responsa, #17)

But there is a second and more fundamental reason why the Rishonim maintain that one cannot do *mitzvot* to help the deceased. One cannot do something to elevate or otherwise benefit someone else's spiritual position, whether they are alive or not. According to Rambam, *mitzvot* affect society, our intellects and our personalities; other authorities express the function of *mitzvot* as creating a relationship with God. Either way, *mitzvot* do not produce spiritual energy, such that one could transfer this to others.

Rashba cites a responsum from Rav Sherira Gaon making this point. Rav Sherira suggests that it might be possible that someone who has passed away can be saved from punishment in the afterlife via the prayers of a righteous person, or via charity, though he stresses that this is not certain. However, he notes that there is no way in which a person can transfer the reward from his *mitzvot* to someone else:

---

[1] Rambam, Commentary to *Avot* 4:22. Note that Rambam was also of the view that mourners do not recite *kaddish* for the deceased. See the later discussion in this chapter regarding *kaddish*.

470

A person cannot merit someone else with reward; his elevation and greatness and pleasure from the radiance of the Divine Presence is only in accordance with his deeds. Even if all the righteous people in the world were to seek mercy for him, and all the righteous acts were to be done in his merit, it would be of no help to him... (Rashba, Responsa, Vol. 7 #539)

Maharam Alashkar cites Rav Hai Gaon who firmly rejects the notion that one can transfer the reward of a mitzvah to another person and explains why this is impossible:

These concepts are nonsense and one should not rely upon them. How can one entertain the notion that the reward of good deeds performed by one person should go to another person? Surely the verse states, "The righteousness of a righteous person is on him," (Ezek. 18:20) and likewise it states, "And the wickedness of a wicked person is upon him." Just as nobody can be punished on account of somebody else's sin, so too nobody can merit the reward of someone else. How could one think that the reward for *mitzvot* is something that a person can carry around with him, such that he can transfer it to another person? (Maharam Alashkar, Responsa #101)

The same position was expressed earlier by Avraham bar Chiyya in *Hegyon haNefesh Ha-Atzuvah*,[2] and later by Rabbi Yehudah HaChassid in *Sefer Chassidim*.[3] It is also implicit in the writings of many other authorities, who speak only about the possibility of descendants and disciples of the deceased being able to benefit them (in a way that we shall later discuss). They make no mention of other people being able to benefit the deceased via studying Torah or performing *mitzvot*, and some of them explicitly state that this would be impossible. Consider the statement of the great halakhist R. Benjamin Ze'ev ben Mattitya of Arta (d. c. 1540):

---

[2] *Hegyon haNefesh Ha-Atzuvah* p. 32. He states that generally, prayers and other deeds performed after a person dies cannot help the deceased, with the exception of returning an item stolen by the deceased, and teaching Torah that originated with the deceased (which is the concept of a merit for the deceased that we shall later explore).

[3] *Sefer Chassidim* 605.

How can the merits of Reuven be of benefit to his brothers Shimon and Levi? What could his *mitzvot* do for them?! (Responsa *Binyamin Ze'ev* 202)

A *Zecher* for the *Neshamah*

Although classical sources maintain that with the exception of descendants and disciples, one cannot perform *mitzvot* to assist the deceased in the next world, this does not mean that we cannot do anything for them. We can express our love towards them and honor their memory by creating a *zecher*, a remembrance, in *this* world. An honor in this world is not to be trivialized. God Himself, when addressing those who faithfully follow His will but are unable to conceive children, does not speak of their reward in the next world, but instead speaks of their *yad vashem*, monument and name, in *this* world:

> And I shall give them, in My House and within My walls, a monument and a name, better than sons or daughters; I will give them an everlasting name, which shall not perish. (Isaiah 56:5)

There are many different ways of remembering and honoring someone, but there are two aspects to providing the greatest honor. One is with regard to the objective value and extent of the honor. The second aspect is that the honor is made more meaningful if it is related in some way to the person who has passed away. Rashi refers to the Geonim as describing how on the anniversary of the passing of a great person, rabbis from all around would gather at his grave and give classes to the public. But instead of saying that this was done to elevate their souls, Rashi says that this was done to *honor* them.[4] A Torah scholar is honored by institutions and lectures of Torah study; a person who helps the community is honored by institutions and deeds of kindness to the community.

---

[4] Rashi to *Yevamot* 122a s.v. *telasa riglei*. See too Responsa Ri Migash 47 and *Nimukei Yosef* to *Bava Kama* 16b, addressing the Gemara's statement that one should not wear *tefillin* and so on at a cemetery, since it is disrespectful to the dead, who can no longer perform *mitzvot*. They rule that one may still hold Torah lectures by a person's grave, since these are being done in his honor. If there was a concept of learning Torah to benefit the soul of the dead, they would surely have mentioned it in this context.

Atonement—Charity and Prayer

Thus far, we have seen that the modern mystical approach is that even those who are not descendants or disciples of the deceased can help them in the next world with every mitzvah, while the classical approach is that they cannot do any mitzvah to help them in the next world. But there is an intermediate position, which maintains that there are two things that anyone can do for the deceased in the next world: prayer and charity. These are presented as being done to atone for the deceased.

The earliest reference to praying on behalf of the deceased is found in the Second Book of Maccabees. This speaks of an incident where people had died as a result of a particular sin. Judah the Maccabee collected money to pay for sin offerings, which is described as being performed as atonement on behalf of those who died.[5] There are also references in the Talmud to praying on behalf of the deceased.[6]

The Midrash *Sifre* discusses the concept of providing atonement for those who have passed away. In discussing the mitzvah of *eglah arufah*—the calf that is sacrificed to atone for an unsolved murder—the Midrash explains that the Kohanim seek forgiveness not only for all living members of the nation, but even for all the members of the nation who have *ever* lived:

> "The priests say, Forgive Your people of Israel, O Lord, [whom You redeemed]" (Deut. 21:8). When it says, "whom You redeemed," this teaches that this forgiveness atones for those who left Egypt. "Forgive Your people"—this refers to those who are alive. "Whom you redeemed"—this refers to those who are dead. This teaches that the dead require atonement; hence, we learn that a murderer effects sin all the way back to those who left Egypt. "Whom you redeemed"—You redeemed us in order that there should not be any murderers among us. (Midrash *Sifre*, *piska* 210 on Deut. 21:8)

However, this Midrash, according to several authorities, is limited to a very restricted context. It is referring specifically to a case of atonement on

---

[5] Book 12:43-45.

[6] See *Makkot* 11b, regarding Moshe praying on behalf of Yehudah. Note that this is praying to God for Him to intervene, not changing the spiritual level of the deceased.

behalf of the entire community for the crime of murder.[7] As the Midrash states, because the Jewish People were redeemed from Egypt with the understanding that they would be a morally upright people, a case of murder calls the entire redemption from Egypt into question; hence, atonement is required.

There is another way in which we see a difference between atoning for a deceased individual and atoning for a community. The Talmud states that if a person was due to bring a sin offering but died, the offering is no longer brought; however, if the sin offering was being brought for the community, it is still brought.[8] It relates this to the view of Rav Pappa, based in turn on the Midrash cited above, that only for a community is it possible to gain atonement after their death.

Accordingly, some authorities maintain that Midrash is only presenting an option (or perhaps: a need) to obtain atonement after death in the case of a community, and according to some, only in the case of atoning for murder. Normally, one cannot benefit the souls of those who have passed away by giving charity on their behalf.[9]

Still, others see charity as always atoning for those who have passed away, regardless of the nature of their sins. A late addition to the Midrash Tanhuma[10] refers to the aforementioned Midrash Sifre and applies the concept to broader circumstances. It states that we mention the dead on Yom Kippur and allocate charity on their behalf. (This is the origin of the custom of Yizkor, which only later spread to the other Festivals.)

---

[7] Maharam Chalavah, ibid; Rabbeinu Avigdor, cited by *Shibbolei HaLeket*, quoted in *Beis Yosef, Orach Chaim* 284:7. Levush, cited by *Pri Megadim* 47:2, suggests that since many people also engage in embarrassing others, which is similar to killing them, it is also appropriate to offer prayers and charity for anyone who has passed away, as an atonement for any acts of embarrassing someone that they may have done.

[8] Talmud, *Horiyot* 6a.

[9] Maharam Chalavah, ibid.; Rabbeinu Avigdor, cited by *Shibbolei HaLeket*, in *Beis Yosef, Orach Chaim* 284:7.

[10] *Tanhuma, Devarim* 32:1. It is presented as being "an additional section." This view is attributed to a Rabbi Shemaryah by *Tashbatz Katan* (#440) and by Maharam Chalavah (who sharply disputes its legitimacy). See too Rabbeinu Bechaya to Deut. 21:8, quoting Midrash Pesikta.

However, several authorities point out that charity is only being mentioned here as a way to save a person from punishment, not as a way to actively provide reward to someone in the next world.[11] In other words, an account of how one can elevate someone from purgatory does not mean that one can elevate a person already in Heaven to higher levels.

It should also be noted that even according to those Rishonim who are of the view that charity benefits the deceased, it is the exception that proves the rule. It is specifically and only charity and prayer that are mentioned as being done in order to atone for those who passed away. No other *mitzvot* are said to be of benefit in this regard.

But why would charity be unique, and what is the mechanism in which it would work? R. Elazar of Worms (known as Rokeach), an important 13th century authority, suggests that giving charity for the dead on Yom Kippur is associated with the half-shekel contribution to the Tabernacle, which is described as a *kofer nefesh*, a ransom for the soul. Rokeach raises the question of how it could help the deceased, and explains it as a form of prayer. One is beseeching God, he says, that God, Who knows everything, surely knows that this person would have given this charity were he still able to do so.[12]

Still, this is very difficult to understand. How is it relevant that the deceased *would have* given more charity if he were still alive? A person who has passed away would certainly have done more good (and bad) deeds if he was still alive, but surely a person is judged based on what they have done in this lifetime, not on what they would have done in further lifetimes. And how does the person giving charity today have any bearing on that?

Whatever the mechanism, we see that the original sources regarding giving charity on behalf of someone who has passed away are very few, limited in scope, and not relevant to other *mitzvot*; in fact, they indicate that other *mitzvot* are *not* of benefit to the deceased. Furthermore, as we have seen, the rationalist Torah scholars rejected any notion of being able

---

[11] This point is explicitly made by Rav Sherira Gaon and *Sefer Hassidim* 605.

[12] *Rokeach* 217, also cited in *Beis Yosef Orach Chaim*, end of 621, and later by *Magen Avraham*.

to perform righteous deeds that would benefit people who have passed away. Nevertheless, others accepted that charity, if not other *mitzvot*, are of benefit. Rashba, for example, says that anyone can pray or give charity to help the deceased.[13]

Eventually it became normative to rate giving charity as appropriate in all cases of people who have passed away. In any case, aside from the concept of atonement, giving charity provides an honor for the person who has passed away.[14]

"A Child Grants Merit to a Parent"

The fourth and final way of doing something on behalf of the deceased is very different from the first three. There is a story in the Midrash about how Rabbi Yochanan Ben Zakkai (or, in another version, Rabbi Akiva) encounters a person undergoing tremendous suffering. The suffering person relates that he is actually dead, and he is suffering for his sins. The person says that he will only gain atonement when his son studies Torah and says *Barchu*. The rabbi finds the man's son and makes it happen, whereupon the man enters Heaven.[15]

Today, this story is commonly cited to show that one can study Torah to benefit the soul of someone who has passed away. However, this story is specifically *not* conveying that idea—note that it was *not* an option for Rabbi Yochanan Ben Zakkai to study Torah and thereby save the man from his suffering.[16] In fact, the story is teaching a different idea: the

---

[13] Rashba, Responsa 5:49. He refers to the Talmud, *Sotah* 10b, about David praying on behalf of Avshalom and raising him from Gehinnom.

[14] With regard to the possibility of giving charity via supporting Torah study, here too there are fundamental differences between various schools of thought among the Rishonim and Acharonim, but this is beyond the scope of our discussion.

[15] The earliest source of this Midrash is in *Tanna Dvei Eliyahu Zuta* 2:17, which mentions Rabbi Yochanan ben Zakkai. In *Masechet Kallah Rabbasi* 2, a similar story is told about Rabbi Akiva. *Menorat HaMaor* (*Klal* I, *Ner* I, 2:1) attributes this story to *Midrash Tanhuma*.

[16] Responsa *Binyamin Ze'ev* 202 points out that it wasn't even an option for Rabbi Akiva to find other relatives. Only the son sufficed.

concept expressed in the Talmud with the phrase "a son can grant merit to the father."[17]

There are several references to people in the Torah receiving a favorable judgment, or a blessing, as a result of their descendants. Noah is said to have been saved from the Deluge in the merit of his descendants;[18] Abraham is said to have been promised the Land of Israel in the merit of his descendants who would bring the Omer offering.[19] In all these cases, the person is being rewarded for the deeds of other people, but this is possible because they are people who exist as a result of him.

Such a merit cannot be provided by people other than descendants.[20] Merits cannot be outsourced, because they are not something that you *give* to the deceased. Rather, it is something that is revealed about what the deceased brought to the world. As Rabbi Yehudah HaChassid explains:

> But how can a deed atone for someone who did not perform that deed while he was alive? …However, thus stated the Holy One: A son provides merit for the father. For example, if the father was a sinner, but ensured that his son studied Torah and performed good deeds, then since it was due to the father that the son thus merited, the son provides merit to the father. If the parents instruct the children to perform [good] deeds after their passing, then when the children perform these deeds, it is as though the parents performed them. (*Sefer Chassidim* 101)

Rabbeinu Yonah likewise writes that the merit of a woman for the next world comes as a result of her children acting appropriately; when they are God-fearing and busy with Torah and *mitzvot*, it is rated as though she is alive and doing this.[21] Several other authorities explain similarly.[22] (Note that the reason why all these justifications/explanations are necessary is

---

[17] Talmud, *Sanhedrin* 104a.

[18] Midrash Rabbah, Bereishis 29:5.

[19] Midrash Rabbah, Vayikra 28:6.

[20] See Rabbi Ben-Zion Uzziel, *Mishpetei Uziel* (Tel Aviv 1935) vol. I *Orach Chaim* 2 pp. 7-14 for extensive discussion of this topic.

[21] Rabbeinu Yonah, *Iggeres HaTeshuvah* 3.

[22] Rashba, Responsa 5:45; Maharsha, *Chiddushei Aggados, Sanhedrin* 104.

that normally it is *not* possible to benefit someone who has passed away; this indicates that they did not believe in the mystical approach of transferring reward from *mitzvot* to benefit the deceased.) The great sixteenth-century halakhist R. Benjamin Ze'ev ben Mattitya of Arta discusses this at length:

> A son provides credit to his father, because the son *is* the father—all the *mitzvot* and good deeds of the son result from him. But the merits and *mitzvot* of other relatives do not assist the sole of the deceased at all. For how can the merits of Reuven be of benefit to his brothers Shimon and Levi? What could his *mitzvot* do for them?! (Responsa *Binyamin Ze'ev* 202)

Merits accrued via the descendants in this way are automatic. There is no need for any declaration to be made that "this mitzvah is being performed as a merit to my ancestor." The achievements of the descendants of the person are automatically a credit to them.

What does "providing a merit" actually mean? There are different possibilities. Some will see it more in terms of providing a favorable judgment in the next world, whereas others will see it more in terms of providing a special form of honor in this world. But, whatever one's approach, the uniqueness of *zechus* is that it only comes about as a result of the person who has passed away. It is not something that can be independently created by someone else.

While the Talmud only describes a child as providing a merit for the parent, this can be understood to likewise encompass anything in this world that exists as a consequence of the person who has passed away. Rabbi Yaakov Skili, a disciple of Rashba, notes that although, generally speaking, someone who has passed away remains in a fixed state according to their character at the time of their passing, their judgment can be changed as a result of the actions of their children or their disciples.[23]

Furthermore, with the story of Rabbi Yochanan ben Zakkai, we see that even though he was unrelated and formerly unknown to the man who died, he was nevertheless able to assist him by bringing to light the latent

---

[23] *Toras HaMincha, Parashas Nitzavim.*

potential of his son. Creating a *zechus* cannot be outsourced in the way that one can outsource a *zecher* and a *kapparah*. But others can enhance and amplify the *zechus* that begins with the descendants or disciples of the person who has passed away. It becomes part of the person's merit, since he/she provided the raw material for others to develop.

Recent and Contemporary Perspectives

As we have seen, according to classical sources, the only people who can benefit the deceased are their descendants and others who are a credit to them. The earliest source stating that *anyone* can do *mitzvot* to credit others, if only with regard to charity, appears to be R. Eliyahu b. Avraham Shlomo HaKohen of Izmir (1659-1729).[24] He states one can give charity as a merit even for a dead person who would not have been charitable when alive, provided that one issues an explicit declaration that one is giving it in his merit and would not give it otherwise. Since the charity is only being given because of the deceased, they receive credit for it.

R. Chaim ibn Attar (1696-1743, the *Ohr HaChaim*), writes that it is "straightforward that a person can give away the merit of a mitzvah and Torah study before he performs it, and the gift is effective."[25] This is strange, because as we have seen, classical authorities to weigh in on this topic not only said that it is not straightforward; they denied that it was at all viable. And the proof that R. Chaim ibn Attar gives for this, regarding the merit acquired by someone who supports Torah study, appears far from sufficient. In that case, it is not that the merit of studying Torah is being transferred from scholar A to supporter B, but rather, that B receives the merit of supporting Torah study.

Rabbi Akiva Eiger (1761-1837), in his will, asked for a notice to be published in newspapers requesting his students and friends to learn Mishnah as a credit to him.[26] This is frequently quoted as a source for the notion that anyone can learn *mishnayot* as an *aliyah* for anybody else. But

---

[24] *Me'il Tzedakah* (Lvov 5609), *siman* 1606. Also quoted approvingly by R. Rahamim Nissim Palaggi, *Yafeh LeLev* III, *Yoreh De'ah* 149:43.

[25] *Rishon LeTziyon, Yoreh De'ah* 249:6.

[26] *Allgemeine Zeitung des Judentums* (1837) 95 p. 378.

this overlooks the difference between people on whom R. Akiva Eiger had an influence—students and friends—and entirely unconnected people. Also, if people were learning for Rabbi Akiva Eiger because he asked them to, then obviously that is due to him; it is not the same as learning for a random person who did not request it.

Chevra Lomdei Mishna is an institution which collects funds in order to support Kollel students studying *l'iluy nishmat* people who have passed away. They also published the popular book *The Neshama Should Have An Aliyah*.[27] This book does not discuss the aforementioned views of the Talmud, Geonim and Rishonim, which show that there is no way to transfer Torah-credits to a stranger. Instead, the earliest source cited in support of the claim that one can transfer the credits for one's mitzvot to any designated person is the work *Sukkat Shalom*, published in 1883 by Rabbi Yisrael Gutmacher of Greiditz.

Acknowledging that it is not straightforward, R. Gutmacher innovates a complicated and difficult combination of arguments in order to explain the mechanism via which this could work.[28] He invokes the suggestion of the Rokeach regarding giving charity for the dead on Yom Kippur; as discussed above, Rokeach explains it as meaning that the deceased would surely have given charity were he still able to do so. This alone, notes R. Gutmacher, is not sufficient to explain how one can transfer the merit of Torah study. And so he also invokes the concept of the Yissacher-Zevulun partnership, whereby one receives reward for enabling Torah study, which, he says, shows that one can divide the reward for a mitzvah with others. Acknowledging that this alone would not suffice in this case—for the deceased has not actually been a partner to this Torah study—he states that the combination of this with the Rokeach's explanation provides the solution. How the two are combined is itself not at all straightforward, and R. Gutmacher has to create a further stretch to Rokeach's explanation; that one is saying to God that were he himself to be dead and the deceased to be alive, the deceased would surely have learned Torah on *his* behalf,

---

[27] Rabbi Tzvi Hebel, *The Neshama Should Have An Aliyah* (Chevrah Lomdei Mishnah/ Judaica Press 2009).

[28] *Sukkat Shalom* pp. 45b-55a.

and so they should be considered true partners, and the reward for the Torah study should be shared between them.

Needless to say, all this is very shaky. Rokeach is suggesting a way to justify a specific custom, of charity on Yom Kippur. To extrapolate a mechanism with far-ranging ramifications, whereby one can perform *any* mitzvah on behalf of *any* designated person, is far-fetched in the extreme. And the notion of creating a fictitious partnership in the Torah study, which enables the reward to be shared, is deeply problematic. With Yissacher and Zevulun, it is not as though there is a pooled reward which is evenly shared. Rather, Yissacher reaps the spiritual benefits of studying Torah, and Zevulun reaps the spiritual benefits of being someone who has supported Torah study. There would not appear to be any mechanism for creating this benefit for someone who didn't actually do anything.

All this takes us back to the discussions by the Geonim and Rishonim that we discussed at the beginning. There is simply no mechanism by which to transfer the reward or credit for a mitzvah to someone who had no fundamentally influential role in that mitzvah being performed. And that is why there is no mention of such a concept in traditional sources; whereas if such a concept were to exist, we would expect it to be very prominent.

At the Entrance to Gehinnom

On the website of Chevra Lomdei Mishna, accompanying some bold claims—"Imagine the merits that can be amassed for your dearly departed loved ones, as well as for yourself and your family, by tapping into the merit of Torah learning by dedicated, serious Torah scholars"—there is a page of sources to back all this up.[29] It is a slim list; just four sources are cited, of which three are contemporary works. The only pre-modern source that they provide is a second-hand citation from a contemporary work, *Pnei Baruch*,[30] which they quote as stating as follows: "Our Sages have said that Asher, son of the Patriarch Jacob, sits at the entrance to

---

[29] https://www.chevrahlomdeimishnah.org/learning-lzecher-nishmas/sources, accessed in June 2018.

[30] Rabbi Chaim Goldberg, *Pnei Boruch* (Jerusalem 1986) p. 422.

Gehinnom (Purgatory), and saves [from entering therein] anyone on whose behalf Mishnah is being studied."

This certainly would be a strong support for the notion that anyone can transfer Torah-credits to anyone else. Yet it seems that no such source actually exists![31] It cannot be found in the Talmud or Midrash or even the Rishonim. The earliest reference appears to be the Chida (1724-1806),[32] attributing it to earlier authorities, yet he too does not provide any source.

However, even more crucially, the statement, as cited both by Chida and in *Pnei Baruch*, does not actually say what Chevra Lomdei Mishnah quotes it as saying. Instead, what it says is as follows:

> Our Sages have said that Asher, son of Jacob, sits at the entrance to Gehinnom, and saves anyone who studies Mishnah. (Rabbi Chaim Goldberg, *Pnei Boruch*, p. 422)

It says that Asher saves *anyone who studies Mishnah*. It does not state that he saves anyone *on whose behalf* Mishnah is being studied!

Now, Rabbi Goldberg does follow this quote with a claim that this would also apply to anyone on whose behalf Mishnah is being studied. Yet this claim, quoted from Rabbi Meshulem Finkelstein (d. 1933),[33] was written with no source or justification. In any case, it is certainly not part of the alleged citation from the Sages.

Kaddish

The above discussion raises questions regarding the recital of *kaddish* for someone who has passed away. What function does it serve? And who can recite it? If there is no relative to recite *kaddish* for someone who has passed away, does it help for a non-relative to recite *kaddish*?

---

[31] Requests to Chevra Lomdei Mishnah to clarify their alleged source met with no response.

[32] Chida, *Moreh B'Etzba* (Livorno 1791) 2.

[33] R. Finkelstein writes it in his appendix to R. Ephraim Margoliyot, *Mateh Ephraim HaShalem* (Warsaw 1920), p. 304.

R. Benjamin Ze'ev ben Mattitya of Arta states that *kaddish* serves to provide a merit for the deceased. Accordingly, he says, there is indeed no purpose in it being recited by anyone other than the descendants.[34]

A more expansive discussion of this topic is given by Rav Ben-Zion Uzziel, who incorporates the concepts that we have discussed.[35] He notes that *kaddish* potentially fulfills several functions. One is to provide a merit for the deceased. This is accomplished via the deceased's descendant reciting a prayer which sanctifies God, especially since it is recited in public and leads the entire congregation to endorse it (via responding *Yehei Shemei…*). This function of *kaddish* can indeed only be fulfilled by a descendant of the deceased,[36] since only such a person is a credit to the deceased. Any other person is not able to effect a merit for the deceased.

However, Rav Uzziel lists two other functions of reciting *kaddish*. One is *tzidduk ha-din*—declaring loyalty to the concept of Divine justice even in the face of suffering. This is a duty that specifically befalls those who have personally suffered as a result of the loss of the person who has passed away. This also applies to relatives other than children.

Another function of *kaddish* is to honor the deceased, in this world. Since the *obligation* to provide honor falls upon the children, they should be the ones to recite *kaddish*. But such honor *can* be provided by anyone. Accordingly, if, for whatever reason, the children are unable to do so, others can provide this honor. (Though presumably this would require it being known that whoever is reciting *kaddish* is doing so on behalf of the deceased.)

Doing *Mitzvot* to Benefit Others

The above discussion is also applicable to the question of whether one can do *mitzvot* to benefit someone who is alive but in need of Divine assistance. In Orthodox Jewish society today, there are often calls for people to do *mitzvot*, such as learning Torah or separating *challah*, as a

---

[34] Responsa *Binyamin Ze'ev* 202.

[35] *Mishpetei Uziel* (Tel Aviv 1935) vol. I *Orach Chaim* 2 pp. 7-14.

[36] Rabbi Uzziel notes that this can be either a son or a daughter, and it can be either a child or a grandchild.

merit for people who are sick. Some even contract out *mitzvot*, requesting financial donations for studying Torah or doing other *mitzvot*, purportedly to help people in need of a *shidduch* or seeking children by transferring the credits for these *mitzvot* to their spiritual bank account. (Taking this logic to its ultimate conclusion, there have even been advertisements from someone offering the opportunity for people to transfer to him the debits in their spiritual bank account—i.e., the punishment awaiting them in the afterlife for their sins—in exchange for their money!)

Campaigning for people to do *mitzvot* on someone's behalf can be beneficial from the point of view of alerting and sensitizing the community to a person's plight. However, in terms of whether a person can actually transfer the reward for their own mitzvah to someone else, we have seen above that there is no basis in classical Judaism for this concept. One cannot transfer the reward for *mitzvot*, or the punishment for sins, to other people.[37] The traditional Jewish response to someone's illness is to pray on their behalf, not to attempt to do *mitzvot* on their behalf. We do not find Avraham Avinu trying to save Sodom, or Moshe Rabbeinu trying to help Miriam recover, by doing *mitzvot* in their merit. Instead, they prayed for them.

Some propose a line of reasoning to justify why it would indeed help to perform *mitzvot* in the merit of a sick person. The argument is that since the mitzvah-performer is only doing it because of the sick person, then the sick person is the cause of this mitzvah being performed, and thus receives reward for it. There would appear to be a basis in the Talmud for this concept:

> Rabbi Abahu says: With anyone who causes another to engage in a matter of a mitzvah, Scripture ascribes him credit as though he performed it himself. (*Sanhedrin* 99b)

---

[37] As discussed above, the concept of the Yissacher-Zevulun partnership is not a contradiction to this. According to the earliest sources, which discuss how the tribe of Zevulun enabled the tribe of Yissacher to spend more time on their Torah study (by marketing the produce that Yissacher farmed), they are praised for this act of support; but it is not as though they receive the actual reward for Torah study.

But if that is indeed what the Talmud is saying, then we have a problem. Pharaoh and Haman are the cause of many *mitzvot* being performed! Do they receive reward for this? Surely not!

The answer is that the Talmud is referring to a situation where person A actively and deliberately causes person B to do the mitzvah. In such a case, it is as though he performed it himself. To a lesser degree, this can be extended to any case in which one person causes another to do a mitzvah. If the mitzvah-performer has been raised, educated or inspired by the sick person, then his *mitzvot* are a credit to that person, but not otherwise. That is parallel to the idea of an ancestor (or teacher) getting a merit from a descendant (or disciple), as discussed above. But all this stands in contrast to the popular notion that *anyone* can be credited with a mitzvah merely by virtue of the person performing the mitzvah designating the reward for him.

Conclusion

As we have demonstrated, the classical, traditional ways of doing something for those who have passed away include commemorating their memory in this world, atoning for their soul via charity and prayer, and providing a merit for them (by doing good deeds) in a case where one is their biological or spiritual descendent. The notion that one can learn Torah or perform a mitzvah as a merit for a complete stranger has no basis in classical Judaism, and indeed is clearly opposed by classical Jewish teachings.

How, then, did it come into being? It appears that it was enabled by continued evolution of mystical notions. A mystical worldview allows for the construct of all kinds of metaphysical possibilities. In this case, it enabled the creation of the notion that *mitzvot* create a form of discrete metaphysical currency, which can be transferred to other people.

But *why* did this view become so popular? There would appear to be two answers to this. One is that it is enormously emotionally comforting for people to believe that they can do something for people that they care about. Being a credit to one's ancestors is often not enough; people are attracted to the idea that they can hire people to perform mitzvot and send the reward for those mitzvot to their loved ones.

Second is that there is a lot of money to be made from it. Many *yeshivot* and *kollelim* find it very hard to obtain financial support. A solution is to convince bereaved people that they can help the deceased by giving money to people who will learn Torah on their behalf. In such a situation, it is all too easy to look away from the fact that this flies in the face of traditional Jewish teachings about such things. "For bribery blinds the eyes of the wise, and distorts the words of the righteous" (Ex. 23:8). Even the wise and the righteous are not immune to being swayed by financial benefits.

Supporting the teaching of study and Torah can be a credit to one's ancestor, but not in the way that is commonly believed. The credit to the deceased is not the Torah that is studied, per se; rather, it is that his descendant is supporting the teaching and study of Torah (assuming that it is an institution and way of life that is worthy of financial support; see chapter V in Part One on the nature of Torah). It is only the descendant's actions that can be a credit to the deceased.

Postscript: Standing for the Siren

Our findings regarding the classical rabbinic views on what a person can and cannot do for someone who has passed away have an interesting ramification regarding the practice in the State of Israel of standing silent during the sirens for the victims of the Holocaust and for fallen soldiers and victims of terrorism. This practice is opposed by many people in the Charedi community, ostensibly due to the belief that this is a modern notion, and/or taken from non-Jews, with no basis in classical Judaism. Some people instead recite Tehillim on behalf of the victims, which they believe to me a more traditional Jewish practice.

The practice of sounding the siren for two minutes of silence has its roots in South Africa. During World War I, a businessman in Cape Town suggested that his church observe a silent pause in memory of those who fell in battle. Subsequently, the Mayor of Cape Town instructed that at noon on May 14, 1918, the daily firing of the Noon Gun (for the ships to set their chronometers uniformly) would serve as the signal to begin two minutes of silence in memory of the fallen. This custom later spread throughout the British Empire, and eventually to many different nations and cultures. The Jews living in Palestine adopted this custom and observed a minute or two of silence in response to tragic events. After the War of Independence, the Rabbinate of Israel decided to set Memorial Day on the day before Independence Day. The newly installed national system of air-raid sirens provided a means to simultaneously alert everyone in Israel to observe the silence at the same time.

There is a prohibition in Judaism of following in the ways of gentiles. But the practice of standing silent for a siren would not fall under that prohibition. The prohibition does not refer to any practice which happens to originate with non-Jews. It only refers to practices which are idolatrous, or a practice for which the reasons are unknown and thus potentially originate in idolatry. Any practice which has a sensible rationale is permitted to be adopted, even if it originates with non-Jews.[38]

This even includes practices which relate to the religious sphere. Ketav Sofer permits the innovative non-Jewish practice of carrying the dead on wagons. In the Orthodox Jewish community today, everyone refers to verses in Scripture via chapter numbers, even though these were introduced by non-Jews. And, of course, we refer to the months of the Hebrew calendar with names that originated in Babylonia. Rabbi Moshe Feinstein even permitted Jewish schoolchildren in public schools to participate with Christian schoolchildren in non-denominational school prayer![39]

Standing silent for the siren may have been introduced into Israel as a copy of procedures done in non-Jewish nations, but it is not a non-Jewish procedure. It is simply a natural human expression of solemnity in the face of tragedy.

In fact, not only is there nothing specifically non-Jewish about the practice, it even has conceptual roots in Judaism. Such a response to death goes back to the Torah itself. When Nadav and Avihu were killed by fire,

---

[38] See Rema to *Shulchan Aruch, Yoreh Deah* 178:1.

[39] *Igrot Moshe, Orach Chaim* 4:24.

it says *vayidom Aharon*, "Aharon was silent." While some see this as meaning that he uttered no complaint about God's judgment, others see it as expressing a natural response in the fact of tragedy. Likewise, we find that Iyov's friends sat in silence with him for seven days. The Talmud says that "the merit of attending a house of mourning lies in maintaining silence."[40] Silence expresses both commiserations and solidarity with others, and contemplating matters in our minds. This is something that is very much part of traditional Judaism.

What about the siren? The siren was instituted simply as a way of alerting everyone to this *avodah*, just like the Shabbat siren. It can even be seen as very similar to the *shofar* blast, another type of horn which sounds and to which in response we stand in silent contemplation.

Standing silent for the siren, then, does not only reflect basic human attitudes, but it even echoes traditional Jewish practices. It is not something that is copying non-Jewish practices of questionable theological basis, like *schlissel challah*, pouring lead, and many other popular rituals in *frum* society.

On the other hand, just how traditional is it to say Tehillim on behalf of the dead, and what does it accomplish? We do not find any mention of such a thing in the writings of Chazal and the Rishonim. In classical Judaism, one gives charity for the dead and one prays (such as with the Yizkor prayer, which is recited at Yom HaZikaron events). For one's ancestors and teachers, one learns Torah and does good deeds as a credit to them. Saying Tehillim for strangers does not appear to have any basis in classical Judaism; as we have seen, the earliest sources to discuss such things indicate that one cannot actually accomplish anything for the deceased in such a way.

So which is the traditional Jewish way of commemorating those who died in tragic circumstances, and which is the meaningless custom of recent origin? Like so many other topics, relates to whether one follows the rationalist approach of the Rishonim or the more recent mystical approach. Similarly, it also depends on whether one defines Jewish

---

[40] *Berachot* 6b. Similarly in *Avot d'Rabbi Natan* 11.

tradition as starting in Biblical times and carrying on through the Sages of the Talmud and the Rishonim, or whether one defines it as starting about a hundred years ago.

Appendix I: What Must A Jew Believe?

Rationalism and Faith

There are serious disputes between rationalists and mystics as to the faith requirements of Judaism. Mystics often demand belief in the absolute truth of every word of the Talmud, along with the Tannaic and ultimately divine origins of the Zohar, and many other texts. Rationalists, on the other hand, usually dispute the divine origin of kabbalistic texts, and also maintain that not every part of the Talmud is divinely-inspired wisdom. These differences can lead to disputes about whether rationalist Jews are heretics. Accordingly, it is beneficial to explore what the requirements of faith actually are.

In addition, as discussed, the rationalist approach is a Pandora's Box. Some people who adopt the rationalist approach find themselves questioning or disbelieving even those tenets of faith that are generally considered to be fundamental within a rationalist approach. Such people may wonder whether they have a place in Orthodox Judaism. The information and insights in this discussion may prove helpful.

The Disputed Fundamentals of Faith

To what extent is faith a component of Judaism? Which articles of faith are obligatory?

It is popularly assumed that the minimum requirements of faith to be a good Jew are the thirteen principles of Rambam. But this is clearly mistaken, for two reasons. One is that a number of important authorities disputed the idea that certain beliefs in Judaism can be rated as more important than others. Second, and more devastatingly, is that as Dr.

491

Marc Shapiro demonstrated in his seminal work *The Limits of Orthodox Theology*, there have been countless dozens of authorities over the ages who argued with Rambam concerning the truth of these principles. There were authorities who maintained that God does or can take on some sort of physical form, that angels may be worshipped, that the Torah in our possession was not entirely transcribed by Moses, and so on. This is brought sharply to light in the case of God's incorporeality, which Rambam argues to be fundamental required belief:

> There are five that are called sectarians: One who says that there is no God… one who says that there is a ruler, but that there are two or more; one who says that there is one God, but He possesses a body and form… (Rambam, *Mishneh Torah, Hilchot Teshuvah* 3:7)

Yet Raavad notes that there are great Torah scholars who disagree:

> "One who says that there is one God, but He possesses a body and form…"—But why did Rambam rate such a person as a sectarian? Surely there were greater and better people than he (i.e. than Rambam) who followed this idea due to what they saw in Scripture, and even more so due to aggadot that corrupt opinions. (Ra'avad, commentary ad loc.)

In fact, it was not only the case that there were great Torah scholars who took a corporeal view of God; they believed that it was in fact Rambam's philosophical belief in an incorporeal God that was heretical! R. Moshe Taku, one of the Tosafists, decries those who believe that God is everywhere as being heretics.[1] God, he insists, is spatially located in the Heavens, not on earth, and certainly not in disgusting places such as toilets.[2]

While Raavad and R. Moshe Taku, along with everyone else, would certainly have demanded belief in God and revelation, there is much dispute as to which beliefs are required beyond that. Clearly, if we are

---

[1] *Ketav Tamim*, in *Otzar Nechmad* (Vienna, 1860)

[2] "…Forfend that the One Who is holy with all types of sanctity should be distilled into unclean places and within statues! And He already wrote for us in the Torah that 'your camp shall be holy; let Him not find anything unseemly among you, and turn away from you (Deut, 23:15)'—thus, the Torah attests that the Holy One, blessed is He, is not found in inappropriate places."

looking for a universal, timeless set of required beliefs, Rambam's list falls short.

The Counter-Argument: They Could Say It, We Cannot

We are faced with the problematic historical fact that there have been radically opposed views in Jewish history—indeed, mutually exclusive views—as to the requirements of Jewish belief. Some attempt to counter this by claiming that even though, historically, there were those who differed with Rambam's principles, it is irrelevant, since their views have been "paskened" (legally ruled) against. It was not heretical for R. Moshe Taku to be a corporealist, but such a view is heresy today. This how some people interpret the phrase "They could say it, we cannot," which was uttered by Rav Elyashiv with regard to the statements of various Rishonim about science that I published in my books, which he banned.

This position is, however, severely problematic. It is true that there is a long-standing dispute about the status of a sincere, Torah-observant Jew, who holds incontrovertibly heretical views but who does so out of innocence (for example, he never grew out of his childhood Bible class which taught him that God possesses physical form). Rambam, who understood that Heavenly reward is a natural consequence of intellectual perfection, was forced to take the view that such a person was tragically still a heretic, doomed to receive no share in the World-to-Come.[3] But one need not adopt such a Maimonidean view of the afterlife in order to maintain that someone who maintains heretical beliefs out of innocence is still a heretic. This position was also maintained by Rabbi Chaim Soloveitchik, who famously stated that someone who is *nebach* (tragically) an *apikorus* is still an *apikorus*. Rabbi Yosef Albo, on the other hand, and several others, stated emphatically that such a person is not to be deemed a heretic.[4] God can, in His graciousness, choose to grant Heavenly reward

---

[3] For a full discussion of Rambam's views, see the appendix "Maimonides on Reward and Punishment," in Menachem Kellner, *Must A Jew Believe Anything?* (London: Littman Library 2006).

[4] Rabbi Yosef Albo, *Sefer ha-Ikkarim*, 1:2; Rabbi Shimon ben Tzemach Duran, *Ohev Mishpat* 15a; Radvaz, *Responsa* 1258 (references from Shapiro p. 10). This is also apparently the position of Raavad.

to whoever sees fit, and would not withhold it from someone who errs out of innocence.

However, regardless of which position one takes in this dispute, it is clear that this dispute is only regarding the treatment of the person who espouses such views. But the views themselves, even if reached in good faith, are still heretical! Even if it is due to an honest misunderstanding that a person concludes that God has physical form, and we do not condemn him for his error, we still maintain this to be an utterly false conception of God. There is dispute about whether *nebach* an *apikores* is indeed an *apikores*, but *nebach* a *kefirah* is most definitely *kefirah*!

Thus, it cannot be said that it was theologically legitimate in antiquity to have certain beliefs which have since been ruled theologically illegitimate. There is, however, a way in which this argument can be modified, to which I shall later return, in which we are not ruling on the innate validity of the belief, but rather on how to treat people who espouse certain beliefs.

Scripture and Beliefs

The first place to look for Judaism's required beliefs is in the foundational text of Judaism, the Written Torah. And yet Scripture does not list required beliefs. Nevertheless, this is understandable. Beliefs are about the nature of God, about certain facts of Jewish history, but these are the very ideas that are part of Scripture itself. In Scripture, there are various beliefs that are taken for granted, since they are part of the history of the Jewish People. These include the existence of God, and the revelation at Sinai. Scripture does mandate loyalty to God and prohibits worshipping other deities, which inherently includes the belief that God is all-powerful. But there is no Code of Beliefs; no Ten Commandments of Belief. Instead, the beliefs form an assumed backdrop to the commandments.

The Mishnah and Beliefs

Moving on to the Mishnah, we notice that while there is a tractate for every topic from blessings to *uktzin* (the impurity of vegetable stems), there is no tractate dedicated to the topic of beliefs. There is not even an individual chapter of any tractate devoted to this topic. Instead, all we have is a single Mishnah in Sanhedrin:

> Every member of Israel has a share in the World-to-Come... But these have no share in the World-to-Come: One who says that the Resurrection of the Dead is not in the Torah; that there is no Torah from Heaven; and an *apikores* (which is defined in the Talmud as someone who shows disrespect to Torah scholars)... (Mishnah, *Sanhedrin* 10:1)

Yet as a code of beliefs, even this Mishnah is problematic on a number of levels.

First of all, there are some important beliefs that are not mentioned here. For example, there is no mentions of beliefs concerning God.

Second, it is rather odd that we only have condemnations of false beliefs, not a list of correct beliefs.

Third, what does it mean that a person loses his share in the World-to-Come? Does this have any ramifications in terms of how the person is to be treated in the community? Can one count such a person for a *minyan*?

Fourth, if the idea of losing one's share in the World-to-Come is taken as some kind of fundamental disqualification from being a Jew in good standing, then this is applied with an astonishingly broad brush. A later Mishnah states that even the generation of the Wilderness—those who reached the heights of revelation at the Red Sea and at Sinai—fall into this category:

> The generation of the Deluge has no share in the World-to-Come... the generation of the Dispersal has no share in the World-to-Come... the Spies have no share in the World-to-Come... the generation of the Wilderness has no share in the World-to-Come... (Mishnah, *Sanhedrin* 10:3)

Menachem Kellner therefore concludes that the expression "losing one's share in the World-to-Come" is simply an expression of disapproval rather than an actual disqualification. I am not absolutely convinced that this is the case; the fact that this expression is used polemically elsewhere does not mean that it is not intended literally here. Still, even if it is taken literally, the aforementioned points still mean that we have something considerably less than a code of beliefs here.

But if this Mishnah is not presenting a list of required beliefs, then what is it doing? A consideration of the listed categories, in the context of other discussions in the Talmud, reveals that it is targeting Sadducean beliefs. It was the Sadducees who denied the authority of the Oral Torah and the Resurrection. Thus, this Mishnah is condemning those who break from Rabbinic Judaism. Note that it refers to someone "who declares," not to someone who thinks or believes. Someone who declares their affiliation with Sadducean beliefs has undermined the community and is condemned.

The Talmud and Beliefs

If the Mishnah does not present a list of required beliefs, then the next place to look is the Talmud, which is far more extensive than the Mishnah. Yet here, too, there is nothing to be found. The Talmud has lists of medical remedies for various ailments, it lists the gestation period and reproductive habits of various animals, yet it does not include a list of required beliefs!

There is one place in particular where we would expect to find a list of required beliefs, and what we find instead is most revealing. This is with regard to the laws of conversion. In order to be accepted as a valid Jew, one must engage in certain education, pass various requirements, and answer certain questions. Yet none of these involve matters of belief:

> The Rabbis taught: If someone comes to convert, we say to him: "Why do you see fit to convert? Do you not know that today, the Jewish People are afflicted, oppressed, downtrodden, harassed, and frequently subject to hardship?" If he says, "I know, and I am unworthy," we accept him immediately. We inform him of a few light *mitzvot* and a few serious *mitzvot*... we do not overwhelm him, and we are not exacting with him... (*Yevamot* 47a)

Now, this is not to suggest that Chazal held other beliefs to be a free-for-all. At that time, many other beliefs could simply be taken for granted. The existence of God and the historical truth of the events in the Torah were automatically assumed. Nevertheless, it is clear that Chazal were not especially concerned with matters of belief, except where they signified a break from the behavioral community.

There is one further passage of relevance in the Talmud. Consider the following discussion about Rabbi Hillel:

> Rabbi Hillel said: There shall be no Mashiach for Israel, because they have already enjoyed him in the days of Chizkiyah. R. Yosef said: May God forgive Rabbi Hillel. *Sanhedrin* 99a)

Rabbi Hillel denied the arrival of the Messiah, directly contravening that which Rambam would later list as a fundamental of faith. The Talmud records R. Yosef as saying "May God forgive him." What does that mean? It seems to mean that Rabbi Hillel's view is wrong, it is a perversion of our deepest beliefs about Jewish destiny. But there is no indication of his being disqualified as a Jew or ousted from the community.

Rambam's Revolution

Moving on to medieval times, Rambam is obviously the figure that requires discussion. For Rambam, beliefs were exceedingly important. But he was clearly making a break from Chazal. Consider how he presents the Talmudic discussion regarding conversion.

> How do we accept righteous converts? When a gentile comes to convert, and investigation shows no ulterior motive, we say to him, "Why do you see fit to convert? Do you not know that today, the Jewish People are afflicted, oppressed, downtrodden, harassed, and frequently subject to hardship?" If he says, "I know, and I am unworthy," we accept him immediately. And we inform him of the fundamentals of religion, which are the unity of God and the prohibition of idolatry, and we dwell upon this at length. And we inform him of a few light *mitzvot* and a few serious *mitzvot*, but we do not dwell upon this at length... (*Mishneh Torah, Hilchot Issurei Biyah* 14:1-2)

The Talmud made no reference at all to the fundamentals of religion. Rambam not only inserts this, but adds that this is something to be dwelt upon at length!

The reason for this is that Rambam was influenced by Greco-Muslim philosophy to believe that the intellectual life is all that counts. The afterlife consists solely of the intellect merging with God. *Mitzvot* have no real rewards; rather, they prepare one's personality so that the intellect can be developed appropriately. With such a worldview, the correct beliefs are critical. Even if one is merely in doubt about these beliefs, one has forfeited one's afterlife.

There are countless authorities who followed Rambam's list of required beliefs, but few are they who adopted the underlying conceptual framework. As noted earlier, Raavad, R. Yosef Albo and countless others, while agreeing with Rambam's prescribed beliefs, did not believe that those who disputed certain of these beliefs are heretics. And there are many authorities who actually disputed the content of some of these beliefs.

Given the widespread opposition to either the content or the necessity of Rambam's list of beliefs, why did they become so popular? The answer is probably that this list was a very useful shorthand yet authoritative way of distinguishing being loyal members of the Jewish community and disloyal members. The Reform movement, for example, clearly disputed Rambam's list of principles. Furthermore, probably due to the influence of non-Jewish society, it became prevalent to think of religion as a set of beliefs. Accordingly, one's membership in good standing depends upon a set of beliefs—and Rambam had written a useful list.

The Preservation of the Community

Based on everything in Torah, Mishnah and Talmud, we see as follows. Clearly, it can't be that beliefs are of *no* significance. On the other hand, there is no reference to, or requirement of, any list of beliefs. And this has caused there to be much subsequent debate regarding not only which beliefs are required, but even as to which beliefs are actually true, which are false, and which are heretical.

The explanation for all this, and for the Mishnah's references to various specific problematic beliefs, must be as follows. The precise nature of beliefs is not as unequivocal and important as is commonly assumed.

What *is* important is strengthening the community rather than undermining it. Judaism is based around the community, not the individual.

There are different ways in which the community can be threatened. Halachic practice plays a major role, since Judaism is primarily a religion of deed rather than creed. Accordingly, any undermining of the halachic system is taken very seriously. The *zaken mamre*—the rebellious elder who goes against the ruling of the Great Beit Din—is put to death for undermining the halachic system. He is permitted to believe himself to be correct—indeed, as Chatam Sofer stresses, he may very well actually *be* correct—but he must not rule that way, due to the practical problem that it creates in terms of weakening the community.[5]

Another example of this is that as Rabbi Dr. Shnayer (Sid) Leiman observes, the Book of Jubilees was excluded from the canon, while Ecclesiastes was allowed in, despite the Talmud observing its theologically problematic statements.[6] The reason is that theologically problematic statements with regard to abstract beliefs do not undermine the community to anywhere near the degree that messing with the halachic calendar system does. Commitment to the halachic community is crucial.[7]

---

[5] See too the earlier chapter, "Arguing With God: When May Students Dispute Teachers?"

[6] Sid Leiman, "Inspiration and Canonicity: Reflections on the Formation of the Biblical Canon," in E.P Sanders, ed., *Jewish and Christian Self-Definition*, Fortress Press: Philadelphia, 1981, vol. 2, pp. 56-63.

[7] At this point I would like to discuss one of the primary resources on the topic of required beliefs, Professor Menachem Kellner's book *Must a Jew Believe Anything?* (second edition, Littman Library of Jewish Civilization 2006). It is an outstanding work upon which I based much of this chapter, and an absolutely essential read for anyone who is interested in such topics, but I must express certain reservations about it.

The book can be divided into two parts. The first six chapters, along with the fascinating appendix, explore the role of faith in classical Judaism and compare it to the role of faith in Maimonidean thought, and is the part which I cannot recommend highly enough. The seventh and final chapter of the book forms a separate unit; it contains Kellner's own view of how the previous discussion can be used to change the way that Orthodox Jews relate to non-Orthodox Jews, and is the part about which I have severe reservations.

But sometimes, expressing problematic beliefs can also undermine the community—such as when these beliefs are held by a rival group. An example is the beliefs that the Mishnah in *Sanhedrin* condemns, which were the beliefs held by the Sadducees. Someone who declares their

---

Kellner's idea is as follows. Once one realizes that defining "being a Jew in good standing" based on adherence to Maimonidean dogma is an aberrant and problematic definition, then we are left with defining a good Jew based on halachic observance. But nobody keeps absolutely every halachah, and nor is there anyone who does no *mitzvot* at all. Thus, we have a continuum of observance, extending over Orthodox, Conservative, and Reform Jews. While we do not agree with the theology of Conservative and Reform, we can increase our cooperation and unity with them via this insight.

Here is where I must part company with Prof. Kellner (notwithstanding my tremendous respect for him and his superb books). My critique is very similar to that raised by Daniel Statman, which Kellner himself cites and discusses in the afterword to the second edition of his book, but to which he does not, in my opinion, present an adequate response. It seems to me that traditionally, Judaism did not define "being a good Jew" either in terms of adherence to Maimonidean-style dogma or in terms of counting how many *mitzvot* one performs. Instead, there was a presumption of certain basic beliefs about God and Torah, but even more significant was *commitment and loyalty to the halachic community.*

There may well be a continuum of halachic observance among all the different flavors of Jews. But there is nevertheless a clear difference between someone who is, in principle, committed to the traditional halachic community (albeit with various lapses) and someone who is not committed to it. (This is not affected by a gray area surrounding the extreme left-wing of Orthodoxy. The gray area simply means that people disagree as to where to draw the line. But all agree that the line itself revolves around commitment to the halachic community.) If a person lapses in his personal observance, he is not undermining the community. But if he supports a rival system (such as the Sadducees and Karaites in ancient times, or Conservative and Reform in modern times), he is undermining the community, and is thus appropriately rejected.

Kellner somewhat acknowledges all this in his discussion of Statman's critique on pp. 136-140, but maintains that there is much to be gained by defining membership in terms of behavior rather than belief, and that excluding people based on their being "public enemies" is untrue to the teachings of Rabbinic Judaism. I must respectfully disagree— I think that this is how Judaism always operated, either consciously or subconsciously.

Again, all this is not to say that I believe Kellner's efforts in the first six chapters to be wasted. On the contrary; I think that they are extremely useful. But in my view, these concepts are useful in a different way than Kellner proposes. They do not provide a way to attain acceptance of other strains of Judaism, but they do provide a way for those who dispute various dogmas of belief to live in the halachic community.

affiliation with Sadducean beliefs has undermined the Rabbinic community and is thus condemned.

Even with Rambam, we must distinguish between two types of beliefs that he lists as being required. There are those that, due to his identification with Greco-Muslim philosophy, he saw as essential for creating the intellectual afterlife—namely, the first five beliefs, concerning the nature of God. These he believed to be absolutely required or else there is simply no way to obtain an afterlife. And there are those that served purposes similar to those of the Mishnah in *Sanhedrin*—maintaining the integrity of the halachic community in the face of a threatening alternate group.

This explains certain of Rambam's stated required beliefs which initially appear strange. For example, Rambam requires the belief that Moshe Rabbeinu's level of prophecy was qualitatively superior to that of every other prophet. Now, suppose someone were to believe that Yirmiyah had the same level of prophecy as Moshe Rabbeinu. Would that really matter? Of course not. But it wasn't people believing that Yirmiyah was as great as Moshe that Rambam was concerned about—it was the risk of their believing in Mohammed.

> ...An *ikkar* does not arise from the fact that its negation is false, but from the fact that its negation undermines the Jewish system of belief. That Moses' prophecy was of a different order than that of other prophets is an explicit verse in the Torah (Numbers 12:7); [but] it was a specific historic context, its denial by Islam, that turned this verse from a religious dictum into an *ikkar*. A belief is an *ikkar* when its content is what differentiates Judaism from the surrounding credal system. (Haym Soloveitchik, "Two Notes on the Commentary on the Torah of R. Yehudah he-Hasid," p. 244)

Another example is that Rambam required the belief that every verse in the Torah is from God. Yet Rambam himself knew of the many textual inconsistencies in various Torah scrolls. However, again, this belief was required in light of the threat of Islam, which claimed that the Torah had become majorly corrupted and that in the original text it was Yishmael that became the Chosen People.

God's Demands, Society's Demands

All this relates to another fundamental point to be acknowledged: that we must distinguish between those beliefs required by God and those required by the community.

In 12th century northern France, there were communities in which it was obligatory to believe in the literal meaning of all aggados, including those describing God in corporeal terms. But in Spain, such beliefs were rated as heresy.

So is such a belief acceptable or not? The answer is simple: According to those who follow the authorities who maintain that it is acceptable, it is acceptable, and according to those authorities who maintain that it is not acceptable, it is not acceptable!

This may sound comical, but it is not. If a belief is true, it is true no matter who says otherwise; if it is false, it is false no matter who propounds it. A person can perform his own analysis of the issue itself, but there is no way of conclusively determining and ruling who is correct.

God Himself is either incorporeal or not. If someone possesses the wrong opinion on this matter, God will deal with him in the way that He sees fit, which we may or may not be able to correctly assess. Our assessment of His response does not determine it. But our assessment of this issue does determine how this person will be treated by us. A declared incorporealist will not be well received in a corporealist society, and vice-versa.

With this in mind, let us turn to the issue of whether one can issue a halachic ruling on beliefs. Rambam states in several places that beliefs are not subject to the procedures of halachic rulings:

> And I have already said many times that when there is an argument between the sages in ideas concerning belief, where its purpose is not in the area of action, we do not say that the halachah is like so-and-so. (*Perush HaMishnayot* to *Sotah* 3:5, stated in regard to whether the waters of a *sotah* are delayed from killing the *sotah* as a result of a merit that she has.)

> I have mentioned to you many times that all arguments that are between sages that do not effect action, but is only a belief in a thing, there is no

reason to decide the halachah like one of them. (*Perush HaMishnayot* to *Sanhedrin* 10:3, stated in regard to the question of whether the ten tribes will ultimately return or are lost forever.)

And in regards to this argument it is not that the halachah is like the words of so-and-so, because it is something that concerns God. (*Perush HaMishnayot* to *Shavuot* 1:4, regarding which public offerings atone for which sins.)

A similar statement is made by Rabbi Chaim David Azulai, the Chida. In the context of establishing that a certain Amora is arguing with all the Tannaim regarding the nature of the Messianic Era, he writes:

It is widely accepted that with anything that has no halachic application, a late Amora can argue with a majority [of Tannaim], for with something that has no halachic application, permission is granted for everyone to speak his own mind. (Responsa *Chaim Sho'al* 98)[8]

There is good reason for this. A belief is either true or false; one cannot change this via a *halachic* ruling. If a rabbi rules that God has physical form, and even if every rabbi were to agree with him, this does not grant Him physical form. Conversely, imagine R. Moshe Taku's reaction to the idea that people have paskened that corporealism is heresy. He would say that it is laughable and offensive for people with their tiny minds to insist that one not believe the plain meaning of revelation.

Now, it is true that in cases of beliefs that may be heresy, there are halachic decisions that have to be taken with regard to these views. Can a person who espouses such views be converted to Judaism? If he slaughters an animal, is it kosher? Can he be counted for a *minyan*? Such rulings, however, are necessary determinations for how to treat such a person; they do not determine the ultimate truth or falsehood of these propositions. To the best of our ability, we will assess whether these beliefs are true, and whether they are fundamental to Jewish theology, and based on this, we will decide upon who is a member of our community in good standing. But if a belief is true, it always has been and always will be true; if it is

---

[8] Rashash to Talmud *Shabbat* 63a states the same, as does Rabbi Shlomo Algazi, *Gufei Halachot* (Izmir 1675), *Klalei Ha-Alef* 35.

false, it always has been and always will be false; we cannot change or resolve this via a *halachic* ruling.

Yet here is where some people err and misunderstand Shapiro's work. The fact that we cannot conclusively arbitrate between authorities does not mean that we will legitimize people adopting whichever of these views they choose. There is such a thing as overwhelming historical consensus, and this renders such views socially unacceptable. If a person wishes to follow those Rishonim who believed that God has physical form, we cannot issue a *halachic* determination regarding God's corporeality, but we can say that since we are overpoweringly of the opinion that this is a gross perversion of Judaism, don't expect to flaunt this view and receive an *aliyah* in *shul*. This view has been overwhelmingly rejected by the historical consensus of the Jewish community, and it will therefore not be tolerated. We declare this view heresy in the sense that it is a drastic break from the beliefs of the community and therefore the person espousing this belief has effectively removed himself from the community.[9] It is not so much a halachic ruling on a belief as it is an observation resulting in a declaration about the person holding the belief. Interestingly, Maharal also applies this in reverse, stating that "someone who separates himself from the ways of the community is [expressing] a view of heresy, since he is removing himself from the group, and scorning the community, and he has no portion in the community."[10]

Some free-thinkers may protest that they have a right to follow the great Rishonim who held this view. Perhaps they do; but the rest of the Jewish community has a right to reject them. Consider someone who sincerely believes that the United States is an evil country which must be destroyed. He can claim a right to his opinion; but he cannot claim that

---

[9] I was tempted to note that in the Pesach Haggadah, we state about the wicked son that "since he excluded himself from the community, he has denied the foundation," explicitly defining heresy in terms of making a break from the community. However, further research revealed that in earlier versions of this text, such as in the Talmud Yerushalmi and Mechilta, it states instead that the wicked son "has excluded himself from the community *and* has denied the foundation."

[10] *Chiddushei Aggadot, Rosh HaShanah*, p. 112.

the United States must grant him citizenship. The United States is equally within its rights to deny his entry into their community.

Thus, when we consider statements by great Torah scholars of history that are at odds with what we would consider to be acceptable doctrine, we cannot use halachic procedures to prove such beliefs wrong, but we can say that we believe them to be wrong and we will not tolerate such beliefs.[11] In severe cases, this can even reach the halachic situation of their being formally excluded from the community of believers.

So can we say, "They could say it, but we cannot"? That depends on what that phrase is intended to mean. We cannot declare that, because it was stated by someone of stature, it must have been a valid belief. *Nebach* a *kefirah* is still a *kefirah*; if a belief is heretical, it is heretical no matter who said it. But we *can* say that authorities of great stature living in certain eras can get away with possessing such beliefs and not being stigmatized to the extent that they are no longer regarded as Torah authorities, especially if their views on these matters are little-known. In this, we need not have any reason to follow Rambam. Rambam was forced to state that anyone espousing heretical beliefs was a heretic, due to his understanding of how intellectual perfection is ultimately the sole purpose of Judaism. Virtually nobody else adopts this approach, and we can be more generous about great people who were a product of their culture and era and therefore held certain beliefs that would be unthinkable today.

R. Moshe Taku was a corporealist; but he lived in a time and place where Rambam's philosophy had not yet penetrated, and we can therefore understand why he took such a view. Today, on the other hand, that belief has been so overwhelmingly rejected that someone who overtly espouses it is making a radical break with the community and will not be tolerated. In that sense, the earlier authorities could say it, but we cannot.

---

[11] While Chatam Sofer (*Yoreh De'ah* 356) does state that the halachic process does apply to beliefs, he does not seem to mean that one can change the status of their truth, but rather that we are guiding people in terms of what they are permitted to believe.

Public and Private Heresies

A corollary of this understanding of the parameters of belief is that the way in which a belief is expressed is of great importance. Practically speaking, heresy means making a drastic break from the beliefs of the community, in such a way as to undermine the stability of the shared belief system. Our concern is the extent to which the espouser of such beliefs is destabilizing the shared belief system; in some cases it may be to such an extent that he can no longer be said to be a part of that shared belief system, and in turn of the community itself.

This in turn depends on how he is expressing his beliefs. Ralbag denied God's knowledge of contingent events, but his commentary is still found in the *Mikraot Gedolot*, since his views are little known. Rambam's *Guide for the Perplexed* contains some absolutely shocking views, but it can be tolerated in a yeshivah library, since its radical positions are relatively inaccessible. But there will never be an ArtScroll elucidated *Guide for the Perplexed*. Publicizing Rambam's astonishing views on creation, miracles, providence and so on would destabilize the shared belief system of the community; someone who overtly promotes these views would be distanced.

Again, according to Rambam himself, it seems that no such distinction can be drawn. Rambam held that the spiritual reward of eternity is contingent solely upon intellectual perfection. It makes no difference whether a problematic belief is held publicly or privately; even if it is only tentatively thought of privately, it damages a person's afterlife. But most authorities do not follow Rambam in this, because they operate from a different framework of the soul and the afterlife. And in any case, designations of somebody as a heretic relate to how we treat the person more than to what his fate in the afterlife will be, which is God's business.

Different Communities

Not only does the mode of expression of a person's belief affect how he will be treated; also of great importance is the community in which this belief is being expressed, because that is also a determining factor in the degree of destabilization. A belief may be of little consequence in an intellectually sophisticated and broadly-learned society, but that same belief may be very damaging in a community that is more limited in its intellectual horizons. There are some communities which are better able to tolerate diverse beliefs than others.

Then there is the factor of sub-communities within the larger umbrella of Orthodox Judaism. Consider the case of Chabad. Rabbi Dr. David Berger has persuasively argued that a substantial portion of the Chabad community possess beliefs that are certainly rated as heretical by many people in the rest of the Orthodox community. And yet, there is no campaign to delegitimize them. According to Berger, this is inexcusable. According to Menachem Kellner, on the other hand, this demonstrates that most people correctly subconsciously adopt what he believes to be the traditional view—that beliefs are of little consequence if they do not affect halachic observance. I would disagree with both of them. The reason why Chabad is tolerated is that they do not affect the rest of the Orthodox community, since they are an entirely separate group and do not attempt to proselytize other Orthodox Jews. It is not that Chabad beliefs are unimportant (as Kellner argues); it is that they are irrelevant to the rest of Orthodoxy.

As an example of the significance of different communities, consider the controversy over my own works, and the position of Rambam and many others that the Sages of the Talmud were not infallible in matters of science. It is clear that if one truly believes this position to be heresy— a fundamental falsification of the nature of the Talmud and the Oral Law—then it is heresy no matter when it was said or by whom. If Natan Slifkin has a horribly perverted understanding of the stature of Chazal and the nature of the holy Gemara in thinking that it could contain scientific errors, then so did Rav Sherira Gaon, Rambam, Rav Hirsch, and the other forty or so authorities who maintained this view. I am not claiming that nobody has the right to make this claim. But most are understandably reluctant to pass such a judgment on such great Torah scholars; and it seems strange to condemn people as disrespectful for saying that the Sages lacked scientific data while simultaneously saying that the Rishonim had perverted *hashkafot*. Yet there are people who seem to think that they can accuse me of such a perverted grasp of the Talmud, and yet not be saying anything disrespectful about Rambam and the others, on the grounds that it has only now been *paskened* to be heretical. I hope that my analysis shows the fallacy of this illusion. If someone is saying it about me, they are saying it about everyone else.

Now, some of the rabbinic opponents of my work, such as Rabbi Moshe Shapiro and Rabbi Elya Ber Wachtfogel, were indeed of this position. They were of the view that someone who ascribes scientific error to Chazal is espousing genuine heresy; that is to say, such a person has a critically perverted understanding of the nature of Chazal and the Talmud.[12] They had no difficulty passing this judgment upon me, but what about the great Rishonim and Acharonim who proposed these views? Since these opponents of mine are from a community in which their understanding of the doctrine of *yeridat hadorot* (the decline of generations) does not permit them to accuse the Torah giants of earlier generations of possessing such a perverted attitude, this put them in a difficult situation. When faced with works written by great Rishonim and Acharonim which state these views,[13] they were thus forced to either denounce these works as forgeries, creatively reinterpret the positions of these authorities, or to backtrack and claim that they were not really condemning my positions, but rather my "tone."[14]

---

[12] Rabbi Moshe Shapiro (*Afikei Mayim, Shavuot*, p. 16) claims that someone who requires empirical confirmation for a statement of Chazal's that seems scientifically impossible is a heretic; at a lecture in London (from which I possess a detailed transcript) he claimed that all Talmudic statements are Torah, and someone who rates a statement in the Talmud as being a scientific error has denied the Torah. The recently published work *Chaim B'Emunatam* by his disciple Rabbi Reuven Schmelczer, bearing effusive approbations from Rabbi Shapiro, Rabbi Wachtfogel and others, is all about how denial of the Sinaitic origins and infallibility of anything at all in the Talmud is heresy and punishable by death. For a review and critique of this work, see www.zootorah.com/-controversy/ChaimBEmunasam.pdf.

[13] Some find it difficult to believe that these great Torah authorities were not aware of these sources to begin with. But these issues are relatively obscure issues of theology; great Talmudists and Halachists are generally not fluent in them.

[14] This claim is deeply problematic for several reasons. First, since most of them did not read my works, they are not in a position to judge the tone. Second, the language used in the text of the ban simply does not reconcile with a condemnation of the tone but not

On the other hand, many of the rabbinic opponents of my work did not consider the position that the Talmud contains scientific errors to be genuinely heretical. They were aware that Torah giants of earlier generations maintained this belief (even if they were unaware of how prevalent this view was), and would not judge it to be fundamentally perverted understanding of the Talmud. Rav Elyashiv fell into this category; indeed, one of his own rebbeim, Rav Yitzchak Herzog, was of this belief, and it seems unlikely that Rav Elyashiv would have considered his rebbe to have possessed a heretical, perverted understanding of the Talmud.

Therefore, when Rav Elyashiv signed a ban which states that books presenting the approach of Rambam are heretical, this is not to be interpreted as meaning that he believes them to be genuine heresy. Rav Elyashiv was of the opinion that the books "could be called" heresy—i.e., using the loose colloquial definition of the term that is so common in the Charedi world. This means that it is a viewpoint that is strongly opposed and is absolutely socially unacceptable. But it is not literally, technically heretical—there is no absolute judgment here that this approach undeniably reflects a fundamental perversion of Chazal. Rav Elyashiv subsequently penned a statement that he only meant that the books were forbidden to be brought into the community—i.e., the Charedi community.[15] "They could say it, we cannot"—it was socially acceptable to say it at other times and places, but not in the Charedi community today.

The leaders of the Charedi community have decided that, regardless of how many Rishonim and Acharonim espoused the rationalist approach,

---

the content. Third, "tone" is something which varies immensely between different times, cultures and communities. Fourth, there has been a conspicuous lack of citation of examples of such problems in "tone." Fifth, since in truth these rabbis really do consider the notion of Chazal's scientific fallibility to be a genuinely heretical belief, they are obviously going to find the tone unacceptable; whereas someone who considers this belief legitimate, and certainly someone who maintains it himself, will have a very different opinion of the "tone."

[15] Rabbi Feldman's letter concerning Rav Elyashiv can be found at www.zootorah.com/-controversy/ravelyashiv.html.

they do not want it legitimized in their community. They have good reason for this; the rationalist approach is a Pandora's Box, which can potentially cause more problems than it solves, and which, on a communal level, demonstrates a tendency to weaken zealous passion for Torah observance and sacrifice. Yet even if one does not agree with this assessment, the Charedi community still has the right to reject whatever and whoever they want. One cannot insist on membership within a club. A person might have every reason to publicly condemn a particular country and its system of government, but he cannot expect to move to that country and receive citizenship. The Charedi community has the right to reject the rationalist approach as a social policy, no matter how superb its rabbinic credentials. It is a treasured belief of Charedi society that one approaches the words of Chazal and Rishonim with unquestioning reverence. Someone who publicly critically evaluates them in light of science is indeed a heretic, in that they are undermining one of the most treasured, foundational beliefs of that society.

What does a Jew need to believe?

The seemingly simply question, "What does a Jew need to believe?" is actually too vague. It could mean, "What does God, and the Torah, according to Jewish tradition, demand a Jew to believe?" It could mean, "What does a Jew need to profess to believe in order to be viewed as a card-carrying member of the Orthodox community in good standing?" It could mean, "What does a Jew need to *actually* believe in order to be viewed as a card-carrying member of the Orthodox community in good standing?" Or it could mean, "What is the minimum belief, as a public, communal idea, that makes Orthodoxy meaningful and viable?" Each has different answers, and so we will have to address each question separately.

What does God, and the Torah, according to Jewish tradition, demand a Jew to believe?

This is precisely what Rabbinic authorities have been arguing about for centuries, and this is not the forum to hash it all out again. But we can make the observation that—putting Rambam's peculiar position aside—God, Chazal and Jewish tradition always seemed to be far more concerned with a person being committed to living their life as an observant Jew, and being a loyal member of the Torah community, rather than with someone's private beliefs. Still, this in turn requires a general commitment to the divinity of the Torah and the truth of its content.

What does one need to publicly profess to believe in order to be viewed as a card-carrying Orthodox Jew in good standing?

In general, one must certainly profess to believe the thirteen principles of faith. Notwithstanding the fact that these have been disputed, in the public eye they are still inviolable. Furthermore, they are a fairly good approximation of normative beliefs. Various communities will also have other tenets that one must profess to believe.

What does one need to actually believe in order to be viewed as a card-carrying Orthodox Jew in good standing?

The simple answer to this question is that one does not need to believe anything at all—as long as you keep your mouth closed. There are people who do not have any beliefs, but still function as members of the Orthodox community. Their observance of halachah may be due to habit, feelings of historic obligation, or respect for the halachic system. However, while such reasons may be sufficient to motivate some people to keep halachah, it would completely undermine Orthodox Judaism to publicly legitimize such beliefs.

What _should_ the Orthodox community demand as its basic beliefs—what is the bare minimum that makes Orthodoxy meaningful and viable?

There is no clear answer to this, because there is no such monolith as "the Orthodox community." The problem is as follows. Suppose that we propose the following as the minimum required beliefs:

- The existence of God
- God as being the God of the Jews

- *Torah Min HaShamayim*—in some meaningful sense. (This would include belief in what the Torah says, such as regarding prophetic revelations.)
- The binding nature of the Halachic system

This is the barest minimum to ensure basic conformity of practice and to give it objective meaning. (There could still be some divergences, e.g. regarding the role of women, but these can't really be changed by theological beliefs; they are more a function of the definition of the halachic community.) But each community will still have other treasured beliefs which, if publicly challenged, undermine the faith of the community and threaten its stability and integrity as a community. Both the nature of these beliefs, and the amount of intellectual divergence that can be tolerated, vary between communities.

Conclusion

Defining what one must believe to be a good Jew is complicated, not least because the Torah, Mishnah and Talmud never took an interest in the matter. Yet this itself teaches us that the precise nature of beliefs is not as unequivocal and important as is commonly assumed. The important point is that one strengthens the community rather than undermining it.

The strengthening of the community primarily involves allegiance to the halachic community. Still, it is also important not to undermine treasured beliefs of the community. Heresy is the expression of a view in a way that undermines especially treasured beliefs—which are those that distinguish the community from others.

God alone determines how He reacts to those who do not possess correct beliefs. But there is the separate issue of how society relates to beliefs. And each society will have its own approach to which beliefs are a treasured component of their identity. In most sectors of Charedi society, to say that Chazal erred in science is heresy. In most sectors of Modern Orthodox society, to say that the Torah was not written by Moshe Rabbeinu is heresy, and on the flip side, to say that Rabbinic leaders are infallible is heresy.

To be a Jew in good standing, one must build up the community, not undermine it. Theologically, this means not challenging precious beliefs in a way that will undermine people's confidence. But in general, building up the community does not refer to matters of belief, but rather to practical acts—the study of Torah, the fulfillment of *mitzvot*, the loyalty to the halachic community. Being a Jew is primarily about how one lives, not how one thinks. And that, in turn, is why rationalists and mystics can co-exist.

Appendix II: The Authenticity and Authority of the Zohar

The Problem of Authenticity

It is popularly believed today that the Zohar was authored by the Tanna Rabbi Shimon bar Yochai (Rashbi), and thus its mystical content is further enhanced by being of Tannaic status. It is often assumed that not only is the Zohar completely the work of R. Shimon bar Yochai, but also that there are no Orthodox Jews who would dream of disputing this. R. Chaim Kanievsky has stated that one who denies that the Zohar was written by R. Shimon bar Yochai is a heretic who cannot be counted for a *minyan*.

Yet the truth is that the claim as to the origin of the Zohar is disputed by all academic scholars—including all Orthodox Jewish academic scholars. It is also disputed even by many prestigious rabbinic authorities of impeccable credentials, although they are often sensibly discrete about this. Some rabbinic scholars, such as Rav Yaakov Emden and Chatam Sofer, were of the view that very little (if any) of the Zohar can be attributed to Rashbi, and while there is a core of material dating back to the Amoraim, there is also plenty of material from the medieval period. Others, while rejecting the Zohar in its entirety, nevertheless believed in the authenticity of other strands of kabbalah. Still others followed Rambam, R. Delmedigo and R. Yehudah Aryeh Modena in denying the authenticity of kabbalah outright. (Note that this does not mean that they see no value in it. R. Yehuda of Modena, while dismissing the Zohar in its entirety as a clumsy fourteenth-century forgery, states that it is nevertheless a praiseworthy work with great inspirational value.)

There are no references to the Zohar in any of the writings of the Tannaim, the Amoraim, the Geonim, or the early Rishonim. The only early testimony of any sort regarding the Zohar is found in *Sefer Yuchasin* by R. Avraham Zacuto. It contains the testimony of R. Yitzchak of Akko who traveled to Spain to discover the origins of the Zohar. He reports that it was published by R. Moshe de Leon, but with regard to the origins of the text itself, he heard different accounts. Some believed that it had indeed been authored by R. Shimon b. Yochai and had been relayed from ancient Israel to Spain by way of Ramban. Others told him that it was not written by R. Shimon b. Yochai, but that it was nevertheless divinely inspired—that R. Moshe de Leon knew by way of the Divine Name to draw out this knowledge, and he attributed it to R. Shimon b. Yochai "in order to sell it for a good price." But another scholar, R. David de Pancorbo, reported that R. Moshe de Leon's wife had said that her husband made it all up, and that when she asked him why he wanted to ascribe it to R. Shimon bar Yochai, he told her that it would sell much better that way.

The problems with accepting Rashbi's authorship of the Zohar are numerous. Aside from the conspicuous lack of historical evidence, and the reports about de Leon's wife's own claim, the internal evidence from the Zohar itself strongly mitigates against having been authored by anyone in the era of Chazal. R. Yaakov Emden marshals some *three hundred* separate arguments to this end, and later scholars amplified these arguments.[1] These can be divided into several categories:

Faulty Biblical Quotations

There are several instances where the Zohar has inaccuracies regarding matters that are in Tanach. For example, the Zohar states that the Omer offering was brought from barley flour, even though the Torah actually says that it was brought from whole kernels. And the Zohar attributes the

---

[1] The most comprehensive listing of the problems with claiming authorship by Rashbi is still that of Rav Yaakov Emden in *Mitpachat Sofrim*. For a more recent and comprehensive discussion, see F. Lachower and I. Tishby, *Wisdom of the Zohar* (Oxford: Oxford University Press, 1989) vol. I, pp. 55–87.

phrase *zachrah li Elokai letova* to Ezra, whereas they were actually uttered by Nechemia—an understandable error if the author lived before the books of Ezra and Nechemia were divided in the 15th century, but still not the kind of error that ought to be made by a Tanna writing with Divine inspiration.

Problematic Citations of Aggadot

The Zohar makes several statements which either contradict or are misquotations of aggadot in the Talmud. For example, the Zohar says that the palm tree bears fruit after seventy years, while in the Talmud this is said about the carob, while the palm tree is said to take one year. The Zohar states that Gehazi received a share in the next world, while the Talmud states that he did not.

Errors Regarding People

The Zohar makes numerous inaccurate statements about Tannaim, including those connected to Rashbi, which would hardly be expected if it was written by Rashbi. For example, it repeatedly presents R. Pinchas ben Yair as Rashbi's father-in-law, and dying before him. In fact, the evidence from the Talmud shows that R. Pinchas Ben Yair was Rashbi's son-in-law, and outlived him. Likewise, the Zohar presents Rav Hamnuna Sava and Rav Yeyva Sava as the teachers of Rashbi, but in fact they lived over a century after him. The Zohar also refers to many different Amora'im—all of whom lived long after Rashbi.

Historical Anachronisms

The Zohar makes a number of allusions to Islam, which only arose long after Rashbi. For example, it notes that the religion of Ishmael is similar to Judaism in being monotheistic, whereas in fact the Arabs only moved to monotheistic Islam long after Rashbi. It also states that the children of Ishmael occupy the Holy Land, which they did not in Rashbi's time, but which they did in de Leon's time. The Zohar also polemicizes against the medieval forms of Christianity. And consistent with how mystics often love to speak about the imminent arrival of the Messiah, there are also references to the Messianic Era beginning in the fourteenth century, 1200 years after Rashbi, but fortuitously in the era of de Leon.

There are many other historical anachronisms. The Zohar refers to the practice of putting on two pairs of *tefillin*—which originated in the dispute between Rashi and Rabbeinu Tam. It also contains extensive discussion about *nikud* (vocalization symbols), and yet *nikud* only originated in the era of the Geonim. The Zohar states that Shemini Atzeres is always Simchas Torah—and yet at the time of Rashbi, through to the medieval period, the custom in the Land of Israel was to complete the Torah over a three and a half year cycle; they did not even acknowledge the division of *parashiyos* over one year that we use today.

Geographical Errors

The Zohar makes many statements about places in the Land of Israel which are incorrect, but which would be perfectly understandable if they were authored by someone living in Spain. For example, in multiple places the Kinneret is described as being in the territory of Zevulun, and as being the source of the *chilazon* that produces *techelet*, even though it was actually derived from the Mediterranean. Lod is described as being situated in the Galileee, and Cappadocia is described as a village near Sepphoris rather than as a province in Asia Minor.

Linguistic Anachronisms

Most of the Zohar is written in Aramaic. In medieval times, this would present an image of an authentic ancient text for scholars; but the fact is that among the Tannaim, Aramaic was spoken by the masses, and Hebrew was the language of scholars. Furthermore, the Aramaic of the Zohar is not ancient Aramaic, but rather bears every appearance of being written by someone who knew little Talmudic Aramaic but much medieval Hebrew. There are also many specific words in the Zohar which are clearly taken from medieval Hebrew translations of Arabic philosophical terms. Even medieval Spanish makes its appearance in the Zohar, which states that a synagogue is known as an "*esh nogah*"—with the word *esnoga* being a Portuguese corruption of the Spanish *synagoga*. The Zohar also adapts countless passages from the writings of the Amoraim, the Geonim, the

Rishonim, including (ironically) the writings of Rambam, and the Spanish poetry of Ibn Gabirol.

Halachic Disputes with the Talmud

There are numerous instances in which the Zohar argues with Talmudic law. Of course, one could argue (as some did) that R. Shimon b. Yochai, as a Tanna, was entitled to dispute the Talmud, especially since he was privy to unique divine inspiration. However, the problem with this is that if he really did have such an advantage, then why is Talmudic law usually decided in accordance with his adversary Rabbi Yehuda? Later halachic authorities—even those who believed in the Tannaitic authorship of the Zohar—did not give the Zohar the same halachic weight. But for many, the very challenges to the Talmud that are contained in the Zohar was another blow to the claims of its authenticity. Furthermore, the opinions in the Zohar appear to reflect a lack of legal skill and unfamiliarity with the Talmud rather than a differing Tannaic opinion. And in some cases, they appear bizarre, such as the statement in the Zohar that one who wears *tefillin* on *chol hamoed* is liable for the death penalty.

Reactions to the Challenges

Needless to say, there have been many committed defenders of the Zohar's antiquity, who provided all kinds of creative responses to these criticisms. However, those not religiously committed to the Zohar's antiquity consider that these responses are forced and unconvincing.

When people today first become aware of the notion that the Zohar was not written by Rashbi, the reaction is usually one of shock and hostility. The most commonly presented counter-arguments are that if the Zohar was accepted by a mystical giant such as the Ari and a universally renowned genius such as the Vilna Gaon, then its authenticity surely cannot be questioned.

In fact, the Ari himself, while widely respected, did not have his teachings universally accepted. Some of his mystical innovations, such as prefacing *brachot* with *LeShem Yichud*, were fought by great rabbinic scholars of later eras such as R. Yechezkel Landau (1713-1793, the *Noda*

B'Yehuda). In addition, the Ari took a highly unusual path with regard to kabbalah and Talmudic studies. The Ari was a largely self-taught kabbalist.[2] His studies under great rabbinic scholars were limited to his youth, and afterwards there is no evidence of him being engaged in Talmudic studies. He wrote no independent works of Talmudic or Halachic scholarship and there is no evidence of his displaying noteworthy erudition in Talmud. His mouthpiece, R. Chaim Vital, stated that the reward for performing mitzvot and studying the revealed parts of Torah is only in "this world and its Gan Eden," and that reward in the Upper World is only received for studying the wisdom of the Zohar.[3]

Regarding the Vilna Gaon, it should be noted that Rav Yaakov Emden and others were well aware of the genius of the Vilna Gaon, and yet they did not see this as a reason to accept the authenticity of the Zohar. Presumably this is because they were aware that the fact of someone being an extraordinary genius does not necessarily mean that he is correct in all his beliefs, because when one is *a priori* committed to certain beliefs, that person's genius is used to rationalize their truth.

Rabbinic Scholars who rejected the Authenticity of the Zohar

R. Yaakov Emden was far from the only rabbinic scholar who did not accept that R. Shimon b. Yochai authored the Zohar. Even R. Moshe Isserles, the Rema, writes in very non-committal language: *"I have heard that the author of the Zohar is the Rabbi Shimon mentioned in the Talmud, who is Rabbi Shimon bar Yochai."*[4]

R. Yechezkel Landau, the *Noda B'Yehuda*, delivered a sermon in which he observed that the Zohar does not have a chain of transmission like the Talmud, and if even with the Talmud there are texts that became corrupted, "then how can we rely on writings which were found many

---

[2] See *Sefer Hakavanot veMaaseh Nissim* by R. Avraham Rosanis, discussed in David Tamar, *"Reshito Shel Ha-Ari B'Mitzrayim," Tziyon* 44 (5739) pp. 229-240.

[3] R. Chaim Vital, preface to *Sefer Etz Chaim* of the Ari.

[4] *Darkei Moshe, Yoreh Deah* 65:12.

hundreds of years after the death of Rabbi Shimon b. Yochai?!"⁵ R. Landau's disciple R. Eleazar Fleckeles writes that one page of the Talmud is more holy than the entirety of the Zohar, and that if the Zohar was indeed authored by R. Shimon bar Yochai, how is it that there is no reference to it by any of the Tannaim, Amoraim, Geonim or Rishonim.⁶

R. Moshe Sofer tells a correspondent that he suspects someone of falsely attributing an opinion to a great authority. He nevertheless states that this person should not be condemned for this, and then refers to R. Yaakov Emden's work *Mitpachat Sofrim*, which "says a great thing in this matter, which will cause astonishment to those who see it, and this is a sufficient allusion for the wise."⁷ In other words, he is alluding to Moses de Leon wanting his ideas to gain acceptance and therefore falsely attributing them to R. Shimon bar Yochai. One of Chatam Sofer's disciples, Rabbi Eliezer Lipman Neusatz, attests to having explicitly heard from Chatam Sofer that "if there were the human ability to establish the *midrashim* of Rabbi Shimon bar Yochai in their pristine state, to pick them out from that which was attached to them from subsequent generations, its entirety would only be an extremely small book, taking up few pages."⁸

More recently, none other than Rav Ovadiah Yosef, as attested by one of his aides, was asked about whether the Darda'im—a Yemenite group, following R. Yichya Kapach, who vociferously denied the authenticity of the Zohar—should be rated as heretics. Rav Ovadiah replied that "it is difficult to say this, since the Zohar was concealed for many years, and after it was found they discovered all kinds of difficulties with it, which seem to contradict that which is stated in the Torah, and they thus cannot be rated as heretics."⁹

---

⁵ *Drashot Noda B'Yehuda*, published in Maoz Kahana and Michael Silber, *Kabbalah* 21 (5770), p. 355.

⁶ *Teshuva Me-Ahavah*, 1:26.

⁷ Responsa Chatam Sofer 6:59.

⁸ R. Eliezer Lipman Neusatz, *Mei Menuchot*, p. 43a.

⁹ R. Yehudah Naki, *Maayan Omer*, vol. I, *Hilchot Beit HaKnesset*, p. 221.

Appendix II: The Authenticity and Authority of the Zohar

There are numerous other rabbinic scholars who rejected the Tannaic authorship of the Zohar either in part or in whole.[10] Nevertheless, while awareness of this is continually spreading, there are still many people who are entirely unaware of it, and it is an extremely sensitive topic in many Orthodox Jewish circles.

---

[10] See Marc Shapiro, "Is There An Obligation To Believe that the Zohar Was Written By Rabbi Shimon ben Yochai?" *Milin Havivin* 5 (2010/11) pp. 1-20 (Hebrew.)

Index

rationalist vs. mystic approach to the
order of nature, 29, 30, 39
required beliefs of Judaism, 507
Sages' powers of life and death, 375
sun's path at night, 266
hishtadlut, 46, 47
A History of the Jews (Johnson), 124
Hiyya, R., 106
Holocaust, 486
Holy City. *see* Jerusalem, Israel
Holy Land. *see* Israel, Land of
Holy Language. *see* Hebrew
Holy of Holies, 62
Holy Temple. *see* Beit HaMikdash
Hool, R. Doniel, 416
Horowitz, R. Yeshaya, 101
Horwitz, R. Pinchas, 452
Hoshea, R., 218
Huna ben R. Yehoshua, R., 198
Huna, R., 382
Hurwitz, R. Pinchas Eliyahu, 287, 288,
289, 370, 419
Hutner, R. Yitzchak, 313

ibn Attar, R. Chaim ben Moshe (*Ohr
HaChaim HaKadosh*), 362, 371, 479
Ibn Ezra, Abraham, 11, 92, 321–22, 323,
391, 389–92, 392, 393
Ibn Gabirol, Solomon, 518
Ibn Kaspi, R. Yosef, 332–33, 336
Ibn Shuib, R. Yehoshua, 323, 324, 325,
327
Ibn Tibbon, R. Shmuel, 37, 253, 254,
387
Idel, Moshe, 378
IDF, 110, 112
idolatry, 48, 50, 61, 105, 125, 416, 487,
497
Igrot Moshe (Feinstein), 428–29
Igroth, 396
ikkar, 224, 236, 256, 501
Ilustriravansk Mir, 427

impurity
evolution of the olive, 215
rabbinic attitudes to demons, 397
rationalist vs. mystic approach to
supernatural entities, 58–61, 65
rationalist vs. mystic approach to the
function of *mitzvot*, 83, 84
required beliefs of Judaism, 494
students disputing teachers, 209
sun's path at night, 251
Independence Day, 487
intellectual submissions to authority, 26–
27
Intelligences, 54
interventions, miracles as supernatural,
177–79, 191
Iron Dome, 111
Isaiah, 170
Isaiah, Book of, 40
Ishmael, 516
Islam
authenticity and authority of the
Zohar, 516
ayin hara, 425
defining rationalism and mysticism, 6
development of the rationalist vs.
mystical divide, 11, 126
rabbinic attitudes to demons, 391
rationalist vs. mystic approach to
supernatural entities, 54
rationalist vs. mystic approach to the
nature of Torah, 95
required beliefs of Judaism, 498, 501
sun's path at night, 255, 258, 277,
292, 301
Israel, Land of
authenticity and authority of the
Zohar, 515, 516, 517
ayin hara, 416, 429
development of the rationalist vs.
mystical divide, 123, 126

Index

ABOUT THE AUTHOR

Born in England, Natan Slifkin moved to Israel for many years of post-high school study in various yeshivot. He received rabbinic ordination from Rabbi Dov Schwarzman and taught for several years at a variety of yeshivot and seminaries. Subsequently he received an MA in Jewish Studies from Machon Lander in Jerusalem, graduating summa cum laude, and then a doctorate in Jewish History from Bar Ilan University.

Rabbi Dr. Slifkin is the author of numerous works on the interface between Judaism and the natural sciences. For over ten years he has written on the topic of rationalism vs. mysticism on his popular website www.RationalistJudaism.com. He has also lectured worldwide on these topics.

Rabbi Dr. Slifkin is the founder and director of the Biblical Museum of Natural History, which recently moved to a new facility next to Beit Shemesh. He lives in Ramat Beit Shemesh with his wife and children.